Social Problems

Social Problems

Michael S. Bassis
University of Wisconsin — Parkside

Richard J. Gelles
University of Rhode Island

Ann Levine

Under the General Editorship of
Robert K. Merton
Columbia University

Harcourt Brace Jovanovich, Inc.

New York / San Diego / Chicago / San Francisco / Atlanta / London / Sydney / Toronto

HM
51
.B33

ISBN: 0-15-581430-3
Library of Congress Catalog Card Number: 81-86532
Printed in the United States of America
Cover: outdoor mural painting by Burnett Hord, Jr., photograph © Philip Pocock

Acknowledgments and Copyrights appear on pages 565–570, which constitute a
continuation of the copyright page.

To Our Parents
Barbara and Lewis Bassis
Clara and Sidney Gelles
Estelle and Louis Sickles

Preface

During the two years we spent writing this text, we often felt that we were being shadowed by the mass media. No sooner had we completed the draft of a chapter than a news magazine printed a cover story on that subject: "Global Negotiations," "The Graying of America," "The Plague of Violent Crime," "The Children of Divorce." Almost every day, the newspapers ran editorials or articles on the problems we were addressing.

There are critical differences between the sociology of social problems and news reporting, however. The news media often fix blame for social problems on particular people and organizations, policies and laws. By implication, if this person were a better administrator, or if that law were changed, the problem would disappear. Other events and trends are reported as if they were inevitable—the deterioration of inner cities, for example. The sociology of social problems seeks to explain how situations that now seem inescapable developed. It shifts attention away from individual "villains," to the social and historical circumstances that create problems.

The central message of this book is that social problems are not caused by bad people, bad government agencies and corporations, bad policies and laws. Nor do they come out of nowhere. They are the product of social forces, of particular kinds of social organization that can only be understood in historical context. Our goal is to show how problems—ranging from famine in Africa, to declining productivity in American industry, to sexual dysfunction, to alcoholism—are *social* in origin.

Part One, "The Sociology of Social Problems," introduces this approach by explaining how sociologists think and work. Chapter 1 uses an extended case study—a flood in Buffalo Creek, West Virginia—to trace the social origins of what was at first described as a "natural disaster." Chapter 2 introduces basic research techniques by presenting three studies that influenced public opinion and social policy and discusses the politics of social research.

Part Two, "The National and International Context," grew out of our belief that the problems and anxieties of the 1980s are global, in origins and consequences. People are accustomed to thinking of such things as unemployment and environmental pollution as national problems, requiring national solutions. In reality, today's social problems do not respect national borders. Chapters 3 and 4 are designed to add global dimension to the study of social problems. Chapter 3 examines such urgent issues as mass hunger and nuclear power in the context of limited global resources, the growing world population, and increasing environmental risks. Chapter 4 analyzes the structure of international tensions, focusing on the emergence of the Third

World and potential sources of East-West and North-South conflict. (Although much of the material in these chapters is new to the social problems course, the tools we use to analyze data are from the sociologist's basic kit.) These chapters lay the groundwork for a re-examination of the U.S. political economy in Chapter 5.

Part Three, "Social Settings in Turmoil," focuses on three social contexts of daily life: the metropolitan community, the workplace, and the family. These chapters trace the historical and social origins of today's concerns. The emphasis is on how problems that seem intractable, such as unemployment and the decline of major cities, come into being, and on how problems of daily life, such as boredom on the job or divorce, are shaped by events and processes that are beyond individual control.

Part Four, "Social Inequality," deals with the sharply uneven distribution of opportunities and rewards in the United States today. This section is organized around a series of puzzles. Why is there poverty in the midst of plenty? Why, when prejudice has declined and discrimination has been outlawed, does racial inequality persist? Why did the Women's Movement take hold in the 1970s? Why is age a liability in our society?

In Part Five, "Private Troubles, Public Issues," we turn to subjects that arouse both public controversy and private anxiety: physical and mental health, crime and violence, sex, and drugs. This section breaks through clichés to consider behavior Americans do not usually think of as social problems, such as the use of prescription drugs, sexual dysfunction, and cigarette smoking.

Three themes run throughout the book. The first is that social problems are interconnected. For example, although poverty, racism, and sexism can be separated for purposes of analysis, in reality they are intertwined. The second theme is the importance of historical perspective. Discovering the way social problems change—or fail to change—over time is the first step toward un-

derstanding them. The third theme is the impact of public perceptions on social problems. In some cases, the public fails to recognize a social problem, to perceive that a problem is socially constructed and could be changed. In other cases, public alarm turns a relatively harmless situation into a harmful one. The complex interplay of social issues and social problems figures prominently in many chapters.

This book is designed both for students who are taking their first and only course in sociology and for sociology majors. Chapter 1 provides a concise summary of basic sociological theories; sociological concepts are highlighted and defined as they appear in the text. In each chapter, we present not only up-to-date information on the dimensions of social problems, but also in-depth sociological analysis. If we succeed, students will come to appreciate the sociological approach, to fit current events in the news and in their own lives into this framework, and to question political slogans implying that everything is black or white.

The Harcourt Brace Jovanovich College Department gave the lie to the notion that writing a book is an isolated and lonely experience. Judith Greissman was a constant source of inspiration, a muse of the social sciences. Her energy, her endless questions, her dislike of simplism and sentimentality, her special combination of biting wit and warm encouragement are unique. Judy is both editor and friend. Claire Thompson was with us every step of the way—and sometimes ahead of us. Her ability to see where the logic failed, to interest the reviewer whose opinion we valued most, and to keep track of the whole when we were immersed in the pieces—all in good humor —was a small miracle of publishing.

There were others. Our copy editor Sandy Lifland's dedication to her job and professional dislike of loose ends almost made her late for her wedding. Elaine Bernstein tantalized us with many more photographs than space allowed us to use. Her talent for translating sociological concepts into images is special. Nancy Kirsh caught the spirit of the book in her interior design, then wrapped it in what we believe is a perfect cover.

When time threatened, Robert Faulkner, University of Massachusetts, Amherst, contributed ideas for the organization of the chapter on the workplace; Carl Gersuny, University of Rhode Island, for the chapter on poverty; and Jeffrey P. Rosenfeld, Nassau Community College, for the chapter on age. Patricia A. Steffan wrote clear, intelligent drafts of the chapters on the workplace and poverty, adding her own considerable insights on the material.

This is the second book on which Sheryl Horwitz has been a member of our team. She is a superb secretary and, more importantly, counseled and tolerated us during the ups and downs of the project. Mary A. Harrison and Claire Pedrick Cornell served as research assistants and fathomed the mysteries of the University of Rhode Island library so well that in the final stages of the book we met each critical deadline. Karen Lee Ginsberg applied the same resourcefulness in New York.

Most of all, we want to thank Robert K. Merton, Columbia University Professor Emeritus and Special Service Professor. Professor Merton's editorial guidance is legendary. His invaluable contributions to the early shaping of this book were equaled only by his critical and constructive reading of each chapter. There is not a page in this book that does not bear his stamp. Working under his editorship was a privileged education for all of us.

Acknowledgments to Reviewers

A number of reviewers read and criticized our manuscript in various drafts. We appreciate the contributions of the following people to the shaping of this book: Richard J. Barnet, Institute for Policy Studies; Robert A. Clark, Gordon College; John A. Clausen, University of California at Berkeley; Lawrence E. Cohen, University of Texas at Austin; John Colombotos, Columbia University; Cynthia Fuchs Epstein, Columbia University; Norman Fainstein, The New School; Marcus Felson, University of Illinois at Urbana; Claude S. Fischer, University of California at Berkeley; Erich Goode, State University of New York at Stony Brook; Joan Huber, University of Illinois at Urbana; Eric Josephson, Columbia University; Benjamin A. Kogan, M.D.; Louis Kriesberg, Syracuse University; Jeylan T. Mortimer, University of Minnesota at Minneapolis-St. Paul; Carole Offir, San Diego Mesa College; David E. Olday, Moorhead State University; Ronald M. Pavalko, University of Wisconsin—Parkside; Letitia Anne Peplau, University of California at Los Angeles; Theresa F. Rogers, Columbia University; Edward Sagarin, City University of New York; John Scanzoni, University of North Carolina at Greensboro; Allan Schnaiberg, Northwestern University; Judith Stacey, University of California at Davis; Paul H. Tress, Mitre Corporation; Eleanor M. Vander Haegen, Keene State College; Joan M. Waring, Equitable Life Assurance Co.; Robert S. Weiss, Harvard Medical School; Marvin E. Wolfgang, University of Pennsylvania.

Michael S Bassis
Richard J. Gelles
Ann Levine

Contents

Preface   vii

PART ONE
The Sociology of Social Problems

One

Perspectives on Problems   3

The Sociological Imagination   4

Buffalo Creek: A Case Study   5
The Destruction of Buffalo Creek   6
Sociological Perspective   7
The Depletion of Natural Resources   9
The Depletion of Human Resources   9

Identifying Social Issues and Social
    Problems   10
Social Issues   11
Social Problems   15
*Connecting Social Issues and Social
    Problems*   18

The Sociological Frame of Reference   18
Culture   19

The Social System   19
The Individual in Society   19

Explaining Social Problems: Theoretical
    Approaches   20
*Social Disorganization: Yesterday's
    People*   20
    Cultural Lag   21
    Alienation   21
Conflict Theory: Black Gold   22
Deviance and Moonshine   26
    Learning Theory   26
    Opportunity Structures   27
    Labeling   27

Social Problems in the 1980s   31

Two

Sociology in Action 39

Generating Knowledge: The Role of
  Research   42

A Survey of Family Violence   42

*A Field Study of Women of the
  Corporation*   45

*An Experiment in Treatment of the
  Mentally Ill*   47

The Ethics of Research   51

Utilizing Knowledge   55

Potential Uses and Users of Sociology   55

Assessing the Scope of Problems   57
Challenging Myths   58
Designing and Evaluating Solutions   59
Broadening Perspectives   60

Obstacles to Use   62

Contradictory Findings   62
Media Distortions   63
Unheeded Results   64

Social Problems and Social Action   64

The Politics of Problems   65

Sociology's Responsibilities   69

PART TWO

The National and International Context

Three

Global Ecology 75

Sociology and Ecology   80

Future Demands   81

Population Patterns   81

Demographic Arithmetic   81
Speeding Fertility Decline   83
Future Prospects   86

Patterns of Consumption   87

Current Patterns   88
Future Trends   89

Global Resources   90

Food Supplies   90

Future Prospects   90
Supply vs. Distribution   91

Energy Resources   93

Nonrenewable Resources   93
Renewable Resources   96
Energy Costs and Energy Profits   96

The Environment at Risk   97

Technological Fallout   98

Air Pollution   99
Water Pollution   100
Ground Pollution   100
Pesticides   101
The Greenhouse Effect   103

The Allocation of Risk   103

The Sociology of Survival   105

Four

International Conflict 111

International Conflict: An
  Overview   115

Nations in an Age of
  Interdependence   116
The Nationalization of Loyalties   116
The Globalization of Interests   117

The Structure of International
  Relations   119
Three Worlds of Development   119
  The First World   122
  The Second World   122
  The Third World   124
  Triad in Turmoil   125

East vs. West   126

Competition for Natural Resources   127
Conflict over Human Rights   129

North vs. South   132
Explaining North-South Inequality   132
*The Role of the Transnational
  Corporation*   133
Third World Strategies   136
  Association with a Major Power   136
  Building Third World Coalitions   137

Toward an International Order   138
Developing Global Perspective   140
Transnational Organizations   141
*More Critical Choices for the United
  States*   143

Five

The Political Economy 149

Corporate Power   152
The Road to Oligopoly   155
  The Capitalist Ideal   155
  Market Domination   156
*The Use and Abuse of Corporate
  Power*   157

The Power of the Federal
  Government   159
The Rise of Big Government   160
  Promoting Economic Security   160

Maintaining the Military
  Establishment   166
Protecting Public Rights   168
A Bureaucracy Out of Control   169
  Organized Inefficiency   170
  Responsive to Whom?   171

Pressure Politics   172
Clash of Interests   173
The Special Interest State   174
In the Public Interest   179

PART THREE
Social Settings in Turmoil

Six

The Urban Crisis 185

Urban America in Transition   189

The Central City   191

Suburbia   192

Sunbelt Cities   192

The Urban Experience   194

Theoretical Perspectives   195

  The Determinist View   195
  The Counterargument   196
  The Subcultural View   198
Assessing the Quality of Urban Life   198

Urban Isolation and Stress   198
Urban Crime   200

Locking the Poor Inside the City   202

Transportation   202

Housing   204

Education   208

Urban Revitalization: Proposals and
  Prospects   211

Inner-City Recommendations   211

Metropolitan Recommendations   213

Seven

The Workplace 223

The Changing Workplace   224

The Global Factory   224

The Post-Industrial Economy   226

  The Change from Goods to Services   226
  Post-Industrial Work: An Assessment   227

Two Labor Markets   229

Work and Its Discontents   230

The Changing Work Ethic   230

Alienation and Job Satisfaction   231

  Blue-Collar Blues and White-Collar
  Woes   233

The Manager's Plight 236
The Happy Worker 236

Unemployment 236

The International Labor Market 237
Migration of Industry and Automation of
    Production 237
Discrimination 238
The Changing Job Market 239

Danger, Disability, and Death on the
    Job 239

Accidents at Work 240
Unhealthy Workplaces 242
Job Satisfaction and Mental Health 243

Reforming the Workplace 244
*The "Work Is Inherently Unpleasant"
    Assumption* 244
*The "Work Is Beneficial"
    Assumption* 246

Eight

The Family 253

The Family: Dying or Developing? 256
Is the Family Dying? 256
The Developing Family 257
The Consequences of Change 259
The Case of Working Wives and
    Mothers 260

Divorce 262
*Divorce in the U.S.: Past and
    Present* 262
Changing Divorce Rates 263
Who Gets Divorced? 264
The Consequences of Divorce 265
The Impact on Adults 265
The Impact on Children 268

Family Violence 270
Family Violence in Perspective 270
The Extent of Family Violence 271

Violence Toward Children 271
Violence Between Spouses 272
Violence Between Siblings 273
Violence Toward Parents 273
The Causes of Family Violence 273
Myths About Family Violence 274
The Structural Causes of Family
    Violence 274
*The Consequences of Family
    Violence* 275
Responses to Family Violence 275
Victims of Child Abuse 276
Victims of Wife Abuse 276
The Prognosis 278

Sexual Abuse of Children 278
*The Incidence of Sexual
    Victimization* 279
Patterns of Father-Daughter Incest 279
The Consequences of Incest 279

PART FOUR
Social Inequality

Nine
Poverty 287

Poverty in the Midst of Plenty   290

The Penalties of Poverty   293
The Poor Get Less . . .   293
. . . And They Pay More   295

Who Is Poor?   296
Female-headed Families   296
Minorities   297
The Aged   298
Regional Poverty   298

Explanations of Poverty   298
The Culture of Poverty   299
The Uses of Poverty   301
The Economics of Poverty   301
Poverty and Power   303

Remedies and Obstacles   304
Social Welfare Programs   304
Social Insurance   304
Cash Assistance   305
In-Kind Aid   307
The Culture of Inequality   307

Ten
Racial Inequality 315

The History of Racism in the United
States   316
Native Americans   318
Black Americans   322
Mexican Americans   324

The Roots of Racism   327
Social Preconditions   327
Racist Ideology   328

Maintaining Racial Inequality   329
Prejudice and Discrimination   329
Institutionalized Racism   335

Contemporary Racial Issues and
Conflicts   338
Actions   338
Southern Protest   338
Chicano and Pan-Indian Movements   340
Urban Riots   341

Reactions 343

   Legislation 343
   Retrenchment 344

The Dimensions of Racial Inequality
Today 345

Eleven

Gender Inequality 353

Explaining Gender Inequality 354

Biology Is Destiny 355

Learned Inequality 356

   Gender Socialization 356
   Mixed Sexual Identities 358
   Cross-Cultural Studies 358

Biology and Learning Reviewed 359

Prejudice 360

Institutionalized Sexism 360

Women and Inequality 361

Women and Families 361

Women and Education 365

Women and Work 367

Men: Dilemmas and Confusion 375

Responses to Inequality 378

*Womanhood in America: A Brief
   History* 378

The Women's Movement Today 380

Responses to Feminism 383

Twelve

Age Inequality 391

The Early Years: Childhood and
   Adolescence 394

Children's Rights 394

   The History of Childhood 394
   Competing Interests 396

Adolescent Turmoil 398

   The Social Origins of Adolescence 399
   The Social Problems of Adolescence 400

The Later Years 403

*Attitudes Toward Aging and the
   Elderly* 404

*The Negative Consequences of
   Aging* 408

   Poverty and Underemployment 408
   Housing Problems 411
   Victimization of the Elderly 413

Problems and Prospects 414

PART FIVE
Private Troubles, Public Issues

Thirteen
Physical and Mental Health 421

Physical Disorders   425

The Medical Establishment   425

  The AMA   426
  Blue Cross   426
  Medical Centers   427
  Professional Autonomy and Social
    Control   428

Escalating Costs   428

  Physicians   431
  Hospitals   431
  Alternative Financing Systems   433

Poverty, Old Age, and Health   435

Mental Disorders   437

The Medical Model   437

  The Freudian Influence   439
  The Mental Hospital   441

The Social Model   442

  Mental Disorders and Social Class   442
  Mental Disorders and Labeling   444

*The Community Mental Health
  Movement*   447

  Deinstitutionalization and the Drug
    Revolution   447
  Community Mental Health Centers   449

Health Care: Toward an Uncertain
  Future   450

Advancing Medical Technology   450

The Politics of Health Care   451

*Preventive Care: Whose
  Responsibility?*   451

Fourteen
Crime and Violence 459

Criminal Behavior   460

What Is a Crime?   460

Patterns of Crime   462

The Costs of Crime   463

Measuring Crime   465

The Extent of Crime   466

  Uniform Crime Reports   466
  National Crime Survey   467

Perpetrators and Victims   467

Causes of Violence 471

Biological Explanations 471

Psychological Explanations 471

Social-Psychological Explanations 472

Social Learning 472
Differential Association 474

Sociological Explanations 474

Social Disorganization 474
Violence and Anomie 475
Opportunity Structures 475
Culture and Violence 476

The Criminal Justice System 478

The Police 480

The Courts 481

Prisons 483

Capital Punishment 483

Deterrence Considered 485

The Social Roots of Crime and
   Violence 486

F i f t e e n

Sexual Behavior 493

Sex and Society 494

Instincts or Social Learning? 494

Variations in Sexual Conduct 496

*Sexual Attitudes and Behavior in the
   United States* 497

The Victorian Influence 497
Science "Discovers" Sex 498
A New Morality? 500

Adolescent Sexuality 503

Teen-age Pregnancy 503

Venereal Disease 506

Marital and Extramarital
   Sexuality 507

The Sociology of Sexuality 508

Learning Sexual Roles 508
Sexual Dysfunction 509

*Alternatives to Monogamous
   Sexuality* 510

The (Clandestine) Affair 510
Sex and Divorce 511

Commercialized Sex 511

Pornography 511

The Legal Dilemma 511
The Public Concern 514
The Future of Pornography 516

Prostitution 517

An Industry in Decline 517
Contrasting Views of Prostitution 517

Homosexuality 520

Problems of Definition 520

Becoming Homosexual 522

The Homosexual "Condition": Biological
   and Psychological Explanations 522
The Homosexual Role: Learning
   Theory 523

The Politics of Homosexuality 523

Gay Liberation 525

A False Dichotomy 526

Social Problems and Social Issues 527

Sixteen

Drug Use 533

Drugs and Their Effects   534

Depressants   534

Stimulants   538

Hallucinogens   540

Drug Use: The Contemporary Scene   542

Patterns of Drug Use   542

Explaining Drug Use   545

The Social Control of Drug Use   549

The Politics of Drug Control   550

Drug Laws and Their Consequences   554

   Intolerance   555

   Tolerance   557

The Drug Problem in Perspective   560

Name Index   571

Subject Index   578

Social Problems

PART ONE

The Sociolgy of Social Problems

Chapter One

Perspectives on Problems

The Sociological Imagination

Buffalo Creek: A Case Study

The Destruction of Buffalo Creek

A Sociological Perspective

The Depletion of Natural Resources

The Depletion of Human Resources

Identifying Social Issues and Social Problems

Social Issues

Social Problems

Connecting Social Issues and Social Problems

The Sociological Frame of Reference

Culture

The Social System

The Individual in Society

Explaining Social Problems: Theoretical Approaches

Social Disorganization: Yesterday's People

  Cultural Lag

  Alienation

Conflict Theory: Black Gold

Deviance and Moonshine

  Learning Theory

  Opportunity Structures

  Labeling

Social Problems in the 1980s

T he parade of issues and events in the news often is bewildering. One week troubles in Eastern Europe capture the headlines; the next week it is Southeast Asia or Latin America. In the national news, conflicts over the defense budget, environmental regulations, the death penalty, and abortion laws compete for space. No one seems to know what to do about inflation or crime in the streets. Racial and sexual inequality resist efforts to correct them. The drug problem refuses to go away. Often the solution to one problem (for example, building nuclear power plants to ease energy shortages) threatens to create new problems.

The Sociological Imagination

The complexity of our times produces a kind of double vision. Some of the problems we face seem remote and intractable. The average person is a spectator at world events, relying on the news media to keep score. Terms like "stagflation" and the "population explosion" hint at vague, impersonal, and uncontrollable forces. Where do they come from? What do they mean to the ordinary citizen? Other problems seem immediate and personal—how to find a job, where to park the car, whether it is safe to walk alone at night, how to pay medical bills, what to do about aging parents. People wonder what is going wrong and why it is happening to them.

In some cases, the connections between private troubles and social trends are clear. A war in the Middle East does not seem remote when gasoline prices at home jump ten cents in a single week. Statistics on the growing number of older Americans do not seem abstract when an elderly relative who requires full-time care is told she must wait two years to get into a nursing home. Discussions of changing sexual behavior take on new meaning when an unmarried teen-age sister becomes pregnant.

Often people fail to see the connections between their private lives and social circumstances, however. Consider unemployment. When a man is fired, he is likely to blame himself, a rival at work, or bad luck. Losing a job feels like a personal problem. But when tens of thousands of workers are laid off (as happened in the U.S. auto industry in the 1970s and early 1980s), we cannot explain the situation in terms of *individuals'* skills or character. We have to look elsewhere—to the tripling of oil prices by OPEC (The Organization of Oil Exporting Countries); a shift in consumer demand from big "gas guzzlers" to smaller, often foreign-made cars; higher interest rates; and other factors beyond the control of workers.

Consider education. When students fail, they are likely to blame themselves for being stupid or not working hard enough. But why tens of thousands of students fail to learn basic reading and writing skills cannot be explained in terms of individual IQs or study habits. We have to look at the educational system as a whole and at the way education is affected by tracking (segregating students according to ability), the "hidden curriculum" (which places more emphasis on obedience than learning), and the low salaries and prestige awarded teachers.

Consider divorce. When two people no longer want to live together, they blame themselves and one another. One or the other was too preoccupied with a career. One or the other was a careless homemaker. Each divorce feels like a uniquely private experience. But when tens of thousands of couples are divorced each year, we cannot explain the situation in terms of individual incompatibility. We have to look at the institution of marriage—at the impact of longer life spans and fewer children on the couple's relationship, at the reasons why working wives still do most of the housework and men are rarely given paternity leave, and at other factors. The trouble may be, not that a man and woman failed at marriage, but that marriage failed them.

In each case, the individuals' troubles are not entirely the result of something they, personally, did "wrong." They result in part from social forces that are beyond individual control. The social conditions that lead to widespread unemployment, breakdowns in the educational system, or comparatively high divorce rates do not spring up overnight. Nor did they always exist. They reflect their time and place. They have a history. Understanding how and why these social conditions developed in a particular time and society is critical.

It takes what C. Wright Mills (1959) called "sociological imagination" to see the connection between private troubles and the sweep of history. *Sociological imagination* is the insight into private troubles that comes from understanding the historical development of social patterns and their impact on private lives. Individuals are both the creators and the creatures of their social worlds. Our "fate" is tied to the society and times in which we live. Biography and history are interconnected; to understand one, we must understand the other.

We believe sociological imagination is critical to an understanding of social problems. To illustrate this approach, this opening chapter focuses on the problems of Buffalo Creek, a small town in Logan County, West Virginia. We chose Buffalo Creek, not because what happened in the town was unique, but because it provides a particularly clear example of how the sociological imagination contributes to our understanding of social problems.

Buffalo Creek: A Case Study

Most of the 5,000 or so residents of Buffalo Creek are descendants of eighteenth-century pioneers (Erikson, 1976; Weller, 1965; Caudill, 1963). Heading west across the Appalachian Mountains, they happened on what is now West Virginia and decided to stay. They were a select sample—men and women who were attracted to the isolation of the mountain hollows and the untamed forest. For over a century, they farmed and hunted the mountains, one generation living much as the last one had. Contacts with outsiders were rare. But the land was rich with timber, and just below the surface lay thick veins of coal—the nineteenth century's "black gold." Appalachia had what the industrial world needed. In the late nineteenth century, the mountain silence was broken by the sounds of progress: falling timber, mine blasts, and railroad clatter.

Buffalo Creek today is very much a coal-mining town (Erikson, 1976). Most of the townspeople work in the mines, live off miners' wages, or draw pensions because of injuries or death in the mines. The size and character of the town have changed with the coal industry. When the first mines were opened, they attracted families from hundreds of miles around. When machines began to replace men underground, and when oil began to replace coal in factories up North, people wandered away and Buffalo Creek shrank.

The town is located in one of the many hollows etched into the plains alongside the Appalachians. It takes its name from the creek that winds seventeen miles through the hollow. Until recently, the most prominent feature in Buffalo Creek had been what local people called the "dam." For almost twenty years, the Buffalo Mining Company had dumped refuse at the top of the hollow, at the rate of about one thousand tons a day. By 1970, a forty-foot-high pile of slag—coal dust mixed with shale and clay—reached from one valley wall to the other, looming over the town. The streams that fed into the creek were clogged, and an artificial twenty-acre, two-hundred-foot-deep lake had formed behind the "dam." Slag is as black as coal and nearly as combustible. It may smolder silently for years, then suddenly become irritated and explode. But the dumping had gone on for years, and residents were accustomed to the steaming, black-water lake.

Like people everywhere, the residents of Buffalo Creek have their share of private troubles. A man loses his job and takes to drink; couples fight; children leave home for the big city. They see these as private troubles. A sociologist looking at Buffalo Creek would see their troubles are not entirely of their own making. There is a pattern of unemployment in Appalachia, for example. Although Buffalo Creek is small and remote, it is part of a nationwide—indeed, a global—economic system. The economic fates of townspeople are tied to the mines. A company decision to open or close a mine, to mechanize the operation, or to shift from underground to strip mining, can put money in their pockets or send them to the unemployment office. Their economic fortunes also reflect energy policies set in Washington, environmentalists' demands for cleaner air (and less burning of coal) in California or New York, the price OPEC sets for a barrel of oil, and the political situation in the Middle East. Thus, remote as they are, the people of Buffalo Creek are pushed this way and that by social forces they only dimly perceive and cannot control.

In the winter of 1972 to 1973, all seemed well in Buffalo Creek. Most of the men in town were earning good wages in the mines. They may not have been wealthy by national standards, but the $30 to $40 they earned for an eight-hour shift was a vast improvement over the $2 to $3 their fathers had taken home for a twelve-hour shift. Most owned their own homes and spent their days off improving them. Their taxes were low. Their union was strong. On the whole, the people of Buffalo Creek felt they led "secure, honest, comfortable" lives (Erikson, 1976, p. 24). Then quite suddenly, the ground was literally swept from under their feet. An unexpected (though predictable) event revealed a web of interwoven social problems.

The Destruction of Buffalo Creek

On the night of February 25, 1973, it rained in Buffalo Creek. Residents closed their windows, locked their doors, and went to sleep as usual. A minute or two before 8:00 the next morning, the "dam" above the town suddenly collapsed. In a matter of seconds, over 130 million gallons of water and debris burst into the hollow. Some people heard a boom that sounded like thunder; others were awakened by the roar of the flood. The word "flood" is inadequate to describe what hit them. A wall of steaming, thundering mud fifteen to forty feet high tore through the town. The maelstrom careened from one side of the hollow to the other—setting off explosions when it swept down power lines, tearing up railroad tracks and twisting them like wire, bouncing trucks and houses into the air "like beach balls." People lucky enough to scramble to high ground in time watched helplessly as relatives and neighbors were pulled under.

By 10:00 A.M., when the water began to subside, Buffalo Creek was utterly destroyed. One hundred twenty-five bodies lay in the wreckage, many unrecognizable. The bodies were swollen and coated with slag; the faces, frozen in terror. Nearly 4,000 of the 5,000 townspeople were homeless. Bits and pieces of their lives were strewn all over the hollow. Familiar landmarks—the gas station down the road, the tree on the corner—had been washed away.

The Buffalo Creek flood headlined that evening's news broadcasts. Disasters are always news, and this was one of the worst in the nation's history (Stern, 1977). TV reporters interviewed bewildered survivors while the camera panned the creek bed, pausing over bodies not yet recovered. The Army Corps of Engineers set up shelters and moved bulldozers in to clear the wreckage. It looked like a war zone. News coverage continued for some days, and public reaction quickly turned from disbelief and sorrow to out-

Battered homes and lives were strewn across the railroad tracks at Buffalo Creek like empty cardboard boxes. The flood was not a "natural disaster"; it was man-made.

rage. Pittston, Buffalo Mining's parent company, maintained that the flood was a natural disaster, "an act of God," but residents had no doubt that the disaster was man-made. It hadn't rained any harder on the morning of February 26 than it usually did during that time of year. The "dam" was in fact a dump and had always been weak. The Buffalo Mining Company had flouted the 1969 Coal Mine Health and Safety Act, which specifically forbids constructing refuse piles that "impede drainage or impound water." In the next few weeks, a U.S. House of Representatives sub-committee convened hearings to determine why this dangerous situation had not been detected and corrected. With the help of Arnold and Porter, a prestigious Washington law firm, 650 survivors sued Pittston for damages and eventually agreed to a $13.5 million settlement out of court (Stern, 1977, p. 301).

A Sociological Perspective

The reason why disaster struck Buffalo Creek seems obvious: The mining company had knowingly violated safety regulations. This is correct as far as it goes. But another, more puzzling ques-

In the Words of Survivors

"People don't know what they want or where they want to go. It's almost as though they don't care what happens anymore."

"[T]here was months and months and months where I felt I was just sitting around waiting to die."

"[Y]ou start to say something and forget what it was, or just walk away while someone is still talking to you."

"Sometimes when you go to sleep and start to relax, the nightmares start."

"My nerves have been bad . . . . My body is one big pain . . . ."

"I don't like being in a crowd of people no more. If I can, I avoid them."

"I just stay mad. Sometimes I think they have brighter people in a nut house than I am."

Source: Kai Erikson, *Everything in Its Path* (New York: Simon & Schuster, 1976), pp. 204, 158, 213, 170, 216.

tion remains. If the townspeople had known the "dam" was dangerous, why hadn't they done something about it? How could they have gone about their daily lives as if nothing were wrong, with millions of gallons of poisonous black water, pushing against a makeshift "dam," poised over their heads? To answer this question, we turn to research by the sociologist Kai Erikson (1976).

The survivors' lawyers asked Erikson to be one of a team of investigators who would study Buffalo Creek in 1973 and 1974. On his first trip to the hollow, Erikson found that the federal government had come to the rescue, supplying mobile homes, medical assistance, and other aid. The place had been cleaned up. But much of the "human wreckage" remained. "[P]eople still looked out at the world with vacant eyes and drifted from one place to another with dulled and tentative movements. They rarely smiled or played" (1976, p. 184). Were the survivors still recovering from the shock of the flood? Erikson distributed questionnaires, conducted interviews, and studied the history and culture of Appalachia. He sought the links between this catastrophe and local social patterns, between people's biographies and Appalachian history.

After a year of study, Erikson concluded that the flood alone had not produced the "human wreckage" in Buffalo Creek. Rather, this sudden shock had brought to the surface a *chronic* (long-term) *condition* that had gathered force slowly and insidiously over generations. The troubles created by the flood were "small" compared with the underlying problems of Appalachia as a whole. Events of the past hundred years had undermined the mountain landscape and the moun-

In a school gymnasium, survivors of the Buffalo Creek flood sit waiting for help.

taineer's life style. Buffalo Creek and towns like it had been systematically stripped of both natural and human resources, leaving the people virtually defenseless.

The Depletion of Natural Resources

Erikson traced the depletion of natural resources back through history. The first European settlers of Appalachia found a rich forest covering mile after mile of rippling hills and valleys. In the eighteenth century, birches and willows lined the creek bank; great poplars and white oaks towered at the base of the hills; armies of hickories, beeches, and evergreen marched up the ridges (Cau-

dill, 1963, pp. 62–63). The forest was alive with bears, deer, and other wild game, rich with nuts and berries and honey for the gathering.

The early settlers cleared patches of forest for homesteads and fields but left much of the land untouched. The first attack on the environment began in the 1870s, with the nationwide lumber boom. Grateful for a little cash, homesteaders sold what they considered worthless timber to outside entrepreneurs. By 1925, 8.5 million acres of virgin forest in West Virginia alone had been stripped bare (Caudill, 1963, pp. 63–64). The rush for coal followed quickly on the heels of the lumber boom. For as little as fifty cents an acre, mining operators purchased the right to hollow out mountains; to take as much timber as they needed for construction; to dump wastes wherever they liked; to dam or divert streams (as in Buffalo Creek); and to "rearrange the lives of persons living on the surface" (Erikson, 1976, pp. 69–70). The final indignity, one that continues today, was strip mining: exposing surface veins of coal with bulldozers and explosives.

Little remains of Appalachia's once-rich natural resources. The landscape has been scarred beyond recognition. "[T]he blacks and grays and rusty reds of the underworld" streak the ridges; the debris of abandoned mining operations spills into the hollows "like ashes from long dead fires" (Erikson, 1976, p. 23). For local people, the exploitation of resources was a *man-made* disaster. Most of the profits from the century-long harvest went to outsiders. Timber and mining operations transformed a naturally rich environment into a lean and hazardous one, where crops refuse to grow and where flash floods and cave-ins are frequent events.

The Depletion of Human Resources

The depletion of natural resources was only part of the problem. The people of Appalachia had also been damaged. According to legend, the early settlers of Appalachia were a special breed — raw, adventuresome, independent men and women who spurned the gentility of town living. In this case, legend may be accurate (Erikson, 1976, pp. 51–78).

Life in Appalachia was hard in the early days. It took a great deal of physical courage and personal competence to hunt and farm the mountains. Families lived off by themselves, separated from other families by miles of steep, slippery trails. Each household had to do its own farming and hunting, carpentry and blacksmithing, weaving and preserving, doctoring and teaching. Each delivered its own justice. The mountaineer of yesterday was "a creature of action rather than contemplation" — famous for "his readiness to protect his home from marauders, his reputation from rivals, and his livelihood from such meddling outsiders as revenue [tax] agents" (Erikson, 1976, pp. 74, 85). The mountaineer of yesterday was self-reliant to a fault.

The spirit of these original settlers has all but disappeared (Weller, 1965, Chapter 3). Visitors take away from towns like Buffalo Creek today an impression of passivity, not assertiveness; dependency, not self-sufficiency; physical disability, not physical strength. Early in the century, the once-proud mountaineers became dependent on the coal companies. In the mining camps, they lived in company houses, bought their food, clothing, and tools from company stores. Their children were delivered by company doctors and taught by company teachers. When they died, they were buried by company undertakers and prayed for by company preachers. Over time, they lost the knowledge and the custom of doing for themselves.

Illness became a way of life in Appalachia. Many people suffered from diseases and injuries contracted in the mines (such as black lung disease). Many also had a variety of psychosomatic ailments — the result, they said, of "bad nerves." Illness provided a rationalization for living off welfare, as many had for generations. When asked what happened to the old mountaineers, local shopkeepers would say, "The welfare done got them all" (Peterson, 1972, p. 114). People in Buffalo Creek no longer felt in control of their own destinies. They knew the "dam" was dangerous, but what could they do? Events of the past century had taken the fight out of them. They lost not only their natural resources but much of their resourcefulness. This debilitation was the heart of the problem, as Erikson saw it. When disaster hit, people had little resistance. The flood had aggravated old injuries.

Identifying Social Issues and Social Problems

The kind of damage Erikson observed is not confined to Buffalo Creek and Appalachia. The same verbal expressions of hopelessness, the same vacant stares, can be found in migrant labor camps, in urban ghettos, in old people's homes, and on mental wards. Buffalo Creek is by no means the only community where mining or manufacturing has threatened people's health and safety. The depletion of natural resources and environmental deterioration are not only local or national problems but global ones. Buffalo Creek is an especially clear illustration of the historical roots of these conditions. To understand the "human wreckage" created by the flood, one must understand the impact of social forces, over time, on the community.

The reaction of Buffalo Creek people to the flood illustrates two overlapping concerns of this book: social issues and social problems. Before the flood, the problems in Buffalo Creek went largely unnoticed. Few Americans knew about conditions in Appalachia's coal-mining towns. The people of Buffalo Creek themselves had grown accustomed to the "dam" that loomed over their town. In this case, a catastrophe brought the situation to public attention.

Social Issues

One of the aims of this book is to explore how conditions that may have existed for some time come to be viewed as social issues. A *social issue* is a condition that captures public attention, generates public concern and controversy, and in some cases, leads to collective action. For a situation to become a social issue, people must believe that it can be changed. And to believe that a condition can be changed, they must see it as the product of human social behavior, not as inevitable. Similarly, to see a situation as *wrong,* people must feel that *rights* are being violated.

In other words, to qualify as social issues, "misfortunes" must be seen as "injustices" in the public mind. Poverty is a classic example. A century ago, most Americans considered poverty, like weather, one of the facts of life. That some people would work long hours at dangerous and degrading jobs, live in squalor, go hungry, and die early was thought inevitable. Poverty was attributed to God's will, lack of ambition, or simply "the breaks of the game." It was only when people began to view poverty as the product of a social system that distributes power and wealth unevenly that it became a social issue.*

Sudden and dramatic change contributes to the emergence of social issues. Chronic problems tend to fade into the background. Like the "dam" looming over Buffalo Creek, they become a fixed part of the social landscape. People know in the back of their minds that a problem exists, but they don't give much thought to it. They take the "dam" for granted. Often it requires a catastrophe—a dramatic event—to move such conditions into the spotlight of public attention. The flood at Buffalo Creek, the urban riots of the 1960s, the Arab oil embargo in the early 1970s are examples. In a vague way, people knew the United States was too dependent on foreign oil for safety, but they weren't overly concerned about it. When OPEC briefly turned off the spigot, the background problem of energy dependency became a social issue.

The identification of "villains" also contributes to the emergence of social issues. When people see a condition as the byproduct of routine, acceptable behavior, they are not likely to get excited about it. Few people are outraged by the annual death toll of 55,000 on U.S. highways, for example. (After all, nobody means to cause accidents.) When people see a condition as the result of deliberate, purposive behavior, they are more likely to demand that something be done. Thus, when the public found that the Buffalo Mining Company had ignored safety regulations, a tragedy became a social issue. When Arab leaders refused to ship oil to Israel's allies, energy dependency became a social issue.

Social issues are controversial, almost by definition. Public opinion is often divided, especially in a heterogeneous country like the United States. The values and interests of different segments of the population are frequently at odds. What conditions trouble people depend in part on where they stand in the social system. For example, from the point of view of blacks, women, and other minorities, the seniority system is unfair. It links job security and promotions to length of time on the job, and most minority members have only recently entered skilled, unionized occupations. From the point of view of white males, however, the seniority system is a basic working man's right, and affirmative action programs, which reserve space for qualified members of minority groups, violate that right. As this example suggests, "one group's solution is often another group's problem" (Merton and Nisbet, 1976, pp. 9–10).

---

*Of course, some segments of the American public still blame poverty on the poor or, if not on the poor, on a welfare system they believe encourages living off the dole.

Changing Public Perspectives

Since November, 1935, the Gallup Poll has queried Americans on the most important problem facing the people of this country. The phrasing of the question has varied slightly. Initially, it was: "What do you regard as the most vital issue before the American people today?" From 1939 on, the question always dealt with the "most important problem" facing Americans, with the typical form being: "What do you think is the most important problem facing this country today?" This open-ended question was asked of "a representative cross-section of the total United States adult, non-institutionalized population." I have tabulated the results of the poll for 1935 and each year thereafter in which the question was asked. Table 1 shows each problem which was named at least five times during the forty year period and the years in which it was named. There are a number of observations we can make from an examination of the table. First, although the number of problems identified varies from year to year (some of this, of course, is due to the omission from Table 1 of problems which were not mentioned in at least five different years), there has been almost continual expression of concern with some problems—war and peace and various economic matters. Second, some problems seem to be identified periodically—taxes, foreign policy, and the lack of religion and morality. Third, some problems appear to have a limited span during which they are identified. They may be transient concerns, such as concern with the atomic bomb from 1945 to 1956, or faddish concerns like that with Communism during certain periods. They may be basically resolved in the public eye—labor problems were identified almost continuously from 1935 to 1958, but have not been mentioned since. Finally, some problems emerge during the period and may either continue or, like labor problems, fade out of the public arena of concern. Thus, crime and delinquency and the race problem were first identified in the 1950s and poverty emerged in 1965; all have remained a public concern through the 1970s.

There appear then, to be at least three different patterns of public concern for social problems. Some problems are of more or less continual concern. Others appear periodically over time. And others have a natural history of emergence and disappearance. As we gather public opinion over a longer time span, of course, these patterns may prove to be somewhat different. . . .

Table 1 not only shows various patterns of public opinion about different problems, but also indicates the kinds of problems that are of concern. If we rank order the problems in terms of frequency of mention during the forty years, war and peace emerges as the greatest concern and farm problems as the least concern. There has been great concern with economic issues. In fact, we could summarize the results of the polls in the statement that the primary concerns over the forty year period have been economic and perceived threats to life and property.

Table 1
Social Problems as Identified by Public Opinion, 1935–1975

Years Problem Named

Problem	1935	1937	1939	1943	1945	1946	1947	1948	1949	1950	1951	1953	1954	1956	1957	1958	1959	1962	1963	1964	1965	1966	1967	1968	1969	1970	1971	1973	1975
1. War and peace (including neutrality)	X	X	X	X	X	X	X	X	X	X	X	X	X	X	X	X	X	X	X	X	X	X	X	X	X	X	X	X	X
2. The economy, including unemployment	X	X	X	X	X	X			X	X	X	X	X	X		X	X	X	X	X	X	X	X				X	X	X
3. High cost of living including inflation						X	X	X	X	X	X	X	X	X			X	X	X	X	X	X	X	X	X	X	X	X	X
4. Taxes	X	X	X	X		X			X	X	X	X					X	X			X								
5. Government spending	X	X	X	X						X	X																		
6. Labor problems	X	X	X	X	X	X	X	X	X	X	X		X	X		X		X											
7. Foreign policy						X	X	X		X		X		X				X	X	X							X	X	X
8. Communism						X	X	X	X			X	X					X	X										
9. Crime and delinquency												X		X	X	X		X			X			X	X	X	X	X	X
10. Civil rights and race											X		X	X	X	X	X	X	X	X	X	X	X	X	X	X	X	X	X
11. Farm problems	X	X										X		X	X														
12. The atomic bomb					X	X	X			X			X		X														
13. Lack of religion and morality	X		X								X				X					X	X					X		X	
14. Poverty																				X	X		X	X		X	X		

Source: Robert H. Lauer, "Defining Social Problems: Public and Professional Perspectives," *Social Problems,* Vol. 24 (October 1976), pp. 122–30.

Like the strip mine looming over this Virginia town, social problems may become so much a part of the landscape that people forget about them. Often it takes a disaster, like the flood at Buffalo Creek, to bring them into focus.

What becomes a social issue depends on public opinion. And public opinion depends, in large part, on second-hand information. People who have never been victims of violent crime, who know nothing about nuclear energy, who have never seen a pornographic film, nevertheless have opinions about these matters. Public evaluations of social conditions depend heavily on information acquired from the media. The media tend to represent special interests, often inadvertently. Certain individuals (for example, the President) appear in the media more often than others. Organized groups, such as labor unions or the National Organization for Women (NOW), are better able to capture media attention than are unorganized segments of the population—like the poor. Moreover, the manner in which the news is presented can create distorted impressions. For example, an eyewitness report on the robbery and beating of an elderly woman is likely to create the impression of a crime wave; an anchor man or woman's statement that the crime rate has dropped is likely to go unnoticed (Davis, 1952). The ebb and flow of public concern, the emergence and disappearance of social issues, is one theme in the chapters to come.

Social Problems

The second and central aim of this book is to examine social problems. A *social problem* is a social condition that has been found to be harmful to individual and/or societal well-being. It is a condition that originates in social behavior and that proves to have harmful consequences.

Social problems are not self-evident. To state that a specific phenomenon is a social problem is to imply that the existing situation violates an ideal state of affairs. For example, the statement that sexual inequality is a social problem is based on the assumption that in an ideal society all people would have equal dignity and opportunity, regardless of their sex. A vision of an ideal society serves as a measuring rod for assessing the status quo and deciding what is or is not a social problem. In other words, the identification of social problems necessarily involves making value judgments.

The values guiding the identification of social problems in this book are based on the Universal Declaration of Human Rights, adopted by the UN General Assembly in December 1948. In the words of Secretary General Kurt Waldheim, the Universal Declaration of Human Rights serves "as a moral imperative guiding the relationship between individuals and their Governments and as a bulwark safeguarding the human rights and fundamental freedoms and the inherent dignity of all members of the human family." Its adoption

in 1948 marked the first time that the world community agreed upon "a common standard of achievement for all peoples and all nations" (Waldheim, 1974, p. iii). (Excerpts on pp. 16–17.) We chose this statement of rights because it is accepted not only in the United States but throughout most of the world. Clearly, the Universal Declaration of Human Rights is utopian. No society, past or present, has lived up to this ideal. Nevertheless, it sets goals for the entire human family and provides a standard for assessing current social conditions.

How do we determine that universal rights have been violated, that a particular social relationship, behavior pattern, or institution is harmful? In this book we will rely on the best available scientific evidence. Scientists strive for a level of objectivity and universality that is often missing from public debate. Scientific investigation transfers such questions as "Is marijuana harmful?" from the realm of speculation into the realm of demonstration (Manis, 1976). Is marijuana addictive? Is it a health hazard? Does it interfere with a person's ability to function effectively in daily life? Does widespread use of marijuana threaten social relationships and institutions? If so, why? Similar questions can be asked about government corruption, crime in the streets, school busing to achieve integration, divorce, mandatory retirement at age seventy, and other social issues. Scientific investigation provides at least tentative answers.

Scientific research provides a guide for distinguishing between major and minor, serious and trivial problems. It directs attention to latent (or publicly unrecognized) problems, as well as to manifest (publicly recognized) problems that have become social issues (Merton and Nisbet, 1976, pp. 13–14). Whereas media reports on the Buffalo Creek flood blamed the mining company for the destruction of a community, Erikson's research uncovered an ongoing pattern of abuse and neglect of Appalachia's resources.

Excerpts from the
Universal Declaration of Human Rights

Article 1   All human beings are born free and equal in dignity and rights. They are endowed with reason and conscience and should act towards one another in a spirit of brotherhood.

Article 2   Everyone is entitled to all the rights and freedoms set forth in this Declaration, without distinction of any kind, such as race, colour, sex, language, religion, political or other opinion, national or social origin, property, birth or other status. . . .

Article 3   Everyone has the right to life, liberty and security of person.

Article 4   No one shall be held in slavery or servitude; slavery and the slave trade shall be prohibited in all their forms.

Article 5   No one shall be subjected to torture or to cruel, inhuman, or degrading treatment or punishment.

Article 6   Everyone has the right to recognition everywhere as a person before the law.

Article 9   No one shall be subjected to arbitrary arrest, detention or exile.

Article 12   No one shall be subjected to arbitrary interference with his privacy, family, home or correspondence, nor to attacks upon his honour and reputation. Everyone has the right to the protection of the law against such interference or attacks.

Article 13   1. Everyone has the right to freedom of movement and residence within the borders of each State. . . .

Article 16   1. Men and women of full age, without any limitation due to race, nationality or religion, have the right to marry and to found a family. They are entitled to equal rights as to marriage, during marriage and at its dissolution. . . .

Article 17   1. Everyone has the right to own property alone as well as in association with others. . . .

Article 19   Everyone has the right to freedom of opinion and expression; this right includes freedom to hold opinions without interference and to seek, receive and impart information and ideas through any media and regardless of frontiers.

Article 20   1. Everyone has the right to freedom of peaceful assembly and association. . . .

Article 22   Everyone, as a member of society, has the right to social security and is entitled to realization, through national effort and international co-operation and in accordance with the resources of each State, of the economic, social and cultural rights indispensable for his dignity and the free development of his personality.

Article 23   1. Everyone has the right to work, to free choice of employment, to just and favourable conditions of work and to protection against unemployment. . . .

Article 24   Everyone has the right to rest and leisure, including reasonable limitation of working hours and periodic holidays with pay.

Article 25   1. Everyone has the right to a standard of living adequate for the health and well-being of himself and of his family, including food, clothing, housing and medical care and necessary social services, and the right to security in the event of unemployment, sickness, disability, widowhood, old age or other lack of livelihood in circumstances beyond his control. . . .

Article 26   1. Everyone has the right to education. Education shall be free, at least in the elementary and fundamental stages. Elementary education shall be compulsory. Technical and professional education shall be made generally available and higher education shall be equally accessible to all on the basis of merit. . . .

Article 29   1. Everyone has duties to the community in which alone the free and full development of his personality is possible. . . .

Source: United Nations Resolutions, Series I, General Assembly VII, 1948–49, ed. and comp. Dusan J. Djonovich (Dobbs Ferry, N.Y.: Oceana Publications, Inc., 1973).

Research does not provide all the answers. Often, scientific opinion is divided. In some cases, different studies produce conflicting findings; in others, scientists interpret the same findings differently. Scientific opinion often changes in the light of new data and new theories. Moreover, in many cases, research is inconclusive. However — an important however — science is guided by techniques specially designed to minimize (if not eliminate) personal bias and to test and retest interpretations. In addition, scientists are responsible for making explicit the limitations of their research and the values that guide their interpretations. In this book we will follow the Universal Declaration of Human Rights, and we will point out when research is inconclusive or conflicting.

Connecting Social Issues and Social Problems

A third aim of this book is to show how social issues (conditions that capture public attention, generating controversy and concern) and social problems (conditions that cause demonstrable harm to individual and societal well-being) are intertwined.

Public opinion plays a key role in the natural history of social problems. If people do not see a problem, they are not likely to press for a solution. In some cases, failure to perceive a problem results in perpetuation of the problem. For example, in the years following World War II, the majority of American men and women subscribed to the ideal of the happy housewife. Most women sought fulfillment in marriage and motherhood, dismissing other ambitions as "unfeminine." Hardly anyone questioned the mutual dependency of husbands and wives on a strict division of labor and power within the family. Unrecognized and unlabeled, the discontent of many housewives was perpetuated.

Public opinion can also turn a minor problem into a major one, or even create a problem where none existed before. In other words, a social issue can become a *self-fulfilling prophecy* (Merton, 1968, Chapter 13). The classic illustration of this took place on Black Wednesday, the eve of the Great Depression. Rumors that banks were on the verge of collapse began to circulate. Acting on these rumors, people flocked to banks by the thousands to withdraw their money before it was too late. In fact, the banks were solvent that morning. But banks do not keep all deposits on hand, locked in vaults. They invest depositors' money, which is how accounts earn interest. The sudden, massive demand for cash caught banks unprepared; they did indeed collapse. Thus "the prophecy of collapse led to its own fulfillment." The study of social problems reveals numerous examples of *false* public perceptions evoking "new behavior which makes the originally false conception come *true*" (Merton, 1968, p. 477).

Finally, proposals to solve social problems depend in large part on public willingness to support collective action. For example, in *The Other America: Poverty in the United States* (1962), Michael Harrington had described Appalachia as "a reservation for the old, the apathetic, and the misfits" (p. 43). In 1966, geologists had singled out the "dam" above Buffalo Creek as being one of the most hazardous of the mine-waste dumps they had studied (Caudill, 1972, p. 16). But neither of these alerts stimulated public concern or action. The story of Buffalo Creek is a clear illustration of how public failure to perceive a problem may make it worse.

The Sociological Frame of Reference

Identifying social problems is the first step; explaining them is the second. Sociologists have developed a number of theories to explain how social problems develop. Each approaches social problems from a different perspective, yielding different explanations. However, all share a common frame of reference. Here we want to introduce a set of key concepts sociologists use to describe the social world and to capture important notions about the nature of social life.

Culture

Virtually everything human beings learn to think and do has cultural underpinnings: how people walk and talk; how they sit and what they sit on; what kind of work they do and how they feel about it; when they play and when they go to war; what makes them laugh or cry or scream; the conditions under which they are born and die; what life and death mean to them. Thus, the term *culture* refers, broadly, to a people's way of life.

People tend to take their own culture for granted, as an expression of human nature. In reality, culture is learned. It is the product of human traditions, imaginings, and innovations, passed from one generation to the next. What one group of people considers "only natural" (eating with utensils, or marrying for love), another may find unthinkable. *Cross-cultural variations* are differences between one society and another. *Subcultures* (such as the Appalachian mountaineer's traditional way of life) are variations on the central themes of a culture that make certain ethnic, religious, regional, or even occupational groups in a society distinctive.

Culture includes both material and nonmaterial elements. The term *material culture* refers to the things people make: pots, plows, clothes, toys, missiles, houses, cathedrals, factories, satellites, saxophones. A people's material culture depends on their technology—on the way they apply what they know to what is available in the natural environment. The term *nonmaterial culture* refers to a people's intangible creations: ideas, beliefs, and values. Values—shared, general notions about what is good and bad, desirable and undesirable—are the heart of nonmaterial culture. They suggest what goals in life are worth pursuing.

The Social System

Institutions are structures that develop to organize important activities in ways that uphold cultural values. (Basic institutions are the economic and political systems, education, religion, and the family.) Institutions translate culture into a social system: an overall blueprint for social relationships and behavior, a society.

A society's institutions establish and maintain shared standards of conduct, rules for what people should and should not think, say, or do in a particular kind of situation. These standards, or *norms*, set forth the legitimate means for pursuing cultural goals. They indicate what we have a right to expect from others, and what others have a right to expect from us. (For example, traditional Appalachian norms said a person should stand up for his or her kin, no matter what.) *Sanctions* are social rewards for abiding by norms and punishments for violating them. Sanctions may be formal (a promotion at work, a prison sentence) or informal (a smile and a pat on the back, a stare and a cold shoulder).

Norms vary not only with the situation (a party or a funeral) but from one person to another. Different norms, and different sanctions, apply to different kinds of people. For example, a man who "cries like a baby" is likely to be ridiculed in American society. A child may be punished for behavior that is considered normal for adults (for example, sexual activity). And while this society's norms support spanking a child, hitting an adult is considered "assault." Why? Because of their different positions in society.

The Individual in Society

Sociologists use the term *position* (or *status*) to refer to the place individuals occupy in society. A position in the social system is something like a position on a baseball team: The catcher has one set of responsibilities; the pitcher, another; the outfielders, still others. Knowing a player's position enables people to predict where that player will be and what actions he or she will take as the game progresses. Moreover, people can make these predictions no matter who (Tom, Dick, or Harry) is playing the position. In much the same way, knowing that an individual is ten years old or forty, a doctor or a rock star, a bachelor or a husband, enables people to predict something about his or her behavior—whatever the person's individual characteristics. And knowing your position tells you what people in other positions expect from you and what you can expect from them. The term *role* describes the set of rights, duties, and expectations that accompany a given position in the social structure. There are, of course, important differences between a game of baseball and the "game of life." In life, the rules are subtler; only some are written down in the form of laws. A person occupies a number of different positions at the same time (for example, female, black, mother, teacher). People change positions: A student becomes a worker; a husband becomes a widower. And the game never stops.

How do people learn to play their roles? Through socialization. *Socialization* is the process of social interaction that immerses individuals in their culture and locates them in the social structure. It is through socialization that individuals acquire values, a set of inhibitions that limit their behavior from the inside, knowledge of the rules and the roles that control behavior from the outside, and a sense of self in relation to others. Families, schoolmates, teachers, the media, bosses and co-workers, spouses and children, all contribute to socialization. The process begins at birth and continues throughout life, shaping and reshaping the individual's identity and behavior.

In attempting to explain social problems, sociologists draw on all of the concepts above. To understand the problem in Buffalo Creek, one has to understand the Appalachian subculture, set against the backdrop of American culture as a whole; the structure of American society and the structure of life in the mountains; and how socialization impresses values, norms, and roles on the individual.

Explaining Social Problems: Theoretical Approaches

Within the broad framework just described, there are a number of theoretical approaches to the explanation of social problems (see Rubington and Weinberg, 1977, Chapter 1). *Theories* are sets of tentative explanations that also act as guidelines for research. They suggest where to look for answers, what to consider, and what to ignore. Where researchers look determines in part what they find. Hence, different theoretical approaches lead to different conclusions, though not necessarily conflicting ones. Here we will examine the contributions of three leading approaches— social disorganization, conflict, and deviance theory—to an understanding of the problems of Appalachia.

Social Disorganization: Yesterday's People

The term *social disorganization* refers to "inadequacies in a social system that keep people's collective and individual purposes from being as fully realized as they could be" (Merton and Nisbet, 1976, p. 26). Theories of social disorganization focus on the workings of the social system. There are a number of variations to this approach (see Rubington and Weinberg, 1977, Chapter 3). One central theme is that social change may lead to a breakdown in traditional norms for regulating behavior. Situations arise for which there are no norms, or people are caught between conflicting norms, or conformity to norms fails to produce expected rewards. Two classic sociological concepts, cultural lag and alienation, shed light on such situations.

Cultural lag Cultural change is rarely steady and systematic. Often one element of culture changes faster than others, throwing the whole system out of phase. As a rule, people are more willing to accept new tools than they are to embrace new ideas. Hence, material culture often leaps ahead of nonmaterial culture. William Ogburn (1922, pp. 199–280) coined the term *cultural lag* to describe situations in which changes in norms and values trail behind changes in technology.

Cultural lag played a central role in the problems of Appalachia. The flow of settlers to the mountains virtually stopped after the Civil War. Visitors from abroad were startled to find Appalachians still living a rugged, pioneer life in the late nineteenth century. Here "in the heart of the bustling, money-making, novelty-loving United States" were people who had never seen a steamship or a railroad and who had rarely seen a dollar bill (Semple in Erikson, 1976, p. 34). To call the mountaineers a living relic of the past was only a slight exaggeration. Time seemed to have passed them by.

Well into the twentieth century, the mountain economy was a subsistence economy: Families produced most of what they needed for themselves and bartered for a few extras. The opening of the coal mines in the 1910s and 1920s brought sudden and uneven change to Appalachia. Almost overnight, a mountaineer became a miner. Working in the mines meant working for wages, and Appalachians had little experience with cash. The mountaineer who moved from a cabin on a ridge to a shack in the camps

> had not realized that he would have to buy all his food. A garden and cornfield had always seemed to him an inseparable part of a house. [In the camp] his cow starves as she roams at large. Milk and butter

> had heretofore seemed almost a part of the landscape. He can keep no bees for the honey. There is no acorn or hickory mast for his hog. . . ." (Raine, 1924, pp. 236–37)

The mountaineers had no norms for handling money (or, for that matter, handling next-door neighbors). They learned quickly that money can be converted into material goods—and that they weren't making very much. But to this day, many haven't developed a "feel" for money. Its more abstract, long-term uses—saving to purchase a secure future, investing money so that it grows—still elude them. Lawyers who came to Buffalo Creek after the flood found it hard to believe that survivors had had four or five television sets in a two-room shack, maybe $40,000 in the trunk of a car.

Nothing in the mountaineers' background prepared them for life in the coal camps. In a sense, their traditions made them willing participants in their own exploitation. We will say more about this in the section on conflict theory. Here we want to consider what happened to the mountaineers' inner lives—that is, to show the connection between social problems and private troubles.

Alienation According to theories of social disorganization, one common response to cultural lag is *alienation:* the sense that one is separated from the society around one. Alienated people feel that they can no longer predict the consequences of their behavior, that what they do or do not do is of little consequence, that they are strangers (aliens) in places and among people who should be familiar, perhaps that they are strangers to themselves. The term alienation is often used to describe the effect of routine, mindless, assembly-line jobs on workers and the effect of the anonymity of life in big cities on their residents. The term also applies to Appalachian mountaineers.

Well into the twentieth century, the main institution in the mountains was the family (Erikson,

1976, pp. 58–59). Each household (typically a couple, ten or twelve children, and one or two aging parents) was "a community unto itself." The family was the only source of social support and identity a person had. There were no public institutions in the mountains—no townships, no lodges or clubs, and few stable religious congregations. The mountaineers were religious folk, but their "convictions were episodic." They would go to meetings one week, spend the next week drinking and dancing and loving, in a cycle of "backsliding and revival" (Erikson, 1976, p. 62). Although extremely fond of the spoken word and great admirers of oratory, the majority of mountaineers were illiterate. (In 1928, one county in Kentucky with a population of 35,000 produced fewer than 100 high school graduates [Caudill, 1963, p. 131].) Formal education had few applications in the mountains. The knowledge needed to hunt and farm the hollows was "born of time and experience," and passed from mother to daughter, father to son. In short, the family was everything to mountaineers: the main source of companionship and partnerships, the only government, church, and school.

Families who had lived off by themselves for generations were wedged tightly together in the coal camps. Too late, they discovered they couldn't go back. Some had signed the rights to their land over to coal companies; others found their old fields and hunting grounds spoiled by mine wastes. With no education or industrial skills, they couldn't move on. In the coal camps how well parents provided for their children depended on the boss, not on their own initiative. Old talents and skills were useless. They couldn't teach their children how to deal with a system they didn't understand themselves. After a fight, men couldn't go their separate ways as before; they had to see each other the next day. Company guards, pastors, and teachers set the rules and enforced them. The strange new world of the mining towns left the mountain people feeling "that the

world operates by a logic alien to their own instincts" (Erikson, 1976, p. 257).

Among mountaineers, alienation took the form of extreme fatalism: accepting whatever happened, good or bad, as somehow inevitable. Fatalism acts as a buffer against disappointments. It allows people to go on thinking that their way of life (their cultural tradition) is fundamentally right, even when nothing seems to go as it should (Weller, 1965, p. 37). Fatalism may protect people from hoping for too much and being disappointed. It may also prevent them from taking action on their own behalf (in Buffalo Creek, from protesting the dangerous dumping of wastes).

In short, the structure of the mining camps made it all but impossible for mountaineers to pursue their collective and individual goals in the ways to which they were accustomed and which they believed to be right. Brought into sudden contact with the industrial world, a traditional culture virtually collapsed—as has happened in many parts of the world. In the camps, mountaineers occupied social positions they could never have imagined; familiar social roles became obsolete; their norms and values applied to a quite different way of life. It was as if they had learned the parts and memorized the lines for one play and found themselves on stage in another play.

Conflict Theory: Black Gold

The view that social problems result from social disorganization rests on certain assumptions about society (Antonio, 1975, pp. 1–12). First, social and individual well-being depends on a degree of consensus, or agreement, about what constitutes right and wrong behavior. People must agree at least on the way things *should* be. No matter what position people occupy in the social structure, all have a set of common, basic, interests. Bankers, bricklayers, and beauticians all have a stake in the smooth functioning of the system. Given these assumptions, a breakdown in social order by definition creates social problems.

The conflict perspective rests on a different set of assumptions. According to this view, the positions people occupy in the social structure cause them to see things quite differently. People in equivalent positions may have similar ideas about the way things should be. But except in very small, traditional societies, a high degree of consensus is rare. Social problems arise from conflicts of interest. They arise from the efforts of those in power to impose on others the definitions of right and wrong that further their own interests.

From the conflict perspective, breakdowns in social order are not the only, or the main, cause of social problems. Indeed, the smooth functioning of the system may create problems. Some conflict theorists argue, for example, that poverty is a necessary part of a capitalist economic system, that it results from the normal functioning of such a system. Breaks with the normal order may be the solution, not the problem. The civil disobedience of black Americans who protested racial segregation laws in the 1950s and 1960s is an example. Of course, not everyone would agree that this was a solution—which is precisely the point being made by conflict theorists. They maintain that people's ideological positions on social problems and social issues are derived from their positions in the social system.

Karl Marx was by far the most influential conflict theorist. Marx was interested in the broad, historical dimensions of social problems— in social problems writ large (see Sprey, 1969; Coser, 1971, pp. 43–57; Duke, 1976, Chapter 2). Three propositions guide the Marxist view of social problems. First, in the words of Marx and his colleague Friedrich Engels, "The history of all hitherto existing societies is the history of class struggles." A *class* is a category of people who occupy similar positions in the social system and have similar economic, political, and cultural characteristics. Different classes have different access to power and resources. In every age, separate and opposing economic interests have led to class conflict. "Freeman and slave, patrician and plebian, lord and serf, guildmaster and journeyman, in a word, oppressor and oppressed stood in constant opposition to one another, carried on an uninterrupted, now hidden, now open fight...."

Second, human societies function under conditions of perpetual scarcity. No society has ever succeeded in meeting the material needs of all of its members, so that everyone could live comfortably. Even if a society did succeed, there are few limits to human ambition. Some groups would try to gain control of more than their economic share. Each group would work to further its own interests at the expense of other groups. Confrontations over scarce resources, controversial means, and incompatible goals are inevitable and continuous.

Third, when one group succeeds in gaining control over resources and, thereby, over social and political power, it tends to use that power in an exploitative way, taking advantage of those with less power to further its own goals. In so doing, Marx argued, the ruling class sows the seeds of its own destruction. Given time, given leaders to make them conscious of their exploitation and of new productive possibilities, the exploited class rebels.

As this brief summary suggests, Marx's interpretation of history was materialistic. He believed that material conditions and the relationships people establish in pursuit of a livelihood shape both history and personal experience. Individuals are assigned to a particular class at birth. This position shapes their opportunities and predisposes them to certain kinds of behavior, whether they realize it or not. Further, Marx argued that different technologies produce different kinds of social relationships. Being a modern factory worker is qualitatively different from being a medieval serf. In modern capitalist societies, according to Marx, those who control the means of production (especially the factories) control the social and political machinery as well. In theory, workers are free to sell or not sell their labor. In practice, they have no choice. Marx also argued that industrialization produces a special form of alienation. In feudal societies, peasants may have little control over their economic situation, but they can take pride in what they produce. They work with their hands and see what they produce with their own eyes. They feel an identity with their neighbors; they know their lord by sight. Not so in industrial societies. According to Marx, the modern worker is alienated not just psychologically but literally — "from the object he produces, from the process of production, from himself, and from the community of his fellows" (in Coser, 1977, p. 51).

The conflict perspective, with its emphasis on opposing interests arising from different economic positions, adds a new dimension to an understanding of the problems of Buffalo Creek. Technically, the mountaineers owned all the coal in Appalachia. It was their land. But the mountaineers did not own the means of production; they did not have the capital and technology to exploit this natural resource. Power passed to those who did. In the 1880s, when gentlemen from the Northeast began appearing at the remotest cabins, the mountaineers welcomed the chance to sit and rest and talk a spell. As the afternoon drawled on, the visitors explained that they hadn't come to buy land. They only wanted to purchase the mineral rights — leaving mountaineers the illusion of ownership, as well as responsibility for taxes. Fifty cents an acre seemed more than fair. Thousands of short forms granting "the usual and ordinary mining rights and privileges" were signed by men who could barely scrawl an X. Years passed before they discovered that the "usual and ordinary rights" meant not only the right to mine but the right to take timber, divert streams, and spill wastes wherever it was convenient. By 1910, close to 85 percent of the mineral rights in Appalachia had been bought up by outsiders. The railroads, which would bring mining technology into the hills and take "black gold" out, were almost completed.

From the beginning, mine owners used their economic advantage to gain social and political control. The mine companies ran the coal camps like medieval fiefdoms. In some cases, they obtained municipal charters and incorporated towns, handpicking the mayor, judges, and other officials. (Having no experience with local government, miners left politics to the bosses.) Elsewhere, they simply hired private guards to provide company-style law and order. Employees were required to live in company houses, for a monthly rent. The company provided stores, doctors, recreation, even burial — profiting from each service. Most of what miners earned went back into company pockets. In some cases, mine companies even produced their own currency — "scrip," or coupons, which were issued as credit on future wages and could be used only in company stores. Miners were encouraged to go into debt so that they couldn't quit if they wanted to (Caudill, 1963, Chapter 10). In the camps as in the hollows, they were isolated from national political and economic currents. In effect, Appalachia was a colonial territory, run by outsiders.

From the Marxist point of view, the companies treated the mountaineers as they treated the mountain — ruthlessly exploiting both. The camps consisted of tight rows of hastily built shacks with crude outhouses. In no time, rain turned the "streets" into hog wallows. Flies multiplied in garbage that piled up behind the shacks. The streams reeked of raw sewage. The air was thick with coal dust. The smell of danger mingled with these human and animal odors (Erikson, 1976, p. 96). Mining was and is an exceedingly hazardous occupation. Since the turn of the century, hundreds of thousands of men have died in the mines and millions more have been incapacitated

(Barnet, 1980). Miners are buried alive by roof falls. Coal dust is highly combustible. Without warning, a spark can set a chain of explosions booming through underground corridors. In some areas, pockets of methane gas are locked in the coal. Long-term exposure to small amounts causes the nervous system to degenerate, causing twitches in the limbs, distorted spasms in the face muscles, and unemployment (Caudill, 1963, Chapter 10). A host of respiratory ailments afflict miners. An estimated 17 out of every 100 die of black lung disease (silicosis) (Barnet, 1980, pp. 62–63). In the early days of coal mining, these deaths were attributed to "natural" causes. People would say of a man, "He just ran out of air" (Erikson, 1976, p. 98). Miners injured on the job were sometimes given a month to clear out; sometimes not.

For most intents and purposes, there were only two classes in Appalachia: the oppressors and the oppressed. As predicted by conflict theory, the miners eventually did rebel. At first, however, the idea of organizing to demand better working and living conditions and higher wages ran counter to the mountain tradition of each man looking out for himself. Individual miners might resist, but they did not fight the company as a group. Union organizers came from the outside and at first found an indifferent audience. If they made a few converts in one camp, they had to start over at the next, with companies threatening to fire and blacklist anyone caught talking to union men. In the 1920s, the price of coal began to drop, pulling miners' wages down with it. Increasing numbers of miners slipped out of the camps at night for secret meetings, swearing blood oaths to the union (Caudill, 1963, Chapter 14). A protest march turned into a full-scale battle on Blair Mountain, near Buffalo Creek. Miners armed with hunting rifles and weapons from World War I dug in on one side; Sheriff Don Chafin and an army of deputies, on the other. Chafin hired two airplanes to drop pamphlets—and small bombs—on

The political struggle in the mines continues today. Here, miners protest 1981 proposals to lower benefits for victims of black lung disease. "With this black lung," a veteran miner explains, "you smother continually, twenty-four hours a day, seven days a week" (in Erikson, 1976, p. 98).

the miners. Before federal troops restored order, forty-seven men had been killed and hundreds wounded (Erikson, 1976, pp. 120–22). Far from disarming the union drive, such violent reprisals increased miner solidarity. By the mid-1930s, most Appalachian coal companies had either signed union contracts or gone out of business.

In a sense, though, miners won the battle but lost the war. In the late 1940s and the 1950s, American industry began converting to oil and gas, which at that time were cheap and readily available. Automation hit the mines in the 1950s, cutting labor requirements by half. When old mines began running out of coal in the 1960s, companies turned to strip mining, which requires only a few men and machines for large-scale operations. New industry did not replace the mines. Instead, welfare became one of the major industries and "employers" in the area. According to conflict theory, the whole range of social problems in Appalachia and Buffalo Creek can be traced to the clash of different groups pursuing their economic self-interest.

Deviance and Moonshine

A third perspective on social problems focuses on behavior. It is concerned, not with the structure and workings of society or with the broad sweep of history, but with how people act and why. *Deviance* is behavior that does not conform to norms and evokes social disapproval. It is behavior that people consider odd, "sick," wrong, threatening. Deviance is relative. What is and is not thought deviant changes over time, varies from society to society and from group to group within a society, and changes according to the situation. Deviance often becomes a social issue, inspiring public controversy and concern. But, in and of itself, the violation of norms is not necessarily a social problem. It depends on the consequences. In some cases (for example, rape), deviance does indeed cause harm. In other cases, however, deviance can be seen as a useful and healthy adaptation. It is more a solution than a problem. (The Civil Rights and Women's Movements, both of which were considered deviant in their early days, are examples.) And in some cases, the fact that people consider behavior deviant (not the behavior itself) creates problems

where none existed or exacerbates minor problems.

Consider the history of moonshine in Appalachia. In the 1920s, during Prohibition, Appalachia was famous for moonshine (homemade corn whiskey) and mayhem (lawlessness) (Caudill, 1963, Chapter 12). The goings-on in these remote mountain hollows were a social issue (just as the sale of marijuana is an issue today). Why did the mountaineers defy the law? Was moonshine a problem or a solution in Appalachia?

Learning theory Common wisdom suggests that there is "something wrong" with people who commit crimes, take drugs, or engage in other forms of deviance, that these people have not been socialized properly. Sociologists take the opposite position: They maintain that deviance usually is a product of socialization, that people learn unconventional behavior in the same way they learn conventional behavior.

Whiskey played a central role in Appalachian traditions. The rules of hospitality said that when someone came to call, the first thing you did was bring out the whiskey. At prayer meetings, people would leave a jar of "spirits" next to the water bucket for the preacher's refreshment (Caudill, 1963, pp. 157–58). Appalachians used whiskey as an all-purpose medicine, much as we use aspirin today. And they made their own, just as they built their own houses, grew their own food, sewed their own clothes. Mountain youngsters grew up watching their mothers pass the jug, following their fathers to the stills, listening to tales of their grandfathers outwitting the law, and dreaming of the day when they would be adults and participate in these honored rituals. Like other elements of culture, making and drinking whiskey seemed "only natural."

According to one view, deviance reflects *differential association* (Sutherland and Cressey, 1966). People adopt deviant values, norms, and roles when their exposure to nonconforming behavior outweighs their exposure to conforming behavior. Their behavior depends on the people with whom they associate and what kind of behavior those people admire and reward.

Opportunity structures Differential association explains *how* people learn to violate norms. The next question is *why*. In "Social Structure and Anomie" (1968, Chapter 6), Robert Merton suggests that the same values that induce most people to conform lead some people to deviate from norms. Which path people choose depends on opportunities. Merton reasons as follows.

Culture defines the goals of life, the things "worth striving for." Culture also establishes legitimate means of working toward those goals. Ideally, the social structure provides ample opportunities for people to realize cultural goals by approved means, what is called the "opportunity structure." However, in some cases, culture and the social structure work at cross-purposes. For example, American culture defines the accumulation of wealth as something "worth striving for." Opportunities for achieving financial success by legitimate means are limited, however. Accepted routes to success are closed to large segments of the population. People feel playing by the rules won't get them anywhere.* The result is *anomie,* or a breakdown in the norms regulating behavior. People feel no obligation or reason to obey the rules. At the social level, anomie causes confusion; at the individual level, it causes feelings of anxiety, isolation, and purposelessness (Merton, 1968, pp. 215–19). Continuity with the past seems broken. "Doing the right thing" does not produce the expected results.

Merton identifies five adaptations to anomie

---

* The same thing would be true if a culture defined artistic creativity, scientific achievements, or religious orthodoxy as paramount goals, and legitimate means of achieving these goals were limited.

(see Figure 1–1): conformity, innovation, ritualism, retreatism, and rebellion. Appalachian moonshiners were innovators on this scale. They accepted the all-American dream of monetary success, but lacking access to legitimate opportunities, they improvised. The soil in the mountains was too thin to grow anything but corn and vegetables for their own use. A man could search the hills for wild plants to sell, float logs downstream, or drive a few cattle down steep trails to a railroad stop. But the risks were high and the profits small. The one thing mountaineers could produce and transport to market for a profit was corn whiskey. For a time, whiskey was their only cash crop (Erikson, 1976, pp. 67–68). Moonshine was a solution to their problems. The fact that whiskey was outlawed by the Volstead Act didn't stop these innovators. In the words of one man, "If it's my corn I've got a right to eat it and I've got a right to drink it and damn the man that says I can't sell it if somebody wants to buy it" (Caudill, 1963, p. 157).

The sociologists Richard Cloward and Lloyd Ohlin (1960) add an interesting twist to Merton's theory. Whether people conform, innovate, or adapt to anomie in some other way, they argue, depends on the availability of *illegitimate opportunities*. Breaking the law doesn't come naturally. It takes skill, contacts, and a market for illegal products or services. And illegitimate opportunities are as unevenly distributed as legitimate opportunities in American society. Many people conform because they lack opportunities to violate norms profitably. (Put another way, deviance is a matter of *differential opportunities*.) By creating a black market for whiskey, Prohibition gave the mountaineers the opportunity to turn private skills into a profitable industry.

Labeling Labeling theory approaches deviance from a rather different angle. Labeling theorists are as interested in the behavior of people who create and enforce norms as they are in the be-

Figure 1-1
Modes of Individual Adaptation

Modes of Adaptation	Culture Goals	Institutionalized Means
Conformity	+	+
Innovation	+	−
Ritualism	−	+
Retreatism	−	−
Rebellion	±	±

Conformists strive to achieve the goals culture defines as desirable by legitimate means, even against the odds.

Innovators are dedicated to the pursuit of culturally defined goals but are willing to use illegitimate means of pursuing them—to break the law, cheat, cut corners, and so on.

Ritualists put all of their energy into abiding by the rules and lose sight of the ultimate goals of their behavior in the process.

Retreatists see little value in the goals culture prizes and pay little attention to legitimate means of striving toward them. They have given up. [Merton cites "psychotics, autists, pariahs, outcasts, vagrants, vagabonds, tramps, chronic drunkards, and drug addicts" as examples. (p. 207)]

Rebels reject culturally established goals and means, substituting new ambitions and new means of achieving them. They seek to change both the culture and the social structure.

Source: Robert K. Merton, *Social Theory and Social Structure,* enlarged ed. (New York: The Free Press, 1968) p. 194.

havior of people who violate them. From this perspective, the central questions are: Why are certain behavior patterns labeled as deviant? Why are certain individuals labeled as deviant? What are the consequences?

According to this view, deviance is in the eye of the beholder. In Howard Becker's words, *"social groups create deviance by making the rules whose infraction constitutes deviance,* and by applying these rules to particular people and labeling them as outsiders" (1963, p. 9). Ideas about what is and is not deviant change over time, as the passage and later repeal of Prohibition illustrates. Moreover, enforcement of norms varies. Everyone breaks the rules on occasion, but only some people are caught and publicly labeled as deviant.

Why does making and drinking whiskey (or any other form of behavior) come to be seen as

In breaking the law during Prohibition, Appalachian moonshiners honored two old American traditions: private enterprise and resisting government interference. Below, a government official destroys a mountain still. Elsewhere in the nation, flouting the law became highly fashionable; the flapper at right conceals a tiny flask of liquor in her garter.

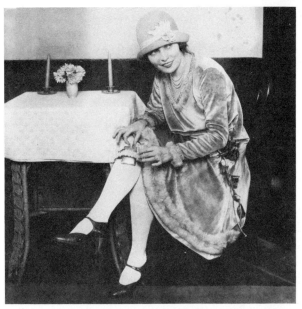

deviant? Labeling theorists answer that it is because someone, or some group, makes it their business to see that the public becomes alarmed and that rules are established and enforced. Becker refers to such people as *moral entrepreneurs*. The women and men who actively and adamantly fought for Prohibition are examples. In most cases, moral entrepreneurs have something to gain from putting other people down. At the very least, moral crusades employ law or norm enforcers (soldiers and saints in the Middle Ages; police, social workers, and others today).

Deviance theorists suggest that whether or not a person has actually violated norms, whether or not the act harmed anyone, being branded as deviant has serious consequences for a person's self-image and further social participation. Someone who has been publicly labeled a "dope fiend," a "whore," or a "lunatic" may be treated accordingly. Respectable people prefer not to associate with them. A deviant label tends to create a *master position* (or master status) that overrides everything else the person is or does (Hughes, 1945). Moonshiners were labeled as criminals. They had shown themselves to be the kind of people who have no respect for the law. That they believed in God, helped their neighbors without being asked, loved their children were discounted.

Labeling can become a self-fulfilling prophecy. For example, a man who has been convicted of crime and sent to prison may find, on release, that he cannot get a regular job. No one wants to hire a "known criminal." Unable to get a job, he may return to crime, embarking on a *deviant career*. Thus the response to nonconforming behavior may turn primary deviance (the original violation of norms) into secondary deviance (the adoption and elaboration of a deviant role) (Lemert, 1972). In other words, labeling behavior as deviant may create a social problem.

The mountaineers bitterly resented being labeled as criminals for making whiskey. As they saw it, Prohibition established a double standard.

If people were so against whiskey, why did they buy it? Moonshiners were fined, arrested, and not infrequently, shot when they tried to resist arrest or the destruction of their stills. In contrast, most people caught drinking moonshine in big city speak-easies were simply sent home. To some extent, labeling Appalachian distillers as "deviant" did become a self-fulfilling prophecy. One student of the region believes Prohibition created an abiding distrust of government, a conviction among the mountaineers that all public officials are dishonest and hypocritical. In using deception to obtain welfare payments later in the century, many felt they were only using the government the way the government had used them (Caudill, 1963, p. 164).

The three theoretical approaches presented here focus on different social processes and thus offer different perspectives on the origins of social problems. Deviance emphasizes patterns of individual behavior; conflict, clashes among groups with different interests and goals and unequal power; social disorganization, the working of the social system and the effects of change. No single approach can account for the range of social problems and social issues we will examine in this book. In some cases, one theoretical perspective is particularly useful. In other cases, a full understanding depends on all three.

Social Problems in the 1980s

In the 1980s, faith in the nation's ability to solve its problems, hope for effective government action, the conviction that progress is guaranteed — all seem to have faded. Is this because the problems Americans face are more complex today than they were in the past? Or because Americans are more aware of the complexity of social problems? The answer is probably both.

In 1788, the year the Constitution was ratified, the population of the United States was about 4 million—less than half the number of people who live in New York City today. There were only two American cities whose entire populations would not have fit comfortably into Yankee Stadium. The majority of Americans lived on the farm and rarely traveled farther than the nearest church or general store. They rarely met a stranger. New products and scientific breakthroughs were even rarer than strangers. The pace of life and the rate of change were leisurely. Social problems were largely local problems.

The rate of change accelerated over the years, until change became a way of life. Americans expect tomorrow to be different from today. Advancing technology is one obvious reason. Technological change not only alters the way people work, it affects the way they relate to one another and think about themselves and the world. For example, television made mass communication possible. The same images were beamed into thousands, then millions of homes every night. In a sense, television made the world smaller. In a few years, however, many Americans will be able to choose their own television shows from a stack of video cassettes, some bought, some homemade. The "mass culture" of the 1950s and 1960s may fade into the past (see Toffler, 1980). Advancing technology multiplies our options and, hence, the decisions we must make. The accelerating rate of change adds to the bewildering complexity of modern times.

The wave of change that hit Appalachia at the turn of the century has affected nearly everyone on earth. Only a few, remote societies lead independent lives today. Nations are more interdependent, and the world is more complicated than it was in 1900, or even in 1950 (see Chirot, 1977, Chapter 1). In 1900, Europeans and their descendants in the United States directly or indirectly controlled most of the earth. One could speak of a global division of labor. The rich, industrialized nations acted as an "international upper class"; the poor, underdeveloped nations, as an "international lower class," supplying cheap labor. Although there are still rich and poor nations, no one bloc rules the world, or even a large part of the world. In a sense, the number of "middle-class nations" has increased, as has their power in international affairs. For example, the price OPEC nations set for a barrel of oil has direct and immediate impact on U.S. and other economies. The future of so-called superpowers depends heavily on their relations with middle-range powers. Both the level of global interdependence and awareness of global interdependence have increased.

Many of today's social problems are global in scale. The case history of Buffalo Creek illustrated this. By contemporary standards, Buffalo Creek is small (5,000 inhabitants) and remote, but it is very much part of the world system. Nearly everyone in town works in the mines or for shops, clinics, and other establishments that serve miners. Hence, their economic situation depends on world patterns of energy use. Coal acquired a dirty reputation in the years following World War II. Mining coal is dangerous to miners and to people who live in the scarred environment around the mines. Burning coal pollutes the air, damaging the health of people who live nowhere near the mines. Oil is much cleaner. However, with the price of oil so high, the cost of cleaning up coal to meet environmental standards seems less prohibitive. Interest in coal is reviving in the 1980s. Indeed, multinational oil companies (Gulf, Exxon, Standard) have been quietly acquiring coal companies and mineral rights (Barnet, 1980). With some of the largest coal deposits in the world, the United States might become a leading exporter of energy—"the Saudia Arabia of coal"—in future decades. How this will affect Buffalo Creek is difficult to predict. The point is that the day Appalachian mountaineers went to work in the mines, their fortunes were tied to work markets and political contests well beyond their control.

Looking Back—25 Years of Social Problems Research

Twenty-five or so years ago, most social problems research was narrowly focused and essentially descriptive. Studies were addressed to assessing the psychological or, sometimes, biological functioning of individuals in some narrowly-defined segment of the population—for example, prisoners, treated addicts, mental patients, "bigoted" whites, or "typical" adult men and women. Findings from such research were often generalized uncritically to a much more heterogeneous population—criminals, drug users, the mentally disturbed, all prejudiced persons, or in the case of sex-role differentiation, humankind. . . .

There has been a dramatic enlargement of perspective in the past few years, not in all research, but certainly in the leading research on social problems. Recent studies explicitly recognize the complex interrelationship of individual, situational field, and broader social structure. And recent research has begun to pay attention to processes of social change. These developments can be illustrated in virtually all fields of social problems research; here are some important examples:

Sex-Role Differentiation

Despite a few notable early studies of cultural variations in sex-role differentiation, the modal work on sex roles of 25 years ago described psychological differences between American males and females, generally students, as evidenced in tests and in experimental situations. The subjects were almost always white and middle class. . . . When these studies dealt with behavior in natural settings, the focus was almost invariably on one institution, the family. . . .

. . . Research on sex roles now includes the analysis of sex-role differentiation and of sexual stratification not only in the family, but also in other spheres of life, notably the occupational, the educational, the political, and the recreational. Description of existing differences in sex roles in middle-class America has turned into comparative study—across cultures, social structures, and historical epochs—of the many arrangements known in human societies. . . .

Source: Melvin L. Kohn, "Looking Back—A 25-Year Review and Appraisal of Social Problems Research," *Social Problems*, Vol. 24, No. 1 (October 1976), pp. 94–112.

Race Relations

. . . A quarter of a century ago, it was widely believed that discriminatory behavior simply reflects prejudiced attitudes; the predominant research emphasis was on the psychodynamics of prejudice. But then it was learned that most discrimination results less from blatant bigotry than from the behavior of people who simply follow standard institutional practices, without being much concerned about, or sometimes even aware of, the discriminatory consequences of their behavior. The questions have more and more become: Why are institutional practices as they are? What forces make for continuity and for change in patterns of race relations? . . .

Poverty

. . . In the recent past, interest was limited for the most part to the psychology of the poor, an underlying and often explicit assumption being that a "culture of poverty," transmitted from generation to generation, keeps the poor from rising in the stratification system. Out of a raging controversy over the validity of such an attribution of cause has come the recognition that the values and attitudes of the poor represent adaptation to a set of *current* social and economic conditions. These values and attitudes can be and often are modified by changing conditions. . . .

Similar illustrations of an expanded perspective could be elaborated in almost every other field of social problems research. . . . The movement is from description to analysis; from the study of individuals already "having" the problem to the study of conditions important in the production of the problem; and from a predominant concern with the individual to a broader concern with the interaction between the individual and the larger social structure.

Along with a growing breadth of perspective *within* each of the specialized fields of social problems research, and of even greater potential importance, is the increasing recognition that social problems are all interconnected, both in their underlying conditions and in their consequences. Each field of social problems research long tended to be an island unto itself, with students of that problem often not even reading the research literature on other problems. . . [O]ur analyses paid too little attention to underlying conditions and to common factors in the development of many of the particular problems. Even when investigators in several areas of social problems research found the same variables to be involved, they often failed to notice the commonalities. The growing awareness of the interconnectedness of social problems must surely be counted as a major conceptual advance.

The social problems of the 1980s reflect the increasing scale and global interdependence of modern societies. It is no longer possible for a society to insulate itself from world events. And events are harder to control. Today's social problems defy both easy explanations and easy solutions. But the fact that there are no *easy* solutions does not mean there are no solutions.

Summary

1. Sociological imagination is the ability to see the connections between private troubles and social problems, to understand the historical development of social patterns and their impact on individuals.

2. The flood at Buffalo Creek exposed chronic social problems. Large-scale lumber and mining operations had depleted Appalachia's natural resources, turning a rich environment into a hazardous one. The exploitation of miners had depleted the region's human resources.

3. A *social issue* is a condition that captures public attention, generating concern, controversy, and in some cases, collective action. A *social problem* is a social condition that causes demonstrable harm to individuals and society. Not all social issues are social problems, and vice versa.

4. Social issues and social problems are connected in three ways: Failure to perceive a problem may make conditions worse; public concern and controversy may create a problem where none existed (the self-fulfilling prophecy); the solutions to social problems require collective action.

5. The sociological framework consists of certain key concepts: culture, institutions, norms and sanctions, positions and roles, and socialization.

6. Theories of social disorganization emphasize inadequacies in the social system that interfere with people's individual and collective purposes. One example is cultural lag, when changes in norms and values do not keep pace with technological change. A second is alienation, the feeling that one is a stranger in one's own social world.

7. Conflict theories emphasize the ongoing struggle for wealth, power, and prestige among different groups in a society. According to Marx, in capitalist societies, the group that controls the means of production (especially factories) controls the social and political machinery as well and is therefore in a position to oppress and exploit workers.

8. Theories of deviance emphasize the origins and consequences of behavior that does not conform to social norms. Deviance may be seen as the product of learning and differential association; as a response to opportunity structures, especially illegitimate opportunity structures; or as both a cause and consequence of labeling.

9. The scale and global interrelatedness of today's social problems defy easy solution.

Suggested Reading

Berger, Peter L. *Invitation to Sociology: A Humanistic Approach.* New York: Doubleday/ Anchor, 1963.

Berger, Peter L., and Hansfried Kellner. *Sociology Reinterpreted: An Essay on Method and Vocation.* New York: Doubleday/Anchor, 1981.

Caudill, Harry M. *Night Comes to the Cumberlands: A Biography of a Depressed Area.* Boston: Little Brown/Atlantic Monthly Press, 1963.

Coser, Lewis A. *Masters of Sociological Thought: Ideas in Historical and Social Context.* New York: Harcourt Brace Jovanovich, 1971.

Erikson, Kai T. *Everything in Its Path: Destruction of Community in the Buffalo Creek Flood.* New York: Simon & Schuster, 1976.

Mills, C. Wright. *The Sociological Imagination.* New York: Oxford University Press/ Evergreen, 1959.

Peterson, Bill. *Coaltown Revisited.* Chicago: Regnery, 1972.

Rubington, Earl, and Martin S. Weinberg. *The Study of Social Problems: Five Perspectives,* 2d ed. New York: Oxford University Press, 1977.

Weller, Jack E. *Yesterday's People: Life in Contemporary Appalachia.* Lexington, Ky.: University of Kentucky Press, 1965.

References

Antonio, R. F. *Social Problems, Values and Interests.* Boston: Allyn and Bacon, 1975.

Barnet, R. J. "The World's Resources, Part I," *The New Yorker,* March 17, 1980, pp. 45–81.

Becker, H. S. *Outsiders: Studies in the Sociology of Deviance.* Glencoe, Ill.: Free Press, 1963.

Caudill, H. M. *Night Comes to the Cumberlands: A Biography of a Depressed Area.* Boston: Little, Brown/Atlantic Monthly Press, 1963.

Caudill, H. M. "Buffalo Creek Aftermath," *Saturday Review,* August 26, 1972, pp. 16–17.

Chirot, D. *Social Change in the Twentieth Century.* New York: Harcourt Brace Jovanovich, 1977.

Cloward, R., and L. Ohlin. *Delinquency and Opportunity.* Glencoe, Ill.: Free Press, 1960.

Coser, L. A. *Masters of Sociological Thought: Ideas in Historical and Social Context,* 2d ed. New York: Harcourt Brace Jovanovich, 1977.

Davis, F. J. "Crime News in Colorado Newspapers," *American Journal of Sociology,* Vol. 57 (January 1952), pp. 325–30.

Duke, J. T. *Conflict and Power in Social Life.* Provo, Utah: Brigham Young University Press, 1976.

Erikson, K. *Everything in Its Path: Destruction of Community in the Buffalo Creek Flood.* New York: Simon & Schuster, 1976.

Harrington, M. *The Other America: Poverty in the United States.* New York: Macmillan, 1962.

Hughes, E. C. "Dilemmas and Contradictions of Status," *American Journal of Sociology,* Vol. 50 (1945), pp. 553–59.

Lemert, E. M. *Human Deviance, Social Problems, and Social Control,* 2d ed. Englewood Cliffs, N.J.: Prentice-Hall, 1972.

Manis, J. G. *Analysing Social Problems.* New York: Praeger, 1976.

Merton, R. K. *Social Theory and Social Structure,* enlarged ed. New York: Free Press, 1968.

Merton, R. K., and R. Nisbet. *Contemporary Social Problems,* 4th ed. New York: Harcourt Brace Jovanovich, 1976.

Mills, C. W. *The Sociological Imagination.* New York: Oxford University Press/Evergreen, 1959.

Ogburn, W. F. *Social Change with Respect to Culture and Original Nature.* New York: Huebsch, 1922.

Peterson, B. *Coaltown Revisited.* Chicago: Regnery, 1972.

Raine, J. W. *The Land of Saddle-bags: A Study of the Mountain People of Appalachia.* 1924; rpt. Detroit, Mich.: Gale Research Co., 1969.

Rubington, E., and M. S. Weinberg (Eds.) *The Study of Social Problems: Five Perspectives,* 2d ed. New York: Oxford University Press, 1977.

Sprey, "The Family as a System in Conflict," *Journal of Marriage and the Family,* Vol. 31, No. 4 (November 1969), pp. 699–706.

Stern, G. M. *The Buffalo Creek Disaster.* New York: Vintage, 1977.

Sutherland, E. H., and D. R. Cressey. *Principles of Criminology,* 7th ed. Philadelphia: Lippincott, 1966.

Toffler, A. *The Third Wave.* New York: Morrow, 1980.

Waldheim, K. *United Nations Action in the Field of Human Rights,* Preface. New York:
United Nations, 1974.

Weller, J. E. *Yesterday's People: Life in Contemporary Appalachia.* Lexington, Ky.:
University of Kentucky Press, 1965.

TIRED OF THE VIOLENCE
AT HOME ?

There is a solution........

ALTERNATIVES TO
DOMESTIC VIOLENCE

Bergen County
Community Action Program, Inc.

Chapter Two

Sociology in Action

Generating Knowledge: The Role of Research

A Survey of Family Violence

A Field Study of Women of the Corporation

An Experiment in Treatment of the Mentally Ill

The Ethics of Research

Utilizing Knowledge

Potential Uses and Users of Sociology

   Assessing the Scope of Problems
   Challenging Myths
   Designing and Evaluating Solutions
   Broadening Perspectives

Obstacles to Use

   Contradictory Findings
   Media Distortions
   Unheeded Results

Social Problems and Social Action

The Politics of Problems

Sociology's Responsibilities

The first issue of the *American Journal of Sociology*, published in July 1895, called for a sociology of action. In the mind of its editor, Albion Small, the discipline of sociology and the effort to solve social problems were tightly linked. "[T]he relations of man to man are not what they should be," he wrote; "something must be done directly, systematically, and on a large scale to fight these wrongs" (in Scott and Shore, 1979, p. 8). Albion Small was not alone. Many of the early American sociologists were social reformers. Ministers or the sons of ministers from rural backgrounds, they were deeply concerned about the impact of rapid industrialization and urbanization on social life (Hinkle and Hinkle, 1954, pp. 3–4). In its early days, American sociology was essentially a moral crusade.

The harsh realities of World War I lowered faith in humanity's ability to find rational solutions to its problems. Rebelling against the idealism of their predecessors, many younger sociologists took refuge in "pure" research. They emphasized statistical methods, quantifiable data, and above all, objectivity. Other sociologists concentrated on developing theories, building a framework for future studies. Together they launched sociology's battle to win recognition as a science. The study of social problems became almost a sideline.

During World War II, interest in social problems was revived. Many sociologists worked for the government, investigating military and civilian morale, ethnic tension and conflict, and other problems that might affect the war effort. Their studies were not only useful to the government but interesting to their academic colleagues. Faith in social scientific research reached a peak in the late 1960s and early 1970s. The following statement was typical of this period:

> We are living in social crisis. There have been riots in our cities and in our universities. An unwanted war [in Vietnam] defies efforts to end it. . . . At the root of many of these crises are perplexing problems of human behavior and relationships. The behavioral and social sciences . . . can help us survive current crises and avoid them in the future. . . ." (National Academy of Sciences, 1969, p. 1)

The difference between the hopes expressed in the first issue of the *American Journal of Sociology* and this statement is that sociologists had gained both knowledge and experience in the interim. Their theories and methods are better informed and more sophisticated.

The practical value of sociology is being questioned again today, however (Scott and Shore, 1979, pp. 27–32). On the one hand, there are those who believe that sociological research is a vital part of the effort to solve social problems. According to this view, many of today's problems result in part from the failure to use sociological knowledge in the past. On the other hand, there are those who argue that sociology has produced little of practical value. According to this view, most sociological research is too specialized or too technical to be of use. In our view, the truth lies between these two extremes. Sociology has a good deal to contribute to the solution of social problems. Its practical applications are limited, however—both by the state of the art and by political forces.

This chapter presents sociology and sociologists in action. We begin with research, with the techniques sociologists have developed for generating knowledge. A survey of family violence, a field study of a corporation, and an experiment in the treatment of the mentally ill illustrate the basic requirements for sound research. In the second section, we will consider the ways in which sociological knowledge may be used—by the general public, practitioners (in social work, health care, and other fields), and public policy makers. We will also suggest some of the reasons why sociological information might *not* be used. This brings us to the third section of the chapter, on the politics of solving social problems. What determines whether action is taken to correct a harmful situa-

The Sociologist's Quadruple Bind: Why You Can't Win

". . . the relations between the socially plausible, in which appearances persuade though they may deceive, and the true, in which belief is confirmed by appropriate observation. . . . The independence of the two confronts the sociologist with some uncomfortable alternatives. Should his systematic inquiry only confirm what had been widely assumed—this being the class of plausible truths—he will of course be charged with "laboring the obvious." He becomes tagged as a bore, telling only what everybody knows.

Should investigation find that widely held social beliefs are untrue—the class of plausible untruths—he is a heretic, questioning value-laden verities. If he ventures to examine socially implausible beliefs that turn out to be untrue, he is a fool, wasting effort on a line of inquiry not worth pursuing in the first place. And finally, if he should turn up some implausible truths, he must be prepared to find himself regarded as a charlatan, claiming as knowledge what is patently false."

		If a widely held assumption is	
		Plausible	Implausible
And his work shows them to be	Actually true	He is a bore, laboring the obvious.	He is a charlatan, claiming obvious falsehoods.
	Actually false	He is a heretic, questioning value-laden verities.	He is a fool, wasting effort on obvious untruths.

The point is, of course, that we don't know in advance of systematic research which widely held beliefs are untrue and which widely rejected beliefs are, in fact, true.

Source: Robert K. Merton, "Notes on Problem-Finding in Sociology," in Robert K. Merton, Leonard Broom, and Leonard S. Cottrell, Jr. (Eds.), *Sociology Today: Problems and Prospects* (New York: Basic Books, 1959), pp. xv-xvi, n. 5.

ation? When does a social problem become a social issue? What role should sociologists play in the politics of problem solving?

Generating Knowledge: The Role of Research

What distinguishes sociologists from the average man or woman is their refusal to rely on common sense. Thoughtful speculation is not enough. They do not accept the obvious explanation or solution of a social problem—unless, of course, a body of research indicates that the obvious is correct (see p. 41).

Sociologists have three basic tools for gathering facts and testing theories: the survey, the field study, and the experiment. Which method researchers choose depends on the kinds of problems they are investigating, the kinds of information they seek, and the opportunities for different kinds of research.

A Survey of Family Violence

A *survey* is a study that uses standardized questionnaires or interviews to collect data from and about people. Surveys are particularly useful in determining the distribution of certain behavior or characteristics in a large population. They enable researchers to identify and measure the dimensions of a problem. Murray Straus, Richard Gelles, and Suzanne Steinmetz's study of violence in American families provides an example.

Events of the 1960s and 1970s (assassinations, riots) brought Americans face to face with the problem of violence in our society (see Stark and McEvoy, 1970). Health and social workers were concerned about child abuse, and feminists were calling for programs to aid battered wives. But no one knew how widespread these problems were. Official records are only the tip of the iceberg.

People are often reluctant to file charges against members of their own family because of shame, fear, and other factors. Moreover, the decision to attribute an injury to child abuse rather than to an accident depends on a health official's judgment, public and political pressures on health agencies, local definitions of abuse, and state and local laws—all of which vary.

Straus and colleagues launched a national survey in 1976 to answer three basic questions: How common is violence in the home? How violent are American families? (The researchers investigated the entire continuum of violence, from spankings to shootings.) What does violence mean to participants? (Do people consider family violence deviant or normal?) They were also interested in finding out what kinds of families engage in violence and why. But their primary goal was to gather information.

Studying violence in America's most private and intimate institution involves special difficulties. Most people are reluctant to discuss their family lives with a stranger. Questions had to be presented carefully and phrased to elicit honest answers. Straus and colleagues used the Conflict Tactics Scale (Figure 2-1), which had been tested in numerous pilot studies. The interviewer made a statement about the kinds of conflicts that may develop in families, then read a list of ways in which family members might have handled them. The list began with rational tactics (such as discussion), then moved through sulks and threats to acts of violence. The person was asked how often family members had used these tactics in the past year, then whether they had ever used them. Each step was calculated. By linking violence to conflict, the researchers legitimized affirmative responses. After all, everybody knows family members quarrel. Each series of questions began with rational solutions to conflict, so that respondents had an opportunity to give "correct" (socially acceptable) answers first. The interview began with questions about fights among chil-

Figure 2–1
Conflict Tactics Scale

Interviewer: In some families where there are children, they always seem to be having spats, fights, disagreements, or whatever you want to call them; and they use many different ways of trying to settle differences between themselves. I'm going to read you a list of some things that (REFERENT CHILD) might have done when (he/she) had a disagreement with the other (child/children) in the family. For each one, I would like to know how often (REFERENT CHILD) did it in the past year.

Referent child–in the past year

		Never	Once	Twice	3-5 times	6-10 times	11-20 times	More than 20 times	Don't know
a.	Discussed the issue calmly	0	1	2	3	4	5	6	X
b.	Got information to back up (his/her) side of things	0	1	2	3	4	5	6	X
c.	Brought in or tried to bring in someone to help settle things	0	1	2	3	4	5	6	X
d.	Insulted or swore at the other one	0	1	2	3	4	5	6	X
e.	Sulked and/or refused to talk about it	0	1	2	3	4	5	6	X
f.	Stomped out of the room or house (or yard)	0	1	2	3	4	5	6	X
g.	Cried	0	1	2	3	4	5	6	X
h.	Did or said something to spite the other one	0	1	2	3	4	5	6	X
i.	Threatened to hit or throw something at the other one	0	1	2	3	4	5	6	X
j.	Threw or smashed or hit or kicked something	0	1	2	3	4	5	6	X
k.	Threw something at the other one	0	1	2	3	4	5	6	X
l.	Pushed, grabbed, or shoved the other one	0	1	2	3	4	5	6	X
m.	Slapped or spanked the other one	0	1	2	3	4	5	6	X
n.	Kicked, bit, or hit with a fist	0	1	2	3	4	5	6	X
o.	Hit or tried to hit with something	0	1	2	3	4	5	6	X
p.	Beat up the other one	0	1	2	3	4	5	6	X
q.	Threatened with a knife or gun	0	1	2	3	4	5	6	X
r.	Used a knife or gun	0	1	2	3	4	5	6	X
s.	Other (PROBE):_____	0	1	2	3	4	5	6	X

Source: Illustration from *Behind Closed Doors* by Murray A. Straus, Richard J. Gelles, and Suzanne K. Steinmetz. Copyright © 1980 by Richard Gelles and Murray A. Straus. Reprinted by permission of Doubleday & Company, Inc.

"Nice," middle-class people who hold responsible jobs and live in good neighborhoods are not immune to family violence. This woman's glazed, uncomprehending stare is typical of battered wives.

dren, which research showed most Americans consider normal. By the time the interviewer came to questions about husbands and wives beating each other, respondents had had practice in answering the questions.

Straus, Gelles, and Steinmetz found that family violence is, indeed, widespread. Although the milder forms of violence are most common, millions of Americans are beaten up by family members each year. Violence seems to beget violence: Often adults who abuse children were themselves abused as children. Many Americans consider family violence regrettable but inevitable. Most see fights between siblings as normal and consider husbands and wives striking one another justifiable on occasion. (The full implications of this survey are discussed in Chapter 8.)

The key to most survey research is sampling. The object of most social surveys is to obtain results that can be generalized to a larger population (e.g., all families in the United States). Since it is usually impractical, if not impossible, to survey all members of a population (e.g., members of all 56 million families is the United States), survey researchers employ samples. A *sample* is a portion of the population about which the investigator wants to generalize. A *representative sample* is a sample in which each member of the population has a chance, and the same chance, of being selected to be part of the sample.

There are two potential sources of sampling error which can affect the accuracy of a survey. The first is sample size: The smaller the sample, the greater the chance of error. Small samples exaggerate individual quirks. If a researcher studying family violence surveyed only ten families and one family was extremely violent, it might skew the results of the study. The larger the sample, the less chance an unusual case will distort the results. The second common error is *response rate.* It is unusual for everyone who is selected to be in a sample to be contacted, agree to participate, or complete the interview or questionnaire. The smaller the response rate (percentage of the sample who complete the survey), the greater the chance of error. This is particularly relevant if the reason people did not participate in the study is related to a key aspect of the study. Suppose a researcher mailed out a thousand questionnaires asking people's opinions of corporal punishment in school. Only 250 questionnaires are returned (a 25 percent response rate), and 90 percent of those returning the questionnaire oppose corporal punishment. People who strongly disapprove of behavior are more likely to respond to a questionnaire than those who approve. Because of the small response rate, a conclusion that most people oppose corporal punishment would be highly distorted. Researchers generally consider a 65 to 85 percent response rate adequate.

The chief advantage of a survey is that it enables researchers to collect data on a large population in a relatively short time. For this reason, it is an economical procedure. A second advantage is that surveys are standardized. All respondents are asked exactly the same questions and, in many surveys, given the same choice of answers. Findings can be quantified (translated into numbers), which enables a researcher to make fairly precise comparisons of different groups and precise measurements of change over time. Standardization is also one of the drawbacks of surveys, however. In phrasing questions and answers in terms anyone can understand, the researcher may oversimplify complex topics. The results may be somewhat artificial. In real life, people's opinions rarely take the form of "strongly agree, agree, disagree, strongly disagree." At best, this format yields an approximate measure of opinion. Moreover, surveys rely on self-reports. Researchers learn what people *say* they do or might do, not what they *actually* do. The fact that people say they favor sexual equality in work, for example, does not mean that they would willingly work for a female boss or hire a male secretary. Thus surveys are only an indirect measure of social behavior (Babbie, 1979, pp. 345–47).

A Field Study of Women of the Corporation

The idea that no one, male or female, likes to work for a woman has long been a cliché. Two somewhat contradictory stereotypes of the female boss seem to be circulating. According to one, women simply do not have what it takes to command. Whereas men tend to be ambitious, task-oriented, and work-involved, women tend to put

personal relationships first. They are less motivated to succeed, less committed to their jobs. The company man is, indeed, a man. These alleged male/female differences are sometimes attributed to biology, sometimes to socialization. A second stereotype holds that women in high positions are bossy, rigid, controlling, and generally unpleasant to work for.

Is there any truth to the above images? Rosabeth Kanter (1977) attempted to answer this question with a field study of Industrial Supply Corporation (Indsco), a major U.S. corporation renamed to protect its identity. Despite the growing number of women in the labor force, changes in the law that forbid discrimination against women in employment, and company efforts to promote women, 96 percent of all managers and administrators in the United States who earned more than $15,000 a year as of the 1970 census were men. Kanter hoped her study would offer practical advice to companies that were implementing "equal opportunity" and "affirmative action" programs.

A *field study* consists of observation of social behavior at the scene of the action. Sociologists use this technique to learn about behavior that can best be understood in its natural setting. Ideally, a field study takes a researcher backstage into people's lives so that he or she can learn what they actually do as well as what they say they do. Kanter found that much of what "happened" at Indsco took place off the record. Often the informal discussions people had in what they designated "social" time were as important as their formal meetings. To capture the complex social reality of the corporation, Kanter employed a wide variety of research techniques. She became a participant observer, sitting in on meetings at the invitation of participants; she held seminars on job satisfaction, men/women relations within the corporation, and work/family issues; she conducted a mail survey designed to measure commitment to the corporation; and she talked with

What is wrong with this picture? There are no women. The fact that more women are being promoted to managerial positions today does not mean that they are invited to go out drinking "with the boys." And many business contacts and contracts are made in informal settings like this.

people, at work and in their homes, in "conversational interviews." Each source of data, each informant (or interviewee), served as a check against the others. Over a five-year period, Kanter spent more than 120 days at the site and collected data on more than 600 employees.

Kanter concluded that there is a *grain* of truth to stereotypes about women in the corporation. Indsco employees overwhelmingly agreed with the statement "men make better supervisors," even though most rejected the idea that it was "unacceptable" or "unfeminine" for women to become managers. Moreover, Kanter's own observations and those of her informants indicated that many female managers fit the stereotype of "mean and bossy."

In Kanter's view, the explanation for her findings lies not in women's biology or upbringing but in the kinds of jobs women usually hold. Traditionally, women have been given low-opportunity jobs where the tasks do not change, there are few opportunities to increase skills or to demonstrate initiative, and there is no established

route out of the job to higher positions. Thus they lack formal power. Kanter suggests that such jobs affect behavior, even personality. People who feel they have little control over their own working lives may compensate by overcontrolling others. They need to be right and become irritable when proven wrong. On the other hand, they don't want to offend their superiors and so play it safe, following the rules to the letter. In short, they become rigid, critical, bossy — the stereotypical female boss. Moreover, women who manage to work their way out of traditional jobs may find they lack the informal power. Because "betting" on a woman is riskier than betting on a man with the same potential, women have a harder time attracting sponsors, collaborators, and protégés to support them. Kanter notes that studies show that men in powerless blue-collar jobs often exhibit what are considered "female" characteristics: "They limit their aspirations, seek satisfaction outside of work, dream of escape, interrupt their careers, emphasize leisure and consumption" (1977, p. 161). Kanter's point is not that these men are feminine. Rather, these traits reflect the kinds of jobs people hold, not their gender. The job shapes the person.

The chief advantage of field studies like Kanter's is depth. Participant observers are able to record subtleties in behavior and attitudes that surveys often miss. The researcher can learn more about the social meanings people attach to events. Another advantage of field studies is flexibility. Interviews can be open-ended. If new questions arise, it is relatively easy for the researcher to change directions in mid-study. Researchers in social problems have found field studies particularly useful in studying deviant, or socially unacceptable, behavior. To learn first-hand what it is like to be an outsider in our society, sociologists have conducted field studies of deviant subcultures (teen-age gangs, prostitutes, and so on).

The main weakness of field studies is that they depend so heavily on the researcher's insights and judgments. Frequent face-to-face contact, joint activities, and intimate revelations may turn an impartial researcher into a friend and advocate. A second problem is that field studies typically rely on small, informal sampling. There is no reliable way of testing whether the event the researcher observes and the people he or she interviews are representative of a larger group. In a sense, the sample is self-selecting, since a researcher usually begins with the people who come forward voluntarily. They may be atypical individuals who hope to gain prestige through association with the newcomer, or have some other ulterior motive. It is difficult to generalize from field studies. For example, Indsco may have hired particular kinds of people who were not typical of all corporations. Finally, there is always a chance that the researcher's presence will influence the way people behave. Events may be staged to please, or perhaps to deceive, the investigator. Field studies, which depend on some improvisation, are particularly hard to replicate. Kanter attempted to overcome these handicaps by using many different informants and sources of data, and by cross-checking. Everything she reported had been corroborated by different informants on several occasions.

An Experiment in Treatment of the Mentally Ill

In 1955, about three-quarters of Americans who had been diagnosed as mentally ill were confined to hospitals (Hilgard, Atkinson, and Atkinson, 1979, p. 482). Although the government was spending almost $1.8 billion a year on treatment of the mentally ill, most of these patients received only custodial care. Forty-five percent had been hospitalized for ten years or more. The state institutions in which most were confined were too large; the staffs were small and poorly trained; knowledge of how to cure mental illness was inadequate. Today, less than 30 percent of Americans diagnosed as mentally ill are confined to hospitals. The average length of hospital stay for psychiatric patients has been reduced to 124 days (U.S. Department of Health, Education, and Welfare, 1979, p. 55). State institutions are being emptied.

Benjamin Pasamanick, Frank Scarpitti, and Simon Dinitz (1967) conducted one of the early experiments on treating psychiatric patients in their homes and communities rather than confining them to hospitals. Pasamanick and colleagues were interested in three main questions: (1) Was home care for schizophrenic (severely disturbed) patients feasible? (2) Was home care a better or worse method of treatment than hospitalization? (3) Would the new drugs that were becoming available help to prevent rehospitalization? At the time, the very idea of treating schizophrenic patients at home was revolutionary. Community treatment had never really been tried in the United States. Indeed, the state hospital in Ohio for which the experiment was planned changed its mind and refused to participate. Louisville,

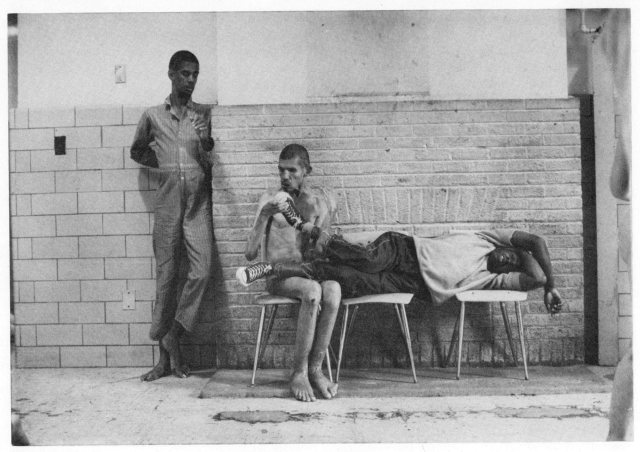

This photograph was not taken in a concentration camp thirty or forty years ago. It was taken in one of today's state mental hospitals. A small percentage of the mentally ill who do not respond to the "miracle" drugs developed in the 1960s, spend much of their lives in wards like this one.

Kentucky, volunteered its services, but many doctors and patients' families were skeptical. Pasamanick and colleagues studied less than half as many patients as they had hoped.

Experiments are most useful to sociologists when their interest is focused on a particular condition whose effects can be measured, as in this case. An *experiment* is a systematic, controlled examination of cause and effect. Experiments are attempts to discover relationships among conditions that can be changed, or what scientists call *variables*. The researcher sets up some of the conditions for an experiment. These are called *independent variables*. (They are independent of the subjects' behavior.) The change in the subjects' behavior that results from the introduction of independent variables is called the *dependent variable*. In this experiment, then, the independent variables were home care and drug therapy. The dependent variable was the patients' behavior, measured through staff evaluations, psychological tests, and rates of return to the hospital.

The success of an experiment depends on the researchers being able to hold variables other than the ones they are studying constant. Patients assigned to the *experimental group* were exposed to the experimental treatment—in this case, home care and drugs. Instead of being hospitalized, they were returned home; visited by a nurse once a week for three months, then once every two weeks; given an appointment with a psychiatrist at least once every three months; and told what they or their families should do in emergencies. If the experiment had stopped here, the results could have been distorted. By chance, the researchers might have studied the least disturbed or the most disturbed individuals in the Louisville system. The results of the study would reflect the patients selected, not home care versus hospitalization. To correct for this, researchers set up a control group. The *control group* was not exposed to the experimental treatment: Patients were hospitalized and treated as they would have been under the usual system. To eliminate the possibility that researchers might unconsciously assign the patients with the most hopeful prognoses to one group or the other, assignments were made at random. Moreover, half of the members of the experimental, home-care group were given appropriate medication (the second experimental condition) and half were given placebos ("sugar pills"). Only the doctor who examined the patients knew which were receiving active medication; the staff and family members who evaluated patient behavior did not.

Pasamanick and colleagues followed 152 schizophrenic patients over periods ranging from three to thirty months. They found that over 77 percent of the home-care patients who also received medication succeeded—that is, remained in the community. Only 34 percent of those receiving placebos remained at home. Nevertheless, the successful home-care patients in both groups were less likely to suffer setbacks than members of the control group who had been hospitalized for an average of about three months.

Two tentative conclusions can be drawn from these data. First, home care plus medication is a vast improvement over traditional treatment (isolating patients in mental wards). Second, hospitalization has a slight *negative* impact on schizophrenic patients: Those who are hospitalized have a smaller chance of returning to the community and remaining there. Pasamanick and colleagues' experiment added to a growing body of research indicating that hospitalization should be the treatment of last resort, used only when mental patients are dangerous or cannot care for themselves (see Chapter 13 for detailed discussion).

The main advantage of experiments over other research methods is control. The researcher attempts to isolate independent variables and measure their impact over time. The use of randomly assigned experimental and control groups is critical to this process. A second advantage of an experiment is that it is usually possible for another researcher to *replicate* or repeat the experiment with other groups of subjects at other times and places. This minimizes the danger that the results of one study are coincidental, or that they apply only to the particular group used as subjects, or that they reflect the personality or preconceptions of the researcher. If other researchers perform the exact same experiment and obtain the same results with different subjects, one can be more confident that the results are accurate.

Like other research methods, experiments have certain built-in drawbacks. First, they are somewhat limited in scope. The most careful experimental design can accommodate only a small number of variables. Second, when experiments are conducted in a laboratory, the results may be somewhat artificial. For example, showing a

Figure 2-2
Research Methods

RESEARCH METHOD	ADVANTAGES	DISADVANTAGES
Survey: A study that uses standardized questionnaires or interviews to collect data.	**Economy:** A researcher can collect data on a large population in a relatively short time. **Comparisons:** Because findings can be quantified, a researcher can make precise comparisons of different groups and precise measurements of changes over time.	**Oversimplification:** Standardized questions may obscure subtle differences **Reliance on Self-Reports:** Surveys measure what people say they do, not what they actually do. Respondents may give "socially correct" but inaccurate answers.
Field Study: Direct observation of social behavior in its natural setting.	**Depth:** A researcher can investigate the social meanings people attach to behavior and events. **Flexibility:** A researcher can change directions if new questions arise.	**Subjectivity:** Findings depend on the researcher's insight and judgments, and may reflect personal prejudices. **Limited Application:** Findings may only apply to the group studied; generalization is risky. **The Observer Effect:** The presence of an observer may alter the way people behave.
Experiment: A systematic, controlled examination of cause and effect.	**Control:** A researcher can isolate variables by using control and experimental groups. **Replication:** Other researchers can repeat the experiment to verify results.	**Limited Scope:** A researcher can manipulate only a small number of variables. **Artificiality:** The situations a researcher creates in a laboratory may not reflect "the real world" outside.

group of white subjects a film on black history might reduce prejudice as measured in the laboratory. This does not mean that showing the film in a neighborhood theater would have the same result (Babbie, 1979, p. 287). Pasamanick and colleagues' field experiment was unusual; most are conducted in laboratories. Finally, many of the conditions and behavior patterns that sociologists study cannot be created experimentally for ethi-

cal reasons. This is particularly true in investigations of social problems.

The development of a foundation of social knowledge depends on adequate sampling, on sound and accurate measurements, and on replicability. Generalizations cannot be drawn unless a sample represents the population under study. The accuracy of research depends in part on the investigator's ability to measure the factors that are important in the study. The final test of research is whether another investigator can replicate the study and obtain the same results.

The Ethics of Research

Whether a researcher is interested in family violence, sex discrimination, treatment of the mentally ill, or another social problem, the subjects of the research are human beings. Moreover, the results of a study may become part of public opinion or public policy or both, influencing real people's life chances. The potential effects of research on human lives give sociologists special responsibilities.

A team of researchers' first responsibility is to their human subjects. The most fundamental ethic of sociological research, and all scientific investigation, is that one should not conduct a study that might cause subjects extreme or lasting physical or psychological pain or humiliation. Simply put, research should not harm people. This ethic is based on values that define the ultimate aim of science as benefiting humankind (Diener and Crandall, 1978, Chapter 2).

Determining whether a procedure might *harm* subjects is often difficult in sociological research, however. For example, in studies of fear, anger, and stress, experimental subjects have been put into situations that were at best uncomfortable. One researcher (Lazarus, 1964) measured subjects' physiological responses while they watched a film of men in an Australian tribe performing painful circumcision rites on adolescent boys; another (Hess, 1965) used a film of bodies piled in a concentration camp. Some researchers have encouraged subjects to do something wrong—for example, agree to participate in a robbery (West, Gunn, and Chernicky, 1975) or administer what they thought were painful electric shocks to another person (Milgram, 1963). (The robbery did not take place, and the shocks were faked.) In a study of self-esteem, another researcher attempted to manipulate female subjects' feelings of self-worth by telling some that tests showed they had extremely healthy personalities and others that they were constricted and unimaginative. Pasamanick and colleagues (1967) took a risk when they asked families of schizophrenic patients to give up hospital care for home care and medication, whose full effects were not known.

A second issue in sociological research is *privacy.* Americans, like others, consider privacy a basic right: Individuals and groups are held to have the right to determine for themselves when, how, and what kind of information about them is communicated to other people (Westin, 1967, p. 7). In some cases, the only way researchers can obtain the information they seek is to penetrate public facades. Family research is an example (LaRossa, Bennett, and Gelles, 1981). Many Americans consider their family their most precious, and private, possession. Yet family members may agree to participate in a study without realizing the consequences. If an interview takes place in the home, for example, a couple may treat the researcher as a guest. After a while, they may feel "what the heck, we're all friends" and disclose more about themselves than they had intended. Or they may feel obligated to answer questions or see the researcher as a therapist. The risk of self-exposure—of learning new things about oneself—is as great as that of public exposure. Seeing one's personal life scrutinized and objectified may be troubling. Although the researcher may use pseudonyms and other devices to disguise personal identities in writing up the study, the subjects are likely to recognize themselves. So are friends and family members who know they participated in the study. The risks to privacy in sociological research depend on the sensitivity of the topic, the number of people who are able to connect private information to personal names, and the setting in which behavior is studied. Family violence is a particularly sensitive topic; people are not proud of family

Innovation and Evaluation:
A 264-Year Time Lag

My topic here is innovation and evaluation. I begin with an early experiment in nutrition. It was designed by Daniel of the Lion's Den, but for humans rather than lions. Daniel was held hostage in Nebuchadnezzar's court and, possibly for religious reasons, disapproved of the rich food, wine, and meat served there. The eunuch in charge feared for his own head if he were to give Daniel and his three friends merely the simple Judean vegetable fare called pulse (such as peas and beans). Daniel asked for a 10-day trial and promised to turn to the court's diet if the Judean hostages weren't then as healthy as the others. To turn to a translation of the original article, Daniel I:12–15:

> Prove thy servants, I beseech thee, ten days; and let them give us pulse to eat, and water to drink.
>
> Then let our countenances be looked upon before thee, and the countenance of the children that eat of the portion of the king's meat: and as thou seest, deal with thy servants.
>
> So he [the eunuch] consented to them in this matter, and proved them ten days.
>
> And at the end of ten days, their countenances appeared fairer and fatter in flesh than all the children which did eat the portion of the king's meat.

Had this study been submitted as a report to *Science,* the reviewer might make the following remarks. First, there is no sampling problem because Daniel needed only to prove that he and his three friends were better off with the diet. He did not have to make the generalization to, say, the entire population of Judea or the human race. This is unusual because ordinarily we *are* trying to make such generalizations. For Daniel it was fortunate as well, because with such a small sample—Daniel, Shadrach, Meshach, and Abednego—the eunuch would have had to insist on using Student's t-test, and this would not be invented for another 2500 years, almost exactly.

Second, the length of the trial, 10 days, is short for a nutrition experiment.

Third, the end point "fairer and fatter in flesh" seems not well defined. Other translations speak of "sleeker" which also is vague.

From the eunuch's point of view, the diet of pulse was an innovation, while the court's regular diet was the standard. And so Daniel designed a comparative experiment, an early evaluation of an innovation.

I turn to a historical, but more policy-oriented example: Another nutrition experiment was carried out by James Lancaster starting in 1601 when the East India Company sent its first expedition to India. He was general of four ships and a victualler. They sailed from Torbay in England in April 1601. At that time scurvy was the greatest killer of the navy and of expeditions and explorations, worse than accidents or warfare or all other causes of death together. More than half a crew might die of scurvy on a long voyage. In 1497 Vasco da Gama sailed around the Cape of Good Hope with a crew of 160 men: 100 died of scurvy.

Lancaster served three teaspoons of lemon juice every day to the sailors on the largest ship of his fleet and few became ill. By the time the fleet got to the Cape of Good Hope, so many sailors on the three smaller ships were sick from scurvy that Lancaster had to send sailors from the large ship to rig the smaller ones. When they reached the Cape of Good Hope 110 men had died, mostly from the 278 men who started on the three smaller ships. Clear evidence that lemon juice prevents scurvy? Maybe. At any rate, the evidence is so strong that the East India Company and the British Navy could surely be expected to follow up this investigation with further research. Not at all! Policy moves more majestically.

About 150 years later, 1747 to be precise, the physician James Lind carried out an experiment consisting of adding something special to the diets of scurvy patients on the ship *Salisbury*. He had six dietary additions:

1) Six spoonfuls of vinegar.
2) Half-pint of sea water.
3) Quart of cider.
4) Seventy-five drops of vitriol elixir.
5) Two oranges and one lemon.
6) Nutmeg.

Lind assigned two sailors ill from scurvy to each treatment. Those who got the citrus fruit were cured in a few days and were able to help nurse the other patients. The supply of citrus fruit ran out in about 6 days.

Lind knew about Lancaster's work as well. With this dramatic and crucial experiment plus the backup of Lancaster's earlier voyage surely the British Navy now will adopt citrus fruit for prevention of scurvy from long sea voyages? No! Forty-eight years later policy caught up. In 1795 the British Navy began using citrus juice on a regular basis and wiped out scurvy in the service. The British Board of Trade followed suit after a delay of only 70 years (1865) and wiped it out in the mercantile marine. We often talk about how slow we are to make use of innovations, but this case study of citrus juice should give us a little encouragement. Today we are worrying about 20-year lags. Here is one of 264 years.

Source: Frederick Mosteller, "Innovation and Evaluation," *Science,* Vol. 211, No. 4485 (February 27, 1981), pp. 881–82.

conflict. Kanter's study of women in a corporation also involved a threat to privacy: Disclosing feelings about company policies and fellow employees to an outsider can be viewed as disloyalty. An informant could be risking his or her job. In both cases, researchers disguised the identities of their informants with pseudonyms and took other steps to protect their anonymity.

In biomedical research, the traditional rule is that research on human subjects is ethical only if subjects have given their *informed consent.* Specifically, the subjects must understand the risks involved, must voluntarily agree to participate, and must know that they are free to withdraw at any point (Diener and Crandall, 1978, Chapter 3). In some research, however, deception is critical. For example, one researcher (Reiss, 1971) was interested in how police treated civilians and whether charges of police brutality were based in fact. He told police officers that he was interested in how citizens treated police, however. He felt that revealing his true purpose would have drastically reduced police assaults on citizens, of which he observed many. As this example suggests, in some cases deception may yield information that would otherwise be unavailable. There are risks, however, even when no harm is involved: Subjects and the public at large may become suspicious of social researchers; the scientists may become cynical about the gullibility of their subjects. A number of researchers make a point of debriefing subjects who have been deceived, informing them about what was done in the procedure and why.

In deciding whether to proceed with a study, sociologists engage in what amounts to cost/benefit analysis. If the expected benefits of the study exceed the risks to subjects, the study is considered ethical. For example, Pasamanick believed the long-term benefits to society of learning about the effects of different kinds of treatment on schizophrenics were worth the risk to a comparatively small number of individuals. Home-care patients and their families received careful instructions and regular visits. The cost/benefit formula does not absolve researchers from responsibility, however. In many cases, it is impossible to predict the effects of a study on subjects. Most researchers take steps to minimize danger and to screen subjects. In addition, many conduct follow-up studies to determine if subjects were troubled by their experience, and in some cases they offer counseling.

The ethics of sociological research also include responsibility to the discipline, to one's colleagues, and to oneself (Zuckerman, 1977). Science is a collective enterprise. No researcher can hope to understand the complex topics of sociological research independently. Every sociologist builds on the discoveries of others. Science depends on accurate, shared information. If research is not conducted objectively and reported honestly, everyone loses. False reports not only send other researchers on wild goose chases; they undermine public faith in the scientific enterprise.

There are a number of incentives for scientists (like business persons or students) to cheat, however. Employment, promotions, and salaries—not to mention the respect of colleagues and national acclaim—are based largely on a scientist's publishing significant research. And periodically, reports of scientific hoaxes appear in the news. In one of the most famous—the Piltdown hoax—the skull of a modern human and the jaw of an ape were doctored to simulate the remains of a prehistoric human. The hoax threw physical anthropology (and theories of human evolution on which definitions of human nature are based) into confusion for years. Quite recently, evidence was uncovered that Sir Cyril Burt, the British psychologist, falsified data that seemed to prove intelligence is hereditary. The consequences of his publications had been far-reaching. The system in British schools is based on the belief in fixed intelligence. In the United States, Burt's data have been cited in studies of racial differences in performance on IQ tests, which have provided ammunition for opponents of school busing to achieve integration.

In summary, there is no ethical alternative to scientists being as honest, accurate, and unbiased as is humanly possible. The ethics of scientific inquiry include an obligation to report biases that cannot be eliminated and data that are not as conclusive as the researcher had hoped they would be.

Utilizing Knowledge

The aim of social research is to add to our understanding of human social behavior: to expand the library of knowledge and to strengthen theory. The hope is that better understanding will lay the foundation for better societies. Sociologists disagree about the extent to which they themselves should become involved in applying sociological knowledge to practical problems (Weiss, 1977, Chapter 1). On the one hand, there are those who feel that a sociologist's first responsibility is to the discipline and that researchers in applied sociology are mere "technicians." On the other hand, there are those who consider "pure" research self-indulgent and argue that sociology must earn its keep in society. In practice, the distinction between pure research (studies designed to advance sociological knowledge) and applied research (studies designed to produce some practical benefit for society) often breaks down. A classic study may become the cornerstone of new government policies or programs; government-commissioned research may add new methods or theoretical perspective to the discipline. Here we will look at the direct and indirect uses of sociological knowledge as a whole, not just at research designed for immediate use.

Potential Uses and Users of Sociology

Who uses sociology? It would be only a slight exaggeration to say "everyone." The general *public* uses sociology both consciously and unconsciously. Over the years, a good deal of sociological data and theory has found its way into the fund of common knowledge, as well as into popular vocabularies. Familiar terms like bureaucracy; upper, middle, and lower class; in-group; minority group; and role playing were coined by sociologists. Sociology enters public thinking by two main routes: education and the media. In 1975, 1.8 million college undergraduates enrolled in sociology courses (*ASA Footnotes,* 1975, p. 4). Sociology is also offered in many high schools and adult education programs. Every week, if not every day, the news media report sociological findings, consult sociologists as experts, or use sociological techniques. The most familiar example is the so-called "public opinion poll" (or survey) used to measure everything from consumer opinions to religious beliefs. In presidential election years, political polls become almost as frequent and about as reliable as weather reports. Like consumers of commercial products, the public sometimes "buys" authentic, well-made packages of sociological knowledge, sometimes shabby imitations and out-of-date models.

A second category of sociological consumers consists of a variety of *practitioners* in fields like social work, health care, city planning, and corrections. Practitioners not only study sociology as part of their training; many consult with sociologists on a regular basis as part of their job.

The third category of sociological consumers is made up of *public policy makers*—people at the federal, state, and local levels of government who are responsible for "decisions that go beyond the routine" (Weiss, 1977, p. 1). Now one knows precisely how many sociologists are studying policy

Disarticulation: One View

CHICAGO—Scholars who are seriously studying the contemporary United States have come to recognize the limitations of "theories" they offer to explain our current difficulties. Moreover, many thoughtful analysts admit that "scientific" approaches frequently are ideological justifications for political goals of particular pressure groups. It is time to realize that universities have entered directly and excessively into the stalemated political process. The public would be better off if the experts concentrated on helping the public understand how society actually operates, and on stimulating political leaders to sharpen their sense of their own—and society's—enlightened interests.

Political leaders and citizens need a broad perspective on the question, "Why don't things work anymore?" Such an outlook must reflect the vast changes of the last half century if it is to be relevant to political democracy. It cannot be held with rigid, fanatical conviction. In particular, society needs an explanation of the fragmentation of our political institutions, a fragmentation that is at the root of our difficulties. . . .

. . . I believe that our social institutions have become disarticulated: By "disarticulated," I mean that the various parts do not fit together effectively, although many of the individual parts are adequate and even highly effective.

The operating room in a modern hospital is extraordinary but the nation's medical-delivery system does not work. The individual farm is highly efficient, but agriculture loses millions of tons of topsoil annually, and the farm-subsidy system is not needed. The junior officer in the Air Force and in the ground-combat arms of the military services is a dedicated professional, highly skilled and prepared to risk his life, but we have serious doubts about the readiness of the military as a whole. . . .

. . . [T]he expert and the policy analyst have contributed to the growth of disarticulation, as they have sought to take over the role, or intrude into the domain, of the elected official. The function of the expert—especially the university expert—is to collect information and to increase our understanding of the whole society and its institutions. It is not to make an effort to offer and implement specific solutions and policies. A "post-industrial" society ruled by experts is a myth, and this idea has proved self-destructive.

In part, "things don't work" because the expert and the scholar have misused their competence to become pressure-group advocates rather than effective teachers, advisers, and "staff officers" for the society as a whole.

Source: Morris Janowitz, "Disarticulation," *The New York Times*, April 26, 1981, p. E23.

Figure 2-3
Sociology's Clientele

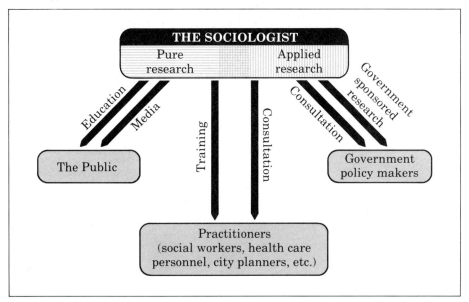

questions, serving as consultants to policy-making groups, or working directly in government-sponsored programs. We do know, however, that in 1971, the federal government spent $89 million for applied research in sociology (Baker, 1975). What are these investigators trying to accomplish? How might their research, and sociology in general, be useful to its different audiences?

Assessing the scope of problems During the 1980 presidential campaign, Ronald Reagan commented, "When I was young . . . this country didn't even know it had a racial problem." The remark was greeted with laughter and scorn, but there is some truth to what he said. Forty or fifty years ago, most white Americans probably did not know the extent of racial inequality in the United States. They did not know a social problem existed or, if they knew, did not realize how widespread or how devastating racial discrimination

was. A sociological classic, Gunnar Myrdal's *An American Dilemma* (1944), is widely credited with making Americans realize that this was not the free and open society it claimed to be, not the land of opportunity for everyone. Myrdal described the impact of segregation on black Americans in concrete terms. He also described the undertow of hypocrisy in a society which preached equality but practiced overt discrimination. Similarly, Michael Harrington's *The Other America* (1962) is credited with bringing poverty in the United States to public attention in the early 1960s, firing the first shot in President Lyndon Johnson's "war on poverty." Harrington emphasized the paradox of poverty in the midst of affluence. He pointed out the social origins and consequences of what many believed to be the personal failures of the poor.

Often neither the public, practitioners, nor policy makers know the magnitude of a problem or even if one exists. The report of the President's

Commission on Population Growth and the American Future (1972) contains many examples of sociologists filling gaps in policy makers' knowledge (Westoff, 1973). Was population growth as big a problem for industrialized nations as for nonindustrial countries? The Commission concluded that the United States was not threatened with an immediate population explosion, but that in the long run unchecked population growth would magnify other social problems. The quality of life might be reduced. The Commission recommended setting a goal of zero population growth. Eliminating *unwanted* births, by itself, would reduce U.S. population growth to zero. No radical changes in family patterns were necessary. (By implication, large numbers of Americans lacked information about or access to birth control devices.) In short, the Commission told the government what the future population would be if X, Y, or Z occurred. It also provided data on attitudes toward family size.

Challenging myths A second function of sociology is to examine the assumptions that guide private, public, and often practitioners' decisions. Sociological research may correct erroneous beliefs, reveal the latent functions and unanticipated consequences of established patterns, disclose complexity where others see easy answers, and otherwise dispel myths about social problems. This is not to say that sociologists are always right and nonsociologists always wrong. But common sense is subject to a number of common errors.

Most people operate on the principle "seeing is believing." We trust the evidence of our own eyes and ears. But our perceptions can be distorted. In an experiment conducted some years ago, researchers showed subjects a headline that read "Black officer opposes war protests." A number of subjects saw "Black officer opposes war *policy*." They assumed that black Americans opposed the war in Vietnam and saw what they expected to see. Often people unconsciously give in to social pressure or confuse what is with what *ought to be.* In another experiment, married couples were asked to fill out questionnaires about who made decisions in their households, and then to participate in decision-making games in the laboratory. In nearly every case, the couple said that the husband made most decisions. In the laboratory, however, the couple shared responsibility. But apparently they believed the husband should be the "head of the family" and thought they acted this way.

Studies of the riots that blazed through the nation's black ghettos in the 1960s are an example of sociological research dispelling myths. Common-sense explanations of the riots drew on the "riffraff" and "rabble-rouser" theories of collective violence. According to the riffraff theory, most rioters were uneducated and unemployed youths with criminal tendencies or recent immigrants from the rural South who had not put down roots in the city. The rabble-rouser theory held that the riots had been deliberately provoked by small bands of organized militants. Nathan Caplan and Jeffery Paige's surveys of Detroit and Newark (1968) challenged both theories. They found that rioters had about the same average income as nonrioters, had significantly *more* education, and tended to be more active in community affairs. Most were long-term residents of the area, not recent arrivals, and most had grown up in stable, intact families. What distinguished rioters was a high degree of black pride. They were more likely than nonrioters to blame their employment problems on racial discrimination, not personal failings (lack of talent or education). There was no evidence of an organized conspiracy in Detroit or Newark. Studies by other researchers in other cities produced similar results. This research did not, of course, justify the rioters' behavior. But it did make it harder for the public and policy makers to dismiss their grievances as the complaints of marginal people or as militant rhetoric.

Serious questions about another myth were raised in Philip Zimbardo and colleagues' prison experiment (Haney, Banks, and Zimbardo, 1973). Everyone knows that conditions in the nation's prisons are deplorable. Common sense blames the violent, dehumanized atmosphere on the "nature" of the people who are confined to prisons, the "nature" of those who run prisons, or both. As Zimbardo points out, these explanations have an appealing simplicity. They locate the source of trouble in certain "bad seeds," not in the condition of the "prison soil." To learn whether this common-sense explanation was correct, Zimbardo had to separate the characteristics of prison environments from those of prison inhabitants and employees. Studying an actual prison population wouldn't do.

Zimbardo set up an experiment in an artificial prison constructed on the campus of Stanford University. Twenty-two law-abiding, middle-class, male college students whom tests and interviews judged to be stable and healthy were enlisted for the experiment. This group was divided at random into "prisoners" and "guards." The day before the prisoners were arrested, the guards were given uniforms, shown around the simulated prison, and assigned the task of maintaining "the reasonable degree of order within the prison necessary for effective functioning." (They were not told *how* to do this.) The student-prisoners were arrested the next day by actual members of the local police force, brought to the prison, assigned cells, given smocks for clothing and numbers to replace names (as in real prisons). Prisoner and guard behavior was observed directly and recorded on video tape. Individual reactions were collected in questionnaires, personality tests, and interviews. Designed to run two weeks, the experiment was terminated after six days. Why? To simplify a bit, the guards became unexpectedly harsh in their treatment of prisoners, and the prisoners were becoming extremely demoralized and disoriented. What Zimbardo and colleagues observed in this brief period convinced them that behavior that is usually attributed to the deviant tendencies of prisoners and/or guards in fact may be a product of "an intrinsically pathological *situation* which could distort and rechannel the behavior of essentially normal individuals" (italics added).

Zimbardo's experiment added to a growing body of research that suggests our penal system may harden rather than rehabilitate convicted criminals. For example, sociologists have documented the ways in which being labeled deviant and stigmatized may push someone into a deviant career (see Chapter 1). They have also described violent prison subcultures. These conclusions echo the report by the Commission on Law Enforcement and the Administration of Justice (1968) and that on the Causes and Prevention of Violence (1969). Both commissions recommended that, whenever possible, people should be diverted from the existing penal system into other systems of social control, particularly if they are young or if they have committed "victimless" crimes (Ohlin, 1975, p. 109). The sociological hypothesis that prisons create as many criminals as they correct or cure — once a radical notion — is finding its way into popular thinking.

Designing and evaluating solutions Sociological research may also be used to identify alternative ways of solving social problems and to measure the results of a policy or program (evaluation research). Pasamanick's experiment with mental patients provided concrete evidence that home care with medication was more successful than custodial hospitalization, for example. This experiment and others led to a radical change in treatment of the mentally ill, as noted above. In some cases, policy makers and practitioners turn to sociology for general information about a problem. In others, research is designed expressly to test a program of social action or to evaluate one that is already in use.

Kanter's recommendations concerning women and job opportunities (1977, Chapter 10) were based on her belief that affirmative action programs will only work if companies address questions of informal as well as formal power. Her suggestions for changes in job opportunities and formal power included: redefining jobs (for example, making managers career counselors as well as supervisors); basing salaries on skills and responsibilities rather than job titles (so that secretaries might advance, for example); posting job opportunities (so that employees can apply for new positions instead of waiting to be noticed); and rotating jobs (so that people do not become more concerned about protecting their turf than about doing their work). Kanter next addressed the question of informal power. Often women are left out of the informal communication networks that keep men informed about what's happening in other areas of the corporation, how to obtain fringe benefits, shortcuts, and the like. She recommended seminars or newsletters to educate everyone about the real workings of the organization. Since women have a harder time than men attracting sponsors, Kanter recommended a formal system of sponsorship with concrete rewards for senior people who develop new talent. She suggested teaching male managers to control unconscious behavior that tends to undermine female peers and subordinates—for example, learning *not* to rush in to help a woman who seems to be struggling and refusing to listen to someone who goes over the head of a woman supervisor. Kanter herself worked on a job training program designed to integrate women into a formerly all-male field. The program emphasized team thinking, rather than individual achievement, to help women make supportive connections with male peers. High-level managers were brought in so that they would develop an early interest in the new employees. To provide role models, the young women were given reasons to interview the few senior women in the corporation. In these ways, Kanter put her ideas to work, in the hope of correcting some of the problems she had discovered through her research.

The data collected by the Commission on Population Growth mentioned above also led to specific policy recommendations. The finding that most Americans could not even guess the size of the U.S. population led to a call for population education. The discovery that most sexually active teen-agers do not practice birth control indicated a need for sex education in high school. The discovery that nearly 50 percent of Americans thought decisions about abortion should be left to individuals and their physicians emboldened policy makers who favored repeal of anti-abortion laws. Thus, data from population studies led in many different directions.

The direct application of sociological findings to problem solving has been called "social engineering" (Janowitz, 1972). The sociologist draws on available knowledge to help policy makers resolve technical problems in social programs. A few years ago, a team of researchers questioned over 200 upper-level officials in the executive branch of government about their use of social science research (Caplan, Morrison, and Stambaugh, 1975). Officials said social science findings played an important role in policy recommendations. Examples cited ranged from recommendations for programs to meet the educational needs of minority children, to the feasibility of an all-volunteer army, the use of federal parkland, and the organization of government agencies.

Broadening perspectives A fourth function of sociology is less visible but perhaps more influential. It is what Morris Janowitz calls "enlightenment": creating the intellectual conditions for problem solving by teaching the importance of the social context. Enlightenment affects the identification and definition of social problems, as

Clinical Sociology: The Sociologist as Practitioner

During the past year there has been a revival of interest in clinical sociology, a form of sociological practice which has existed for half a century. In the broadest sense, clinical sociology is the bringing of a sociological perspective to intervention and action for change. The client may be an individual, family, school system, medical center, work group, or the like, and the task may involve a redefinition of self, situation, or the creation of healthier and more humane environments.

Clinical sociology is an enlightening process, a recognition and clarification of alternatives, thus helping clients to formulate their own solutions and learn problem-solving in the process. This model for change underlies many schools of education and psychotherapy—existential, client-centered, humanistic— where the therapist or change agent plays a supportive role or is a catalyst or clarifier of social reality rather than a dictator of change. The sociological clinician pays particular attention to those problems which have their source in social interaction rather than in individual personality. The question of what institutional changes are needed to foster a climate for human growth and well-being is a guideline for both short- and long-range efforts in this field.

A small but growing number of sociologists are identifying themselves as clinicians and can be found working in a variety of health care, organizational, educational, and community settings. The newly formed Association of Clinical Sociologists is concerned with expanding employment and training opportunities in clinical sociology and in spreading the idea that a sociological perspective is useful and valid in facilitating many change efforts.

Clinical sociology can serve as a link between the creation of knowledge (research) and its utilization (intervention), thus helping to close the rift between theoretical and applied sociology. The development of clinical sociology offers new opportunities for training social scientists in practice roles and gives sociology a revitalization it sorely needs by bringing back its humanistic tradition of serving humanity.

Source: John Glass, "Renewing an Old Profession," *American Behavioral Scientist,* Vol. 22, No. 4 (March/ April 1979), pp. 513–29.

well as informing solutions. "The impact is not measured and judged in terms of specific assignments and specific recommendations, but in the broader intellectual climate it seeks to engender" (1972, p. 3).

For example, sociological theory and research have shaped the "ecological" approach most social workers take in their work with the elderly (Kirschner, 1979). Traditionally, social workers treated the elderly as individual patients. Sociology teaches that aging is not a disease. It is a normal stage in the life cycle, but one that is ill-defined in contemporary American society. Although the number, and proportion, of elderly people in this country is growing, there is still no clear role for retirees. (What are they supposed to do with themselves?) Our notions of disease and our medical system are designed to deal with acute problems of the earlier years, not the chronic physical disabilities of old age. Perhaps most troubling, individuals and their families rarely prepare for old age. The ecological approach to social work with the elderly embraces these interrelated problems: the client's psychological reaction to aging, tensions that the new role of parents' caretaker creates for adult sons and daughters, and what is in many cases an unresponsive environment (federal bureaucracies, remote landlords, lack of convenient transportation). The emphasis is on assisting the individual to develop social resources. This approach is based not on one particular piece of research but on a new perspective that emerged from a host of sociological studies conducted over many years.

Sociology provides a fragmented society with a common vocabulary (Weiss, 1977, p. 17). It gives names to conditions that have not been recognized before, such as "mid-life crisis" and "white flight." Concepts like social role, class conflict, labeling, and anomie tell people what to pay attention to in the confusion of everyday events. Sociological theories provide syntax, or rules, for

combining and ordering these bits and pieces. In sum, sociology gives policy makers, practitioners, and the general public a conceptual map. "Not here the imminent decision, the single [fact], the weighing of alternative options, and shazam! Officials apparently use social science as a general guide to reinforce their sense of the world and make sense of that part of it that is still unmapped or confusing. A bit of legitimation here, some ammunition for the political wars there, but a hearty dose of conceptual use to clarify the complexities of life" (Weiss, 1977, p. 17).

Obstacles to Use

Clearly sociology can be useful—in assessing the scope of social problems, challenging popular assumptions, designing and evaluating programs, and putting social issues and problems into perspective. There are a number of obstacles to applying sociological knowledge, however. Some lie within the discipline itself; some lie outside.

Contradictory findings In many areas, sociological knowledge is limited. At best, sociologists can make an educated guess as to why a problem developed or what can be done to solve it. Often different studies produce contradictory results. The "white flight" controversy is an example. In 1975, Coleman, Kelly, and Moore published data indicating that school desegregation was causing white families to move out of integrating school districts or to withdraw their children from public school. By implication, school desegregation programs were self-defeating. Less than a year later, Farley (1976) and Pettigrew and Green (1976) released data indicating that school desegregation had "no discernible effect" on white enrollment. Soon other researchers were lining up on either side of the white flight debate. Which researcher was right? All of them in their own ways. The researchers had used different methods to study different aspects of the white flight hypothesis and, as a result, drew different conclusions (Farley, Richards, and Wurdock, 1980). Desegregation does seem to affect enrollment within school districts, but does not explain differences between districts. On the average, desegregation is associated with a short-term decline in white enrollment, but has little or no long-term effect. These averages conceal wide variations among districts. Moreover, many questions remain unanswered. For example: How do different types of integration plans (voluntary versus court-ordered busing) influence white enrollment? What kinds of white families leave the district or the school? There isn't any simple answer to the question of whether school desegregation causes white flight. People's responses to desegregation are complex and varied. It may take years of research to discover an overall pattern, if one exists. The discipline of sociology thrives on this kind of debate, but policy makers are less than thrilled with apparently contradictory findings.

Contradictory findings are not peculiar to the social sciences. For over ten years, scientists have argued about whether marijuana does or does not cause physical harm to users (Zinberg, 1976). Claims have seesawed back and forth. In 1970, for example, the National Clearing House for Drug Information reported that marijuana users do about as well academically as nonusers. Within a month, the Federal Bureau of Narcotics and Dangerous Drugs issued a report stating the opposite. In March 1971, the president-elect of the American Medical Association claimed that marijuana had been shown to cause sterility and birth defects; a month later he reversed himself. Some researchers have found evidence that marijuana causes psychosis, brain damage, a breakdown in the body's immune responses, and sexual impairment. Other researchers have rejected every one of these claims. According to Norman Zinberg (1976), not one study showing marijuana is harmful has been consistently replicated. (This is not to say marijuana is harm*less*; its long-term effects are not known.) But as Zinberg points out, research condemning marijuana makes headlines. Papers questioning methods and studies that show little or no effect do not make news.

Media distortions Most people get the majority of their information on social problems from news reports in the mass media. News reports may be accurate in every detail, but still create distorted impressions. There are three ways in which the media may inadvertently slant the facts. First, they tend to define "news" as the unique event or personality. The emphasis is on dramatic action. Gradual, cumulative changes and complicated situations do not make as good a story; they are difficult to capture in a three-minute TV news slot or in two columns of a newspaper. Second, there is a bad-news bias in media reporting. As one TV producer put it, "All journalists assume that the Boy Scouts and the churches are operating normally; our job is to cover what goes awry" (in Gans, 1970, p. 40). Unscheduled, unexpected events are covered; the routines of everyday life are not. Third, the media present information bit by bit. They focus on the isolated incident, on the particular scientific report. There is little attempt to put people, events, or research findings in social and historical context. Consumers get the "who, what, when, and where" of a story, but not the "why." Watching the evening TV news broadcasts is a little like watching a play with many characters and scenes, but virtually no plot. The effect can be misleading.

Consider crime. What people see on TV and read in the newspapers strongly influences their impressions of crime and law enforcement (Wheeler, 1968). A classic study in this area showed that public estimates of the amount of violent crime and theft in a city reflected the number of crimes in the news, not the actual crime rate (Davis, 1952). The mass media give considerably more attention to the details of specific crimes than to trends. Even if the anchor person reads data on the crime rate, pictures of the scene of a crime, the victim, and their families are more likely to impress viewers. Often the media fail to explain the reasoning behind official actions. For example, the evening news may tell viewers that a suspect was released on a technicality, but not that this "technicality" is designed to minimize the possibility of innocent people being sent to prison. (Releasing people arrested on scant evidence, like sending criminals to prison, is designed to protect the public). In emphasizing the individual case over the crime rate, the specific act over the reasoning, the media inadvertently create distorted impressions. And in deciding public policy, officials respond more to public sentiments and fears—as shaped by the media— than to research findings.

Unheeded results Even when the government itself has commissioned research, it is under no obligation to heed the results. Often public officials ignore the findings of their own commissions. The story of the President's Commission on Obscenity and Pornography (1970) is a classic. The Commission conducted an extensive review of data collected both here and abroad. It found "no evidence that exposure to or use of explicit sexual materials plays a significant role in the causation of social or individual harm such as crime, delinquency, sexual and nonsexual deviancy or severe emotional disturbance . . ." (p. 58). The Commission's recommendation that laws banning the sale of pornography to adults be repealed was rejected outright, however. In the sociologist Otto Larsen's words, "The Commission on Obscenity and Pornography was conceived in Congress, born in the White House, and after twenty-seven months of life, was buried without honor by both parent institutions. Now, three years later, it is clear that the third branch of government [the Supreme Court] is not interested in its resurrection. . . . In effect, then, a serious social

and behavioral science effort has been deemed irrelevant for national policies in the area" (1975, p. 5). Indeed, the report boomeranged, causing a flurry of anti-pornography pronouncements and activities in government. This was not an isolated instance. The recommendations of the Commission on Population Growth, mentioned above, were also rejected. President Nixon declared that making contraceptive information and services available to teen-agers would seriously weaken the family. Other recommendations were simply ignored. In the next section, we examine some of the reasons for this.

Social Problems and Social Action

It is tempting to think of social problems as engineering problems. "If societies were really 'things,' we could locate the offending part and replace it, or redesign and reshape the entire assembly of 'parts.' But . . . the 'parts' are people and groups, with ideas, needs, interests, and above all plans of their own" (Rule, 1978, p. 173). Policy makers are under constant pressure from groups that have a vested interest in their decisions. Often they are inundated with data and competing claims to expertise. Moreover, decisions are fragmented in our system of government. There is no one, authoritative policy-making board. The many officials who participate in the policy process have different roles, constituencies, interests, values, and abilities. They may respect scientific research or debunk it. They may see commissioning a study primarily as a way to delay a decision. They may brandish research supporting their view at opponents like a loaded weapon. In short, decisions about whether and how to use sociological research are basically political decisions. They are part of an adversary process in which resolving conflicts with minimal pain tends to override scientific or "rational" decision making.

The Politics of Problems

For people to demand action, a social problem must become a social issue (see Chapter 1). People must become concerned about a condition they see as harmful or offensive; they must believe that something can and should be done. (If they see nothing wrong with existing conditions or feel nothing can be done to change them, they do not press for action.) Ideas about what is undesirable are grounded in people's values and interests. In a heterogeneous society such as ours, consensus is rare. People disagree about what is and is not a social problem and what should be done about it, if anything. Often one group's problem is another's solution (Merton and Nisbet, 1976, p. 10). At the local level, for example, some adults feel sex education is part of the solution to the problem of unwanted teen-age pregnancy; others feel that this will encourage sexual activity and so contribute to the problem. At the national level, senators from states with large aerospace plants see defense spending as the solution to the problem of unemployment; senators from states with large welfare rolls see defense spending as contributing to the problem by diverting funds from job training programs and the like.

Social issues are an integral part of politics. At any given time, a huge number of diverse groups are pressing claims on the government, demanding that it do something about what they see as a problem. Most of these complaints are disposed of — ignored, cooled out, bargained away, or bought off. Which ones lead to social action? Malcolm Spector and John Kitsuse (1973) suggest that group pressure leads to social action only if four conditions are met. First, a private trouble must be translated into a social problem. People must learn that their troubles are shared. Second, discontent must be focused on a specific complaint for which there is a specific remedy. A group that is vague about who or what is causing harm, and that has no idea what to do about it, is unlikely to inspire action. Third, the group must capture public attention, usually by capturing media attention. One common technique is to violate norms in some dramatic way. The fourth and critical condition is power. The group must be able to overcome indifference or outright opposition. "Other things being equal, groups that have more membership, greater constituency, more money, greater discipline and organization will be more effective in pressing their claim . . ." (Spector and Kitsuse, 1973, p. 149).

A brief history of the abortion controversy illustrates the complex politics of social action (Schur, 1980, pp. 45–59). In the mid-1950s, most American states had laws banning abortions unless "necessary to protect the life of the mother." At that time, the risk of pregnancy was considered

Figure 2–4
Conditions for Social Action

I. REDEFINITION	II. FOCUS	III. ATTENTION	IV. POWER
Private troubles, or "facts of life," are redefined as social problems.	Discontent is focused on a specific complaint for which there is a specific remedy.	The pressure group captures public attention, usually through the media.	The pressure group has sufficient membership, organization, and funds to overcome indifference or opposition.

one of the facts of life. It was part of being a woman. An unwanted pregnancy was considered a private trouble. The decision to have an abortion was made in secrecy and shame. Abortion was something people did not talk about. Women who had to choose between having an unwanted child or an illegal, often dangerous abortion blamed themselves and their husbands or lovers, not the social system.

The first call for reform of abortion laws came not from women but from doctors. Medical advances had made existing laws problematic. Modern medicine had reduced the risks of childbirth to the point where the mother's life was rarely in danger. (The laws were obsolete.) Modern medicine had also identified the sources of a number of birth defects, such as German measles. Many physicians felt abortions were justified in these circumstances. But most were reluctant to terminate a pregnancy for fear of prosecution. Some did stretch the law by claiming a female patient's mental health was in jeopardy, but they were on shaky legal ground. The doctors' complaint was not that anti-abortion laws limited women's options but that the laws prevented physicians from practicing good medicine.

In the late 1950s and early 1960s, many hospitals set up committees to review applications for "therapeutic abortions." Medical associations called for reform of abortion laws. The prestigious American Law Institute joined them, calling for laws permitting abortions when the mother's mental health or the baby's health was in danger, or when pregnancy resulted from rape, incest, or illicit sex with a minor. Numerous medical and legal associations held conferences and issued reports on abortion during this period.

Meanwhile thousands of American women continued to seek illegal abortions. Estimates are that at least 200,000, and perhaps 1.2 million, abortions were performed each year under less than optimal conditions, and that as many as 10,000 women died each year as a result (Schur,

1980, pp. 48–49). Anti-abortion laws had two side effects. First, the quality of the abortion a woman received, and hence the risk she took, depended on her income. Wealthy women were able to obtain safe, legal abortions abroad, or safe abortions here. Second, abortions were not subject to formal or informal social controls. Women who obtained illegal abortions were not likely to report malpractice to the police—or to anyone else.

The medical/legal drive to reform abortion laws met three of Spector and Kitsuse's conditions. It raised a specific complaint and offered a specific remedy; it captured public attention; and it had the power to overcome opposition. But it did not meet the first condition. The AMA and other associations defined abortion as a medical problem, not a social problem. They sought legalization of therapeutic abortions, not abortions by choice. Opinion on the issue was divided. It was the Women's Movement that tipped the balance in favor of repeal. The Women's Movement redefined abortion as a flagrant example of sexual politics. Under existing laws, women did not control their own bodies. Predominantly male legislators and doctors decided whether women could have legal abortions, but it was women who became mothers and primary caretakers or took the risks of illegal abortions (usually performed by males). In the words of Simone de Beauvoir:

> Men universally forbid abortion, but individually they accept it as a convenient solution of a problem; they are able to contradict themselves with careless cynicism. But woman feels these contradictions in her wounded flesh; . . . she regards herself as the victim of an injustice that makes her a criminal against her will, and at the same time she feels soiled and humiliated. (1953, p. 491)

Abortion gave the Women's Movement a specific complaint and remedy (the second condition for social action). The Women's Movement provided pro-abortion forces with membership, organization, and funds (the fourth condition). Each needed the other. Moreover, the drive to legalize abortion took place in a climate of approval (Granberg and Granberg, 1980, p. 252). The relaxation of constraints on extramarital sex, the rising number of consensual unions (unmarried couples living together), the postponement of marriage, the decline in the desired family size, and the rising divorce rate combined to make abortion more acceptable.

In 1970, several states repealed anti-abortion laws. In 1973, the U.S. Supreme Court ruled that a state could not intervene if a woman and her doctor decided on abortion in the first trimester of pregnancy, that the state could set safety standards for abortions performed in the second trimester, and that it could ban abortions in the third trimester (*Roe* v. *Wade*). The Court decision was based on the argument that an abortion is a personal, private matter—a civil right or liberty—not to be interfered with by the state. One might think the decision resolved the issue. It didn't. Rather, it served to polarize opinion on abortion. The Right-to-Life Movement began to

In the past, all-male legislatures and courts declared abortions illegal in the United States. Today the abortion issue has set women against women.

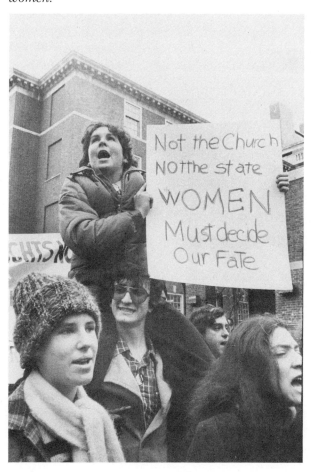

Table 2–1
Percentage of U.S. Adults Approving of Legal Abortion in Various Circumstances,*
Various Years, 1965–1980

"Please tell me whether *you* think it should be possible
for a pregnant woman to obtain a *legal* abortion:

Circumstance	1965	1972	1973	1974	1975	1976	1977	1978	1980
(1) If the woman's health is seriously endangered by the pregnancy	73	87	92	92	91	91	90	91	90
(2) If she became pregnant as a result of rape	59	79	83	86	84	84	84	83	83
(3) If there is a strong chance of a serious defect in the baby	57	79	84	85	83	84	85	82	83
(4) If the family has a very low income and cannot afford any more children	22	49	53	55	53	53	53	47	52
(5) If she is not married and does not want to marry the man	18	43	49	50	48	50	50	41	48
(6) If she is married and does not want any more children	16	40	48	47	46	46	46	40	47
For any reason	na	na	na	na	na	na	38	33	41
Average approval for the six specified reasons	41	63	68	69	67	68	68	64	67

*All percentages are based on the number of those answering yes or no. Respondents who said they did not know or who did not give a yes-or-no answer were excluded from the analysis.

Note: na = question not asked in that year.

Source: D. Granberg and B.W. Granberg. "Abortion Attitudes, 1965–1980: Trends and Determinants," *Family Planning Perspectives,* Vol. 12, No. 5 (September/October 1980), pp. 250–61.

gather momentum and to call for abortion repeal in the press, in the courts, and at the polls. It practiced single-issue politics: selecting light voting districts and turning out its supporters for anti-abortion candidates. Bowing to pressure from the Right-to-Life Movement, Congress passed the Hyde Amendment, which prohibits the use of Medicaid funds for abortions unless a mother's life is in danger. In 1981, Congress held hearings on the question of when life begins. If a law were passed stating that life begins at conception, abortion (and perhaps some form of birth control) would be legally defined as murder. The debate continues. Interestingly, neither side in this controversy uses the word "abortion." One calls itself the Right-to-Life Movement; the other, the Pro-Choice Movement. Both emphasize "horrible consequences." Both are led by women. But where one equates abortion with infanticide, the other sees abortion as a matter of personal choice. The dispute today focuses on abortions for minors, a husband's or parents' consent or notification, a requirement of pre-abortion counseling, performing abortions in public hospitals, public funding, and — once again — abortion itself (see Table 2-1).

Meanwhile, public approval of legal abortion has increased more or less steadily over the last fifteen years. People who approve of abortion usually express a commitment to civil liberties and women's rights; those who disapprove tend to express moral conservatism and a commitment to the Catholic or fundamentalist Protestant religions.

Sociology's Responsibilities

These political realities give sociologists special responsibilities. There is enormous potential for both the use and *abuse* of sociological findings in the political arena we've been describing. The knowledge gathered through research can aid the general public, practitioners, and policy makers in separating fact from fiction. The same knowledge can be used as ammunition in political battles between opposing interests. Tentative findings may be blown up out of proportion and cited as "the truth." Bits and pieces of research may be taken out of context and used to mislead.

Traditionally, sociologists and other scientists took an active role in the search for knowledge but a passive role in determining how society used that knowledge (Diener and Crandall, 1978, p. 197). This position was based on the belief that knowledge is ethically neutral and that the scientist has no special expertise in ethics. Today, however, more and more scientists feel an active responsibility to see that their work is not misused. Obviously, scientists cannot control the use of published research. But they can make an effort to see that the public receives correct information and is informed on all sides of an issue. Scientists can speak out publicly, as individuals and through professional organizations, when they see that officials are ignoring or misinterpreting scientific findings.

The social sciences rarely produce the clear-cut findings that are possible in the physical sciences. Sociological findings are not as readily transformed into practical applications. There are no laws of human behavior as there are laws of physics. Admitting this to the agencies that commission and fund research, and to a public that wants answers, is sometimes difficult. Scientists have a responsibility to admit the limitations of their knowledge. We shall make a determined effort to live up to this obligation in this text.

Summary

1. The role of research in sociology is to collect data and to test theories. Sociologists have three basic research tools: surveys, field studies, and experiments.

2. A *survey* uses standardized questionnaires or interviews to collect information from and about people. Sampling is critical to this procedure. The chief

advantages of surveys are economy and precise comparisons and measurements of change. The chief disadvantages are oversimplification and reliance on self-reports.

3. A *field study* employs direct observation of social behavior in its natural setting. The chief advantages of field studies are depth and flexibility; the chief disadvantages, reliance on the observer's insights, limited application, and the observer effect.

4. An *experiment* is a systematic, controlled examination of cause and effect. The use of experimental and control groups helps to eliminate bias, but the ultimate test of experimental findings is replication. The chief advantage of experiments is control. The chief disadvantages are limited scope and, especially in sociological experiments, artificiality.

5. Scientific researchers have an ethical responsibility not to harm or humiliate their subjects. The issues of privacy and informed consent raise difficult questions for sociologists. Scientists also have an ethical responsibility to their discipline.

6. The public, a variety of practitioners, and public policy makers are all "consumers" of sociology.

7. Social problems research is used to assess the scope of social problems, to examine popular assumptions, to design and evaluate solutions to social problems, and to broaden perspectives.

8. There are obstacles to using sociology, however. Research may produce contradictory findings; the media may unintentionally distort results; and policy makers may ignore results.

9. Discontent is most likely to lead to social action if private troubles are recognized as a social problem, discontent is focused on a specific complaint for which there is a specific remedy, the groups that favor action capture public attention, and these groups have the power to overcome public indifference or opposition.

Suggested Reading

Kanter, Rosabeth M. *Men and Women of the Corporation.* New York: Basic Books, 1977.

Komarovsky, Mirra (Ed.). *Sociology and Public Policy: The Case of Presidential Commissions.* New York: Elsevier, 1975.

Pasamanick, Benjamin, Frank R. Scarpitti, and Simon Dinitz. *Schizophrenics in the Community: An Experimental Study in the Prevention of Hospitalization.* New York: Appleton-Century-Crofts, 1967.

Rule, James B. *Insight and Social Betterment: A Preface to Applied Social Science.* New York: Oxford University Press, 1978.

Scott, Robert A., and Arnold R. Shore. *Why Sociology Does Not Apply: A Study of the Use of Sociology in Public Policy.* New York: Elsevier, 1979.

Straus, Murray A., Richard J. Gelles, and Suzanne K. Steinmetz. *Behind Closed Doors: Violence in the American Family.* Garden City, N.Y.: Anchor/Doubleday, 1980.

References

Babbie, E.R. *The Practice of Social Research,* 2d ed. Belmont, Cal.: Wadsworth, 1979.

Baker, K. "A New Grantsmanship," *The American Sociologist,* Vol. 10 (November 1975), pp. 206–18.

Caplan, N., and J. Paige. "A Study of Ghetto Rioters," *Scientific American,* August 1968.

Caplan, N., A. Morrison, and R.J. Stambaugh. *The Use of Social Science Knowledge in Policy Decisions at the National Level.* Ann Arbor, Mich.: Institute for Social Research, University of Michigan, 1975.

Coleman, J.S., S.D. Kelly, and J.A. Moore. *Trends in School Segregation, 1968-73.* Washington, D.C.: The Urban Institute, 1975.

Davis, F.J. "Crime News in Colorado Newspapers," *American Journal of Sociology,* Vol. 57 (1952), pp. 325–30.

de Beauvoir, S. *The Second Sex.* New York: Knopf, 1953.

Diener, E., and R. Crandall. *Ethics in Social and Behavioral Research.* Chicago: University of Chicago Press, 1978.

Farley, R. "Is Coleman Right?" *Social Policy,* Vol. 6 (1976), pp. 1–10.

Farley, R., T. Richards, and C. Wurdock. "School Desegregation and White Flight: An Investigation of Competing Models and Their Discrepant Findings," *Sociology of Education,* Vol. 53 (1980), pp. 123–39.

Gans, H.J. "How Well *Does* TV Present the News?" *The New York Times Magazine,* January 11, 1970, pp. 31–45 passim.

Granberg, D., and B.W. Granberg. "Abortion Attitudes, 1965–1980: Trends and Determinants," *Family Planning Perspectives,* Vol. 12, No. 5 (September/October, 1980), pp. 250–61.

Haney, C., W.C. Banks, and P.G. Zimbardo. "Interpersonal Dynamics in a Simulated Prison," *International Journal of Criminology and Penology,* Vol. 1 (1973), pp. 69–97.

Harrington, M. *The Other America: Poverty in the United States.* New York: Macmillan, 1962.

Hess, E.H. "Attitude and Pupil Size," *Scientific American,* Vol. 212 (1965), pp. 46–54.

Hilgard, E.R., R.L. Atkinson, and R.C. Atkinson. *Introduction to Psychology,* 7th ed. New York: Harcourt Brace Jovanovich, 1979.

Hinkle, R., and G.J. Hinkle. *The Development of Modern Sociology.* New York: Random House, 1954.

Janowitz, M. *Sociological Models and Social Policy.* Morristown, N.J.: General Learning Press, 1972.

Kanter, R.M. *Men and Women of the Corporation.* New York: Basic Books, 1977.

Kirschner, C. "The Aging Family in Crisis: A Problem in Living," *Journal of Contemporary Social Work,* Vol. 60, No. 4 (April 1979), pp. 209–18.

LaRossa, R., L.A. Bennett, and R.J. Gelles. "Ethical Dilemmas in Qualitative Family Research." Paper presented at National Council on Family Relations, Boston, 1979. In *Journal of Marriage and the Family,* Vol. 43, No. 2 (May 1981).

Larsen, O.N. "The Commission on Obscenity and Pornography: Form, Function, and

Failure." In M. Komarovsky (Ed.), *Sociology and Public Policy: The Case of Presidential Commissions.* New York: Elsevier, 1975.

Lazarus, R.A. "A Laboratory Approach to the Dynamics of Psychological Stress," *American Psychologist,* Vol. 19 (1964), pp. 400–11.

Merton, R.K., and R. Nisbet (Eds.). *Contemporary Social Problems,* 4th ed. New York: Harcourt Brace Jovanovich, 1976.

Milgram, S. "Behavioral Study of Obedience," *Journal of Abnormal and Social Psychology,* Vol. 67(1963), pp. 371–78.

Myrdal, G. *An American Dilemma.* New York: Harper & Row, 1944.

National Academy of Sciences. *The Behavioral and Social Sciences: Outlook and Needs.* Englewood Cliffs, N.J.: Prentice-Hall, 1969.

Ohlin, L.E. "Report on the President's Commission on Law Enforcement and Administration of Justice." In M. Komarovsky (Ed.), *Sociology and Public Policy: The Case of Presidential Commissions.* New York: Elsevier, 1975.

Pasamanick, B., F.R. Scarpitti, and S. Dinitz. *Schizophrenics in the Community: An Experimental Study in the Prevention of Hospitalization.* New York: Appleton-Century-Crofts, 1967.

Pettigrew, T.F., and R.L. Green. "School Desegregation in Large Cities: A Critique of the Coleman 'White Flight' Thesis," *Harvard Educational Review,* Vol. 46 (1976), pp. 1–53.

Reiss, A.J. *The Police and the Public.* New Haven: Yale University Press, 1971.

Rule, J.B. *Insight and Social Betterment: A Preface to Applied Social Science.* New York: Oxford University Press, 1978.

Schur, E.M. *The Politics of Deviance.* Englewood Cliffs, N.J.: Prentice-Hall, 1980.

Scott, R.A., and A.R. Shore. *Why Sociology Does Not Apply.* New York: Elsevier, 1979.

Spector, M., and J.I. Kitsuse. "Social Problems: A Re-formulation," *Social Problems,* Vol. 21, No. 2 (Fall 1973), pp. 145–59.

Stark, R., and J. McEvoy III. "Middle-Class Violence, *Psychology Today,* Vol. 4 (November 1970), pp. 52–65.

Straus, M.A., R.J. Gelles, and S.K. Steinmetz. *Behind Closed Doors: Violence in the American Family* Garden City, N.Y.: Anchor/Doubleday, 1980.

U.S. Department of Health, Education, and Welfare, National Center for Health Statistics. *The Nation's Use of Health Resources.* Washington, D.C.: U.S. Government Printing Office, 1979.

Weiss, C.H. *Using Social Research in Public Policy Making.* Lexington, Mass.: Lexington/Heath, 1977.

West, S.G., S.D. Gunn, and P. Chernicky. "Unbiquitous Watergate: An Attributional Analysis," *Journal of Personality and Social Psychology,* Vol. 32 (1975), pp. 55–65.

Westin, A.F. *Privacy and Freedom.* New York: Atheneum, 1967.

Westoff, C. "The Commission on Population Growth and the American Future: Its Origins, Operations, and Aftermath," *Population Index,* Vol. 39, No. 4 (October 1973), pp. 491–507.

Wheeler, S. "Crime and Violence." In F.T.C. Yu (Ed.), *Behavioral Sciences and the Mass Media.* New York: Sage, 1968.

Zinberg, N.E. "The War over Marijuana," *Psychology Today,* Vol. 10, No. 7 (1976), pp. 44ff.

Zuckerman, H. "Deviant Behavior and Social Control in Science." In E. Sagarin (Ed.), *Deviance and Social Change.* Beverly Hills, Cal.: Sage, 1977, pp. 87–138.

PART TWO

The National and International Context

Chapter Three

Global Ecology

Sociology and Ecology

Future Demands

Population Patterns

Demographic Arithmetic
Speeding Fertility Decline
Future Prospects

Patterns of Consumption

Current Patterns
Future Trends

Global Resources

Food Supplies

Future Prospects
Supply vs. Distribution

Energy Resources

Nonrenewable Resources
Renewable Resources
Energy Costs and Energy Profits

The Environment at Risk

Technological Fallout

Air Pollution
Water Pollution
Ground Pollution
Pesticides
The Greenhouse Effect

The Allocation of Risk

The Sociology of Survival

In March 1981, the United Nations sounded a "global alert." An estimated 150 million Africans faced immediate and severe food shortages. In the preceding year and a half, as many as 30,000 nomads had starved to death in one remote district of Uganda. Unless the UN could rapidly collect and distribute 2.7 million tons of emergency food, many more would be doomed. The UN attributed the famine in Africa to too little rain, too many babies, the rising cost of oil, and the shift in farming from food to cash crops to pay for oil. In Kenya, for example, the average woman has eight children, and the population is expected to double in the next seventeen years. Only 12 percent of the land is arable, and half of that is planted with coffee and tea for export. Kenya already spends 60 percent of its foreign income for oil, and this is likely to increase. In addition to oil, Kenyans burn 27 million tons of wood for heating and cooking each year. At this rate, the country will be out of wood by 1995 (*The New York Times,* March 25, 1981, p. A2).

The world may face a water crisis in the near future. As things stand, 80 percent of the people in the world do not have access to clean tap water. An estimated 5 million people die from water-borne diseases each year. Irrigation accounts for 80 to 90 percent of the water people use today, and estimates are that twice as much irrigation water will be needed in the year 2000 (*The New York Times,* March 14, 1979). Where will it come from? The supply of usable water, like the supply of oil, is limited. Most is in the ocean and is too salty for drinking or irrigation. The United States is not immune from this problem (*Newsweek,* February 23, 1981). Much of the water Americans use for irrigation, power, drinking, and bathing comes from underground reserves (aquifers) that were deposited during the Ice Age and are not refilled by rain. Quite simply, we are taking water from these underground reserves at a faster rate than nature can replenish them. The situation is analogous to withdrawing money from a checking account faster than you make deposits. Sooner or later the balance will read zero (see Figure 3–1).

In the early morning hours of March 28, 1979, the nuclear power plant at Three Mile Island, near Harrisburg, Pennsylvania, was performing the routine task of boiling water to produce steam and thereby generate electricity when an accident took place (Ford, 1981). A chain reaction of human and mechanical errors turned a minor mishap into a major one. Within minutes of the accident, the uranium fuel rods in the core overheated, swelled, and ruptured. Boiling radioactive water poured into the containment building. Invisible clouds of radioactive steam escaped into the atmosphere. It was two days before officials on the scene could determine what had happened inside the plant. Although no one was seriously injured at Three Mile Island, the reactor came perilously close to a "meltdown," in which a mass of white-hot, molten, radioactive uranium would have eaten through the bottom of the reactor tank into the ground. The effect would have been equivalent to that of dropping a small atomic bomb on Harrisburg. This was not the first accident at a nuclear power plant in the U.S. (Perrow, 1979).

The question is whether famine in Africa, natural and man-made droughts around the globe, and the accident at Three Mile Island are previews of worse things to come. Has the human population outgrown the earth's ability to sustain it? Is modern technology a "Frankenstein's monster" that threatens to destroy its creators? There is much disagreement about where we stand and what the future holds. Two opposing views prevail, the Limits Thesis and the Cornucopian Thesis (Ridker and Cecelski, 1979, pp. 3–4).

The *Limits Thesis* is based on four assumptions: (1) Because the earth is finite, there are definite limits to both population and economic growth. There is only so much air, water, land, and fuel on

Figure 3–1
Our Water Account

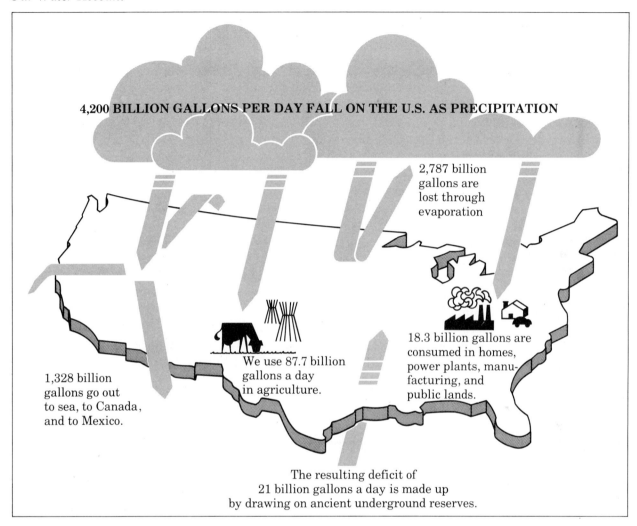

4,200 BILLION GALLONS PER DAY FALL ON THE U.S. AS PRECIPITATION

2,787 billion gallons are lost through evaporation

18.3 billion gallons are consumed in homes, power plants, manufacturing, and public lands.

We use 87.7 billion gallons a day in agriculture.

1,328 billion gallons go out to sea, to Canada, and to Mexico.

The resulting deficit of 21 billion gallons a day is made up by drawing on ancient underground reserves.

Source: Data from U.S. Water Resources Council.

"the spaceship earth." Moreover, the earth can absorb only so much waste. (2) We are about to approach these limits. (3) If we expand any more than we already have, world death rates will soar. (4) Even if the limits are farther away than we believe, we *ought* to cut back—because after a certain point, the production of material goods reduces the quality of life; because we are wasting resources that ought to be conserved for future generations; and because if rich nations consume less, there will be more for the poor nations of the world. According to this view, "small is beautiful"; the way to improve society is to limit growth.

Disaster Forecasts: A Cornucopian Perspective

Statement: The supplies of natural resources are finite. This apparently self-evident proposition is the starting point and the all-determining assumption of such models as *The Limits to Growth* and of much popular discussion.

Response: Incredible as it may seem at first, the term "finite" is not only inappropriate but is downright misleading in the context of natural resources, from both the practical and the philosophical points of view. As with so many of the important arguments in this world, this one is "just semantic." Yet the semantics of resource scarcity muddle public discussion and bring about wrongheaded policy decisions.

A definition of resource quantity must be operational to be useful. It must tell us how the quantity of the resource that might be available in the future could be calculated. But the future quantities of a natural resource such as copper cannot be calculated even in principle, because of new lodes, new methods of mining copper, and variations in grades of copper lodes; because copper can be made from other metals; and because of the vagueness of the boundaries within which copper might be found—including the sea, and other planets. Even less possible is a reasonable calculation of the amount of future services of the sort we are now accustomed to get from copper, because of recycling and because of the substitution of other materials for copper, as in the case of the communications satellite.

Even the total weight of the earth is not a theoretical limit to the amount of

---

Advocates of the Limits Thesis cite population growth, current energy and food shortages, and environmental damage as evidence that we are approaching a crisis point. The Club of Rome, an international organization of business leaders, scientists, and scholars, sounded the alarm in 1972 (Meadows et al.). A report entitled *The Limits to Growth* warned that if current trends continued, critical resources would begin to run out in the year 2000, causing a sharp drop in industrial and especially food production and a dramatic global decline in standard of living. Others have suggested that we are past the point of no return and are about to enter a New Dark Age (see Heilbroner, 1974; Vacca, 1974; Hirsch, 1976; Brown, 1978).

Opponents of this view see little reason to be pessimistic about the future. The *Cornucopian Thesis* is based on three assumptions: (1) Science and technology have gone beyond the old limits. The earth is not really finite, for technology *creates* new resources. (2) Even without further advances in scientific knowledge, the limits to growth are remote. Humans have only scratched the surface of the earth. New untapped resources can be substituted for old ones that are running copper that might be available to earthlings in the future. Only the total weight of the universe—if that term has a useful meaning here—would be such a theoretical limit, and I don't think anyone would like to argue the meaningfulness of "finite" in that context.

With respect to energy, it is particularly obvious that the earth does not bound the quantity available to us; our sun (and perhaps others suns) is our basic source of energy in the long run, from vegetation (including fossilized vegetation) as well as from solar energy. As to the practical finiteness and scarcity of resources—that brings us back to cost and price, and by these measures history shows progressively decreasing rather than increasing scarcity.

In summary, because we find new lodes, invent better production methods, and discover new substitutes, the ultimate constraint upon our capacity to enjoy unlimited raw materials at acceptable prices is knowledge. And the source of knowledge is the human mind. Ultimately, then, the key constraint is human imagination and the exercise of educated skills. Hence an increase of human beings constitutes an addition to the crucial stock of resources, along with causing additional consumption of resources.

Source: Julian L. Simon, "Resources, Population, Environment: An Oversupply of False Bad News," *Science,* Vol. 208 (June 27, 1980), pp. 1435–36.

low; growth can continue into the foreseeable future. (3) Economic growth is good—because no society has yet succeeded in satisfying its material needs; because growth is the only practical way to alleviate poverty; and because growth challenges people, sparking creativity, adventure, a sense of purpose, and hope. According to this view, "big is better"; the way to improve society is to stimulate growth.

Advocates of the Cornucopian Thesis cite history as their best evidence. Looking back, they see a steady march of progress in science and technology; looking forward, they see no reason why this should be halted. In the words of one, "Atoms and molecules and their energies, not fields and trees and fossils [fossil fuels such as petroleum] are the building blocks of our time" (Barnett, 1967, p. 8). According to this view, scientific knowledge and technological change are our most important resources and the most precious gift one generation can pass on to the next (see Kahn, 1976; Novak, 1978).

In this chapter, we examine the available evidence on these issues from a sociological point of view. We begin by laying the sociological foundations for the study of global ecology. In the two sections to follow, we attempt to estimate the supply of the earth's energy and food resources, relative to the kinds of demands that humanity is likely to make on those resources in the coming decades. We will show that both supply and demand are governed to a great extent by social factors. Estimates are that the global population will reach 6 billion before 2000. And 6 billion people will need more food, water, and other goods than the 4.4 billion alive today. But how much people take from the global store also depends on life styles, on patterns of consumption. With food and energy supplies, it is clear that there are limits to the amount of land available for farming and the amount of oil under the ground. To some extent, however, technology can offset these limits. For example, new agricultural technology may enable farmers to produce more food from an acre of land. There is a catch, however, as we illustrate in the fourth section of the chapter. Modern technology is a double-edged sword. It has enabled people to live longer and materially better lives than ever before. But it has also accelerated the rate at which people use up the earth's limited resources—oil, for example—and has created new threats to health in the form of nuclear accidents, polluted air and water, almost indestructible poisons, and potential changes in the climate. The final section of the chapter discusses how social mechanisms relate to the environmental problem. The evidence presented in this chapter suggests that both the Limits Thesis and the Cornucopian Thesis are exaggerated. Simply put, we are not doomed, but we have reason for concern. Population and demand are growing, some critical resources are running short, and the environment is in jeopardy.

Sociology and Ecology

The French teach schoolchildren this riddle: *If the lilies in a pond double each day, and the pond is full on the thirtieth day, on what day is the pond half full?* (Brown, 1978). The answer is, on the twenty-ninth day. Children (and adults) are often amazed at how fast change can happen. One day there seems to be plenty of room for growth; the next day the pond is filled to overflowing. By analogy, the lilies stand for the world population; the pond represents world resources and the environment; and the question becomes, Is humanity in its twenty-ninth day? (Advocates of the Limits Thesis say yes; supporters of the Cornucopian Thesis say no.)

An understanding of the problems of population growth, dwindling resources, and environmental deterioration begins with an understanding of ecology and the human species' place on earth.

Relationships in our biological community, the "ecosphere," are both complex and delicate. Seemingly minor disturbances in one part may have significant, and perhaps delayed, effects on others far distant. One goal of this chapter is to describe what people put into the ecosphere, what they take out, and what the consequences are. To do this we will draw on *ecology*, the study of how animals, plants, and microbes interact with the physical environment and with one another in the processes that sustain life.

Human beings occupy a special place in the ecosphere. Unlike members of other species, people adapt to the environment not only with the biological equipment nature provides but also through culture—traditional ways of thinking and behaving that are taught by one generation to the next. We do not communicate, use energy, eat, or breed quite like other creatures. We have languages, make fires and nuclear reactors, refine the art of cooking, make love. People are "cultural animals" (Fox, 1970). We not only adapt to environments, we create environments. The impact of material culture on the ecosphere is most obvious. With technology, people reshape the landscape. But nonmaterial culture also has an impact. Norms and values determine what people do with their knowledge and tools. And understanding this requires sociology.

Returning to the riddle of the lilies and the pond, human beings complicate the answer. People do not multiply in predictable, biologically set patterns. People demand more from the earth than simple nourishment. And through technology, people may expand the pond, postponing the twenty-ninth day. We can—and have—fouled the water. Thus, the future of humanity cannot be reckoned simply in terms of numbers of people and amounts of available resources. Complex social factors intervene. For example, global statistics indicate that providing people with modern birth control devices does not, by itself, slow population growth. The number of children a couple wants seems to reflect their economic circumstances. Data on today's food shortages indicate that the problem is one of distribution, not supply. Enough food is produced today to provide everyone on earth with three square meals a day, but not everyone gets enough to eat. Similarly, we have the technology to supply all of humanity's energy needs but lack the social machinery to put this technology to work.

To find out whether humanity is in its twenty-ninth day, we have to examine the institutions that translate culture into organized patterns of social behavior. The key question is whether institutions that developed when the world was less crowded and life was simpler can help people adapt to changing social conditions. Or are we entering a period of *global* disorganization?

Future Demands

It is possible to think of demand as population (the number of lilies in the pond) multiplied by consumption (how much each lily takes out of the pond). While recent studies suggest that fears of runaway population growth and insatiable consumer demand may be exaggerated, there is no doubt that demands on the earth's resources will increase substantially in future years.

Population Patterns

The human population of the earth today is approximately 4.4 billion, and increasing by about 74 million a year. At current rates, we add another million people every five days. In the last minute, about 120 people died and 190 babies were born, for an increase of 70. Barring massive famines or nuclear holocaust, the world population will reach 6.2 billion in the year 2000 and will continue to climb.

Current population growth is all the more remarkable when you consider the past. There are four times as many people alive today as *ever lived* before 1830 (Barnet, 1980, p. 163). For the hundreds of thousands of years our ancestors lived off the land, as hunters and food gatherers, the population was comparatively small (about 10 million), stable, and dispersed. When people discovered how to cultivate plants and domesticate animals (about ten thousand years ago), population size and density increased. The Agricultural Revolution set off the first population explosion: By A.D. 1, the number of people on earth had grown to about 300 million. But as we shall soon see, the current population explosion is as different from the first one as nuclear war is from conventional warfare.

Demographic arithmetic Demography (from the Greek words for "measuring the people") is the scientific study of population. Demographers use a variety of standard measures to translate the number of babies born in a particular village, city, or country, the number who die, and the number who moved in or out, into general statistics.

The *fertility rate* for an area is the average number of children its women can be expected to have in their lifetimes. The *birth rate* is the actual

Figure 3-2
Population Age Pyramids: Developed and Developing Regions, 1975 and 2000

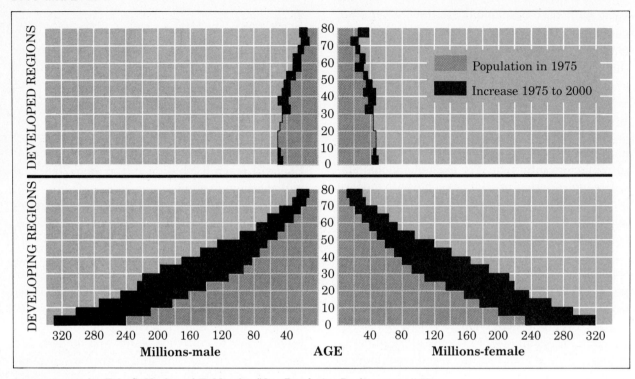

DEVELOPED REGIONS

DEVELOPING REGIONS

Population in 1975
Increase 1975 to 2000

320 280 240 200 160 120 80 40

40 80 120 160 200 240 280 320

Millions-male   **AGE**   **Millions-female**

Source: J. van der Tak, C. Haub, and E. Murphy, "Our Population Predicament: A New Look," *Population Bulletin,* Vol. 34, No. 5 (Washington, D.C.: Population Reference Bureau, December 1979), p. 6.

number of births per 1,000 women. Thus the fertility rate measures potential increase; the birth rate reflects such social factors as the number of children couples want and whether they are able to control fertility. The *death rate* is the number of deaths per 1,000 people. And the annual *growth rate* for the world population is the number of births minus the number of deaths per 1,000, expressed as a percentage.* In calculating the growth rate for a particular country, demographers also consider the *migration rate:* rela-

tively permanent moves into or out of a country. What do these statistics tell us?

The best way to grasp the implications of a particular rate of growth is to consider *doubling time,* the number of years it will take a population growing at a given rate to double. At a 1 percent growth rate, a population doubles every 69 years; at 2 percent, every 35 years; at 4 percent, every 17 years. (Remember the lilies in the pond.) At the current growth rate (1.7 percent), the world population will double in forty years. This figure conceals wide variations, however. The population is growing much faster in some parts of the world than in others. The United States and other developed nations have reached *zero*

---

*For example, in 1977 the world birth rate was 28 per 1,000; the death rate was 11 per 1,000. Subtracting 11 from 28 gives a growth rate of 17 per 1,000, or 1.7 percent.

population growth: their birth rates have declined to replacement levels (the average woman has only two children, "replacing" herself and her husband). This does not mean that the population in these countries will not continue to expand for some time. Population growth often has a built-in *momentum factor* determined by the age structure of the population. This momentum factor is considerably greater in the cases of developing nations because their populations have such a high proportion of young people (see Figure 3–2). Between 40 and 50 percent of their people are in, or about to enter, their childbearing years (compared to about 25 percent in developed countries). Even if couples in developing nations decide *tomorrow* to limit themselves to two children, it will take a century or more for their populations to stop growing.

In 1981, the World Fertility Survey, a multinational research project, announced that population growth rates had dropped significantly in the last decade. But for the reasons we have just described, this does *not* mean that the population problem is fading. Far from it. It is important to remember that even though a population's growth *rate* declines, the actual *number* of people added each year may increase (see Figure 3–3).

Speeding fertility decline What can be done to defuse the population explosion? In the last decade, a number of developing nations have launched birth control programs with mixed results. Family planning techniques, by themselves, can reduce only the number of *un*wanted births. People need to be motivated to use these techniques.

Through most of human history, disease, droughts, and food shortages slowed population growth. "Nature" held in the reins. Abraham Lincoln's family was typical of families in preindustrial societies (Heer, 1975, p. 56). Lincoln's mother died when she was thirty-five years old and he was nine. Of the four children Mrs. Lincoln

Figure 3–3

Population Growth Rates versus Actual Increase: Though the Rate Falls, the Number of People Added Goes Up.

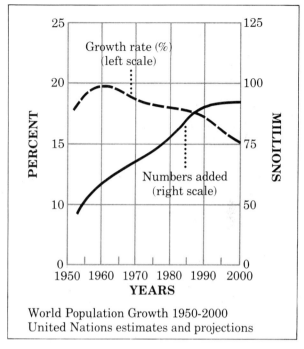

World Population Growth 1950-2000
United Nations estimates and projections

Source: J. van der Tak, C. Haub, and E. Murphy, "Our Population Predicament: A New Look," *Population Bulletin,* Vol. 34, No. 5 (Washington, D.C.: Population Reference Bureau, December 1979), p. 5.

had before she died, one son died in infancy, a daughter at age twenty. Lincoln's first love, Ann Rutledge, died at age nineteen. Only Lincoln survived to maturity.* It was common for young people to die before they could raise families themselves. Birth rates were high, but so were death rates, leaving population more or less stable. Then, rather suddenly, things changed.

Population growth began to accelerate in Western Europe in the early nineteenth century; toward the middle of the century in North America.

---

*If all of Mrs. Lincoln's children had lived and had had four children themselves, she would have had sixteen grandchildren and sixty-four greatgrandchildren.

Some Keys to Success in Family Planning

In many places, the introduction of modern birth control methods has met with unanticipated success in slowing runaway population growth (van der Tak, Haub, and Murphy, 1979, pp. 33–36). The most impressive success story comes from the People's Republic of China, where large families have been revered for centuries. One-fifth of all the people in the world (some 960 million) live in China. Thus, what happens there has considerable impact on the future size of global population. In a mere ten years, China has cut its annual population growth rate almost in half, to 1.2 percent (the same as in the United States). To accomplish this, the government dispensed free contraceptives through local teams of paramedics (teams that always included a woman); enlisted local groups in establishing and maintaining birth quotas; encouraged late marriage; and took steps to involve women in all aspects of community life, not just child rearing. With the goal of achieving zero population growth by the year 2000, China is considering proposals to reward one-child families with child-care subsidies, priority in housing and schools, and generous pensions when parents retire.

The relationship between economic, social, and cultural factors and human reproduction is only poorly understood. We do not know what it is that makes people want larger or smaller families. Three tentative conclusions can be drawn, however. First, family planning programs can work, particularly when designed to fit local traditions. Many couples want smaller families but lack birth control information and devices. Expanding and improving family planning services should be a top priority. Second, there seems to be a connection between the status of women and the birth rate. Where women are confined largely to the roles of wife and mother and are limited in their social contacts and communications networks, birth rates tend to be high. Where women are receiving education and opportunities, birth rates tend to be lower, in part because they delay marriage. Improving the status of women might have a direct impact on birth rates. Third, as long as there are numerous economic incentives for having large families (extra income, security in old age) and few incentives (such as those being considered in China) for limiting family size, it seems likely that population growth will continue.

Agricultural innovations provided the spark. Increased food supplies made for better nutrition, which increased resistance to disease. Improvements in transportation made it possible to transfer food from regions with a surplus to regions with a shortage, thereby averting famines. Advances in sanitation and medicine—better sewage disposal, cleaner water, pasteurized milk, and medicines that controlled such ancient killers as yellow fever and cholera—improved public health. Birth rates were high, more infants lived, and more children survived to become parents. The populations of Western Europe and North America spiraled upward.

Toward the end of the century, however, the spiral began to reverse. Gradually, small families with only two or three children became the norm. Today one or two children are the norm in much of Europe and the United States. Most demographers attribute the declining birth rate to industrialization, urbanization, and increased education. In an industrial economy, children are an economic burden. They do not do productive work, as they do in preindustrial societies, and they are financially dependent on their parents for an extended period. It costs money to raise them and put them through school. Thus the fewer children in a family, the higher its standard of living. What this suggests is that birth rates drop when a country reaches a "threshold" in industrialization, urbanization, and literacy. Only then do a majority of couples see an advantage in having small families. Only then *is* there a direct advantage.

Demographers refer to this pattern as the *demographic transition.* The demographic transition occurs in three stages. In Stage I, the death rate drops, but the birth rate remains high, causing the population to grow. In Stage II, the birth rate begins to drop, and the mortality rate remains low. The population continues to grow, but more slowly. In Stage III, the birth rate stabilizes at or below replacement levels (women have no

Figure 3–4
The Demographic Transition

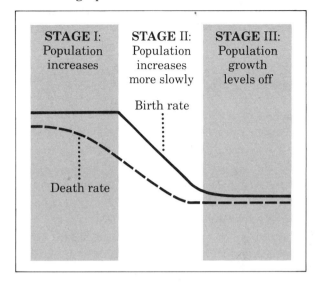

more than two children), so that birth and death rates begin to balance (see Figure 3–4). The demographic transition is complete when low or zero population growth is achieved.

Most developed nations are in Stage III of the demographic transition. The picture in developing nations is quite different. The death rates in Latin America, Africa, and Asia began to drop after World War II, but not because of gradual social and economic change, as in Europe and North America. This decline in mortality was the result of imported technology applied almost overnight (van der Tak, Haub, and Murphy, 1979, pp. 8–10). International health agencies and foreign aid programs supplied instruction in public sanitation, antibiotics, immunizations, insecticides, and, in many nations, food. As a result, demographic changes that occurred over a century ago in the West were telescoped into two decades. In the words of an old man who lives in a village near Calcutta, "When I was a boy, they took away forty or fifty bodies after a cholera epidemic. It happened every five or ten years. Now they come and vaccinate our children. I have lived here almost seventy years. The biggest change in my time is health. We've learned to keep from dying" (Evans, 1961, pp. 79–80). The lowering of death rates in developing nations was nothing short of miraculous. But an unintended consequence of introducing modern medicine without modern birth control was a population explosion. The populations of developing nations are increasing at an average rate of 2.1 percent a year, compared to an average of 0.7 percent in developed nations (van der Tak, Haub, and Murphy, 1979, pp. 4–6). Developing nations are in Stage I of the demographic transition: Death rates have dropped but birth rates are still high. Moving into Stages II and III, toward zero population growth, seems to depend on economic development.

At the 1974 World Population Conference in Bucharest, the rallying cry for Third World nations was "Development is the best contraceptive." But the fact that these nations are already overcrowded makes development an uphill fight. Whatever economic gains they make are literally eaten up by their growing populations. Funds that might be used for investment in economic development are spent on survival. From the individual's point of view, moreover, children are the only form of capital. They can be put to work on family fields or hired out to big landowners. Ten children bring in twice the income of five. Often, children are the only form of social security. They are culturally obligated to support their parents in old age, and no one else will. (In China, where a government-sponsored social welfare system has replaced the traditional family welfare system, birth rates have declined significantly.) It's not simply that people want and enjoy large families. The short-term advantages of more children outweigh the long-term, abstract advantages of limiting births.

Success stories in family planning are few and far between. The International Planned Parenthood Federation (1978) estimates that only 20 percent of couples in developing nations use contraceptives (compared to 65 percent in developed nations). Moreover, the number of potentially fertile women *not* practicing family planning rose from 342 to 361 million between 1971 and 1976. The World Fertility Survey, funded by the United Nations and the U.S. Agency for International Development and launched in 1971, is revealing. Ultimately the survey will cover forty developing and twenty developed nations. To date, fifteen developing countries have been studied (Kendall, 1979). Over 75 percent of the women surveyed had heard of at least one method of birth control, but less than half the women in ten countries had ever used contraception. Nearly 50 percent of married women said they did not want to have more children, but only half of these women were using contraception. Thus there seems to be a wide gap between the knowledge and practice of family planning.

Future prospects The rate of world population growth seems to have peaked in the mid-1960s. The birth rate has fallen much more rapidly than anyone would have predicted ten years ago, particularly in Asia and some Latin American nations. Family planning programs have had some impact. In many developed nations, the growth rate has declined to replacement levels, in part because more women are working outside their homes. Though the data are encouraging, the population problem remains serious. Even at reduced rates, the global population is expected to reach 6.2 billion in the next two decades, and most of the increase will take place in the nations least able to support more people. Even though the *rate* of increase is slowly and grudgingly declining, the sheer *size* of the global population will place increasing pressures on material resources, the environment, and the social fabric.

A human traffic jam in Shanghai. The rate *of population growth may have slowed in recent years (especially in China), but the absolute number of people on earth is still a severe problem.*

Patterns of Consumption

The number of people on earth today and expected tomorrow does not tell the full story. Each of the 74 million people who will join the world population this year will need food, clothing, and shelter, at a minimum. Necessity is a matter of social definition, however. What people consider a decent home, a fine set of clothes, a hearty meal varies from place to place and changes over time. Future demands on the earth's resources will depend not only on the size of the population but also on patterns of consumption. Modern communication systems that beam images of Western abundance to all corners of the earth have raised expectations. To some extent, desires have been globalized. People everywhere want shoes, radios, jeans, and white bread.

Current patterns There is a wide gap between levels of consumption in developed and developing nations. A young man from Mozambique said, "I simply do not understand America. It is the moon. The rest of the world is dealing with problems of production and distribution and you Americans seem threatened by waste, by disposal. Tell me, do you really have twelve different kinds of toothpaste? Why?" (*The New York Times*, December 30, 1979). Here we'll look at the consumption of two critical resources, energy and food.

With just over 5 percent of the world's population, the United States consumed 32 percent of the world's commercial energy in 1972 (Ridker and Watson, 1980, Tables 2-4, 5-6).* One American uses as much commercial energy as two Englishmen, three Swiss or Japanese, nine Mexicans, fifty-three Indians or Indonesians (Independent Commission on International Development Issues, 1980, p. 162). Although the United States is by far the most extravagant consumer of energy in the world, all industrial nations consume disproportionate amounts of energy in terms of their population.

In contrast, the developing nations, with 71 percent of the world's population, used only 16 percent of all commercial energy in 1972 (Ridker and Watson, 1980, Tables 2-4, 5-6). In many of these countries, 90 percent of the population is still living in the "wood age" (Barnet, 1980, p. 73). They use no fossil fuel (oil, gas, or coal) whatever. They burn wood for heat, light, and cooking, and use human and animal muscle power for transportation and work. For developing nations, mass electrification, like mass education, is still largely a dream.

Global inequalities in food consumption are just as great. The average person in developed countries consumes about 3,380 calories per day; the average person in developing nations, about 2,210 calories (van der Tak, Haub, and Murphy, 1979, p. 25). The food gap is wider than these figures indicate, however, for there are differences in the quality as well as the quantity of food. In many developing nations, especially Africa, the majority of the population lives on roots and coarse grains that are low in vitamins and protein, supplemented by some wild fruits and vegetables and occasional Coca-Colas. The more nutritious foods grown in these countries are usually grown as cash crops, not for local consumption. The staple in Asia and Latin America — rice — is highly nutritious *if* it is served with green vegetables and fish, beans, or potatoes. Often it is not (Barnet, 1980, pp. 175–79). Moreover, the figure for average calories conceals the fact that in many places the elite eat well while most people are chronically hungry (van der Tak, Haub, and Murphy, 1979, p. 25). (Of course, there also are inequities in the rich nations. Many Americans are undernourished, as Chapter 9 will show.)

In contrast, the average diet in developed nations is high in animal protein. North America, Europe, and, increasingly, the Soviet Union are carnivorous islands in a vegetarian world. The average American today eats about 120 pounds of meat a year. It takes about 7 pounds of grain to produce a single pound of meat. Thus meat eaters consume more of the world's food supply than simple calculations of calories indicate. The United States and Canada use more than 1,800 pounds of grain per person per year, with all but 100 pounds going for cattle and chicken feed. Iran, Pakistan, Morocco, India, and Thailand use only 400 pounds of grain per person, nearly all in the form of bread or cereal. Including indirect calories, the average American consumes 8,825 calories a day (Barnet, 1980, pp. 182–83; Ayres, 1979, pp. 179–82).

Are these patterns likely to continue? If so, what impact will they have on future demands?

---

*For the first time in a quarter of a century, energy use in the United States declined in 1979, but only by a fraction of 1 percent.

Future trends Common sense suggests that the demand for food, energy, and other material goods in developing countries will "explode" in coming decades—in part because of population growth and in part because of industrialization. Developing nations' incomes are so low, however, that it seems unlikely that they will consume a large portion of the global pie for many years to come (Ridker and Cecelski, 1979, p. 20). Data from the People's Republic of China support this. Between 1975 and 1976, China increased its use of petroleum by 30 percent and still, with one-fifth of the world's population, used only 2.5 percent of global energy supplies (Barnet, 1980, p. 36). What happens in developed nations will have far more impact on future demands.

There are already signs of a slowdown in consumption in developed nations, and this seems likely to continue (Ridker and Cecelski, 1979, pp. 20–24). There are two basic reasons. First, personal income will probably decline, since increased expenditures for new forms of energy and environmental protection are taking money out of consumers' pockets. Second, there are limits to the number of cars, houses, refrigerators that one person can *conveniently* own. Things like campers, cameras, and roller skates compete for a person's time. Moreover, when the Joneses keep catching up, enjoyment of material goods diminishes. Most people will not enjoy their vacation home, their CB radio, their snowmobile so much if everyone else is doing the same thing. Clutter and congestion are slowing consumption in developed nations (Hirsch, 1976).

All this suggests that the rate of growth in demands for world resources will decline somewhat in future decades. According to one projection, the growth rate in energy consumption will drop from 4.6 percent a year in 1975 to 3 percent in 2025 (Ridker and Watson, 1980, Tables 2-4, 5-6). But even if the *rate* of growth slows, the absolute amount of resources needed will increase dramatically. In all likelihood, people will require

Figure 3–5
World Energy Consumption: 1975, 2000, 2025, and 2050

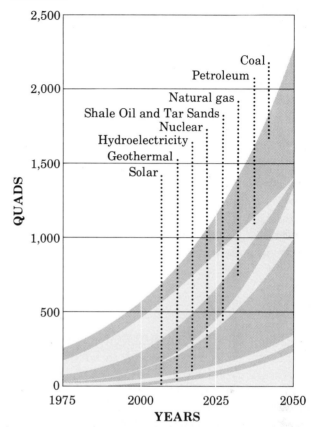

Source: R.G. Ridker and W.D. Watson, Jr., *To Choose a Future: Resources and Environmental Problems of the United States, a Long-Term Global Outlook* (Baltimore, Md.: Johns Hopkins Press, 1980), p. 23.

five times as much energy in 2025 as they do now (see Figure 3–5). In 1985, people will need 44 percent more food than they did in 1970. Over the next quarter century, developing nations will have to produce or buy 600 million tons of grain, in addition to the 400 million they use now, just to maintain their current standard of living. In short, although the rates of population growth and consumption are slowing down, the sheer number of people who need food every day and want hot showers (and more) will be staggering. The lilies in the pond continue to multiply, and what they collectively take from the pond is increasing.

Global Resources

Are the earth's resources adequate to meet future demands? Is the pond wide and deep enough to support the blossoming population? Geologists' estimates of the earth's riches provide only part of the answer. It also depends on what people *make* of global resources. Estimates of future supplies must take into account new technology and how technology and its products are distributed. Thus questions about the size of the pond are in large part sociological questions. Here, again, we'll look at food and energy.

Food Supplies

In 1798, Robert Thomas Malthus, the British mathematician and clergyman, declared, "Man is necessarily confined to a room" (the ecosphere) and lives in constant danger of eating himself out of house and home. Malthus held that sexual appetites drive human beings to increase much faster than the food supply. Population increases geometrically (2,4,16,256—multiplying like the pond lilies), while the food supply increases only arithmetically, field by field (2,4,6,8). Malthus saw population and food supply as a kind of seesaw. When the food supply is high and people are eating well, they have many healthy babies who live to have more babies, who have more babies. As the population rises, however, the amount of food available for each person goes down. Eventually there are so many mouths to feed that the amount of food available for each person plummets. Famine sets in. Death from starvation lowers the population. The food supply begins to go up, and the whole process starts

again. Malthus believed humanity was strapped onto this seesaw of feast and famine.

Malthus made two miscalculations. First, he did not consider the possibility that people could or would control population growth. Upon reading an article on contraception, Malthus exclaimed, "I profess not to understand . . ." (Kroedel and van de Walle, 1979, p. 229). Second, he assumed that there were only so many acres of land available for farming and that an acre could produce only so much food. He allowed for small increases in food production, but not for giant leaps.

Malthus failed to predict the *Green Revolution*, a series of supply-boosting agricultural innovations. The first shot in the Green Revolution was fired at a research center in Mexico in the late 1950s by the geneticist Norman Bourlag. Bourlag developed a strain of "miracle wheat" that doubled or even tripled the yield per acre. (The miracle wheat is in fact a dwarf plant whose thick, short stem can support larger quantities of ripe grain without breaking [Harris, 1975, p. 450].) This led to the engineering of miracle rice and, most recently, miracle beans, all designed specifically to reduce hunger in developing nations. From World War II to the present, food production actually has grown faster than population (van der Tak, Haub, and Murphy, 1979, pp. 24–25). With the help of scientists, farmers broke the Malthusian supply barrier.

Future prospects The question remains whether agricultural production can continue to expand, and expand enough to feed 6.2 billion people in the year 2000. There are four possible ways to increase food supplies: adding to the land now under cultivation, increasing the yield per acre, farming the sea, and developing new food sources (Ehrlich and Ehrlich, 1972; Mesarovic and Pestel, 1974). Each approach has problems as well as potential.

Estimates are that 7.86 billion acres of the earth are arable (suitable for farming)—more than three times the number being cultivated today (Ehrlich and Ehrlich, 1972, p. 113). However, over 4 billion acres lie in the tropics, where the soil is too thin and the rains too heavy for growing anything but low-protein and non-food crops (palm oil, bananas, coffee) with today's technology. Much of the remaining land is now desert or savannah and would have to be irrigated. Irrigation has been a spectacular success in many places: Southern California, now the nation's fruit and vegetable basket, was once a desert. But the supply of water is limited, as suggested in the beginning of this chapter, and after a time, irrigation causes minerals to build up so that the soil has to be "dry cleaned" (taken out of cultivation).

A second strategy for winning the race between population growth and food supply is increasing the yield per acre—the promise of the Green Revolution. The "miracle" plants are richer than traditional varieties; several crops can be grown in a single season. World production of wheat, rice, and other cereals has doubled since pre-Green Revolution days (Ridker and Cecelski, 1979, p. 15). When these plants were introduced to India and Pakistan, the harvest increased by a third in a single year (Ehrlich and Ehrlich, 1972, p. 120).

The Green Revolution is not without problems, though. The high-yield plants require large amounts of water, heavy doses of chemical fertilizer, and regular baths with insecticides, all of which are expensive. (The fertilizers are made with petroleum.) To join the Green Revolution, a country needs capital. Nations that have already mortgaged their futures to keep hunger at a "tolerable" level go further into debt. In addition, the Green Revolution encourages planting large tracts of land with a single crop, and a region that depends on a single plant is extremely vulnerable. If there appears a new plant disease for which there is no known cure or a pest for which there is no poison, the entire harvest may be destroyed. Thus the price of high yield is high risk.

Except for a few experiments, human beings have not even begun to farm the ocean. The French and Italians herd mussels and oysters into underwater "pastures." But by and large, we are in the hunting and gathering stage on the ocean. Even so, seafood supplies one-fifth of the world's protein, and the harvest could be doubled with current technology. There are two basic obstacles to farming the ocean. The first is pollution, not only from industrial wastes but also from the fertilizers and pesticides farmers use to boost food production on land. The second obstacle is political. No one owns the high seas. An attempt to establish ocean plantations by one nation is sure to be met with opposition by others. (We will discuss conflicts over the ocean in some detail in Chapter 4.)

A fourth solution to food supply would be synthetic or unorthodox foods, such as protein supplements made from soy and cottonseed oil (Ehrlich and Ehrlich, 1972, pp. 134–37). One problem here is that people may not like the taste.

There is room for optimism concerning increases in the food supply. If all the land in temperate climates yielded as much as the corn fields in Iowa, there would be enough food to provide 7.5 billion people with 2,500-calorie diets. If the problems of farming in the tropics were solved, 38 to 48 billion people could enjoy 4,000- to 5,000-calorie diets (Revelle, 1975). These are big *ifs*. Nevertheless, it is possible that everyone will have enough to eat in the next century. The central problem may not be supply but distribution.

Supply vs. distribution "The most serious energy crisis in the world," writes Richard Barnet of the Institute for Policy Studies, "is the depletion of human energy because the brain receives too few calories or too few proteins to think and the body too few to act" (1980, p. 161). An estimated 1.3 billion people are chronically hungry today. As many as 462 million are starving, over half of them small children. Hunger is especially com-

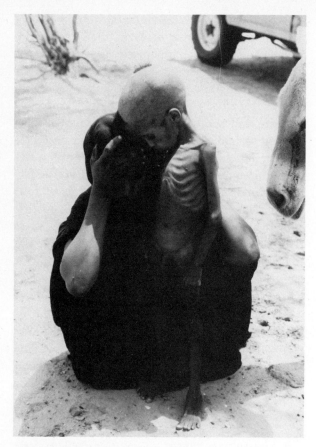

This child is one of an estimated 12 million children under age five who die each year from starvation or because they are too undernourished to resist diseases like measles. Malnutrition leaves as many as 300 million who survive childhood mentally retarded.

mon in the developing nations of Africa, Asia, and Latin America. This human energy crisis is not the result of inadequate supplies. Enough grain is produced today to provide every man, woman, and child on earth with 3,000 calories every day — not counting meat and fish, fruits and vegetables. Why then do people go hungry? In Barnet's words, "because they no longer grow [food] themselves and they do not have the money to buy it" (1980, p. 151).

Food production has become increasingly commercial, mechanized, and internationalized. In traditional agricultural societies, most people live on what they grow themselves or trade at local markets. Peasant communities are largely self-sufficient. Often land is communally held. The exchange of goods and services is governed by traditional social obligations, not profits. Participation in such a community protects individuals from failure, to some extent. The commercialization of agriculture — the shift from village-based food production to a money-based private-property system — changes the structure of food distribution (Chirot, 1977, pp. 122–26). A commercial farmer's livelihood depends on the unpredictable whims and tastes of people who have no obligation to buy his produce, on the availability and cost of transportation, and on what farmers in other places independently decide to grow. The individual farmer may profit from this system in ways that are not possible in a peasant economy, but the individual may also lose. As a rule, it is large landowners who profit and landless peasants who lose.

The commercialization of Third World agriculture dates back to the nineteenth century, when European nations began to industrialize and acquire colonies on a large scale. Colonial powers encouraged the shift from growing food for local consumption to growing cotton, coffee, and other commodities for export.

Commercialization has accelerated in recent years. In the last two decades, the production of cash crops for sale in the global market has increased twice as fast as the production of food for consumption in developing countries. At least fifteen nations devote more acres to exports than to vegetables and fruits that might feed their people. As a result, food has to be imported. While the well-fed nations import animal feed and non-essentials (coffee, sugar, bananas) from hungry nations, the hungry nations import staples (wheat, corn, rice). For example, on land that was used for growing black beans, a peasant staple, Brazil now grows soybeans to export as cattle feed. It imports black beans at prices the poor can't afford. A former president of Brazil comments, "Brazil is doing well but the people aren't" (Barnet, 1980, p. 256). Thus one of the unintended consequences of the commercialization of agriculture has been a decline in food self-sufficiency.

The mechanization of agriculture has contributed to inequality within nations and among nations. Modern agricultural technology has encouraged the replacement of small farms with large ones, human labor with machines. The Green Revolution has played a role in this. In many places, wealthy landlords were the only ones who had the cash or credit to join the Green Revolution. Seeds, fertilizer, and water all cost money. When small farmers were given supplies, many sold them on the black market to meet their immediate food needs. In Punjab, a center of the Green Revolution, 50 percent of agricultural jobs have been eliminated. Countless peasants have been evicted. Cut off from their traditional food sources, these refugees from the Green Revolution migrate to already overcrowded cities, are unable to find jobs, and join the crowds of urban scavengers. More food is being produced, but the people who need it can't buy it. The Green Revolution, a technical solution to the problem of food supply, has caused unanticipated social dislocation.

Thus, hunger in the world today is not the fulfillment of Malthus's prophecy. There is enough food to go around. Nor is hunger the result of scheming or callousness in government and the corporations that dominate agribusiness. No one has a calculated plan to profit from malnutrition. The international supply and distribution of food is lopsided. As things stand, people are concentrated in some parts of the world and food production capacity is concentrated elsewhere. The bridges between them—the global institutions to achieve some balance in food supply—have not been built.

Energy Resources

If food shortages are the most urgent problem facing developing nations, energy shortages are the most urgent problem facing developed nations. Energy "is the resource for gaining access to all other resources" (Barnet, 1980, p. 19). It is the key to opening new land for cultivation, desalting sea water for irrigation, producing fertilizer, mining ores, recycling metals, and generally maintaining a decent standard of living. We have already experienced energy shortages. What does the future hold?

In estimating future energy supplies, it is important to distinguish between resources, current reserves, and prospective reserves. *Resources* are all the materials that may someday be used to provide energy, including new discoveries and technology. *Current reserves* are resources that are known and recoverable with current technology at current prices. Data on current reserves are available but are probably incomplete—because corporations under-report and because some areas have not been thoroughly explored. *Prospective reserves* are known and suspected resources that are likely to be used during the next twenty-five years as current reserves run out, people are willing to pay more for energy, and/or new, less costly technology is developed. If current rates of growth in population and consumption continue, known reserves of many energy resources will, indeed, run out within a few decades (Ridker and Cecelski, 1979, pp. 24–26). Energy resources will not be exhausted, however.

Nonrenewable resources Nonrenewable resources are finite materials that can be used only once. Oil, gas, coal, and uranium are all nonrenewable. While current reserves are almost exhausted, prospective reserves are abundant.

The world consumes almost 30,000 gallons of petroleum each *second* (Barnet, 1980, p. 21). Western nations depend on oil for almost half

Protest spans the globe. Indian agricultural workers displaced by the Green Revolution demonstrate in New Delhi; in Washington, D.C., American farmers protest the low price of farm products and the high price of oil.

their energy needs; natural gas supplies another quarter of these needs. There may be as many as 6 trillion gallons of oil still underground. Most of this resource will never be used, however. It is trapped in pockets, like water in a sponge. And long before the last drop is squeezed from the earth, the cost of extracting oil will far exceed its value. The same is true for natural gas, a first cousin to oil often found in the same deposits. We are fast approaching this point of diminishing returns. The most optimistic estimates indicate that both oil and natural gas will be essentially exhausted in the next fifty to seventy-five years (Ridker and Cecelski, 1979, p. 33).

All is not lost, however. Oil can also be extracted from *shale* and *tar sands,* which are found all over the globe, often in huge quantities. North America, with some of the largest deposits, has an estimated 600-year supply. Already a plant in Alberta, Canada, is producing 50,000 barrels of oil a day from tar sands. It takes 1.7 tons of shale to produce a single barrel of oil, however, so that waste disposal is a problem. The extraction process requires huge amounts of water, and the largest deposits are found in regions where water is in short supply. Finally, the cost of starting up a new fuel industry, almost from scratch, would be enormous.

Coal is everybody's least favorite fuel. Mining it is dangerous; transporting it is unwieldy; burning it is toxic. Although production has declined in recent years, coal is making a comeback, and the reason is supply. There is enough coal in the ground to supply the energy needs of 10 billion people for several hundred years. Coal can be burned directly, or it can be pulverized, mixed with steam and oxygen, and turned into a gas or liquid fuel. Again, there are problems and again, the first is cost. The price tag for opening enough mines and building enough conversion plants to supply U.S. needs would be at least $150 billion. This figure does not include the cost of converting factories that switched from coal to oil or gas (when they were cheap) back to coal. A second problem is transportation, particularly in the United States. Antiquated railroads would have to be refurbished. The third and most difficult problem is environmental pollution. Mining operations can cause irreversible damage to the environment, as described in Chapter 1. And burning coal can cause irreversible damage to people's health through lung diseases and cancer. Researchers are working on new "scrubbers" that would eliminate some of the effects of a shift to coal, but only some.

Nuclear power plants are fueled by *uranium,* another nonrenewable resource. The seventy-two nuclear power plants now operating in the United States produce about 12 percent of the nation's electricity, or the equivalent of 1 million barrels of oil a day. Ninety-four additional nuclear plants are under construction (*U.S. News & World Report,* August 13, 1979, p. 39). Estimates of both the world supply of uranium and future demands are sketchy. We might use up 30 to 85 percent of uranium reserves by 2025, depending on which technology we use (Ridker and Cecelski, 1979, p. 33). Breeder reactors generate more energy than nuclear fission plants do from the same amount of uranium, but they have the disadvantage of producing plutonium as a byproduct. Plutonium is the basic ingredient for an atom bomb.

The construction of nuclear power plants creates a number of hazards (Barnet, 1980, pp. 85–97). The first and potentially most catastrophic is the possibility of a meltdown. The second hazard is death from low-level radiation. Uranium miners, plant operators, and the people who live near nuclear power plants are exposed to this all of the time. Current standards for safe level exposure are largely guesswork. Because the cancer caused by radiation exposure may not appear for twenty or more years, no one really knows what is safe. The third hazard comes from the disposal of nuclear wastes. A typical plant produces about 2,400 tons of waste a year, and this material will remain radioactive for *thousands* of years to come. Two additional dangers are theft and sabotage. The technology for producing an atom bomb is an open secret. The only way to control the production of bombs is to control the materials. According to a House subcommittee report, 50 tons of nuclear material, including 6,000 pounds of weapons-level material, have already been "lost." It takes only about 20 pounds to make a bomb.

Renewable resources Given the limits, dangers, and cost of nonrenewable fuels, renewable sources of energy are looking more and more attractive. In many ways, solar energy seems an obvious choice: Each day enough sunlight falls on the earth to supply it with fifteen years of power. Sunlight drenches the earth's 800 million square miles of desert. If only 0.4 percent of this area were covered with solar collectors, we would have all the energy we needed—forever (Tuve, 1976, p. 77). The problem is that deserts are almost always in the wrong place—miles from population centers, industry, and agriculture. In the right places, where people live and farm and work, sunlight is highly variable. The amount changes from season to season, hour to hour. Clouds can suddenly turn off the switch. So can air pollution. And although solar energy is abundant, the technology for collecting, storing, transporting, and converting solar power to practical use is only now being developed. With current technology, solar energy is useful only on a small scale.

Other renewable sources of energy include "energy plantations" to convert sugar cane residues, kelp, or even garbage to alcohol fuels; hydroelectric energy; geothermal resources (hot springs and geysers); and giant windmills. Some are already being used. Brazil uses sugar cane wastes to produce gasahol for its cars. Iceland gets most of its winter heat from hot springs. The town of Boone, North Carolina, constructed a 150-foot windmill that provides power to 300 homes. Alone, none of these resources provides a great deal of energy. In combination, however, they could make a sizable dent in the world's oil bill.

Energy costs and energy profits The immediate energy problem facing the United States and other Western nations is dependence on oil from a politically unstable part of the world. Even if this were not the case, oil is a finite resource and the supply is running short. The long-term problem is making an orderly transition from a system based on one set of energy resources to a system based on another.

Technologically, energy self-sufficiency is within our grasp. Why, if renewable and domestic sources of energy are available, has the United States staked so much on oil? Why haven't we developed alternative energy sources? There is no one answer to these questions.

A number of obstacles block the path to energy self-sufficiency (Thurow, 1980, pp. 35–40). First, each alternative energy source available to the United States contains hidden costs. Coal, for example, is a relatively cheap source of energy—if you don't care about the environmental damage that occurs wherever it is mined or burned. If you value a clean environment, however, and insist on pollution controls, coal becomes expensive. A shift to coal might provoke serious regional conflicts in the United States. To power automobiles, coal would have to be converted to liquid or gas fuel, a process that requires a great deal of water. The states with the most abundant coal reserves (Montana and Wyoming) are short on water. Either the coal would have to be moved to the water, or the water to the coal. Who wants to give up their water? Who is willing to have the slag heaps from coal plants dumped on their land? No one. Second, the shift from one energy source to another will take time (fifteen to twenty years at least) and money. And while the benefits of energy independence lie in the distant future, the price would have to be paid now. Under our election system, politicians who pressed the nation into costly investments probably would not be here to claim the credit when those investments paid off. Third, the international situation creates *dis*incentives for private companies that might invest in alternative energy sources. The high price of oil today is not the result of natural scarcities; it is man-made. It only costs about 40¢ to produce a barrel of oil. OPEC, which controls most of the world's petroleum, keeps prices high by withholding supplies. Suppose that the price of imported oil is $30 a barrel. A private investor develops a process that produces synthetic fuel for $25. OPEC would simply reduce its price to $24.99, and the investor would be left with a worthless production plant. Finally, the high profits still to be made from depleting the earth's remaining oil reserves create an incentive to *delay* the development of alternative energy sources (for example, purchasing the patent on solar equipment, then not producing it).

The obstacles to energy self-sufficiency are built into our political and economic systems. Our political system enables organized groups of people who do not want to live next door to heaps of coal slag or a nuclear reactor to veto such plans. Our economic system leaves energy development in corporate hands, so that decisions are based on today's profits, not long-term national goals. The international situation encourages economic competition rather than cooperation for energy resources. This is not to say that there are no solutions to the long-term energy problem, but that none of them are simple.

In summary, the Limits Thesis (resources are almost exhausted) and the Cornucopian Thesis (resources are virtually inexhaustible) are both overstatements. There is no guarantee that nations will be able to maintain even their current standards of living in the future. With food, the problem is not only supply but also distribution. With energy, the key problem is not lack of alter-natives but lack of incentives. Thus social patterns of use and distribution will play a critical role in future supplies. One thing seems clear: Supplies will not meet future demands without the aid of new technology, and technology almost always holds risks.

The Environment at Risk

A decade ago, Barry Commoner wrote, "The environment has just been rediscovered by the people who live in it" (1972, p. 1). Since then, discoveries of the damage people have done to the planet have appeared at an accelerating rate. It is as if we thought we were guests at a global banquet, then suddenly were presented with a staggering bill: pollution, unleashed poisons with no known antidote, unpredictable changes in the climate. To explain how the human race ran up this bill we turn to ecology.

Barry Commoner has outlined four informal laws of ecology (1972, pp. 29–41):

1. *Everything is connected to everything else.* The global ecosystem consists of many interrelated parts that act upon one another. Change in one part of the system causes change in others.

2. *Everything must go somewhere.* There is no such thing as "waste" in nature. What one organism expels, another takes up. Nothing "goes away"; it can only be moved from one place to another or transformed from one type of molecule to another.

3. *Nature knows best.* Commoner compares the ecosystem to a watch. Suppose you opened the back of your watch, closed your eyes, and poked a pencil into the works. There is a *tiny* chance that a random poke would make the watch work better, but this is extremely unlikely. The workings of the ecosystem are far more complex than those of a watch. The odds that "poking around" in the ecosystem will by harmful are overwhelming.

The Nature of Ecosystems

Ecologists see the earth and its inhabitants as a limited but self-renewing system. All life depends on energy from the sun that penetrates the atmosphere, is absorbed by green plants and algae, and thus enters *food chains.*

Plants use light to produce carbohydrates and other compounds. Herbivores, (from caterpillars to elephants) are the next link in the chain. These animals eat plants and retain some of this energy in their bodies. The next link is forged when carnivores (robbins, lions, spiders, people) eat them. Some energy is lost with each move up the chain, but the sun keeps up the supply. There is no extraterrestrial source of supply for other essential ingredients of life, including carbon, hydrogen, oxygen, and nitrogen. These substances must be continually *recycled.* Nitrogen, a vital part of proteins, enzymes, vitamins, and hormones, illustrates this. Most of the nitrogen on earth (80 percent) is in the air. Certain bacteria and algae capture airborne nitrogen and fix it in the soil. There, other bacteria turn the nitrogen into nitrates, which are absorbed into the roots of plants, which use it to make protein and more. The animals that eat these plants return some of the nitrogen to the soil as wastes. Some is returned through decay. The nitrogen-fixing bacteria replace whatever is lost in this process, keeping the cycle in motion. The flow of energy from the sun through food chains and the recycling of elements are what keeps life going.

4. *There is no such thing as a free lunch.* Commoner borrows this expression from economics. The point is that every gain exacts a price. Payment can be delayed, but it cannot be avoided.

Commoner argues that people have violated and ignored these laws for so long that the global ecosystem is in extreme peril. A decade ago this was a minority view. No longer.

Technological Fallout

Like all animals, humans have an impact on their environment. We consume oxygen, water, plants, and so on, participating in food chains and the recycling of minerals. But technology amplifies human beings' impact on the environment. For example, our distant ancestors used only the oxygen needed for respiration. Today we build fires, power plants, and chemical processors that consume vast amounts of oxygen. In addition, we've added new substances to the environment that nature never intended—plastics, radioisotopes, insecticides, and most recently, new organisms produced through genetic engineering. Some of the effects of our activities are clearly visible; some are only shadows and whispers.

Twenty-five years ago, few people were concerned about the disposal of industrial wastes. Emissions from factory smokestacks drifted away; human and industrial refuse could be flushed down rivers; fertilizers and insecticides disappeared after they had done their jobs—or so we imagined. In fact, we didn't dispose of anything if by dispose we mean "get rid of." Everything goes somewhere (Law 2). We are paying now for treating the air, water, and land as if they were free (Law 4), and the price is pollution. Pollution occurs under two conditions: when the amount of waste produced exceeds the ecosystem's ability to absorb and recycle; when people create substances that are not degradable (cannot be recycled) by natural means.

Air pollution The word "smog" (a combination of smoke plus fog) was coined in England in 1952 to describe a thick, brownish cloud that enveloped London for five days. It was the worst air pollu-

A foggy day in London town? Not exactly. This is the great smog of 1952—a blanket of choking sulphur dioxide that killed 4,000 Londoners.

tion disaster ever recorded: 4,000 people died. Sulphur dioxide, a gas that attacks the lining of the lungs and reduces resistance to infection, is a byproduct of burning coal and oil (Commoner, 1972, pp. 64–65). Since 1952, many other sources of air pollution have been discovered. For example, automobile exhausts contain carbon monoxide, a deadly gas used in many Hollywood portrayals of suicide in the garage. The combination of engine heat and sunlight sets off chemical reactions that produce still more dangerous compounds. Photochemical smog, as this is called, has killed over a million trees in California and is causing the Italian city of Venice to crumble. Smog is visible. But invisible substances (mercury vapors and asbestos fibers, to name two) also contaminate the air. Damage is not confined to the area where pollutants are released. Once in the air, their movement is unpredictable. For example, radioactive fallout from an atomic bomb test in China reached Brookhaven, Long Island, only nine days after the test (Woodwell, 1967, p. 26). Some particles are taken up by clouds and deposited on land as "acid rain." Some are breathed in by humans and deposited in the lungs. In 1970, the Department of Health, Education, and Welfare calculated that breathing the air in midtown Manhattan during rush hours was equivalent to smoking two packs of cigarettes a day. That year, U.S. automobiles, electric power plants, and industries were releasing one ton of air pollutants *per person*. The Clean Air Act of 1970 requires emission controls on factories and cars, but standards have to be continually upgraded to compensate for the addition of new cars and new factories.

Water pollution Industrial and human wastes also cause water pollution. They are not the only sources of this pollution, however. Consider Lake Erie (Commoner, 1972, Chapter 6). When fish began to disappear from the lake in the first half of this century, the problem was blamed on sew-age from surrounding cities and towns. Sewage promoted the growth of bacteria, which used up so much oxygen that many fish couldn't breathe. The logical solution was to build sewage treatment plants. A jeweler might as well have poked a pencil into a watch in an attempt to fix it (Law 3, Nature knows best). The treatment plants used phosphates, a chemical detergent, to turn sewage into inorganic material, including nitrates. But since both phosphates and nitrates are fertilizers, this caused a population explosion among the algae. Soon there were too few nutrients for the algae, and they began to die. This in turn caused the bacteria to multiply still faster, using up still more oxygen. To further complicate matters, nitrogen fertilizer from nearby farms had begun to seep into the lake. By the late 1960s, most of Lake Erie was lifeless.

The problem of water pollution does not stop at the shores of a lake. Water from contaminated lakes and rivers makes its way to the ocean. Pollutants spread along the shores, attacking marine life. The remains of oil spills and chemical wastes collect on the surface, shutting out sunlight. The ocean may seem like a bottomless pit, but in fact, it is just another lake, landlocked on every side (Heyerdahl, 1975).

Ground pollution In the late 1970s, Americans discovered a "new" environmental problem at Love Canal: ground pollution. The canal was built in the late nineteenth century by William T. Love as part of a model city (Brown, 1980). Some years later, the Hooker Chemical Company bought the canal and began filling it with wastes from their plants—including such substances as dioxin, a chemical defoliant that was created for use in the Vietnam war but banned when it was found to cause birth defects. (The Army called it Agent Orange.) Hooker closed the dump, covered it over with a layer of dirt in 1953, and deeded it to the local school board for $1. By then, a number of people had built homes in the area. In a few

At a dump site in Sorrento, Louisiana, a local official examines rotting drums of hazardous chemicals. Ten years ago there was no law against trucking wastes to a dump site. Many of the companies that did so are out of business today. Who should pay for cleaning up?

years, strange things began to happen. On humid, moonlit nights, a greenish luminescent haze hung over the canal. Trees shed their leaves overnight. But it was years before residents made the connections between these events and birth defects, liver and kidney damage, respiratory ailments, and cancer. Chemical residues, including many poisons like Agent Orange, had escaped the dump, invaded neighboring yards and houses, and found their way into the bodies of residents. After a ten-year struggle, residents captured public and government attention. The immediate area was evacuated. In 1980–81, the trench was sealed with a tile barrier. But even so, 355 of 550 homeowners took advantage of a government offer to buy their homes and moved away (*Newsweek*, September 14, 1981, pp. 13–14).

There are three interrelated problems here. First, modern technology has created a wide array of artificial substances (plastics, synthetic fabrics, food preservatives) that nature is incapable of recycling. Second, it is only in the last five years that ground pollution has become a social issue. Sites like Love Canal are the result of a combination of ignorance and lack of concern about the environment. Third, in many cases the companies that produced and dumped toxic substances have vanished. Who should pay for cleaning up? The Environmental Protection Agency proposed that chemical companies be taxed to create a $4 billion Superfund to handle "orphan" dumps. The chemical industry objected to what it saw as retroactive punishment. In one spokesman's words, "It's like saying it's illegal to do something yesterday" (*The New York Times*, June 8, 1980, p. 5).

Pesticides According to UN statistics, the world produces 1.3 billion pounds of pesticides each year (in Heyerdahl, 1975). In the San Joaquin Valley of California alone, farmers use about 250 million pounds each year (Boraiko, 1980, p. 146). The creation of artificial toxins creates special environmental hazards (see p. 102). Pesticides are poisons. No poison is totally safe. The use of DDT was banned in the United

A Solution Becomes a Problem—DDT

DDT—a man-made chemical that attacks insects' nervous systems—is a classic example of a solution that became a problem. When first introduced in the early 1940s, it was hailed as a miracle. It saved the cotton belt from the boll weevil, an insect that had migrated to the United States from Mexico and had been eating into the South's economy for decades. All over the world, DDT halted epidemics. The annual number of malaria cases in Sri Lanka alone dropped from nearly 3 million to 7,300 in ten years after the introduction of DDT.

But the magic didn't last. DDT soon began to exact a price. In addition to the insects at which it is aimed, it kills beneficial insects, such as spiders and assassin bugs, which prey on cotton bollworms. In other words, it wipes out natural pest controls. Moreover, the target insects themselves become immune to the poison in a short time. DDT never succeeds in killing off all members of the offending species. A few odd ones, resistant to the insecticide by genetic chance, survive and breed quickly. Farmers end up having to use more and more DDT to maintain only partial control. As Barry Commoner has suggested, artificial pesticides are like an addictive drug. Using them creates a need for more (1972, p. 151). An estimated four hundred species of insects and mites are resistant to all the pesticides we have in our arsenal today, twice the number that were outwitting us in 1965.

There is more. DDT is an almost unbreakable compound that remains intact and active for years after application. One Long Island marsh that was sprayed for twenty years accumulated thirty-two pounds per acre. Estimates are that more than a billion pounds are now circulating through the ecosystem. Even if DDT were never used again, it would remain there for many years to come (Curtis, 1975, p. 982).

DDT is highly mobile. A type sprayed on crops in East Africa traveled 4,000 miles to the Bay of Bengal in only a few months. It has been found in the brains of Arctic polar bears, in the blubber of whales, and in Eskimo mothers' milk (Heyerdahl, 1975). Moreover, there is evidence that high concentrations of DDT interfere with reproduction in birds. Estimates are that the average person in the world today has about eleven parts per million DDT in his or her body. What effects DDT may have on human beings, and at what concentrations, is not known.

States in 1972; other insecticides have been taken off the market. However, to ban pesticides altogether might be a disaster. Insects damage or devour about a third of U.S. crops each year, at an estimated cost of $9 billion. Without insecticides, these figures might double. Thus, we're left with a choice between two evils: hazards to the environment and to human health if we use pesticides, a decline in food supplies if we don't. Experiments with natural pesticides (including the use of natural predators like grasshoppers) are being conducted (Boraiko, 1980). Natural pest control has not been developed for much the same reason that alternatives to fossil fuels haven't been developed: There are still enormous profits to be made from synthetic pesticides.

The greenhouse effect Perhaps the most serious problem with the environment is that we simply do not *know* how much damage has already been done. The effects of introducing new substances into the environment are often delayed.

The carbon dioxide problem illustrates the extent of our ignorance about environmental consequences. Since the beginning of the Industrial Revolution, the amount of carbon dioxide in the atmosphere has increased by about 10 percent (Hobbs, Harrison, and Robinson, 1974, p. 911). Some of this increase is a byproduct of burning fossil fuels; some, the result of deforestation. (Green plants convert carbon dioxide to oxygen.) A number of scientists are concerned about the possible "greenhouse effect." The glass in a greenhouse admits sunlight, which is absorbed by the soil and converted to heat. The heat rises but bounces back when it hits the glass, keeping the greenhouse warm. A blanket of carbon dioxide in the atmosphere *might* have the same affect. The global temperature might rise by as much as 3 degrees Celcius. This seemingly small increase would force plants, animals, and people to relocate. Storm belts would shift, turning jungles into

deserts and vice versa. Eventually the polar ice caps might begin to melt, raising the sea level and flooding many of the world's major cities. Estimates of when there will be enough carbon dioxide in the atmosphere to create a greenhouse effect vary widely. Some scientists have predicted the opposite effect: air pollution might increase cloudiness, block incoming heat, and lower global temperatures. We simply do not know (Ridker and Cecelski, 1979, p. 37).

The Allocation of Risk

A list of known and potential threats to the environment could go on for pages. The key point is that technology is a double-edged sword. Technology has enabled us to lengthen the human life span and to increase food and energy production to meet the demands of a growing world population. At the same time, technology has created new threats to life and health, and has consumed and damaged irreplaceable resources. Life on earth has always been risky. Humans have always lived with the threat that a drought, a volcanic eruption, or a tidal wave would destroy them. What has changed is that many of the environmental threats we live with today are manmade. Technology has given human beings the power to allocate risks—but not to avoid them. Three Mile Island illustrates this.

Charles Perrow (1979) characterizes what happened at Three Mile Island on March 28, 1979, as a *normal accident*—the kind of accident that cannot be prevented and is virtually certain to occur again. Perrow contrasts this to other kinds of accidents. The term "unique accident" refers to such things as the collapse of a skyscraper during an earthquake. In everyday conversation, we call them "freak accidents" or "acts of God." No one can be held responsible for unique accidents. There is no way to protect against them. Moreover, they are so rare we don't have to worry about them. "Discrete accidents" are mishaps that result from one or two pieces of equipment failing or an operator making a mistake. Discrete accidents are comprehensible. Something went wrong, but the problem can be identified and corrected. It won't happen again. The system does not have to be abandoned. A third type of accident results from "calculated risks." The manufacturer or operator gambled and lost. For example, the Ford Motor Company gambled on not spending an extra $16 per car to make the gas tanks in Pintos safer. After numerous preventable accidents, the cars were recalled. As in this case, calculated risks are often hidden from the public.

By contrast, normal accidents occur in systems that are so complex that it is not possible to design or build them in ways that will anticipate all eventualities. Normal accidents emerge from the characteristics of the systems themselves. They are *built into* complex technological equipment like nuclear power plants. In a sense, the more technologically advanced a society becomes, the more accident-prone it becomes.

Perrow argues that the accident at Three Mile Island was a normal accident. Signals that might have enabled plant operators to avert the accident were only interpreted as warnings in retrospect. For example, an engineer with the TVA had sent a technical report to the Nuclear Regulatory Commission (NRC) predicting almost exactly what happened at Three Mile Island. The report was never circulated — not because of carelessness but because of choice. The NRC is inundated with warnings. It receives 3,000 to 4,000 detailed reports of plant mishaps each year. If it turned every report it received into regulations, the entire system would be paralyzed. In order to operate at all, managers and designers have to select and focus on a limited number of possible dangers. In fact, most hypothetical accidents do *not* occur. But the NRC only learns it has made a poor choice when something goes wrong. At Three Mile Island, so many alarms were sounding and blinking on March 28, operators had to turn them

off. In retrospect it is possible to say which of the alarms were significant and which were not; at the time, it was not possible. The liability is built into complex systems.

According to Perrow, the accident at Three Mile Island was not preventable. Moreover, such accidents are bound to occur in complex technological systems. They are "normal." We would like to think that we can prevent such occurrences through better training, design, and construction, that we can localize and minimize the dangers through better safety systems. This is wishful thinking. In fact, we are taking a risk. Nuclear technology may be an extreme example. But burning coal, damming rivers, and even cutting down forests all involve risks. Often we do not know what the dangers are until after the fact.

One additional point about technological risks deserves mention. The risks of normal accidents and environmental deterioration are not distributed evenly among all segments of society. For example, the miners in Buffalo Creek (Chapter 1) risked their lives every time they went into the mines. Many lost their lives and homes in the flood. The directors and stockholders in the Buffalo Mining Company were not exposed to these dangers. They derived benefits in the form of income but did not pay costs in terms of their health. Cost-benefit analysis of the exploitation of natural resources and the free use of the air and water for disposal of wastes indicates that, overall, the affluent have derived maximum benefits for minimum costs (Schnaiberg, 1980). They profit from environmentally dangerous or degrading industrial enterprises both as owners and stockholders and as consumers. When the air, water, and land become polluted, the affluent can move to a cleaner environment, vacation in a remote wilderness, visit health spas, and purchase escape in other ways. In contrast, the poor have derived minimum benefits for maximum costs from industrial enterprises. The poor are trapped. They cannot afford to move away from towns like Buffalo Creek or to leave jobs that endanger health. And they pay a proportionately larger share of the cost of cleaning up pollution. For example, when a power company is allowed to charge higher rates for electricity because it installs anti-pollution equipment, the higher bills have a greater impact on the poor than on the rich.

The Sociology of Survival

Global industrialization has been functional in the sense of raising the standard of living for large numbers of people, but dysfunctional in stimulating population growth, rapid consumption of limited resources, and environmental pollution. Moreover, the pace of change has been so rapid we have not developed the social mechanisms to protect the environment, or ourselves, from technological fallout. The ecosphere is both complex and fragile. The unchecked growth of population, industrialization, and pollution threaten the delicate balance of nature and humanity's survival on earth.

The ecological problems we face today cannot be blamed on greedy people, corporations, or nations. Nor are they inevitable. They are the products of what Allan Schnaiberg describes as the *treadmill of production* (1980, pp. 228–29). For almost two centuries, Western industrial nations have been committed to economic growth. In capitalist societies, everyone has something to gain from economic expansion. For business, increased production means increased profits; for labor, more jobs and more consumer comforts; for government, increased revenues from taxes that enhance government's ability to satisfy public demands. This coalition of interests sets the treadmill of production in motion. The main strategy for increasing production has been investing in technology, which substitutes inanimate sources of energy for human labor. In other words, machines replace people. This strategy produces immediate gains but long-term problems. Unemployment rises, creating labor unrest and increased demands that the government take care of people's needs. One solution is for government to assist business in expanding production, which creates new jobs and also generates new tax revenues for the government. (The treadmill picks up speed.) New profits are invested in more complex technology that produces more goods. This creates a new kind of problem for business. To sell all of these goods either new consumers have to be brought into the market, or workers have to be paid more so that they can buy more. The solution, again, is to increase production. (The treadmill goes into high gear.)

The important points here are, first, that industrialized production tends to develop a momentum of its own. Once set in motion, it is difficult to slow down. Second, business, labor, and government all have a vested interest in keeping the treadmill going. All thrive on economic growth. There is a catch, however. Each acceleration of the treadmill requires larger inputs of energy (larger doses of fuel) and produces larger outputs in terms of environmental pollution. Shifting from products made from wood and metal to plastics is an example. Plastic is made from petroleum, requires high-energy technology, and is not naturally degradable.

The dilemma for the United States is whether or not to continue on this path of economic growth. On the one hand, growth tends to compound our problems by using up more resources and causing more environmental pollution. On the other hand, economic growth adds to our capacity for solving problems, by providing funds to search for and implement new solutions (Ridker and Cecelski, 1979, p. 38).

On the international level, this dilemma is writ large. The world is entering a transitional period.

At the very least, we will have to shift our dependence from oil to other fuels in the next quarter century. Just as shifts in the earth's geological plates cause volcanic eruptions, so shifts in the resource base may cause social tensions to burst to the surface. In choosing whether to reinvest in coal or take the nuclear alternative, whether to plant crops for cash or local consumption, people are making decisions about how dependent their society will be on others, how much energy and water it will use, what kinds of jobs will be created, which cities and regions will prosper and which fall behind (Barnet, 1980, pp. 97–98). These are not technical choices; they are social choices. Environmental uncertainties and risks make these choices all the more critical.

Summary

1. The riddle of the lilies in a pond illustrates how a population may suddenly outstrip the environment's ability to support it. According to the Limits Thesis, humanity is in its twenty-ninth day. According to the Cornucopian Thesis, technology can expand the pond indefinitely. Both are oversimplifications.

2. Future demands on the earth depend not only on population but also on patterns of consumption.

3. At current rates, the world population is doubling every forty years. Population growth is not distributed evenly around the world. Developed nations are in Stage III of the demographic transition: Birth rates have fallen to replacement levels. Developing nations are in Stage I: Death rates have dropped, but birth rates are high. Their growing populations are literally "eating up" their economic gains.

4. Although the *rate* of population growth has slowed in the last decade, the *number* of people born each year is increasing.

5. Patterns of consumption around the world are lopsided. Developed nations consume more energy, more food, and higher-quality food than developing nations. Although the rates of consumption may slow down, demands on the earth's resources will increase.

6. Future supplies depend not only on resources but also on technology. Malthus's predictions of global famine did not take into account modern birth control or agriculture technology.

7. New technology may increase food production, but the history of the Green Revolution suggests that technological solutions to the problem of the food supply can have unanticipated social consequences.

8. People go hungry today because of the system of food distribution, not supply. The commercialization, mechanization, and internationalization of food production and distribution have reduced food self-sufficiency.

9. Nonrenewable energy resources (oil, gas, coal, uranium) will not run out as quickly as some forecasters have predicted, but using these fuels entails environmental risks. Renewable energy resources (solar, water, and wind power) may supply the future.

10. The immediate problem facing the United States and other Western nations is reliance on oil from a politically unstable part of the world. The long-term problem is making an orderly transition to new sources of energy.

11. The air, water, and land become polluted when people create more wastes than the ecosystem can absorb or create new substances that are not biodegradable. We do not know what the long-term effects of toxins on the human body, or industrial byproducts on the climate, will be.

12. Modern technology has given human beings the power to allocate risks. The accident at Three Mile Island can be characterized as a "normal accident," as a risk that is built into complex technological systems and cannot be prevented by human or mechanical means.

13. Environmental risks are not distributed evenly. Poor people and poor countries pay more for environmental exploitation, but derive minimum benefits for maximum costs.

14. The current situation can be traced to the treadmill of production in capitalist industrial nations, which depend on economic growth. Once set in motion, this treadmill develops a momentum of its own.

Suggested Reading

Barnet, Richard J. *The Lean Years: Politics in the Age of Scarcity.* New York: Simon & Schuster, 1980.

Brown, Lester R. *The Twenty-Ninth Day.* New York: Worldwatch Institute, Norton, 1978.

Morgan, Dan. *Merchants of Grain.* New York: Viking, 1979.

Odum, Eugene P. *Fundamentals of Ecology,* 3d ed. Philadelphia: Saunders, 1971.

Ridker, Ronald G., and Elizabeth W. Cecelski. "Resources, Environment, and Population: The Nature of Future Limits." *Population Bulletin,* Vol. 34, No. 3 (August 1979).

Van der Tak, Jean, Carl Haub, and Elaine Murphy. "Our Population Predicament: A New Look." *Population Bulletin,* Vol. 34, No. 5 (December 1979).

References

Ayres, R.U. *Uncertain Futures: Challenges for Decision-Makers.* New York: Wiley, 1979.

Barnet, R.J. *The Lean Years: Politics in the Age of Scarcity.* New York: Simon & Schuster, 1980.

Barnett, H.J. "The Myth of Our Vanishing Resources." *Transaction,* Vol. 4, No. 7 (June 1967), pp. 7-10.

Boraiko, A.A. "The Pesticide Dilemma." *National Geographic,* Vol. 151, No. 2 (February 1980), pp. 145-83.

Brown, L.R. *The Twenty-Ninth Day.* New York: Worldwatch Institute, Norton, 1978.

Brown, M. *Laying Waste: The Poisoning of America by Toxic Chemicals.* New York: Pantheon, 1980.

Chirot, D. *Social Change in the Twentieth Century.* New York: Harcourt Brace Jovanovich, 1977.

Commoner, B. "Evaluating the Biosphere." *Science Journal,* Vol. 5A, No. 4 (1969), pp. 67-72.

Commoner, B. *The Closing Circle: Nature, Man and Technology.* New York, Bantam, 1972.

Curtis, H. *Biology,* 2d ed. New York: Worth, 1975.

Ehrlich, P.R., and A.H. Ehrlich. *Population, Resources, Environment: Issues in Human Ecology,* 2d ed. San Francisco: Freeman, 1972.

Evans, R., Jr. "India Experiments with Sterilization." *Harper's Magazine,* Vol. 225, No. 1338, (1961), pp. 79-80.

Ford, D. "Three Mile Island." *The New Yorker,* April 6, 1981, pp. 49-120; April 13, 1981, pp. 46-109.

Fox, R. "The Cultural Animal." *Encounter,* Vol. 35, No. 1 (July 1970), pp. 31-42.

Harris, M. *Culture, People, Nature,* 2d ed. New York: Crowell, 1975.

Heer, D. M. *Society and Population,* 2d ed. Englewood Cliffs, N.J.: Prentice-Hall, 1975.

Heilbroner, R. *An Inquiry into the Human Prospect.* New York: Norton, 1974.

Heyerdahl, T. "How to Kill an Ocean." *Saturday Review,* November 29, 1975, pp. 12-18.

Hirsch, F. *Social Limits to Growth.* New York: Twentieth Century Fund, 1976.

Hobbs, P.V., H. Harrison, and E. Robinson. "Atmospheric Effects of Pollutants." *Science,* Vol. 185, No. 4128 (March 1974), pp. 909-15.

Independent Commission on International Development Issues. *North-South: A Program for Survival.* Cambridge, Mass.: MIT Press, 1980.

International Planned Parenthood Federation. "International Planned Parenthood Survey of Unmet Needs in Family Planning." *People,* Vol. 5, No. 3 (1978).

Kahn, H. *The Next 200 Years: A Scenario for America and the World.* Hudson Institute. New York: Morrow, 1976.

Kendall, M. "The World Fertility Survey: Current Status and Findings." *Population Reports,* Series M, No. 3 (July). Baltimore, Md.: Johns Hopkins University Press, 1979.

Knoedel, J., and E. van de Walle. "Lessons from the Past: Policy Implications of Historical Fertility Studies." *Population and Development Review,* Vol. 5, No. 2 (June 1979), pp. 217-45.

Meadows D.H. et al. *The Limits to Growth: A Report for the Club of Rome's Project on the Predicament of Mankind.* New York: Universe Book, 1972.

Mesarovic, M., and E. Pestel. *Mankind at the Turning Point: The Second Report to the Club of Rome.* New York: Dutton/Reader's Digest, 1974.

Novak, J. "Beyond North and South: The Second Coming of the World Economy." *Worldview* (March 1978).

Perrow, C. "Three Mile Island: A Normal Accident." Unpublished ms. Stony Brook, N.Y.: SUNY Sociology Department, 1979.

Revelle, R. "Will the Earth's Land and Water Capacity Be Sufficient for Future Populations?" In *The Population Debate: Dimensions and Perspectives, Papers of the World Population Conference, Bucharest, 1974,* Vol. II. New York: United Nations, 1975.

Ridker, R.G., and E.W. Cecelski. "Resources, Environment, and Population: The Nature of Future Limits." *Population Bulletin,* Vol. 34, No. 3 (August 1979).

Ridker, R.G., and W.D. Watson, Jr. *To Choose a Future: Resources and Environmental Problems of the United States. A Long-Term Global Outlook.* Baltimore, Md.: Johns Hopkins Press, 1980.

Schnaiberg, A. *The Environment: From Surplus to Scarcity.* New York: Oxford University Press, 1980.

Thurow, L.C. *The Zero-Sum Society: Distribution and the Possibilities for Economic Change.* New York: Basic, 1980.

Tuve, G.L. *Energy, Environment, Populations and Food.* New York: Wiley, 1976.

U.S. Department of Health, Education, and Welfare. "Programs in the Prevention and Control of Air Pollution." Third Report of the Secretary of HEW to the Congress of the United States. Senate Document No. 91-64. Washington, D.C.: U.S. Government Printing Office, 1970.

Vacca, R. *The Coming of the Dark Age.* New York: Anchor, 1974.

Van der Tak, J., C. Haub, and E. Murphy. "Our Population Predicament: A New Look." *Population Bulletin,* Vol. 34, No. 5 (December 1979).

Woodwell, G.M. "Toxic Substances and Ecological Cycles." *Scientific American,* Vol. 216, No. 3 (March 1967), pp. 24-31.

Chapter Four

International Conflict

International Conflict: An Overview

Nations in an Age of Interdependence

The Nationalization of Loyalties

The Globalization of Interests

The Structure of International Relations

Three Worlds of Development

  The First World
  The Second World
  The Third World

Triad in Turmoil

East vs. West

Competition for Natural Resources

Conflict over Human Rights

North vs. South

Explaining North-South Inequality

The Role of the Transnational Corporation

Third World Strategies

  Association with a Major Power
  Building Third World Coalitions

Toward an International Order

Developing Global Perspective

Transnational Organizations

More Critical Choices for the United States

The post–World War II dream of a stable world order based on a balance of power among nations seems a distant memory today. Crosscurrents of international suspicion, shifting coalitions, sudden racial and ethnic storms, and the undertow of desperate poverty threaten everyone on earth. The arms buildup over the last three decades provides a dramatic illustration of the level of international tension. Humanity may well be arming itself to death. On a world average, one tax dollar out of every six is spent on armaments, for an annual military bill of $450 billion (ICIDI, 1980, pp. 117, 124). Nearly half of the scientists and engineers in the world devote their skills to military research (Tinbergen, Dol-

man, and van Ettinger, 1976, p. 25). Although the United States and the Soviet Union are by far the biggest spenders, Third World countries devote large amounts of their limited budgets to arms. In 1978, developing nations spent $14 billion on weapons (ICIDI, 1980, p. 120). In developed nations, arms sales to other countries have become a major industry. An estimated 350,000 Americans' jobs depend on military exports (Klare, 1979, p. 26) (see Table 4–1).

The destructive capacity of modern nuclear weapons stretches the imagination. Only recently have humans become such efficient killers (Sherrill, 1978, pp. 513–19). When eleven German planes bombed London on October 1, 1916 (in one

Table 4–1
Weapons Sales to the Third World*
(in millions of current U. S. dollars)

	1974	1975	1976	1977	1978	1979
Total	23,521	22,329	21,394	27,356	24,198	29,978
Non-Communist total	16,581	17,979	14,254	17,606	20,458	19,258
United States	11,921	11,614	10,669	9,976	11,268	10,388
France	2,030	2,300	1,025	2,800	2,500	4,000
Britain	760	1,400	630	1,550	1,800	2,420
West Germany	725	790	360	1,170	2,220	400
Italy	425	990	220	960	1,360	360
Other	720	885	1,350	1,150	1,310	1,690
Communist total	6,940	4,350	7,140	9,750	3,740	10,720
Soviet Union	5,900	3,600	5,900	9,000	2,900	9,800
Other	1,040	750	1,240	750	840	920
Dollar inflation index (1974 = 100)	100	109	118	127	136	148

*Foreign data are for calendar year; U.S. data for fiscal year. Prices include sale of weapons, construction, military assistance, and spare parts. Third World category excludes Warsaw Pact, NATO countries, Europe, Japan, Australia, and New Zealand.
Source: *The New York Times,* June 21, 1981, p. E1.

Table 4–2
The Nuclear Club
(countries which appear technically capable of detonating a nuclear bomb within the next decade)

Who has it	Within 3 years	4 to 6 years	7 to 10 years
United States (1945)	Australia	Argentina	Finland
Soviet Union (1949)	Canada	Austria	Iraq
Britain (1952)	West Germany	Belgium	Libya
France (1960)	Israel	Brazil	Roumania
China (1964)	Italy	Czechoslovakia	Yugoslavia
India (1974)	Japan	Denmark	
	Pakistan	East Germany	
	South Africa	Netherlands	
	Spain	Norway	
	Sweden	Poland	
	Switzerland	South Korea	
	Taiwan		

Source: *The New York Times,* April 26, 1981, p. E3. Data based on U.S. Government Estimates.

of the earliest air raids), one person was killed. On August 6, 1945, one U.S. plane carrying a single bomb killed 100,000 or more residents of Hiroshima, Japan, leveling most of the city. At that time, the atom bomb was described as a "psychological weapon," a threat no one would ever again use. To set off a nuclear war would be insanity. Atomic weapons were billed as "deterrents"; a balance of terror would replace the balance of power. By this curious twist of logic, the U.S. and U.S.S.R. began stockpiling atomic weapons with the stated aim of preventing, not winning, wars. Once started, the arms race developed a momentum of its own. Between them, these two nations now have over a million Hiroshima-size bombs, with enough "overkill" capacity to destroy the entire human population twelve times (Tin-

bergen, Dolman, and van Ettinger, 1976, p. 295). The major powers have not been able to control the spread of nuclear weapons, as they had once hoped they could. The so-called nuclear club is known to include only Britain, France, China, and India. But by the year 2000, thirty to forty nations may have the capacity (the knowledge and materials) to produce nuclear weapons, intensifying the dangers of regional conflict (ICIDI, 1980, p. 122) (see Table 4–2).

Although no nation has used its nuclear weapons since World War II, in a sense the killing has already started. The arms race consumes funds that might otherwise be used to ease poverty, hunger, and disease. The world spends 150 times as much on armaments as it does on peace and development through the United Nations (Tin-

The Effects of Nuclear War

Now appears to be the time to say it again: the entire industrialized world could be destroyed in 24 hours through nuclear war. Everyone in his fifties or older saw this grim situation of opposing "deterrents" emerge during his adult life. Those in their forties or older, remember real life nuclear war scenarios: the Berlin crisis and the open threats of nuclear use in the Cuban missile crisis. But those in their twenties have largely escaped confrontation with this reality. And some of their elders may have forgotten it.

The situation, in brief, is this. One bomb can destroy one city. A large warhead with 25,000,000 tons of TNT equivalent (25 "megatons") will level homes 13 miles in all directions from its ground zero. The Soviet Union is ready to deliver 100 to 200 bombs of this size. One such bomb would level the largest city, e.g. New York. A five megaton bomb will do the same for cities with a radius of 7.5 miles. The Soviet Union is ready to deliver 400 such weapons. Warheads of about 1 megaton could level cities that are four miles in radius. The Soviet Union has 6,000 warheads in that range. The U.S. has only 2,000 cities over the minimal size of 10,000 persons. All of those could therefore easily be destroyed.

In 1959, Congressional hearings suggested nuclear war would kill (deaths within 30 days only) 40 million of the 150 million people in 71 urban areas with only 1,500 megatons. Today, in a world of many more missile carrying MIRVed warheads, and of *10,000* megatons on the Soviet side, the official estimates are that between 70 million and 160 million people would die—and 20 to 30 million more if the Soviet Union's targeters really tried to kill people per se. America's population stands today at 226 million. Thus, 30% to 70% of the population would die promptly. Tens of millions more would die from non-existent medical care, from unchecked disease, from low temperatures when winter arrived, and from agriculture failures.*

Recently, the medical doctors have begun to show the concern which only physicists showed in earlier times—to communicate this danger. They note how little blood plasma would be available and how much medical care is required for a single victim of burns. This seems to get through to people. At the other analytical extreme, economists can describe the difficulties which would attend any post-attack economic recovery at all.

Indeed, for the 1980s and beyond, the question will not be how much of the country is destroyed in nuclear war, but how much is left and even whether a functioning country will re-emerge.

*In the 200 years of this nation's history, "only" 1.05 million Americans have been killed in wars.
Source: *F.A.S. Public Interest Report*, Vol. 34, No. 2 (February 1981), (Washington, D.C.: Federation of American Scientists), pp. 1–2.

bergen, Dolman, and van Ettinger, 1976, p. 25). One-half of what we now spend on arms each year would be enough to provide for the nutritional and health needs of everyone on earth for an entire decade. Half a *day's* military expenditures would give the World Health Organization the funds to wipe out malaria. For the cost of a single jet fighter, we could establish 40,000 village pharmacies; for the price of a single tank, storage facilities for 100,000 tons of grain or classrooms for 30,000 children (ICIDI, 1980, p. 14). By using up funds, the arms race wages a hidden, unacknowledged war against the world's poor. The millions who die from hunger are the hostages and victims of international tensions as surely as if they died at the point of a gun.

Human misery and hostility are by no means twentieth-century inventions. They have occurred throughout history. Yet the scale of today's problems exceeds anything humanity has ever known. These problems involve and implicate every nation on earth, rich and poor.

This chapter begins with an overview of international conflict. In the second section, we analyze the clash between the reality of global interdependence and national loyalties. There is a familiar sociological paradox here: By acting in their own best interests, nation-states may undermine their own security (and that of humankind). The third section of the chapter describes the uneasy triangle that structures international relations today. Communications among the so-called Free World, the Soviet bloc, and the Third World are complicated by their different histories and concerns. Next we examine tensions between the East and West, looking at conflicts over both resources and values. The fifth section analyzes conflicts between the rich, industrialized nations of the Northern Hemisphere and the poor, underdeveloped nations of the Southern Hemisphere. We consider what changing perceptions have contributed to changing relations between the Northern and Southern Hemispheres. The final section of the chapter suggests what we, as citizens of the United States and of the world, might do to avert global crisis.

International Conflict: An Overview

Following the sociologist Louis Kriesberg (1973, 1981), we define *international conflict* as a relationship between two or more nations who believe (or whose spokesmen believe) that their goals are incompatible (1973, p. 17). Each believes that it can achieve its goals only at the expense of the others. Belief is a key word in this definition. Conflicts grow out of different nations' *perceptions* of their own best interests and worst enemies. In some cases, these perceptions are realistic: One nation wants or needs what the other has. In other cases, however, conflict is unrealistic: A nation seeks compensation for a grievance from the wrong adversary, or adversaries overlook the interests they have in common. For example, many Americans believe that the taking of American hostages in Iran in 1979 was an erroneous reprisal against the United States for Iran's internal problems. Most international disputes include both realistic and unrealistic elements.

International conflicts are caused by three factors today. The first is competition for the limited resources described in the preceding chapter, especially food and energy. The awareness that these resources may become more scarce heightens international tensions. For example, dependence on oil from Iran tempered European nations' responses to the hostage crisis. The second factor is global inequalities in the distribution of wealth, power, and prestige. The perception of injustice underlies many conflicts in the world today. Third, nations frequently have different interests and values. Some disputes grow out of conflicts of interest: Two or more nations pursue the same goal in the belief that only one can win. Other disputes grow out of conflicts of values: Because their ideas of what is desirable differ, one nation makes unacceptable claims on another. For example, many Americans supported the goal of modernization pursued by the former Shah of Iran. Islamic conservatives within Iran evaluated his activities from quite a different perspective and saw modernization as foreign and evil. While Americans viewed the Shah as a "progressive," many Iranians considered him a "satan." As the Iranian case suggests, competition for limited resources, feelings of injustice, and conflicts of values make international relations extremely complex. In the next section, we will examine the global context in which conflicts among nations develop.

Nations in an Age of Interdependence

More than any other recent events, the oil embargo of 1973 and the rise in oil prices over the next decade made Americans aware of global interdependence. Nations we once considered small and insignificant now seem able to threaten our standard of living. Neither the United States nor any other nation on earth is wholly self-sufficient today. Yet we enter the age of global interdependence with nationalist ideals and loyalties that create serious obstacles to global cooperation. Nationalist ambitions and frustrations set the stage for much international tension in today's world.

The Nationalization of Loyalties

Nationalism is a world view that places the interests of one's own nation above the common interests of all nations and supports efforts to achieve national advancement or independence. Under the banner of nationalism, states claim the sovereign right to freedom of action within their borders and on the world stage. The proper concern of the state is defined as the welfare of its *own* peo-

ple. In times of crisis, concern for the rights of others and for humanity as a whole takes second place.

The nationalization of loyalties is a comparatively modern phenomenon. Two hundred years ago the nation of Germany, for example, did not exist in the modern sense. What is now Germany was a patchwork of feudal territories. People were loyal to the Church or to the local baron, not to the Holy Roman Empire or the Hapsburgs. They identified themselves as Wurttembergers or Bavarians, not as Germans. Italy, France, and England were all loosely united kingdoms until recently. The rise of nationalism in Europe was associated with the replacement of a feudal order, in which kings reigned by virtue of religious authority, with secular, centralized states (Ayres, 1979, p. 85). The rise of nationalism in the United States and other countries is associated with the fight for independence. Before the war with Britain, people considered themselves citizens of Massachusetts or Virginia, not Americans. (States' rights, as opposed to federal authority, are still an issue in this country.)

On one level, nationalism is often a unifying force that promotes cooperation, order, and prosperity. Nationalism overrides the local and tribal loyalties that divide people. The basic unit of social loyalty is expanded. This opens economic opportunities that are not available when people are loyal to competitive, mutually suspicious villages or tribes. It can promote cooperation, particularly when people are struggling to defend or enlarge their territory.

On the international level, however, nationalism can be a disintegrating force, creating misunderstandings and conflict. According to an old European saying, "a nation is a group of persons united by a common error about their ancestry and a common dislike of their neighbors" (Deutsch, 1969, p. 3). Nationalism promotes feelings of cultural superiority, the belief that "our way is best" and that "what is good for us must be good for them."

> Nations see themselves as the centre of the universe. They tend to worry about all manner of threats because they implicitly or explicitly see behavior elsewhere being directed towards themselves. They interpret the actions of adversaries in terms of their own problems and vulnerabilities. . . . They see the world as a wheel, and themselves as the hub. (Booth, 1979, p. 34)

Leaders of different nations see the same events from different points of view. What looks like "aggression" to one appears as "self-defense" to another; what one calls "repression" another calls "re-education." Part of being a French or Italian or Chinese is entertaining a particular set of notions about human rights, the proper role of government, and the sources of war and peace.

Cultural differences are most likely to stir international conflict when people do not understand that they are not understanding one another. For example, the so-called cold war between the U.S. and the U.S.S.R. was based in part on misunderstandings. John Foster Dulles, the U.S. Secretary of State during the Eisenhower administration, was convinced that the Soviet goal in international relations was expansion and that the Soviets knew this was how the West perceived them. Furthermore, Dulles believed that the Western goal was consolidation, not expansion, and that the Soviets perceived this. In fact, Soviet beliefs were a mirror image of Western beliefs. They were convinced that the *Western* goal was expansion, that their own goal was consolidation, and that Western leaders *knew* this, whatever they said publicly (Gamson and Modigliani, 1966).

International affairs are projections of national interests into the world arena. It is extremely rare for a nation to base decisions on global concerns, unheard of for a nation to sacrifice its own interests for global well-being. The content of international negotiations is nearly always *internal* affairs of particular nations, not global cooperation (Cleveland, 1979). Negotiators for each nation attempt to change the others in ways that benefit themselves. The aim is to alter the other's government policies, business activities, or even the way citizens behave. No one acknowledges this openly. If one nation accuses another of attempting to intervene in its domestic affairs, the other is sure to reply "Certainly not!" though both know this is the intention. But because the norms of nationalism are so strong, each maintains the "mandatory lie" of not wishing to intervene.

The Globalization of Interests

Global interdependence has increased substantially in the decades since World War II. It is no longer possible for a nation to pursue its national goals independently, without the cooperation of other nations. The distinction between domestic and international affairs has become blurred. Issues that used to be considered purely domestic have taken on global significance; global issues have clear domestic implications. The rules of international relations (rules based on the principle of national sovereignty) have not changed, but the game has.

Changes in the world economy provide clear examples of the globalization of national interests. There is nothing new about international trade. The Phoenicians were obtaining tin from Britain in 1000 B.C. (Manning, 1976, p. 283). But the peoples of the world have never been as economically interdependent as they are today. Virtually every nation is dependent on other nations to provide both natural resources for its industries and markets for its products. Distant events have a direct impact on national employment, interest rates, and buying power. For example, when the Polish government announced that it was raising food prices in 1970, dock workers rebelled, burning party headquarters in Gdansk and seizing control of the shipyards in Szczecin. The government backed down and subsidized food prices. Two years later, the Soviets decided to import grain for the first time, in order to provide more meat for consumers and avoid a similar situation. The decision was a boon to U.S. grain companies but not to U.S. consumers. Between 1972 and 1975, the food bill in this country rose by $54 billion (Morgan, 1980, pp. 38–39). In this way, a strike in Poland was heard halfway around the world. (Dissatisfaction with government policy resurfaced in Poland in 1980–81, again with global implications.) The globalization of economic activities makes it increasingly difficult for national governments to fulfill their role as managers of their economies. Many of the factors that affect investment, employment, and prices are beyond their control.

New categories of problems and issues have arisen for which national governments have few precedents and little experience. Many defy independent national solutions. The clearest examples of this are the ecological problems described in the preceding chapter. The United States may invest in technology to reduce the buildup of carbon dioxide in the atmosphere as a result of burning fossil fuels. But this will not eliminate the threat of climatic changes unless Brazil establishes a policy of reforestation in the Amazon. Brazil's efforts will be ineffective if the United States does not cooperate. The problems of population, food distribution, energy supplies, and monetary stability all require international solutions.

Awareness of global interdependence is increasing and there are more attempts to collaborate in solving global problems, but the globalization of interests has not been matched by a globalization of loyalties. Nations still act as if they were independent of one another, and to a

These children are not playing. The scene is Belfast, Northern Ireland, where youngsters are sometimes sent to the front line in riots in the hope that this will make soldiers reluctant to shoot. Irish nationalists have been fighting British rule for centuries.

large extent their citizens accept this fiction. Moreover, there has been a resurgence of nationalism and ethnic self-identification (Manning, 1976, pp. 284–85). Some of the resurgence is occurring in developing nations that are newly independent or struggling to overcome tribal and religious conflict within their borders. But nationalist movements are also appearing in older, developed nations, as groups like the Basques in Spain, the Catholics in Northern Ireland, French Canadians, and Native Americans in the United States struggle to keep their separate national identities. Thus, although nationalism may not fit the reality of today's global interdependence, it remains a powerful force.

One way to think about the situation we are describing is to use an analogy called "the tragedy of the commons" (Hardin, 1968). A commons is a tract of land owned jointly by all members of a community. Anyone who wishes may pasture his cattle on the commons. Guided by the desire for personal gain, each man strives to increase the size of his herd. For a time, this system works to everyone's advantage. But the commons can support only a limited number of animals. The day will come when the addition of more cattle will damage and ultimately destroy the resource on which everyone depends. Even though each man knows this, it is still in his rational self-interest to continue adding to his own herd. The personal benefits outweigh the costs, which are divided among all who use the commons. Moreover, if he doesn't add to his herd, others will add to theirs. As a result, the commons is destroyed. By analogy, the earth is humanity's commons. Acting in national self-interest, each country strives to "increase its herd," to get as much from the earth as it can. Short-term profits and national interests are valued over long-term productivity and global benefits.

The Structure of International Relations

Nationalism has contributed to the emergence of new nations and to a new structure of international relations, one quite different from that of 1900 or even 1950. At mid-century, the United States was the undisputed leader of the so-called Free World—that is, of Western, democratic, capitalist nations. The Soviet Union led the Socialist bloc—the communist nations of Eastern Europe and Asia. The two had squared off in a twenty-year cold war, in which other nations were pressed to take sides. For most intents and purposes, the Third World—today's nonaligned, developing nations—did not exist. Many of the peoples of Africa and Asia still lived under colonial rule and had no political voice. Other Third World nations (such as Korea) were considered only to the extent that they figured in struggles between the two superpowers. Third World nations began to gain independence in the years following World War II and to gather political force in the late 1960s and early 1970s. Thus, there are more independent nations in the world today. (There are almost three times as many nations in the UN today as when it was founded in 1945.) And these new nations are not willing to accept marginal status in one or the other superpower camps. As a result, the structure of international relations has shifted from what the German sociologist, Georg Simmel (1950) called a dyadic (two-party) relationship to a triadic (three-party) balance of power.

Three Worlds of Development

There are a number of different ways of sorting the nations of the world (Ray, 1979, pp. 154–62). The sociologist Daniel Chirot (1977), for example, distinguishes between what he calls "core societies" and "peripheral societies." Core societies are the rich, economically diversified, industrial European nations that dominated the world scene in 1900. Peripheral societies are the poor nations that remained on the outer edge of the world system in terms of power and wealth, providing the core societies with cheap labor, raw materials, and some agricultural products. Here we follow the sociologist Irving Horowitz (1972) who divides nations into three categories: the *First World* (sometimes called the "Free World"), the *Second World* (the Soviet bloc), and the *Third World* (developing, nonaligned nations). We have chosen this approach because it focuses on the different

The Continuing Enigma of China—a View from the U.S.

China has for centuries been an object of fascination, bewilderment, and concern to the Western world. The Communist regime which came to power in 1949, following a century of political and social decay, imperialist exploitation, and protracted violence, continues to attract and bemuse statesmen, scholars, and Westerners in general. It is this aura, the universal perception that major historical forces are at work for all to see on one-fourth of humanity, and the astonishingly limited amount of elemental information available about the society, much less a sophisticated grasp or feeling for what is transpiring, that must be noted before any effort is made to set forth generalizations about the directions of change in China. . . .

Past efforts by American specialists to understand the most basic political features of the Communist government offer scant encouragement. During the 1950s there were virtually no dissenters from the view that China was an integral part of a Soviet dominated monolithic Communist bloc. Following the Sino-Soviet split, conventional (scholarly) wisdom saw Peking as a radical nationalist regime with no serious domestic political instabilities now that the Great Leap Forward program was ended. This judgment collapsed with the Cultural Revolution, an event that led to yet another interpretation, China beset by internal problems was an unpredictable and potentially disruptive revolutionary force in international affairs. Within four years, China was in the United Nations, had been effectively accepted within the international political community, and had welcomed the president of the United States to Peking. This ushered in the development era, that is, a period in which the overwhelming majority of China specialists saw the Chinese as concerned primarily with internal economic growth and having a nonexpansionist foreign policy essentially directed against the threat from the Soviet Union. Within three weeks after the death of Chou En-lai, the pragmatists were

social problems these nations face today and on the historical development of these problems.

The three-world approach has a number of limitations. The First World is deeply divided on many issues, not the least of which is the role the United States should play in world affairs. Neither Western European nations nor Japan unquestioningly follows the American leader. There is dissension also within the ethnically diverse population of the Soviet Union, as well as among under attack and, to the astonishment of almost all observers, the new premier was a man (Hua Kuo-feng) about whom only the scantiest information was available. In retrospect, what passed for scholarly wisdom was more like a filmstrip chronicle of the passing scene which took on the form of an intellectual *opera buffa*. The problem was partly a lack of evidence, but more basically the failure lay in not asking the appropriate (i.e., critical) questions about Chinese society. . . .

[T]he leaders of China are divided over the question of whether development should be the primary goal of the government or whether equalitarian political and social goals should receive priority. These divisions are likely to persist and if there continues to be recurrent political turmoil the economic problems will worsen. To this I would add that the intense politization of the Chinese masses (in comparison, say, with India) raises the potential for truly disruptive repercussions if a breakdown rooted in overpopulation should occur.

If China grows at 5 to 7 percent per year over the next twenty-five years, it is still unlikely to be a major force in international trade, but will make significant progress in building a military force. China will be constrained for at least a decade or so by budgetary limitations, but the capacity to become a global strategic power and to establish the capacity to defend its territory alone is clearly within reach. . . .

China will remain a major participant in regional and global international politics, and a major challenge for American foreign policy is how to cope with the Chinese enigma in establishing our strategic priorities. . . .

Source: Donald C. Hellmann, "Introduction: Toward a New Realism," in Donald C. Hellmann (Ed.), *China and Japan: A New Balance of Power, Critical Choices for Americans*, Vol. XII (Lexington, Mass.: Heath, 1976), pp. 13–17.

its allies in the Second World. The term "Third World" spans a wide range of cultures, political and economic systems, levels of development, and resource bases. The rich, sparsely populated kingdom of Saudi Arabia and the crowded, pov- erty-ridden nation of Haiti, for example, are as different as two nations could be. Nationalism prevents Third World countries from speaking with a single voice. Moreover, the People's Repub- lic of China does not fit neatly into any of these categories.* Nevertheless, the three-world view shows how different histories and concerns shape international relations.

The First World The First World consists of the cluster of European and North American nations that transformed themselves from feudal, agrarian states (or in North America, colonies) into parliamentary, industrial states before the twentieth century. These nations share a capitalist orientation: Most of the instruments and means of production (natural resources, farms, factories, banks) are owned by private individuals or corporations. Their political and economic machinery are geared to use technology "for private enrichment and public welfare in uneven doses" (Horowitz, 1972, p. 5). They are egalitarian in ideology, consumer- and commodity-oriented in practice. Capitalism, industrialization, and democracy are the cornerstones of the First World.

What distinguishes the First World from the other two is that these nations' transformation from traditional, agrarian states into modern, industrial ones was internally generated. Change came from the inside, not from the outside, through conquest or influence. Then with a relatively small technological advantage and an almost messianic belief in progress, European nations conquered much of the world in the eighteenth and nineteenth centuries. They were interested not so much in power as in obtaining raw materials and opening new markets. (Only the United States and Canada, economically self-sufficient until recently, did not become major colonial powers.) The development of the First World was "unplanned" in the sense that it was guided by what Adam Smith called the "invisible hand" of free enterprise.

In the post-World War II period, the First World enjoyed unparalleled economic growth and prosperity. Fed by cheap supplies from the Third World (including oil), world production tripled between 1950 and 1970, and most of the profits went to Europe and North America. It was a period of material prosperity and scientific and technological achievement for the First World. In the early 1970s, however, the tide seemed to turn. The international monetary system created after World War II began misfiring. Wages were rising faster than productivity (workers received more wages for the same work). Inflation rates climbed. The Organization of Petroleum Exporting Countries (OPEC) raised the price of oil. In September of 1975 alone, 17 million workers lined up in the unemployment offices of the richest nations in the world. Environmental problems became more visible. In a relatively short time, cumulative prosperity led to anxiety. The commitment to economic growth and the ever-increasing demand for scarce resources created doubt about the future. A central concern of the First World today is that the good times may be over (Tinbergen, Dolman, and van Ettinger, 1976, pp. 11–15).

The Second World The Second World consists of the Soviet Union and its allies and satellites in Eastern Europe and Asia. The Second World is communist in orientation. The instruments and means of production are publicly owned and state controlled. Individuals are not supposed to own factories, large farms, or other means of production (though some do) or to accumulate private wealth. The elites of the Second World do enjoy such privileges as cars and summer cottages. But these privileges are attached to a person's job and cannot be sold or inherited. They are more like expense accounts than like private wealth in the Western sense (Chirot, 1977, p. 237). In these nations there is one center of power, the party—

---

*We have not included the People's Republic of China in this discussion for two reasons. First, from 1949, when the revolutionary government took power, to the 1970s, China conducted its economic development largely in isolation from the international economic order. Second, because it has been isolated, data on economic development in China are difficult to acquire and verify.

If the Achilles' heel of the First World is oil, that of the Second World is food. Here, Americans line up to buy gasoline; Poles line up to buy food.

unlike the First World, where government, business, labor, and so on all have power. Second World economies are centrally planned, with the emphasis on heavy industry rather than on consumer goods and services.

The development of the Second World was condensed into a relatively short period of time and was government directed. Changes that emerged from individual enterprise and popular demand in the First World were brought about by revolution, conquest, and programming in the Second. In 1900, Russia was a poor and backward nation by Western standards. After 1928, when the U.S.S.R. had repaired some of the damage from World War I and the Russian Revolution, the nation began to industrialize on a large scale. Between 1929 and 1940, industrial production in the U.S.S.R. tripled. The percentage of Soviet citizens who worked in agriculture dropped from 81 percent to 59 percent. This progress was the result of forced industrialization, directed by the government, and exacted a high price "in terms of human lives and freedoms" (Chirot, 1977, pp. 112–13). An estimated 5 million peasants were shot or sent to Siberia for resisting the move to collective farms in this period. The slaughter of livestock by resisters and noncooperation on collective farms dealt a blow to Soviet agriculture—one from which the U.S.S.R. has never completely recovered.

From the beginning, the goal of Soviet planning was to catch up with industrialized Western nations. As Joseph Stalin put it at the First Conference of Russian Managers held in 1931, "[T]he backward are always beaten. But we do not want to be beaten. . . . The history of old Russia is the history of defeats due to backwardness. . . . We are fifty to a hundred years behind the advanced countries. We must cover this distance in *ten* years. Either we do this or they will crush us" (in Horowitz, 1972, p. 13). Ten years later, Germany crossed the Russian frontier and the Soviet Union was not beaten. To this day, catching up with the

First World is a central concern in the Second World. The Soviets won the first lap of the technological race to put a satellite in space when they launched Sputnik in 1957. Some experts believe that the Soviets may have achieved military parity (or equality) with the United States. But the goal of material abundance for the people has proven to be elusive. Technological and military achievements were won at the cost of neglecting consumer demands. (They gave up "butter" for "guns.") The per capita GNP in Eastern Europe is roughly $1,000 to $3,000; in Western Europe, $2,500 to $6,000. Manufactured goods account for only 20 percent of Eastern Europe's exports, whereas machinery accounts for 40 percent of its imports (Tinbergen, Dolman, and van Ettinger, 1976, pp. 17–18). This imbalance has economic, political, and ideological consequences. "The legitimacy of the Soviet state and other [communist] regimes depends on delivering the promise of equality, but an equality of abundance, not poverty" (Barnet, 1980, p. 300).

The Third World The Third World consists of 100 or more nations in Latin America, Africa, and Asia that are politically independent. They do not belong to either the U.S.-NATO alliance or to the Soviet Warsaw-pact group. Most Third World nations were colonies until after World War II. (India won independence in 1947; Angola in 1974.) The legacy of colonialism in the Third World includes a period of 100 to 600 years of political nonparticipation; a heightened desire for modern goods but a lack of modern facilities for producing them; and boundaries drawn by colonial powers, often without regard for ethnic or tribal groupings. Most Third World nations draw their technological aspirations from the First World and their ideological inspiration from the Second. These "imports" are combined with local traditions and values (with Islam in some of the Arab nations, for example) in distinctive ways. Most Third World nations endorse central planning but have mixed economies, with both state-controlled and private enterprise. Many hold democratic ideals, but see authoritarian rule as a temporary necessity.

What unites the Third World is, in Horowitz's words, "the fact and the shame of backwardness" (1972, p. 4). With 70 percent of the world's population, the Third World earns only 11 percent of its total income. The current income gap between the rich and poor nations has been estimated at $8,000 per person, per year, and shows few signs of closing (*U.S. News & World Report,* July 31, 1978, pp. 55–56). A number of factors are involved here. Many Third World nations export raw materials and import manufactured goods. Because raw materials are in greater supply, this trade is uneven. (Oil exports are a notable exception.) From colonial times, many Third World nations have specialized in a single crop, such as peanuts or coffee. Cash crops take land out of agricultural production, forcing them to import food. Cash crops also make Third World nations dependent on the unpredictable, fluctuating prices of the world market. Copper, like coffee, tends to go through booms and busts. Because Third World nations do not have the purchasing power to influence world prices, the so-called free market works to their disadvantage. (Again, the OPEC nations are an exception.) Unfavorable geography, population pressure, and rapid urbanization complicate these problems. As things are structured, Third World nations have to compromise between the desire for self-sufficiency and the need for aid from the First and Second Worlds.

The central concern of the Third World today is moving from political to economic liberation, achieving a decent standard of living. As stated in a report to the Club of Rome, "They have discovered that political liberation does not necessarily bring economic liberation and that the two are inseparable: that without political independence it is impossible to achieve economic independence; and without economic power, a nation's political independence is incomplete and insecure" (Tinbergen, Dolman, and van Ettinger, 1976, p. 15). The United Nations has become the main forum in which the Third World articulates its position.

In summary, the First World is struggling to maintain its high standard of living; the Second World, to catch up; the Third World, to get started.

Triad in Turmoil

Sociological analysis suggests that the emergence of the Third World has altered the structure of international relations. From the end of World War II to about 1960 or 1970, the structure of international relations was *dyadic,* or two-part. The world was effectively divided into two camps; the U.S. and the U.S.S.R., and their respective allies. In a dyad, everything depends on the relationship between the two parties. Three things may happen: The parties may maintain a balance of power; one may dominate the other; or they may engage in open conflict, with the aim of establishing a new balance of power or a new dominant party. The addition of a third party changes this.

A *triad* consists of three parties that are related in a persistent situation. It is less stable than a dyad. The outstanding characteristic of triads is their tendency to divide into coalitions of two against one (Caplow, 1968). If the situation *requires* all members of a triad to interact with one another, coalitions will form and dissolve at different times and in different situations. No alliance is permanent. This is precisely what is happening in international relations today. The globalization of interests requires the three worlds to interact with one another. There is no out. But patterns of interaction are constantly shifting.

The international situation is complicated by inequalities among nations. A nation's power in international relations depends on population size, industrial capacity, the size and quality of its military, the possession of natural resources, and geographic advantages, such as ports (Ray, 1979, pp. 100–02). These assets are not distributed evenly among nations. The struggle to maintain the current distribution of assets, or to change it, creates a permanent state of flux, prompting conflict in some situations and cooperation in others. Sociological analysis suggests why.

Imagine a game in which player A has resources equal to 45, player B's resources equal 40, player C's 15, and it takes resources of 50 or more to win (Ray, 1979, pp. 168–69). There are three possible winning coalitions in this game: AB, AC, or BC. Thus although player A has many more resources than player C, player A cannot win alone. Neither can player B. This gives player C considerable *pivotal power.*

Translating to the current world situation, the First World (player A) has a slight advantage. The Second World (led by the U.S.S.R.) seeks coalitions with the Third World to assist in its goal of catching up. Threatened by coalitions and fearful of losing its dominant position, the First World also seeks coalitions with Third World nations. Note that although the Third World is the weakest member of this triad, it is in a pivotal position. Neither A nor B can afford to have C form a coalition with the other. In real world terms, this may lead the superpowers to court Third World nations. It may also prompt them to invade and take over these nations, militarily or economically.

Nationalism further complicates international relations. All three parties in the global triad would prefer to have full independence of action. The First World does not want the Third World to be telling it what to do, and vice versa. Still, the only way to "win" is to form a coalition. If a coalition succeeds in overpowering the opponent, the weaker partner will then fall under the domination of the stronger. In the game, if B and C form a coalition and defeat A, player C loses his pivotal power. Similarly, if the Third and Second Worlds joined forces and succeeded in depriving the First World of resources and driving it out of the "game," the Third World would be subject to Soviet domination and have nowhere to turn for help. The same would be true if a coalition of the First World and the Third World forced the Second World out of the game. For this reason, long-term, stable coalitions are rare. The three worlds coexist in a precarious balance of power. Within this unsteady triad, there are two major currents of tension: East-West conflict and North-South antagonisms.

East vs. West

The future of world events will be determined in part by relations between the United States, the dominant power in the First World and the West, and the Soviet Union, the dominant power in the Second World and the East. These two superpowers are separated not only by the Atlantic and Pacific Oceans but by their different histories and international concerns (as described above).

In recent years, the U.S. and U.S.S.R. have been described as "hobbled giants." Neither superpower dominates other nations as it once did. In spring of 1980, for example, the U.S.S.R. attempted to use military force to keep Afghanistan in its orbit as a satellite state. It encountered strong, religiously backed resistance from the Afghans. When the U.S. responded by calling for a boycott of the Moscow Olympic games by Western nations, it found its allies less than eager to fall into line. Some joined the boycott; many did not. But despite some loss of control, it seems doubtful that another state will attain the status and power of these two superpowers in the near future. The potential for violent conflict between the U.S. and the U.S.S.R. remains.

To date, the U.S. and U.S.S.R. have avoided direct military confrontation (Miller, 1980). Both have taken risks—for example, in the 1962 Cuban missile crisis and the 1973 Middle East war. They have confronted one another indirectly, through well-equipped allies and proxies—for example, in Vietnam. Until recently, their access to raw materials and markets seemed assured, reducing the threat that either superpower would use force for economic reasons. This may change. Moreover, each tends to draw "worst case" conclusions about the other's actions. Here we will examine potential East-West conflicts of interest and conflicts of values.

Competition for Natural Resources

Both the U.S. and the U.S.S.R. are amply endowed with natural resources (Arad et al., 1979, Chapter 3). The Soviet Union has more oil than Saudi Arabia and leads the world in deposits of strategic minerals (minerals needed for industrial and military uses). The United States ranks second in these resources, but has superior technology. Both nations have enormous agricultural potential, though the U.S. produces more. Nonetheless, the two superpowers use considerably more natural resources than they possess within their borders, and their needs are growing. For example, the U.S. depends on other nations for many minerals that are essential to its industry and defense (see Table 4–3). Hence the scramble for world resources is a potential source of East-West confrontation. Competition for strategic raw materials is both offensive and defensive in design, as each superpower seeks to secure and maintain its own access to resources and to deny access to the other. The most likely points of conflict are the Persian Gulf region (with its huge deposits of oil and natural gas), Southern Africa (with its abundant and scarce minerals), and the

ocean. In a number of ways, the ocean is a special case.

Two-thirds of the planet lies under the ocean (Tinbergen, Dolman, and van Ettinger, 1976, Annex 10). The undersea world has all the features of dry land: plains, mountains and valleys, mineral resources, and a wide variety of plants and animals. The ocean is the last and perhaps most valuable source of raw materials on earth, one humans have only begun to tap. A Pacific rectangle about 12,000 miles long and 4,000 miles wide contains at least 10 billion and perhaps 500 billion tons of manganese, nickel, copper, and cobalt (Barnet, 1980, p. 128). The tiny crustaceans called "krill," found in the water between Antarctica and South America, could supply twice the present *total* world fish catch (Kemp, 1977, p. 54). In addition, the sea is one of the gray areas on the world's political map, a region that is still "open for grabs." The traditional law of the sea combines the two principles of sovereignty and freedom. Nations claimed territorial rights to a narrow belt of sea along their coasts, but freedom reigned on the high seas (subject only to enforced respect for the freedom of others). This era may be drawing to a close, however. One reason is technology. Modern fishing fleets range far from their native shores, harvesting vast quantities of marine life. The technology for offshore drilling already exists, and the technology for mining the seabed is in the development stages. The questions of how far national sovereignty extends into the sea and who owns the seabed in what are still open territories have taken on new meaning.

The two superpowers have different but equally compelling interests in the future of the ocean. If the Achilles heel of the West is its need for oil, that of the East is its need for food (Kemp, 1977, p. 50). The increasing dependence of the United States on imported oil has been well documented. Control of transportation routes for supertankers is of immediate importance to the U.S. In the next

Table 4–3
Where America Falls Short

Mineral	U.S. Imports*	Major Sources
COLUMBIUM	100%	Brazil
STRONTIUM	100	Mexico
INDUSTRIAL DIAMONDS	100	Ireland, South Africa
MANGANESE	98	South Africa, France, Japan
TANTALUM	96	Thailand, Canada, Malaysia
BAUXITE	93	Jamaica, Guinea, Surinam
COBALT	90	Zaire, Belgium, Zambia
CHROMIUM	90	South Africa, Philippines, U.S.S.R.
PLATINUM GROUP	89	South Africa, U.S.S.R.
ASBESTOS	85	Canada
TIN	81	Malaysia, Thailand, Indonesia
NICKEL	77	Canada
CADMIUM	66	Canada, Australia, Mexico
ZINC	62	Canada
MERCURY	62	Algeria, Spain, Italy
TUNGSTEN	59	Canada, Bolivia, South Korea
SELENIUM	40	Canada, Japan, Yugoslavia

* Latest estimates

Source: *Newsweek*, November 10, 1980, p. 98. Data based on figures from the U.S. Bureau of Mines, Sinclair Group Cos.

decade, offshore drilling may account for as much as 50 percent of petroleum production (Arad et al., 1979, p. 79). Therefore, control of the waters off West Africa (to name one spot) may become as important to the U.S. as relations with Saudi Arabia are today. This area is also of vital concern to the U.S.S.R. West Africa's coastal waters are rich in marine life. Food production has not kept pace with consumer demand in the East (Holsti, 1979). In the spring of 1980, for example, food shortages inspired at least four walkouts and shutdowns of major factories—extremely rare events in the Soviet Union. Fishing is more important to the U.S.S.R. than to any other industrial nation save Japan. In recent years, it has obtained 15 percent of its protein supply from the sea (Kemp, 1977, p. 53). With more nations declaring 200-mile offshore fishing limits, this critical food supply is being threatened. Oil and food are only part of the story. Conflicts may also develop over minerals, especially in the Pacific. The Pacific is dotted with uninhabited islands that do not "belong" to anyone. East-West conflict in this area seems likely, if not inevitable. For some time, the United States has regarded the Pacific as an "American lake," but in recent years, the Soviets have been sending increasing numbers of ships into the area (Arad et al., 1979, pp. 81–85).

The United Nations Conferences on the Law of the Sea (UNCLOS) are an attempt to resolve disputes over ocean resources and to create international machinery for managing the sea. To date, UNCLOS has not produced firm agreements, though it has given tacit endorsement to the concept of 200-mile exclusive offshore economic zones. Ironically, the signing of a treaty on the Law of the Sea might intensify rather than avert conflict—setting off a scramble to secure sovereign rights over every one of the thousands of tiny islands in the Pacific and elsewhere. Equally ironic, the U.S. and U.S.S.R. often find themselves on the same side in UNCLOS debates. The Third World is pressing for the ocean to be recognized as the common heritage of humankind. These nations want to establish an independent, international authority over the ocean, and to create public, international corporations to exploit and distribute the sea's resources. In contrast, the U.S. and U.S.S.R. favor issuing licenses to private companies or national governments, respectively. For the moment, this triadic power struggle—East-West conflict, balanced by Third World pressure—seems to be maintaining a degree of stability on the high seas.

A key point here is that the distribution of resources, and hence the "distribution" of potential and actual conflicts, changes. Ten or twenty years ago, the ocean floor was not a source of international conflict for the simple reason that no one had the technology to collect or mine minerals buried under water. A hundred years ago, the oil in the Middle East was not a source of political conflict because the technology for using petroleum and hence the demand for oil had not developed. Changing technology has made the ocean floors a potential battleground. (Figure 4–1 shows how competition for resources in the Persian Gulf led to an arms buildup, greatly increasing the potential for armed conflict. The Middle East today is a powder keg.)

Conflict over Human Rights

Competition for natural resources is only one source of East-West tension. The clash of values has been just as intense—often more so. The human rights issue is a clear illustration of this. Historically there have been two basic variations on the concept of human rights (Pagels, 1979). On one side are cultures holding that the individual has certain intrinsic rights and that society is morally obliged to protect those rights. According to this view, ultimate value resides in the individual. On the other side are cultures holding that society has the intrinsic right to make demands of the individual, and the individual has a moral obligation to live up to those demands. According to this view, ultimate value resides in society. The United States, with its emphasis on political and civil rights, exemplifies the first view. The Soviet Union, with its emphasis on social and economic rights, exemplifies the second. These different cultural definitions of human rights have led to frequent misunderstandings, with each side accusing the other of inhumane and inconsistent behavior. As a result, the clash between them often has been portrayed as that of competing moral crusades.

The American definition of human rights emphasizes personal liberty; the right of individuals to physical security and freedom of thought, conscience, and speech (Hauser, 1979). The central aim of our Bill of Rights (1791) was to protect individuals from arbitrary, tyrannical government. To this end, the United States and other Western societies have focused on developing procedures to limit the power of the state. The centerpiece of this system is the right to due process under the law. Americans have provided for due process with an independent judiciary, the right to legal counsel, the right to a fair and public trial by a jury of one's peers, protection against arbitrary imprisonment, and the prohibition against cruel

Figure 4-1

Pressure on the Persian Gulf—How Competition for Oil Translates into an Arms Buildup

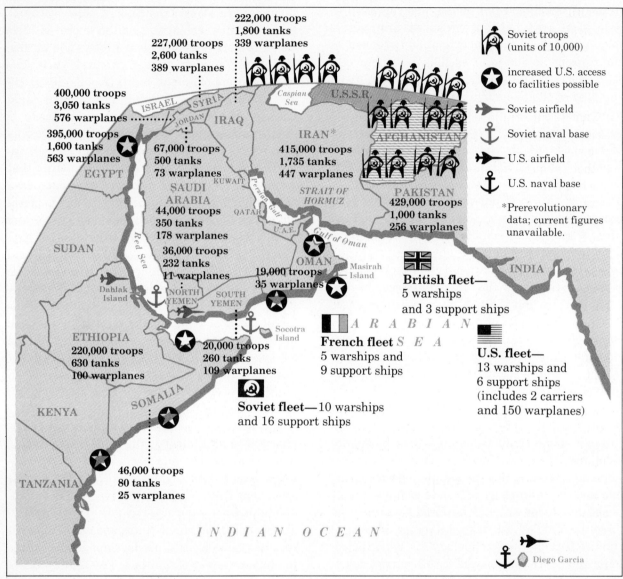

Source: *Newsweek,* July 14, 1980, p. 32.

and unusual punishment. These rights are basic to the American sense of justice. It was not until the twentieth century that Americans also sought to institutionalize economic security, free education, health and old age insurance, and similar guarantees of well-being. To some extent, Americans still regard these as privileges, not rights. (Indeed, social guarantees are still controversial in the United States, for they require a degree of government intervention.) Americans tend to put political and civil liberties first, social and economic rights second.

Although the Soviet Constitution includes most of the freedoms laid down in the American Bill of Rights, the emphasis is on the public good, not private freedom (Reddaway, 1979). In the words of one Soviet leader, "We do not have, and cannot have, freedom to struggle against communism" (*Pravda,* December 22, 1962). In Soviet law and practice, freedom of expression is permitted only when it is considered to be of positive value, according to official Party policy. (Article 70 of the Soviet criminal code prohibits "anti-Soviet agitation and propaganda"; Articles 190 and 191 prohibit the circulation of fabrications that defame the Soviet system. Violations are punishable by three to seven years in prison or five years' exile.) Limitations on personal freedom are justified on the grounds that the rights of working people, by definition, cannot be violated by a people's government. The state is a dictatorship, but a "dictatorship of the proletariat." In Soviet thinking and practice, economic and social rights come first; political and civil liberties are secondary. The Constitution of the U.S.S.R. emphasizes the right to work, to education, to leisure, and to social security. Without these rights, Soviets argue, personal liberties are meaningless.

On August 1, 1975, U.S. President Gerald Ford, Soviet Premier Leonid Brezhnev, and the heads of thirty-two European nations plus Canada signed a declaration of intention known as the Helsinki Agreement (Robertson, 1979). It was the culmination of twenty years of negotiation, initiated by the U.S.S.R. The Soviets saw the agreement as a diplomatic coup. For the first time, non-communist European and North American nations formally recognized the borders the U.S.S.R. had established during World War II. The non-communist nations saw the agreement as a first step toward ending the cold war. As it turned out, the Helsinki Agreement served to underline basic disagreements about the meaning of human rights. It accentuated, rather than defused conflict.

At Helsinki, participating nations agreed to respect one another's borders; to discuss arms limitations; to engage in scientific, cultural, and economic exchange; and to respect — indeed, promote and encourage — "human rights and fundamental freedoms, including the freedom of thought, conscience, religion, or belief, for all without distinction as to race, sex, language, or religion." The signing of this agreement caused a stir, particularly in the East. In Czechoslovakia, 500 intellectuals signed the "Charter 77" and vowed to monitor human rights violations in their country. Similar groups formed in East Germany, Poland, Roumania, and in the U.S.S.R. (this one chaired by Youri Orlov, assisted by the renowned Soviet physicist Andrei Sakharov). The Soviets moved quickly to isolate these "dissidents" through house arrest, exile, and imprisonment. The West (led by the U.S.) responded by declaring support for dissidents, officially (President Carter's letter to Sakharov) and unofficially (through private groups). From the Western point of view, the Soviets were engaging in flagrant violation of the Helsinki Agreement. To many American citizens, it was one more sign that the Soviets could not be trusted. From the Eastern, Soviet point of view, the U.S. was engaging in flagrant violation of the provisions not to intervene in another state's internal affairs. The U.S. was encouraging Soviet citizens to violate the people's rights, as defined by the Party. Given their quite different cultural definitions and social systems, the issue of human rights is likely to generate East-West conflict for some time to come.

North vs. South

Much as an iron (military) curtain separates East and West, a curtain of poverty divides the North and South. Most of the rich, developed, First World countries are found in the Northern Hemisphere; most of the poor, developing, Third World nations in the Southern Hemisphere. We use the terms "North" and "South" here to emphasize this economic division. To be sure, a few Southern nations (mainly the oil exporters) have higher per capita incomes than some Northern nations, but they are exceptions.

The nations of the South share a common predicament. Although they have achieved political independence, they remain economically dependent on the North and unequal to it. With a quarter of the world's population, the North (excluding Eastern Europe) earns four-fifths of its income. The three-quarters of the world's population in the South lives off one-fifth of the world's income. The average person in the North can expect to live for seventy years, to eat every day, and to receive at least a secondary (high school) education. In the South, life expectancy for most people is only fifty years; one out of four children dies before age five; over a fifth of the Southern population is chronically hungry; almost half have little hope of escaping illiteracy. It is not only that the North is richer. Over 90 percent of all industries are located above the equator. Transnational corporations based in the North control many of the world's patents on new technology, dominating world trade. And this gives the North the power to set the rules and regula-

tions for the global economic system (ICIDI, 1980, pp. 31–32; Dadzie, 1980). How did these inequalities develop? Why are the nations of the South so poor?

Explaining North-South Inequality

In the 1950s and early 1960s, many social scientists attributed the inequalities between the North and South to internal, national characteristics (Chirot, 1977, p. 2). According to this view, the nations of the North were more advanced because they had developed a rational, modern approach to business; a strong Puritan ethic that encouraged people to save and invest (rather than spend); and strong educational systems. The nations of the South were poor because the people were bound by tradition; labored under outdated political systems that did not respond to popular demand and economic systems that discouraged ambition; and lacked the educational systems to provide skilled workers. According to this view, it is all but impossible to graft technology developed in one cultural and social system onto another.

To be sure, there are cultural differences between the North and South, but do these differences alone explain underdevelopment? The sociologist Daniel Chirot thinks not. By 1900, the capitalist nations of the North directly or indirectly controlled most of the world. The South "had already experienced prolonged and extremely unsettling contact with the highly modernized, industrialized, and politically dominant Western world" (Chirot, 1977, p. 7). They were part of what Chirot and others have called "the capitalist world system." And their poverty and backwardness have to be explained in terms of their weak position in this system. According to this view, there was a deliberate attempt to withhold technology from the South.

Chirot argues that the colonial period created what amounted to a global division of labor and a global system of social stratification. The rich, economically diversified, industrial powers of the North acted as an international upper class; the poor nations of the South, which provided cheap labor, raw materials, and some agricultural materials, became the international lower class. Economic activities within the rich nations benefited from a more or less free market. In the colonies, Northern powers monopolized trade and exchange. The colonies became overspecialized (overly dependent on one, or a few, exports) because the industrial nations ran them like plantations, for their own profit. (It was not that the South did not develop; it was developed in a specific direction, to serve the needs of the North.) Like workers in a migrant labor camp or a coal-mining town (described in Chapter 1), the peoples of the South had no choice but to buy at the "company store" (from Northern nations). Like these workers, their wages were kept low so that they had to buy on credit, to live in perpetual debt. Political independence did not liberate Southern nations from economic dependence. Most are still overspecialized, still dependent on loans and aid. A new actor on the world stage, the transnational corporation, plays a significant role in perpetuating Southern dependency.

The Role of the Transnational Corporation

Transnational (or multinational) corporations are companies that are owned and directed by people from one country but have factories, land, and other investments in many countries. Strictly speaking, transnationals are not new. The East India Company, chartered in England in 1600, was one. At one point, it effectively ruled 250 million people, had its own army, and even employed its own bishops (Barnet and Müller, 1974, p. 72). Oil and grain companies have been operating internationally since the beginning of the

century. But the scale, sophistication, and impact of transnational corporations have increased dramatically in the post–World War II era. Transnationals control at least a quarter and probably a third of all world production. (Corporate secrecy makes it hard to say exactly.) The total sales of their foreign affiliates were estimated at $830 billion in 1976—as much as the combined GNP of *all* developing nations except the oil exporters (see Table 4-4). The marketing, processing, or production of a number of commodities—including oil, bauxite, copper, iron ore, nickel, lead, zinc, tin, tobacco, bananas, and teas—is dominated by transnationals (ICIDI, 1980, p. 187).

One might think that major corporations investing in the South would speed development and boost the Southern nations' economies. Many transnationals claim they do this. Richard Barnet and Ronald Müller (1974) argue that global corporations in fact perpetuate dependency by controlling finance capital, technology, and marketing. Transnationals claim to provide the poor countries of the South with a vital source of finance capital (investment funds). In fact, when global corporations establish operations in a foreign country, they are more likely to use local capital than to invest foreign money (Barnet and Müller, 1974, pp. 152–62). Not surprisingly, local banks would rather lend money to Sears, Roebuck or General Motors than to local entrepreneurs. Thus transnationals deprive local developers of funds. Some of the money transnationals borrow is invested in building new factories and the like, but a substantial portion is used to buy up local firms. This makes good business sense for the corporation; it reduces competition. But a transfer of ownership does not contribute to the host country's development. In addition, much of their trade takes place *within* the corporation. Transnationals buy and sell to their own affiliates, raising the cost of imports for Southern nations and lowering the price of exports to maximize cor-

Table 4–4
The Fifty Largest Economic Units in the Global System, 1970

Country or Corporation	Gross National Product or Gross Annual Sales *(millions of dollars)*	Country or Corporation	Gross National Product or Gross Annual Sales *(millions of dollars)*
1 United States	974,100	26 Pakistan	17,500
2 Soviet Union	497,000	27 South Africa	16,690
3 Japan	197,180	28 **Standard Oil (N.J.)**	16,550
4 West Germany	186,300	29 Denmark	15,600
5 France	147,500	30 **Ford Motor Company**	14,980
6 United Kingdom	121,000	31 Austria	14,300
7 China (PR)	120,000	32 Hungary	14,300
8 Italy	93,200	33 Norway	13,400
9 Canada	84,700	34 **Royal Dutch Shell**	10,800
10 India	52,920	35 Venezuela	10,300
11 Poland	39,400	36 Philippines	10,230
12 Brazil	35,440	37 Finland	10,200
13 Mexico	33,000	38 Iran	10,180
14 Australia	32,990	39 Bulgaria	9,800
15 Sweden	32,600	40 Greece	9,500
16 East Germany	32,300	41 Turkey	9,000
17 Spain	32,300	42 **General Electric**	8,730
18 Netherlands	31,200	43 South Korea	8,213
19 Czechoslovakia	30,500	44 Indonesia	7,600
20 Belgium	25,700	45 **Mobil Oil**	7,260
21 **General Motors**	24,300	46 Colombia	7,070
22 Argentina	23,830	47 **Chrysler**	7,000
23 Roumania	22,300	48 **Unilever**	6,880
24 Switzerland	20,500	49 Chile	6,670
25 Yugoslavia	19,000	50 Egypt	6,580

Source: Marshall R. Singer, "The Foreign Policies of Small Developing States," in James N. Rosenau, Kenneth W. Thompson, and Gavin Boyd (Eds.), *World Politics* (New York: Free Press, 1976), pp. 265–69. Copyright © 1976 by The Free Press, A Division of Macmillan Publishing Co., Inc. Reprinted with permission.

porate profits and, in some cases, evade taxes. "Transfer prices," as these are called, differ from the price raw materials or finished products might obtain on a free market. Julius Nyerere, President of Tanzania, describes the impact of these practices on developing nations:

> The dominant philosophy of international exchange which we met at independence—and which still prevails—is that of a "free market." In theory this means unfettered competition and bargaining between equals, with prices being the combined actions and wishes of sellers and buyers. . . . Unfortunately the theory bears little relation to fact. Equality between nations of the modern world is only a legal equality. It is not an economic reality. . . . The price of manufactured goods is fixed by producers; if any competition enters into the situation at all, it is between giant firms like Ford, General Motors, and Volkswagen. . . . Conversely, the price of primary products [raw materials] is fixed by the purchasers. The producers put on the market whatever they have managed to grow or mine in that year; the goods are often perishable, and in any case the poor nations are desperate for foreign exchange and have no facilities for storage—known

facts which further weaken their bargaining position! A small number of purchasers then decide how much they will buy, at what price. . . . The poor nations of the world remain poor because they are poor, and because they operate as if they were equals in a world dominated by the rich." (In Barnet, 1980, p. 147)

Control of finance is only part of the problem. Transnationals argue that they encourage economic development by sharing advanced technology with the South. Barnet and Müller found that the technology they share is often outdated and overpriced (1974, pp. 162–72). For example, shops in Bangkok and Accra offer 1950s model refrigerators and washing machines, at today's prices. When transnationals do introduce new technology, they usually retain control. A 1964 UN study showed that almost 90 percent of the patents in India, Turkey, the United Arab Republic, Pakistan, and Trinidad were owned by foreigners. Moreover, much Western technology is designed to save costs by reducing labor requirements. (It is capital-intensive rather than labor-intensive, requiring large financial investments but few

The globalization of tastes: Coca-Cola opens a plant in Peking. The Chinese word for Coke translates as "tasty happiness" in English.

workers.) The nations of the South have limited funds but many workers. Capital-intensive technology "tends to convert their human resources, which are their biggest assets, into social liabilities" (Barnet and Müller, 1974, p. 166). For example, although manufacturing has increased dramatically in Latin America in recent decades, the percentage of the labor force employed in manufacturing is lower than it was fifty years ago. New technology has increased, not decreased, employment problems.

Finally, transnationals use the considerable marketing and communications skills of Madison Avenue to shape tastes and values in the South (Barnet and Müller, 1974, pp. 172–84). Advertisements are designed to stimulate demand, to create desires. Often the effect is to upset cultural and even nutritional balances. For example, studies in rural Mexico show that many peasants prefer white bread to nutritionally superior tortillas and sell the few eggs and chickens they raise to buy Coca-Colas.

In recent years, transnational corporations have begun to act like independent nations with their own "state departments," ambassadors, intelligence gathering, and private foreign policies (Bock, 1974; Kraar, 1980). Because they have bases in many nations, global corporations are able to act with some autonomy in their home and host nations. Corporate interests are not only different from national interests, they are sometimes directly competitive with them. For example, Gulf Oil has been pumping approximately 150,000 barrels of oil a day from wells off the shores of the African nation of Angola since 1968. When civil war broke out in Angola in 1975, the U.S. government sent guns and money to guerilla groups that opposed the Popular Movement for the Liberation of Angola (the MPLA). The MPLA was backed by Cuban troops and thus indirectly by the Soviet Union. Gulf predicted—correctly— that the MPLA would win the war and began ne-

gotiations with them to continue drilling. At one point, the CIA had budgeted $31.7 million to stop the MPLA, while Gulf was offering them $200 million in royalties. Today a shaky MPLA government is installed in the Angolan capital and Cuban troops are guarding Gulf Oil's installations (Barnet, 1980, p. 228). Global economics makes strange bedfellows.

Third World Strategies

The leaders of the nations of the South find themselves in a delicate situation. Rapid economic development is their top priority. They seek economic self-sufficiency and equality, but they are dependent on the North. For this reason, influencing international affairs is also a top priority. Like all government leaders, they seek national autonomy and security, and they worry about external threats. Like all leaders, they are also concerned about threats to their governments from within. To achieve their goals, the leaders of Southern nations have employed two major strategies: association with a major power and/or building coalitions within the Third World (Wriggins, 1978).

Association with a major power Particularly during the cold war years, a number of Southern nations sought to strengthen their position by establishing links to the U.S. or U.S.S.R. (Wriggins, 1978, pp. 77–85). For example, Pakistan, Taiwan, South Korea, Iran, and Turkey signed treaties with the U.S.; Cuba, Egypt, Syria, and Somalia had similar ties to the U.S.S.R. (Note that these examples are drawn from the 1960s; many have since changed.) The advantages of association with a major power are obvious. The smaller nation receives aid in the form of food, technical assistance, and funds for building roads, communication systems, schools, and other facilities that promote development. Often this not only boosts the economy, it helps the government to deal with internal opposition and thus remain in power. Typically the smaller nation also receives military aid and training.

The liabilities of association with a major power—whether communist or capitalist—are as clear as the advantages. The smaller nation may find that it loses both autonomy in foreign affairs and control over its own economic development. It may be spurned by other Third World nations. Moreover, the balance of internal politics may be altered. For example, military aid may put the army in a position to dominate domestic affairs.

Building Third World coalitions In the last decade, coalitions among Southern nations have become an increasingly viable alternative to association with a major power. Quite simply, the nations of the South have begun to mobilize their collective bargaining power vis-à-vis the North. W. Howard Wriggins (1978, pp. 43–76) distinguishes among three types of coalitions: commodity, regional, and universal coalitions.

Commodity coalitions are based on the locations of strategic resources and transcend regional and cultural differences. The outstanding example is OPEC—a cartel of oil exporters founded in Baghdad in 1960. It is, in the words of a Venezuelan oil minister, "a very exclusive club." Commodity coalitions influence international affairs by withholding resources until prices go up and/or until importing nations agree to their political demands. The power of commodity coalitions depends, first, on the global demand for their resources, and second, on the members' ability to do without earnings until the loss is felt. The OPEC nations may be uniquely favored; coalitions based on phosphates, copper, and tin have been less successful.

Regional coalitions are based on the common economic and political interests and cultural ties of neighboring countries. Examples are the

Organization of African Unity (OAU), the Association of Southeast Asian Nations (ASEAN), and the Andean Pact. Regional associations in the South are designed to reduce local conflicts, as well as to formulate joint international policies.

Universal coalitions are associations of all or most Southern nations that act as generalized pressure groups on behalf of the Third World (Wriggins, 1978, pp. 63–76). To a large extent, their influence is based on the sheer strength of numbers. Leading examples are the Non-Aligned Nations, a coalition formed at the height of the cold war, and Group-77, which grew out of the UN Conference on Trade and Development (UNCTAD). To date, these organizations "deal largely in words, resolutions, and symbolic positions" (Wriggins, 1978, p. 73). Although they have won few concrete concessions from the North, their symbolic victories should not be undervalued. Through organized pressure, they have succeeded in altering the agenda of international meetings, shifting the focus from East-West security problems to North-South economic problems. In part because of influence "borrowed" from OPEC, they have made the North listen. For example, in a Declaration of a New International Economic Order, UNCTAD called for international machinery for stabilizing the prices of minerals and the other commodities, for a lowering of tariffs that limit the South's outlets for manufactured goods in Northern markets, and for renewed financial aid, including debt relief.

Two general conclusions emerge from a review of Southern strategies. First, the South is not as helpless as it once seemed; second, Southern nations are no longer forced to choose between the East and West. New economic and political backing is available—from the OPEC nations, the European Common Market, and Third World coalitions, for example. What does this mean for coming years? In Wriggins's words, "The world of the 1980s . . . is not likely to fit the convenient,

International Terrorism

The growth of political terrorism into a trans-national phenomenon has been greatly facilitated through a revolution in communication—radio, satellite television, air travel, and tourism. Terrorist acts committed in the remotest parts of the world now receive instant coverage and their "propaganda by deed" is exploited to full advantage. . . .

Terrorism's emergence as a self-sufficient tool to achieve political objectives is largely due to the vulnerability of our modern urban civilization. While Mao Tse Tung emphasized rural, peasant-based guerrilla warfare and thought in terms of an ultimate, armed and open revolutionary conflict to attain victory, today's urban guerrillas view the modern city as the new battleground. . . .

Political terrorism essentially is *propaganda by deed.* Consequently, advertising the movement becomes an integral part of its tactics. The weak, who generally resort to terrorism as a weapon, have a great need for their cause to be widely noticed. . . .

During the past few years the communication media have reported a wide variety of politically motivated terrorist acts designed both to gain publicity and to build organizational morale. The P.F.L.P.'s [Popular Front for the Liberation of Palestine] simultaneous skyjacking and subsequent destruction of four international airliners in September 1970, the Palestine Liberation Organization (P.L.O.) Commando's seizure of a Jewish high school at Maalot in May 1974 resulting in the death of two dozen children, and the death of some twenty innocent pedestrians in May 1974 when stolen cars packed with time bombs exploded in downtown Dublin, are but a few grim reminders of this tactic. However, to create a favorable image, such acts must be carefully targeted and efficiently executed, otherwise they may create an unfortunate first impression of the group and antagonize the populace. The so-called Symbionese Liberation Army's mindless abduction of Patricia Hearst followed

tidy, and rather nostalgic model of global bargains or nicely balanced [exchanges]. It is far more likely that it will be disorderly, messy, and punctuated by periodic disorders . . ." (1978, p. 116).

Toward an International Order

The need for international cooperation—and the potential for conflict and misunderstandings among nations—has never been greater. An un-by confused political rhetoric and material demands, exemplifies the latter result. . . .

The individual political terrorist . . . articulates himself through group participation. Group acts enhance his sense of political purpose and direction, his dignity and identity. Individual consciousness is welded into a group ideology that provides needed social and political supports. . . .

The dominant forms of political terrorism today are but a reflection of the politics of our time. As the national independence movements were the natural products of colonialism, the contemporary political terrorists symbolize, often mistakenly, resistance against discrimination, exclusion, suppression, and abusive power and privilege all too manifest in social, economic, ethnic, cultural, and political spheres of society. . . .

. . . The sociological and psychological research dealing with the individual actors who participate in this form of political violence is sketchy at best. This much, however, is known: most contemporary terrorists, or at least the leading figures among them, are persons of intellect and come from comfortable socio-economic backgrounds. This is true of most of the present-day groups including the *P.L.O.,* Uruguayan *Tupamaros,* the Brazilian disciples of Marighella, the West German *BaderMeinhoff,* the Japanese Red Army, and the I.R.A. . . .

Political terrorism occurs as the result of a conscious decision by ideologically inspired groups to strike back at what their members may perceive as "unjust" within a given society or polity. The answers to contemporary political terrorism, therefore, would have to be found within this larger social, economic, political, and psychological context.

Source: Baljit Singh, "An Overview," in Yonah Alexander and Seymour Maxwell Finger (Eds.), *Terrorism: Interdisciplinary Perspectives* (New York: John Jay Press, 1977), pp. 7–15.

easy triadic balance of power exists among the First, Second, and Third Worlds today. Conflicts of values compound conflicts of interests. Competition for resources and incompatible standards of social justice pit East against West. The struggle for economic liberation continues in the South. It is not a conventional war. The "enemy" is difficult to identify and confront. New situations are arising for which there are no rules of international conflict. Tensions are likely to mount as the world confronts the interrelated problems of population growth, hunger, dwindling resources, and environmental deterioration, described in Chapter 3 of this book. As shown in that chapter, these are global problems, requiring global solutions. They will not be solved through traditional means of arbitration among nation-states.

Norms for international relations do exist. There are, for example, widely agreed-upon rules of war. [This is one reason why terrorism is so disturbing. Terrorists violate international norms (see page 138).] But norms are effective only if they are shared by a significant proportion of the actors in an international conflict and if they are backed by sanctions (rewards and penalties). This is one reason why the United Nations is not more effective (Ray, 1979, pp. 211–13). Although all member nations are committed to peace, there is no universally agreed-upon definition of aggression. The norms are vague. Moreover, norms espoused in the UN General Assembly are not backed by sanctions. When the Soviets invaded Hungary in 1956, for example, and when the United States invaded the Dominican Republic in 1965, there was little the United Nations could do. There is no final political authority in international affairs as there is within nation-states, no institutions or political machinery for enforcing decisions. It is as if we lived in a global city where each person (each nation) is intent on his own destination, each one is in a hurry, and there are no traffic regulations (norms) or police officers with tickets (sanctions) to enforce them.

Developing Global Perspective

The sociologist Robert Angell (1979) believes that the establishment of a world order geared to seeking common solutions to common problems depends on the development of *enlightened patriotism:* a pride in country grounded, not in what the nation accomplished for one's ancestors or promises one's descendants, but in what the nation contributes to "the welfare of the global human enterprise" (pp. 51–52). Enlightened patriotism is loyalty to one's fellow citizens without the nationalistic sentiments that separate "us" from "them." It is a sense of responsibility for all humankind.

Angell's research indicates that a few nations have achieved this kind of global perspective, but only a few. Angell ranked 114 nations in terms of a number of indicators, including their contributions to the United Nations and its specialized agencies; their participation in UN activities (voting, supplying troops for peacekeeping operations); and the percentage of their GNP donated to the International Committee of the Red Cross. According to this scale, Switzerland, Denmark, Sweden, and Norway are pioneers in support for world order. Many other nations are "underachievers" on Angell's scale. Judging by the level of education in these nations, the number of citizens who participate in nongovernmental international organizations, their involvement in foreign trade, and other measures, one might expect them to be committed to world order. But their actions indicate their concern for global welfare is halfhearted.

The United States is one of the underachievers on Angell's list. Until quite recently, the United States government led the world in the amount, and perhaps the quality, of foreign aid. This assistance took the form of aid to war-torn countries of Europe and Japan in the late 1940s, military support during the cold war in the 1950s, and help for economically weak nations beginning in the 1960s. The Fulbright Program, the Peace Corps, Radio Free Europe, and the Asia Foundation are all examples of attempts to build constructive international relationships. Today the United States lags behind other nations in foreign aid (see Figure 4–2). Even so, polls in-

Figure 4–2

*U.S. Official Development Assistance in Comparison with That of Other Development Assistance Committee Countries**

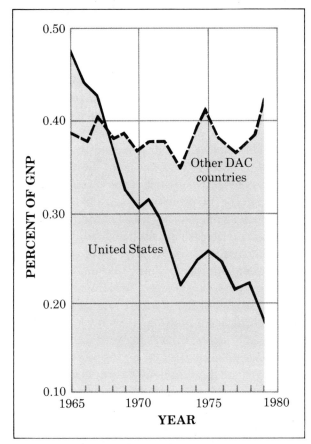

*DAC countries include Australia, Austria, Belgium, Britain, Canada, Denmark, Finland, France, West Germany, Italy, Japan, Netherlands, New Zealand, Norway, Sweden, and Switzerland.

Source: Based on data from the Overseas Development Council.

dicate that more Americans feel that we spend too much on foreign aid than feel that we spend enough or too little (Roper, 1979). As one congressman put it, many Americans think the world is "ripping this nation off" (*U.S. News & World Report,* March 31, 1980).

There may be a number of cultural barriers to enlightened patriotism in the United States (Rhinesmith, 1979). Americans like to think of themselves as rugged individualists. They dislike feeling dependent, or inextricably involved, with others. Americans willingly engage in cooperative ventures only when they believe they have the option of withdrawing. The very idea of global interdependence may make Americans uneasy. The ability to see the interconnectedness of things, or *systems thinking,* is a special skill (Kerr, 1979). Typically, American schoolchildren are taught to isolate a problem, attack it frontally, and seek the simplest solution. They are rarely encouraged to look for complexities or for the "concealed wiring." The emphasis on specialization in higher education reinforces this narrow focus. In a world where so many problems have global origins and consequences, this approach to education may be dysfunctional. This is not to say that Americans are uniquely nationalistic; different cultures create different obstacles to enlightened patriotism.

Transnational Organizations

Most discussions of the international situation focus on the behavior of nations and the relationships among them. There are a number of other actors on the world stage, however: organizations whose activities involve people and resources in different nations and who are not formally associated with any national government (Ray, 1979, p. 220). The number of transnational organizations has grown in recent years (see Table 4–5), and rapid and inexpensive transportation and communication have made them more effective. If this trend continues, transnational organizations might establish a network of relationships that

Table 4-5
The Number of Transnational
Nongovernmental Organizations, 1909-1972

1909	1951	1954	1958	1960	1964	1966	1970	1972
176	832	1008	1073	1268	1718	1935	2296	2470

Source: Union of International Associations, *Yearbook of International Organizations,* 15th ed. (Brussels, Belgium, 1974), p. s33.

would crosscut national boundaries and hence ease tensions among nations.

We described transnational corporations earlier in this chapter. Not surprisingly, labor unions have sought international connections. The International Confederation of Free Trade Unions (ICFTU), the World Federation of Trade Unions (WFTU), and the World Confederation of Labor (WCL) are concerned with all kinds of crafts and industrial activities. Other transnational unions, such as the International Federation of Airline Pilots and the International Metalworkers Federation, are organized around specific kinds of work. There are a number of structural obstacles to worldwide labor unions, however (Ray, 1979, pp. 247-50). For example, in Europe, unions tend to be centralized at the national level but decentralized at the plant level. Most pipe fitters belong to a single union, so that the workers at a single plant are represented by different unions. In the United States, the reverse is true. Most trade unions in Europe are communist; most American unions, aggressively anticommunist.

International unions are only one type of transnational organization. Religion is another basis for global connections. The Roman Catholic church, for example, has perhaps 560 million members, a professional staff of 1.6 million, a diplomatic corps, and even a small military force. In recent years, some members of the Catholic church have been quite active in the political affairs of Latin America. The World Council of Churches is another religiously based transnational. Amnesty International (AI), established in London in 1961-62, is dedicated to seeking the release of political prisoners all over the world and to ensuring humane treatment of those it cannot get released. AI was created in large part because modern technology (surveillance equipment, psychoactive drugs, sensory deprivation chambers, and so on) make it so easy for governments to identify political dissidents and to extract information from prisoners. AI attempts to maintain political neutrality, selecting equal numbers of cases from First, Second, and Third World nations. Another transnational, the Red Cross, was founded in Switzerland in the 1860s. The scientific community has always had a transnational character, in part because the goals and methods of science serve as an international language. Transnational scientific organizations, led by the International Council of Scientific Unions, organize international conferences and set international standards for the collection and presentation of data. In recent years, a number of these organizations have set up committees to study global problems. Two transnational organizations that deserve special mention are the World Order Models Project (WOMP) and the Club of Rome. The first is dedicated to exploring "preferred worlds" for the 1990s in its journal *Alternatives* and annual *State of the Globe* message. The Club of Rome, which grew out of a private meeting called by an Italian industrialist, uses computers to simulate the future consequences of current trends. Its first report, *The Limits to Growth,* called worldwide attention to the dangers of exponential growth (described in the preceding chapter of this book).

Whether transnational organizations represent the wave of the future or a passing fad is impossible to say (Ray, 1979, pp. 265–66). At present, they play only a marginal role in international affairs, while nations remain the most important actors on the global stage. As things stand, nations will decide the future.

More Critical Choices for the United States

The biologist Garrett Hardin (1968) describes the choices facing the United States today in a parable. He sees the nations of the world as a number of lifeboats afloat in the sea. Some of the boats (the rich nations) have room to spare: They can support their own populations and then some. Others (the poor nations) are already filled to overflowing. Hardin portrays Americans as fifty people on a boat with a capacity for sixty. One hundred swimmers who have been forced off their own boats are begging to come aboard. As Hardin sees it, Americans have three choices. First, they could permit all those who ask to get on board. This would result in "complete justice [but] complete catastrophe." The boat would sink and everyone, including the original passengers, would drown. Second, Americans could allow ten swimmers on board. This would raise troubling questions about whom to save. It would also sacrifice the margin of safety for the original passengers. The third choice would be to admit no one, ensuring the survival and comfort of the original passengers.

Hardin draws an analogy between these choices and decisions about food policy. The United States could (1) provide food for all the hungry people in the world, (2) give assistance to only a few, select nations, or (3) deny all requests and take care of its citizens only. Hardin ad-

vocates the third choice, or what has become known as a "lifeboat ethic." He argues that if the United States supplied food to even a few hungry nations, it would encourage them to allow their populations to grow. It would remove what Hardin sees as the crucial motivation for population control: hunger. He argues that each nation is intrinsically responsible for the welfare of its own people. For rich nations to assist poor nations in evading that responsibility is a threat to everyone. Mass starvation is sure to result. For Hardin, isolationism is the most responsible choice.

There are a number of flaws in Hardin's reasoning (Soroos, 1979). First, he does not take into account the different size and weight, and different eating habits of the boats' occupants. If people in the larger boats (the rich nations) were to reduce their consumption of meat, give up such luxuries as strawberries and asparagus, or even keep fewer household pets, the carrying capacity of the boats—and the earth—would increase. Second, Hardin limits his discussion to food supplies. If lifeboat ethics were applied to energy resources, the American boat might be among the first to sink. Third, no nation is self-sufficient today. A more accurate description of the world would be one lifeboat with food but little water, another stockpiled with cans of water but no food, and a third with the only tool for opening the containers. The only way occupants of any of these boats can survive is by sharing resources. Finally, it seems unlikely that occupants of the smaller boats will sink without protest. Hardin does not consider the possibility that desperate, armed "swimmers" will capsize the American boat.

Hardin's description is useful, however, in underlining the life-or-death nature of the choices this and other nations face. Real interests, not imaginary ones, are at stake. Choosing enlightened patriotism over isolationist lifeboat ethics would mean significant readjustments in the way Americans think and live. The alternative—

aggressive (military) pursuit of the national interest, alone or with other members of the First World — would also mean drastic changes. The next chapter, which examines the distribution of power and decision making in the United States, suggests how these choices will be made.

Summary

1. International conflict develops when two or more nations believe their goals are incompatible.

2. Nationalism fuels international conflict. The globalization of interests has not been met by a globalization of loyalties. As a result, humanity faces "the tragedy of the commons."

3. The structure of international relations has changed from a dyadic (two-party) standoff to an uneasy triadic (three-party) balance of power.

4. The First World — Western, parliamentary, capitalist nations that industrialized gradually, in response to internal pressures — is concerned with maintaining its position in international relations.

5. The Second World — Eastern, one-party, communist nations whose industrial development was centrally planned — is concerned with catching up.

6. The Third World — nonaligned, developing nations that share a legacy of colonial domination — are concerned with starting up.

7. Instability is built into triads, which have a tendancy to divide and redivide into coalitions of two against one.

8. The East (the Second World, led by the U.S.S.R.) and West (the First World, led by the U.S.) are divided by conflicts of interest and values. Their competition for the mineral resources in the ocean floor and incompatible definitions of human rights are potential sources of conflict.

9. A curtain of poverty divides the North (the First World) and South (the Third World). Cultural differences alone do not explain the underdevelopment of the South. These nations have been exploited by colonial powers and, more recently, transnational corporations. To achieve economic liberation, they have associated with major powers and/or formed commodity, regional, and universal coalitions.

10. The norms regulating international relations are not shared by all actors on the world stage or backed by sanctions. Enlightened patriotism is not widespread. Transnational organizations play a minor role in world events. Both offer hope, however.

11. The U.S. may have to choose between "lifeboat ethics" and difficult readjustments in thinking and life styles in the future.

Suggested Reading

Angell, Robert C. *The Quest for World Order.* Ann Arbor, Mich.: University of Michigan Press, 1979.

Barnet, Richard J., and R.E. Müller. *Global Reach: The Power of the Multinational Corporations.* New York: Simon & Schuster, 1974.

Chirot, Daniel. *Social Change in the Twentieth Century.* New York: Harcourt Brace Jovanovich, 1977.

Independent Commission on International Development Issues. *North-South: A Program for Survival.* Cambridge, Mass.: MIT Press, 1980.

Kriesberg, Louis. *The Sociology of Social Conflicts.* Englewood Cliffs, N.J.: Prentice-Hall, 1973.

Ray, James L. *Global Politics.* Boston: Houghton Mifflin, 1979.

Sampson, Anthony. *The Arms Bazaar.* New York: Viking, 1977.

References

Angell, R.C. *The Quest for World Order.* Ann Arbor, Mich.: University of Michigan Press, 1979.

Arad, R.W. et al. *Sharing Global Resources.* McGraw-Hill, 1980s Project Council on Foreign Relations, 1979.

Ayres, R.U. *Uncertain Futures: Challenges for Decision-Makers.* New York: Wiley-Interscience, 1979.

Barnet, R.J. *The Lean Years.* New York: Simon & Schuster, 1980.

Barnet, R.J., and R.E. Müller. *Global Reach: The Power of the Multinational Corporations.* New York: Simon & Schuster, 1974.

Bock, P.G. "The Transnational Corporation and Private Foreign Policy." *Society,* Vol. 11, No. 2 (January-February 1974), pp. 44–49.

Booth, K. *Strategy and Ethnocentricism.* New York: Holmes & Meier, 1979.

Caplow, T. *Two Against One: Coalitions in Triads.* Englewood Cliffs, N.J.: Prentice-Hall, 1968.

Chirot, D. *Social Change in the Twentieth Century.* New York: Harcourt Brace Jovanovich, 1977.

Cleveland, H. "The Internationalization of Domestic Affairs." *Annals of the American Academy, AAPSS,* Vol. 442 (March 1979), pp. 125–137.

Dadzie, K.K.S. "Economic Development." *Scientific American,* Vol. 243, No. 3 (September 1980), pp. 58–64.

Deutsch, K.W. *Nationalism and Its Alternatives.* New York: Knopf, 1969.

Gamson, W.A., and A. Modigliani. "Knowledge and Foreign Policy Opinions: Some Models for Consideration." *Public Opinion Quarterly,* Vol. 30 (Summer 1966), pp. 187–99.

Hardin, G. "The Tragedy of the Commons." *Science,* Vol. 162 (December 13, 1968), pp. 1243–48.

Hauser, R.E. "A First World View." In D.P. Kommers and G.D. Loescher (Eds.), *Human Rights and American Foreign Policy.* Notre Dame, Ind: University of Notre Dame Press. 1979, pp. 85–89.

Holsti, O.R. "Global Food Problems and Soviet Agriculture." In D.W. Orr and M.S. Soroos (Eds.), *The Global Predicament: Ecological Perspectives on World Order.* Chapel Hill, N.C.: University of North Carolina Press, 1979, pp. 150–75.

Horowitz, I.L. *Three Worlds of Development: The Theory and Practice of International Stratification,* 2d ed. New York: Oxford University Press, 1972.

ICIDI (Independent Commission on International Development Issues). *North-South: A Program for Survival.* Cambridge, Mass.: MIT Press, 1980.

Kemp, G. "The New Strategic Map." *Survival,* Vol. 19, No. 2 (March 1977), pp. 50–59.

Kerr, C. "Education for Global Perspectives." *Annals of the American Academy, AAPSS.* Vol. 442 (March 1979), pp. 109–16.

Klare, M.T. "The Arms Overstock." *Harper's,* Vol. 259 (November 1979), pp. 24–29.

Kraar, L. "The Multinationals Get Smarter About Political Risks." *Fortune,* March 24, 1980, pp. 86–100.

Kriesberg, L. *The Sociology of Social Conflicts.* Englewood Cliffs, N.J.: Prentice-Hall, 1973.

Kriesberg, L. "Peace Promotion." In M. Olsen and M. Micklin (Eds.), *Frontiers of Applied Sociology.* New York: Holt, Rinehart and Winston, 1981.

Manning, B. "246 Years of American Foreign Policy: Doric, Ionic—and Corinthian?" In I. Kristol and P. Weaver (Eds.), *The Americans: 1976/Critical Choices for Americans,* Vol. II. Lexington Mass.: Heath, 1976, pp. 253–91.

Miller, L.B. "Superpower Conflict in the 1980s." *Millennium: Journal of International Studies,* Vol. 6, No. 1 (1980), pp. 45–63.

Morgan, O. *Merchants of Grain.* New York: Penguin, 1980.

Pagels, E. "Human Rights: Legitimizing a Recent Concept." *Annals of the American Academy, AAPSS,* Vol. 422 (March 1979), pp. 57–62.

Ray, J.L. *Global Politics.* Boston: Houghton Mifflin, 1979.

Reddaway, P.B. "Theory and Practice of Human Rights in the Soviet Union." In D.P. Kommers and G.D. Loescher (Eds.), *Human Rights and American Foreign Policy.* Notre Dame, Ind.: University of Notre Dame Press, 1979, pp. 111–29.

Rhinesmith, S.H. "Americans in the Global Learning Process." *Annals of the American Academy, AAPSS,* Vol. 442 (March 1979), pp. 98–108.

Robertson, A.H. "The Helsinki Agreement and Human Rights" In D.P. Kommers and G.D. Loescher (Eds.), *Human Rights and American Foreign Policy,* Notre Dame, Ind.: University of Notre Dame Press, 1979, pp. 130–49.

Roper, B.W. "The Limits of Public Support." *Annals of the American Academy, AAPSS,* Vol. 442 (March 1979), pp. 40–45.

Sherrill, R. *Governing America.* New York: Harcourt Brace Jovanovich, 1978.

Simmel, G. *The Sociology of George Simmel.* K.H. Wolff (Ed. and trans.). New York: Free Press, 1950.

Soroos, M.S. "Lifeboat Ethics Versus One-Worldism in International Food and Resource Policy." In D.W. Orr and M.S. Soroos (Eds.), *The Global Predicament: Ecological Perspectives on World Order.* Chapel Hill, N.C.: University of North Carolina Press, 1979, pp. 131–49.

Tinbergen, J., A.J. Dloman, and J. van Ettinger. *Reshaping the International Order: A Report to the Club of Rome.* New York: Dutton, 1976.

Wriggins, W.H. "Third World Strategies for Change" In W.H. Wriggins and G. Adler-Karlsson (Eds.), *Reducing Global Inequities.* New York: McGraw-Hill, 1980s Project/ Council on Foreign Relations, 1978, pp. 21–117.

Chapter Five

The Political Economy

Corporate Power

The Road to Oligopoly

  The Capitalist Ideal
  Market Domination

The Use and Abuse of Corporate Power

**The Power of the Federal
  Government**

The Rise of Big Government

  Promoting Economic Security

Maintaining the Military Establishment
Protecting Public Rights

A Bureaucracy Out of Control

  Organized Inefficiency
  Responsive to Whom?

Pressure Politics

Clash of Interests
The Special Interest State
In the Public Interest

The Arab oil embargo of 1973–74 has been compared to a first, mild heart attack (Thurow, 1980, p. 3). Just as a first heart attack forces a person to confront the fact of his mortality, so the oil embargo forced Americans to confront their economic vulnerability. Were this nation's days as the economic leader of the world numbered? The lines that formed once again at gas stations in 1979, when revolution halted oil production in Iran, were not reassuring.

Americans' initial reaction to the Arab oil embargo was indignation mixed with disbelief. Was it possible that a small number of desert sheiks could force *us* to wait on gasoline lines and threaten *our* standard of living? Apparently, yes. In the late 1970s, the evidence mounted that the United States was losing its competitive edge in world markets. As recently as 1960, U.S. manufacturers had produced one-fourth of all industrial exports in the world market and supplied 98 percent of the goods in the American market. In the 1970s, the United States lost 23 percent of its share of world industrial markets, at an estimated cost of $125 billion and perhaps 2 million jobs (*U.S. News & World Report,* June 30, 1980). At the same time, the number of imports in American stores increased (Figure 5–1). One-fourth of the cars purchased in California in 1980, for example, were imports. A shopper looking for an American-made radio or tape recorder had trouble finding one. Virtually all of these products were made abroad. Prior to 1970, the U.S. had not run a deficit in foreign trade for fifty years. In 1978, the U.S. trade deficit to Japan alone was $13.5 billion (Fallows, 1980). Whereas Japan and Germany forged ahead in the 1970s, in the United States, the rate of investment in research and development, the construction of new plants and purchase of new equipment, and worker productivity had all slowed down. The American economy, which for decades had produced the highest standard of living in the world,

Figure 5–1
The Shrinking Share of U.S. Manufacturing in Domestic and Foreign Markets

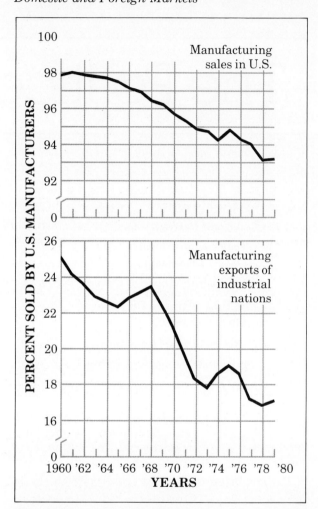

Source: *Business Week,* June 30, 1980, pp. 58–59. Data based on Commerce Department figures.

slipped to fifth place on the list of non-oil-exporting nations (International Monetary Fund, 1979).

Oil shortages and rising prices were not the only symptoms of disease in the American economy. The 1970s had brought chronic high inflation. Inflation means, simply, a general rise in prices, which leads to a decline in purchasing power. What used to cost $1.00 now costs $1.20 or $1.50. Economists consider a 2 to 4 percent annual rate of inflation "normal." In the 1970s, however, the rate reached 11 percent. At the same time, the U.S. economy seemed to be in a recession. Unemployment rose. In 1980, over 7.3 million Americans were out of work; each week, 600,000 applied for unemployment compensation. According to traditional economic theory, this should not happen (Samuelson, 1980, pp. 236–37): When wages rise, prices go up. When prices get too high, however, people stop buying, producers cut back, and workers are laid off. When production slows down, wages drop because workers are competing for fewer jobs, and prices drop because producers are competing for fewer consumers. People start buying and the cycle of inflation/recession begins again. In other words, booms should follow busts in succession. To say that the economy is going through recession *and* inflation is roughly equivalent to saying that a heart patient is suffering from high *and* low blood pressure. According to traditional economic theory, inflation and recession cannot occur at the same time. But what cannot happen in theory did happen in fact. At a loss to explain this, economists searched for new diagnostic terms: The most popular was "stagflation," combining *stag*nation in production and employment and in*flation* of prices (Samuelson, 1980, p. 766).

Experts disagree sharply over where the problem with the U.S. economy lies. Conservative economists blame the current economic crisis on too much government (see Friedman and Friedman, 1980). According to this view, the federal government is undermining the free-enterprise system with high taxes on corporate profits and capital gains (which discourage investment), complicated regulations (such as pollution controls and equal opportunity requirements), and its own spending policies (particularly for social welfare). In contrast, liberal economists blame the current economic crisis on too *little* government (see Galbraith, 1973). According to this view, too many of the decisions that shape society are made in private by the heads of corporations who are more concerned with profits than with the national welfare.

There are two points on which liberals and conservatives agree, however. First, many of our current problems derive from centralization and the concentration of power. Liberals are concerned about the size and power of corporations, and their potential for exploiting the public. Conservatives worry about the size and power of the federal government, and its potential for destroying private enterprise. Second, liberals and conservatives agree that the way the government manages (or fails to manage) the economy is largely responsible for the nation's current problems. The subject of this chapter, then, is the political economy. The term *political economy* refers to the interrelations of politics and economics and their mutual influence on other areas of life. In the first two sections of the chapter, we look at big business and big government, show how they acquired their size and power, how they are intertwined with one another, and what the consequences are for individuals and for society. A decade ago, the chapter might have ended here. New concerns have emerged, however.

American society has become increasingly differentiated. The nation is divided by numerous special interests. Business and labor, farmers and physicians, New Englanders and Californians, stockholders and welfare recipients, women, retirees, and numerous other special interest groups — all press competing claims on the government. As often as not, one group's solution is another group's problem. Often, they work at cross-purposes. The prosperity of the 1950s, followed by the successes of the Civil Rights and other movements in the 1960s and 1970s, raised group expectations. But the economy didn't grow as fast in the 1970s as it had in preceding decades. Rising expectations collided head-on with declining abundance. In the last section of this chapter, we consider the possibility that competing special interest groups have paralyzed the political economy, at least temporarily.

Corporate Power

The size and grasp of America's major corporations have been well documented. According to a study conducted by the Senate Government Operations Committee (1974), eight institutions, including six major banks, dominate American business through their stock holdings. The two hundred largest corporations control two-thirds of the nation's manufacturing assets (Mintz and Cohen, 1971, p. 35). The oil industry is controlled by the "seven sisters"; the grain trade, by five companies; the automobile industry, by four. A number of these corporations are the economic equivalent of nation-states. General Motors, for example, employs as many people as work for the federal government in the Washington, D.C., area (800,000). In the 1970s, GM's income exceeded the Gross National Product (the total goods and services produced by everyone) of many nations (*Fortune,* May 1975) (see Table 4–4).

How powerful are American corporations? Power, like love, is a word people use every day, understand intuitively, but have difficulty defining (see Martin, 1977, pp. 35–58). *Power* is the ability to control what other people and organizations do, whether or not they agree with one's goals and means (Weber, 1964, p. 152). Sometimes power is coercive, as when the threat or use of physical injury, confinement, or deprivation forces people to comply with a command. Not all power emanates from the barrel of a gun, however. Sometimes people obey commands willingly. Nobody likes to pay income taxes, for ex-

ample, but few people question the government's right to collect them or refuse to pay them. *Authority* is power exercised in ways that people consider legitimate and proper (Lipset, 1959, p. 51).

If power is the ability to command, authority is the acknowledged right to do so. American corporations have both. An incident in Detroit, Michigan, illustrates this. In 1974, the Federal Mogul Corporation shut down a roller bearing plant on Detroit's east side (Stillman, 1980). In so doing, the corporation demonstrated its power over workers' lives. More than 2,000 men and women were laid off permanently. Many had spent most of their working lives at the factory and had planned to remain there until they retired. The average age of the employees was fifty-one, and the average seniority was twenty-one years. The $5,800 the average worker received in severance pay and pension benefits would not last long. And finding a job at age fifty-one isn't easy, particularly in Detroit. (Between 1970 and 1976, there were at least 278 plant shutdowns in that city, displacing as many as 50,000 workers.) Some Federal Mogul employees found other jobs (usually for less pay), some retired, and some are still unemployed. Some died. Research has shown that plant closures affect physical and mental health. The incidence of heart disease, hypertension, diabetes, peptic ulcers, depression, anxiety, alcoholism, and sexual dysfunction are all higher among displaced workers than among control groups. Their suicide rate is thirty times the national average (*U.S. News & World Report,* June 23, 1980). Eight former Federal Mogul employees took their own lives after the shutdown. "When . . . executives signed the shutdown directive, the workers were robbed of the future they had earned—not with a six-gun, but with a fountain pen" (Stillman, 1980, p. 88).

The impact of plant shutdowns does not stop with employees. There is a "ripple effect"; the economic security of entire communities may be

Owned outright by the Draper textile mills for more than 120 years, Hopedale, Massachusetts, used to be known as the Cadillac of mill towns. Draper shut down in 1980. Since then, the town has not been able to afford a full-time fire department, and the school system has fired 20 percent of its teachers.

threatened. Small businesses located around factories or dependent on workers for their incomes, such as coffee shops and clothing stores, are hurt. The city is deprived of corporate tax revenues, and citizens have to pick up a larger share of the cost of such things as education and police and fire protection. The mere *threat* of relocation may lead to changes in local laws to accommodate large employers and concessions from unions at the bargaining table. The coercive power of corporations is clear. But American business does not have to depend on coercion.

Few question the legitimate right of companies to decide where to locate, what to produce, and so on. In the United States, corporations have the authority, as well as the power, to take actions that affect many people's lives. Definitions of legitimacy differ from society to society. In West Germany and Britain, for example, companies must obtain government approval to transfer work or to open new factories. Relocations must also be negotiated with employees. In the United States, corporations can write off the cost of closing a plant against their taxes (making relocation profitable). In Sweden, a company can receive tax credits only if it demonstrates that a decision will have social benefits (such as providing work to a region whose people have been underemployed). In the United States, corporations have enormous authority as well as coercive power over individuals' lives and community well-being. We consider decisions based on the profit motive legitimate. How did this come about?

Mental Health and the Economy

Each day's news contains stories about the real and obvious material costs of unemployment and increased prices. But does our economic situation create other problems, as real but perhaps not as obvious? Namely, does it affect our mental health? Researchers at ISR [Institute for Social Research] who have studied work and job stress say that it does. . . .

Several years ago . . . an ISR research team conducted an in-depth study of what happens to workers who lose their jobs when a plant closes. This project, known as the "Termination Study," showed that job loss caused both psychological and physiological problems, as well as economic deprivation. The terminated workers in this study suffered increased psychological problems such as anxiety, tension, pessimism, depression, and insomnia. Their increased physical problems included cases of arthritis and heightened cholesterol; there were also some cases of high blood pressure, diabetes, peptic ulcers, and heart attacks.

Interestingly, the impact of job loss on health was most acute from the time the workers heard about their impending job loss through the time the jobs actually ended. In other words, the anxiety and uncertainty of an unknown and possibly jobless future produces as many or more health problems than the actuality of being unemployed. . . .

James House, who also works with SRC's [Social Research Council's] Social Environment and Mental Health program, has had a particular interest in work, stress, and social support. He recently finished a project which studied occupational stress and the mental and physical health of factory workers. These findings, combined with results from the research of Cobb and others, have led House to believe that social support can and does buffer the effects of stress.

"Japanese society," House points out, "has long recognized the value of social support to weathering uneven economic tides. In Japanese culture there is traditionally much social support from family and friends. Companies, too, have traditionally tried to minimize the effects of economic downturns on workers by reassigning workers to different jobs rather than resorting to layoffs and terminations, and, where possible, have absorbed losses rather than pushing the burden of loss onto the individual workers." He suggests that in the United States we may be able to help ourselves by moving toward these ways of thinking.

Source: "Faltering Economy Takes Its Toll on Americans' Mental Health, ISR Social Psychologists Say," *Institute for Social Research Newsletter* (Autumn 1980), p. 3.

The Road to Oligopoly

In 1776, the year of the Declaration of Independence, the Scottish philosopher Adam Smith published *The Wealth of Nations,* the "bible" of capitalist economic systems. The system of production Smith extolled played a major role in the Founding Father's thinking. Thus, the authority enjoyed by U.S. business today can be traced back to the early days of the nation.

The capitalist ideal In *The Wealth of Nations,* Smith argued that the pursuit of self-interest under conditions of free competition produced the best of all possible economic systems. In Smith's view, the cornerstones of capitalism are the pursuit of personal profit and open competition. In other economic systems, all but a few personal and household goods are owned by the tribe, the village, or the state. In premodern societies, the goal of economic activity (farming, manufacturing, trade) is defined in traditional terms, as an obligation to the gods or a chief. In socialist societies, these activities are viewed as contributing to the welfare of society. These are the culturally given reasons why people work. In capitalist societies, property is privately owned and the goal of economic activity is defined as making a profit. Hence, the driving force in capitalist economies is self-interest. What transforms the pursuit of self-interest into a working economic system is competition. To simplify a bit: In the pursuit of profits, capitalists strive to discover what consumers need and want. When one entrepreneur discovers or creates a need or desire for a product (say, frozen, precooked dinners), other producers are drawn to the market. In the effort to win consumers, manufacturers compete by striving to make a better product for a lower price. Competition ensures, first, that people's needs are met (where there's a need, there's a profit) and second, that the quality of goods and efficiency in production are always improving.

The system is self-correcting. The forces of supply and demand combined with the profit motive ensure that wasteful economic activities and wasteful producers are eliminated. All in the name of self-interest!

Adam Smith argued, in effect, that there was virtue in acquisitiveness. Rags and riches are not distributed indiscriminately; the rewards go to the economically virtuous (those who are most efficient, producing the best goods for the lowest price). "Without intending it, without knowing it," Smith maintained, when we pursue private gain, we are participating in a design that is larger than our own. We are guided by Smith's "invisible hand." The only requirement is "an obvious and simple system of natural liberty." Smith believed that attempts by government to interfere with open competition, to regulate the free market, would disrupt the entire system. In particular, he believed that controlling the demand or supply of goods or controlling prices would destroy the motive to produce (personal gain). Smith was a strong advocate of *laissez-faire* ("let it be" or "hands off") economic policy. So, in theory, were the founders of this nation. What they wanted most from government was to be left alone.

Smith's ideal capitalist system had obvious appeal to colonists who were struggling to free themselves from the tyranny of foreign rule — and from such impositions as the salt tax and tariffs that favored British shippers. Smith was recommending economic democracy. Just as the citizens of the new nation could control the government by voting officials in or out of public office, so consumers could control business by "voting" with their dollars. The different vested interests of producers and consumers would act like the checks and balances in government. Most important, the signers of the Constitution — all men of wealth and property — would be free to profit. The lack of economic specifics in the U.S. Constitution is a tribute to Adam Smith's capitalist vision.

Whether the ideal capitalist system ever existed in fact is debatable. There was a period of rough-and-tumble competition in the years after the Civil War (Berg, 1968, pp. 182–87). The U.S. economy was booming, railroads were cutting paths to new sources of raw materials and new markets, and entrepreneurs of every sort were trying their luck. Before long, however, the competition became *too* rough. The orgy of freewheeling competition in the post–Civil War years was followed by an orgy of protective consolidation and merger (Sherrill, 1978, p. 572). The era of free enterprise drew to a close, though the ideal of free enterprise lingered.

Market domination Open competition is risky business. A manufacturer has to bid against other manufacturers for raw materials. The price of finished goods depends on distributors as well as consumers. If a company buys up competing companies plus suppliers and distributors, consolidating the entire operation, it can obtain a measure of control and security. The bigger the share of the market a business controls, the better. The process of consolidation and merger that began in the late nineteenth century continues today. (For example, in 1904, there were thirty-four automobile manufacturers in the United States; in 1921, eighty-eight; today, there are only four, and three dominate the market.) Consolidation and merger are American business strategies for ruling the market rather than being ruled by it (Berg, 1968, p. 184). As a result, competition is limited and the U.S. free-enterprise system is something less than free. (The government has also intervened in the economy, as we'll discuss later in the chapter. Here we want to focus on business.)

The domination of an industry by a small number of large firms creates an *oligopoly* (from the Greek for "few sellers"). Oligopoly in American business developed as a response to anti-trust legislation, beginning with the Sherman Anti-Trust Act (1890), which outlawed *monopolies* (the control of an industry by a single firm). Oligopolistic corporations escape the market forces Adam Smith idealized by avoiding (rather than eliminating) competition. The basic technique is called "parallel pricing" or "price leadership." The leaders of top industries do not meet behind closed doors to set prices (as the leaders of OPEC nations do, for example) or sign agreements about shares of the market. Secret agreements aren't necessary. Rather General Motors or U.S. Steel or Proctor & Gamble announces a price increase through the media; within days other manufacturers in their fields follow suit. No formal conspiracy to fix prices has occurred, but the effect is the same. Consumers are deprived of the voting power of their dollars. The reason why corporations collaborate is simple. Price wars would be disastrous to all of them. Avoiding competition is far more profitable. Oligopolies have been compared to exclusive clubs whose members compete according to well-established but unspoken rules and informal agreements. (They have an informal social structure.) Except in limited ways, price competition is considered "antisocial"; introducing radically new technology would not be "sporting." The main criterion for membership in these clubs is size (Barnet and Müller, 1974).

The most familiar and conspicuous oligopolistic industries in the United States are automobiles, aluminum, tires, soaps, cigarettes, and light bulbs (Green, 1972, p. 7). But there are others. Consider food (Hightower, 1980). Food is very big business in the United States—bigger than automobiles, oil, or steel. In 1977, Americans spent $223 billion on this most basic commodity. According to Adam Smith's model, the price of food should be determined by farmers competing for consumer dollars. It isn't. About sixty cents of every dollar spent on food today goes to middlemen, chiefly food processors. And although there are 30,000 food processing companies in the United States, 50 companies control 90 percent of the market. Packing and labeling disguises the food processing oligopoly. For example, Beatrice Foods Company (hardly a household name) owns more than a hundred brands, including Dannon Yogurt, LaChoy, Sunbeam Bread, Meadow Gold milk, Louis Sherry ice cream, and Rainbo pickles. In 1979, this almost unknown company's sales receipts were $6.4 billion. As a result of consolidation and mergers in the food processing industry, "there is considerably less competition than meets the eye in the supermarket" (Hightower, 1980, p. 11). Competition among major food processors is largely limited to packaging. Huge advertising budgets effectively prevent small companies from getting into the game. Similar stories could be told about the replacement of "Mom and Pop groceries" with supermarkets and the growing fast-food industry.

Two new types of corporate giants, conglomerates and transnationals, have emerged in recent years. Whereas the firms we have been describing are huge companies that dominate a single industry, *conglomerates* are large corporations with holdings and subsidiaries in many different industries (Pertschuk and Davidson, 1980). For example, Gulf & Western owns Madison Square Garden, produces movies at Paramount, publishes books at Simon & Schuster, weaves cloth, makes cigars, rolls steel, and lends money—among other business activities. Gulf & Western has over 100 subsidiaries, employs over 100,000 workers, and produces earnings of over $4 billion annually. The power of oligopolistic corporations is limited by the size and importance of their single industry. GM, for example, has no direct impact on the supply and price of food. The conglomerate, with interests in many unrelated industries, has no such natural boundaries. Diversification also protects conglomerates from the worst effects of failure or decline in one industry, adding another protective wall between the company and the market.

The fastest-growing institution in business today is the *transnational,* a corporation with holdings and subsidiaries in many different nations (Barnet and Müller, 1974). As explained in Chapter 4, transnationals create global factories by organizing capital from one region, natural resources from another, and labor from still another. For example, from its headquarters in Canada, Massey-Ferguson directs the assembly of transmissions made in France, axles produced in Mexico, and engines from Britain at a plant in Detroit. Typically, transnationals recruit top management from the First World and hire cheap labor in the Third World. Because of their size and reach, transnationals are able to play the world money and commodity markets, diverting resources that might go to local producers. A key to the transnationals' success is their ability to buy and sell to their own subsidiaries in different countries, avoiding price competition (the same company is buyer and seller) and avoiding tax laws in the nations in which they operate without quite breaking them. Transnationals thus add a third protective wall between the company and the market: avoidance of government interference. Although not an exclusively American phenomenon, 60 percent of transnational investment abroad is made by companies based in the United States (Ray, 1979, p. 223).

The concentration of economic activity in the hands of a small number of large corporations through consolidation and merger has taken much of the risk out of business by reducing competition. Today's corporate capitalism is not as Adam Smith envisioned. What are the consequences for American consumers and American society?

The Use and Abuse of Corporate Power

The benefits of corporate capitalism are all around us. Despite current economic problems, Americans still enjoy one of the highest standards of living in the world. Despite inflation, the real income or purchasing power of the American family has risen. In the 1960s, when riots broke out in the nation's ghettos, 88 percent of black families owned TV sets. In the 1970s, when talk of a taxpayers' revolt began, Americans were paying the second-lowest tax of the thirteen leading industrial nations. Although over 30 million Americans are classified as poor, the standard by which this is judged is far higher than in most parts of the world (Sherrill, 1978, p. 549). In short, corporate capitalism has produced a high level of prosperity, by any measure. The mass production and distribution of goods by giant corporations provides Americans with abundant food and consumer items. In the summer of 1980, when Americans were complaining about the rising cost of meat, the government of Poland was shaken, in part because of a shortage of meat. In other parts of the world (especially Africa and Asia), the problem was a shortage of all kinds of food, not just meat. Corporate capitalism has led to technological innovations that improve the quality of life—from penicillin to transistors. This is not to say "What's good for General Motors is good for the United States" (to quote President Eisenhower's Secretary of Defense, Charles Wilson).

In Chapter 3, we discussed at length one of the costs of economic expansion: environmental degradation. Until quite recently, American businesses often treated the environment as if it were a free waste disposal system. It was free only in the sense that corporations didn't pay the cost. Rather, consumers and communities paid—with their health, damage to their property and surroundings, and their dollars. According to one estimate, in 1977, air pollution alone cost Americans $23 billion in damage to health and property (Nader, Green, and Seligman, 1976, p. 8).

American corporations' safety record has not been impressive, in terms of either product safety or safety in the workplace. The 1966 Traffic Safety Act led to the recall of 35 million cars in just ten years; how many deaths and injuries were caused by unsafe automobiles before then is unknown. Estimates of the number of people who die because of overprescription of drugs promoted by pharmaceutical companies range from 60,000 to 140,000 each year. Hundreds of thousands of workers have been routinely exposed to hazardous chemicals on the job, even when the hazards were known and safety procedures available (Nader, Green, and Seligman, 1976, pp. 18–19, 25).

The size and scope of America's largest corporations produces special costs. Oligopolies, conglomerates, and transnationals undermine consumer sovereignty (the consumer's ability to influence business by voting with their dollars) in two ways. The first, as we've suggested, is reducing price competition. Reduced competition leads to overpricing, at an estimated cost of $48–$60 billion each year. (When the market on quinine was cornered in the 1960s, for example, the price rose from 37¢ to $2.13 an ounce [Green, 1972, pp. 3, 14].) The second way corporations undermine consumer sovereignty is by *creating demand.* The average American is exposed to about 40,000 TV commercials a year. In 1974, the nation's top advertisers spent $3.6 billion to improve their images and influence consumer decisions (Nader, Green, and Seligman, 1976, pp. 24–25). Soap and detergent companies plow 20 percent of their earnings back into advertising; drug companies spend four times as much on advertising as they do on research (Green, 1972, p. 13). Only a small part of this advertising provides consumers with information about products or prices. The bulk is devoted to "product differentiation"—to convincing consumers that essentially similar products are different. In simple language, ads are usually designed to convince the public that buying this or that brand will make them happier, healthier, sexier, more successful, more "with it." *Planned obsolescence* is another technique for creating demand. Products are designed so that they will wear out or fall apart quickly or, in a more benign form, so that they will quickly become dated and unfashionable.

Finally, today's corporations exercise far more *political power* than the nation's founders could have envisioned. The problem is not simply that corporations are able to hire lobbyists to promote their interests (and write the cost off their taxes), contribute to political campaigns (directly and legally, or not), or hold hostage communities that depend on them for employment. "That most businesses are not overtly greedy or cruel is beside the point. It is also irrelevant that many businesses devote substantial time, effort, and talent to public causes" (Pertschuk and Davidson, 1980, p. 487). The problem is that the sheer size of today's corporations tips the political scales. For example, in a campaign to postpone safety and emission standards, GM solicited support by writing to its 13,000 dealers, 19,000 suppliers, and 1.3 million stockholders. Few other organizations can marshal such numbers. Mergers have compounded the problem by reducing the number of business voices that seek to influence government. For example, Montgomery Ward was one of a few major companies to actively support the creation of a Consumer Advocacy Agency. When Montgomery Ward merged with Mobil Oil, this independent and dissenting business voice was muted.

What we have described so far conforms, in a most general way, to Karl Marx's predictions for the future of capitalism. Marx argued that free enterprise and open competition inevitably would give way to "monopolistic capitalism." A small elite would gain control of the market, using resources and workers for personal gain. Capitalism contained the seeds of its own destruction, Marx argued, for this system would create a class of exploited workers who would in time rise up and overthrow their oppressors. What Marx did not foresee was that the government would intervene. Neither did the signers of our Constitution.

A young man from Mozambique (quoted in Chapter 3) exclaims, "I simply do not understand America. Tell me, do you really have twelve different kinds of toothpaste? Why?

The Power of the Federal Government

The founders of this nation envisioned that government would play a very limited role in citizens' lives. In Thomas Jefferson's words, "a wise and frugal government . . . shall restrain men from injuring one another [and] shall leave them otherwise free to regulate their own pursuits." In recent years, big government has consistently ranked second or third in Gallup polls of what people consider the nation's "most important problems." Small wonder. In Jefferson's day, the federal government employed a total of 2,120 people—as customs officers, tax collectors, Indian commissioners, marshals, lighthouse keepers, and clerks. Today there are nearly 5 million Americans on Uncle Sam's payroll.

When Jefferson was President, there were three executive departments: State (with nine employees under the Secretary), War, and Treasury. Today there are 13 departments and about 100 operating agencies, boards, and commissions (Cummings and Wise, 1981).

For the first 140 years of this nation's history, federal expenditures never rose above 3 percent of the GNP except during wars. In 1929, the federal budget was 2.5 percent of the GNP; in 1980, it was over 20 percent. Up until 1930, federal income taxes were little more than a symbolic nuisance. In 1981, the federal government collected an estimated $274.4 billion in individual income taxes (*Budget of the United States Government. Fiscal Year 1981,* pp. 60, 61).

In the early part of this century, Washington, D.C., seemed remote to most Americans (Sherrill, 1979, pp. 332–33). People thought of government largely in terms of city hall, the county jail, the state insane asylum. Their only contact with the federal government was through the post office. Today the word "government" evokes images of the Pentagon or the massive Department of Health and Human Services (neither of which existed in 1930). The federal government seems to be everywhere.

The Rise of Big Government

The U.S. government did not grow by accident. The emergence of big government can be traced to population growth, increasing social differentiation, and the demands of an ever-expanding number of interest groups. In particular, the Great Depression of the 1930s laid the foundation of a "welfare state"; the partnership of government and business during World War II gave birth to the military-industrial establishment; and the public rights movement of the 1960s and 1970s (comprising the Civil Rights Movement, which spread from blacks to women and other minorities, and the consumer and environmental protection movements) added new demands for government to take on added responsibilities. Each gave the growth of government a boost.

Promoting economic security The Great Depression caught the nation off guard. In 1929, the rich in America were very rich. Interest rates on investments were high and income taxes, low. There were 513 millionnaires in the U.S.—more than ever before. And "a million stock market speculators were glad that the rich were rich, because they expected to be rich soon themselves. Millionnaires were being made every day. It was as if a fairy godmother had decreed a coach for every Cinderella" (Bird, 1966, pp. 3–4).

Then, on October 29, 1929, the bottom fell out of the stock market. By the end of the day, $4 billion in stock values had disappeared into thin air. In the next two weeks, another $26 billion disappeared, and this was only the beginning. When the stock market crashed, it took the entire economy down with it. In their worst forecasts, the nation's leaders could not have imagined how poverty would spread in the years to come. At the height of the Great Depression, between 12.5 and 17 million Americans—over a third of the labor force—were unemployed. Those lucky enough to have jobs were earning 40 to 60 percent less than they had in the spring of 1929 (Cole, 1969, p. 240ff). Food riots swept Oklahoma City, Minneapolis, and New York City. Perhaps a million homeless men wandered aimlessly from place to place, begging food and sleeping in boxcars. A sudden decline in the marriage and birth rates gave mute testimony to the degree to which Americans had lost faith in themselves and the future.

The Government and You

If you were born in a hospital, it was probably a hospital built wholly or in part with federal funds. Poor or rich, as soon as you appeared in this world, the government permitted your parents to count you as a tax deduction.

When you went to school, your lunch was probably subsidized to some extent by the U.S. Department of Agriculture. Your school was built with tax dollars (if it was a public school), and your books were bought with tax dollars. You walked to school on sidewalks, or drove to school on streets, paid for with tax dollars. . . .

All your life you have eaten food from cans or boxes or wrappers that bore descriptive labels imposed by government decree. The meat you eat was first passed by government inspectors. The orange juice you drink came from oranges picked by workers who lived in camps that had to meet government-set sanitation standards.

If you or your parents borrowed money from the bank to pay your way through college, the interest rate was influenced by the government. When you deposit money in the bank, the government guarantees that your money (up to a certain amount) is safe, even if the bank goes out of business.

If you traveled to college by plane or train, you were using a vehicle that operates according to a government schedule and is subsidized generously by the government.

When you go to work, the government will require you to get a Social Security number and pay a certain amount each week into the Social Security Trust Fund. It will also require your employer to withhold income tax from your paycheck. As for your employer, there is a good chance that part of his or her income is from government contracts or government subsidies or government tax rebates (incentives).

If you fail to find employment—and if there are enough others who have your bad luck—the government will probably spend millions of dollars in make-work projects to give you employment. Or, if you lose your job, the government will pay unemployment compensation for a time.

When you retire you can begin drawing monthly checks from the Social Security system and, when sick, help from the Medicare system. And when you die, the government will tax your estate. If you were a veteran, it will help pay for your burial.

Source: Robert Sherrill, *Why They Call it Politics* (New York: Harcourt Brace Jovanovich, 1979), pp. 296–97.)

The bread lines of the 1930s seem like ancient history. Yet the jobless rate among black teen-agers today is higher than the unemployment rate during the Great Depression.

The trauma of the Great Depression transformed the relationship between the government and the economy. Before 1930, the government's official policy toward the economy was that of *laissez faire*. When President Franklin D. Roosevelt took office in 1933, this changed. Henceforth the government would take responsibility for economic stability. With strong support from Congress, Roosevelt set up federal machinery for managing the economy and for guaranteeing individual economic security. Much of what we think of as "big government" was created in the 1930s.

When the Great Depression hit, most Americans had nothing to fall back on—no unemployment compensation, no welfare, no federal training or hiring programs. All that stood between a jobless person and hunger was private charity. Under Roosevelt's New Deal, the government became the "employer of last resort," creating jobs for millions of unemployed Americans through the Works Progress Administration (WPA). The 1935 Social Security Act created Social Security itself (a compulsory insurance program, in theory financed by employers and employees, to provide income to the elderly, later extended to survivors and the disabled); set up three public assistance or "welfare" programs (financed in part through federal grants to states); and required states to provide unemployment compensation (financed through state and local taxes on employers). In addition, the New Deal gave the federal government the authority to support agriculture, guarantee bank deposits, regulate the sale of securities and stocks, and set a minimum wage.

A new generation of social programs was created in the 1960s under President Lyndon Johnson's administration. In large part, the New Deal had been designed to protect the middle class, to secure their homes and farms and savings. Johnson's Great Society was aimed at bringing the poor into the economic mainstream. Programs organized under the Office of Economic Opportunity (OEO) included Head Start for young children; the Job Corps for high-school dropouts; and Community Action, designed to involve the poor in planning and fighting the war on poverty. National health insurance for the elderly and the poor (Medicare and Medicaid) were part of the plan. Between 1964 (when Johnson was elected) and 1975, federal spending for health, education, and welfare tripled. The number of people receiving food stamps grew from 500,000 to nearly 20 million. Each new program added millions of dollars to the federal budget and thousands of workers to the federal bureaucracy (see Figure 5–2).

The government has also been called upon to

Figure 5–2

The Growth of Government Bureaucracy, 1940–1975

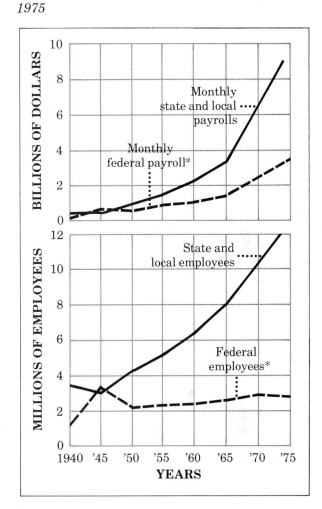

*Excluding uniformed military.

U.S. Bureau of the Census, *Statistical Abstracts of the United States,* various issues.

protect individuals and small firms from "big business." Congress passed the Sherman Anti-Trust Act in 1890, in response to public pressure. The act prohibited "every contract, combination . . . or conspiracy in restraint of trade" and made it criminal to "monopolize or attempt to monopolize" commerce within the United States. Antitrust legislation has been weakly interpreted and enforced, however (Nader, Green, and Seligman,

Government and the Economy

Government management of the economy usually takes two forms: monetary policy (regulating the supply of money and credit) and fiscal policy (government spending and taxation). The Federal Reserve System, established in 1913, controls monetary policy. The Federal Reserve is a banker's bank. It is where banks go to borrow money, which they then lend to individuals and corporations. When the Federal Reserve lends money, in effect it creates money. By lowering interest rates it can stimulate or "heat up" the economy. This encourages borrowing, spending, increased production, the creation of new jobs, and higher prices. By raising interest rates, the Federal Reserve can "cool down" the economy, discouraging expansion, spending, and price hikes. Members of the Federal Reserve Board of Governors are appointed by the President for fourteen-year terms. This, plus the fact that it has its own funds, makes the "Fed" largely independent of both the White House and Congress.

Fiscal policy is controlled by the President and Congress, who decide what the government will collect and spend. A cut in taxes or an increase in government spending can heat up a sluggish economy; an increase in taxes or a cutback in government spending can cool down an overheated, inflationary economy. The theory that a government can spend its way out of a depression and generate prosperity was developed by the British economist John Maynard Keynes. Economists refer to the basic strategy as "priming the pump." When a pump stops drawing water, mechanics pour water in, the sucker expands, and the level of water in the well rises. Keynes advocated pouring money into the sinking U.S. economy of the 1930s. Roosevelt practiced what Keynes preached, using federal money to create jobs for the millions of unemployed.

The emphasis in Keynesian economics is on demand and purchasing power. According to this view, inflation occurs when "too many dollars are chasing too few goods." When wages rise faster than productivity, companies can charge more for the same goods because consumers have more to spend.

1976, Chapter 1). Shortly after the Act was passed, the Supreme Court ruled that only "unreasonable" restraint of trade was illegal. In bringing corporations to trial, the government had to prove *intent* to monopolize. Moreover, the penalties for violating anti-trust laws are relatively mild—as of 1974, a maximum fine of $1 million for corporations and three years in jail for individuals (the latter rarely imposed). For major corporations, this is part of the cost of doing business —a cost passed on to consumers.

Many government activities seem designed

According to this view, the government's job is to keep supply and demand in balance. The government may take purchasing power out of the hands of consumers by either taxing more or spending less, thus easing demand for the limited supply of goods. Or it may tax less or spend more, increasing purchasing power, stimulating demand and, ultimately, output and employment.

"Supply-side" economics, endorsed by the Reagan administration, suggests a different view. The emphasis is on production (or supply), not on demand and purchasing power. According to this view, government constraints on economic activity are a leading *cause* of economic problems. Supply-siders see the economy as a coiled spring, held down by government weight. Remove government restraints and the economy will bounce back (Heilbroner, 1981). They offer two main prescriptions for the nation's economic ills. The first is to relieve inflation by cutting taxes, especially on investments. Supply-siders argue that if the government took a smaller share of profits, big companies would expand, more small businesses would be started, individuals would work harder, and productivity would rise. Critics argue that we have no reason to expect either businesses or individuals to respond to tax cuts as predicted. People might invest their extra dollars (the supply-siders hope), or they might work fewer hours, or spend the extra money, feeding inflation. Second, supply-siders advocate an overall reduction in government activity, which they regard as a wasteful use of economic resources. Critics argue that supply-siders fail to distinguish between private and public benefits. For example, if judged solely in terms of profits, the U.S. space program is hugely wasteful. If judged in terms of scientific productivity (adding to knowledge) or in terms of propaganda value (demonstrating American technological skills), it might be considered a huge success. The government is terribly wasteful only if it is measured by the same criteria as business. This debate is likely to continue for some time.

more to protect the welfare of business than to protect individuals from business. In addition to showing leniency in the courts, the federal government has subsidized big business—directly, through low-cost loans, and indirectly, through tax breaks. Federally guaranteed loans saved Lockheed and Chrysler from bankruptcy. The oil and natural gas industries, in particular, have been granted outright tax breaks (Stern, 1974, Chapter 11). One is the depletion allowance, which allows oil and gas companies to receive 22 percent of their income tax-free. The second is the deduction for "intangible drilling expenses" (wages, fuel, machine, and tool costs). In 1974, the combined cost of business subsidies and tax breaks to the government—and taxpayers—was estimated at $95 billion a year (*Washington Post*, October 16, 1974).

The New Deal and Great Society programs described above were designed to protect individual economic security; the oil depletion allowance and similar legislation, to protect individual industries. In addition, the federal government has assumed responsibility for the economy as a whole (see page 164). Some of the growth of the federal government, then, can be traced to demands from the public for protection from financial disasters, to demands from business for protection from free and risky competition, and to their combined demand for general economic stability.

Maintaining the military establishment A second wave of government expansion can be traced to the growing size and importance of the military. On December 7, 1941, the Japanese attacked Pearl Harbor, drawing the United States into World War II. There is some evidence that the war did as much to pull the economy out of the Great Depression as did the New Deal. Big government and big business became partners during World World II, under a War Production Board created to coordinate and direct industry. Defense spending climbed. Virtually everyone (including women) went to work.

Something odd happened after World War II, however (Lieberson, 1971, p. 573). After other wars in the nation's history, the draft was ended and military spending dropped. In contrast, after World War II, the draft was suspended but then revived (from 1948 to 1973). Military spending slipped a bit, then began to climb—pushed by the cold war and the fear of communism, pulled by the Truman Doctrine which declared the United States the policeman of the world.

Figure 5–3

A Breakdown of U.S. Defense Spending

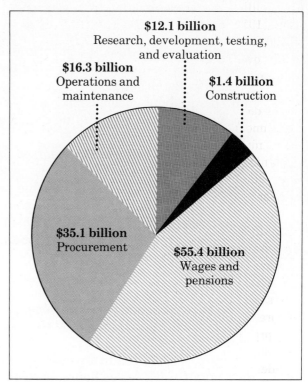

Source: L.J. Korb, "The Price of Preparedness: The FY 1978–1982 Defense Program," *American Enterprise Institute Defense Review,* Vol. 3 (1977), pp. 8–17.

The United States spends twice as much on arms and soldiers today as it did at the peak of World War II (see Figure 5–3). The Department of Defense consumes one-fourth of the federal budget and 5.6 percent of the GNP. Almost 80 percent of the people who work for the federal government are employed by the Pentagon. In 1979, there were over 2 million military personnel, 1 million civilians, and 850,000 military reservists and National Guard on the Pentagon payroll, making it the largest employer in the nation. The more sophisticated military hardware becomes, the more it costs. A single B-1 bomber costs $94 million today; a single Trident submarine, $1.6 billion. The defense budget continues to climb, in war and peace. In 1978, the U.S. spent $110 billion on arms and military personnel (Korb, 1977, pp. 5, 7, 16, 17). In 1980, Pentagon officials argued that it would take more than $1 *trillion* over the next five years to keep the nation from becoming a "second-class" military power (*U.S. News & World Report,* July 21, 1980).

Why does the nation need so vast a military establishment? The obvious reason is defense. The nation must be prepared for an attack by the Soviet Union or another major power, and also for a lesser power interfering with vital sea and air lanes or resource supplies. (As the Pentagon puts it, we need to be prepared for one-and-a-half wars.) In theory, a strong military also acts as a deterrent, discouraging attacks, especially from the Soviet Union. The arms race with the Soviet Union has built-in momentum. The Pentagon discovers or suspects the Soviets are producing new or more weapons; in self-defense, we increase military production; seeing this, the Soviets build up their supplies; and so on. Virtually every recent presidential election has focused on the arms race. The "bomber gap" of the Eisenhower years was followed by the "missile gap" of the Kennedy years, the "megatonnage gap" in Barry Goldwater's campaign, the "security gap" in Nixon's 1968 campaign, the "loss of momentum" in 1972, the "loss of military superiority" in 1980. Defense spending is a bottomless pit. At what point do we achieve military security? There is no concrete answer.

A second reason for maintaining the military is that the U.S. economy depends on the military establishment. The roughly 4 million Americans who work directly for the Pentagon are only the tip of the iceberg. Indirectly, millions more depend on military spending. The Pentagon helps to support 120,000 companies. The partnership between government and industry created during the war was not dissolved. Defense contracts for aircraft and missiles kept many companies alive

in the late 1940s and early 1950s. As part of the cold war, the government spent $30 billion to put a man on the moon, with most of the money going to private contractors. Up to 1976, it spent $1.9 billion on nuclear research, with much of the work being given to Westinghouse and General Electric (Barber, 1966, p. 20). This military-industrial partnership remains intact.

Five thousand cities and towns depend on defense plants and contractors. According to one estimate, the Pentagon feeds one American in five (Sherrill, 1978, p. 562). When Lockheed, a major defense contractor, was threatened with bankruptcy, the official justification for bailing the company out with a guaranteed loan was that Lockheed was essential to the nation's defense. More candidly perhaps, then Secretary of the Treasury John Connally told a Senate committee, "We are guaranteeing them basically a $250 million loan. What for? Basically so they can . . . minimize their losses, so they can provide employment for 31,000 people throughout the country at a time when we desperately need that type of employment. That is basically the rationale and justification" (in *The Nation,* August 7, 1972). Simply put, more missiles, more bombs, and more tanks mean more jobs. Some argue the economy cannot do without these jobs.

Powerful cliques in the military and industry pressure Congress into granting funds. Although many officials move back and forth between jobs in the Pentagon and jobs with contractors, empirical studies have failed to find evidence of a clear military-industrial conspiracy in the United States (Lieberson, 1971; Cobb, 1976). Nevertheless, the large number of corporations and communities with vested interests in maintaining the military establishment undoubtedly influence political decision makers. What might be equally significant is that no special interest group has a vested interest in stopping or cutting back defense spending (Cobb, 1976, pp. 180–81). There are huge profits to be made in building up the military establishment, but few profits to be made from breaking it down.

The central point here is that the expansion of the military establishment, in partnership with big business, adds enormously to the size of the government.

Protecting public rights A third wave of government expansion came in response to growing public awareness that social problems that had long been taken for granted were neither inevitable nor uncorrectable. Racial injustice, sexual inequality, environmental degradation, health and safety on highways and in the workplace, and honesty in promotion of consumer products all became social issues in the 1960s and 1970s. In this case, it was social activists—the leaders of the Civil Rights, Women's, Environmental, and Consumer Movements—that prodded the public into awareness and the government into action.

The ideal of equality is a centerpiece of the Declaration of Independence and the U.S. Constitution. It is one of the things Americans hold sacred. Except for the brief Reconstruction period after the Civil War, however, equality was not an object of active government concern (Pole, 1978). The government position on equality was essentially that of "hands off." Under pressure from the Civil Rights Movement, this changed. In 1957, President Eisenhower sent federal troops into Little Rock, Arkansas, to put down a state rebellion against the Supreme Court's order to desegregate schools (*Brown* v. *Board of Education*, 1954). In 1964, Congress passed the Civil Rights Act, which outlawed discrimination in public accommodations, education, employment, and federally funded programs. At the time, public attention was focused on discrimination against black Americans. Later the Act would play an important role in the fight to end discrimination against women and other minorities who saw themselves as victims of inequality. Once the administrative machinery for enforcing these laws

was set up (especially the Equal Employment Opportunity Commission), the goal widened. The federal government would not only protect equal rights for blacks, women, and other minorities, but it would actively promote equal *opportunity*. The leading edge of this effort is affirmative action: programs designed to give minority members some preferential treatment to compensate for discrimination in the past. The government has used both the courts and its power to withhold funds and contracts in pursuit of this goal.

In recent years, Congress has also passed a number of laws designed to protect public health and safety and the environment. Whereas there is little organized opposition to the military, industry has mounted powerful obstacles to government regulation in these areas. Many of the environmental and safety laws are the product of behind-the-scenes bargaining and compromise, and enforcement has proven to be slow and difficult (Lave, 1980). The Occupational Safety and Health Administration (OSHA), created in 1970, for example, requires employers to provide a workplace that is "free from recognized hazards." What is and isn't hazardous is not always clear, however. If rats exposed to 100 parts per million of benzene develop cancer, are 10 parts per million safe for humans? OSHA skirted this issue by adopting some 7,000 standards, most borrowed from industry. It has only 400 inspectors to cover nearly 5 million places of work. To date, only a few "willful" violators have been punished with fines. In some ways, regulating the automobile industry has proved easier than monitoring other industries. The National Highway Traffic Safety Administration has only a few firms to deal with (the major auto and tire manufacturers). Hazards can easily be measured in terms of statistics on highway accidents. Congress has ordered the agency to set standards for fuel emissions and economy in addition to safety. All have proven controversial. Consumers objected to mandatory seat belts, and the requirement was withdrawn. The auto industry argued that meeting fuel economy deadlines would hurt an already ailing industry that employs thousands, and won postponements. Delays, confusion, and disagreements have also interfered with attempts to regulate air and water pollution. Laws to protect consumers were also passed in the 1960s and 1970s—for example, the Truth-in-Packaging law (1966), which requires manufacturers to label products more clearly, and the Truth-in-Lending law (1968), which requires merchants to provide full information on credit terms, in understandable language.

With each new law, the number of government regulations—and regulators—grew. So did costs (see Table 5-1). The federal government has established a foothold in areas that were previously unregulated (ungoverned)—just as it did during the Great Depression with the New Deal and during the cold war when the arms race began.

A Bureaucracy Out of Control

Big government developed gradually over a number of years, in response to new problems and new demands. The question today is whether the government has become so huge that it is both ineffective and unresponsive. Critics argue that the federal bureaucracy is out of control, that it is spreading like a weed, strangling initiative and consuming talent and money that are badly needed elsewhere.

A main product of the growing federal bureaucracy seems to be paper. The list of government programs and regulations published each year in the *Federal Register* takes up 60,000 pages of fine print. According to one writer, reading the regulations issued in a single week by the former Department of Health, Education, and Welfare would have been equivalent to reading *War and Peace* twice (Sherrill, 1978, p. 416). When Eli Lilly & Company sought approval from the Food and Drug Administration for a new arthritis med-

Table 5-1
Costs of Health, Safety, and Environmental Regulations, 1978
(in millions of dollars)

Agency	Budget Allocation
Consumer Product Safety Commission	$40.6
National Highway Traffic Safety Administration	54.6
Federal Railroad Administration	7.3
Federal Aviation Administration	203.7
National Transportation Safety Board	15.4
Occupational Safety and Health Administration	136.6
Occupational Safety and Health Review Commission	7.2
Mine Safety and Health Administration	99.3
Department of Agriculture	206.5
Food and Drug Administration	288.7
Nuclear Regulatory Commission	141.4
Environmental Protection Agency	643.5

Source: *Study on Federal Regulation*, Vol. 6, *Framework for Regulation*, Senate Committee on Governmental Affairs (Committee Print) 95 Cong. 2 sess. (U.S. Government Printing Office, 1978), pp. 36–37.

icine, the application was 120,000 pages long. It took two trucks to carry the forms, in duplicate and triplicate, to Washington. Lilly estimated the cost to the company at $15 million, which in turn cost consumers an extra 50¢ per prescription (Simon, 1978, p. 21). The Office of Management and Budget calculates that, all told, administering and complying with federal regulations costs Americans $100 billion each year—almost as much as the nation spends on defense.

Government waste and inefficiency are a large problem. Consider defense spending (Fox, 1974). In 1962, the Pentagon ordered 1,726 F-111 bombers at $2.8 million each. The actual cost, in 1970, turned out to be $14.7 million. As a result, the Air Force reduced its order to 519 planes. Meanwhile, the Navy had realized that the plane would be too heavy for carrier landings and canceled its order. This apparent inefficiency is built into the military-industrial system. The military depends on private industry for weapons; a number of industries depend on the military for work. The relationship between them is tangled. Contracts for military production are obtained, not through competitive bidding, but through a process euphemistically referred to as "negotiation." What happens, in essence, is this: The Pentagon and one or more of its business partners collaborate on the design and planning of a new weapons system. They do not negotiate cost and schedule until after a design is approved. Given the size of defense contracts, manufacturers have a good deal of incentive to underestimate costs and time during negotiation in order to win the contract. Once a weapons system is in production, the Pentagon is committed. Given the urgency of military schedules, it is unlikely to start over with a new contractor because of cost overruns or less-than-perfect results. Finally, military technology is constantly changing, so that current weapons quickly become obsolete. Creating new weapons systems means retooling plants, constructing new installations, and retraining personnel, in addition to purchasing actual equipment. Lack of competitive bidding, cost overruns, and obsolescence all raise the cost of the peacetime military. The key question is not whether government procedures and regulations are wasteful and inefficient. The question is, Why? Part of the problem can be traced to the structure of the federal bureaucracy, part, to the actors within the federal bureaucracy and to the audiences to which they play.

Organized inefficiency The classic description of an ideal bureaucracy comes from Max Weber (1925). He characterized bureaucracy as a highly formal and strictly rational organization (in contrast, say, to a family). Activities in a bureaucracy are governed by written rules and regulations (hence the volumes of paper work). These are designed to apply to categories of events and thus to eliminate the need to make decisions regarding every new situation. Clients are treated as "cases," not individuals. Positions in a bureaucracy are strictly defined and limited. Each position has its set of responsibilities and privileges. Authority is vested in the position, not in the person who happens to occupy it. Ideally, positions in bureaucracy are assigned on the basis of technical qualifications, not personal liking or connections. In most cases, a position implies lifelong tenure, with regular promotions based on performance and seniority. By and large, choosing staff according to technical qualifications should put the right people in the right jobs. Tenure and regular promotions inspire loyalty to the organization. Adherence to rules and regulations ensures impartiality. In these ways, nonrational decisions based on personal biases or whims are minimized. The great advantage of bureaucracy, in Weber's view, is its efficiency in dealing with the coordination of large-scale activities. Why does the operation of the federal government (or other bureaucratic organization) seem to differ so markedly from the ideal? Why has the term "bureaucracy" become synonymous with *in*efficiency?

Part of the problem is that the federal government developed piecemeal. Departments, bureaus, and agencies were created at different times, in response to different problems and demands. Thus the federal government consists of not one but numerous bureaucracies. Each has its own objectives and ways of doing things. The goals of different federal agencies often overlap and sometimes contradict one another. For example, the Environmental Protection Agency (EPA) is working for tighter air pollution controls, while the Energy Department is urging industries to switch to coal, which is dirtier to burn. The National Highway Traffic Safety Administration orders safety devices that add weight to cars; the Transportation Administration orders lighter vehicles to conserve fuel. It is not simply that "one hand doesn't know what the other is doing." There are hundreds of "hands"—hundreds of more or less independent agencies—in the federal government.

Much of the problem derives from the nature of bureaucracy itself. In some ways, the strengths of bureaucracy are also its weaknesses (Merton, 1968, pp. 249–60). Bureaucrats are rewarded (with job security and promotions) for abiding strictly by the rules. The result can be what Thorstein Veblen called *trained incapacity*. In learning to apply the rules impartially and to abide by the regulations no matter what, bureaucrats learn to overlook the details of particular cases and to dismiss their own perceptions and feelings. In effect, they are trained to wear blinders. But when circumstances change, such habits of mind can become a liability. There is always a danger of overconformity in bureaucracies. Abiding by the rules may become an end in itself. The reasons why the rules were created and the goals of the agency may be forgotten or even subverted.

Bureaucratic regulation has another built-in dilemma. Often regulations that make good sense in one context are nonsense in another. For example, in an area of truck farming, where there are many workers, it makes sense to require one toilet per forty acres. It makes no sense to require an equal number of toilets on a Montana ranch where there are thousands of acres that rarely see an agricultural worker. Yet, a set of government regulations for toilet facilities that would cover every kind of farm would run to hundreds, even thousands of pages (Thurow, 1980, p. 131). Compromises (something between one rule and hundreds) inevitably produce cases of silliness. In other words, the kinds of bureaucratic activity that make for efficiency in general make for inefficiency in particular cases.

Finally, one of the goals of bureaucracy is to handle large amounts of work in a routine, impartial manner. What the bureaucrat sees as routine, however (an income tax ruling, a Medicaid check, or a zoning regulation), is often of intense personal interest to a client of the agency. If officials fail to acknowledge the special nature of a problem or to give it special handling, the client is likely to feel abused. After all, government officials are supposed to be "servants of the people." On the other hand, bureaucrats who do make exceptions are likely to be accused of favoritism—or worse (Merton, 1968, pp. 256–59). Thus they are "damned if they do, damned if they don't."

Responsive to whom? One of the most common complaints about bureaucracies in general, and government agencies in particular, is that they are unresponsive. They pay little or no attention to people's needs. A closer look suggests that federal bureaucracies are responsive, though not necessarily to "the people." For example, responding to pressure from a chairman of the House Agricultural Subcommittee, the Agricultural Department spent $10 million on a campaign against fire ants that scientific evidence predicted would fail. (It did.) Responding to pressure from the food industry, the FDA allowed monosodium glutamate and cyclamates to be marketed, despite tests challenging their safety. In both cases, the agency responded—not to "the people," but to special interests. The reason is not simply that bureaucrats are corrupt (Salamon and Wamsley, 1975). The need to deal with special interests is built into their jobs.

It takes a broadly based coalition and popular support to pass the legislation establishing a new federal agency through Congress. Once the agency is established, however, popular support often diffuses, and the agency finds itself in face-to-face combat with organized opposition (for example, the auto industry's opposition to stiff fuel emission standards). Lacking organized support, it has to establish its authority (its legitimate right to issue or enforce orders) and to develop allies if it is to fulfill its goals. Typically this means establishing good working relationships with the heads of congressional committees and leaders of the businesses and industries it is supposed to oversee (Salamon and Wamsley, 1975). For example, the Federal Housing Administration (FHA), created in 1934 as part of the New Deal, was authorized to guarantee private, low-interest, long-term loans to potential home buyers. The FHA soon discovered it could accomplish nothing without the cooperation of the construction industry on the one hand, private banks on the other. The FHA "played ball." It adopted a standard of economic soundness. Loans were to be granted only if the applicant could demonstrate the ability to pay and the home was sure to last the lifetime of the mortgage. To simplify a bit, middle-income people who wanted homes in the suburbs got loans; low-income people who sought homes in "risky" urban neighborhoods were turned down. Thus, the FHA was responsive—not to the need for low-cost housing and urban renewal, but to the desires of bankers and the construction industry. This is not to suggest a deliberate, organized conspiracy among FHA bureaucrats, bankers, and the heads of construction companies. However, the FHA did tend to recruit staff from the real estate and banking communities, who were sympathetic to their needs. There was a "revolving door" between them (people moved from the agency to the industries the agency was supposed to regulate, or vice versa). Good working relationships and cronyism simply made the FHA's work easier.

Federal agencies exhibit one additional flaw that is common to all bureaucracies. Although they are usually created in response to popular pressure, once in place, they tend to take on a life of their own. Instead of serving the public, they tend to serve themselves. Officials have a vested interest in maintaining, or better, expanding the power of their agencies. (Not only are many federal workers career bureaucrats; making a name for oneself and the agency may bring offers of better jobs outside government.) Loyalty to the agency may override commitment to the goals for which it was created. Officials also have access to information that isn't readily available to the general public. They are in a position to control the flow of information. (The media seek them out.) They can hire people who share their views. As a result, power tends to become concentrated in the hands of a few top officials. J. Edgar Hoover, for example, was able to run the FBI almost like a private agency by capitalizing on the public's desire for law and order, employing such publicity gimmicks as the "Ten Most Wanted" list, and using his position to cement relationships with local law enforcers and Congress through various favors. The transformation of bureaucracies into oligarchies—organizations ruled by a few top officials—may not be an "iron rule," as Robert Michels argued (1911). But the incentives and the opportunities are there. Thus federal officials and workers must be counted among the special interest groups that exert pressure on the government.

Pressure Politics

Polls indicate that Americans have lost confidence in government since the mid-1960s. Only 10 percent of the respondents in a 1978 poll considered it "very likely" that government "will actually be able to do" something about the nation's problems. Meanwhile the percentage who believe the nation is in deep and serious trouble has risen from 30 percent in the early 1970s to 70 percent (Yankelovich, 1980). Is big government, in league with big business, to blame? Are the problems themselves unsolvable?

In *The Zero-Sum Society* (1980), the economist Lester Thurow argues that there *are* solutions to all of our problems—to inflation and recession ("stagflation"), energy shortages and fuel dependency, environmental deterioration. What all the solutions have in common, however, is that they will cause for some group a large reduction in its standard of living. Thurow describes the situation as a zero-sum game. In a zero-sum game, gains on one side are met by losses on the other. For one team to win, another must lose. There are no winners without losers. (Most sports events are zero-sum games.) Similarly, in the stagflation, energy, and environmental "games," some groups must lose if others are to win. No one is volunteering for a place on the losing team. And although some groups are clearly stronger than others, no one group has the power to overcome opposition and impose solutions. As a result, we have reached a stalemate (the point in a game of chess when neither player can move).

Clash of Interests

Underlying most of the demands made on government today is the drive for economic security. "Economic security is to modern man what a castle and moat were to medieval man" (Thurow, 1980, p. 19).

The demand for economic security is a modern phenomenon. In pre-industrial societies, people tend to accept economic losses as part of the nature of things—as, indeed, they are. When the weather is bad, the standard of living drops. No one is to blame; nothing can be done. In industrial societies, economic setbacks are caused by "identifiable human actions" (Thurow, 1980, p. 20). Someone can be blamed, and something can be done. (For example, if sales of American TV sets are declining because Japanese sets are less expensive, the imports can be taxed or barred.)

Thus, in industrial societies, economic setbacks are viewed as social problems, and economic security becomes a realistic objective.

The central problem today, as Thurow puts it, is that "Each of us wants what is collectively impossible" (1980, p. 15). The nation's energy problems illustrate this dilemma. Everyone wants energy independence in the abstract. But each route to energy independence is blocked by some group whose income would decline if that route were taken. One group's solution is another's problem. As a result, each proposed solution is vetoed and the government is paralyzed. Here we will look at what the nation has done, what it might do, and why it hasn't.

In early 1973, the United States consumed more energy than it produced, but a cheap and abundant supply of Middle Eastern oil kept this from seeming a problem. Then, late in the year, OPEC tripled the price of oil, and the nation's dependency became suddenly and graphically apparent. The U.S. government responded by adding regulation to regulation, with only partial success (if that). To begin with, it froze the price of domestic oil. This created two additional problems. First, with prices frozen, domestic producers had no incentive to look for new energy. To solve this, the government added still another regulation, which allowed domestic producers to charge world prices for new oil (encouraging deception). Second, the government reduced the price of imported oil for consumers so that they had little incentive to conserve. To encourage conservation, even more regulations were put into place (reduced speed limits, mileage standards for cars, temperature limits for public buildings, and so on). This web of regulations became cumbersome, limiting the nation's ability to adjust to shocks like the war between Iran and Iraq in 1980–81. It barely put a dent in energy dependency. What could be done?

One solution is to let the price of energy rise with the world market, to adopt a free-market plan. Ideally higher prices would encourage both domestic production and conservation. Of course, someone would have to pay. The cost to consumers would be, roughly, $150 billion, or 7.5 percent of the GNP at 1978 prices. Average income would drop by about 7.5 percent. But the cost would not be shared equally. The poor spend proportionately more of their incomes on energy than the rich do (directly, for gasoline and home heating, and indirectly, for products that take energy to produce). Thurow calculates that the incomes of the poor would drop by 34 percent; those of the rich, by 5 percent. The decline would be 30 percent greater in the Northeast than in the West. Thus if this game plan were adopted, the public—especially the poor in the Northeast— would be losers. Who would win? Domestic oil producers, whose profits would increase by about $120 billion if they were allowed to charge world prices. This free-market solution is vetoed by virtually everyone except the major oil companies.

A second solution would be nationalization: the government taking over existing facilities and developing new ones. Even if there weren't strong ideological opposition to nationalization and deep distrust of government efficiency—which, of course, there are—this would be vetoed on purely economic grounds. Who would volunteer, for example, to pay the costs of compensating hundreds of thousands of oil company stockholders?

A third solution to the problem of energy dependency is to develop alternate sources of energy—coal, nuclear power, solar energy, and so on. Technologically this is within reach. The United States has abundant coal reserves, enough to supply us for many years. We have the nuclear know-how. But here again every path is blocked by groups whose real standard of living would decline if that path were taken. The costs of developing alternate energy sources are complicated by environmental considerations. Coal is cheap if you don't care about the environment in which it is mined and burned, but expensive if you want to repair the damage done by mining and install "scrubbers" on smoke stacks. (Recall the environmental destruction of Buffalo Creek, described in Chapter 1.) To turn coal into gas or liquid requires water. And while coal is abundant in the West, water is not. "Who is willing to stop earning their living and give up their water to make energy for the needs of the country?" (Thurow, 1980, p. 37). The answer is no one. Developing each alternate energy source is vetoed by some group that fears a decline in its standard of living—and its fears are not imaginary.

On the average and in the long run, the gains from alternate energy sources would exceed the losses. This fact supplies little comfort, however. Developing new energy takes time. There would be a substantial lag between the point at which sacrifices were made and the point at which benefits were realized. This creates a classic political problem. The political leaders who take the first step will pay in lost votes for imposing the sacrifices on the electorate; they will not be around to receive the credit when those sacrifices pay off. Moreover, average gains conceal the fact that some groups will suffer real and immediate losses. No group is willing to take the risk or the loss. It is a zero-sum game in which the government is expected to act as referee.

The Special Interest State

John Gardner, a former Secretary of Health, Education, and Welfare and the founder of Common Cause, a citizens' lobby, explains how this zero-sum game translates into politics:

> By the end of World War II, an inescapable fact of life for Americans was the existence of a huge central government capable of facilitating or obstructing an enormous range of activities. And in the decades following the war there emerged a multitude of organized groups that became quite skilled in coping with that government. Far from submitting pas-

sively to an ever-larger government, these groups went on the offensive. They created the Special Interest State. (1980, p. 13)

There is nothing new about special interest groups putting pressure on government, or lobbying. (The term "lobbying" comes from the custom of waiting in the lobbies and halls of government to corner officials.) The First Amendment to the Constitution supports the right of citizens "to petition the Government for a redress of grievances." Up through the nineteenth century, the only groups to make concerted and effective use of this right were merchants and big landowners. In the early part of this century, they were joined by agriculture and labor. After World War II, the number of groups organizing to influence government began to grow. In recent years, it has exploded. Business lobbies, in particular, have become more active and more coordinated. So have public rights lobbies. The House Select Committee on Lobbying Activities estimates that the number of lobbyists is about 15,000 (or 30 lobbyists for each member of Congress). Eighty percent of the nation's 1,000 largest corporations and 50 trade and professional associations have representatives in Washington. An estimated $2 billion is spent each year to influence the government.

The range of special interests represented in Washington is wide (Green et al., 1979, Chapter 2). The military lobby is a collection of forty-one private, tax-exempt organizations (ranging from the American Legion to the Aerospace Association) that claim a membership of 6 million and have a combined annual budget of about $38 million. Working for business, the U.S. Chamber of Commerce has an annual budget of $20 million and claims to be able to mobilize 7 million Americans through its local chapters. The Business Roundtable (an organization of 190 top corporate executives) is the business lobby that succeeded in defeating a labor reform bill and a consumer

advocacy agency in recent years. The AFL-CIO maintains a staff of 300 lobbyists in the capital. Doctors were among the first professionals to take the political offensive, through the American Medical Association (AMA). In only three years, the AMA spent over $3 million to block the passage of Medicare (Thayer, 1974, pp. 211–12). The bill eventually became law, but the AMA had blocked its passage for a full generation. The National Rifle Association, one of the most effective lobbies in the country, has blocked gun control legislation for decades, despite public pressure after three political assassinations (John and Robert Kennedy and Martin Luther King, Jr.). In the late 1960s, cities joined the parade to Washington, organizing the U.S. Conference of Mayors. At the same time, public interest lobbies began to multiply. Among other victories, the environmental lobby succeeded in stopping a government subsidy of the SST (supersonic transport) and in getting Congress to pass a strip mining bill requiring most land to be returned to its original condition. There are also a number of single-issue lobbies—for example, the anti-abortion, anti-ERA, anti-SALT, and anti-busing groups.

How do lobbyists work? How do special interest groups pressure the government? Humorist Will Rogers once quipped, "Congress is the best money can buy." The FBI's Abscam investigation suggested that some legislators are happy to accept bribes. But outright bribes are not necessary. Special interest groups can attempt to influence legislators by contributing to their campaigns, or threatening not to. There are legal limits to the amount individuals or groups can contribute to a given campaign, and candidates are required to report the source of contributions. Still, with campaign costs high, every contribution helps. All public officials, elected or appointed, are forbidden by law from accepting gifts that might raise conflicts of interest. However, there is little to prevent officials from accepting favors—rides on airplanes, weekends at hunting lodges, lunches

Violence and Political Power

Most political scientists view the American system as a pluralist democracy. The image is of a contest, carried out under orderly rules. "You scratch my back and I'll scratch yours"; "If you want to get along, go along"; "Don't make permanent enemies because today's adversary may be your ally next time around."

It's a contest for power and recognition that any number can play. If you've got a problem, get organized, play the game and work for change. Don't expect to win every time or to win the whole pot; compromise is the lifeblood of pluralist politics. More likely than not you'll find some allies who are willing to help you because they think you can help them, now or in the future.

Of course, some people won't play by the rules. Instead of bargaining for advantages, forming coalitions with the powerful, writing peaceful propaganda and petitioning, some groups get nasty. Contestants who misbehave, who resort to violence and, perish the thought, try to eliminate other contestants, must be excluded from the game. . . .

In recent years the body of criticism about the assumptions of pluralist theory has grown. Critics such as C. Wright Mills, whose *The Power Elite* was one of the earliest and most vocal attacks on the theory, deny the pluralist premise that America has no single center of power. "The flaw in the pluralist heaven," writes political scientist E. E. Schattschneider, "is that the heavenly chorus sings with a strong upper-class accent. Probably about 90 percent of the people cannot get into the pressure system."

To know who gets into the system, and how, is to understand the central issue of American politics. In the last 200 years, hundreds of previously unorganized groups here challenged the existing powers. Many of them collapsed quickly and left no trace, some died and rose again from the ashes. Some were pre-empted by competitors, some won the trappings of influence

and dinners, theater tickets, what have you. Lobbyists mobilize grass-roots support for or against a bill, organizing letter-writing campaigns. Few elected officials have the confidence to ignore thousands of letters from constituents. Perhaps the lobbyists' most important resource is information. As one lobbyist put it, what motivates Congressman X is doing a good job (Green et al., 1979, p. 30). No legislator can be expected to have enough information to make intelligent decisions about everything from nuclear fission to sex education. Lobbyists are walking encyclopedias of information on their specialties. When a congressman or woman wants to make a speech or propose without its substance. Some shoved their way into the political arena yelling and screaming, some walked in on the arm of powerful sponsors, some wandered in unnoticed. The fate of these challenging groups reveals just how permeable the American system is.

To see which groups make it, and what factors contributed to their success, I picked a random sample from the hundreds of challenging groups that surfaced in America between 1800 and 1945. I drew the line after World War II because the outcomes for current protest groups are still unclear. . . .

[The] data undermine the pluralist argument that violence is the product of frustration, desperation, and weakness, that it is an act of last resort by those who are unable to attract a following and achieve their goals. Violence, pluralists assume, is unsuccessful as a tactic because it simply increases the hostility around it and invites the legitimate action of authorities against it.

My interpretation is nearly the opposite. . . . The successful group in American politics is not the polite petitioner who carefully observes all the rules. It is the rambunctious fighter, one with limited goals, that can elbow its way into the arena. But the willingness to fight is not enough. A group must be able to fight; it needs organization and discipline to focus its energies. . . .

Perhaps it is disconcerting to discover that the meek do not inherit the earth—or at least that part of it presided over by the American political system. But those rambunctious groups that fight their way into the political arena escape misfortune because they are prepared to withstand counterattack, and to make it costly to those who would keep them out.

Source: William A. Gamson, "Violence and Political Power: The Meek Don't Make It," *Psychology Today*, Vol. 8 (July 1974), pp. 35–41. Copyright © 1974 Ziff-Davis Publishing Company.

legislation or simply to decide how to vote, he or she can turn to a trusted lobbyist for data. (Often lobbyists draft speeches or legislation.) Trust is crucial. It is in a lobbyist's interest to provide accurate information in order to maintain a good relationship. Thus much of the lobbyists' influence derives from the expansion of government into new and complex areas, creating an information gap. Lobbyists stepped into the gap.

Special interest groups have always sought to influence government, as noted above. The impact of special interests on government has increased for three reasons. First, the number and diversity of pressure groups has grown. This is largely a

Modern technology increases the impact of special interest groups. A master of computerized politics, Richard A. Viguerie is able through direct mailings to marshall the support of 5 million "right of center" Americans and 20 million more who respond to various conservative appeals.

function of the increasing complexity of American society, which promotes the emergence of different values and interests. To simplify somewhat, in a society where most people earn their living by farming, people have many more common causes than they do in a society where people engage in hundreds of diverse specialized occupations. Class, regional, ethnic, and other interests compound these occupational differences. Second, expectations have risen. Few groups are willing to accept inequality or sacrifice. And although they may not be able to get exactly what they want, they are able to delay and sometimes block programs that they believe would hurt them. They can veto proposed solutions. Third, demands are increasing faster than the economic resources to satisfy them. Economic growth has slowed. Abundance is declining. As a result of these three factors, the government often seems paralyzed.

The fate of the National Energy Act proposed to Congress by President Carter in 1977 illustrates the combined effect of multiple special interest pressures (Green et al., 1979, pp. 56–59). The act included five bills dealing with energy conservation, utility rates, natural gas policy, coal conversion, energy taxes, and tax credits. Each bill was controversial; each would have threatened some group's economic security. No sooner was the act proposed than the lobbyists descended. The American Gas Association saw the chance to press for price decontrol. Consumer and labor groups argued for utility rate reform and against price decontrol. The American Bus Association urged a $1 billion tax credit for "low income people who ride buses." A council of major industries was created to oppose charging large consumers the same rate as small, private consumers. Truckers even sought a tax credit for windscreens they claimed reduced wind resistance and therefore saved fuel. The struggle eventually came down to deregulation of natural gas. To save other sections of the bill, President Carter reversed his original position and supported price decontrol. Thus lobbyists pushed the administration to an about-face.

John Gardner returns to the image of a game to

summarize what happens in a special interest state (1980, p. 14). Think of a government official as a checkers player surrounded by interested bystanders. One bystander puts a thumb on a checker and says, "Go ahead and play, but don't touch this one." Another bystander puts a thumb on a second checker with the same warning, then another, and another. It is not that the bystanders don't want the player to win. To the contrary, all of them want the government to solve the energy (and other) problems. It's just that they don't want their own, particular checker moved, their interests threatened. The more complex a society becomes, the more "bystanders" there are, bystanders with different interests, values, and expectations.

In the Public Interest

Discussions of the problems in the nation's political economy tend to focus on the relative power of different groups *within* it. The emphasis is on the strategies and tactics of conflict, on which groups are most successful at getting their way and why, on who gets the biggest slice of the pie. The implication is that A can only acquire power by overcoming the resistance of B, and that inevitably B's interests are sacrificed in the process. Here we want to consider the collective power of the system as a whole. Talcott Parsons defines *collective power* as "the capacity to mobilize the resources of society for the attainment of goals for which a general 'public' commitment has been made, or may be made" (1960, p. 221). From this perspective, A and B acquire power by collaborating on mutually beneficial activities. The critical question today is whether this capacity is fading. In the special interest state, the parts are at war against the whole. So many groups are fighting for a piece of the pie, the pie itself may crumble.

The sociologist Arthur Vidich (1980) summarizes the changing problems in the U.S. political economy from this perspective. Today's problems are both external and internal. We have entered an age of global interdependence that has seriously weakened the nation-state. Our political and economic machinery are less and less able to direct the economy. Economic theories based on a world order that no longer exists (as suggested in Chapter 4) are obsolete. At the same time, the nation has become increasingly fragmented into regional, occupational, class, ethnic, life style, and countless other special interest groups. These divisions may have existed in the past. But never before have so many groups been aware of their special interests and organized to protect those interests. Small groups can bring the entire society to a halt. And each group is demanding more, or at least not less, of a shrinking pie.

Vidich identifies two urgent political tasks in this age of declining abundance. The first is the management of special interests—or more accurately, the management of social resentments, of "intergroup hostility, hatred of leaders, and disgust with the system as a whole" (1980, p. 648). The second is finding "nonmaterial means for satisfying competitive claims." In the years following World War II, many Americans acquired homes in the suburbs, education for their children, and other material benefits. Expectations among other, less prosperous groups rose as they adopted these benefits as their standard of American living. Now all are on the defensive. The smaller the pie seems, the fiercer the competition. One possibility would be to de-escalate material expectations, to redefine the common good. The danger, as Vidich sees it, is that the nation will turn to solving economic problems by non-economic means—renewed discrimination and prejudice, abandonment of the poor, nationalism, isolationism, and "lifeboat ethics." "It remains to be seen how . . . this nation will use its power for the future reshaping and reorganizing of a world of inevitable frustrations in which it cannot prevail on its own terms" (1980, pp. 648–49).

Summary

1. The term *political economy* refers to the interrelations of politics and economics.

2. Business has both power (the ability to control what other people and organizations do, despite resistance) and authority (the socially approved right to exercise power) in American society.

3. Adam Smith was a strong advocate of *laissez faire* ("let it be") economic policy, claiming that a free market is self-regulating. The founders of this nation supported this view.

4. In practice, the market has never been free. Monopolies, oligopolies, and most recently, conglomerates and transnationals are economic organizations designed to avoid the selective effects of free and open competition.

5. American business has used its power to create one of the highest standards of living in the world. It has also abused its power (with environmental irresponsibility, a poor safety record, overpricing, creating demands through advertising, and political influence).

6. Population growth, social differentiation, and the demands of an increasing number of special interest groups have complicated the business of government.

7. The size of the federal government today reflects demands for economic security, for a strong military establishment, and for government protection of "public rights."

8. Some of the waste and inefficiency of the federal government is a byproduct of the bureaucratic form of organization (trained incapacity, routine treatment of particular and "special" cases). Some results from the vested interests of bureaucrats.

9. The proliferation of special interest groups has created a "zero-sum society." Each group wants what is collectively impossible. For one group to win, others must lose.

10. Rising expectations and declining abundance complicate the zero-sum game. As a result, the collective power of the political economy—the ability to mobilize society's resources for collective goals—is threatened.

Suggested Reading

Barnet, Richard J., and Ronald E. Müller. *Global Reach.* New York: Simon & Schuster, 1974.

Bell, Daniel. *The Cultural Contradictions of Capitalism.* New York: Basic Books, 1976.

Berg, Ivar. *The Business of America.* New York: Harcourt Brace Jovanovich, 1968.

Green, Mark J. et al. *Who Runs Congress?*, 3rd ed. New York: Bantam, 1979.

Nader, Ralph et al. *Taming the Giant Corporation.* New York: Norton, 1976.

Stern, Philip M. *The Rape of the Taxpayer.* New York: Random House, 1974.

Thurow, Lester C. *The Zero-Sum Society: Distribution and the Possibilities for Economic Change.* New York: Basic Books, 1980.

References

Barber, R.J. "The New Partnership: Big Government and Big Business." *The New Republic,* August 13, 1966, pp. 17–22.

Barnet, R.J., and R. Müller. *Global Reach.* New York: Simon & Schuster, 1974.

Berg, I. *The Business of America.* New York: Harcourt Brace Jovanovich, 1968.

Bird, C. *The Invisible Scar.* New York: Longman, 1966.

Cobb, S. "Defense Spending and Defense Voting in the House." *American Journal of Sociology,* Vol. 82, No. 1 (July 1976), pp. 163–82.

Cole, C.L. *The Economic Fabric of Society.* New York: Harcourt Brace Jovanovich, 1969.

Cummings, M., and D. Wise. *Democracy Under Pressure,* 4th ed. New York: Harcourt Brace Jovanovich, 1981.

Fallows, J. "American Industry: What Ails It, How to Save It." *The Atlantic,* Vol. 246, No. 4 (September 1980), pp. 35–54.

Fox, J.R. *Arming America: How the U.S. Buys Weapons.* Boston: Div. Research, Graduate School of Business Administration, Harvard University, 1974.

Friedman, M., and R. Friedman. *Free to Choose.* New York: Harcourt Brace Jovanovich, 1980.

Galbraith, J.K. *Economics and the Public Purpose.* New York: Signet, 1973.

Gardner, J.W. "The American Political System: Is It Coping with the Problems of Our Society?" Public Affairs Conference at Brown University, *Providence Journal-Bulletin.* (March 23, 1980), pp. 13–15.

Green, M.J. et al. *Who Runs Congress?,* 3rd ed. New York: Bantam, 1979.

Green, M.J., with B.C. Moore, Jr., and B. Wasserstein. *The Closed Enterprise System.* New York: Grossman, 1972.

Heilbroner, R.L. "The Demand for the Supply Side." *The New York Review of Books,* June 11, 1981, pp. 37–41.

Hightower, J. "Food Monopoly." In M. Green and R. Massie (Eds.), *The Big Business Reader.* New York: Pilgrim, 1980, pp. 9–18.

International Monetary Fund. *International Financial Statistics,* Vol. 32, No. 4 (April 1979).

Korb, L.J. "The Price of Preparedness: The FY 1978–1982 Defense Program." *American Enterprise Institute Defense Review,* Vol. 3 (1977), pp. 2–43.

Lave, L.B. "Health, Safety, and Environmental Regulations." In J.A. Pechman (Ed.), *Setting National Priorities: Agenda for the 1980s.* Washington D.C.: The Brookings Institution, 1980.

Lieberson, S. "An Empirical Study of Military-Industrial Linkages." *American Journal of Sociology,* Vol. 76, No. 4 (January 1971), pp. 562–84.

Lipset, S.M. "Some Social Requisites of Democracy." *American Political Science Review,* Vol. 53 (March 1959), pp. 69–105.

Martin, R. *The Sociology of Power*. London: Rutledge & Kegan Paul, 1977.

Merton, R.K. *Social Theory and Social Structure*, Enlarged edition. New York: Free Press, 1968.

Michels, R. *Political Parties*. New York: Free Press, 1967.

Mintz, M., and J.S. Cohen. *America, Inc.* New York: Dell, 1971.

Nader, R., M. Green, and J. Seligman. *Taming the Giant Corporation*. New York: Norton, 1976.

Parsons, T. *Structure and Process in Modern Society*. New York: Free Press, 1960.

Pertschuk, M., and K.M. Davidson. "What's Wrong with Conglomerate Mergers?" In M. Green and R. Massie, Jr. (Eds.), *The Big Business Reader*. New York: Pilgrim, 1980, pp. 484–97.

Pole, J.R. *The Pursuit of Equality in American History*. Berkeley, Cal.: University of California Press, 1978.

Ray, J.L. *Global Politics*. Boston: Houghton Mifflin, 1979.

Salamon, L.B., and G.L. Wamsley. "The Federal Bureaucracy: Responsive to Whom?" In L. N. Reiselbach (Ed.), *People vs. Government: The Responsiveness of American Institutions*. Bloomington, Ind.: Indiana University Press, 1975, pp. 151–88.

Samuelson, P.A. *Economics*, 11th ed. New York: McGraw-Hill, 1980.

Sherrill, R. *Governing America*. New York: Harcourt Brace Jovanovich, 1978.

Sherrill, R. *Why They Call It Politics*, 3rd ed. New York: Harcourt Brace Jovanovich, 1979.

Simon, W.E. *A Time for Truth*. Berkeley, Cal.: Berkeley Publishing Corp., 1978.

Smith, A. *The Wealth of Nations*. 1937; rpt. New York: Modern Library, 1965.

Stern, P.M. *The Rape of the Taxpayer*. New York: Random House, 1974.

Stillman, D. "The Devastating Impact of Plant Relocations." In M. Green and R. Massie, Jr. (Eds.), *The Big Business Reader*. New York: Pilgrim, 1980, pp., 72–90.

Thayer, G. *Who Shakes the Money Tree?* New York: Simon & Schuster, 1974.

Thurow, L.C. *The Zero-Sum Society*. New York: Basic Books, 1980.

Vidich, A.J. "Inflation and Social Structure: The United States in an Epoch of Declining Abundance." *Social Problems,* Vol. 27, No. 3 (June 1980), pp. 636–49.

Weber, M. *The Theory of Social and Economic Organization*. 1925; rpt. New York: Free Press, 1964.

Yankelovich, D. "The Public Must Realize that Sacrifices Must Be Made." *Brown Alumni Monthly* (May 1980), pp. 37–38.

PART THREE

Social Settings in Turmoil

Chapter Six

The Urban Crisis

Urban America in Transition

The Central City

Suburbia

Sunbelt Cities

The Urban Experience

Theoretical Perspectives

  The Determinist View

  The Counterargument

  The Subcultural View

Assessing the Quality of Urban Life

  Urban Isolation and Stress

  Urban Crime

Locking the Poor Inside the City

Transportation

Housing

Education

Urban Revitalization: Proposals and Prospects

Inner-City Recommendations

Metropolitan Recommendations

Americans are ambivalent toward cities and city life (Palen, 1981, pp. 72–95). We praise cities as centers of enterprise, vitality, artistic creativity, excitement, and bright lights; denounce them as breeding grounds for crime, pollution, and decadence. We think of cities as exhibiting our best and worst (see Table 6-1). Good, clean country living is still contrasted with the squalor of dirty, noisy, crowded, crime-ridden cities; down-home country hospitality contrasts with both the cold impersonality and superficial glitter of city life. Americans idealize rural living. Our folk heroes are cowboys, not factory workers. But although we choose to glorify the country, we choose to live in and around cities.

The United States has become an overwhelm-

Table 6-1
Americans' Images of Cities, Suburbs, and Rural Areas
(percentages of a sample of 7,074 people surveyed)

Which Type of Community Has	Cities	Suburbs	Small Towns/ Rural Areas	There Is No Difference/ Not Sure	Total
(A) Negative Attributes					
The most crime	92	1	1	6	100
The worst place to raise children	83	2	4	11	100
The worst housing	64	4	14	18	100
The worst public schools	63	3	15	19	100
The highest divorce rate	58	8	1	33	100
The highest taxes	58	19	4	19	100
The greatest amount of racial discrimination	45	14	18	23	100
The worst shopping facilities	14	6	66	14	100
(B) Positive Attributes					
The most plays, museums, and cultural opportunities	90	4	—	6	100
The best public transportation	81	8	2	9	100
The best selection of movie theaters	78	12	1	9	100
The best selection of restaurants	77	14	2	7	100

ingly urban society. There have been three stages in the urbanization of America. The first stage was the emergence of big cities in the nineteenth century. After the War of 1812, towns on the coast and inland waterways—Boston, New York, Philadelphia, New Orleans, St. Louis, and Cincinnati—began to establish themselves as vital ports, collecting raw materials and dispensing manufactured goods. In 1800, most Americans (94 percent) had lived on farms or in towns with populations of 2,500 or less (U.S. Bureau of the Census, 1960, p. 14). The largest cities in the nation then were Philadelphia (pop. 70,000) and New York (pop. 60,000)—small compared to Paris (pop. 500,000) and London (pop. 800,000) (Schlesinger, 1940). As the century progressed, rural people

Table 6-1
(continued)

Which Type of Community Has	Cities	Suburbs	Small Towns/ Rural Areas	There Is No Difference/ Not Sure	Total
(B) *Positive Attributes*					
The best clinics, hospitals, health care facilities	73	15	4	8	100
The best employment opportunities	72	13	3	12	100
The best colleges and universities	67	13	4	16	100
The best shopping facilities	47	32	9	12	100
The best public services (garbage collection, fire and police protection)	39	33	15	13	100
The widest range of housing that you can afford	32	27	23	18	100
The least amount of racial discrimination	29	12	35	24	100
The best public schools	23	39	24	14	100
The greatest number of people who have attitudes similar to yours	23	24	33	20	100

Source: M.D. Abravanel and P.K. Mancini, "Attitudinal and Demographic Constraints," in D.B. Rosenthal (Ed.), *Urban Revitalization* (Beverly Hills, Cal.: Sage, 1980), p. 33.

flocked to cities. New waves of immigrants from Europe further swelled urban populations, particularly after the Civil War. By 1890, New York had outgrown Paris. By 1900, a third of all Americans lived in cities.

The second stage in urbanization, which began around the turn of the century, was the growth of metropolitan regions. Cities not only continued to grow in terms of population, they expanded geographically. Innovations in transportation and communications restructured urban life styles. The horse-drawn streetcar (circa 1870), the electric trolley (1880), commuter trains, and finally the automobile (1900) linked cities with surrounding towns and enabled people to commute to work and shopping districts. In 1860, the predominant mode of urban transportation had been walking. By 1930, automobile registrations averaged one per household (though not all families owned a car) (U.S. Bureau of the Census, 1960). Telephones, regular radio broadcasts, and newspaper deliveries allowed people to be part of the city without actually living in it. By 1950, almost half the U.S. population lived in what the Census Bureau calls Standard Metropolitan Statistical Areas (SMSAs).*

The third stage of urbanization began in the 1950s, when cities began to run together. The growth of suburbs; the construction of shopping centers, medical centers, and office complexes; the relocation of industry; and superhighways all contributed to the emergence of the megalopolis. A *megalopolis* is a continuous strip of urban and suburban settlements, with a high concentration of population and business activity. "Boswash," the 500-mile chain of cities and suburbs that stretches from Boston to Washington and includes about 42 million people, or 19 percent of the nation's population, is an example (see Figure 6–1). Today two out of three Americans live in one of the nation's "strip cities."

Urbanization has affected the entire globe (Golden, 1981, p. 137). In the last 200 years, the percentage of the world population living in urban areas has increased from 3 percent to nearly 45 percent; the size of the urban population has grown from about 30 million to 1,400 million; the number of cities with 100,000 or more residents has multiplied; and the populations of London, Tokyo, New York, Calcutta, Bangkok, and Shanghai (to name the world's largest cities) have swelled (see Table 6–2).

Table 6–2
World Urbanization, 1800–2000

	Percentage of World's Total Population			
Year	In All Urban Places	In Places 20,000+	In Cities 100,000+	In Cities 1 Million+
1650	*	*	1.8	—
1700	*	*	1.7	—
1750	*	*	1.6	—
1800	3.0	2.4	1.7	.1
1850	6.4	4.3	2.3	.4
1900	13.6	9.2	5.5	.9
1950	28.2	22.7	16.2	.3
1970	38.6	32.3	23.8	12.3
1980	46.0	41.0	32.0	22.0
2000	51–61	42–51	34–42	22–27

*Indicates that no estimates are available.
Source: H.H. Golden, *Urbanization and Cities* (Lexington, Mass.: Heath, 1981), p. 139.

---

*An SMSA must include "(a) One central city of 50,000 inhabitants or more, or (b) two cities having contiguous boundaries and constituting, for general economic and social purposes, a single community with a combined population of at least 50,000.... The SMSA includes the county in which the central city is located, and adjacent counties that are found to be metropolitan in character and economically and socially integrated with the county of the central city" (U.S. Bureau of the Census, 1971, p. 829).

Figure 6–1

Megalopolises in the United States

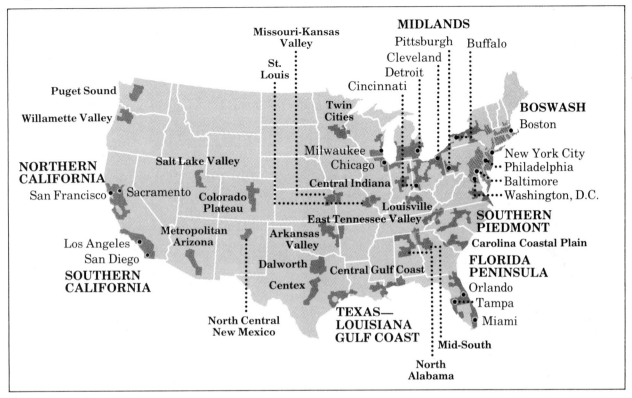

This chapter focuses on the urban crisis in the United States and its impact on entire *metropolitan communities* (cities and their suburbs). In the first section, we look at changes in urban patterns across the United States and at the problems these changes have created, especially for cities in the Northeast and North Central states. In the next section, we consider the impact of urban living on people's behavior and the quality of life. (Is urban life dehumanizing? Do cities "breed" crime? Sociologists disagree on the answers.) In the third section, we show why many of the nation's poor are locked into central cities: Programs designed to solve problems in transportation, housing, and education have caused unanticipated problems for cities and their resi-

dents. In the last section of the chapter, we look at proposed strategies for revitalizing cities and suggest why they are difficult to implement.

Urban America in Transition

The face of urban America has changed in two important ways in recent years. First, the movement from central cities to the suburbs, which began in the 1950s, has accelerated in the last ten years. Substantial numbers of people began leaving the metropolitan region altogether, for homes and jobs in the country. Second, growing numbers of people and jobs began moving from the older urban regions of the Northeastern and North

The Exurban Migration

Since the early 1970's, census estimates have been showing a spreading out of the American population from the cities and suburbs to the countryside, a trend so widespread that authorities now view it as a major national phenomenon with broad economic, social and political implications.

From 1970 to 1980, areas outside the orbit of the cities showed a net gain of about three million people, growing more rapidly than metropolitan areas or the population as a whole, according to the latest estimates by the Bureau of the Census. For most of this century, it was the metropolitan areas that grew.

"With the possible exception of a brief period during the heart of the Great Depression, we do not appear in the modern history of our country ever to have had a previous time when nonmetropolitan population growth rates exceeded metropolitan rates, wrote Calvin L. Beale of the population studies group in the Department of Agriculture. . . .

President Carter acknowledged the back-to-the-land movement . . . when he announced his "small community and rural development policy."

"The demographic trends of the 1950's and 1960's, the migration of people from the rural areas into the cities, has reversed, he said. "Since 1970 the population of the rural areas has increased 40 percent more than has the population in our urban centers. The rural economy is growing. It's become more diverse." . . .

The movement is fueled not by agriculture but by industrial, mining and service jobs, retirement pensions and easy access to highways. The new growth areas cannot be classified as rural, suburban or urban in the way most people think of those terms; they are a mixture of all three. . . .

Not all rural counties are growing. About one-fifth of them, mostly in the Great Plains and in the Corn Belt, where big farms and fertile land predominate, have continued to lose population. But on the whole, according to 1978 estimates, the nonmetropolitan counties in every region showed substantial population gains. . . .

The new growth of communities in the hinterlands, divorced from the cities, is evident in such diverse regions as southern New Hampshire, where houses are lined up like boxcars along once remote roads; central Illinois, where factories have sprung up in the cornfields; the Ozark mountains, where retirement, industry and recreation have brought an economic bonanza, and the hardscrabble counties of West Virginia and Wyoming, where mining is expanding.

Source: John Herbers, "Urban Centers' Population Drift Creating a Countryside Harvest," *The New York Times,* March 23, 1980, pp. 1, 50.

Central states to the South and West. *The President's National Urban Policy Report* (1980) characterized these changes as the "spreading out" of urban America. Spreading out has created problems for the older snowbelt cities, for the suburbs, and for the growing sunbelt cities.

The Central City

In the 1970s, the number of people moving out of central cities exceeded the number of people moving in for the first time. Between 1970 and 1978, 9.7 million Americans left the city. The populations of large cities (1 million or more) declined by over 7 percent (*The President's National Urban Policy Report*, 1980, Chapter 1). People seemed to be moving as far from the city as they could get. The populations of *non*metropolitan counties (counties with no city of 50,000 or more) increased by about 4 percent; metropolitan counties (cities and their surrounding suburbs), by less than 3 percent (*The New York Times*, May 18, 1975, p. 44). Today 40 percent of Americans live in the suburbs, 32 percent in rural areas, and 28 percent in central cities (*The New York Times*, November 3, 1980, p. 2E). As far back as 1948, polls showed that most Americans would prefer to live outside the city. It seems that more people are able to realize this dream today than in the past.

For a variety of reasons, business and industry have also been leaving the central city — and taking jobs with them (Kasarda, 1978, pp. 36–37). As recently as fifty years ago, most goods were shipped by rail or water. Downtown city streets were designed to lead to a port or station, not to handle today's trucks plus automobiles. The multistory loft buildings in central cities are not suited to today's assembly-line production techniques, which require horizontal space. Thus technological changes have contributed to the decline of the city industry. Moreover, suburbs now offer backup services (power, water supplies, sewage and garbage disposal, police and fire protection) to rival those of cities. Sixty percent of all manufacturing operations are located outside central cities today. Three of every five people employed in sales work outside the cities. New York City alone lost 600,000 jobs (with an estimated tax loss of $500 million) in the 1970s, even though professional, clerical, and managerial jobs in the city increased (President's Commission for a National Agenda for the Eighties, 1980, p. 30). Snowbelt cities lost jobs to the suburbs, to the South and West, and also to factories in other countries. (See Chapter 7 on the globalization of labor.) Thus emigration from cities has overtaken immigration to them; decentralization has replaced the concentration of business and industry. The old industrial cities of the Northeast and North Central states have been hardest hit.

The urban exodus has been highly selective. Most of the people leaving the city are middle-income, white-collar workers. They are being replaced by low-income groups with blue-collar skills. For every household with an income of $15,000 or more that moved into the city in the 1970s, three such households moved out (President's Commission for a National Agenda for the Eighties, 1980, p. 30). At the same time, the number of blue-collar jobs in the city has been declining and the number of white-collar jobs rising. The city labor market has shifted from predominantly blue-collar industries to specialized goods and services that require white-collar workers (for example, advertising agencies, brokerage firms, government agencies, and professional centers). There is a growing *mismatch*, then, between the employment opportunities available in the city and the skills of its residents. The most obvious result of these social patterns is increased unemployment. The number of people unemployed for fifteen weeks or more in a year doubled in Baltimore, New York, Philadelphia, and Chicago in the mid-1970s (*The President's National Urban Policy Report*, 1980, p. 4-5). Today's urban blacks and Hispanics do not have access to the kinds of unskilled and semiskilled jobs that were available to earlier generations of urban immigrants. The job-skills mismatch also means that the city depends on commuters to fill many white-collar jobs.

Political structure has not kept pace with these socioeconomic changes. Metropolitan regions are fragmented into antiquated collections of politically independent villages, townships, and other administrative territories, with no overall authority. City governments bear most of the resulting strain. The exodus of middle-income families, retail trade, and industry has undermined the city's tax base. Cities are caught in a bind: If they raise taxes to meet expenses, they are likely to drive away more households and businesses; if they do not raise taxes, they may not be able to pay their bills. The growing number of poor people in central cities has increased the need for social services, adding to the financial strain. (Four of ten poor families in the United States today live in central cities [*The President's National Urban Policy Report,* 1980, p. 4-1].) In addition, the flow of suburbanites in and out of the city each day raises its operating costs. Commuters add significantly to the cost of providing sanitation and protection, and of maintaining streets, parks, and museums. User fees (such as an entrance fee for a museum) provide only token compensation for the amount cities spend on general services. In short, the demands on the city have risen at a time when its financial resources are declining. This is particularly true in Northeastern and North Central cities.

Suburbia

Suburbs are not problem-free, however. Rising energy costs have been particularly hard on suburbanites who must heat large private homes and who rely on automobiles for transportation. Although crime rates are higher in central cities than in suburbs, the crime rate is growing faster in many suburban areas than in large cities. In 1977, although many of the nation's poor were crowded into central cities, 7 percent of suburbanites (over 5.6 million people) were living below the poverty line (*The President's National Urban Policy Report,* 1980, p. 1-13). Zoning restrictions, minimum lot sizes, bans on sewer construction, and other laws designed to maintain a high standard of living in the suburbs have created a housing squeeze. Prices have soared. As a result, many middle-income suburban home buyers get in over their heads financially. The Mt. Vernon Center for Community Mental Health in Fairfax County, Virginia, found that financial strain was contributing to marital problems, divorce, alcoholism, and child-rearing problems. Like the problems inside cities, suburban problems result in part from unanticipated changes in the suburban population. One difference is that the myth of suburbia tends to obscure these problems. The suburban poor, for example, are largely invisible.

Sunbelt Cities

Not terribly long ago, the sunbelt was seen as a dependent colony of the industrial Northeast. No longer. The population of the sunbelt states grew at twice the national rate in the 1970s, largely because of migration from the snowbelt states. The South alone accounted for 40 percent of all new housing construction in this period. In 1960, the Northeast was the industrial center of the nation, with the North Central region ranking second. Today there are more manufacturing jobs in the South than in either of these regions. Between 1960 and 1978, employment rose 88 percent in the South, 93 percent in the West. Nine out of ten new jobs created in the United States in the past five years were in the sunbelt (*The President's National Urban Policy Report,* 1980, Chapter 1).

Businesses are attracted to the sunbelt because of lower taxes, lower wages, lower rates of unionization, and lower energy costs. The "good business climate" attracts labor-intensive, low-wage industries, such as textiles and garments, and also the newer, leading-edge industries, such as small-parts electronics. Over 50 percent of the people who move to the sunbelt cite job-related reasons. Other reasons include the lower cost of living, the mild climate, and the casual outdoor life style. The migration of jobs and people tends to be self-reinforcing. People follow jobs and jobs follow people.

The rapid growth of sunbelt cities has created its own set of problems. Their roads and water and sewage systems were not designed for large populations. They have little experience dealing with traffic jams and air pollution. They are under pressure to expand educational facilities, housing construction, and social services. At the same time, they are under pressure to keep taxes low. Sunbelt officials "are caught between contradictory expectations of northern-level services and southern-level taxes" (Palen, 1981, p. 97). Surprisingly, the "crime capital" of the United States is not New York, or Washington, D.C., or

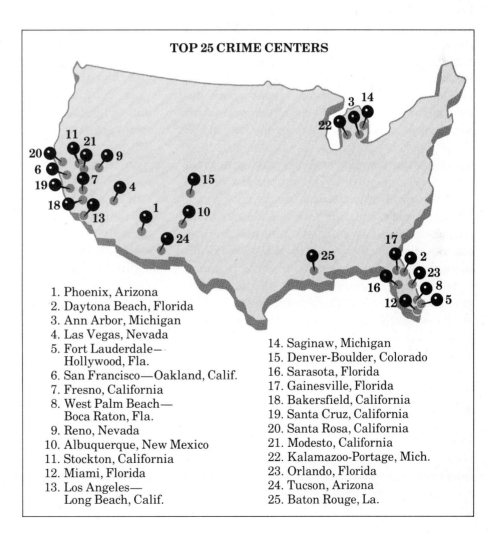

TOP 25 CRIME CENTERS

1. Phoenix, Arizona
2. Daytona Beach, Florida
3. Ann Arbor, Michigan
4. Las Vegas, Nevada
5. Fort Lauderdale—
   Hollywood, Fla.
6. San Francisco—Oakland, Calif.
7. Fresno, California
8. West Palm Beach—
   Boca Raton, Fla.
9. Reno, Nevada
10. Albuquerque, New Mexico
11. Stockton, California
12. Miami, Florida
13. Los Angeles—
    Long Beach, Calif.
14. Saginaw, Michigan
15. Denver-Boulder, Colorado
16. Sarasota, Florida
17. Gainesville, Florida
18. Bakersfield, California
19. Santa Cruz, California
20. Santa Rosa, California
21. Modesto, California
22. Kalamazoo-Portage, Mich.
23. Orlando, Florida
24. Tucson, Arizona
25. Baton Rouge, La.

Figure 6–2

Crime in the Sunshine (cities with the 25 highest crime rates per 100,000 people)

Source: E. Lendler, "Crime in the Sunshine," *New Times,* May 2, 1975, p. 123. Based on the FBI Crime Index, 1975.

Detroit, but rather Phoenix, Arizona (Lendler, 1975). Population changes and even the mild climate contribute to high crime rates in sunbelt cities (see Figure 6–2). The mild climate attracts criminals as well as noncriminals. With thousands of new residents arriving each week, people do not know their neighbors. They may assume that men loading furniture and appliances into a truck are movers. Fear of crime is not as great in the sunbelt as in the snowbelt. People do not talk about crime as much; they are not afraid to go out alone at night; they do not take precautions. As a result, they are more susceptible to victimization. Thus the qualities that attract people to the sunbelt may invite the problems they associate with the snowbelt cities.

In this chapter, we will focus on the problems of the older cities of the Northeast and North Central states, which have been hurt by both the move to the suburbs and the migration to the sunbelt. When Americans talk about an "urban crisis" they are referring to these older cities. The phrase "urban crisis" conjures up images of broken-down neighborhoods, crime in the streets, gang violence, drug addicts and winos, mean-tempered traffic jams, air pollution, and a host of other ills. These are *symptoms* of the urban crisis, not the disease. Cleaning up cities—removing these surface blemishes—would not cure them. Here we are concerned about the underlying problem. The heart of the urban crisis is "the inability of many [cities] to maintain viable economic and social bases for the well-being of their citizens" (Palley and Palley, 1977, p. 4).

The Urban Experience

Modern cities and the discipline of sociology are both children of the Great Transformation that took hold of Western societies in the nineteenth century (Fischer, 1975; 1976). The Industrial Revolution—flanked by urbanization and bureaucratization—was changing the shape of society. The scale and pace of social life were changing. Sociology was born of the effort to understand the impact of these changes on people's mental and social lives. How would modern civilization differ from civilizations of the past? How would new structures affect the social order? What new ways of life and new types of people would emerge? These were the questions that occupied the early sociologists (Marx, Durkheim, Weber, Simmel, Tönnies, and others).

Ferdinand Tönnies, for example, contrasted *Gemeinschaft,* or the traditional community, with *Gesellschaft,* or modern society (1957). *Gemeinschaft* is a small, stable, close-knit community of people with close personal ties of kinship and friendship. They do similar kinds of work, try to raise their families as their parents did, and participate in many joint activities. The social glue that holds *Gemeinschaft* together is a sense of collective *identity* (Coleman, 1976). A man cooperates with his neighbors because he feels their fate is his fate and that helping them will promote their mutual well-being. *Gesellschaft* is a large, complex society whose members have many different histories and life styles. Work in *Gesellschaft* takes the form of specialized tasks, not subsistence activities. Individuals pursue different careers and see the world from different angles. The roles people play in one another's lives are not ordained by tradition, but are variable and changing. What holds the *Gesellschaft* together is *interdependence*. Specialization forces people to cooperate in the pursuit of self-interest. For example, countless people the ballet dancer does not know personally build the theater, set the stage, and fill the audience. The question Tönnies and others asked was: Will the new social glue hold?

The early sociologists saw the city as modern society or *Gesellschaft* in microcosm. In cities the

Great Transformation was displayed in bold relief. The pioneer of urban sociology in the United States, Robert Ezra Park, described the city as "a laboratory or clinic in which human nature and social processes may be conveniently and profitably studied" (1916, p. 130). As Chairman of the Department of Sociology at the University of Chicago, Park practiced what he preached, encouraging students to conduct theoretical and empirical studies of their urban environment. In 1938, Louis Wirth summarized the thinking that emerged from these studies in a classic essay entitled "Urbanism as a Way of Life."

Theoretical Perspectives

Wirth (1938) defines a *city* as "a relatively large, dense, and permanent settlement of socially heterogeneous individuals" (p. 8). Size, density, and heterogeneity are the key points in this definition. What makes the city different from other social settings is not simply the number of people but the number of people with *diverse* traits living in such *close quarters.* "Cities generally, and American cities in particular, comprise a motley of peoples and cultures, of highly differentiated modes of life between which there often is only the faintest communication, the greatest indifference and the broadest tolerance, occasionally bitter strife, but always the sharpest contrast."

What impact, if any, does the urban environment have on social life? Here we'll look at three theoretical views.

The determinist view The main theme of Wirth's *determinist theory* is that the urban environment, in and of itself, changes people's mental and social lives. People think and feel and act differently, simply because they live in the city. The impact of cities is largely negative in Wirth's view. Indeed, he believes that cities promote both social and personal disorganization.

Wirth argues that cities tend to divide people. Geographically, they are cut up into distinct districts—residential neighborhoods, a downtown business district, a section of wholesale food markets, a student quarter, and so on. The patterns of people's lives reflect this geographical fragmentation. City dwellers live in one part of town, work in another, play and shop in still others. With each change in setting and activity, the cast of characters changes. People play different roles with family members, neighbors, co-workers, friends they meet at a club. Their knowledge of one another is limited to one small portion of their lives. As a result, their lives are disconnected. Their time and attention are divided among many places and people. No one group commands their total loyalty and allegiance. The fact that city residents come from diverse backgrounds and do not have a shared set of values and norms adds to these divisions. Neighbors quite literally may not speak the same language.

Wirth believes that urban segmentation weakens the traditional bonds of social solidarity. Kinship becomes less compelling when kin do not live and work together. Neighborliness fades when people spend only a few hours each day around home. "[T]he sentiments arising out of living together for generations under a common folk tradition" are missing. Urbanites substitute formal social controls for the bonds of tradition. For example, when teen-agers misbehave, a neighbor calls the police instead of talking to them or their parents (Fischer, 1976, p. 33). Urbanites have many secondary relationships (impersonal, instrumental acquaintances) but few primary relationships (close, intimate, ongoing ties). They join many voluntary groups but participate in limited ways. City dwellers are free from the constraints that prevent people in small communities from experimenting, but they lack the social supports that catch people in small communities when they fall.

Wirth maintains that the urban environment creates personal as well as social problems. Simply put, the city is too much for people. There are too many sights and sounds, too many people making too many demands, too many possibilities for a person to take in. If city dwellers paid attention to everything going on around them, their sensory apparatus would overload. Their fuses would blow. To protect themselves from this onslaught, they develop a psychological coat of armor. They become aloof, detached, cool, and calculating. In protecting themselves, urbanites gain a degree of personal freedom but lose "the spontaneous self-expression, the morale, and the sense of participation that comes from living in an integrated society." Moreover, in many cases, the armor doesn't work. Wirth suggests that mental breakdowns, suicide, and general psychological disorganization are more common in cities.

In short, Wirth argues that the urban environment weakens the bonds that support families, neighborhoods, and communities, setting individuals adrift. People are freer in cities than in small communities, but the price they pay for that freedom is social and personal disorganization.

The counterargument Not surprisingly, Wirth's position on urban living has provoked debate. Two of Wirth's most severe critics are Herbert Gans and the late Oscar Lewis. Both argue that Wirth's description applies only to the run-down, inner districts of cities where disturbed and otherwise handicapped people are trapped by economic circumstances. Their behavior and attitudes are a reflection of those unhappy circumstances, not of the urban environment per se. Indeed, Gans and Lewis argue that the city has little if any impact on social life.

First, they believe that Wirth exaggerated the differences between urban and rural social patterns. Lewis (1965) points out that living in a small, stable community does not guarantee that someone will be personally involved with and committed to the community. '[P]easants can live out their lives without any deep knowledge or understanding of the people whom they 'know in face-to-face relationships' (p. 61). While in some rural communities the extended family cares for its members—economically and emotionally—all their lives, in others a couple and their young children lead the kind of private, detached lives Wirth associates with cities. Divorce—often characterized as a modern, urban phenomenon—is quite common in many traditional societies. Gans (1962) points out that urban and suburban people have numerous *quasi-primary* relationships—with their druggist, their doorman, their hairdresser, or bartender. While Wirth suggests that the many voluntary organizations urbanites join are purely instrumental (means to an end) and therefore impersonal, Gans argues that often these associations are merely excuses for sociability—as anyone who vainly attempts to stick to "business" discovers. Gans sees "little anonymity, impersonality, or privacy" in urban neighborhoods. To the contrary, everyone minds everyone else's business. Whereas Wirth implies that cities are like giant hotels filled with strangers, Gans compares city blocks and suburban streets to college dormitories.

Second, Wirth's critics feel that his portrait of urban life is overgeneralized. In Gans's words, "people do not live in cities or suburbs as a whole, but in specific neighborhoods." Many bring their traditions and their families with them (think of a city's "Little Italy" or "Chinatown"). Many only venture out of their immediate milieus for specific purposes and short periods of time. They know little of the city's possibilities beyond their families, neighbors, and church. Lewis concurs. Most of the people he studied in Mexico City married someone from their own *colonia,* or district, spent much of their time visiting kin, kept up their religion, and continued to prefer folk

The worst and the best of urban living. Where else but in a city would passers-by pay no attention to homeless, elderly women who sleep on the streets (the so-called shopping-bag ladies)? Where else could a person find any number of chess partners at almost any time of day?

remedies imported from the countryside to modern medicine. In short, city dwellers are "urban villagers."

According to Gans and Lewis, urban life styles are determined by economic condition, cultural background, and stage in the life cycle. The city itself has little impact. Gans (1967) argues that the apparent differences between city and country people are largely the result of *self-selection.* They occur because certain kinds of people choose to reside in cities.

The subcultural view Wirth believed that the urban environment weakened the social bonds of group life, with negative consequences for individuals. Gans and Lewis argued that the city has little or no effect on people's relationships, attitudes, or behavior. Claude Fischer (1976) has challenged both of these views.

Fischer agrees with Wirth that cities have direct impact on social life. He challenges Wirth's description of that impact, however. Fischer's *subcultural theory* is that cities help to create and strengthen social groups by promoting diverse subcultures (1976, p. 36). First, the size of big cities permits "what would otherwise be only a small group of individuals to become a vital, active subculture" (1976, p. 37). For example, in a town of 5,000, there might be 5 kindergarten teachers. In a city of 1 million, there may be 1,000 — enough to form an organization, to take joint action in their own behalf, and to develop a distinct identity. The same is true for newspaper reporters, singles, bird watchers, dope dealers — and for racial and ethnic minorities. Second, the density of the city brings these varied groups into frequent contact. Wirth and others have argued that exposure to different values and life styles tends to dilute traditions and weaken group bonds. Fischer (1980) concedes that in some cases this may be true. In many cases, however, contact with diverse groups intensifies subcultural identity.

The presence of groups that seem peculiar, offensive, or perhaps even threatening causes people to cling even more strongly to their own social worlds. Far from becoming detached and indifferent, urbanites are likely to become more passionately committed to "their own kind."

Assessing the Quality of Urban Life

The central question in the debate we've described is whether the social structure of cities reduces the quality of life. Here we will look at the research inspired by this debate.

Urban isolation and stress Determinists argue that urban living weakens social bonds — particularly close, primary bonds — and thus creates isolation and stress. Simply put, when neighbors do not speak to one another, when family members drift apart, when people are crowded together with strangers, individuals and society suffer. What are the facts?

Research indicates that city dwellers are, indeed, less likely than rural people to know their neighbors personally and to interact with them socially. Jacqueline Zito (1974), for example, conducted a survey of an eight-building, high-rise apartment complex in Manhattan that houses roughly 12,000 people. Most of the residents were middle-aged, married, and middle class (with incomes in the $15,000 to $30,000 range). Zito found that only a few residents (8 percent) could recognize everyone who lived on their floor, and fewer still knew everyone's family name. More than half had a "nodding relationship" with some people on their floor. They chatted in the elevator or the mail room. But most had no specific knowledge of their neighbor's occupation or life style. And most did not consider these people "friends." Many had one or two friends in the apartment complex, but nearly all had made these friends before moving in. Most (68 percent) said they would prefer making friends outside the complex. The exceptions to this rule were nonworking mothers and older people. Mothers met other mothers in the playground and visited one another's apartments several times a week. However, they rarely went places together (shopping or to a museum with the children) and rarely visited in the evenings with their husbands. Older people wanted, and found, friendly relations, especially with one another. They would stop to chat with almost anyone and seemed to know as much about what was happening in their buildings as the doormen. They met often on outdoor benches or in the lobby, where they exchanged gossip about the buildings and stories about their children and grandchildren. They were, however, exceptions. The norm for most residents was "benign neglect." Even introducing oneself was considered a violation of privacy.

On the surface, Zito's research seems to support the view that cities promote anonymity. But there is another way to interpret these findings. The lack of neighboring in these buildings can be explained in terms of the kinds of people who live there. Most of the wives in the building worked, and so were away from home most days. Many couples had moved to the complex after their children had grown up and left home. Some had no children. One professional couple noted, "We work most of the day, often go out in the evening, have no children and go away often on weekends. When do we have time to *see* our neighbors, even if we did want to?" (in Zito, 1974, pp. 73–74). Those residents who were at home during the day, who were raising children, and who had common needs and interests (both mothers and older people) were neighborly. People in the suburbs and small towns are more likely to be neighborly because of their life styles. For example, full-time suburban housewives have numerous opportunities, and reasons, to interact with the people next door. In small towns, people who live next door are likely to have gone to the same school, or to work for the same company, or to know people who do. This brings them together. Zito found that despite the lack of sociability in the Manhattan complex, people expressed a high degree of satisfaction with their living conditions. Loneliness was quite uncommon.

How does the city affect family life? Determinists have argued that urban living weakens the home by depriving "the family of some of its more vital functions" (Wirth, 1938, p. 161). For example, city people do not have to turn to their families for help during an emergency; there are hospitals and social agencies to assist them. They don't have to turn to their families for a job, a meal, advice, or a good time. Urbanites can get all these outside the home. As a result, determinists argue, the urban family is a hollow shell of what it once was. Research indicates there are differences between urban and rural families (summarized in Fischer, 1976, pp. 141–49). Urban families tend to be smaller and less likely to have members of the extended family (grandparents, aunts, or uncles) in the household than are rural families. Urbanites are a bit more likely to live alone or to be divorced, separated, or widowed. These differences are slight, however. What is remarkable is that despite intense competition for the individual's attention and loyalty, the family remains so strong in the city (Greer, 1962; Morris, 1968). When in trouble, urbanites turn first and most often to their families. They see relatives more than they do their friends, neighbors, or coworkers, and care more about their relatives. In short, it seems that the other relationships available in the urban environment do not replace those found in rural environments. Rather, they *add* to the individual's social ties.

What impact does the city have on people's inner lives? Wirth argued that the many voluntary relationships urbanites form do not "insure the consistency and integrity of the personalities. . . . Personal disorganization, mental breakdown, suicide, delinquency, crime, corruption, and disorder might be expected . . ." (1938). Wirth was not alone in suggesting that the city is harmful to mental health. What does research show? Surveys indicate that rates of mental illness, both treated and untreated, are slightly higher in urban than in rural areas (Srole et al., 1975). Some of this difference may be due to the fact that urbanites are more likely to label problem behavior a psychological disorder. And some may be due to the diversity of subcultures in cities: Behavior one group considers quite normal, another labels "crazy." Finally, in surveys, urbanites express slightly higher levels of discontent than rural people do. The reasons for their discontent are quite concrete: They are unhappy with their schools, housing, taxes, and lack of safety (Fischer, 1980).

A number of studies have focused on the effects of crowding on behavior. Popular wisdom holds that overcrowding creates stress and tensions that build inside a person until he or she has to find relief, through either aggression or withdrawal. Most of the research supporting this view has been from studies of animals, not people. For example, rats forced to live in congested cages become aggressive because they are unable to carry on genetically programmed mating and nesting behavior. Other evidence for this view comes from studies of people in atypical situations. For example, a person is likely to feel threatened if a stranger sits down right next to him or her in an almost empty library. However, most people do not become upset if someone pushes against them in a crowded bus or in a discothèque. Crowding, by itself, does not upset most people. It depends on the social situation. Large numbers of people in small places tend to make pleasant situations more pleasant and disagreeable situations more disagreeable. In other words,

crowding intensifies the perceived characteristics of a situation (Freedman, 1975).

Urban crime Cities and crime—especially violent crime—are intertwined in most people's minds. City dwellers are more likely than other Americans to fear being assaulted, robbed, raped, or murdered in their homes or on the street. They are more likely to keep their doors locked, to dress plainly to avoid attracting the attention of criminals, and to decide not to go somewhere because of fear of personal safety (Figgie Report, 1980). Ninety-five percent of the respondents in Zito's survey (1974) gave "security" as a main reason why they had moved into the apartment complex; "lack of security" was the disadvantage mentioned most often. Clearly, safety was a prime concern. How much truth is there to the link between cities and crime? A good deal (Scherer et al., 1975, pp. 221–28). The rates of virtually all crimes increase with community size in the United States. In 1970, the rate of violent crimes in U.S. cities was almost ten times that in rural places. Rates of property crime were five times higher in cities. Rates of arrest for victimless crimes or "vice" (such as prostitution) in cities were eighty-six times those in small towns. The crime rate is rising faster in the sunbelt cities, which most people consider safe, than in the older snowbelt cities, which many people consider unsafe, however.

The determinist view attributes high urban crime rates to a breakdown in social restraints. The urban environment creates a state of anomie, or normlessness; people feel no reason or obligation to abide by the rules. Personal disorganization further weakens restraints. There are fewer inner inhibitions on mugging, robbery, or embezzlement. The subcultural view maintains that high urban crime rates "are largely a result not of the breakdown of community but—quite the opposite—of the *creation* of communities that support criminality" (Fischer, 1976, p. 94). Like other businesses, crime requires a "market" of victims and/or customers. Like other professions, crime requires learning. People are not born criminals. Professional criminals especially depend on associations and organizations. They need organized markets ("fences") for stolen goods, organizations to protect them and to train new people, and so on. The city provides the critical mass for crime to flourish. It provides enough potential clients (customers for drugs or prostitutes), enough potential victims (the affluent, for example, and the elderly), enough corruptible police and politicians — largely because of critical mass. In addition, the city may sustain or create "subcultures of violence" (for example, ethnic groups that endorse family feuding and the like). The combination of professional and traditional criminal subcultures inflates the urban crime rate by providing social support for illegal activities.

There is some evidence that the physical structure of cities contributes to high crime rates. In *The Death and Life of Great American Cities* (1961), Jane Jacobs argues that most of the policing of city streets is done not by police officers, but by ordinary people. "The safety of the street works best, most casually, and with the least taint of hostility or suspicion precisely where people are using and most enjoying the city streets voluntarily and are least conscious, normally, that they are policing" (p. 36). To be safe, city streets must be thronged with people who keep a watchful eye on what goes on. High-rise buildings, such as those Zito studied, tend to destroy street life. Most people do not know enough neighbors to tell whether a person belongs in their building or not. There aren't enough shops, restaurants, and the like in the immediate vicinity to attract people to the streets. Designs that limit the number of families using an entrance so that they come to recognize one another, and that at-

tract people to outdoor areas and lobbies, might reduce some forms of crime.

We will discuss some of the interacting factors that lead to high crime rates in U.S. cities in Chapter 14. A key point here is that crime and cities do not necessarily go together. In some historical periods, the urban environment has fostered murder and mayhem; in others, not (Mulvihille and Tumin, 1969). A study of crime statistics for Massachusetts in the nineteenth century, for example, suggests that cities had a "settling" influence in that period. In the old American South, violence was a distinctly rural tradition from which cities provided a safe harbor (Scherer et al., 1975, pp. 222–23). Today crime rates in some of the world's largest cities (Tokyo, Rome) are below those in American small towns. Thus the city itself seems to be a minor factor in crime.

The population size, density, and heterogeneity of cities thus have mixed effects on the quality of life. The city seems to strengthen some social bonds and weaken others, to provide opportunities for criminal activity in some times and places but to limit them in others. What seems clear is that, for better *and* for worse, urban living is different. The city does have an impact.

The research reviewed here applies primarily to inner cities. In recent decades, the shape of the nation's metropolitan regions has changed. Some groups have had the resources to take the best of city life (the excitement, the varied social and cultural opportunities) and leave the worst behind. The exodus to the suburbs and beyond is a classic example of a *self-fulfilling prophecy*. Fearing the deterioration of cities, the affluent fled — taking with them their lower crime rate, their tax and consumer dollars, and many of their companies and jobs. The city was left with decreasing resources to provide for an increasingly dependent population. Both the social and physical conditions of inner cities are deteriorating as a result. Much of what the affluent feared has come true.

Crowding and Crime

Most of the research on the effects of density in the real world has dealt with the assumption that crowding causes people to be aggressive. The notion of territoriality is that when people are too close together, it causes an instinctive arousal of aggressive feelings and attack by the person who is crowded. Explanations in terms of adrenal activity also suggest that aggression occurs because of overactive adrenal glands, heightened reactivity to external stimuli, and general nervousness and suspiciousness. . . . If crime and juvenile delinquency are regarded as direct effects of aggressiveness, this notion can be tested fairly easily. If crowding does cause increased aggressiveness, more crime and juvenile delinquency should be found in those areas that have a higher population density.

It is easy to understand why people think that crowding causes crime. In the United States there is no question but that more crimes are committed in large cities than in small cities or rural areas. This is hardly a startling finding—practically anyone alive in the United States today could tell you that you are more likely to be robbed in New York than you are in Greenwich, in Los Angeles than in Los Altos Hills, in Philadelphia than in Haverford. Although these observations are based largely on hearsay, for once "common knowledge" happens to be correct. The crime rate per 100,000 people is approximately 1000 crimes per year in rural areas, 2300 in the suburbs, 3400 in small cities, and 5300 in larger cities. The rate of major crimes in the big cities is more than five times as great as in small cities, eight times as great as in the suburbs, and 11 times as great as in rural areas. Crimes, particularly major crimes, occur largely in areas of high population.

Locking the Poor Inside the City

Conditions in the nation's older cities are in large part the *unanticipated consequences* of programs that had no apparent connection to cities. They resulted from developments in transportation, housing, and education that were not intended to weaken urban centers but were designed without thought to the potential impact on cities.

Transportation

Northeastern and North Central cities, especially, are living museums of the history of transportation in the United States. The tight clusters of buildings around the port or the railroad station are relics of the days when the most convenient way to transport people and goods long distances was by ship and, later, by rail. Narrow,

But the subject under discussion is the effect of high population density, not large populations. The population of a city is quite a different matter from its density. The largest cities are not necessarily the most crowded, nor do small cities always have low population density. The fact that large cities have more crime than small cities is not a basis for concluding that crime rate is also associated with high density. . . .

. . . [W]hen areas within a city are equated on income, crowded neighborhoods produce no more crime than uncrowded ones. In fact, in lower-income areas, there is actually less crime when there is high density. Poor neighborhoods have more crime than rich ones. Poor people tend to commit more crimes than people with money. Drug addicts commit a high percentage of serious crimes in the major cities. But there is no evidence that crowding causes crime. Neighborhoods in which houses are close together or where there are many tall apartment buildings, thus producing a high population density, have the same rate of crime as neighborhoods in which the buildings are spaced farther apart or there are fewer tall apartments. Neighborhoods in which there is relatively little space in the apartments themselves, in which people do not have large living quarters, have no more crime than neighborhoods in which the apartments are more spacious. There are a great many reasons why people commit crimes, many factors in modern, complex society that cause crime, but there is no evidence that crowding is one of them.

Source: Jonathan L. Freedman, *Crowding & Behavior* (San Francisco, Cal.: Freeman, 1975). Copyright © 1975. Reprinted by permission of the publisher and the author.

winding streets in these downtown areas are reminders of the time when people traveled by foot. Rings of housing just outside this core are monuments to the introduction of electric trolleys and streetcars just before the turn of the century. Beyond this ring, the highways bear witness to the age of the automobile. Highways are the city's lifeline today. More than half of the land in downtown Los Angeles is paved with freeways, parking lots, and garages. Los Angeles may be an extreme case, but New York City is the only U.S. city in which more than 25 percent of workers use mass transit (Schwirian, 1977, p. 380). Almost four in every five people in most cities drive to work (President's Office of Emergency Preparedness, 1972, p. C-9). Despite the rising costs of vehicles and fuel, by 1990, about 36 million new cars and trucks are expected to have joined the

134 million jamming the nation's roads in 1975 (*U.S. News & World Report,* August 16, 1976, p. 48).

The development of highways and promotion of automobiles—to the neglect of mass transit—were not part of a deliberate, conscious plan. Rather, they are the result of many independent, private, and public decisions that have accumulated over the years. Cars have a number of advantages over other forms of transportation, including a guaranteed seat, privacy, storage space, and freedom from fixed schedules and predetermined routes. Without good roads, however, cars are little more than a diversion—an adult toy. It was the highways that converted Americans to automobiles (Palley and Palley, 1977, pp. 216–18). The first federal highway act, passed in 1916, was designed to provide farmers with access to urban markets. The Bureau of Public Roads was located within the Department of Agriculture; towns with populations of more than 2,500 were not eligible for funds. Then a 1944 act provided federal funds to connect major cities to one another with highways; a 1956 act established the Federal Highway Trust Fund. All taxes collected from the sale of gasoline were to be set aside for the construction of an interstate highway system. Not surprisingly, these programs were backed by the powerful automobile, oil, and farm lobbies.

Meanwhile, mass transit languished. Nearly all bus lines, commuter trains, and subways were either privately owned or financed locally. They received no federal aid. Many cities had minimal systems. Those with established transit systems did little to update them, for a number of reasons. It costs considerably more to build and maintain a commuter rail line than a highway. With each new interstate highway, more riders abandoned mass transit. With patronage declining, the funds for maintaining mass transit declined. Service deteriorated. And the worse service became, the more riders abandoned mass transit. Many mass transit systems fell into disarray. Not until the early 1960s did people begin to realize that the best-laid highways cannot handle the transportation needs of today's metropolis. As of 1974, urban mass transit was receiving $1 billion a year in federal assistance—a modest sum considering that it costs about $4.5 billion to construct a rapid transit system in just one city (Palley and Palley, 1977, pp. 229–30).

The emphasis on private transportation in the United States has had an enormous, unanticipated impact on the city. Suburbanization and the depletion of the city's human and financial resources are most obvious, but there are other effects. Land that might be put to other uses and generate tax revenues is consumed by roads and parking lots. Highways cut across the city, destroying valued neighborhoods. Much of the air and noise pollution in cities is caused by automobiles. And dependence on automobiles severely limits some segments of the population—especially the poor, the elderly, the handicapped, children, and many women. Because they cannot drive or do not own cars, they miss opportunities for jobs, cultural events, bargains, and other goods that are scattered around metropolitan regions. Transportation is one reason why many of the poorest Americans are locked inside cities.

Housing

The housing situation in central cities shows how solutions can become problems. Urban housing became a social issue in the United States in the early nineteenth century when fires and cholera epidemics convinced people that slums were a hazard to public health and safety. The first housing ordinances required all new tenements to have toilets, fire escapes, and garbage receptacles (Palley and Palley, 1977, pp. 161–63). With the 1949 Federal Housing Act, the idea that every American family has a right to "a decent home and suitable living environment"—regardless of its ability to pay—became law. State and local building and housing codes translated "decent" into specifics: sound construction, hot running water and a private flush toilet, no more than one person per room. Elsewhere in the world (Japan, for example), whole families are content to share a single room, and flush toilets are a rarity. Not so in the United States, where middle-class housing requirements set the standard (Glazer, 1967).

Ironically, these high standards are in part responsible for the deterioration of central-city housing. In effect, building codes make it illegal to construct low-quality, low-cost housing in the United States; housing codes make it illegal to occupy or maintain them. The cost of meeting minimum standards is high. As a result, most new housing units are too expensive for low- or moderate-income families.

Anthony Downs (1973) describes metropolitan housing patterns as a *trickle-down* process. A group of houses is built on land at the edge of the city by one or more developers. The houses are similar in design, quality, and price, and they attract a homogeneous group of upper-income families. As time passes, the houses begin to age. Fashions change; new conveniences are developed. These older houses lack such modern features as built-in appliances and family rooms. Other housing developments have sprung up around them, so that they feel less private and exclusive. Families whose incomes have risen move on to newer houses and "fancier" neighborhoods, farther from the center of the city. The families that replace them see the houses as a definite improvement over their former homes. The new residents tend to have larger families and to have less money for home maintenance than the original occupants. Often they are from recent immigrant groups. Over time the housing becomes older and less desirable. The second group moves on, and the process continues. Owners may move on themselves but divide their

old homes into rental apartments. Buildings slide from chronic to acute disrepair. Only those who cannot afford to move, those who have no choice, remain. Thus the housing has trickled down from the top to the bottom of the socioeconomic ladder. Downs estimated the trickle-down process takes from thirty to sixty years. He notes that housing in especially desirable locations (for example, near a lake or a university) may escape the downhill trend.

This process is carried one step farther with *disinvestment*—the abandonment of buildings that are structurally sound and could be renovated. Landlords find that demand for housing in what used to be middle-income neighborhoods has fallen off. Since they can no longer obtain rents that keep pace with inflation (especially rising fuel costs), they cut back on upkeep and services and buildings deteriorate. If tenants stop paying their rent, or if the city insists that violations be corrected, the landlords simply abandon the buildings. In New York City, disinvestment occurs at the rate of about 30,000 housing units a year (*The New York Times,* June 1, 1980).

Downs emphasizes that there is nothing "natural" or inevitable about the trickle-down process and disinvestment. The inside-outward pattern of urban development is not universal. In Paris, the affluent have held onto inner-city housing and the poor live on the outskirts of the city. Neither are cities universally divided into rich and poor neighborhoods. In Caracas and Lagos, Rio and Bombay, the poorest shacks are built on patches of unused land around the most luxurious homes (Downs, 1973, p. 2). In most U.S. cities, however, housing trickles down from the highest to the lowest income groups. The poor inherit what no one else wants.

Substandard housing is not merely unpleasant. It can be lethal. One direct consequence is death, injury, and loss of property through fire. Approximately seven out of ten fires in buildings in this country (700,000 each year) occur in residential

The South Bronx has become the symbol of urban decay. More than 1,200 buildings stand empty, gutted, torched, and abandoned. Firemen are called to some 3,500 fires each year. The devastation now covers more than 2,000 square blocks, and the area is increasing by 4 blocks a week.

structures. The United States has the highest rate of death from fire of any industrial nation. Deteriorating buildings, lack of fire safety devices, the use of unsafe heaters and other appliances (because boilers are not kept up), and unattended children all contribute to this problem. A second direct consequence of substandard urban housing is lead poisoning of small children. Even though lead paint hasn't been used indoors in the United States since the late 1940s, new paint may peel from the walls, exposing toxic layers. A pilot study of poor children conducted in New York City in 1966 showed that more than 18,000 were suffering from lead poisoning (Dentler, 1977, pp. 219–20). Both lead poisoning and deaths by fire are housing-specific problems—that is, they would be extremely rare if all city people lived in safe housing.

Unwittingly, federal and local governments have contributed to urban housing problems. For decades, the federal government has subsidized private homeownership. While reformers and analysts talked of the problems of slum tenements, political officials and most of the public gave their attention to single-family dwellings. To Americans, a home is a house — specifically, a free-standing, owner-occupied, single-family house with a piece of land around it. The federal government has been preoccupied with this dwelling — with "getting it built, getting it financed, saving it from the banks, reducing its costs, increasing its amenities" (Glazer, 1967, p. 29). The Federal Housing Authority (FHA) and the Veterans Administration (VA) were given the power to assist families in buying their own homes. One unanticipated consequence of promoting home-ownership was to hasten the exodus of middle- and working-class families to the suburbs. No one at the FHA or VA planned this. Promoting suburban development at the expense of cities was not official policy. To the contrary, virtually no one thought about the long-range consequences. FHA and VA officials (many of whom were former real estate agents and brokers) considered newly constructed suburban homes much safer investments than central-city dwellings, and therefore promoted them. Zoning regulations forbade the construction of multistory, multifamily apartment buildings in the suburbs. Thus government policies encouraged the middle-class to leave the city but effectively locked the poor inside. A second consequence of government policy was to institutionalize racial segregation of metropolitan areas. In both its 1935 and 1950 official handbooks, the FHA discouraged banks from granting mortgages in racially integrated neighborhoods, which it believed to be unstable (Glazer, 1967, p. 41). Whites could only obtain federal assistance to buy homes in white neighborhoods; blacks, in black neighborhoods. Moreover, because more blacks than whites had low incomes, few could afford to move to the suburbs. As a result, blacks and other minorities tend to be concentrated in central cities, while suburbs are predominantly white (see Table 6–3).

With the Housing Act of 1949, the federal government turned its attention to central-city housing problems and *urban renewal*. Inner cities were to be revived. The basic strategy was to tear down old buildings and construct new ones. The emphasis was on construction, not rehabilitation. However well-intentioned, urban renewal actually destroyed many old and stable (if poor) neighborhoods. Often the poor could not afford to move into new housing constructed on their old home sites. The chief beneficiaries were middle-class people who could afford the new housing and the new theaters and shops (Solomon, 1974, p. 8). A number of public housing projects to provide the urban poor with safe, low-cost housing were also constructed in this period. From the beginning, however, public housing was beset with problems. Occupancy was limited to the poorest (and often most troubled) families. Restrictive, bureaucratic rules about not painting walls and the like made residents feel as if they were living in jail. And living in a housing project was a stigma, a visible brand of poverty. Most projects were located in run-down neighborhoods, in the hope that new housing would upgrade the surroundings. Often the reverse proved true. Many projects became reservations for the poor, totally cut off from middle-class areas and influence. Proposals to scatter low-income housing through middle-class, suburban areas have met with stiff community resistance (Palley and Palley, 1977, pp. 168, 170). Attempts to insure mortgages for low-income families who want to rehabilitate older urban housing, on the FHA model, have had only mixed success. But urban renewal and public housing are small matters compared to the promotion of private home construction and ownership. Since the federal government became involved in housing, 600,000 units have been built under the public housing program and 80,000 under urban renewal, compared to *5 million* with FHA mortgages.

Indirectly, government policy encouraged eco-

Table 6–3
Characteristics and Spatial Distribution of the Population, 1977

	Places of Residence		
	Central City	Suburban	Non-Metropolitan
Population Group	Percentage	Percentage	Percentage
Total population	28.2%	39.1%	32.7%
White population	24.4	41.9	33.7
Black population	55.0	18.7	26.3
Hispanic population	49.4	34.8	15.8
Female-headed households	41.1	30.4	28.5
Median Family Income			
White	$15,069	$17,371	$13,318
Black	9,361	12,037	7,435
Hispanic	9,391	12,624	9,069
Female-headed households	6,658	8,539	6,542
Percentage Below Poverty Level*			
White	11.3%	5.9%	11.4%
Black	31.0	21.5	38.2

*Data available only for whites and blacks.
Source: *The President's National Urban Policy Report, 1980* (Washington, D.C.: U.S. Department of Housing and Urban Development, August 1980), p. 10-3). Data based on U.S. Bureau of the Census figures.

nomic and racial segregation of metropolitan regions. One way to understand how this came about is to look at who has benefited from housing policies: banks (recipients of FHA guarantees), construction companies, trade unions, and large numbers of the middle and working classes who can afford homes. The value of real estate keeps rising, so that homes can be sold at a substantial profit. Moreover, homeowners get numerous tax advantages. In short, many people have benefited from the unofficial policy of subsidizing the con-struction of single-family homes. The losers are cities.

Education

The economic gap between the central city and the suburbs and unofficial racial segregation of metropolitan regions create two interrelated problems for urban education. The first is the continuing struggle to integrate schools. Seventy to eighty percent of the students in Chicago, Detroit,

Los Angeles, Houston, and St. Louis are non-white (*The New York Times*, August 24, 1980, p. E5). The percentage of white students in central-city schools is declining (see Figure 6-3). Busing

Figure 6–3
Declining White Enrollment in Detroit's Central-City Schools

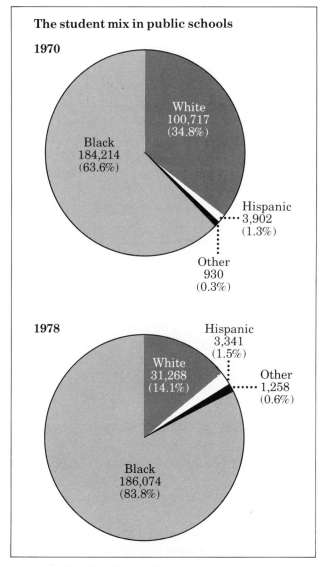

The student mix in public schools

1970

White
100,717
(34.8%)

Black
184,214
(63.6%)

Hispanic
3,902
(1.3%)

Other
930
(0.3%)

1978

Hispanic
3,341
(1.5%)

White
31,268
(14.1%)

Other
1,258
(0.6%)

Black
186,074
(83.8%)

Source: *The New York Times*, August 24, 1980, p. E5. Data based on figures from the Detroit Board of Education.

youngsters to schools in other neighborhoods to achieve racial balance is, to say the least, controversial. The second problem is financing urban education. At a time when the city's financial resources are declining, the cost of educating urban students is rising. Many central-city youngsters are socially disadvantaged and have special needs. City schoolteachers are unionized; they demand and get higher salaries. And city schools must compete with other social services for scarce municipal funds. Financial strain interacts with, and compounds, racial isolation.

Racial segregation of metropolitan areas is carried over into schools and reinforced. In the historic *Brown* v. *Board of Education* decision (1954), the Supreme Court cited research by the psychologist Kenneth Clark which suggested that segregation inflicted serious damage on black children's self-esteem. The Court urged ' all deliberate speed ' in ending school segregation. The 1964 Civil Rights Act provided funds for a more thorough study of the matter. The Office of Education asked the sociologist James Coleman to lead the investigation. The results of the Equal Educational Opportunity Study, or the Coleman Report, were published in 1966. Coleman compared the levels of achievement of black and white students in underequipped, predominantly black schools and in well-equipped, predominantly white schools. He found that the differences in performance among students at the same school were as great or greater than differences between schools. By far the strongest influence on student achievement was family background (economic level, parents' education, and parents' interest in student's academic achievements and aspirations for them). This is not to say that school doesn't matter. Coleman found that the quality of the school had more impact on poor students than on middle-class students. So did the level of other students' achievements and aspirations. For children with few educational resources at home, school and peers made a crucial difference. Coleman compared the poor, minority child in a predominantly white, middle-class school to an English-speaking child at a French school. Just as the latter learns French quickly to get along with peers, so the minority student picks up middle-class educational values to be one of the crowd (Coleman, 1968, p. 25). In particular, Coleman found that black children who attended predominantly white schools had a greater sense of control over their environment and futures than did children in predominantly black schools, and that this feeling of self-direction was related to higher achievement.

The Coleman Report was highly controversial. It provided advocates of school desegregation with concrete proof of the value of mixing black and white students. But the finding that the most significant influence on students is family background gave ammunition to opponents of court-ordered desegregation, by suggesting that schools had relatively little impact on student achievement.

Less than a decade later, Coleman and associates issued a caveat that was as controversial as the original report (Coleman, Kelly, and Moore, 1975; Ravitch, 1978a and 1978b). A new study indicated that school busing was contributing to the *re*segregation of cities by accelerating "white flight" to the suburbs. White families with an opportunity to enter their children in racially and economically homogeneous schools elsewhere were abandoning city school systems. Coleman saw this as an unintended consequence of school desegregation policies. In his words, "in the long run the policies that have been pursued will defeat the purpose of increasing overall contact among races in schools . . ." (in Ravitch, 1978a, p. 135). (See Chapter 10 for other views.)

Resegregation of urban schools is a nationwide phenomenon. Between 1968 and 1976, the percentage of white students in fourteen city public school systems dropped by over 40 percent. As of 1976, twenty-one of the nation's twenty-nine big-city school districts had a majority of nonwhite students and three were about half-white, half-nonwhite (Ravitch, 1978a, pp. 146–47). With little public support for busing students across city-county lines, and with the percentage of minorities in cities growing, the prospects for desegregating city schools are poor. The social structure of metropolitan regions has been an obstacle to achieving the national goal of school desegregation.

The second major problem facing city schools today is money. About half of the more than $60 billion Americans spend on education each year is raised locally, through property taxes and bond issues. This means that the amount a school district spends per pupil depends on residents' ability to pay taxes. States provide financial aid to local school districts. In most cases, however, these state funds are distributed evenly, which does not take into account the fact that it costs city schools more than suburban schools to provide identical services, or that city schools have more disadvantaged students who require special services than do suburban schools. City-suburban inequality is thereby perpetuated.

Some reforms have been made, though. In a landmark decision (*Serrano* v. *Priest,* 1971), California's Supreme Court declared that its method of financing education was unconstitutional because it denied poor school districts the freedom to adopt policies and programs available to more affluent districts. California adopted a "power equalizing" approach: The state ensures that districts which tax residents at the same rate have the same amount to spend per pupil, regardless of their tax base. Over twenty states have followed California's example. Whether these reforms will survive the next decade remains to be seen.

One central theme emerges from the examination of urban transportation, housing, and education. There is nothing inevitable about the decline of central cities. They have fallen into disrepair because demands for services (including education) have grown just when their resources have been declining. The flight to the suburbs would not have occurred, or occurred so rapidly, if the federal government had not subsidized highway construction and guaranteed home mortgages. Neither of these programs was intended to lure the middle class out of cities or to lock the poor inside. Many of the city's problems are the *unintended consequences* of technology, policies, and programs designed to improve the overall quality of life in the United States.

Urban Revitalization: Proposals and Prospects

In 1968, the National Advisory Commission on Civil Disorders appointed by President Johnson to investigate the urban riots of the early 1960s, warned:

> The nation is rapidly moving toward two increasingly separate Americas. Within two decades, this division could be so deep that it would be almost impossible to unite: a white society principally located in suburbs, in smaller central cities, and in the peripheral parts of large central cites, and a Negro society largely concentrated within large central cities. The Negro society will be permanently relegated to its current status, possibly even if we expend great amounts of money and effort in trying to "gild" the ghetto. In the long run, continuation and expansion of such a permanent division threatens us with two perils. The first is the danger of sustained violence in our cities. . . . The second is the danger of a conclusive repudiation of the traditional American ideals of individual dignity, freedom, and equality of opportunity. (pp. 225–26)

The clear implication is that the city is becoming a reservoir for the nation's social ills. Given the trends described in the preceding section – deteriorating mass transit, disinvestment in urban real estate, and the resegregation of schools – this view is hardly surprising. Some of the nation's cities are booming, particularly in the sunbelt, but they are exceptions. Most of our cities are in serious trouble. What can be done to revitalize urban America? There are no quick or easy solutions.

Inner-City Recommendations

One possible solution to the urban crisis would be to lure the middle class, with its tax and consumer dollars, back into cities. Some observers believe that this is already happening, that the middle and upper-middle classes are returning to the city on their own initiative (see Cincin-Sain, 1980). Journalists have labeled this phenomenon variously as the "back-to-the-city" movement, "the urban renaissance," and the "gentrification" of the city. Possible explanations include: a growing shortage of affordable suburban housing even for the middle class (which makes renovating inner-city houses more attractive); the coming of age of the post–World War II baby-boom generation; the emergence of new life styles and family forms that are better suited to urban living (childless couples, single parents, and so on); and the energy crisis, which has raised the cost of commuting to the suburbs and heating large, detached homes. In the words of one author, "the evidence of the late 1970s suggests that the [city] of the 80s and 90s will no longer be a magnet for the poor and homeless, but a city primarily for the ambitious and educated – an urban elite" (Fleetwood, 1979).

A recent survey conducted for the Department of Housing and Urban Development (HUD) indicates there is a grain of truth to these observations – but only a grain (Abravanel and Mancini, 1980). HUD researchers questioned a cross-section of people who had recently moved into cities, recently moved out, or were contemplating a move in one direction or the other. The survey indicated that cities attract a mix of Americans.

Although urban poverty is worldwide, economic segregation of cities is not. In Bombay, squatters live in the shadow of luxury apartment buildings.

Some identified themselves as working class, were unemployed at the time of the survey, and had never earned very much. Others were young, single, well-educated, and ambitious—and their numbers seem to be growing. (Interestingly, both groups see the city as the place to get ahead.) Comparisons of those planning to move into the city with those planning to move out were revealing. Twice as many future city dwellers had college degrees; a third more earned at least $20,000 a year and described themselves as upper-middle or upper class. These individuals' plans do not add up to a general trend, however. The number of middle-class professionals living in the city will continue to decline.

A second sign that the urban crisis may be waning is the revitalization of urban neighborhoods (Cincin-Sain, 1980). Neighborhood revitalization is the opposite of disinvestment. Whereas in some areas landlords are abandoning buildings, in others private homeowners are buying and renovating old, dilapidated buildings, often turning "slums" into chic residential districts. Almost half of cities with populations over 50,000 report private, nonsubsidized investment in housing in older neighborhoods. Between 1968 and 1975, 50,000 urban housing units were renovated. Between 1970 and 1975, the number of urban homeowners increased significantly, and city dwellers' median expenditures for home improvements exceeded those of suburbanites for the first time in many years. The largest numbers of renovations are taking place in big cities in the North and South. Neighborhoods that are close to central business districts or some other location of interest (a park or museum), that have received a historic designation, or that contain run-down housing originally built for upper-income families are the most likely to attract the urban pioneers. With one exception, these homesteaders fit the media stereotype: They tend to be professional, affluent (often childless) couples; both husband and wife work. Contrary to popular impressions, though, they are not part of a back-to-the-city movement. Rather, most are part of a "stay-in-the-city" movement: former urban renters who are purchasing their first homes. Moreover, the number of housing renovations is small when one considers urban housing as a whole. Neighborhood revitalization has attracted attention largely because it is so visible.

Suppose, however, that the urban renaissance were real, that the number of affluent professionals moving back into cities and renovating old buildings were increasing steadily. Luring the middle class back into cities might create as many problems as it solved. What would happen to the people who occupied the buildings before they were renovated? Where would they go? One group's solution is often another group's problem. The neighborhood revitalization of the 1970s and 1980s, like the urban renewal of the 1950s and 1960s, tends to displace the poor (Cincin-Sain, 1980). The first people forced out when a neighborhood begins to change are renters. Often the rents they pay are so low they barely cover the cost of maintenance. Moreover, an empty building is easier to sell. For this reason, landlords may push tenants out by refusing to renew leases or cutting back on services. A second wave of displacement occurs when other affluent buyers follow the pioneers into the area. Long-term residents who have watched the neighborhood deteriorate over a period of years may not realize that the value of their property is now rising and may sell too quickly. Those who remain may not be able to afford the increases in property taxes that result when the value of their homes goes up and when new neighbors demand better services. Often it is elderly couples and members of low-income ethnic and racial minorities who are displaced. These groups have special problems relocating. Female-headed households may experience discrimination when they attempt to rent or buy elsewhere; the elderly may not find affordable homes that are easily accessible to shopping, medical facilities, and other necessities. Often people who are displaced move into nearby housing, the revitalization movement spreads, and they are displaced again.

Metropolitan Recommendations

Part of the urban crisis derives from the fact that the political structure of metropolitan regions does not reflect social and economic realities. Metropolitan regions are divided into numerous competitive, and sometimes overlapping, political jurisdictions (see Table 6-4). As a rule, the poor are concentrated in the inner city, and financial resources have moved beyond city limits. Some recommendations for revitalizing urban America focus on the metropolitan region as a whole, on

Bringing the Middle Class Back to the Cities

As the cities' financial difficulties continue, proposals are beginning to surface once again to bring the suburban middle class back to the city, and to push out—or disperse—the urban poor. A returning middle class, it is thought, will revitalize the urban economy, and if poor people can be encouraged to leave, the cost of running the city will decline.

But why should middle-class people come back to the cities? They moved to the suburbs mainly to get a single-family house, and by now almost all of the commercial, cultural and other facilities they need, including job opportunities, have followed them there. To them, cities mean old apartments, noice and congestion, as well as high rates of crime and violence, all of which are to be avoided; and the few cities that provide excitement and unusual entertainment can be visited on weekends or during vacations. . . .

The idea of dispersing the poor out of the city is equally illusory. The suburbs have the power to refuse them entry, and there are no jobs for them in the Appalachians, the South, Puerto Rico and Mexico, from which most have come. Besides, the poor are not as costly a drain on the city treasury as is commonly thought, since the funds for servicing them come increasingly from the Federal Government. Indeed, returning suburbanites might cost the city more, for they will demand more municipal services than the poor.

Still, no one, including the poor, would disagree that a middle-class city is superior to one inhabited mainly by poor people; the quality of services and of urban life is then higher for everybody. But the solution is not to beg or bribe the middle class to come back; it is to make the poor themselves middle class.

Despite all the verbiage about their cultural deprivation, the vast majority of poor people share middle-class values, and would live by them if they could afford to do so. Nor are they inherently prone to crime and violence. Most poor people are as law-abiding as everyone else, and the high rates of crime and violence associated with poverty are produced by a relative handful, some pathological, others desperate or angry because they cannot get jobs. Just as the European immigrants, who were once called the dangerous classes, stopped being dangerous and became middle class when they obtained economic security, so would today's poor: white, black, Hispanic.

Source: Herbert J. Gans, "Why Exurbanites Won't Reurbanize Themselves," *The New York Times,* February 12, 1977, op ed page.

Table 6–4
Fragmentation of Local Government, 1967

SMSA	1967 Local Governments			1970 Population (thousands)		
	Total	CC	OCC	Total	CC	OCC
Chicago, Il.	1,113	12	1,101	6,979	3,367	3,612
Philadelphia, Pa.-N.J.	876	5	871	4,818	1,949	2,869
Pittsburgh, Pa.	704	11	693	2,401	520	1,881
New York, N.Y.	551	3	548	11,572	7,895	3,677
St. Louis, Mo.-Il.	474	6	468	2,363	622	1,741
Portland, Or.-Wa.	385	17	368	1,009	382	627
San Francisco-Oakland, Ca.	312	18	294	2,988	956	2,032
Indianapolis, In.	282	7	275	1,110	500	610
Kansas City, Mo.-Ks.	272	22	250	1,254	502	752
Denver, Co.	269	6	263	1,228	515	713
Seattle-Everett, Wa.	268	12	256	1,238	401	837
Cincinnati, Oh.-Ky.-In.	266	6	260	1,385	453	932
Peoria, Il.	261	12	249	342	127	215

CC: central city; OCC: outside central city
Source: A.K. Campbell and J.A. Dollenmayer, "Governance in a Metropolitan Society," in A.H. Hawley and V.P. Rock (Eds.), *Metropolitan America in Contemporary Perspective* (New York: Sage/Wiley, 1975), p. 363.

revising the structure "to reflect the actual geographic area of economic interaction" (Campbell and Dollenmayer, 1975, p. 355).

One proposal is to unite city and suburbs under a single metropolitan government (sometimes called metropolitanism). As things stand, metropolitan government is fragmented to the point of chaos. The San Francisco Bay area, for example, has 8 counties, 73 cities, and 201 special districts (such as school districts)—not to mention over 80 planning commissions. This patchwork is a carryover from the early days of statehood when the only way to get things done was to organize locally. Fragmentation was perpetuated because it suited special interests (Hawkins, 1976, p. 210). But the tasks these governments face today (in-

cluding mass transit, pollution control, civil defense, water supply) defy purely local solutions.

Many local governments have adopted metropolitan solutions to some of their problems in an informal way (Zimmerman, 1975). According to a survey of 6,000 municipalities, a significant number have joint service agreements whereby one local government purchases services from the other or they collaborate on projects. In the mid-1960s, the federal government encouraged the formation of Councils of Governments (COGs)—voluntary associations of local officials. COGs have provided a forum for discussion of area-wide problems. They have helped local governments to coordinate their activities to lobby together at the state and federal levels. Because they are voluntary, they are not seen as a threat by local politicians or neighborhood groups. They suffer the same disadvantages the United Nations experiences in attempting to solve world problems, however. COGs depend on cooperation. They have some control over the "carrot" of federal grants, but no stick (no negative sanctions). Cities and towns need not join and need not follow COG recommendations. COGs have not been able to resolve city-suburban conflicts. Many are little more than debating societies.

Attempts to reorganize metropolitan political structures in the United States have rarely succeeded (Campbell and Dollenmayer, 1975, p. 383). No matter how small or large, no matter how financially burdened, few municipalities want to give up "home rule." Almost 1,500 of the municipalities in the survey mentioned above said that they did not even want to enter into service agreements with other jurisdictions. When asked why, nearly half checked "limitations on independence of action" before "inequitable apportionment of cost" and "adverse public reaction" (Zimmerman, 1975, pp. 446–47).

A decade ago, most of the opposition to metropolitan mergers came from the political right (Campbell and Dollenmayer, 1975, pp. 384–85; Hawkins, 1976). Conservatives argued that there was little evidence of bigger government's greater efficiency, effectiveness, or responsiveness. Today, however, much of the opposition comes not from the right but from black Americans. Having gained a majority or near majority in a number of cities, many blacks do not want their political voice muted by merger with predominantly white suburbs. It seems unlikely, then, that either urban or suburban voters will accept metropolitan merger in the near future.

A second metropolitan recommendation for the urban crisis is to open up the suburbs—to increase opportunities for low- and moderate-income households to live there (Downs, 1973). At the present time, inexpensive housing, low-skill jobs, and the kinds of social services on which the poor depend hold low-income people in the city. In addition, zoning laws that deliberately raise the cost of housing to protect "the investments and environments of non-poor suburbanites" keep low-income families out of suburbs (Downs, 1973, p. 39). Zoning laws may set a minimum size for building lots, housing units, and rooms within the unit. They may also establish standards for construction materials and methods. Many suburbs prohibit mobile home developments (one form of low-cost housing) and prohibit or limit apartment construction. These laws (plus high interest rates on mortgages) raise the cost of suburban housing beyond the means of many families.

Opening up the suburbs might solve a number of interrelated problems (Downs, 1973, Chapter 4). First, it would ease the job-worker mismatch by giving low-income workers better access to expanding suburban job opportunities. Second, it would reward people who are now locked inside cities for holding jobs and making small advances up the occupational ladder with nicer homes and neighborhoods, at a moderate price. Third, it would give more children from low-income households the chance to attend better schools with children from middle-class households (definite pluses according to the Coleman Report). Fourth, it would distribute the financial and social costs of dealing with metropolitan poverty more evenly. Finally, it would reduce the possibility of conflict between the "two separate Americas" described in the Report of the Commission on Civil Disorders.

The idea of opening up the suburbs is extremely threatening to most affluent residents, however. They fear declining property values, rising crime rates, and lower-income children "flooding" schools and lowering standards. Anthony Downs argues that these fears cannot be dismissed outright. Violent crime rates *are* higher in the inner city than in the suburbs. In Down's view, the explanation lies in the *concentration* of poverty in the inner city, not in the mere presence of low- and moderate-income families. He argues that the solution is dispersal: opening up the suburbs but keeping the proportion of poor and troubled households in any one area small. "[D]iluting urban poverty by spreading it over a much broader landscape might produce qualitatively different—and much less forbidding—problems than concentrating urban poverty in a few highly deprived areas" (Downs, 1973, p. 41). A few steps have been made in this direction (Rubinowitz, 1977). For example, the 1974 Housing and Community Development Act tied federal funds for such things as street repair or purchasing parks to the development of local plans for low-income housing.

Critics of Downs's position argue that dispersing urban populations would merely perpetuate existing trends (see Smith, 1979, Chapter 6). Some groups might be helped, but the city would continue to decline. Suburban sprawl, with its needless consumption of energy and destruction of natural (unpaved, unpeopled) habitats, would continue. In time, the inner city might be wholly transformed from a place to live to a place to work or to be entertained, and a "dumping ground" for those Downs calls the left-behind poor—people who, for whatever reasons, have given up any hope that they will become full-fledged members of society.

Any plan to restructure metropolitan regions is likely to run into powerful and organized opposition from those who have prospered from suburbanization: suburban homeowners, land developers, mortgage banks, the "auto-highway-rubber-oil-asphalt industrial complex" (Smith, 1979, p. 240). A conflict perspective on urban problems suggests that current social and economic patterns are in large part the result of corporate decisions, combined with the self-interest of land speculators, builders, highway engineers, and construction unions, and are often subsidized by government. People tend to go where the jobs are. A job is the most common reason for moving. And concentrating labor and production in cities, around ports and train depots, is no longer profitable. Profits drew corporations away from the older cities of Northeastern and North Central America to suburbs around those cities and to the South and Southwest. Population followed corporations. "Neither random citizen choice nor public planning has determined the basic pattern of population distribution; rather, employers pursuing criteria of profit, economic efficiency, and internal convenience have set the pattern" (Smith, 1979, p. 239).

Summary

1. The movement of people from central cities to suburbs, from the older cities of the Northeastern and North Central states to the South and West, and from metropolitan regions to the country has created problems for all of these communities.

2. The combination of growing demands and dwindling resources is the core of the problem in the nation's older snowbelt cities.

3. Sociologists disagree on the impact of cities on residents. Determinists maintain that the urban environment encourages both social and personal disorganization.

4. The counterargument says cities have little or no impact on behavior. City dwellers are simply "urban villagers."

5. Subcultural theory holds that cities promote the development of subcultures, with mixed effects.

6. Anonymity, broken or weakened families, overcrowding, and crime are not uniquely urban phenomena.

7. The transportation problems of central cities are largely the unanticipated consequence of government subsidies for automobiles and highways.

8. Urban housing trickles down from the top to the bottom of the socioeconomic ladder in the United States; government support of private homeownership indirectly promoted both economic and racial segregation.

9. The social structure of metropolitan regions has proven to be an obstacle to the national goal of school integration and to the equal education of city and suburban youngsters.

10. Inner-city recommendations for urbanization focus on luring the middle class back to the city, which might have negative consequences for the poor.

11. Metropolitan recommendations, which emphasize breaking down the political barriers between central cities and suburbs, are opposed by those who have an investment in the status quo.

Suggested Reading

Fischer, Claude S., *The Urban Experience*. New York: Harcourt Brace Jovanovich, 1976.

Gans, Herbert J. *The Urban Villagers*. New York: Free Press, 1965.

Hawley, Amos H. and V.P. Rock (Eds.). *Metropolitan America in Contemporary Perspective*. New York: Sage/Wiley, 1975.

Jacobs, Jane. *The Death and Life of Great American Cities*. New York: Random House, 1961.

Lewis, Oscar. "Further Observations on the Folk-Urban Continuum and Urbanization, with Special Reference to Mexico City." In P.M. Hauser and L.F. Schnore (Eds.), *The Study of Urbanization*. New York: Wiley, 1965.

Rosenthal, Donald B. (Ed.). *Urban Revitalization*. Beverly Hills, Cal.: Sage, 1980.

Schwartz, Barry (Ed.). *The Changing Face of the Suburbs*. Chicago, Ill.: University of Chicago Press, 1976.

Wirth, Louis. "Urbanism as a Way of Life." *American Journal of Sociology*, Vol. 44 (July 1938), pp. 3–24.

References

Abravanel, M.D., and P.K. Mancini. "Attitudinal and Demographic Constraints." In D.B. Rosenthal (Ed.), *Urban Revitalization.* Beverly Hills, Cal.: Sage, 1980, pp. 27–47.

Campbell, A.K., and J.A. Dollenmayer. "Governance in a Metropolitan Society." In A.H. Hawley and V.P. Rock (Eds.), *Metropolitan America in Contemporary Perspective.* New York: Sage/Wiley, 1975, pp. 355–96.

Cincin-Sain, B. "The Cost and Benefits of Neighborhood Revitalization." In D.B. Rosenthal (Ed.), *Urban Revitalization.* Beverly Hills, Cal.: Sage, 1980, pp. 49–75.

Coleman, J.S. "Equality of Educational Opportunity." *Integrated Education,* Vol. 6, No. 5 (September-October 1968), pp. 19–28.

Coleman, J.S. "Community Disorganization and Urban Problems." In R.K. Merton and R. Nisbet (Eds.). *Contemporary Social Problems,* 4th ed. New York: Harcourt Brace Jovanovich, 1976, pp. 557–601.

Coleman, J.S. et al. *Equality of Educational Opportunity.* Washington, D.C.: U.S. Dept. of Health, Education, and Welfare, 1966.

Coleman, J.S., S.D. Kelley, and J. Moore. "Trends in School Segregation, 1968–73." Washington, D.C.: Urban Institute Working Paper, 1975.

Dentler, R.A. *Urban Problems.* New York: Rand McNally, 1977.

Downs, A. 1973. *Opening Up the Suburbs.* New Haven: Yale University Press, 1973.

The Figgie Report on Fear of Crime: America Afraid. Part I: The General Public. Willoughby, Ohio: A-T-O, Inc., 1980.

Fischer, C.S. "The Study of Urban Community and Personality." *Annual Review of Sociology,* Vol. 1 (1975), pp. 67–89.

Fischer, C.S. *The Urban Experience.* New York: Harcourt Brace Jovanovich, 1976.

Fischer, C.S. "US Versus THEM: Public and Private World of City Life." Working Paper 319. Berkeley, Cal.: Institute of Urban and Regional Development, May 1980.

Fleetwood, B. "The New Urban Elite and Urban Renaissance." *The New York Times Magazine,* January 14, 1979, pp. 16–20ff.

Freedman, J.L. *Crowding and Behavior.* New York: Freeman, 1975.

Gans, H.J. "Urbanism and Suburbanism as Ways of Life: A Re-evaluation of Definitions." In A.M. Rose (Ed.), *Human Behavior and Social Processes.* Boston: Houghton Mifflin, 1962, pp. 625–48.

Gans, H.J. *The Levittowners.* New York: Vintage, 1967.

Gans, H.J. "Why Exurbanites Won't Reurbanize Themselves." *The New York Times,* February 12, 1977, p. 21.

Glazer, N. "Housing Problems and Housing Policies." *The Public Interest,* No. 7 (Spring 1967), pp. 21–51.

Golden, H.H. *Urbanization and Cities.* Lexington, Mass.: Heath, 1981.

Greer, S. *The Emerging City.* New York: Free Press, 1962.

Hawkins, R.B., Jr. "Regional Versus Local Government: The Lessons for National Planning. In B. Bruce-Briggs et al., *The Politics of Planning.* San Francisco: Institute for Contemporary Studies, 1976, pp. 209–23.

Hawley, A.H., and V.P. Rock (Eds.). *Metropolitan America in Contemporary Perspective.* New York: Sage/Wiley, 1975.

Jacobs, J. *The Death and Life of Great American Cities.* New York: Random House, 1961.

Kasarda, J.D. "Urbanization, Community, and the Metropolitan Problem." In D. Street and Associates (Ed.), *Handbook of Contemporary Urban Life,* Vol. 4. San Francisco: Jossey-Bass, 1978.

Lendler, E. "Crime in the Sunshine." *New Times,* May 2, 1975, pp. 25–28.

Lewis, O. "Further Observations on the Folk-Urban Continuum and Urbanization, with Special Reference to Mexico City." In P.M. Hauser and L.F. Schnore (Eds.), *The Study of Urbanization,* New York: Wiley, 1965, pp. 491–517.

Morris, R.N. *Urban Sociology.* New York: Praeger, 1968.

Mulvihille, D.J., and M.M. Tumin. *Crimes of Violence: A Staff Report to the National Commission on the Causes and Prevention of Violence,* Vol. 12. Washington, D.C.: U.S. Government Printing Office, 1969.

Palen, J.J. *The Urban World,* 2d ed. New York: McGraw-Hill, 1981.

Palley, M.L., and H.A. Palley. *Urban America and Public Policies.* Lexington, Mass.: Heath, 1977.

Park, R.E. "The City: Suggestions for Investigation of Human Behavior in the Urban Environment." 1916; rpt. in R. Sennett (Ed.), *Classic Essays on the Culture of Cities.* New York: Appleton, 1969, pp. 91–103.

Parkinson, M. "Dilemmas for the City Schools: Racial Isolation and Fiscal Stress." In G.A. Tobin (Ed.), *The Changing Structure of the City.* Beverly Hills, Cal.: Sage, 1979, pp. 157–75.

President's Commission for a National Agenda for the Eighties. *Urban America in the Eighties.* Washington, D.C.: U.S. Government Printing Office, 1980.

The President's National Urban Policy Report. Washington, D.C.: U.S. Government Printing Office, 1980.

The President's Office of Emergency Preparedness. *The Potential for Energy Conservation.* Washington, D.C.: U.S. Government Printing Office, 1972.

Ravitch, D. "The 'White Flight' Controversy." *The Public Interest,* No. 51 (Spring 1978a), pp. 135–49.

Ravitch, D. "A Response. . . ." *The Public Interest,* No. 53 (Fall 1978b), pp. 109–15.

Rosenthal, D.B. (Ed.). *Urban Revitalization.* Beverly Hills, Cal.: Sage, 1980.

Rubinowitz, L.S. "The Problem of Metropolitan Housing Choice: Who Gets To Live Where?" In J. Walton and D.E. Carns (Eds.), *Cities in Change: Studies on the Urban Condition,* 2d ed. Boston: Allyn and Bacon, 1977.

Scherer, K.R., R.P. Abeles, and C.S. Fischer. *Human Aggression and Conflict.* Englewood Cliffs, N.J.: Prentice-Hall, 1975.

Schlesinger, A.M. "The City in American History." *Mississippi Valley Historical Review,* Vol. 27 (June 1940), pp. 43–66.

Schwirian, K.P. (Ed.). *Contemporary Topics in Urban Sociology.* Morristown, N.J.: General Learning Press, 1977.

Smith, M.P. *The City and Social Theory.* New York: St. Martin's Press, 1979.

Solomon, A.P. *Housing the Urban Poor.* Cambridge, Mass.: MIT Press, 1974.

Srole, L. et al. *Mental Health in the Metropolis.* New York: McGraw-Hill, 1975.

Tönnies, F. *Community and Society.* C.P. Loomis (Ed. and trans.). East Lansing, Mich.: Michigan State University Press, 1957.

U.S. Bureau of the Census. *Historical Statistics of the U.S., Colonial Times to 1957.* Washington, D.C.: U.S. Government Printing Office, 1960.

U.S. Bureau of the Census. *Statistical Abstracts of the U.S.: 1971,* 92d ed. Washington, D.C.:
  U.S. Government Printing Office, 1971.
Wirth, L. "Urbanism as a Way of Life." *American Journal of Sociology,* Vol. 44 (July 1938),
  pp. 3–24.
Zimmerman, J.F. "The Patchwork Approach: Adaptive Responses to Increasing Urbanism."
  In A.H. Hawley and V.P. Roch (Eds.), *Metropolitan America in Contemporary
  Perspective.* New York: Sage/Wiley, 1975, pp. 431–73.
Zito, J.M. "Anonymity and Neighboring in an Urban, High-Rise Complex." *Urban Life and
  Culture,* Vol. 3, No. 3 (October 1974), pp. 243–63.

Chapter Seven

The Workplace

The Changing Workplace

The Global Factory

The Post-Industrial Economy

  The Change from Goods to Services
  Post-Industrial Work: An Assessment

Two Labor Markets

Work and Its Discontents

The Changing Work Ethic

Alienation and Job Satisfaction

  Blue-Collar Blues and White-Collar Woes
  The Manager's Plight
  The Happy Worker

Unemployment

  The International Labor Market
  Migration of Industry and Automation of
    Production
  Discrimination
  The Changing Job Market

**Danger, Disability, and Death on the
  Job**

Accidents at Work

Unhealthy Workplaces

Job Satisfaction and Mental Health

Reforming the Workplace

*The "Work Is Inherently Unpleasant"
  Assumption*

The "Work Is Beneficial" Assumption

Employers complain about undependable workers. Workers complain about boring jobs. Executives suffer from ulcers and heart disease. Consumers suffer from badly made and unsafe products. Everyone laments that no one seems to care about doing a good job any more. These complaints are signs of serious problems in the workplace.

Other signs appear in the daily newspapers. The automobile industry, long the symbol of American ingenuity and enterprise, reported record financial losses in 1980 and declining sales in the world market. During the 1970s, unemployment hovered between 7 and 8 percent; in human terms, at least 7 million people couldn't find a job. Millions more were statistically rated as underemployed, working at a job for which they were overqualified.

In Western societies, work is the single most important activity of most people's lives. Not only does working take most of our time and energy, but the kind of work we do affects how we live and how we feel about ourselves. Serious social problems arise when there is not enough work to go around or when the only available jobs are boring, dangerous, or so menial that they offer few opportunities for advancement.

Many of the social problems discussed in this book can be traced back to the workplace. Unsafe working conditions mean that more tax money has to be set aside to compensate workers for job-related injuries and illness. When people are bored by their jobs, American industry must pay the cost of low productivity and shoddy workmanship. Problems in the workplace also spill over into other areas of social life. People who are frustrated by monotonous, dead-end work have higher than average rates of alcoholism, drug abuse, and mental illness. In sum, nearly every social problem of modern industrial societies is connected in some way to the ordinary, everyday business of making a living.

This chapter begins with a discussion of the transformation of the workplace in the twentieth century, taking into account the place of the United States in the world economy, the changing nature of work, and the demand for new kinds of workers. Then we will look at how people feel about their jobs and analyze the chronic U.S. unemployment problem. Next we will discuss the hazards of the workplace and the way people adapt to dangerous occupations. The chapter ends with some recent suggestions for making work in America more satisfying and productive.

The Changing Workplace

In just the past twenty-five years, the worldwide spread of industrial development has transformed the location and the nature of work. Today, a new division of labor is taking place across the globe: More and more of the world's goods are being produced in the developing nations of the Third World, and fewer are being manufactured in the highly industrialized countries of Western Europe, Japan, and the United States. Instead of goods, these fully developed economies are providing services—managerial, financial, and technical—to the rest of the world. The result is what Richard J. Barnet has called a "global factory," with its brain in the banks and corporate headquarters of London, New York, and Tokyo, and its hands in the plants and factories of the poor countries of Asia, Africa, and Latin America. In the following section, we will examine some of the implications of this arrangement (1980, pp. 239–58).

The Global Factory

The problems of the American workplace are closely intertwined with these developments in the world economy. Since manufacturing operations can be set up in any part of the world, the global factory is able to choose locations that offer the most attractive tax incentives and the cheapest and most productive workers. Textile workers in New York and South Carolina must therefore compete for jobs with workers in Hong Kong and Manila. Since the market for goods is worldwide, American corporations are competing for business with their European and Japanese counterparts in nearly every major industry.

The United States no longer has a competitive edge in the global market for goods and labor. In 1959, an American company was the largest producer in eleven out of thirteen of the world's basic industries — aerospace, automobiles, chemicals, electronics, food, machinery, iron and steel, metal products, paper, oil, drugs, textiles, and banking. In 1976, only seven of these industries were dominated by American companies. In six of the industries, the number of European and Japanese firms in the top twelve equaled or exceeded the number of American firms.

The extraordinary recovery of Western European and Japanese industry after World War II is partly responsible for their larger share of the world market. The phenomenal growth of Japanese steel provides one historical example. Japan's steel industry, demolished in the war, was rebuilt with plants and equipment more modern and energy-efficient than U.S. prewar technology. As latecomers to industrial development, the Japanese did not have to spend time and money on research; they could copy or license the latest technology from other countries. During the 1960s and early 1970s, their low wage rates and an overvalued dollar gave Japanese goods a price advantage over American products in the world market. In 1947, American companies produced 60 percent of the world's steel; by 1975, they produced only 16 percent. Even the United States was importing large quantities of Japanese steel, as well as TV sets, radios, and automobiles.

The market for goods has also undergone a dramatic shift in the world economy of the 1980s. A good example of this trend is the automobile business. In the United States, the domestic market has nearly reached its saturation point, and it is not expected to grow much in the next decade. The markets for automobiles in Asia and Latin America, however, are expected to double, and the African market to triple, by 1990. Thirteen European companies, the Japanese, and the Americans are battling for these markets with various forms of a small, energy-efficient "world car." To protect themselves from competition and achieve economies of scale, the companies have resorted to mergers and joint ventures: Peugeot and Citroen joined forces, then took over Chrysler's operations in Europe; Ford buys parts from Fiat; and Mitsubishi makes the engines for Chrysler's K cars. The fiercer the competition, the more consolidated the industry, and the more likely the giants will drive their weaker competitors out of business.

In this highly competitive situation, corporations cut production costs by relocating their plants and factories in the low-wage areas of the world. When it becomes less profitable to make a certain product in one place, then manufacturers move to another: from the high-wage labor markets of the United States to Mexico (where the average *daily* wage is $5), South Korea (where two out of five textile workers earn less than $62 a month), or the Philippines (where assembly-line workers receive $1.50 a day). In an age of jet air-cargo carriers and worldwide communications, highly specialized operations can be performed in different parts of the globe, not just different sections of the same factory. Leather covers, yarn, and glue are routinely shipped to Haiti, for example, where local women, working for a few cents an hour, assemble them into baseballs for the all-American sport. The result is chronic unemployment among unskilled American workers in the older industrial cities that economic and technological change have left behind.

The Post-Industrial Economy

During the first century of its existence, the United States was a society of farmers, trappers, and fishermen. In this pre-industrial economy, most people made their livings by extracting goods from the land, primarily through agriculture. For the rest of the world, America was a principal source of cotton, wheat, and other raw materials. With the rise of industrialization, however, Americans began to leave the farm for the factory. By the end of the nineteenth century, more workers were engaged in manufacturing and its related services (banking and transportation, for example) than in agriculture. The United States had become an industrial society, producing more fabricated goods, such as clothing, steel, and locomotives, than raw materials. During the first half of the twentieth century, a huge demand for American products—from automobiles and refrigerators to nylon stockings and cigarettes—spread the conveniences of machine technology throughout the world. In the 1950s, the American economy began to turn another corner. A growing proportion of the labor force was employed in clerical and other service occupations. In 1979, for the first time more than 50 percent of the employed labor force were white-collar workers. Less than 3 percent were farm workers, down from 8 percent in 1960 (U.S. Bureau of the Census, 1980). On the world market, the United States had become an importer of goods and an exporter of professional services and technical expertise to the developing nations of the globe. As we shall see, the emergence of a *post-industrial,* or service-oriented, society has

had enormous consequences for the experience and meaning of work.

The change from goods to services The rise of a service economy brought not only a new kind of economy but new kinds of services as well. In pre-industrial societies, services are largely domestic: Most "service workers" are household servants. In industrial societies, new services develop to meet the demand of manufacturing concerns for such aids as secretarial help, telephones, and advertising. The post-industrial society, however, demands "human services"—health care, education, government—and professional and technical services—scientific research, computer systems, corporate planning. The result is a decline in blue-collar factory and manual work and an expansion of white-collar jobs that require education and managerial skills. In the mid-1970s, professional, technical, and managerial occupations made up 26 percent of the American labor force, clerical workers 18 percent, semiskilled workers 17 percent, and skilled workers only 13 percent. Since 1970, clerical jobs have been the largest single occupational category, and their number is expected to grow to nearly 20 million by 1985 (Ritzer, 1977, pp. 14, 17).

As the site of the workplace changed from farm to factory to office, the character of work was transformed. As the sociologist Daniel Bell puts it, work in the pre-industrial world is "a game against nature" (1976, p. 126). Using sheer muscle power, in most cases, the worker must contend with uncertain elements like weather and soil conditions. Most of the people in the world still work this way.

In the goods-producing societies of the industrial world, work is a game against things. The worker is up against the methodical and predictable forces of the machine. The spontaneous efforts of the farmer and fisherman are replaced by eight-hour shifts and time clocks, and the natural

Table 7–1
The Shift from Working with Things to Working with People

Occupational Group	Percentage of the Labor Force				
	1900	1930	1960	1970	1974
White-collar	17.6%	29.4%	40.8%	45.6%	47.9%
Service	9.1	9.8	11.6	11.8	13.4
Manual	35.8	39.6	36.4	33.4	35.4
Farm	37.5	21.2	6.2	2.9	3.4
Not reported	–	–	5.0	6.3	–
Total	100.0	100.0	100.0	100.0	100.1

Source: G. Ritzer, *Working: Conflict and Change,* 2d ed. (Englewood Cliffs, N.J.: Prentice-Hall, 1977), p. 14.

pace of work is made routine, systematic, mechanical. These working conditions are typical of the mills and factories of industrial nations like the Soviet Union and Japan.

Work in the post-industrial society is largely "a game between persons." The manager's office, the classroom, and the laboratory are social worlds from which both natural forces and fabricating machinery are excluded. The product of work is not goods, but information, recreation, or assistance. The typical worker is a professional with specialized knowledge whose job involves intangible and uncertain relationships with other people. The setting for post-industrial work is often a large bureaucracy.

Post-industrial work: An assessment In his influential work, *The Coming of Post-Industrial Society* (1973), Daniel Bell predicted that the shift from producing goods to producing services signaled the decline of industrial society. He argued that there are three features of the industrial workplace: The corporation is the predominant form of organization; machine technology con-

trols the work process; and social relations are based on class conflict between labor and capital. All three features are markedly changed in the post-industrial society.

Industrial economies are typically dominated by highly concentrated industries controlled by a few giant corporations. Multinational enterprises like General Motors, Nestlé, and Phillips Petroleum have billions of dollars in assets and hundreds of thousands of employees. The distinctive feature of the service sector of the economy, in contrast, is the small size of each company. Although huge corporations do exist in utilities (American Telephone & Telegraph), banking (Bank of America), insurance (Metropolitan Life), and retail trade (Sears, Roebuck), most service firms employ under 1,000 people. There are fewer economies of scale in service businesses, and therefore fewer incentives to enlarge the operations of a hospital, a barber shop, or a real estate agency.

Bell acknowledges that the rhythms of the machine are still prevalent in the post-industrial economy of the United States. Much office work,

Mechanized canning procedures existed at the turn of the century when this photograph was taken, but it was cheaper to put women and children to work trimming green beans under the close supervision of "the boss." Child labor laws, unions, and the minimum wage have changed the economics of green beans.

for example, is as routine and dronelike as assembly-line production: filing and keypunching are also repetitious, mechanical tasks. What is new, he says, is the element of encounter or communication in service occupations:

> From the irritation of a customer at an airline-ticket office to the sympathetic or harassed response of teacher to student . . . . the fact that individuals now talk to other individuals, rather than interact with a machine, is the fundamental fact about work in the post-industrial society. (Bell, 1976, p. 163)

Finally, Bell finds that the antagonism between worker and boss, which was the central conflict of industrial societies for over 100 years, no longer dominates social relations. In many cases, competition for jobs has divided the work-

ing class along racial and ethnic lines. Furthermore, labor-management conflict has been institutionalized so that wages and working conditions are issues for negotiation between more or less equal parties. Bell concludes that the "old" industrial problems—the impersonality of the huge corporate bureaucracy, the dehumanizing effects of machine technology, and the struggle between capital and labor—have all been relieved in the post-industrial setting.

Bell's view has been opposed by Harry Braverman, who denies that the service economy is eliminating disagreeable and degrading jobs. In *Labor and Monopoly Capital* (1974), Braverman argues that control of the work process is crucial to profit making in service industries as well as manufacturing. The faster filing clerks file or textile workers sew, the more productive and profitable they are. The necessity of controlling how efficiently work is done leads to a greater division of labor, more automation, and ever more complex hierarchies of supervision. The shift to the service economy, or what Braverman calls "nonproduction," has created a small proportion of technical jobs, most of them oriented to management, and a larger proportion of routine or unskilled clerical jobs. Computers and other technical machinery have downgraded service work so that it is just as repetitious and mindless as old-fashioned manual labor. Like blue-collar factory workers, white-collar typists and keypunchers are paid, not to think, but to operate machines with all possible speed and dexterity. "For this reason," he writes:

> [T]he traditional distinctions between "manual" and "white-collar" labor, which are so thoughtlessly and widely used in the literature on this subject, represent echoes of a past situation which has virtually ceased to have meaning in the modern world of work. (1974, pp. 325–26)

From the capitalist employer's viewpoint, Braverman notes, *all* forms of labor are treated the same way on the balance sheet. The clerk, no less than the textile worker, can be exploited to achieve the highest profit at the lowest cost. Both manual craftsmen and white-collar secretaries have had their skills downgraded by technological change and the demands of efficiency. Where Bell saw less class conflict and better working conditions in the service economy, Braverman sees more of the same old problems that plagued the industrial workplace.

How much has work really changed in the post-industrial society? The physical setting of the workplace is obviously better on the whole, and workers have more legal rights and union protection. Compared with the horrifying conditions in the coal mines and steel mills of the early industrial era, modern offices and factories are indisputably safer and more comfortable places to work.

And on the whole, as Bell suggests, the trend toward working with people instead of things has probably made work more satisfying and enjoyable.

In other respects, however, white-collar service workers are no better off than blue-collar industrial workers. As Braverman argues, the post-industrial economy has not changed the exploitation of labor for profit, and many office workers have jobs that are just as dull and demeaning as factory work. Finally, the shift to a service economy has not improved the employee's traditionally weak bargaining position.

Two Labor Markets

During the 1970s, employment in the United States expanded at an astonishing rate. Between 1973 and 1979, nearly 13 million new nonagricultural jobs were created, a figure the size of Canada's entire labor force (U.S. Department of Labor, 1980). These new jobs, however, were not spread out evenly over the working population. More than 70 percent were concentrated in services and retail trade, especially eating and drinking places, health services, and such business services as data processing, personnel, and janitorial help. In 1979, services and retail trade alone accounted for 43 percent of all Americans employed in private, nonagricultural occupations. Most of these millions of service jobs are part of the post-industrial economy's growing "secondary labor market."

In economic terms, the U.S. labor market—the kinds and numbers of jobs the economy offers—is divided into two sectors. In the primary market, jobs pay well, working conditions are good, employment is generally stable, and the opportunities for promotion are rather equally distributed. These jobs are found in large corporations, where profits are high and demand for the company's products is stable. Since employers in this sector are assured of a steady business, they are willing to pay good wages to reliable workers. Primary market jobs are also found in unionized industries, such as automobiles and steel; in skilled trades, such as plumbing and printing; in technical occupations like engineering; in government agencies; and in the professions. To enter the primary labor market, workers must have educational credentials or technical qualifications.

The secondary labor market, in contrast, offers badly paid or temporary jobs, poor working conditions, and little job security or opportunity for promotion. These jobs are typical of nonunion manufacturing companies, personal service occupations (waitresses, parking lot attendants), low-level clerical work (cashiers, sales personnel), and seasonal migrant farm labor. These jobs demand few skills and no formal qualifications.

As the dual labor market becomes more pronounced in the post-industrial economy, individual opportunities become more restricted. In spite of the chronic shortage of qualified personnel in many occupations, movement from the secondary to the primary market is rare. Low-level clerical and secretarial jobs hardly ever lead to supervisory or managerial positions. In assembly-line plants, there are few skilled jobs open to unskilled workers, and no normal ladders of promotion. Employees are usually hired to do a particular job and expected to stay in it (Kanter, 1977, p. 140–41).

In a society that values the American dream of success, and where unlimited opportunities are supposed to be open to all, economic change has trapped millions of hardworking men and women in menial, dead-end jobs that provide very low wages, no security, and little hope of improvement. Rather than blaming the economy for failing to produce better jobs, most of these workers believe their troubles come from their own personal failings or bad luck. If Americans are unable to achieve the American dream, they tend to "blame the victim"—themselves.

Work and Its Discontents

The modern view that work should be satisfying and self-fulfilling is rather new. For most of the world's history, endless and backbreaking work was the only means of sustaining life. Early Judeo-Christian tradition held work to be "Adam's curse" and no one expected it to be interesting.

After the Protestant Reformation, hard work began to be considered a virtue. Calvinist reformers saw worldly success as a sign of divine favor and regarded idleness and extravagance as sinful. Working became associated with serving God. According to the sociologist Max Weber, this Protestant ethic was the "spirit of capitalism"; its emphasis on hard work and the accumulation of wealth laid the necessary moral foundation for modern economic development. The Industrial Revolution, which transformed the nature of work, thus changed its meaning and purpose as well. Today there are signs that the work ethic is changing again.

The Changing Work Ethic

The American view of work has always been greatly influenced by the Protestant ethic. The Calvinist values of thrift and self-discipline have been part of the American culture since colonial times. Parents today still teach their children Benjamin Franklin's precepts: "A penny saved is a penny earned," "Time is money," "Never leave to tomorrow what you can do today." Americans believe that everyone (or at least every man) should work for a living, and they tend to admire "self-made men" and to disapprove of "bums" and "good-for-nothings." Many people are so uncomfortable doing nothing that they use their time away from work for purposeful activity—running for exercise, do-it-yourself projects, sports, and hobbies.

According to pollster Daniel Yankelovich (1974), the American work ethic is based on four cultural values:

1. Americans tend to equate masculinity with being a good provider. Men are the traditional breadwinners, and a "real man" is one who can take care of his family.
2. Americans believe in "standing on one's own two feet." A paying job is the way to freedom and independence; having to depend financially on others makes most adults uncomfortable.
3. Americans admire material success: a prestigious job, a large income, expensive possessions, the achievements of one's children.
4. Americans believe in "doing a good job." Work is a source of self-respect. People who work hard and do their jobs well have greater self-esteem than those who do not or cannot work.

On the basis of the same opinion survey, however, Yankelovich found that these traditional attitudes toward work changed in the 1970s. New definitions of success began to emerge—particularly among young, well-educated, and "liberated" Americans—as work became more important for its personal than for its material rewards. Fewer people appeared willing to do any job, no matter how dull and menial, and more people wanted their work to be fulfilling, creative, and challenging. Yankelovich (1981) predicts that the 1980s will witness something of a retreat from this ideal as people try to maintain their standard of living in the face of more austere economic conditions.

Other studies show that the necessity of making a living is only one reason people work (Slocum, 1966; U.S. Dept. of Health, Education, and Welfare, 1973; Kaplan, 1978). A job is the basis for social relationships among employees with common interests and goals. Work is also a source of identity. When people are asked who they are, they usually answer with what they do—"I'm an accountant," "I'm a teacher," "I'm a cop." Work gives daily life purpose, meaning, and content. "A job tells the worker day in and day out that he [or she] has something to offer. Not to have a job is not to have something that is valued by one's fellow human beings" (U.S. Dept. of Health, Education, and Welfare, 1973, p. 14). Discontent with work comes from the frustration experienced by people who do not feel that their jobs are challenging or useful.

Alienation and Job Satisfaction

One measure of job satisfaction is the answer to the question: "Would you choose the same type of work if you could start all over again?" Among the white-collar workers polled in this way, only 43 percent said they would choose the same job (although professionals expressed a high degree of satisfaction). Even fewer (24 percent) blue-collar workers wanted to get into the same type of work again (see Table 7–2). Other surveys have shown that even generally satisfied workers are unhappy about certain aspects of their jobs— especially the monotony, the constant supervision, and the few chances for promotion. *Work in America,* a special task force report to the Secretary of Health, Education, and Welfare, concluded that

> Significant numbers of American workers are dissatisfied with the quality of their working lives. Dull, repetitive, seemingly meaningless tasks, offering little challenge or autonomy, are causing discontent among workers at all occupational levels. . . . Many . . . feel locked-in, their mobility blocked, the opportunity to grow lacking in their jobs, challenge missing from their tasks. (U.S. Dept. of Health, Education, and Welfare, 1973, p. 16)

In Search of a Calling

She is twenty-eight. She is a staff writer for an institution publishing health care literature. Previously she had worked as an editor for a corporation publishing national magazines.

Jobs are not big enough for people. It's not just the assembly line worker whose job is too small for his spirit, you know? A job like mine, if you really put your spirit into it, you would sabotage immediately. You don't dare. So you absent your spirit from it. My mind has been so divorced from my job, except as a source of income, it's really absurd. . . .

. . . When I first went there, I came in early and stayed late. I read everything I could on the subject at hand. I would work a project to the wall and get it really done right, and then ask for more. I found out I was wrecking the curve, I was out of line.

The people, just as capable as I and just as ready to produce, had realized it was pointless, and had cut back. Everyone, consciously or unconsciously, was rationing his time. Playing cards at lunch time for three hours, going sun bathing, or less obvious ways of blowing it. I realized: Okay, the road to ruin is doing a good job. The amazing, absurd thing was that once I decided to stop doing a good job, people recognized a kind of authority in me. Now I'm moving ahead like blazes.

I have my own office. I have a secretary. If I want a book case, I get a book case. If I want a file, I get a file. If I want to stay home, I stay home. If I want to go shopping, I go shopping. This is the first comfortable job I've ever had in my life and it is absolutely despicable.

I've been a waitress and done secretarial work. I knew, in those cases, I wasn't going to work at near capacity. It's one thing to work to your limits as a waitress because you end up with a bad back. It's another thing to work to your limits doing writing and editing because you end up with a sharper mind. It's a joy. Here, of all places, where I had expected to put the energy

The sources of this widespread dissatisfaction lie in the modern work setting. The structure of most offices and factories is geared not to the worker but to the demands of efficiency and modern technology. Highly specialized and impersonally controlled jobs lead to *alienation:* the feeling of separation from one's work and from one's own group or the larger society. Karl Marx used the term to refer to the situation of factory workers under capitalism. "The alienated character of work for the worker," he wrote in 1844, "is shown by the fact that the work he does is not his and enthusiasm and the gifts that I may have to work—it isn't happening. They expect less than you can offer. Token labor. What writing you do is writing to order. When I go for a job interview—I must leave this place!—I say, "Sure, I can bring you samples, but the ones I'm proud of are the ones the Institution never published."

It's so demeaning to be there and not be challenged. It's humiliation, because I feel I'm being forced into doing something I would never do of my own free will—which is simply waste itself. It's really not a Puritan hang-up. It's not that I want to be persecuted. It's simply that I know I'm vegetating and being paid to do exactly that. It's possible for me to sit here and read my books. But then you walk out with no sense of satisfaction, with no sense of legitimacy! I'm being had. . . .

. . . The level of bitterness in this department is stunning. They take days off quite a bit. They don't show up. They don't even call in. They've adjusted a lot better than I have. They see the Institution as a free ride as long as it lasts. I don't want to be party to it, so I've gone my own way. It's like being on welfare. Not that that's a shameful thing. It's the surprise of this enforced idleness. It makes you feel not at home with yourself. I'm furious. It's a feeling that I will not be humiliated. I will not be dis-used.

I'm coming to a less moralistic attitude toward work. I know very few people who feel secure with their right just to be—or comfortable. Just you being you and me being me with my mini-talents may be enough. Maybe just making a career of being and finding out what that's about is enough. I don't think I have a calling—at this moment—except to be me. But nobody pays you for being you, so I'm at the Institution—for the moment.

Source: Nora Watson, "In Search of a Calling," in Studs Terkel, *Working* (New York: Avon, 1975), pp. 675–79.

own, but another's, and that at work he belongs not to himself, but to another" (in Pavalko, 1971, p. 182). Today, Marx's statement applies not only to blue-collar factory workers but also to many white-collar workers in offices and service businesses. Both report feelings of powerlessness, meaninglessness, isolation, and detachment from their work (Blauner, 1964, Chapter 2).

Blue-collar blues and white-collar woes Workers in modern societies rarely have a chance to decide how they will work. They usu-

Table 7-2
Percentages in Occupational Groups Who Would Choose Similar Work Again

Professional and Lower White-Collar Occupations	%	Working-Class Occupations	%
Urban university professors	93	Skilled printers	52
Mathematicians	91	Paper workers	42
Physicists	89	Skilled autoworkers	41
Biologists	89	Skilled steelworkers	41
Chemists	86	Textile workers	31
Firm lawyers	85	*Blue-collar workers, cross section*	*24*
Lawyers	83	Unskilled steelworkers	21
Journalists (Washington correspondents)	82	Unskilled autoworkers	16
Church university professors	77		
Solo lawyers	75		
White-collar workers, cross section	*43*		

Source: U.S. Department of Health, Education, and Welfare, *Work in America: Report of a Special Task Force to the Secretary of HEW* (Cambridge, Mass.: MIT Press, 1973), p. 16.

ally do not share the responsibility for completing a task, and they may not even know the importance or meaning of their work. In a typical factory or office, jobs are so highly specialized that each person performs only a single operation on a continuous flow of parts or papers. The extreme example of mechanical, repetitious work is the moving assembly line. At General Motors's Lordstown, Ohio, plant, for example, 101 cars an hour pass by. The worker has exactly thirty-six seconds to complete just one task, turn around, and be ready to do it again on the next car. Business machines have brought the assembly line's impersonal control into the office. As word processing systems replace secretaries, letters are dictated to a tape recorder and delivered to a typing pool. Each typist receives a steady flow of work and must complete a specified number of lines a day. Instead of a highly skilled secretary with varied responsibilities and routines, there is a semiskilled, low-paid typist whose working pace and output are impersonally controlled. This condition of being treated as a mechanical device—as just a tool to be used for someone else's purposes—is the essence of alienation.

When the worker's self is not in his or her work, it is somewhere else. The stevedore in the television commercial thinks about the beer he will drink at "Miller time," and the steelworker fantasizes about "February in Miami" (Terkel, 1975,

p. 6). Sociological research has uncovered similar means of escape. In Eli Chinoy's classic study, *Automobile Workers and the American Dream* (1955), assembly-line workers daydreamed about leaving the plant to start their own businesses, but most never took any realistic steps to do so. They considered their present jobs only a means of buying leisure activities, or a new car, or a color TV set.

In *Men and Women of the Corporation* (1977), Rosabeth Kanter reported that people who are trapped in low-level, dead-end jobs look for satisfaction outside of working hours. When they cannot get organizational recognition through raises and promotions, they substitute other forms of social recognition. Men and women who have little hope of advancement, for example, seem to find their greatest satisfactions at work in their friendships with their fellow workers.

The bureaucratic emphasis on specialization and rational control is sometimes self-defeating. People who lack commitment to their work are not likely to take pride in the quality of the product they are making or the service they are providing. A young clerical worker in an insurance company explains why she refused to take any responsibility to correct an error she found:

> The other day I was proofreading an endorsement and I noticed some guy had insured his store for $165,000 against vandalism and $5,000 against fire. Now that's bound to be a mistake. They probably got it backwards.
>
> I was just about to show it to Gloria [the supervisor] when I figured, Wait a minute! I'm not sup-

Would this woman choose the same job if she could start all over again? Does she daydream of starting a new career? Would a breakdown of the equipment (through accident or sabotage) enliven her day?

posed to read these forms. I'm just supposed to check one column against another. And they do check. So it couldn't be counted as my error.

Then I thought about this poor guy when his store burns down and they tell him he's only covered for $5,000. But I figured, the hell with it. . . . They don't explain this stuff to me. I'm not supposed to understand it. . . . If they're gonna give me a robot's job to do, I'm gonna do it like a robot! (Garson, 1973, p. 11)

People who are treated like robots are also unlikely to identify their interests with the goals of the organization for which they work. On the contrary, they sometimes assert their own dignity and individuality by rebelling against the organization. Slowdowns, sabotage, and absenteeism are well-known responses to alienating working conditions. Ironically, the organization of work for maximum efficiency has often had the opposite effect.

The manager's plight Job satisfaction is generally higher in white-collar occupations, perhaps because working with people is more rewarding than working with machines. Nevertheless, managerial jobs have their own discontents. Many supervisors are "people in the middle." They must represent the organization and carry out its policies, yet they have no authority to make or change those policies. Middle-level administrators are more constrained in their behavior than manual workers; since they lack technical skills, their main contribution to the firm is their personal loyalty and cooperation. Even when an executive disagrees with company policy, "whistle blowing"—the public exposure of foolhardy, dangerous, or even criminal behavior—is extremely rare (Nader et al., 1972).

Job dissatisfaction also comes from the conflicts inherent in being caught between lower-level employees and top management. Middle-level managers are required to enforce unpopular rules, but they need the cooperation of the people below them to succeed. They must constantly coordinate their activities with other managers, but they must also compete with them for the rewards and support that top management can give. Mutual hostility and jealousy are common, but in order to survive managers must maintain an outward appearance of friendliness and courtesy. No wonder executives in their forties so often feel exhausted, uncreative, "burnt out."

The happy worker Not everyone is miserable at work. Surveys of job satisfaction report that professionals and higher-level executives are the happiest workers—for good reasons. Doctors, scientists, and top managers are likely to be deeply committed to their work. They also have the best-paid, most-respected, and most independent of all jobs. Moreover, higher-level professionals are among the hardest workers. One study found that the great majority of lawyers and professors work more than forty-five hours a week. "Workaholics" who work constantly, enjoying nothing else so much as their jobs, are not uncommon at upper occupational levels (Wilensky, 1963; Whyte, 1967).

A substantial proportion of blue-collar workers also say they like their jobs, but for different reasons. When intrinsic rewards are not available, job satisfaction appears to depend on such extrinsic factors as pay, working conditions, and companionship at work. When low-level workers say they are happy with their jobs, their response seems to reflect the fact that they don't expect to get a better one, not that they wouldn't want more interesting work (Gruenberg, 1980).

Unemployment

For many Americans, the most serious problem of the workplace is not how they feel about their jobs but whether they can get one at all. During the recessions of the 1970s, about 8 percent of the labor force—or 8 million people—could not find a job. Even during more prosperous times, national unemployment hovers around 6 percent, and in some areas, the rate is much higher.

Grim as these figures are, the official definition of unemployment hides millions of other citizens who are actually out of work. To be classified as "unemployed" by the Bureau of Labor Statistics, a person must not have worked at all during the week before the survey and must also have tried to get a job during the previous four weeks. The government's figures thus leave out those "discouraged workers" who have given up looking for work. A black teen-ager in a city where over half the black youths can't find work, for example, is no longer considered unemployed when he or she gives up hope and stops looking for a job. Perhaps a million unemployed people are left uncounted in this way, most of them in groups where recorded unemployment is already high: teenagers, older workers and minorities.

The official statistics also ignore underemployment. An unemployed person who works a few hours at a part-time job during the period of the survey is counted as "employed." So are seasonal and migrant workers, even if they are not currently working. Also excluded are millions of potential workers—housewives, students, elderly, and disabled people—who would like to have a job if they could get one that fit their special circumstances. If this disguised unemployment were taken into account, an estimated 4 million people would be added to the officially jobless (Ad Hoc Committee, 1964, p. 4).

Since work is so highly valued in American society, losing a job or failing to find one has a devastating effect. Most people want to work and feel useless and inadequate when there is no work available. Men who cannot support their families feel especially worthless, but women also find their independence and self-esteem threatened by the loss of a paycheck. Every day about 10 million Americans are up against this frustrating, emotionally unhealthy situation.

The reasons for the continuously high rate of unemployment in the U.S. are complex. Some have to do with international developments, some with purely domestic ones.

The international labor market Since the United States is part of the global labor market, the American economy is feeling the effects of a world employment crisis. Every year between now and the end of the century, 36 million people will enter the labor force, most of them in the Third World. Although the market for goods is also growing in developing countries, it is not growing fast enough to support an equivalent number of jobs (Barnet, 1980, p. 258). Furthermore, since modern agricultural and industrial methods make every pair of hands more productive, the process of industrialization has already produced a huge labor surplus in Third World countries. Millions of these surplus laborers become immigrants—legal and illegal—to the United States.

Migration of industry and automation of production As competition increases on a worldwide scale, corporations are forced to cut costs by moving to cheap labor markets: from the industrial cities of the Northeast and Midwest to the sunbelt of the South and West, and, increasingly, to the low-wage areas of the globe.

The alternative to the global factory is to stay home and automate production. Some experts believe that increasingly sophisticated mechanical devices, such as the latest computer-controlled, or "smart" robots, could replace three-quarters of today's factory work force. General Electric has already begun a major automation program to replace half of its 37,000 assembly-line workers with robots (*Business Week,* June 9, 1980, p. 62). Many service jobs are also threatened by new data processing technologies. In about ten years, a German electronics firm estimates that 40 percent of all office work now done by human beings will be done by machines. A

French government report states that microprocessors could eliminate 30 percent of the jobs in banking and insurance (Barnet, 1980, p. 279).

Large multinational corporations usually cut production costs both ways. A combination of automation and the migration of industry has boosted unemployment, particularly in the older industrial cities of the Northeast and Midwest. Ironically, at the same time there are critical shortages of skilled workers in regions that attract new industry. When Litton opened a new microwave oven factory in Sioux Falls, South Dakota, for instance, the company had 10,000 applicants for 600 assembly-line jobs but could not find enough candidates in the local community for technical and managerial positions. The United States appears to be trapped between a growing shortage in one labor market and a growing surplus in the other (Barnet, 1980, pp. 277–78).

Discrimination Unemployment is not spread out evenly over the whole work force but is concentrated in certain groups. Unskilled workers, as we have seen, have been the principal victims of economic change, while technicians and professionals have been the principal beneficiaries. The hiring and firing of workers is also influenced by discrimination on the basis of race, gender, and age.

Members of racial and ethnic minorities are the first casualties of the workplace. Out of every three minority workers, one is an unemployed, irregularly employed, or "discouraged" job seeker. In 1979, when the national unemployment rate was 5.8 percent, only 4 percent of white male workers were jobless, compared to 7.8 percent of black men and 10.6 percent of black women (*The New York Times,* February 3, 1979, p. 1). A second one of the three minority workers has a full-time job, but it is a poorly paid manual or service

A clerical worker waits to file an unemployment claim at an office in Michigan, where the unemployment rate was twice the national average in 1980. What kind of future will her daughter see for herself?

job (Hiestand, 1972). As a result, members of minority groups earn much less than other workers. In 1978, the median income for white men was $11,453, compared to $8,541 for black men; white women had a median income of only $4,117, but minority women fared even worse: Their median income was $3,707 (U.S. Bureau of the Census, 1980, p. 462). In spite of the passage of federal laws requiring equal opportunity in employment, the disparity between black and white workers' earnings has hardly changed at all over the last decade.

The burden of unemployment also falls more heavily on women. In the recession year of 1975, the rate of joblessness for all female workers was 9.3 percent, compared to 7.9 percent for males; in more prosperous 1978, it was still 7.1 percent for women and 5.5 percent for men (U.S. Bureau of the Census, 1978, p. 399). The lost income that these figures represent is not "pin money." Most single women work because they have to; most married women work because their husbands don't earn enough to support their families.

Finally, age is a factor in unemployment. Teenage workers have the highest unemployment rates in the country. They are three times more likely to be out of work than the average person. Young black workers have the worst prospects. From 1977 on, the official unemployment rate for black teen-agers was over 40 percent, and in some cities it was more than 50 percent.

Older workers also have trouble finding jobs. Although the Federal Employment Act prohibits discrimination on the basis of age, many firms still refuse to hire the middle-aged. Most workers are encouraged or forced to retire at age seventy. In 1979 only one out of five men over age sixty-five was employed, and even fewer were working full time.

The changing job market At the same time as immigration increases the competition for jobs in the secondary labor market, a less prosperous economy is making higher-level work more difficult to get. Economic recession and uncertainty have led to cutbacks in many professional service jobs, especially in the so-called helping professions — social workers, psychological counselors, medical therapists, and so on. Moreover, the expansion of the educational system, which opened up so many jobs in the 1960s, ended when the postwar generation of babies graduated from college. Teachers, administrators, and researchers now find themselves in a shrinking job market. As a result of these trends, many young people now investing in graduate education will find that they are trained for careers that are rapidly disappearing.

Finally, the post-industrial service economy is on the threshold of revolutionary change. Microprocessing technology could soon eliminate the jobs of hundreds of thousands of white-collar workers in the United States — not only jobs now held by clerks and secretaries but also many supervisory positions as well.

Danger, Disability, and Death on the Job

According to the official statistics, every year more than 12,000 workers in the United States are killed on the job and another 2.2 million are injured in work-related accidents (National Safety Council, 1972). Untold millions of other people work in environments that are dangerous to their health. The risk of lung disease and cancer has recently been shown to increase significantly in occupations where the worker is exposed to coal dust, asbestos fibers, chemical fumes, and insecticides. The Public Health Service estimates that there are 390,000 new cases of occupational disease every year and that as many as 100,000 deaths result from them (U.S. Dept. of Labor, 1972). Stress is also an occupational hazard. Emotional pressure and physical exhaustion at work are linked to strokes, heart disease, and poor mental health. In terms of human suffering, threats to life and health in the workplace are surely one of American society's most serious social problems.

An Organizational Response to Occupational Hazards

When the United States declared its intention to stimulate a domestic uranium potential in 1946, occupational safety and health specialists were confident that such a development would not result in an occupational health tragedy. The hazards of mining uranium arise from its radioactive decay products which irradiate sensitive lung tissues when inhaled and produce lung cancer effects. . . . This was documented in published articles showing that miners in central Europe who handled uranium-bearing ore suffered elevated risks of lung cancer. . . . Also published in the journals were descriptions of ventilation techniques that had been devised for the successful control of airborne radioactivity in Czechoslovakian mines in the early 1930s. . . . It seemed certain that [in the U.S.] radiation standards would be quickly imposed and remedial technology adopted on a nationwide basis. . . .

Today, the uranium mining population in the United States is experiencing what has been termed a "lung cancer epidemic." The initial expectations of the occupational health specialists for speedy preventive action proved to be very wrong.

The chronology of radiation hazard raises many questions. For example, why was the industry begun when evidence pointed to a health hazard? Why weren't remedial techniques employed sooner? Why was there a 20-year lag in imposing a federal standard when the hazard had been documented and remedial technology had been developed? In short, why did organizations fail to act in a matter so gravely affecting human life? . . . [A] combination of history and interviewing research revealed that the ebb and flow of organizational action about the radiation hazard was affected by at least three factors. Each served, initially, to obstruct the control process.

Source: Jessica S. Pearson, "Organizational Response to Occupational Injury and Disease: The Case of the Uranium Industry," *Social Forces*, Vol. 57, No. 1 (September 1978), pp. 25–35.

Accidents at Work

For many people, working involves the risk of life and limb. Firemen and policemen obviously have hazardous jobs, but so do miners and machinists, pilots and construction workers, truckers and tree surgeons, football players and window washers. Moreover, job-related injuries are increasing rapidly, rising nearly 29 percent between 1961 and 1970 (Ashford, 1975, p. 5).

How can people work in such dangerous jobs? Sociological studies have shown that it is not

1. *The Intensity of National Needs for Uranium Ore*
   Uranium was a critical component of the United States weapons program of the late 1940s and early 1950s. . . . For many years, concern with national security dominated the thinking of policy-makers associated with the industry to the exclusion of almost any other concern. . . .

2. *The Invisibility of the Hazard*
   Radiation is a health hazard which is impossible to detect with the naked sense. It was also difficult to monitor with measuring devices. Its symptoms in human beings are slow to manifest themselves and difficult to diagnose. As a result, notions that it was lethal met with widespread disbelief. . . .

3. *Industry Instability*
   Sustained by government bonuses and subsidies, uranium mining in the early years of the industry was highly speculative. The industry was unstable, companies came and went, and the high risk, speculative operators tended to resist efforts to restrict their daily entrepreneurial and operational freedoms. . . .

   National needs for uranium ore during the national security crisis of the late 1950s, the invisibility of the radiation hazard, and the transient and speculative nature of the early uranium mining industry all distracted attention from the damaging effects of radiation. . . . As demand for the ore waned (price dropped), as the industry became more large-scale and stable (domination by single largest firm), and as lung cancer damage to miners became more visible (through deaths and compensation claims), the government became more active. It stepped up its program of inspections and sanctions. As a result, mine radiation levels dropped.

because workers in high-risk occupations don't know the chances they are taking. In *Men in Crisis* (1969), Rex Lucas found that coal miners were all well aware of the dangers they faced. To deal with the constant threat of death, the mining community developed special kinds of behavior. Within each work group, for example, the miners tried to prevent accidents by maintaining strict control over work routines and enforcing safety rules. Long years of experience and knowledge also gave the men a feeling of control over the predictable dangers of cave-ins and explosions. As for the unpredictable dangers beyond human control, the miners used a number of mechanisms to deal with their fears. The miner's code of behavior did not permit any expression of anxiety or even any discussion of the risks they took. Any admission of fear was weak, shameful, unmanly. Other defensive responses included staying away from work (in spite of the harsh regulations, absenteeism in the mine ran between 10 and 20 percent), fatalism ("You're going to die when your time comes"), and superstitions (belief in "unlucky days" and omens). These adaptations were so successful that the miners were a jolly group, constantly joking and gossiping with each other. Similar social norms and protective arrangements have been noted among paratroopers (Stouffer et al., 1949, p. 206) and among the high steel construction workers who build bridges and skyscrapers (Haas, 1977, pp. 147–70). By making some of the same attempts to control the situation, the average person is also able to live with danger. In spite of the high statistical chances of being killed or injured in automobiles, for example, most people are able to go on driving because they believe in their own ability to avoid accidents, they trust other drivers to obey the rules, and they refuse to admit their fears openly.

Unhealthy Workplaces

In addition to the threats to physical safety on the job, the workplace frequently represents a threat to health. The leading cause of death in the United States is heart disease, which claims about 750,000 lives a year. There is much evidence to show that stressful work increases the risk of heart disease, as well as other illnesses. One study reported a high incidence of hypertension among telephone operators who must complete a specific number of calls within a short space of time (Mjasnikov, 1961). Air traffic controllers, who work under extreme time pressure and are responsible for hundreds of lives, run a high risk of hypertension and stomach ulcers (Cobb and Rose, 1973). Stress is particularly notable because it affects so many workers: The clerk and the waitress, as well as the doctor and the corporate executive, frequently suffer from long hours, incessant deadlines, and emotional strain. Stress also contributes to numerous illnesses, from headaches and indigestion to strokes and heart attacks.

The inhalation or absorption of toxic or carcinogenic (cancer-causing) chemicals and dusts, which leads to lung disease, cancer, poisoning, and neurological damage is also a common job-related health hazard. In contrast to accidental injuries, which are immediate and obvious, the harmful effects of these substances are usually slow to develop, irreversible, and complicated by nonoccupational factors. Cancer today is the second leading cause of death and appears to be on the rise (330,000 deaths annually). An estimated 80 to 90 percent of cancers are caused by environmental factors, of which half are probably related to occupations. Lung cancer has now reached epidemic proportions among uranium miners, who breathe in radioactive particles at work (Pearson, 1978, p. 23), and employees in chemical plants show high rates of liver and bladder cancer (Wolf et al., 1978, p. 47). In some high-risk occupations, the probability of dying from cancer may be just as high as that of a worker's being injured in an industrial accident (Ashford, 1975, p. 5).

Given the size of the occupational health and safety problem, why has so little been done to protect the worker? There appear to be two answers to this troublesome question. The first has to do with economic considerations. When employers are not held financially responsible for treating a job-related disease or compensating a worker for an injury, they have little incentive to increase their costs by taking safety precautions. Moreover, most protective legislation is designed to eliminate the obvious, immediate safety hazards, rather than the invisible, long-run health hazards. The Occupational Safety and Health Act of 1970, which requires employers to take preventive measures, has led to a dispute over the definition of safe and healthy working conditions. This problem of definition is the second reason why current health and safety standards are so inadequate. When there is no undisputed evidence showing the relationship between health and working conditions, it is difficult to link the two—to decide whether lung cancer, for example, results from inhaling asbestos particles at work or whether it is caused by a combination of many unrelated environmental and genetic factors (Ashford, 1975, pp. 3-5).

Job Satisfaction and Mental Health

In all the research on occupational health, the most startling finding of all may be the evidence that how long you live depends not on the kind of work you do but whether you are happy doing it. In a fifteen-year study of aging (Palmore, 1969), the people who lived longest rated highest in job satisfaction. Happiness at work, together with a high score on "overall happiness," predicted longevity better than general physical health, or use of tobacco, or genetic inheritance. Furthermore, the prevalence of fatal heart attacks in industrialized societies appears to be related to working more and enjoying it less (Wolf, 1969, pp. 74–83). Many less serious illnesses—among them ulcers, colitis, and asthma—have also been linked to dissatisfaction and frustration at work (Hinkle et al., 1960, p. 1327).

Unhappiness at work can also have a devastating effect on mental health. In a series of studies conducted by the University of Michigan's Institute for Social Research, job dissatisfaction contributed to a number of mental health problems, including psychosomatic illnesses, low self-esteem, anxiety, worry, tension, and unsuccessful personal relationships (U.S. Dept. of Health, Education, and Welfare, 1973, p. 82).

Arthur Kornhauser's classic work, *The Mental Health of the Industrial Worker* (1965), was among the first to establish the link between job satisfaction and mental health. A surprising 40 percent of his sample of automobile workers had mental health problems that grew out of the conditions of their work. Kornhauser found that higher-level workers were happier with their jobs and had better mental health than unskilled workers; the least-satisfying jobs were dull, repetitive, unchallenging, and low-paying; dissatisfied workers off the job were passive and escapist, watched television a lot, did not vote, and did not belong to community organizations; and, finally, the workers' self-esteem was closely tied to their happiness at work. Kornhauser concluded that mental health problems occur whenever a person cannot attain the goals on which his or her sense of identity as a worthwhile person depends:

> Persistent failure and frustration bring lowered self-esteem and dissatisfaction with life, often accompanied by anxieties, social alienation and withdrawal, a narrowing of goals and curtailing of aspirations—in short, . . . poor mental health. (1965, p. 269)

Some workers use drugs and alcohol to cope with boredom and frustration. The researchers for *Work in America* uncovered a shocking amount of drug use on the job, especially among assembly-line workers and long-distance truck drivers (U.S. Dept. of HEW, 1973, pp. 85–86). Another study found that 15 percent of the 3,400 workers in one automobile plant were addicted to heroin (Special Action Office for Drug Abuse Prevention, 1972). Certain working conditions can also lead to excessive drinking. Meaningless jobs in which the worker gets little appreciation or sense of accomplishment seem to cause the kind of anxiety that leads to alcoholism (Roman and Trice, 1970).

In sum, wherever people spend their working day making the same motions or processing the same endless forms, and whenever they have little chance of taking individual responsibility or initiative, they usually feel little interest in doing a good job. And no matter how clean and comfortable the office or factory, people working under these conditions won't be healthy or happy. Can this kind of modern work ever be improved?

Reforming the Workplace

Bored and apathetic workers are not only less healthy, they are less productive. Since satisfied workers have lower absentee rates and turn out higher-quality work, making work more interesting and rewarding usually makes it more profitable as well. Reform of the workplace has therefore come from two directions—from the top, from managers who want to improve productivity, and from the bottom, from workers who want to improve working conditions.

Attempts at reform have largely been based on one of two theories of human nature: (1) that people don't like to work, so work can be improved only by making less of it; or (2) that people like to work, but they don't work well when they hate their jobs. In *The Human Side of Enterprise* (1960), the psychologist Douglas McGregor called these two opposing views of work Theory *X* and Theory *Y*. Traditional organizations operate according to Theory *X*, which assumes that people dislike work and prefer to avoid responsibility, and that the desire to do a good job depends on extrinsic rewards like promotions and bonuses. Theory *Y*, in contrast, assumes that people like to work, enjoy responsibility, and are motivated by the intrinsic rewards of doing a good job. McGregor believed that bossy, authoritarian *X* managers were creating a self-fulfilling prophecy: By preventing people from using their full potential, they were turning them into indifferent and unimaginative workers. He thought that an organization based on Theory *Y* would lead to more flexibility and innovation. Two different kinds of reform movements have grown out of these opposing theories of work and motivation.

The "Work Is Inherently Unpleasant" Assumption

Over the course of the twentieth century, most attempts to improve work were based on the assumption that work was an unpleasant necessity. Indeed, industrial work was frequently dirty, noisy, exhausting, and dangerous. Reformers therefore aimed at ending the abuse of the worker and enforcing better working conditions. One way of improving this kind of work was to make less of it. From the start, labor unions have fought for shorter hours and longer vacations. In the 1890s, most industries adopted the ten-hour day and the six-day week; in the 1930s, the normal week was forty-eight hours; and in the 1970s, the average worker had a forty-hour week. Before 1940, only managers were entitled to paid vacations; by 1970, two-thirds of all non-farm workers had an average of two weeks of paid vacation a year (Bell, 1975, pp. 55–57).

Another way to improve inherently unpleasant work is to make it better paid. Labor unions have therefore supported minimum wage laws, Social Security pensions for retired workers, overtime pay, and a variety of benefits ranging from coffee breaks to health insurance plans.

Now that the five-day, forty-hour week has been achieved, and wages and working conditions are much improved, some attempts are being made to make these standard working patterns more flexible. The entrance of millions of wives and mothers into the labor force brought new support for alternatives to the eight-hour day. One result has been the rapid increase in permanent part-time jobs: About one in eight workers is now a part-timer. Another result is the new interest in *flex-time,* an arrangement that permits workers to choose their own working hours within certain limits. The official workday might begin at any

Revitalizing the Bureaucracy

Bureaucracy has been long and accurately criticized for its lack of both external and internal responsiveness. Yet in the 1980s both external and internal pressures are sure to increase. Externally, the 80s will demand that bureaucracies respond to turbulent environments of high uncertainty, rapid change, and permeable boundaries. The oil crisis, growing inflationary pressures, market uncertainties due to foreign competition, regulatory constraints, and an antigrowth bias mean that even "mature" organizations (such as the auto industry), with mechanisms to stabilize their environments, face the need to respond more flexibly and rapidly to these environments by solving a continuing series of new problems and changing their traditional internal focus to a more external one. Internally, the 80s will demand that bureaucracies meet the rising expectations of a drastically changing labor force in a slower growth economy. These expectations will include a demand for more opportunity . . . from a wider range of employees, including growing numbers of educated workers and women, and for more power. . . .

We believe that these trends of the 1980s will show that the issue will be not how to *replace* bureaucracy, but how to *supplement* it. . . . The task in the 80s is to permit bureaucracy to function well where it can while finding a different structure capable of dealing effectively with the tasks and conditions for which bureaucracy is not suitable. The structural form emerging in the next decade that meets this criterion is what Howard Carlson at General Motors has called the "parallel organization." . . .

The parallel organization . . . is change oriented. . . . People are grouped temporarily in a number of different ways as appropriate to the problem-solving tasks at hand. They are not limited by their position in the hierarchy. A different set of decision-making channels and "reporting relationships" operates, and the organization as a whole is more flexible and flat. In this more fluid, parallel structure, opportunity and power can be expanded far beyond what is available in the bureaucratic organization. The main task of the parallel organization is the continued re-examination of routines; exploration of new options; and development of new tools, procedures, and approaches. It seeks to institutionalize change. As their utility is demonstrated, the *new* routines can be transferred into the bureaucratic organization for maintenance and integration.

Source: Barry A. Stein and Rosabeth Moss Kanter, "Building the Parallel Organization: Creating the Mechanism for Permanent Quality of Work Life," *The Journal of Applied Behavioral Science*, Vol. 16, No. 3 (1980), pp. 371–85.

time between 7:30 A.M. and 9:30 A.M., for example, and end between 4:00 P.M. and 6:00 P.M. Employees are usually expected to work forty hours a week, but they can accumulate extra hours to earn time off in the future. Flex-time began in West Germany, where it was designed to reduce rush-hour traffic jams, and later spread to other industrial countries. By 1972, 5 percent of the German work force and 30 percent of Swiss workers were choosing their own hours. In addition to relieving traffic congestion, flex-time schedules have increased productivity and lowered absenteeism wherever they have been adopted (Dickson, 1975, pp. 228–29).

The movement for greater freedom in working hours has also brought the four-day, forty-hour week. Over one million workers in about 2,000 American companies have this compressed time schedule.

These changes in traditional patterns of work have not changed the character of work itself. As one job consultant put it, four days in a lousy job is better than five, but it's still a lousy job (Dickson, 1975, p. 59). The bridge toll collector and the insurance clerk can be well paid and have every kind of employment benefit, but they are only being compensated for tedious occupations. Other reform movements have sought not better wages and schedules, but a radical change in the nature of work.

The "Work Is Beneficial" Assumption

There is much evidence to suggest that people truly like to work. In survey after survey, the great majority say that they would keep on working even if they inherited enough money to live comfortably. When asked why, most replied, "to keep occupied" (Morse and Weiss, 1955, pp. 191–98). This urge to get out of the house, to meet people, and to do something worthwhile and important keeps people working even when they could retire.

How hard and how carefully people work is something else again. If people are motivated not just by economic necessity but also by the need to feel important and to have human companionship, they will be frustrated by jobs in traditional bureaucracies. A hierarchical organization in which workers are interchangeable cogs doing meaningless, low-skilled work, where they are socially isolated and controlled by dozens of petty rules, does not offer much sense of accomplishment or self-fulfillment. As we have seen, the cost of alienation from work is absenteeism, high turnover, low productivity, and poor workmanship.

Most organizations are based on Theory X's assumption that people work most productively when they are rigidly controlled; new work organizations have recently put into practice Theory Y's assumption that people work best when they are allowed to be creative and independent. The reformers' most daring attack has been on the most inhuman and mechanical workplace of all — the automobile assembly line. Volvo's new plants in Sweden, for example, have introduced a measure of industrial democracy. Cars are built by small work groups of up to nine workers. After it is given a work assignment, the team decides who will do what job, elects its own foreman on a rotating basis, and does its own training. Production problems are discussed with managers at monthly meetings (Mire, 1974, p. 6).

Industrial democracy at Volvo (and at Saab, another Swedish automobile company) has been inspired not by idealism so much as by astronomical rates of turnover and absenteeism. In 1966, when the demand for labor was especially high, Saab reported that it had to replace *100 percent* of its assembly-line workers every year. In 1972, Volvo admitted that it was keeping one-seventh of its work force in reserve to fill in for workers who didn't show up. The experiment with industrial democracy has relieved these problems so successfully that Volvo is now fully committed to

In a Nikon factory in Japan, management designs and schedules exercise breaks for employees. In a Volvo plant in Sweden, teams of workers are responsible for assembling a given number of cars. Who does which jobs and how they organize their time is up to them. Which of these companies operates on Theory X? Which operates on Theory Y?

the new system. In 1974, the company opened a new $20 million plant in Kalmar, Sweden—the world's first large-scale automobile assembly plant without an assembly line (Dickson, 1975, pp. 30–32).

Industrial democracy attempts to break down the authoritarian structure of the workplace by giving workers responsibility for managerial decision making. A second type of reform, called *job enrichment,* aims at rebuilding the fragmented structure of modern work.

In one of a series of experiments with job reform at American Telephone & Telegraph, a simplified job broken down into several parts was put back together again to form a meaningful unit of work. A group of forty men had the job of connecting telephone wires, one step in the process of installing new circuits for customers. Each three-man team had a few specific tasks, but no one had complete responsibility for getting the job done. The men usually had no idea whether they had made the right connections, since their work was checked by another type of team on the next shift. Still another team had taken the order, so the men also didn't know who the customer was or what purpose the new connection served. These "framemen," who called themselves "frame apes," were notorious for their high rate of errors, low quality of work, low productivity, and high number of grievances. Job enrichment in their case consisted of combining three specialized operations into one assignment. New teams were organized to do all the work on a single order, from writing it up to delivering a new connection to the customer. The result of this experiment was a dramatic reduction in errors (which dropped to one-quarter of their original level) and grievances (from one a week to none at all during the experimental period). In addition, the team gained a sense of identification with their work, referring to "my circuit" and "my customer" (Dickson, 1975, pp. 53–54).

As this experiment indicates, redesigning work can lower business costs as well as improve the working lives of millions of people. The evidence suggests that as much as 40 percent of the worker's productivity is currently untapped and could be released under different conditions (Walton, 1972). Although not all of the experiments in reorganizing work have been equally successful, the results generally have been encouraging enough to lead to further innovations. The future role of the United States in the world economy depends in part on such attempts to improve the efficiency and quality of American products and services by reforming the workplace.

Summary

1. American industry has lost its competitive edge in the global market. As the competition between industrial nations becomes fiercer, corporations are cutting production costs by moving their operations from the high-wage labor markets of the United States to low-wage areas around the globe.

2. Worldwide industrial development has created a global factory, in which the developing nations of the Third World manufacture goods and the highly industrialized countries of Western Europe, Japan, and the United States provide services (finance, technical expertise, management).

3. The United States is now a post-industrial economy which produces more services than goods. The kind of work most people do has changed from a game against nature (weather, soil conditions) and things (machines) to a game

between persons. As a result, blue-collar manual work has declined, and white-collar office work has expanded enormously.

4. The service economy has made the workplace more comfortable, but much work is still boring and dehumanizing.

5. The expansion of food, health, and business services has led to a more pronounced dual labor market. In the primary market, jobs are well paid, working conditions are good, and there is job security and a relatively equal chance of promotion. The secondary market, in contrast, offers badly paid, temporary, and dead-end jobs.

6. Having a job is a very important source of identity and self-respect. However, the American work ethic, with its emphasis on the value of work and material success, appears to be changing. Work is becoming more important for its intrinsic rewards, and more people want their jobs to be challenging and interesting.

7. Discontent with work comes from the frustration of this desire to be useful and creative. Alienation, the feeling of separation from one's work and from society, is widespread among both blue-collar and white-collar workers. Highly specialized, impersonally controlled jobs are less satisfying than more independent managerial and professional work.

8. The United States has a "normal" unemployment rate of 6 percent, but hidden unemployment raises the rate. Unemployment is caused by the migration of industry to cheaper labor markets; automation; government economic policies; discrimination on the basis of race, sex, and age; and by a worldwide surplus of labor.

9. Thousands of workers die from job-related accidents and occupational diseases, and millions more are injured every year. Poor mental health, drug abuse, and alcoholism are also related to job dissatisfaction.

10. Bored and apathetic workers are less productive, so reformers of the workplace are trying to make work more enjoyable and rewarding. Most reformers assume that work is always an unpleasant necessity and have tried to improve jobs by increasing the pay and benefits and making working hours shorter and more flexible. Others assume that people really like to work and have redesigned work so that people are allowed to be more independent and creative.

Suggested Reading

Bell, Daniel, *The Coming of Post-Industrial Society.* New York: Basic Books/Colophon, 1976.

Garson, Barbara, *All the Livelong Day: The Meaning and Demeaning of Routine Work.* New York: Penguin, 1975.

Kanter, Rosabeth Moss, *Men and Women of the Corporation.* New York: Basic Books, 1977.

Kerr, Clark, and Jerome M. Rosow (Eds.). *Work in America: The Decade Ahead.* New York: Van Nostrand, 1979.

Rothschild, Emma, *Paradise Lost: The Decline of the Auto-Industrial Age.* New York: Random House, 1973.

Terkel, Studs, *Working.* New York: Avon, 1975.

References

Ad Hoc Committee. "The Triple Revolution." *Liberation* (April 1964).

Ashford, N.A. "Worker Health and Safety: An Area of Conflicts." *Monthly Labor Review,* Vol. 98 (September 1975), pp. 3–11.

Barnet, R.J. *The Lean Years.* New York: Simon & Schuster, 1980.

Bell, D. "Work and Its Discontents." In *The End of Ideology.* Glencoe, Ill.: Free Press, 1960.

Bell, D. "The Clock Watchers: Americans at Work." *Time,* September 8, 1975, pp. 55–57.

Bell, D. *The Coming of Post-Industrial Society.* 1973; rpt. New York: Basic Books/Colophon, 1976.

Blauner, R. *Alienation and Freedom.* Chicago: The University of Chicago Press, 1964.

Braverman, H. *Labor and Monopoly Capital.* New York: Monthly Review Press, 1974.

Chinoy, E. *Automobile Workers and the American Dream.* Garden City, N.Y.: Doubleday, 1955.

Cobb, S., and R. Rose. "Hypertension, Peptic Ulcer and Diabetes in Air Traffic Controllers." *Journal of the American Medical Association,* Vol. 224 (1973), pp. 489–92.

Dickson, P. *The Future of the Workplace.* New York: Weybright and Talley, 1975.

Garson, B. "Women's Work." *Working Papers,* Vol. 1, No. 3 (Fall 1973) pp. 5–14.

Gruenberg, B. "The Happy Worker: An Analysis of Educational and Occupational Differences in Determinants of Job Satisfaction." *American Journal of Sociology,* Vol. 86, No. 2 (September 1980), pp. 247–71.

Haas, J. "Learning Real Feelings: A Study of High Steel Ironworkers' Reactions to Fear and Danger." *Sociology of Work and Occupations,* Vol. 4, No. 2 (May 1977), pp. 147–70.

Hiestand, D. "Obligations of Employers and the Society to Minority Workers." 1972; cited in U.S. Dept. of HEW, *Work in America,* Cambridge, Mass.: MIT Press, 1973, p. 205.

Hinkle, L.E. et al. "An Examination of the Relation Between Symptoms, Disability, and Serious Illness in Two Homogeneous Groups of Men and Women." *American Journal of Public Health,* Vol. 50, No. 9 (1960), pp. 1327–36.

Kanter, R.M. *Men and Women of the Corporation.* New York: Basic Books, 1977.

Kaplan, H.R. *Lottery Winners.* New York: Harper & Row, 1978.

Kornhauser, A. *The Mental Health of the Industrial Worker.* New York: Wiley, 1965.

Lucas, R. *Men in Crisis.* New York: Basic Books, 1969.

McGregor, D. *The Human Side of Enterprise.* New York: McGraw-Hill, 1960.

Mire, J. "Improving Working Life – The Role of European Unions." *Monthly Labor Review* Vol. 97, No. 9 (September 1974), pp. 3–11.

Mjasnikov, A. "Discussion in Proceedings of the Joint WHO-Czech Cardio Society Symposium on Pathogenesis of Essential Hypertension." Prague, 1961.

Morse, N.C., and R.S. Weiss. "The Function and Meaning of Work and the Job." *American Sociology Review,* Vol. 20 (April 1955), pp. 191–98.

Nader, R. et al. (Eds.). *Whistle Blowing: Report of the Conference on Professional Responsibility.* New York: Grossman, 1972.

National Safety Council. *Accident Facts.* Chicago, 1972.

Palmore, E. "Predicting Longevity: A Follow-up Controlling for Age." *Gerontologist,* Vol. 9, No. 401 (Winter 1969) pp. 247–50.

Pavalko, R. *Sociology of Occupations and Professions.* Itaska, Ill.: Peacock, 1971.

Pearson, J.S. "Organizational Response to Occupational Injury and Disease: The Case of the Uranium Industry." *Social Forces,* Vol. 57, No. 1 (September 1978), pp. 25–35.

Ritzer, G. *Working: Conflict and Change,* 2d ed. Englewood Cliffs, N.J.: Prentice-Hall, 1977.

Roman, P.M., and H.M. Trice. "The Development of Deviant Drinking Behavior." *Archives of Environmental Health,* Vol. 20, No. 3 (March 1970) pp. 424–35.

Rothschild, E. "Reagan and the Real America." *The New York Review of Books,* February 5, 1981.

Slocum, W. *Occupational Careers.* Chicago: Aldine, 1966.

Special Action Office for Drug Abuse Prevention report. 1972; cited in U.S. Dept. of HEW, *Work in America,* Cambridge, Mass.: MIT Press, 1973, p. 86.

Stellman, J.M., and S.M. Daum. *Work Is Dangerous to Your Health.* New York: Vintage Books, 1973.

Stouffer, S.A. et al. *The American Soldier,* Vol. 2. Princeton, N.J.: Princeton University Press, 1949.

Terkel, S. *Working.* New York: Avon, 1975.

U.S. Bureau of the Census. *Statistical Abstract of the United States, 1978.* Washington, D.C.: U.S. Government Printing Office, 1978.

U.S. Bureau of the Census. *Statistical Abstract of the United States, 1980.* Washington, D.C.: U.S. Government Printing Office, 1980.

U.S. Department of Health, Education, and Welfare. *Man's Health and the Environment— Some Research Needs: Report of the Task Force on Research Planning in Environmental Health Science.* Washington D.C.: U.S. Government Printing Office, 1970.

U.S. Department of Health, Education, and Welfare. *Work in America: Report of a Special Task Force to the Secretary of HEW.* Cambridge, Mass.: MIT Press, 1973.

U.S. Department of Labor, Health, Education, and Welfare, and Occupational Safety and Health Review Commission. *The President's Report on Occupational Safety and Health.* Washington, D.C.: U.S. Government Printing Office, 1972.

U.S. Department of Labor. *Employment and Earnings* (March 1980), Tables B-1 and B-2.

Walton, R. "Workplace Alienation and the Need for Major Innovation." Cambridge, Mass.: Harvard Graduate School of Business Administration, 1972.

Whyte, W.H., Jr. "How Hard Do Executives Work?" In G.D. Bell (Ed.), *Organizations and Human Behavior.* Englewood Cliffs, N.J.: Prentice-Hall, 1967, pp. 272–81.

Wilensky, H.L. "The Uneven Distribution of Leisure." In E.O. Smigel (Ed.), *Work and Leisure.* New Haven: College and University Press, 1963, pp. 107–45.

Wolf, S. "Psychosocial Forces in Myocardial Infarction and Sudden Death." *Circulation,* Supplement 4 to 40, No. 5 (1969), pp. 74–83.

Wolf, S., J.G. Bruhn, and H. Goodell. *Occupational Health as Human Ecology.* Springfield, Ill.: Charles C. Thomas, 1978.

Yankelovich, D. "The Meaning of Work." In J.M. Rosow (Ed.), *The Worker and the Job.* Englewood Cliffs, N.J.: Prentice-Hall, 1974.

Yankelovich, D. *New Rules: Searching for Self-Fulfillment in a World Turned Upside Down.* New York: Random House, 1981.

Chapter Eight

The Family

The Family: Dying or Developing?

Is the Family Dying?

The Developing Family

The Consequences of Change

  The Case of Working Wives and Mothers

Divorce

Divorce in the U.S.: Past and Present

  Changing Divorce Rates

  Who Gets Divorced?

The Consequences of Divorce

  The Impact on Adults

  The Impact on Children

Family Violence

Family Violence in Perspective

The Extent of Family Violence

  Violence Toward Children

  Violence Between Spouses

  Violence Between Siblings

  Violence Toward Parents

The Causes of Family Violence

  Myths About Family Violence

  The Structural Causes of Family Violence

The Consequence of Family Violence

Responses to Family Violence

  Victims of Child Abuse

  Victims of Wife Abuse

The Prognosis

Sexual Abuse of Children

The Incidence of Sexual Victimization

Patterns of Father-Daughter Incest

The Consequences of Incest

The White House Conference on Families was held in 1980. The goal was to explore Americans' attitudes toward the family and to learn how people think the government, business, the media, and other institutions help or hurt or ignore their families. Hearings were held at three sites across the country; more than 100,000 people participated in regional and local discussions; the Gallup Organization conducted a national poll. From the beginning, the conference served as a lightning rod for a storm of controversy over modern families. Organizing first and fastest, conservatives captured the early elections of state delegates to the conference—prompting many governors to try to establish balanced delegations, including representation from racial minorities, single households, families with incomes of $10,000 or less, and families with handicapped members. Midway through the first meeting, a self-styled "pro-family" coalition of thirty delegates stormed out when the meeting voted down motions against abortion, the Equal Rights Amendment, and homosexual rights. Delegates could not even agree on a definition of the family.

American Families in 1980 — A Survey

The overall objective of the survey was to explore American attitudes toward families and the relationship of family life to government, business, media, and other major institutions. . . .

The survey is based on in-person interviews with 1,592 adults, interviewed in more than 300 scientifically selected localities in the nation during the period March 21 through 24, 1980. . . .

Any belief that Americans do not place top priority on the family and family life is completely refuted by the results of this survey. The findings represent a ringing endorsement of the importance of the family in American life.

No fewer than *eight in ten persons* interviewed say their family is either the "most" or "one of the most" important elements of their lives. Only 7 percent say the family is only a "fairly unimportant" or "very unimportant" element.

Solid and similar majorities of women and men, whites and non-whites make the family the centerpiece of their lives. Nor is there much difference by education level, region of the nation, age or income.

Furthermore, an earlier Gallup survey showed an overwhelming majority (91 percent) of Americans saying they would welcome more emphasis on "traditional family ties" in the coming years.

Among the most satisfying things about marriage to most people are children, closeness, caring, companionship and a loving atmosphere. . . .

Although Americans place great stock in the family, and women like the role of wife and mother as much as ever, as many as half are less than fully satisfied with their own family life at this time. . . .

Conservatives proposed "People related by heterosexual marriage, blood, or adoption," thus excluding unmarried couples. A homosexual delegate proposed defining the family as "two or more persons who share resources, responsibility for decisions, values and goals and have commitment to one another over time." Both definitions were defeated. Pickets for and against this or that appeared at every hearing. The family conference became a family feud.

Clearly, the family is a social issue. Discussions of the family and social problems are almost always heated and political. There is much disagreement about whether American families are in trouble, how much trouble, or what the trouble is. In the first section of this chapter, we ask whether the family, as an institution, is dying. We show that ideas about what is right or wrong with and within families depend in part on how one defines a family. Then we turn to private troubles that occur within families and have an impact on both family members and society as a whole. Virtually all of the problems considered in this book affect the family; poverty, crime, gender

---

Looking to the future, nearly four in ten (37 percent) of the total sample say they are "not satisfied" with the future facing them and their families. . . .

Nearly unanimous agreement among all segments of society is found regarding the most important problem facing families. Fully eight in ten name the high cost of living, far ahead of the problem named next most often—energy costs, cited by 53 percent. . . .

Americans clearly have a high degree of confidence in the potential strength of the family in our society, but at the same time see the family threatened on all sides. And they are ready to admit that they need help in building a stronger family and marriage. . . .

Five basic mandates for the federal government emerging from this survey are:

1. Greater assistance in terms of the health care of the elderly.
2. Tax breaks for parents of handicapped children.
3. Assistance in child care and in other ways for working mothers.
4. Provide help for poor families.
5. Government should become overtly aware of its own impact upon families, and act with that in mind.

Source: *American Families—1980*. Report submitted to the White House Conference on Families by the Gallup Organization, Inc. (Princeton, N.J., 1980).

inequality, drug abuse, mental and physical health all create troubles for families. Here we ve selected three topics: divorce, family violence, and sexual abuse of children. Why have divorce rates risen? What effect does divorce have on the couple and on children? How common are family violence and sexual abuse of children? What are the consequences for individuals, families, and society as a whole?

The Family: Dying or Developing?

In every known society, the family has played a central role in social organization. The family is a *social institution*—an established, patterned, routinized way of carrying out important social activities. What happens within families affects the shape of society. The fact that most elderly Americans do not live with their middle-aged children, for example, has created a demand for retirement communities, nursing homes, and cost-of-living adjustments in Social Security benefits. Larger social forces, in turn, affect what happens within families. For example, when unemployment rates rise, a father loses his job; a mother goes back to work full time; they may be unable to keep up mortgage payments on their house and move in with in-laws; or they may move to the Southwest where jobs are plentiful. Relationships among family members and daily activities change dramatically. The institution of the family thus connects individuals and society. The question social scientists ask is whether the changing family can continue to play its key role in social organization.

Is the Family Dying?

It has become almost commonplace to assert that the family, as an institution, is dying. In 1928, the behavioral psychologist John Watson predicted that it would be extinct by 1977. Ten years later, Pitirim Sorokin warned that the family was becoming "a mere overnight parking space" (1937, p. 109), and in 1977, Amitai Etzioni predicted that not one American family would be left in 1990. These exaggerated statements were intended to call attention to the possibility that the family of the future will be unrecognizable as a result of the rapid changes in family structure and functions.

The structure of the family consists of certain positions (for example, wife) and roles (behavior expected of those who occupy the positions). When the structure of the family changes, behavior changes. When a couple are divorced and the children live with the wife during the week and the husband on weekends, she plays the roles of father and mother during the week; he, on the weekends. When a wife and mother goes to work, her position in the family changes. She is no longer totally dependent on her husband's income; she may expect him to contribute more to housekeeping and child care. Urie Bronfenbrenner (1977) is concerned about the effects of changing family structure. He believes that the growing number of single-parent families and working mothers is creating problems for individuals and for society. The trouble with the family, he argues, is that nobody is home. Too many young people return from school each day to empty houses. Too many are being "raised" by television and by their peers. Bronfenbrenner traces a host of problems—including reading difficulties, school dropouts, drug addiction, and childhood depression—to children being left to their own devices. He also suggests that children who are not cared for do not learn to care for others.

The functions of the family are also changing. Traditionally, the family functioned as an economic unit. In pre-industrial societies, members of families often work together, pooling their talents, labor, and harvest. Industrialization removed work from the home, but until recently husband and wife were still economically interdependent. A woman depended on her husband's income, a man on his wife's domestic and child-rearing services. With more and more wives working outside the home, this is no longer the case. Traditionally, the family had primary responsibility for socializing children. This, too, is changing. School and television compete with parents today. The average child spends over thirty hours a week watching TV. This represents a dramatic change since the 1950s, when home TV sets first became available. Moreover, the average child spends almost twenty hours a week in school. Children start school earlier and stay in school longer today than in the past (Bane, 1976b, p. 15). In addition, peers, and to some extent, family experts dilute parents' influence over children. One function the family retains, however, is socio-emotional gratification (Goode, 1963; Nimkoff, 1965; Winch, 1970; Skolnick, 1978). People feel they have a right to expect love, affection, and companionship at home.

The Developing Family

The argument that the family is dying seems to receive a good deal of support from statistics: rising divorce rates, declining birth rates, increasing numbers of women working outside the home. But Mary Jo Bane (1976a) has pointed out that a close examination of the data suggests a different interpretation—that the family is "here to stay."

Much of the worry about the family is concern about future generations. How are changes in the structure and functions of the family affecting children? Are children less well cared for today than in the past? Bane thinks not. The falling birth rate is frequently cited as evidence that Americans do not want and value children as much as they once did. In fact, the birth rate is low not because fewer people want children, but because people want to have fewer children. Indeed, childlessness has declined since the 1930s, largely because of improvements in general health and new treatments for sterility and infertility. Voluntary childlessness has increased slightly, but involuntary childlessness has almost disappeared, so that a higher percentage of women have children today. They simply have fewer—one or two instead of six or seven. On the whole, small families seem to be good for children. They receive more attention, and their families are better off economically.

The parent-child bond seems as strong as ever. In fact, more children live with at least one parent than was true in the past. There are two reasons for this: Fewer children lose a parent through death, and more widowed or divorced women are able to keep their children with them. Although the effects on children of having only one full-time parent are not fully understood, one parent is probably better than none. The mother-child bond also seems strong. Many more women are working outside their homes today, but the available evidence suggests that these mothers spend as much or more time in planned activities (such as reading to their children) as nonworking mothers do. And they probably spend considerably more time with each individual child than mothers of five or six children did three generations ago. In summary, there is little evidence that the family's role in caring for children has declined (Bane, 1976a, Chapter 1).

The trend most frequently cited as evidence of the decline of the family is the rising divorce rate. In the minds of most Americans, lifelong, monogamous marriage is the cornerstone of the family. What distinguishes marriage from transient, changing "dating" relationships and friendships is permanent commitment. Most Americans see "the transformation of marriage into a short-lived, fair-weather friendship" as a serious threat to family life. Eighty percent of those divorced remarry within three years, however. This indicates that they were dissatisfied with a particular marriage, not with the institution of marriage. If one includes statistics of marriages

interrupted by death, the percentage of disrupted marriages has not changed substantially. More people lost a spouse through early death in the past; the difference is that the ratio of voluntary to involuntary disruption has increased. In general, married people are more likely than single, divorced, or widowed people to describe themselves as "very happy." And even when a marriage was unsatisfactory, both partners usually experience grief and distress after divorce (Weiss, 1975, 1979). Marriage is still exceedingly important to Americans, even though it may be harder to sustain today than in the past (Bane, 1976a, Chapter 2).

Why do social scientists draw different conclusions from the same data? Much of their disagreement centers on the definition of a family. The view that the family is "dying" is based on the assumption that the ideal family is a *nuclear family* —a breadwinning husband, a homemaking mother, and their dependent children living under the same roof. According to this view, a one-parent household is a "broken home"; a childless couple is an "incomplete" family; a woman

who works cannot be a "good" mother; a couple who live together but are not married do not qualify as a family at all. In 1960, almost two out of three U.S. households conformed to the nuclear ideal (Weitzman, 1978, p. 64). Today, however, traditional nuclear families are a statistical minority. In fact, less than a third of American households consist of a husband, a wife, and their children.

The fact that the family is changing does not necessarily mean it is in trouble. Rather, the variety of arrangements for living and loving practiced in the United States today can be seen as evidence of the adaptability and vitality of the family. For example, if staying together at all costs is considered evidence of a healthy marriage and a healthy society, divorce will be viewed as a problem. If the goal of marriage is seen as establishing a secure and pleasant environment for adults and children, divorce will be seen as one possible solution to the problem of ongoing conflict between a husband and wife. Twenty-five years ago, most Americans considered the nuclear family the only natural and right way for

Figure 8–1

The Changing Family

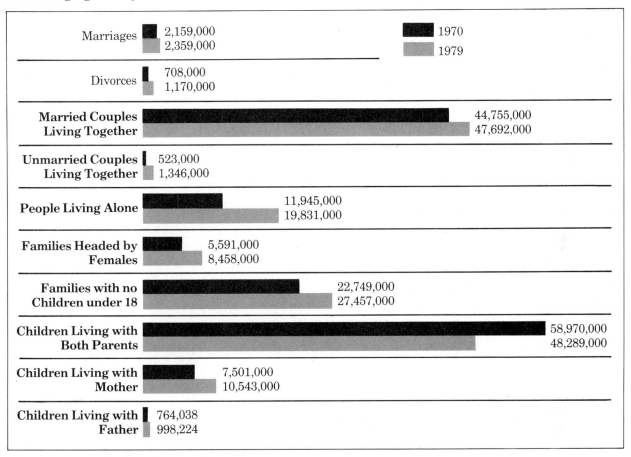

	1970	1979
Marriages	2,159,000	2,359,000
Divorces	708,000	1,170,000
Married Couples Living Together	44,755,000	47,692,000
Unmarried Couples Living Together	523,000	1,346,000
People Living Alone	11,945,000	19,831,000
Families Headed by Females	5,591,000	8,458,000
Families with no Children under 18	22,749,000	27,457,000
Children Living with Both Parents	58,970,000	48,289,000
Children Living with Mother	7,501,000	10,543,000
Children Living with Father	764,038	998,224

Source: U.S. Bureau of the Census, *Statistical Abstract of the United States, 1980* (Washington, D.C.: U.S. Government Printing Office, 1980).

people to live. Other household arrangements were considered deviant. Although most Americans still view the nuclear family as the ideal, many accept variations on that standard. Today we have not one but many types of families. In Alice Rossi's words, "What we defined a decade ago as 'deviant' is today labeled 'variant,' in order to suggest that there is a healthy, experimental quality to current social explorations into the future 'beyond monogamy,' or 'beyond the nuclear family' " (1978, p. 1).

The Consequences of Change

Changes in family structure and function are clearly a social issue. They arouse concern and controversy, as the White House Conference described at the beginning of this chapter illustrated. Modern families and modern styles of child rearing are nearly always measured against families of the past—and found wanting. In contrast, modern technology is nearly always seen as an advance over earlier times. "In technology,

Table 8-1
In One Decade — 10 Ways Families Have Changed

	1970	Latest	Percentage Change
Marriages performed	2,159,000	2,317,000	Up 7.3%
Divorces granted	708,000	1,170,000	Up 65.3%
Married couples	44,728,000	47,662,000	Up 6.6%
Unmarried couples	523,000	1,346,000	Up 157.4%
Persons living alone	10,851,000	17,202,000	Up 58.5%
Married couples with children	25,541,000	24,625,000	Down 3.6%
Children living with two parents	58,926,000	48,295,000	Down 18.0%
Children living with one parent	8,230,000	11,528,000	Up 40.1%
Average size of household	3.3	2.8	Down 15.2%
Families with both husband and wife working	20,327,000	24,253,000	Up 19.3%

Source: *U.S. News & World Report,* June 16, 1980, p. 50. Data based on U.S. Department of Commerce figures.

progress is the standard. In social institutions, continuity is the standard, and when change occurs, it is seen as a decline rather than an advance," (Bane, 1976a, p. 3). The fact that families are changing, however, does not in itself constitute a social problem. Some changes appear to be beneficial.

Paul Glick (1977), senior demographer of the U.S. Bureau of the Census, believes that family life has gotten better, not worse, in recent years. The fact that Americans are marrying at a later age than in the past increases the chance that they will make rational, mature choices of marriage partners. (Early marriages tend to be unstable.) The fact that people delay having their first child and have fewer children increases the amount of time they can devote to each, as noted above. Glick believes that it is also good for the family that women are working. The time a working woman spends with her family is ' a change of pace and more enjoyable than if the woman were always at home. Hours spent with children

are more "play" than "work." On a large scale, smaller families help to reduce population pressure on the environment.

The case of working wives and mothers Some changes in family arrangements, like divorce, can be extremely painful for individuals. In most cases, however, the effects of change are mixed. Consider the case of working wives and mothers. Women have always worked, in the sense that the female of the species has been expected to be economically productive in most societies and times. Typically, women s work (for example, gardening) did not take them far from home. If it did, there were other relatives at home to care for small children. What has changed is that nearly all jobs today require one to be away from home for most of the day, and few households include relatives who might care for children. In the early days of industrialization, poor women (and children) were prominent among factory workers. Today, wives of white-collar and blue-collar husbands are going to work (Hoffman and Nye, 1974, p. 226). A majority of American wives and mothers have jobs. What effect does working have on women themselves, on their marriages, and on their children?

Working may have positive or negative effects on marriage. On the one hand, the fact that a woman can support herself and derive satisfaction and self-esteem from a job may reduce her desire to get married. Kristin Moore and Sandra Hofferth call this the "independence" effect (1979, p. 28). On the other hand, a working woman might be more likely to get married. First, with two salaries, she and her boyfriend might be better able to afford marriage (the "income" effect); second, having an income makes a woman more attractive to men (the "dowry" effect); third, a working woman has more opportunities to meet men than if she were not working (the "access" effect). Statistics indicate that the fact that women are working may play a role in delaying marriage but has not dampened enthusiasm for it.

What happens when a woman continues to work after she is married? Estimates are that housework consumes between forty and seventy hours a week, despite modern conveniences. All available evidence indicates that working wives continue to bear the traditional responsibility for domestic chores. Men are contributing more to housework, not because their wives are working, but because attitudes are changing—younger men are less reluctant than older men to help with domestic chores. Nevertheless, housework is still primarily women's work. By becoming more efficient or lowering their standards, working wives reduce domestic work to about twenty-six hours a week. Still, the average American wife works sixty to seventy-five hours a week (job plus housework)—eight hours more than her husband (Moore and Hofferth, 1979, pp. 30–31). Surprisingly, a major reason for this seems to be women's —not men's—attitudes. According to one poll, 47 percent of women do not agree that "men should

share the work around the house with women" (Mason and Bumpass, 1975).

How happy are working wives with their jobs and their marriages? How do their husbands feel? A woman's attitude toward work seems to depend on the kind of work she does; on her husband's, friends', and relatives' attitudes toward her working; and on her reasons for working. Not surprisingly, well-educated wives who work out of choice, have interesting jobs, and can afford domestic help are more content than wives who do routine, low-paying work out of financial necessity. In contrast, men of all social classes seem to accept their wives' working only grudgingly. They expect women to put their families first. Husbands of working women report lower marital satisfaction than husbands of full-time housewives. But despite overwork and apparent strain in the husband-wife relationship, working wives seem as happy with their lives as housewives, or happier (Moore and Hofferth, 1979, pp. 33–34).

With divorce as with marriage, female employment seems to have competing effects. On the one hand, the fact that a couple can be financially independent of each other may encourage divorce. (She doesn't feel as dependent; he doesn't feel as guilty.) On the other hand, the wife's income raises the family's standard of living and may increase marital stability. To date, there is no evidence that the chances of a couple seeking divorce are increased by the woman's working (Hoffman and Nye, 1974).

What effect does a mother's working have on her children? According to one poll, most parents (69 percent) believed that a mother of small children should not work unless she absolutely must. Working mothers themselves were divided on this question: 49 percent said children are better off if their mothers work; 48 percent said that children are worse off (Yankelovich, Skelly, and White, 1979, p. 128). What is the evidence?

There is ample documentation of the fact that a child's emotional development depends on the opportunity to form close, personal attachments in infancy (Hoffman, 1979). Babies need intimate interaction, verbal and visual stimulation, and direction. They need care. But it is not clear whether an infant's caretaker has to be the mother, or whether being cared for by other people interferes with an infant's attachment to the mother. Some studies show little difference between working and nonworking mothers in the amount of one-to-one mother-infant contact. Working women seem to compensate for the time they spend away from home by devoting more of the time they are at home to their babies.

With school-aged children, there is some evidence that mothers' working has different effects on girls and boys. Daughters of working mothers seem to admire their mothers more than do daughters of nonworking mothers. They tend to be higher achievers. Sons of working mothers seem to have less stereotyped notions of men's and women's roles. But some research indicates that lower-class sons of working mothers are less admiring of their *fathers* than other boys and that middle-class sons of working mothers score lower on intelligence tests than do sons of nonworking mothers. With adolescents, these sex differences fade. It seems that working women are better able to cope with adolescents' struggles over identity, autonomy, and sexuality than nonworking mothers. They are more likely to accept and encourage teen-agers' desire to become independent. Nonworking mothers struggle not only with their adolescents' troubles but also with the threat that their own major role in life, being a mother, is coming to an end.

This is not to say that a working mother is an unqualified blessing for a child. The evidence is far from complete. However, there is little indication that a woman's having a job, by itself, harms children. And there is some evidence that overmothering has as many negative consequences for child development as part-time mothering (Hoffman, 1979). Because two-career families are

comparatively new, both men and women are going through a period of adjustment. Some may experience considerable difficulty, particularly if the wife seeks independence and equality but the husband prefers more traditional arrangements. In some families, a woman's going to work will create tension and conflict, and perhaps even contribute to divorce. The effects of changing family styles are highly variable, as the case of working wives and mothers shows. Even so, people are generally satisfied with their families and think their families are in better shape than the nation is. Given the popularity of marriage and the importance most people attach to families, it seems unlikely that large numbers of people will give up the struggle (Bane, 1976a, p. 36).

Divorce

In 1980, a record 1.18 million couples were granted divorces in the United States—more than twice the number granted twenty years earlier. Estimates are that nearly 40 percent of women now in their twenties will end their first marriages in divorce (Glick and Norton, 1977). This does not mean that Americans are giving up on marriage. As we noted earlier, most of these people will remarry. Americans apparently want to be married as much as they ever did. The trouble seems to be that in many cases their marriages are not working out. Why is the divorce rate so high? What is the impact of divorce on ex-husbands and wives, and on children?

Divorce in the U.S.: Past and Present

People give a variety of reasons for getting divorced. Quarrels over money, children, or in-laws; alcoholism, gambling, or infidelity; the feeling that the marriage has grown stale or that one partner has outgrown the other—all may precipitate divorce. To the couple, divorce seems like a personal problem. Changes in the divorce *rate,* however, show it to be more than a private matter. The high divorce rate in the United States today is a social fact that requires sociological explanation.

Changing divorce rates In the 1920s, the divorce rate in this country was between 10 and 15 per 1,000 married women per year. The rate dropped off sharply during the Great Depression (the cost of obtaining a divorce and setting up new households seems to keep people together during periods of economic hardship), then rose to almost 25 per 1,000 in the mid-1940s. Except for that brief surge immediately following World War II (wartime marriages are often unstable), the divorce rate remained constant and even declined in the 1950s. Then it began to climb. Between 1965 and 1975 alone, the divorce rate doubled, going above 30 per 1,000 in 1975 (Glick and Norton, 1976), and reaching 38 in 1978 (Espenshade, 1979). The remarriage rate declined somewhat during this period, increasing the proportion of divorced men and women in the population. The proportion of divorces involving children also increased, and the number of female-headed households grew from 4.5 million in 1960 to 8.5 million in 1979 (Espenshade, 1979) (see Figure 8–2).

Why is the divorce rate so high? One factor is that many of the legal barriers to divorce have been lowered. Through the 1960s, most states would grant divorces only on grounds of desertion, nonsupport, adultery, or physical or mental cruelty. (Until 1949, North Carolina did not permit divorce on any grounds.) Today about half the states have adopted "no fault" laws that allow a couple to obtain a divorce by mutual consent. Whether more liberal laws are a cause or an effect of changes in attitudes toward divorce, however, is difficult to say (Bane, 1976a, p. 32). In California, for example, the number of divorces increased the year after a new law was passed (perhaps because couples delayed filing until the

Figure 8–2

Rates of Divorce and Remarriage for U.S. Women, 1921–1977

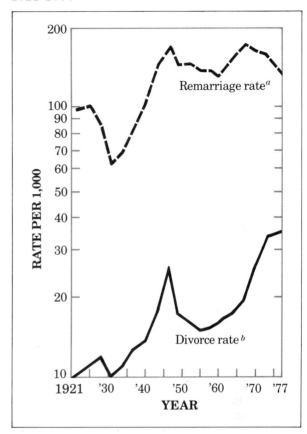

[a]Remarriages per 1,000 widowed and divorced women 14 to 52 years old.
[b]Divorces per 1,000 married women 14 to 44 years old.

Source: Adapted from Hugh Carter and Paul C. Glick, *Marriage and Divorce: A Social and Economic Study,* rev. ed. (Cambridge, Mass.: Harvard University Press, 1976), p. 394. Computations for 1975–77 from Paul C. Glick and Arthur J. Norton, "Marrying, Divorcing and Living Together in the U.S. Today," *Population Bulletin,* Vol. 32, No. 5 (October 1977), pp. 2–29.

new law was enacted), then returned to the old level.

Perhaps more significantly, economic barriers to divorce have been weakened. Through the

1950s, the great majority of married women in the United States were financially dependent on their husbands. After a divorce, most women were forced to move back into their parents' households or to live with siblings; most men had to pay alimony for the rest of their lives. No longer. Not only have job opportunities opened up for women, but most women have work experience before and during marriage. Women's fear of divorce has lessened. Indeed, there is some evidence that the higher a woman's income, the greater the probability that she and her husband will separate (Ross and Sawhill, 1975). Economic barriers to divorce have also been lowered for men (Goode, 1976, p. 530). At the turn of the century, it was extremely difficult for a man to get along without a wife, particularly if he lived on a farm, as many did. In urban settings, with modern conveniences, this is no longer the case. And if a man's ex-wife works, the divorce court may not require him to pay alimony.

Attitudes toward both marriage and divorce have changed (Weiss, 1975, pp. 5–10). Through the 1950s, most Americans viewed marriage almost as a religious calling, as a service to society. Marriage was considered the foundation of all Western civilization. Today, however, marriage is regarded more as a source of individual pleasure and enrichment than as a social responsibility. Not terribly long ago, divorce was a scandal. In gossip sheets and novels, divorced people were portrayed as selfish, irresponsible, disreputable. Divorce nearly always spelled the end of a political career. Although divorce is still considered regrettable, it is no longer a social disgrace.

Underlying these changes is a conflict between what the sociologist Robert Weiss calls "the ethic of self-realization" and the constraints imposed by commitment to marriage and a family. Industrial societies require mobile and adaptive citizens whose first loyalty is to the development of their individual capabilities. Self-realization is almost a duty. Americans are particularly resis-

tant to attempts to place restrictions on their private lives. We claim a "right to the unimpeded pursuit of happiness" (Weiss, 1975, p. 8). As Margaret Mead put it, "All persons should be allowed to move if they don't like their present home, change schools, change friends, change political parties, change religious affiliations. With freedom to choose goes the freedom to change one's mind. . . . [W]hy should marriage be the exception?" (1949, p. 334). The clash between self-fulfillment and family commitment explains the apparent paradox that although most Americans consider marriage critical to their well-being, divorce rates have climbed. The desire and even duty to find happiness makes Americans less willing to tolerate an unhappy, unsatisfying marriage. This plus the fact that barriers to divorce have decreased and opportunities for a decent life after divorce have increased explains current trends.

Who gets divorced? Divorce is not distributed evenly through American society. Certain segments of the population are more likely to divorce than others, and certain kinds of marriages are more likely to break up than others. A profile of divorce-prone marriages suggests how social forces work for and against marriage. The following factors have been associated with divorce (based on Goode, 1976; Norton and Glick, 1976; Reiss, 1976; and Glick and Norton, 1977):

Residence: Urban couples are more likely to get divorced than couples who live in rural areas.

Age at Marriage: Divorce rates are twice as high for men married before age twenty and women married before age eighteen than for people who marry later in life.

Length of Acquaintance: Couples who knew each other for at least two years before getting married are more likely to remain married.

Income: Divorce rates are highest in the lower-income brackets and lowest in the upper-income brackets. (One reason may be that the social and financial consequences of divorce are greater for upper-income couples, who are more likely to be involved with one another's kin and to have property investments that are difficult to divide.) In recent years, however, the divorce rate has been increasing faster in upper- than in lower-income groups, so that the two rates are beginning to converge.

Education: Men who have graduated from college or gone to graduate school have the lowest divorce rates. For women, the reverse is true. Those with the most education (college degrees and graduate school) have the highest divorce rates. This may be because they have more options or because training removes them from the marriage market. In recent years, however, the education gap, like the income gap, has been closing.

Religion: Divorce rates are higher for Protestants than for Jews or Catholics; higher for people who do not attend church regularly than for those who do; and highest for couples of different faiths. (The principle of homogamy—like marrying like—seems to hold.)

Family and Friends: A couple whose family and friends approve of their marriage, share their attitudes toward marriage, and view their marriage as stable is more likely to remain together than those who risk social disapproval with their choice of mate and life style.

We do not mean to suggest that knowing a couple's background and social environment enables one to predict whether their marriage will last. But certain types of marriages are higher risks than others.

The Consequences of Divorce

A marriage has been going badly for months, even years. Finally the day comes when he packs his things and moves to a new apartment, or she collects the children and drives to her mother's or sister's house. In some cases, the husband and wife agree that they would be happier apart and plan the separation together. In other cases, one spouse plans the separation alone and the other comes home to an empty house. What happens next?

The impact on adults Robert Weiss's interviews with separated and divorced men and women suggest that nearly all go through a period of emotional and social upset (1975). Usually the couple's fondness for one another erodes before they separate. Trust has given way to mistrust, identification to alienation, desire to anger. They see each other's faults all too clearly. Yet even though love has faded, attachment—the feeling of being emotionally bound to the other person—persists. Most of the people Weiss interviewed experienced "separation distress." For a time, all their attention was focused on the lost spouse, and the inaccessibility of that person caused intense discomfort, anxiety, even panic. Many had difficulty sleeping or concentrating on their work. Severe depression is much more common among recently separated individuals than among other people of the same age and socio-economic position (Paykel, 1969). Whether depression is a cause or an effect of separation is difficult to say: Emotional disturbances may lead to divorce or vice versa. Not everyone experiences separation distress, however. Some individuals become euphoric. Suddenly life feels like an adventure; anything seems possible; they are elated to discover that they can do very well on their own. Over time, both separation distress and euphoria give way to loneliness. At times, they feel empty and isolated, without hope of finding someone who cares and whom they can care for. Weiss suggest that the impact of divorce on adults depends in part on whether they see themselves as having initiated the separation or as having had divorce imposed upon them. Individuals who were caught off guard—who thought they had a reasonably satisfactory marriage until their spouse unexpectedly announced that the

Mitigating the Negative Economic Impact of Divorce: Public Policy Recommendations

Were it not for the financial disadvantages that being a member of a female-headed family entails, this phenomenon [a rising divorce rate accompanied by a falling rate of remarriage] might not have attracted much attention. But these families run a disproportionately high risk of being poor. In 1977 the median income for families headed by males was $17,517 in contrast to $7,765 for female-headed families. Moreover, whereas female-headed families comprised 14.4 percent of all families, they accounted for almost half (49.1 percent) of the families in poverty. . . .

In light of the fact that many American children will spend some part of their youth in single-parent families, usually headed by their mothers, and that these families often suffer economic deprivation, the high incidence of divorce makes this problem a candidate for policy action.

1. It is recommended that the economic effects of divorce on older women who have not worked outside the home during the marriage be studied and appropriate action taken if necessary to assist this group in becoming economically self-sufficient. . . . Programs might involve job guidance, training, day care for children, and temporary income maintenance. Other suggestions include equal pay for equal work, equal credit rights, higher welfare benefits, low-cost housing, and low-cost legal services. . . .

marriage was over—seem to suffer most. The ground has been swept from under their feet. They expect disasters in other areas of their life and begin to doubt their own judgments and perceptions.

Divorce creates social as well as emotional troubles. The loss of a spouse may be compounded by the perceived or actual loss of social standing; loss of friends (either because they "took sides" or because the individual now feels uncomfortable with married couples); material losses (income, savings, a home, a car, possessions); and perhaps loss of access to children. More subtly, when a couple divorces, both partners lose the social definitions that accompany being married and settled. A woman may lose the identity she had through vicarious participation in her husband's occupation (for example, the identity of "doctor's wife"). A man may lose his children's daily confirmation of his social role as father. Both partners may feel as though they are not quite the same people as when they were married. And adjusting

2. It is recommended that more effective means be sought to ensure full compliance with child support and alimony awards. Consideration might be given, for example, to the development and implementation of a federal law requiring child support deductions from wages. Such a system could be cost-effective in terms of its welfare cost savings and would also reduce the physical and emotional stress on custodial parents. If fathers are in partial or total noncompliance, mothers have an array of enforcement mechanisms from which to choose. Many women, however, fail to utilize them, in part because of the cost in terms of both time and money. . . .

3. It is recommended that standards be developed to aid the courts in awarding reasonable and fair amounts of child support and alimony. For child support, these criteria should include, among other things, the number and ages of dependent children and the joint resources of all members of the previously intact family. . . . [One] formula recognizes both the mother s and father s earnings as relevant in determining how much the father should pay. The formula also includes adjustments for economies of scale, child-care expenses, income taxes, changes in economic status after a divorce, economic needs of a new family, and long-run opportunity costs of marriage and children.

Source: Thomas J. Espenshade, "The Economic Consequences of Divorce," *Journal of Marriage and the Family,* Vol. 41, No. 3 (August 1979), pp. 615–25.

to divorce depends on social as well as emotional resources. Adequate financial resources, loyal relatives and friends, and the wife's job skills and husband's homemaking skills all make a difference.

When children are involved, these troubles are compounded. Here we will look at just one source of trouble, finances. Over 90 percent of the children living with only one parent in this country live with their mothers. Divorce nearly always means a reduction in their standard of living. Indeed,

female-headed families are far more likely to be living in poverty than male-headed families (see box above). Although it is true that a higher percentage of low-income than middle- or upper-income couples get divorced, this is only part of the reason. Suppose that a middle-income couple bought a modest house in the suburbs and the wife quit her job to be at home with their small children (Weiss, 1979, pp. 15–16). In the divorce settlement, he agrees to give her the house plus half of his $1,500 monthly salary. This is a generous settlement, more than U.S. courts usually award. Nevertheless, it means an immediate reduction in income of 50 percent. Although the husband's departure reduces family income, it does not reduce expenses by very much. Mortgage payments, taxes, heat, and light for the house might add up to $650 a month. This leaves her $100 a month for all other expenses. The obvious solution is for her to get a job, but if she has been out of the labor market for some time, there is little chance of her earning enough to make up for the reduction in income. Indeed, getting a job may create additional expenses—for baby-sitters, or perhaps for a car or a new wardrobe. There is no guarantee that he will continue to send her half of his income, especially if he remarries. (Support payments are difficult to collect.) A recent survey of divorced mothers showed that their incomes go down while their needs rise (Duncan, 1976, p. 87). Moreover, the higher a mother's standard of living before divorce, the greater the discrepancy between her post-divorce income and needs (Weiss, 1979, p. 16). This decline in standard of living affects children as well as adults.

The impact on children The proportion of American children living with only one parent more than doubled between 1960 and 1978. About one child in six (or 12 million youngsters) lives in a single-parent household today. Estimates are that nearly one in two children who are now infants will see their parents separated or divorced before they reach age eighteen (Weiss, 1979, pp. ix–x).

Fifteen or twenty years ago, conventional wisdom held that divorce was always bad for children. Parents were advised to remain in unhappy marriages "for the sake of the children." So-called broken homes were held responsible for psychological problems, antisocial behavior, learning difficulties, and other childhood problems. Today, many people believe that quarreling parents are

worse for children than divorce is. What are the facts?

In 1971, Judith Wallerstein and Joan Kelly launched the Children of Divorce Project in Marin County, California. Members of sixty families that had recently been dissolved through divorce were given in-depth interviews by members of a team of psychologists and social workers. Follow-up interviews were conducted eighteen months later and again after five years. The children in the study were essentially healthy, happy youngsters. The majority were selected from middle-class, suburban families to control for the possibility that the effects of chronic poverty or urban living on children would be confused with the effects of divorce.

Wallerstein and Kelly's findings were mixed (Kelly and Wallerstein, 1976; Wallerstein and Kelly, 1976). For nearly all of the children, divorce had hit like a bolt of lightning. In one child's words, "We were sitting in the dark with candles. Then they [her parents] told us suddenly about the divorce. We didn't have anything to say, and so we watched TV." The children were totally unprepared. They saw their families as no better but no worse than other families around them. None of the children experienced divorce as a solution to unhappiness.

The immediate impact of divorce varied with the child's age. Pre-schoolers tended to pretend that their families were not breaking up. School-aged youngsters, seven to ten, reacted as they might to a death. "I have to hold it in, 'cause I'd be crying all the time," one seven-year-old boy told the interviewer. Many experienced loss as insatiable hunger; many were afraid of being forgotten by the parent who moved out (usually the father). Older children tended to react with shame and anger. They were ashamed that their family was breaking up, ashamed of their parents' behavior, ashamed of the implied rejection of themselves. "She's acting just like a college student, at age thirty-one—dancing and dating and having to be with friends," one girl said of her mother. A number were morally indignant. They saw no justification for the divorce and blamed one parent or the other. (Few blamed themselves, contrary to widespread belief.)

Five years later, Wallerstein and Kelly (1980) found that 28 percent of the children strongly approved of the divorce in retrospect; 30 percent still strongly disapproved; 42 percent were in the middle. Most harbored fantasies of magically reconciling their parents. About 29 percent were doing reasonably well. Their teachers considered them "average," but spells of sadness, insecurity, and anger punctuated their lives. Roughly 39 percent were moderately to severely depressed. Loneliness was their main complaint. Thirty-four percent were thriving. Having survived the divorce seemed to have increased their self-sufficiency. They felt highly competent at school, on the playground, and at home. Most of the children, however, had suffered.

Wallerstein and Kelly found that the crucial factors in a child's adjustment were a stable, loving relationship with *both* parents, a predictable visiting pattern with the parent who did not have custody, and lack of friction between parents. Several factors they expected to influence adjustment did not, including grandparents who accepted the divorce, friends, and whether or not the mother worked. When one or both parents remarried, after an initial period of friction (particularly if the new mate assumed the role of parent too quickly), most children accepted the stepparent without renouncing their feelings for their real parent. Asked about his father, one ten-year-old boy responded, "Which dad do you mean?" Children whose parents tried to turn them against their ex-spouse suffered the most. Wallerstein and Kelly conclude that "a divorced family per se is neither more nor less beneficial for children than an unhappy marriage. Unfortu-

nately, neither unhappy marriage nor divorce is especially congenial for children" (1980, p. 76).

Richard Farson of the Humanistic Psychology Institute in San Francisco (1978) has argued that the data show that most children (the 34 percent who are thriving and the 29 percent who are average) adjust well to divorce, without the suffering described by Wallerstein and Kelly. He believes that all children have spells of turmoil, grief, and anger, that it's part of living. He argues that given the cultural notion that divorce is a tragic event, it is hardly a surprise that questioning children about their parents' breakup elicits "pathetic responses" from them. They are reflecting their culture and the attitudes of adults: They say what they have learned they are expected to say. Farson holds to the "calamity theory of development": that adversity makes children stronger.

What can be done to reduce any negative impact of divorce on children? One possibility is joint custody: giving the mother and father equal legal rights and responsibilities for children so that neither becomes a "weekend parent." The children live with one parent one week (or semester), the other parent the next, visiting in between. Ideally, this would reduce the child's sense of loss and prevent parents from using children as pawns in their own disputes (Dullea, 1980). In most cases, however, custody is awarded to the mother, and the economic problems of a female-headed household compound the social and emotional troubles of divorce. In Sweden, the government resolves this by guaranteeing divorced mothers who do not work an income, assuming responsibility for collecting child-support and alimony from the father, and providing inexpensive day care for all parents who work (Bane, 1976b). Although divorce is not a social disgrace in the United States today, it has not been accepted to the point where society assumes responsibility for all divorced mothers.

Family Violence

Through the 1960s, most people considered family violence a rare phenomenon, confined to mentally disturbed or poor people (Gelles, 1980). Research based on official statistics or clinical studies tended to support this impression. Although medical and mental health professionals were concerned about child abuse, other forms of family violence were largely ignored. Several factors contributed to the emergence of family violence as a high-priority social issue in the 1970s. First, both social scientists and the general public became increasingly sensitive to violence. The war in Vietnam, political assassinations, urban riots, and the rising homicide rate made the nation self-conscious. One black militant quipped, "Violence is as American as cherry pie." Second, the Women's Movement called attention to battered wives. It provided a forum where women could discuss their special problems and it publicized the results of these discussions. Third, new research (Gil, 1970; Gelles, 1974) suggested that family violence was widespread and that it could not be explained solely in terms of psychological factors or income.

Family violence continues to be a social issue because there is little agreement about where to draw the line between the legitimate use of force and illegitimate acts of violence in the family. Most Americans approve of the use of certain kinds of physical force on family members in certain situations. For example, most people think spanking a child on occasion is normal, necessary, and good (Straus, Gelles, and Steinmetz, 1980). One in four men and one in six women even say it is acceptable for a man to hit his wife under some circumstances (Stark and McEvoy, 1970). A number of studies show that bystanders, agents of social control (such as police or social workers), and victims of family violence accept behavior among family members that would be considered illegitimate violence if it occurred between strangers. It is "OK" for a parent to smack a child. But is it OK for a stranger to do so, or a teacher? At what point does physical punishment become child abuse? The lack of agreed-upon norms governing the use of force in the family is one reason why bystanders and even victims are reluctant to report family violence to officials, and officials are reluctant to label injuries evidence of abuse. Lack of consensus tends to cover up, and even perpetuate, family violence.

Murray Straus and colleagues (1980, pp. 20–22) distinguish between normal and abusive violence as follows: "Normal violence" refers to acts that are intended to cause physical pain, but have wide social approval, such as a slap or a spanking. They characterize these acts as violent because they do not believe the utility of spanking or slapping should be taken for granted. There is some evidence that approval of milder forms of violence in the family encourages children to use more abusive forms of violence as adults. "Abusive violence" refers to acts that have a high potential for injuring a family member, such as kicking, beating up the person, hitting the person with a hard object, shooting or trying to shoot, stabbing or trying to stab a family member.

Family Violence in Perspective

Violence toward children dates back to pre-Biblical times. Five thousand years ago, the Sumerians appointed an official to whip young boys who misbehaved. In medieval times, Christians commemorated the anniversary of King Herod's Slaughter of the Innocents by whipping children. In colonial America, the Puritans took the Biblical dictum "Spare the rod and spoil the child" quite literally. Parents felt a moral obligation to "beat the devil" out of their children (Radbill, 1974). For most of history, wives have also been on the receiving end of the stick. According to the Biblical story of creation, it was Eve who brought sin and sorrow on humankind by eating the forbidden fruit. Women have been considered inherently evil, and deserving of punishment, ever since. The expression "rule of thumb" is said to come from British common law, which stated that a husband must not beat his wife with a rod thicker than his thumb. The law was intended to "protect" wives from excessive punishment (Davidson, 1977).

Family violence is found in most contemporary societies. Wife-beating has been found in affluent German families (Haffner, 1978); linked to both traditional patterns and changing family roles in Africa (Mushanga, 1978); and associated with notions of male honor in Mediterranean and Arab nations (Loizos, 1977). In parts of Italy and India, small children are sold to landlords and treated as chattel. Elsewhere, children are commonly used as soldiers and as beggars (and sometimes mutilated to make them more effective at the latter) (Taylor and Newberger, 1979). How widespread is family violence in the United States today?

The Extent of Family Violence

Victims of family violence are among the "missing persons" in official crime statistics. People are unlikely to report that someone who is supposed to love them has physically hurt them. To overcome this statistical deficit, the sociologists Murray Straus, Richard Gelles, and Suzanne Steinmetz conducted a national survey in 1976 (as described in Chapter 2). A representative cross-section of 2,143 American families was interviewed. Each person was asked how he or she dealt with family conflicts and given a choice of eighteen responses. Seven of the items described acts of normal or abusive violence. The others described rational discussions or arguments, and verbal or

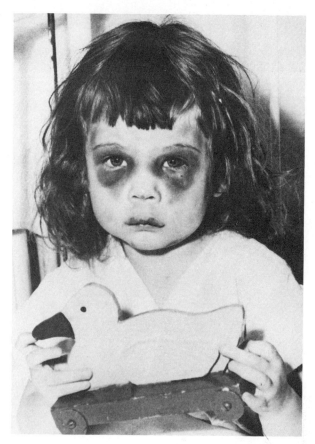

In most cases, a severe beating is not an isolated incident but part of a pattern of child abuse.

nonverbal expressions of hostility (such as insults or smashing objects). This survey found that family violence is surprisingly common (Straus, Gelles, and Steinmetz, 1980).

Violence toward children About seven in ten parents said they had used some form of violence on a child during the preceding year. In most cases, the punishment was relatively mild—a slap, a shove, a spanking. But many admitted to abusive violence. At some point, nearly 8 percent had kicked, bitten, or punched a child; slightly more than 4 percent had beaten up a child; and almost

Table 8-2
Frequency of Parental Violence Toward Children

| Violent Behavior | Percentage of Occurrences in Past Year | | | | Percentage of Occurrences Ever Reported |
	Once	Twice	More Than Twice	Total	
Threw something at child	1.3	1.8	2.3	5.4	9.6
Pushed, grabbed, or shoved child	4.3	9.0	18.5	31.8	46.4
Slapped or spanked child	5.2	9.4	43.6	58.2	71.0
Kicked, bit, or hit child with fist	0.7	0.8	1.7	3.2	7.7
Hit child with something	1.0	2.6	9.8	13.4	20.0
Beat up child	0.4	0.3	0.6	1.3	4.2
Threatened child with knife or gun	0.1	0.0	0.0	0.1	2.8
Used a knife or a gun on child	0.1	0.0	0.0	0.1	2.9

Source: Adapted from R.J. Gelles, "Violence in the Family: A Review of Research in the Seventies," *Journal of Marriage and the Family,* Vol. 42, No. 4 (November 1980), p. 877.

3 percent had threatened a child with a knife or gun. In many cases, the situation was chronic: Children who were beaten were beaten an average of every other month. Projecting these figures onto the U.S. population as a whole, as many as 1.9 million children are kicked, bitten, or punched by a parent each year; as many as 750,000, beaten up; and about 46,000, threatened with a knife or gun (see Table 8–2).

Violence between spouses In one of every six families interviewed, the husband or wife had committed at least one violent act toward his or her spouse during the preceding year (see Table 8–3). One in three had used violence at some point in their marriage. Almost 4 percent of wives had been beaten up by their husbands that year. Most

surprising, given the belief that males are the more aggressive half of the species, was the finding that 4.6 percent of husbands had been hit by their wives. This is not to say that the problem is as serious as that of battered wives. There is evidence that women are more likely to be severely injured than are men and that many wives become violent in self-defense (Gelles, 1979). Conjugal violence does not necessarily stop with punches and kicks. One of twenty-seven people interviewed had been threatened with a knife or gun by a spouse. Moreover, spouse abuse was not an isolated event. Over half the couples who reported violence said beatings took place an average of three times a year. In most cases, both the husband and the wife used violence.

These figures suggest that each year, over 1.8

million American wives are beaten, and 1.7 million are threatened with a knife or gun by a spouse. It seems that for many Americans, a marriage license is a hitting license.

Violence between siblings Although parent-child and husband-wife violence have received the most attention, physical fights between brothers and sisters are by far the most common form of family violence. Four out of five children ages three to eighteen who had a sibling at home had tried to hurt a brother or sister in the preceding year. Fights between siblings go well beyond "fun and games," or normal violence. Forty-two percent of children had kicked, punched, or bitten a brother or sister; 40 percent had hit a sibling with an object; 16 percent had beaten up a sibling. These were not isolated events. For example, among fifteen- to seventeen-year-olds who were violent, fights broke out about every three weeks. The survey found that boys are more violent than girls, but only slightly so. The rate of sibling violence does decrease with age, but incidents may still occur among siblings in their twenties. All told, the survey indicates that each year, 19 million American youngsters commit at least one violent act that would be considered assault if not directed at a family member. One reason for this high rate of violence is that parents consider fights among siblings inevitable: "Kids will be kids."

Violence toward parents Interviews revealed that children not only fight with one another; they attack their parents. Each year between 750,000 and 1 million American teen-agers commit a violent act toward a parent. As many as 2,000 parents are killed by their own children each year. The elderly do not escape family violence. An estimated 500,000 persons over age sixty-five who live with younger family members are abused each year. Abuse of the elderly includes violence (beatings, punching, scalding,

Table 8–3
Comparison of Husband and Wife Violence Rates

	Incidence Rate (%)	
	H. to W.*	*W. to H.**
a. Threw something at spouse	2.8	5.2
b. Pushed, grabbed, or shoved spouse	10.7	8.3
c. Slapped spouse	5.1	4.6
d. Kicked, bit, or hit spouse with fist	2.4	3.1
e. Hit or tried to hit spouse with something	2.2	3.0
f. Beat up spouse	1.1	0.6
g. Threatened spouse with knife or gun	0.4	0.6
h. Used a knife or gun on spouse	0.3	0.2
Spouse-Beating (Includes *d* through *h*)	3.8	4.6
Overall Violence Index (Includes *a* through *h*)	12.1	11.6

*H. to W.: husband to wife; W. to H.: wife to husband.
Source: Adapted from R.J. Gelles, "Violence in the Family: A Review of Research in the Seventies," *Journal of Marriage and the Family,* Vol. 42, No. 4 (November 1980), p. 878.

burning with a cigarette), neglect (withholding food or refusing help in getting to the bathroom), and extortion (taking checks or other assets by force or threat) (see Chapter 12).

The Causes of Family Violence

Why is the American family the scene of so much violence? Let's begin with what does *not* cause violence in the home.

Myths about family violence Many people believe that someone who beats his or her spouse or child must be "sick"—psychologically disturbed. The earliest research on family violence concluded that wife- and child-beaters were suffering from personality disorders. However, these conclusions were based on *post hoc* studies of a limited number of cases (Spinetta and Rigler, 1972). For example, a researcher might interview a parent after he or she had been identified as a child abuser by hospital staff. The interview might suggest the person was suffering from paranoia. But did the parent abuse the child because he or she was paranoid, or did the parent become paranoid because he or she was accused of child abuse? (Gelles, 1979). Current research indicates that the rate of psychological disturbance in violent families is no higher than that in the population as a whole (Straus, 1980).

Another common myth is that family violence is confined to the lower classes. It isn't. Abusive violence is found in every class and at every income level. The impression that the poor are violent comes from the fact that poor people are more likely to go to clinics, to come to the attention of authorities, and to be recorded in official statistics. This is not to say that family violence is distributed evenly through society, however. Rates of family violence are highest among urban families, members of racial minorities, people with no religious affiliation, people with some high-school education, low-income families, blue-collar workers, people under age thirty, and families in which the husband is unemployed. Far from explaining family violence, this list of characteristics raises new questions for research. For example, the most violent husbands and fathers in this survey were men with high-school educations. Grammar-school dropouts and college graduates were far less likely to be violent. Does this mean that having some education is more stressful than having no education (Straus, Gelles, and Steinmetz, 1980, pp. 146–47)?

The structural causes of family violence Straus, Gelles, and Steinmetz (1980) concluded that violence is built into the family system, that the structure of American families tends to encourage violence. They identify four factors that contribute to violence. The first is *intimacy*. Family members spend more time with one another than with anyone else. The range of their activities is much greater than that with non-family members. They are committed to one another—often involuntarily. (One can divorce one's spouse, but not one's parents or children.) Family members get to know each others' likes and dislikes, strengths and weaknesses, loves and fears. This information can deepen relationships, but it also provides ammunition for vicious attacks. A cutting remark by a family member hurts more than the same remark by an outsider—and is more likely to lead to violence.

A second factor is *privacy*. As the saying goes, "A man's home is his castle." What happens within the walls of a castle is shielded from outside observers. The very word "castle" connotes freedom from outside intervention. Neighbors, friends, and police are reluctant to invade family privacy. Often they pretend not to notice violence. Moreover, when disputes occur within the family, there is no disinterested third party to act as a referee. This is particularly true in nuclear families.

Third, cultural *norms* support and even mandate the use of violence on family members. Often victims of conjugal violence say they deserved a good crack; they "had it coming." Support for using violence on children is even stronger. Seventy percent of parents in the survey said it was necessary or good to slap or spank a twelve-year-old (1980, pp. 47, 55). Many parents feel it is their duty to spank children, that it is for the children's own good, and that they are glad their parents used corporal punishment on them (Gelles, 1977). Another survey (Stark and McEvoy, 1970) found that 70 percent of Americans believe it is "very important" for a boy to have a few fist fights while he is growing up. Often the fight is between siblings. Thus it seems that Americans consider the use of physical force on family members normal. Violence is an accepted solution to conflicts.

An incident reported to one researcher shows how norms relating to violence operate. A marriage counselor was seeing a couple in which the husband had hit his wife on several occasions. Each time, he had apologized with apparent sincerity, explaining that he had "lost control." In his mind, the act was almost involuntary. During one session, the counselor asked why he hadn't stabbed his wife. The husband looked at the counselor as if he were crazy. The counselor's point was that the man was in fact operating under the norm that it is acceptable to hit your wife, but not to stab her. If he had been truly out of control, the norm against stabbing would not have operated (Straus, Gelles, and Steinmetz, 1980, p. 45).

Finally, the process of *socialization* teaches many people to associate violence with the family. The family is the place where most people have their first experience of physical coercion. More importantly, violence acquires emotional and moral meaning from the family context. Parents spank children for their own good, because they love them. The use of physical punishment conveys three hidden messages. Lesson one is that those who love you most are also those who hit you—which implies that the people you love are the ones you hit. Lesson two is that hitting someone is morally right if it is for a worthy purpose. After all, parents hit children to correct their behavior or to teach them to avoid injury. Lesson three is that when all else fails, violence is permissible. When a parent says, "Johnny, I've told you ten times . . ." a smack or spanking is likely to follow (Straus, Gelles, and Steinmetz, 1980, pp. 102–04). In short, a slap or spanking carries more than one message. Corporal punishment, however, may accomplish the opposite of what the parent intends: When a parent spanks a child for hitting a sibling, the child may "learn" that hitting is an acceptable way of trying to control another's behavior.

The Consequences of Family Violence

The harm family violence causes individuals is obvious. Each year, an estimated 1.5 to 2 million children are abused and 1,500 to 2,000 are killed by their parents (Straus, Gelles, and Steinmetz, 1980). Domestic disputes account for over 30 percent of aggravated assaults and over 33 percent of homicides in the United States. More police officers are killed answering calls about family disturbances than responding to holdups, robberies, or any other type of crime (Gelles, 1979).

Family violence also has negative consequences for society as a whole. Violence in the home spills over onto the streets. Abused children are more likely to become child abusers themselves. Many murderers and assassins had extremely violent childhoods. Arthur Bremer, who attempted to assassinate Alabama Governor George Wallace, wrote in his diary, "My mother must have thought I was a canoe, she paddled me so much" (Button, 1973). A study of violent inmates of San Quentin found that all had been severely abused between the ages of one and ten (Maurer, 1976). Family violence also exacts a toll from society in terms of police deaths and injuries, court time and expense, and social services. In short, battered children, wives, and husbands are not the only victims. Society as a whole pays for family violence.

Responses to Family Violence

Family violence presents American society with a dilemma (Newberger and Bourne, 1978). On the one hand, norms protect the family from outside intervention. Traditionally, parents have been granted autonomy in rearing children. What happens between a husband and wife is a private matter. On the other hand, norms hold society responsible for protecting people (especially children) from physical harm. Abiding by one set of norms (protecting family privacy) means violating the other (protecting individuals who cannot protect themselves). Abusers also create a dilemma for society. An adult who abuses a child or, to a lesser degree, a man who abuses a woman may be seen as the lowest kind of criminal. Many people find the act so repulsive that they assume there must be something wrong with the person. This in turn activates another view that defines child and wife abusers as sad, needy, deprived people who deserve help. The plights of victims of family abuse—and the victimizers—reflect these contradictory norms.

Victims of child abuse When a battered child comes to official attention, social service agencies essentially have one of two choices. They can take the child away from his parents, or they can return him to his parents and provide the family with social support (counseling, day care, and the like). Neither solution is ideal. Often no relatives or foster homes are available for children who need care, and there is little monitoring of children who are placed in other homes. Moreover, most children either do not think of themselves as abused or believe they deserved it. When taken from their parents, they think they are being given away because they were bad. Family services are also limited. After six months or a year, the family may be declared capable of managing on its own or may simply drop out of counseling. Overburdened and underfinanced, social service agencies rarely follow up on such families. Given the risks of either course, agencies usually end up trying to select the least detrimental alternative as they consider each case.

Victims of wife abuse Why does a woman who is being physically abused remain with her husband? This question complicates the problems of battered wives. Many people accept the myth of the masochistic woman—the belief that on some level, the woman enjoys or needs to be beaten. In interviews with battered wives here and in Britain, however, Lenore Walker (1978, 1979) found no evidence that women enjoyed being hurt. They stayed with their husbands because they didn't know how to support themselves, because of their children, because they had no safe place to go, and out of fear.

Walker found that many abused wives suffer from "learned helplessness." They've come to believe that nothing they do matters, that they have no control over their lives.* She suggests that this is an exaggeration of the female role, which casts women as totally dependent on men. Many abused wives saw their only goal in life as making a successful marriage. They were embarrassed by their home lives and went to great lengths to cover up family violence. Nothing they did pleased their husbands or changed their situation. They ceased trying to escape.

What can an abused wife do? One possibility is to call the police. Usually this provides only temporary relief. The police can either attempt to restore calm or arrest the husband. If they make an arrest, if the case goes to trial, if the man is found guilty, he is usually required to pay a fine or peace bond and released. All of these are "if's," however. The police can make an arrest only if the wife swears out a complaint, but wives often fear that this will only provoke another beating. A vicious cycle begins: Police see one wife after another back off; the police lose sympathy for the women; the women come to see the police as indifferent.

A second possibility is for the wife to go to a

---

*Learned helplessness has been demonstrated with laboratory animals that are given random shocks from which they cannot escape. After a time, the animals become totally passive and make no effort to avoid pain, even when presented with obvious escape routes.

The Chiswick Women's Aid Center in England was one of the first to provide sanctuary to abused women and children. The only men at the center are children's play-group leaders, who teach the youngsters that men can be warm and gentle.

shelter—if there is one nearby and she knows about it. Shelters not only provide physical protection from a violent mate, they provide social support—the company of other women with similar experiences, help in dealing with social service agencies, and so on. Shelters, however, are basically emergency services. In most cases, they do not deal with the husbands. And there are only about 300 shelters in the entire country, though the number is growing.

The third and perhaps most obvious possibility is for the wife to get a divorce. Walker found, however, that many abused wives so isolate themselves from friends and family that they do not realize how bad their situation is. They lie so much to others that they become confused themselves. Moreover, the violence isn't constant. It comes in cycles. Tension builds, the husband explodes, and after the battering there is often a calm, loving period. Many women keep hoping this will last (Walker, 1978, p. 532). More concretely, many women simply do not know how to go about getting a divorce or how to support themselves alone.

The Prognosis

Although the problem has existed for centuries, only in recent years have victims of family violence been recognized or asked for recognition. Slowly, services are becoming available. Shelters, hot lines, and self-help therapy groups (such as Parents Anonymous, for abusive parents) are examples. New York City has set up a program to train police in family intervention and mechanisms to refer families to social agencies (Bard, 1969). In Kansas City, police determined that in over 85 percent of domestic assault and homicide cases, they had been called to the address at least once before the fatal incident. They are now working on ways to analyze data from disturbance calls to predict family violence (Stephens, 1977). Programs to strengthen the family in times of stress are also helpful in treating family violence — for example, family planning (to prevent unwanted children), day care (to relieve mothers of twenty-four-hour duty), and education in parenting (abusers often expect too much from children).

These programs may be useful in treating people *after* they have become victims. But Straus, Gelles, and Steinmetz maintain that the *prevention* of family violence would require major changes in both society and the family. Spankings, the use of corporal punishment in schools (allowed in forty-six states), the death penalty (the use of violence by the state), and private ownership of guns all teach that in certain circumstances violence is acceptable. Unemployment and underemployment weaken already fragile families by denying large segments of the population the resources to create comfortable homes. Violent families tend to be isolated families. Businesses that shift personnel or relocate, government rearrangement of neighborhoods, and other policies tend to deepen isolation. Finally, gender role stereotypes that define housekeeping and child care as women's work (confining women to the home) and define men as the dominant sex tend to encourage *physical* battles between the sexes and the generations. Until these things change, the cycle of violence is likely to continue unbroken. Without domestic disarmament, the level of violence in American homes and American society is likely to remain high.

Sexual Abuse of Children

One reason that family violence was not brought to public attention sooner was that the subject was "taboo." People were reluctant to admit the problem. The taboo against sexual relations between children and adults, especially if they are related, is even stronger. People would like to believe that incest is exceedingly uncommon. The subject has rarely been discussed outside the closed doors of therapists' offices. Studies of the social dynamics of incest typically have focused on small, premodern societies. Anthropologists report that the incest taboo is universal. With rare exceptions,* all societies prohibit sexual relations between close family members, although who is defined as "close family" varies. (The taboo may or may not include various degrees of cousins.) Anthropologists have also suggested that violation of the incest taboo is common. Because of the taboo, research on incest in the United States is still in the "brainstorming" stage (Finkelhor, 1978).

Sexual abuse of children is "the involvement of dependent and developmentally immature children and adolescents in sexual activities that they do not fully comprehend, to which they are unable to give informed consent, or that violate social taboos of family roles" (Kempe, 1978). Sexual abuse of children can be distinguished from both rape and physical abuse. Unlike rape, sexual victimization does not necessarily involve inter-

---

*Brother-sister incest was permitted in ancient Egyptian, Hawaiian, and Incan royal families.

course. Although coercion may be used, it usually does not take the form of physical force or violence. Often children passively submit. Whereas rape is an isolated occurrence, sexual victimization (particularly incest) may continue for months and even years (Finkelhor, 1978, 1979b). How widespread is sexual abuse?

The Incidence of Sexual Victimization

Although more common among rural and poor people, the rate of sexual victimization is surprisingly high in urban and suburban middle and upper classes, according to David Finkelhor's surveys (1979b). Questioning undergraduate sociology students, Finkelhor found that one in five women and one in eleven men had been sexually victimized as children. In most cases, children were victimized by members of their families or by family friends. Sexual relations between a father or stepfather and daughter are the most common.

Patterns of Father-Daughter Incest

Finkelhor has identified six sociocultural factors associated with incest. First, the father exaggerates the male gender role. Often the men are tyrannical. Demanding sexual relations with a daughter is part of a pattern of intimidation. (Other men are shy, ineffectual, and apparently unable to find sexual partners, however.) A second factor is role confusion in the family. Often the mother is withdrawn and depressed, and sexual relations between the husband and wife have ceased. The daughter assumes the mother's responsibilities for the home, the care of small children, and the sexual satisfaction of the father. A mother who suffers from learned helplessness and makes no effort to protect her daughter leaves the younger woman doubly vulnerable. Third, incest is associated with a pattern of abandonment. The cast of characters in the family is constantly shifting. The father and/or daughter may see sexuality as their last resource for holding the family together. Isolation (from social controls and from other sexual partners), overcrowding (so that family members do not or cannot observe the norms of privacy), and opportunity may also facilitate incest. For example, an unemployed father has the time and opportunity to initiate sexual relations with a daughter.

The Consequences of Incest

What is wrong with sexual relations between children and adults? When David Finkelhor (1979a) asked this question, most people responded that they believe it is wrong but aren't clear why. One argument is that it draws children into a world they aren't ready for, that sex in childhood is premature. There is abundant evidence, however, that children are extremely curious about sex and frequently experiment with one another. The asexuality of childhood is largely a myth. A second argument is that children are frightened by sexual advances and that early experience may cause sexual problems later in life. This may be true. Clinical studies indicate that some children are harmed by early encounters. But because of the taboo on researching this question, there is little evidence to say that all or even most children are harmed by sex with adults.

In Finkelhor's view, the central issue is consent. To consent to an activity, a person must know what it is that he or she is consenting to and must have true freedom to say yes or no. Children in our society lack the knowledge to make an informed decision about sexual matters. They don't know the cultural meaning of sexuality, the rules and regulations of intimate relationships, or how other people are likely to react to their behavior. Moreover, a child does not have true freedom to say yes or no to an adult, particularly to a family member. Adults control all manner of things children require (food, shelter, toys, and so on). Often children consent to sexual advances because they have been taught to obey adults. Such consent is neither informed nor free. Of course, a wife may not feel free to refuse her husband's sexual advances, or a secretary her boss's overtures, but at least both have some knowledge of what is going on. Children may not know the cultural implications of sexual experiments with one another, but at least they are equals in their sex play. The *combination* of lack of knowledge and lack of power on the part of the child distinguishes child-adult sexual relations from other forms.

Incest illustrates a theme that has run throughout this chapter. Two of the things people value most in their families—privacy and intimacy—contribute to both private troubles and social problems. To a large degree, contemporary families are insulated from social controls and social assistance. They are not surrounded by kin and neighbors who are as close as family. Norms of privacy often prevent people from discussing family troubles with outsiders and prevent outsiders from "interfering." People experience incest, abuse, and the loneliness of divorce as private troubles. The personal history of their troubles tends to blind them to the social origins of their experience (such as age and gender inequality). Moreover, the conditions that promote intimacy, warmth, and support—privacy, time spent together, deep emotional involvement, in-depth knowledge of one another—also create the potential for incest, for family violence, and for emotional dislocation during a divorce.

Summary

1. The family is a social institution—an established, patterned way of carrying out social activities—that links individuals to society.

2. The changing structure and functions of American families have led some sociologists to conclude that the family, as an institution, is "dying."

3. Other sociologists conclude that although voluntary childlessness and marital disruption have increased, Americans care as much for children and consider having a family as important as ever. Variations on the traditional nuclear family can be seen as healthy adaptations, although they may cause temporary problems of adjustment.

4. Today's high divorce rate can be traced to the lowering of legal and economic barriers to divorce, changing attitudes toward marriage and divorce, and the conflict between the ethic of self-realization and family commitment.

5. Divorce may cause adults emotional and social dislocation—including separation distress, loneliness, changes in social identity, and financial stress. The impact of divorce on children depends in part on their age and continuing relationships with both parents.

6. Family violence is not a rare phenomenon. Both "normal" and "abusive" violence are found at all levels of society and affect husbands as well as wives, parents as well as children.

7. To some extent, violence is built into the family. The intimacy and privacy of family life, cultural norms that support the use of force, and early socialization set the stage for physical abuse of family members and complicate society's response to family violence.

8. The combination of lack of knowledge and lack of power on the part of the child distinguishes adult-child sexual relations from other forms. Although this taboo subject is difficult to research, the available data indicate that sexual abuse of children may be common.

Suggested Reading

Bane, Mary Jo. *Here to Stay: American Families in the Twentieth Century.* New York: Basic Books, 1976.

Hoffman, Lois W., and F. Ivan Nye. *Working Mothers: An Evaluative Review of the Consequences for Wife, Husband, and Child.* San Francisco: Jossey-Bass, 1974.

Straus, Murray A., Richard J. Gelles, and Suzanne K. Steinmetz. *Behind Closed Doors: Violence in the American Family.* New York: Anchor/Doubleday, 1980.

Weiss, Robert S. *Going It Alone: The Family Life and Social Situation of the Single Parent.* New York: Basic Books, 1979.

References

Bane, M.J. *Here To Stay: American Families in the Twentieth Century.* New York: Basic Books, 1976a.

Bane, M.J. "Marital Disruption and the Lives of Children." *Journal of Social Issues,* Vol. 32, No. 1 (Winter 1976b), pp. 103–15.

Bard, M. "Family Intervention Police Teams as a Community Mental Health Resource." *Journal of Criminal Law, Criminology, and Police Service,* Vol. 60, No. 2 (1969), pp. 247–50.

Bronfenbrenner, U. "Nobody Home: The Erosion of the American Family." *Psychology Today,* Vol. 10, No. 12 (May 1977), pp. 41–47.

Button, A. "Some Antecedents of Felonious and Delinquent Behavior." *Journal of Clinical Child Psychology,* Vol. 2 (Fall 1973), pp. 35–38.

Davidson, T. "Wifebeating: A Recurring Phenomenon Throughout History." In M. Roy (Ed.), *Battered Women: A Psychosociological Study of Domestic Violence.* New York: Van Nostrand Reinhold, 1977, pp. 2–23.

Dullea, G. "Is Joint Custody Good for Children?" *The New York Times Magazine,* February 3, 1980, pp. 32 ff.

Duncan, G.J. "Unmarried Heads of Households and Marriage." In G.J. Duncan and J.N. Morgan (Eds.), *Five Thousand American Families,* Vol. 4. Ann Arbor, Mich.: Institute for Social Research, 1976, pp. 77–107.

Espenshade, T.J. "The Economic Consequences of Divorce." *Journal of Marriage and the Family,* Vol. 41, No. 3 (August 1979), pp. 615–25.

Etzioni, A. "The Family: Is It Obsolete?" *Journal of Current Social Issues* (Winter 1977), pp. 4–9.

Finkelhor, D. "Psychological, Cultural, and Family Factors in Incest and Family Sexual Abuse." *Journal of Marriage and Family Counseling,* Vol. 4 (October 1978), pp. 41–49.

Finkelhor, D. "What's Wrong With Sex Between Adults and Children?" *American Journal of Orthopsychiatry,* Vol. 42, No. 2 (October 1979a), pp. 692–97.

Finkelhor, *Sexually Victimized Children,* New York: Free Press, 1979b.

Gelles, R.G. *The Violent Home: A Study of Physical Aggression Between Husbands and Wives.* Beverly Hills, Cal.: Sage, 1974.

Gelles, R.J. "Violence in the American Family." In J.P. Martin (Ed.), *Violence and the Family.* New York: Wiley, 1977, pp. 169–82.

Gelles, R.J. "The Myth of Battered Husbands and New Facts About Family Violence." *Ms.,* October 1979, pp. 65–73.

Gelles, R.J. "Violence in the Family: A Review of Research in the Seventies." *Journal of Marriage and the Family,* Vol. 42, No. 4 (November 1980), pp. 873–85.

Gil, D.G. *Violence Against Children: Physical Child Abuse in the United States.* Cambridge, Mass.: Harvard University Press, 1970.

Glick, P.C. "Updating the Life Cycle of the Family." *Journal of Marriage and the Family,* Vol. 39 (1977), pp. 5–14.

Glick, P.C. "Future American Families." *Coalition of Family Organizations Memo,* Vol. 2, No. 3 (Summer/Fall 1979).

Glick, P.C., and A.J. Norton. "Number, Timing, and Duration of Marriages and Divorces in the U.S.: June 1975." *Current Population Reports,* Series P-20, No. 297. Washington, D.C.: U.S. Government Printing Office, 1976.

Glick, P.C., and A.J. Norton. "Marrying, Divorcing, and Living Together in the U.S. Today." *Population Bulletin,* Vol. 32, No. 5 (October 1977), pp. 2–39.

Goode, W.J. *World Revolution and Family Patterns.* New York: Free Press, 1963.

Goode, W.J. "Family Disorganization." In R.K. Merton and R. Nisbet (Eds.), *Contemporary Social Problems.* New York: Harcourt Brace Jovanovich, 1976, pp. 511–54.

Haffner, S. "Wife Abuse in West Germany." *Victimology,* Vol. 2 (1978), pp. 472–76.

Harris, Louis, and Associates, Inc. *The General Mills American Family Report 1980-81: Families at Work.* Minneapolis, Minn.: General Mills, 1981.

Helfer, R.E., and C.H. Kempe. *The Battered Child,* 2d ed. Chicago: University of Chicago Press, 1974.

Hoffman, L.W. "Maternal Employment: 1979." *American Psychologist,* Vol. 34, No. 10 (October 1979), pp. 859–65.

Hoffman, L.W., and F.I. Nye. *Working Mothers: An Evaluative Review of the Consequences for Wife, Husband, and Child.* San Francisco: Jossey-Bass, 1974.

Kelly, J.B., and J.S. Wallerstein. "The Effects of Parental Divorce: Experiences of the Child in Early Latency." *American Journal of Orthopsychiatry,* Vol. 46, No. 1 (January 1976), pp. 20–32.

Kempe, C.H. "Child Abuse—The Pediatrician's Role in Child Advocacy and Preventive Pediatrics." *American Journal of Disease in Children,* Vol. 132 (1978), pp. 255–60.

Loizos, P. "Violence in the Family: Some Mediterranean Examples." In J.P. Martin (Ed.), *Violence and the Family*. New York: Wiley, 1977, pp. 183–96.

Martin, J.P. (Ed.). *Violence and the Family*. New York: Wiley, 1977.

Mason, K.O., and L.L. Bumpass. "U.S. Women's Sex Role Ideology." *American Journal of Sociology*, Vol. 80 (1975), pp. 1212–19.

Maurer, A. *Physical Punishment of Children*. Paper presented at the California State Psychological Convention, Anaheim, 1976.

Mead, M. *Male and Female: A Study of Sexes in a Changing World*. New York: Morrow, 1949.

Moore, K.A., and S.L. Hofferth. "Effects of Women's Employment on Marriage: Formation, Stability, and Roles." *Marriage and Family Review*, Vol. 2, No. 2 (1979), pp. 1, 27–36.

Mushanga, T.M. "Wife Victimization in East and Central Africa." *Victimology*, Vol. 2 (1978), pp. 479–85.

Newberger, E.H., and R. Bourne. "The Medicalization and Legalization of Child Abuse." *American Journal of Orthopsychiatry*, Vol. 48, No. 4 (October 1978), pp. 593–607.

Nimkoff, M.F. *Comparative Family Systems*. Boston: Houghton Mifflin, 1965.

Norton, A.J., and P.C. Glick. "Mental Instability: Past, Present, and Future." *Journal of Social Issues*, Vol. 32, No. 1 (Winter 1976), pp. 5–20.

Paykel, E.S. et al. "Life Events and Depression." *Archives of General Psychiatry*, Vol. 21 (December 1969), pp. 753–60.

Radbill, S.X. "History of Child Abuse and Infanticide." In R.E. Helfer and C.H. Kempe (Eds.), *The Battered Child*, 2d ed. Chicago: University of Chicago Press, 1974, pp. 3–21.

Reiss, I.L. *Family Systems in America*, 2d ed. Hindsdale, Ill.: Dryden, 1976.

Ross, H.L., and I.V. Sawhill. *Time of Transition: The Growth of Families Headed by Women*. Washington, D.C.: The Urban Institute, 1975.

Rossi, A.S., J. Kagan, and T.K. Hareven (Eds.). *The Family*. New York: Norton, 1978.

Roy, M. *Battered Women: A Psychosociological Study of Domestic Violence*. New York: Van Nostrand Reinhold, 1977.

Skolnick, A. *The Intimate Environment: Exploring Marriage and the Family*. Boston: Little, Brown, 1978.

Sorokin, P.A. *Social and Cultural Dynamics*. New York: Dutton, 1937.

Spinetta, J.J., and D. Rigler. "The Child-Abusing Parent: A Psychological Review." *Psychological Bulletin*, Vol. 77 (April 1972), pp. 296–304.

Stark, R., and J. McEvoy. "Middle Class Violence." *Psychology Today*, Vol. 4 (November 1970), pp. 52–65.

Stephens, D.W. "Domestic Assault: The Police Response." In M. Roy (Ed.), *Battered Women: A Psychosociological Study of Domestic Violence*. New York: Van Nostrand Reinhold, 1977, pp. 164–72.

Straus, M.A. "A Sociological Perspective on the Causes of Family Violence." In M.R. Green (Ed.), *Violence in the Family*. Boulder, Col.: Westview Press, 1980, pp. 7–31.

Straus, M.A., R.J. Gelles, and S.K. Steinmetz. *Behind Closed Doors: Violence in the American Family*. New York: Anchor/Doubleday, 1980.

Taylor, L., and E.H. Newberger. "Child Abuse in the International Year of the Child." *New England Journal of Medicine*, Vol. 301 (November 29, 1979), pp. 1205–12.

Walker, L.E. "Battered Women and Learned Helplessness." *Victimology*, Vol. 2, Nos. 3–4 (1978), pp. 525–34.

Walker, L.E. *The Battered Woman.* New York: Harper & Row, 1979.

Wallerstein, J.S., and J.B. Kelly. "The Effects of Parental Divorce: Experiences of the Child in Later Latency." *American Journal of Orthopsychiatry,* Vol. 46, No. 2 (April 1976), pp. 256–69.

Wallerstein, J.S., and J.B. Kelly. "California's Children of Divorce." *Psychology Today,* January 1980, pp. 67–76.

Watson, J.B. *Psychological Care of Infant and Child.* New York: Norton, 1928.

Weiss, R.S. *Marital Separation.* New York: Basic Books, 1975.

Weiss, R.S. *Going It Alone: The Family Life and Social Situation of the Single Parent.* New York: Basic Books, 1979.

Weitzman, M.S. "Finally the Family." *Annals of The American Academy of Political and Social Science,* Vol. 435 (January 1978), pp. 61–82.

Winch, R. "Some Speculations as to the Family's Future." *Journal of Marriage and the Family,* Vol. 32 (1970), pp. 133–43.

Yankelovich, Skelly, and White, Inc. *The General Mills American Family Report 1976-77: Raising Children in a Changing Society.* Minneapolis, Minn.: General Mills, 1979.

PART FOUR

Social Inequality

Chapter Nine

Poverty

Poverty in the Midst of Plenty

The Penalties of Poverty

The Poor Get Less . . .
. . . And They Pay More

Who Is Poor?

  Female-headed Families
  Minorities
  The Aged
  Regional Poverty

Explanations of Poverty

The Culture of Poverty

The Uses of Poverty
The Economics of Poverty
Poverty and Power

Remedies and Obstacles

Social Welfare Programs

  Social Insurance
  Cash Assistance
  In-Kind Aid

The Culture of Inequality

Everyone knows that poverty exists, but few people realize how extensive it is in such a wealthy and powerful country as the United States. Middle-class commuters rush past the slums in their cars or trains, catching only a glimpse of the littered streets and crumbling houses. Few tourists visit isolated rural villages, and fewer still stop to notice the sickly children or the tar-paper shacks that are without heat and running water. Indifferent city dwellers look hastily away from the ragged derelicts and homeless bag ladies who sleep in neighboring parks and doorways. As a result of this widespread ignorance and neglect, most Americans know little about the invisible world in which at least 25 million of their fellow citizens live.

Having assumed that government welfare programs eliminate at least the worst aspects of poverty, the comfortable television viewer is shocked to learn that in the "other America," babies are dying of malnutrition and elderly citizens are surviving by eating dog food. As a believer in the American dream of success through hard work, the average person finds it hard to believe that among certain social categories, many people cannot find jobs, and that many people who do work do not earn enough to support their families.

Such shock and disbelief echo through the testimony of Robert Coles before a U.S. Senate committee in February 1969. Coles, a research psychiatrist and Pulitzer-prize-winning author, reported having witnessed

> not only extreme poverty, but gross, clinical evidence of chronic hunger and malnutrition—evidence that we as doctors found it hard to deal with ourselves, let alone talk about, because we had been unprepared by our own medical training for what we saw. Today's American physicians are simply not prepared . . . to find in this nation severe vitamin deficiency diseases, widespread parasitism, and among infants, a mortality rate that is comparable, say, to the underdeveloped nations of Asia or Africa.
>
> Why . . . must these children go hungry, still be sick? . . . Why do American children get born without the help of a doctor, and never, never see a doctor in their lives? It is awful, it is humiliating for all of us that these questions still have to be asked in a nation like this.

The poverty that Coles describes usually is defined as absolute deprivation, or lack of the basic necessities of life. To be sure, poverty in the United States is not the same as poverty in the underdeveloped nations of the world. In terms of absolute deprivation, poor Americans are undoubtedly better off than the destitute millions who live on the edge of starvation in Asia, Africa, and Latin America. The poverty of developing nations is discussed in Chapters 3 and 4; this chapter considers poverty within a rich country, the United States. In both cases, poverty is a social problem because it increases human suffering and denies millions of people the chance of a healthy and satisfying life. Moreover, poverty is associated with many other social problems, from crime and political unrest to mental illness and family troubles.

This chapter begins with a discussion of the extent of poverty in the United States. It then examines some of the effects of poverty on the lives of the poor. Next it considers the question of who is poor and shows that the odds of being poor are much greater in certain categories of the population. The main theories explaining the incidence and persistence of poverty are covered in the fourth section. Finally, we weigh the effectiveness of current poverty programs and note the strong opposition to the continuation of efforts to end poverty.

Two Nations: 1840s and 1960s

In the 1840s, Benjamin Disraeli wrote of the constrast between the lives of the rich and poor:

"Well, society may be in its infancy," said Egremont, slightly smiling; "but, say what you like, our Queen reigns over the greatest nation that ever existed."

"Which nation?" asked the younger stranger, "for she reigns over two."

The stranger paused; Egremont was silent, but looked inquiringly.

"Yes," resumed the younger stranger after a moment's interval. "Two nations; between whom there is no intercourse and no sympathy; who are as ignorant of each other's habits, thoughts, and feelings, as if they were dwellers in different zones, or inhabitants of different planets; who are formed by a different breeding, are fed by a different food, are ordered by different manners, and are not governed by the same laws."

"You speak of—" said Egremont, hesitatingly.

"The Rich and the Poor."

In the 1960s, when poverty was receiving much attention in the United States, little had changed. Echoing Disraeli's thoughts, Michael Harrington wrote:

The United States in the sixties contains an affluent society within its borders. Millions and tens of millions enjoy the highest standard of life the world has ever known. This blessing is mixed. It is built upon a peculiarly distorted economy, one that often proliferates pseudo-needs rather than satisfying human needs. For some, it has resulted in a sense of spiritual emptiness, of alienation. Yet a man would be a fool to prefer hunger to satiety, and the material gains at least open up the possibility of a rich and full existence.

At the same time, the United States contains an underdeveloped nation, a culture of poverty. Its inhabitants do not suffer the extreme privation of the peasants of Asia or the tribesmen of Africa, yet the mechanism of the misery is similar. They are beyond history, beyond progress, sunk in a paralyzing, maiming routine.

. . . [T]his country seems to be caught in a paradox. Because its poverty is not so deadly, because so many are enjoying a decent standard of life, there are indifference and blindness to the plight of the poor.

Source: Benjamin Disraeli, *Sybil: Or the Two Nations* (1845; rpt. London: Oxford University Press, 1969), p. 67; Michael Harrington, *The Other America* (Baltimore: Penguin, 1963), p. 169.

Poverty in the Midst of Plenty

How many individuals in the United States are poor? Is the extent of poverty declining? Answers to these questions depend on how poverty is defined. In the statistics kept by the U.S. Government, the *poverty line* determines who is or is not classified as poor. In 1978, the official poverty line for an urban family of two adults and two children was set at an annual income of $6,662, or about $128 a week (U.S. Bureau of the Census, 1979c). Only families with less income than that are considered unable to acquire the basic necessities of food, clothing, and shelter. According to the government's figures, 11.4 percent of the population was living below the poverty line in 1978—more than one out of ten Americans, 25 million people, whose physical needs were not being met (U.S. Bureau of the Census, 1979c).

In 1980, however, New York City's Department of Consumer Affairs estimated that an average family of four in the city spent about $100 for their weekly "food basket." If an average diet cost $100 a week, a family whose income was slightly above the poverty line ($6,800) would have had only $30 a week left to spend on other essentials —rent, utilities, clothing, transportation, medical care, and taxes. To make ends meet on $130 a week, this family would have had to cut back drastically on food expenses, give up going to the dentist and the doctor, and do without new clothes and decent housing. Nonessentials—life insurance, birthday presents, an automobile, an occasional movie—would be out of the question. By the standards of most Americans, members of this family would be deprived of the goods and services anyone needs for a decent life. Yet by the official definition, they would not be poor. The government's definition of poverty appears to be unrealistically low.

Upon close inspection, other problems with the government's poverty line become evident. The

This elderly gentleman, begging on the streets of the richest nation in the world, shows that the "social safety net" has holes.

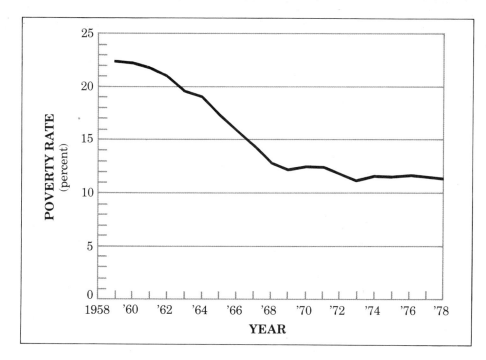

Figure 9–1
Persons Below the Poverty Level, 1959–1978

Source: U.S. Bureau of the Census, *Social Indicators III* (Washington, D.C.: U.S. Government Printing Office, December 1980), Table 9/24.

official poverty line is calculated on the assumption that a poor family spends a third of its income on food. If, as the U.S. Department of Agriculture estimates, a "nutritionally adequate" diet for a family of four costs $2,000 a year, then the threshold of poverty is a $6,000 income. But since the non-food expenses for poor families rose much faster than did food costs during the last few decades, it would be more accurate to count food as one-fourth of today's subsistence-level budget. If this four-to-one ratio were used, the number of the "officially poor" would increase substantially.

Overall, the standard of living for Americans — including the poor — has clearly risen over the last generation. Economic growth has roughly doubled real family disposable income (corrected for inflation) throughout the income scale (U.S. Bureau of the Census, 1975, pp. 17, 18). The greatest gains were made during the 1960s, when a booming economy and new social welfare programs increased job opportunities and public assistance for the poor. During the same period,

there was a sharp rise in the number of dwellings with indoor plumbing, in the sales of automobiles and TV sets, and in private home ownership — all signs of a higher standard of living for every income group. In 1959, over 22 percent of the population was officially poor; by 1969, only 12 percent was (Okun, 1975, p. 69) (see Figure 9–1).

While incomes generally have risen, the distribution of income has not changed since the end of World War II. Families in the top fifth of the income range have consistently received over 40 percent of all income; families in the bottom fifth have received between 4 and 6 percent. Today, the richest 10 percent of U.S. households receive 26.1 percent of all income, while the poorest 10 percent receive 1.7 percent, mostly in the form of Social Security and other transfer payments (Thurow, 1977, p. 11). Using wealth instead of income as a measure of distribution shows that the top 20 percent owns three-quarters of everything that can be privately owned in the United States (stocks, bonds, real estate, and so on), and the bot-

Figure 9–2

The Distribution of Wealth and Income in the United States

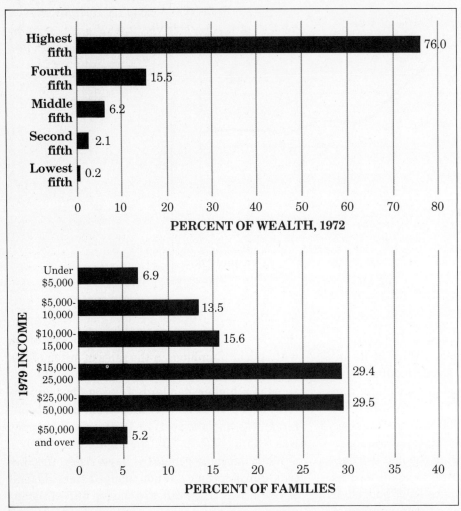

Source: Executive Office of the President, Office of Management and the Budget, *Social Indicators, 1973* (Washington, D.C.: U.S. Government Printing Office, 1973), Chart 5/15; U.S. Bureau of the Census, *Statistical Abstract of the United States, 1980* (Washington, D.C.: U.S. Government Printing Office, 1980), p. 450.

tom 20 percent owns almost nothing. No matter how it is measured, economic inequality is very great in the United States (see Figure 9–2). Furthermore, welfare spending and income taxes have hardly changed the situation over the last thirty years. Although the income pie has grown, the relative size of the slices given to the rich and the poor is about the same.

This tremendous inequality of wealth and income has led some social scientists to suggest an-

Table 9-1
"Optimistic" Budget for a Family of Four
at Approximately Half the Median Income
(150% of the current official poverty line)

Category	Annual Cost	Interpretation
Food	$2,485	$48 per week or $11.95 per person for a week's food (30 percent lower than intermediate budget)
Housing	$1,239	$103 per month for rent, utilities, and furnishings
Transportation	$ 455	$38 per month or 31¢ per day per person
Clothing	$ 660	$14 per month per person
Personal care	$ 186	89¢ per week per person
Medical care	$ 737	$61 per month for all doctor visits, prescriptions, and health insurance
Family consumption	$ 294	$1.41 per week per person
Other costs	$ 327	$27 per month (50 percent lower than intermediate budget).
Compulsory Social Security and disability insurance	$ 472	6.4 percent of total income
Personal income tax	$ 520	7.1 percent of total income
	$7,375	

Source: K. Keniston and the Carnegie Council on Children, *All Our Children* (Harcourt Brace Jovanovich, 1977), p. 30.

other way of defining poverty. Rather than calculating a level of absolute deprivation, the alternative definition conceptualizes poverty in relative terms. Specifically, it has been suggested that half the median income would be a more accurate poverty line. In 1976, the median income was $14,960: Half the families in the United States earned more than that amount, and half earned less. Poverty, defined in relative terms as less than half the standard income for the whole society, would thus be a family income under $7,480. While this figure is about 150 percent of the current official poverty line, it is barely adequate as a family budget (see Table 9–1). Most people agree that this definition produces a truer measure of poverty. When Americans are asked how much money one needs "to get by," they consistently name an amount that is about half the U.S. median income (Rainwater, 1973). Using this amount as a poverty line, however, means that 20 percent of American families in 1976 did not have enough to get by. By this measure, 45 million Americans are poor (U.S. Bureau of the Census, 1978a).

The Penalties of Poverty

Social class standing has a profound and pervasive effect on an individual's life chances, or the opportunities to get a college education, good medical care, a comfortable home, and a well-paying job. Membership in the lowest class brings so many disadvantages that the life chances of the poor — including the chance of surviving at all — are severely limited.

The Poor Get Less . . .

The penalties imposed on the poor begin even before birth. In many cases, poverty means being born to a mother whose nutrition and health care have been poor and who is younger than a middle-class woman when she has her first child and older when she has her last. These conditions are closely correlated with the higher incidence of premature births and mental deficiency that is found among the poor (Hurley, 1969, p. 55). The odds of survival also are affected: Infant mortality at the lowest income levels is nearly 40 percent higher than it is at the middle-income level (U.S. Department of Health, Education, and Welfare, 1972).

This history of illness continues as poor children grow up. Medicaid, a national health program for the poor, has significantly improved medical services in recent years, so that poor children now visit a doctor nearly as often as other children do. Nevertheless, the health of poor children is still much worse: Study after study shows that children in poor families have many more serious health problems, ranging from dental cavities and bad eyesight to tuberculosis and amebic dysentery. Moreover, serious mental illness is diagnosed more often among the poor, and the poor are more likely to be hospitalized than are middle-class patients (De Lone, 1979, pp. 12–13).

Poor families also suffer from unhealthy living conditions. Compared with better-off families, they are more likely to live in crowded and dilapidated housing, whether in farm shacks or in city tenements. In addition, the Census Bureau reports that poor tenants live in neighborhoods that have less police protection and fewer outdoor recreation areas, hospitals, and shopping centers than do the neighborhoods of middle- and upper-class families (U.S. Bureau of the Census, 1979a).

Even when they are healthy, poor people lead dangerous lives. As children, they are more often the victims of child abuse; as adults, they are more often killed or injured in violent attacks (see Chapters 8 and 14). When they fought for their country in Korea and in Vietnam, soldiers from poor families were almost twice as likely as soldiers from middle- and upper-class families to be casualties of war (Mayer and Hoult, 1955, pp. 155–59; Zeitlin, Lutterman, and Russell, 1973, pp. 313–28; Baskir and Strauss, 1978, pp. 6–13). Considering their unhealthy and risky living conditions, it is not surprising that the poor die at an earlier age. The average life expectancy for men and women in the lowest income group is six years shorter than it is for those in the highest group (Antonovsky, 1972, p. 472).

Perhaps the most tragic effect of such deprivation is the limits it imposes on the education that poor children get and, later on, on the income they will earn. Richard H. De Lone, in a report for the Carnegie Council on Children, describes the arithmetic of inequality:

> Jimmy and Bobby are second-graders in the same town, but at different schools. Both boys like school and pay attention in class. Their test scores show that they are both reading slightly above grade level and have slightly better than average I.Q.s. In spite of their similar abilities, Bobby is certain to go to college—more than 4 times as likely as Jimmy—and almost certain to finish—more than 12 times as likely as Jimmy. As a result, Bobby will probably have 4 years more schooling than Jimmy. Bobby is also *27 times* as likely to get a job which will put him in the top 10% of all incomes in the country by the time he is in his late forties. Jimmy has about one chance in 8 of earning even a median income.
>
> These unequal futures of two equally bright students are forecast on the basis of just two facts: Bobby's father is a lawyer making $35,000 a year; Jimmy's father is a high-school dropout who works as a part-time messenger or janitor and earns $4,800 a year. (1979, pp. 3–4)

De Lone concludes:

> In the United States . . . it is a penalty to be born to parents with little education. It is a further penalty to be born to parents who are frequently unemployed and whose employment opportunities are limited to relatively uninteresting, dead-end jobs. . . . Some of the penalties are immediate—the physical

deprivations of poor nutrition, poor health, poor housing, inadequate medical care; some accumulate slowly, influencing the development of adult skills, aspirations, and opportunities. Together, they produce the odds that make Bobby's probable future a vista rich with possibilities and Jimmy's probable future a small door into a small room. (1979, p. 4)

. . . And They Pay More

The penalties of poverty do not end with lack of money and opportunity. The poor pay more for the things they are able to buy: They pay proportionately higher taxes, and they must also pay the hidden psychological costs of being considered failures by the rest of society.

In good economic times, poor families have to struggle to make ends meet. In bad times, when the rate of inflation or unemployment goes up, poor families suffer more than others from rising prices and run the greatest risk of losing their jobs. In a study of the effect of inflation and recession during the 1970s, David Caplovitz concluded that both of these recent economic ills have had the greatest impact on the same kinds of people — "the poor, the poorly skilled, the poorly educated, and members of minority groups" (1979, p. 36).

Since the poor have no disposable income (money left after necessities are paid for), they are hit hardest by increases in the cost of living. According to the Department of Agriculture, feeding a non-farm family of four costs about $2,200 a year. Food costs thus represent 33 percent of a poor family's budget of $6,600, but only 14 percent of the budget of a family living on the median income of about $15,000. If food prices rise 25 percent, the additional cost ($550) represents a much larger share of the poor family's income (8.3 percent) than of the median family's income (3.7 percent). Inflation thus has a disproportionate effect on the lowest income groups.

Rising food costs in the 1970s were partially off-set by raising the poverty line, but higher non-food costs were not taken into account. For example, when the cost of energy doubled in the 1970s, the lowest income groups paid a much higher proportion of their income for heating and gasoline than other groups did (see Table 9–2). When the price of heating oil and gasoline doubled, the impact was thus almost seven times greater for the poor than for the rich (Thurow, 1980, p. 29).

For the same reasons, the burden of certain taxes falls most heavily on people in the lower income groups. Since poor families spend a higher proportion of their income on goods and services, sales and excise taxes account for over 9 percent of family income at the bottom of the income scale, but only about 1 percent at the top (Pechman and Okner, 1974, p. 58). All in all, effective tax rates are highest for the very rich, who pay proportionately more in graduated income taxes, and for the very poor, who pay proportionately more in regressive state and local sales taxes.

The poor not only pay relatively more of their income for basic necessities, they also often pay absolutely more for the things that they buy. Poor families often lack the time and information necessary to shop around for bargains, and they are usually unable to save enough cash to get the benefits of buying in large quantities. Since the cost of doing business is higher in low-income neighborhoods, the poor are often charged higher prices for goods and credit. Finally, slum dwellers are more likely to fall prey to unscrupulous merchants who sell them expensive but inferior products (Caplovitz, 1967, pp. 15–20, 28–31).

The poor must also carry the tremendous emotional burden of continually losing the struggle to feed a family and hold down a menial job. They must suffer as well the contempt of the more prosperous, who consider them "bums" and "welfare chiselers." The daily degradation of poverty was directly experienced by one researcher in disguise:

Table 9-2
The Poor Pay More: Percentage of
Income Spent on Gasoline and
Other Energy Consumption

Population Segment	Gasoline Consumption	Home Energy Consumption	Indirect Energy Consumption	Total
Lowest tenth	9.6%	20.2%	4.3%	34.1%
Second	5.8	10.4	3.9	20.1
Third	5.6	7.4	3.5	16.5
Fourth	5.2	5.6	3.1	13.9
Fifth	4.8	4.7	2.7	12.2
Sixth	4.5	3.9	2.3	10.7
Seventh	3.8	3.9	2.0	9.7
Eighth	3.7	3.3	1.7	8.7
Ninth	3.1	3.0	3.1	7.4
Tenth tenth	2.2	2.0	1.0	5.2

Source: L.C. Thurow, *The Zero-Sum Society: Distribution and the Possibilities for Economic Change* (New York: Basic Books, 1980), p. 30. Estimated from data in U.S. Department of Labor, *Consumer Expenditure Survey,* Series 1973–74, and from input-output tables of U.S. Department of Labor.

At Union Station, while I still had on a conventional business suit, I stopped at a busy orange drink stand and asked the young girl to change a dollar bill. She did and handed me the change with a pleasant, "yes sir." Twenty minutes later I came back in paint-splotched shoes, old black trousers, khaki shirt, and ragged sweater, a wrinkled threadbare raincoat, the part out of my hair, carrying an old brown canvas zipper bag. I asked the girl for an orange drink and she served me, holding the drink until I had put the money on the counter, her face frozen and hostile and never looking directly at me. I already felt the blank wall between me and respectable society by which a man can walk as though invisible. If he asks directions he may get no answer, as though his voice made no sound, or he may get a flash of fear and revulsion in the eye of the man he asks. It is remarkably easy to become an emotional exile from one's own society. (Bagdikian, 1969, p. 20)

Who Is Poor?

Although poverty can happen to almost anyone, the odds of being poor are much greater in certain population groups.

Female-headed families The feminization of poverty is one of the most striking social developments of the last decade. In 1976, for the first time since the Census Bureau began keeping statistics, more poor people were living in families headed by women—widowed, separated, divorced, or unmarried—than in families headed by men. Today, nearly one out of three female-headed households is poor, compared with about one in eighteen male-headed households. The main reasons for this shift are the increasing number of single-parent families (from 11 percent of all families in

1970 to 20 percent in 1978) and the poor job opportunities and inadequate social services that are available for single mothers. When child care is unavailable or expensive, and when the only jobs for unskilled women are low paying, working at all is difficult and often is not worth the trouble. The majority of female heads of families with children do work at least part time, but their earnings are so low that over one-third of single, full-time working mothers of pre-school-aged children are still poor. Nevertheless, single working mothers are much better off than are mothers who depend on welfare: A shocking nine out of ten single, nonworking mothers of small children have incomes below the poverty line (National Advisory Council on Economic Opportunity, 1981, p. 166).

The poverty of fatherless children has increased along with the poverty of their mothers. Of all age groups in the United States, children are the most likely to be poor: About 40 percent of all poor people are under eighteen years of age. More than half of these 10 million children live in female-headed families, and four-fifths of them depend on welfare support to survive (U.S. Bureau of the Census, 1979b). By the official definition, about 16 percent of all American children are poor; by the relative definition of having less than half the median income, more than 25 percent—one out of four—of the children in the United States are paying the penalties of poverty (De Lone, 1979, p. 7).

Minorities The majority of the poor are white, as are most of the families who receive welfare payments. Nevertheless, a greater proportion of blacks and other minority groups are poor. Black Americans make up less than one-eighth of the total population, yet they are almost one-third of the poor population; 31 percent of black families and 22 percent of Hispanic families have incomes below the official poverty line, compared with 9 percent of white families. Disproportionate numbers of Native Americans also are poor: About one-third of Indian families live in poverty, most of them on isolated reservations. Even when minority members are not poor, they still earn less than do members of the white majority (U.S. Bureau of the Census, 1979c, p. 1-3).

These dismal statistics are the product of several social factors. One penalty of being born poor is receiving less education than those born better off. Blacks in the United States are much less likely than whites to finish high school and attend college. In 1978, among people over fourteen years of age, 63 percent of the white population, but only 45 percent of the black population, were high-school graduates; 28 percent of white men and women, but only 17 percent of blacks, had attended college (U.S. Bureau of the Census, 1979b). While the inequalities are still striking, legal efforts to end racial discrimination have recently improved the educational situation for minorities. In 1977, among older blacks (in the over-twenty-five population), only 2 percent had attended college and only 28 percent had finished high school (U.S. Bureau of the Census, 1978b, p. 143).

A second factor that affects the poor is lack of employment opportunities. Even among the college educated, blacks earn only 80 percent as much income as whites earn—a sign that racial discrimination is affecting blacks' chances for better-paying jobs. Moreover, many blacks live in the center of older industrial cities, which were hit hardest by the decline of the U.S. automobile and steel industries. In the large cities of the Northeast and Midwest, unemployment was estimated to be at least 40 percent among black teen-agers in 1977, and the number of black families living below the poverty line increased by 21 percent during the 1970s (U.S. Bureau of the Census, 1978, p. 408; *The New York Times,* September 29, 1980).

Another factor that affects the poor is the higher proportion of female-headed households among the black population. In 1967, the odds that a single black woman with a family would be poor were seven and a half times as great as the odds for a white man; by 1977, the odds were ten and a half times as great (National Advisory Council on Economic Opportunity, 1981, p. 167). This rapid deterioration in the situation of black women affects nearly all statistics on U.S. poverty.

The aged One of the largest groups among the poor are people over sixty-five years of age, who make up about 13 percent of the total. The majority of the aged poor are elderly couples, and the rest are nearly all widows. The economic position of the aged has improved considerably since 1975, when Social Security pensions were automatically tied to rises in the Consumer Price Index. In 1981, the average retired worker's monthly check was increased by $374, and the average couple's check to $640 (*The New York Times,* April 24, 1981). Apart from this subsistence-level income, the aged have few financial resources. Older workers often are required to retire before they are ready, and they find that getting other jobs is difficult. As a result, more than half of the "senior citizens" in the United States live in poverty or at a level not far above it.

Regional poverty Poverty used to be a mainly rural problem, but it is becoming an urban one. While 42 percent of poor families still live in the largely rural South (compared with 30 percent of the total population), the social programs of the 1960s' War on Poverty were far more effective in the Southern states and in other rural areas than they were in the urban North and West. Approximately 14 million fewer people were poor in 1977 than in 1959; of this total, non-metropolitan areas lost 12 million poor, and the South lost 9 million. Moreover, while the rate of Southern poverty has continued to fall since 1969, the rate of poverty in the North and West has risen. In fact, the rate of

urban poverty was higher in 1977 than it had been ten years before (National Advisory Council on Economic Opportunity, 1981, p. 165). In the 1960s, the worst poverty was in depressed agricultural areas, but now most of the chronically poor and unemployed reside in the central cities.

Who, then, is poor? As we have seen, the overwhelming majority of the poor are people who cannot earn the money necessary for subsistence. Many people are poor because they are too old, too young, or too sick to work or because they are single mothers who are not able to hold a full-time job and care for young children at the same time. Instead of being an accident, which happens to individuals at random, poverty is mainly the result of social circumstances that stack the deck against certain groups of people. Far from being only the result of personal failings, poverty is more likely to be the result of social inequality—being born into a poor family, or in a depressed section of the country, or into a deprived racial or ethnic group. For these reasons, explanations of poverty should focus not on individuals but on the impersonal forces of economic change, on the competition for power, and on the effect of cultural beliefs and attitudes.

Explanations of Poverty

In poor countries, poverty is an attribute of the whole society. Except for a wealthy elite, the vast populations of the underdeveloped world survive at subsistence level. Overpopulation and lack of capital account for the slow economic growth that keeps much of Asia, Africa, and Latin America on the edge of starvation. In the highly developed industrial nations of the West, however, poverty stems from different causes. Theories of poverty try to explain why poverty is so persistent even in wealthy societies and why it is concentrated among certain categories of people.

The Culture of Poverty

The easiest answer to the question of why some people are poor is, "It's their own fault." If the poor cannot get a job, or if they have more children than they can support, then it must be because they do not have the same ambitions and interests as other people. Many Americans see the poor as individuals who "don't want to try to better themselves" and whose "mother and father didn't try to teach them anything . . . [or] set an example" (Coleman and Rainwater, 1978, pp. 196–98). In scholarly terms, the poor are thought to have different cultural values and expectations, which they pass on to their children, creating a permanent, isolated underclass.

From his studies of poor communities in Latin America and New York, the anthropologist Oscar Lewis developed the concept of a *culture of poverty* (1959, 1966). Lewis concluded that this culture—or, more properly, this subculture—appears in societies like that of the United States, where the following conditions are found: (1) a persistently high rate of unemployment and low wages for unskilled labor; (2) few political or social organizations that support the lower class; and (3) values in the dominant culture that stress material success and blame individual incompetence or inferiority for failure. In such a situation, Lewis finds, the poor are excluded from the major institutions of society. Out of suspicion or apathy or because of lack of money or discrimination against them, people who live in the culture of poverty

> have a low level of literacy and education, do not belong to labor unions, are not members of political parties, generally do not participate in the national welfare agencies, and make very little use of banks, hospitals, department stores, museums, or art galleries. They have a critical attitude toward some of the basic institutions of the dominant classes, hatred of the police, mistrust of government and those in high position, and a cynicism which extends

even to the church. . . . A minimum of organization beyond the . . . family . . . gives the culture of poverty its marginal and anachronistic quality in our highly complex, specialized, organized society. (Lewis, 1970, p. 71)

Typically, the family in the culture of poverty is dominated by the mother or another woman. Rates of illegitimate births and desertion by fathers are higher than average. Close family relationships are emphasized, but they are often undermined by competition for maternal affection and the very limited supply of material goods.

On the individual level, the members of the culture of poverty feel rejected, helpless, dependent, and inferior; they have little ability to plan ahead or to put off immediate gratification for later rewards. In the face of repeated failure, feelings of resignation and a low level of aspiration are common (Lewis, 1970, pp. 72–73).

Lewis distinguishes between poverty and the culture of poverty. He believes that the latter affects only about 20 percent of the officially poor population of the United States. Although the culture of poverty was originally a response to the frustrations of failing to reach middle-class goals, Lewis argues that it has become a way of life that influences the character and expectations of the children who grow up in it. For that reason, Lewis finds that eliminating poverty through better economic opportunities would not eradicate the culture of poverty (1970, pp. 77–79).

The concept of a subculture of poverty has been subjected to devastating criticism. The most telling points were scored by Charles A. Valentine, who argued that the so-called cultural traits of the poor were the external symptoms, not the underlying causes of poverty (1970, pp. 135–40). Valentine writes that lack of work and low wages are conditions of the environment to which the poor must adapt, conditions that are determined not so much by the behavior and values of the poor as by the economic and political actions of the non-poor. Hostility toward the dominant institutions, low levels of aspiration, and an inclination to live for the present instead of the future —these values and attitudes seem to Valentine to be almost inevitable emotional responses to deprivation and lack of opportunity.

Whether the poor actually violate the norms of honesty and hard work more often than those better off is open to question. Cheating on welfare occurs far less frequently than cheating on income taxes, and several studies have concluded that

If deprivation is blamed on "the culture of poverty," how do we explain how some of the poorest groups, such as Italian Americans photographed here at the turn of the century, escaped the slums?

the rate of white-collar crime is probably as high as that of the more visible crime committed by the poor (see Chapter 14). Lack of prudence and self-discipline is not limited to the lowest class. The "idle rich" have long been known for their self-indulgence and dislike of work. Furthermore, much evidence shows that the poor are as hardworking and ambitious as anyone else. A study of workers in Houston, for example, found no significant differences between the poor and the non-poor in "intrinsic work motivation," commitment to "work and achievement" rewards, or "time orientation." In fact, the ethnic minorities with high levels of poverty expressed greater support of the work ethic than did the white majority. Among blacks and Anglos, the poor were less likely to be employed than the non-poor, but the Chicano poor were employed almost as often as the Chicano non-poor (Davidson and Gaitz, 1974, pp. 229–45).

Other critics have argued that poverty is not a permanent culture but a largely temporary condition. In a recent study of poverty conducted by University of Michigan economists, only about 22 percent of the people surveyed were persistently poor; the others slipped below the poverty line or rose above it from year to year. Most of the persistently poor were simply unable to work: They were either elderly, physically handicapped, or mothers of pre-school-aged children (*The New York Times*, July 17, 1977).

The culture of poverty theory has also been attacked as a sophisticated version of what William Ryan has called "blaming the victim" for social problems. If the causes of poverty and unemployment are assumed to rest in lower-class culture, Ryan argues, then the solution to these problems is supposed to lie in changing those cultural values and attitudes that are handicapping the lower class (1976, pp. 117–41). According to this popular application of Lewis's theory, poverty could be eliminated if the poor were taught the "middle-class" virtues of being responsible, sober, well educated, steadily married, and socially acceptable in every way. Thus to the injury of being poor is added the insult of being thought mentally or morally defective.

Emphasis on the cultural characteristics of the poor, whatever they may be, distracts attention from the basic cause of poverty—lack of money. Other explanations of poverty turn to the economic and political arrangements that produce inequality in American life.

The Uses of Poverty

To explain the persistence of poverty even in wealthy societies, functional theorists argue that inequality is both inevitable and necessary to maintain society. The classic statement of this position was made forty years ago by Kingsley Davis and Wilbert E. Moore, who argued that social stratification—the unequal distribution of prestige and material rewards—ensures that the most important positions are filled by the most qualified persons (1945, pp. 242- 44). If it were not for the social prestige and substantial income that come from practicing medicine, for example, enough talented people would not undertake the years of training and make the effort necessary to be a doctor. A garbage man's position, on the other hand, requires little effort and sacrifice, carries little prestige, and pays a low salary.

The functional theory of stratification has been questioned on several grounds. First, the importance of one occupation over another is often impossible to evaluate. Since garbage men protect clean water supplies and provide sanitary living conditions, for example, they have probably saved more lives than have doctors. Many would argue that some rewarded positions (prostitute, bookmaker) contribute little to society, while others are given higher rewards than their importance or training seems to deserve (movie stars, models, athletes). It also is hard to argue that a vice-president of General Motors must be paid fifty times as much as a schoolteacher in order to ensure an adequate supply of corporate executives.

Functional theorists assert that inequality benefits an entire society by ensuring that the most talented and hardworking people will fill the most important positions. Herbert J. Gans uses the same logic to show how inequality provides additional benefits for certain groups (1973, pp. 102–12). Gans illustrates how many groups have practical "uses" for other people's poverty. First, poor people subsidize many activities that benefit the non-poor: the hiring of low-paid domestic workers frees their employers to get jobs, take on civic duties, and pursue selfish interests. In the United States, the poor wages paid to migrant farm workers benefit consumers by keeping the prices of fruits and vegetables low. Poverty also creates jobs for the social workers, police officers, and pawnbrokers who serve the poor, as well as the racketeers and loan sharks who victimize them. An impoverished class at the bottom of the social hierarchy confirms the status of privileged groups, who can reinforce their own values by comparing themselves with the "shiftless," "irresponsible," and "corrupt" poor. Gans lists ten more social functions of poverty, from providing a market for inferior goods (day-old bread, second-hand clothes) and inferior services (incompetent doctors and teachers) to supporting a stable political system (by giving the Democratic party a dependably loyal constituency). By pushing the functionalist argument to its logical absurdity, Gans demonstrates a tragic irony: Most of society has a personal stake in maintaining a permanently poor underclass.

The Economics of Poverty

The economics of the labor market offer another explanation of poverty. Instead of a single market, in which each worker competes with every other worker for jobs and each employer competes with every other employer for workers, there are

Why don't "they" get a job? When Western Electric advertised for workers in Oklahoma City newspapers, the line began forming at 11:30 A.M. By dawn the next morning, the crowd of job applicants had grown to 2,000. Institutional barriers, not lack of effort or ambition, explain poverty and unemployment in the United States.

actually separate markets for manual, white-collar, and professional labor (Kerr, 1954, pp. 92–97). Furthermore, barriers prevent competition between workers within even these separate markets. There are the preferences of individual workers, who might not want to move to another kind

of job or to another part of the country, and the preferences of individual employers for a certain kind of worker. Institutional barriers are set up by labor unions, professional organizations, and the government so that workers who do not have the right credentials cannot get certain jobs. Some workers lack seniority, for example, or a law or business degree; others may not work because they are not U.S. citizens or because they are under legal working age. As a result:

> [P]ainters do not compete with bricklayers, or typists with accountants, or doctors with lawyers; nor individuals in Portland, Maine, with those in Portland, Oregon. . . . Beyond the specificity of skills and the money costs of physical transfer, lie such various but no less important impediments to competition as lack of knowledge, the job tastes of workers, their inertia and their desire for security, and the personal predilections of employers. (Kerr, 1954, pp. 94–95)

Since workers do not or cannot compete across these barriers, a shortage of labor in one market can exist side by side with an oversupply in another, and the low-paid worker will not be able to take advantage of the higher wages that are being offered in other kinds of jobs. In the current U.S. labor market, it is virtually impossible for laid-off automobile workers in Ohio to become plumbers in Florida or for high-school dropouts in St. Louis to meet the demand for clerical workers in Houston.

In discussing unemployment, economists sometimes refer to a *dual labor market* (see Chapter 7). Jobs in the primary market offer good wages and working conditions, security, and a fair chance of promotion. The typical employer is a large corporation, and the typical employee has specialized skills or education. Jobs in the secondary market, in contrast, are characterized by low wages, poor working conditions, a high rate of turnover, and hardly any chance of advancement. Here the typical worker is part time, unskilled, and non-union; most of the jobs offered are in service industries (nursing homes, fast-food restaurants, data processing) and manufacturing "sweatshops" or as migrant farm labor. Women and minorities make up the majority of the work force.

The roots of poverty are in the secondary market, where unemployment and underemployment are high. Since workers rarely move from one labor market to another, the poor are trapped in the secondary market of badly paid, seasonal, and dead-end jobs.

Poverty and Power

Economic theories explain poverty in terms of the job opportunities that are created by impersonal economic forces. The conflict theory of poverty starts from another premise: that the labor market is essentially a structure of power (Giddens, 1975, pp. 100–03). Relationships within the market are based on the relative bargaining strengths of different groups of workers and employers.

All in all, the poor have little bargaining power in an economy where there is an oversupply of unskilled labor and in a political system that is dominated by the affluent majority. Furthermore, the poor in the United States find organizing as a political bloc to be difficult. The poor are not a homogeneous group with common interests, and many of them do not vote. The result is a vicious cycle: Poor people have little incentive to vote because politicians do not pay much attention to their problems, and politicians do not pay much attention to the problems of the poor because the poor do not vote. Since the poor are discouraged from participating in conventional politics, their principal power, often unrecognized and unused, is in their ability to force concessions by disrupting the social order with demonstrations and various forms of unruly political protest (Gans, 1981, pp. 40–42).

The National Welfare Rights Organization (NWRO) is the first organization to attempt to organize the poor into a separate interest group. Founded in 1966 to protect the poor by making welfare agencies stick to their own rules, the NWRO has won some significant legal victories. One Supreme Court ruling, for example, upheld welfare recipients' right to privacy against unwarranted inspection of their homes by public officials. Many other organizations—including the Urban League and the United Farm Workers' Union—represent the poor primarily, but their interests are so varied that their political effect has been limited.

Powerful groups also discriminate against the poor in their hiring practices. In every society, low-status people do the low-status work. In the United States, women, young and old workers, and minorities fill most of the part-time, domestic, and menial jobs. These "peripheral workers" are often considered mentally or physically unfit for doing regular work (Morse, 1969, p. 66). It is no coincidence, of course, that these "inferior" groups have the same population characteristics as the poor.

Laws forbidding discrimination against minorities and women already exist, but they are not enforced strictly enough to end many racist and sexist practices that handicap the poor. Moreover, reducing discrimination can help poor workers only in an expanding economy; in a static or shrinking job market, more employment for minorities just means more unemployment for other groups.

The unskilled also face a number of institutional barriers to employment, including the college or high-school diploma that is required for many low-level jobs and the restrictive rules for union apprenticeship. Lowering the barriers to allow the poor to compete for these jobs, however, would undoubtedly be protested loudly by the employees and trade unions concerned.

Poverty is a complex social problem with many different roots. No single theory can explain all its causes, but each one illuminates a different aspect of inequality. Efforts to eliminate poverty must also take different directions, from attempts to remedy its most obvious characteristic—lack of money—to attacks on the underlying social and economic causes.

Remedies and Obstacles

In the space of a single decade, total spending on social welfare in the United States quadrupled—from $77.2 billion in 1965 to $286.5 billion in 1975. These enormous expenditures have succeeded in reducing but not eliminating poverty. In 1965, 33 percent of the poor were raised above the poverty line by cash welfare; by 1972, the proportion had risen to 44 percent. In that year, welfare payments and Social Security benefits had reduced the number of poor people from nearly 40 million to about 23 million. These programs, however, do not reach all the poor. In 1975, only about 60 percent of the non-aged poor were receiving any welfare benefits at all, and only about 35 percent received cash assistance. In many cases, the stigma attached to welfare is so great that large numbers of needy persons are too proud to "go on relief" and so never claim the benefits to which they are entitled (Rodgers, 1978, pp. 254–55).

The main reason why so many of the poor fall through the "safety net" can be traced to the inefficiencies and ineffectiveness of current government income-support policies. In fact, welfare is not a single program, but a patchwork quilt of many different federal and state programs, each designed for different purposes and built on different assumptions. Sometimes referred to as the "welfare mess," the variety of these programs makes it difficult for those in need of public assistance to find out how to get it, requires a great deal of money and bureaucratic effort to administer, and by and large neglects a sizable proportion of the needy—the working poor.

Social Welfare Programs

Social welfare spending falls into three main categories: social insurance, cash assistance, and in-kind aid.

Social insurance Social Security pensions, veterans' pensions, and unemployment insurance are designed to replace income that is lost through retirement, disability, or temporary unemployment. All of these programs require contributions from employees and employers (usually through payroll taxes) and pay benefits that are related to past earnings. These programs together paid out $124 billion in benefits during 1976, or about 68 percent of all government transfer payments. Only a third of this money went to families in the lowest fifth of the income scale (Congressional Budget Office, 1977, p. xiii).

Social Security is by far the largest and probably the most successful government income-transfer program. Since its payments increase automatically with rises in the Consumer Price Index, and since every year the number of its elderly recipients grows, Social Security is primarily responsible for the skyrocketing costs of social welfare. Yet, technically, Social Security is not welfare at all (see Chapter 12). Although it produces a huge redistribution of income from the young to the aged, Social Security benefits people at all income levels, not just the poor. Moreover, it is a social insurance program that is financed by regressive taxes: It costs the poor proportionately more but provides them with lower benefits because their earnings are lower. Nevertheless, Social Security has brought the United States a long way toward ending poverty for the aged.

Unemployment insurance and workman's compensation also benefit the better off as well as the poor. These programs serve an important purpose for the people they reach, but since their benefits last only a few months, they tend to miss helping the long-term and chronically unemployed. In

The Dual Welfare System

Two welfare systems exist simultaneously in this country. One is well known. It is explicit, poorly funded, stigmatized and stigmatizing, and is directed at the poor. The other, practically unknown, is implicit, literally invisible, is nonstigmatized and nonstigmatizing, and provides vast but unacknowledged benefits to the non-poor—whether working class, middle class or well to do. . . .

. . . "Social insurance," the heart of the welfare system for the non-poor, has been constructed to be legitimate, to protect the integrity and dignity of the people involved. To a large extent, this legitimacy is provided by some form of camouflage—by protective nomenclature such as "parity," "compensation" and even "social insurance"; by the paraphernalia of private programs, such as Social Security account numbers; and by burying welfare programs in tax laws.

"Public charity," or the welfare system for the poor, has been constructed to be illegitimate. Thus it too leaves the ideology intact. The illegitimacy of poor people's welfare is multifold. There is, first, the illegitimacy of dependency— living off the incomes of others. Second, there is the separate illegitimacy of apparent idleness and the usual association with sin. And third, there is the inherent illegitimacy of government spending, financed by taxation.

Source: A. Dale Tussing. "The Dual Welfare System." *Society*, Vol. 11, No. 2 (January/February 1974), pp. 50–57.

1976, a special survey by the U.S. Bureau of Labor Statistics found that only 36 percent of the unemployed in their sample were receiving unemployment insurance, and even fewer (25 percent) received other kinds of public assistance. In most states, unemployment benefits are minimal in any case: In September 1979, the average weekly payment was $89.10—about $27 less than full-time work at the minimum wage and nearly $40 below the poverty line for a non-farm family of four (National Advisory Council on Economic Opportunity, 1981, p. 167).

Veterans' programs offer pensions and disabil-ity insurance, but they too benefit only a fraction of the poor.

Cash assistance In comparison with Social Security benefits, which represent over two-thirds of government transfer payments, the amount spent on welfare is rather small. Aid to Families with Dependent Children (AFDC) and Supplementary Security Income (SSI) provided $18 billion in cash benefits to the poor in 1976, or only about 10 percent of total government transfer payments (Congressional Budget Office, 1977, p. 2).

AFDC is the most controversial of all welfare

programs. It has been criticized by liberals for not doing enough to protect children and for violating the privacy of its recipients, and it has been attacked by conservatives for being too expensive and for harboring cheaters. By extending benefits primarily to destitute single women and their children, AFDC has also been accused of breaking up families and discouraging parents from working.

The states share the costs of AFDC with the federal government and determine the need of recipients. Statistics for 1975 show that 81 percent of the money went to female-headed families; intact husband-wife families are eligible for aid in only twenty-eight states (Rodgers, 1978, p. 255). The size of the payments varies irrationally from state to state: On average, Mississippi pays $50 per month per family, while New York pays $346

(Keniston and the Carnegie Council on Children, 1977, p. 101). In all, during 1972, over 3 million families received $7 billion in benefits (Council of Economic Advisers, 1974, pp. 168–69).

Since its benefits are set arbitrarily low, the AFDC program is not meeting its explicit goal of supporting children. Families who receive aid often do not get enough to reach the official poverty line, and less than half the children of families living in relative poverty (less than half the median income) receive any benefits at all (Keniston and the Carnegie Council on Children, 1977). Moreover, AFDC is expensive to administer. Elaborate efforts to weed out "chiselers" increase costs and humiliate those in genuine need.

Despite recent reforms, AFDC usually pays more to a fatherless family than to a family with a father who cannot support it. Husbands in desperate financial straits thus have an incentive to move out (or to pretend to), and divorced mothers have little incentive to remarry. The program also discourages the poor from working, since they lose their benefits even at very low income levels. Parents who earn $4,000 a year, for example, are eligible for AFDC in most states; but if in one year they work more hours and earn $5,000, they might lose as much as $600 in benefits, making a net gain of only $400—hardly enough to cover the extra income taxes and expenses involved (Keniston and the Carnegie Council on Children, 1977).

Public assistance to adults is federally funded by the SSI program. It reaches those people who cannot work: the blind, the permanently and totally disabled, and the indigent aged.

In-kind aid Help in acquiring basic necessities is provided by food stamps, subsidized housing, and medical care programs. In 1976, these in-kind aids accounted for $41 billion, or the remaining 23 percent, of government transfers (Congressional Budget Office, 1977, p. 2).

The food stamp program has been one of the most successful aid programs, providing food at lower than usual cost, based on a sliding scale according to income. It is the only poverty program that helps the working poor and near poor and does not stop abruptly when income reaches an arbitrary level. However, partly because food stamps must be bought with one lump sum at the beginning of the month, a substantial number of people who are eligible for the program do not participate in it.

Medicare for the aged is tied to Social Security and helps rich and poor alike. Medicaid, a program specifically for the poor, has undoubtedly improved health care while contributing to the spiraling costs of medical services (see Chapter 13). As we have seen, the medical care of poor children and the maternal health care programs for the poor are still far from adequate.

Finally, most states provide in-kind aid in the form of housing subsidies for poor families.

The welfare dilemma comes from the difficult trade-off among three considerations: providing minimal living standards for the poor who cannot work encouraging those who can work to do so, and paying the cost of public assistance. Adequate aid programs remove the incentive to work, but inadequate aid denies the poor, especially poor children, the basic requirements of a decent life. Direct cash grants for families below half the median income level, sometimes called an "income floor" or a "negative income tax," have been suggested as a means of eliminating the patchwork of different programs and their cumbersome bureaucracy. Work incentives would be maintained, for example, if no one lost more than 50 percent of their higher income in reduced benefits.

The Culture of Inequality

Granting the right to a decent life is well within the power of the affluent United States. About $9 billion a year would bring the incomes of the non-aged poor (who do not already receive Social Security benefits) above the poverty line; about $25 billion a year would lift the income of non-aged families above half the median. In other words, much less than 1 percent of the Gross National Product would close the poverty gap, and less than 2 percent would raise every family of working age to a decent living standard (Okun, 1975, p. 108). The total annual outlay would be far less than the $55 billion that is given to the rich in tax exemptions on income from capital gains and municipal bonds.*

Many more modest attempts to eliminate poverty, however, have met strong opposition. Any

---

*Total 1967 tax revenue lost through these exemptions (calculated in Pechman and Okner, 1974).

Welfare Myths

Hostility toward welfare programs gives rise to a number of misconceptions about government transfer payments to the poor—what they are, who gets them, and how effective they are in relieving poverty.

Myth: Welfare families are loaded with kids, and they have more children just to get more money.

Fact: Over half—54.2 percent—of welfare families have one or two children. The usual increase for an additional child is $35 a month—much less than the cost of raising a child.

Myth: Most welfare families are black.

Fact: Whites are the largest racial group on welfare; 48.3 percent of welfare families are white, 43.3 percent are black, and 8.4 percent are Native Americans and other racial minorities. Over two-thirds of all poor people are white.

Myth: Why should people work if they can live it up on welfare?

Fact: In 1972, welfare payments for a family of four with no other income ranged from a low of $197 a month in Mississippi to a high of $463 a month in Alaska. In all except three states, payments for basic needs are below the poverty line.

Myth: Give them more money, and they will spend it on drink and big cars.

Fact: Most welfare families say that any extra money they received would be spent on essentials. Among welfare mothers, nearly half say they would spend the money on food.

Myth: Most welfare children are illegitimate.

Fact: About 70 percent of the children on welfare are legitimate. In recent years, family planning services have been made available to welfare families.

Myth: Once people go on welfare, they remain on welfare.

Fact: Half the families on welfare have been receiving assistance for less than twenty months, and two-thirds have been on the welfare rolls less than 3 years.

Myth: Welfare people are cheats.

Fact: All welfare claims are checked for possible fraud, and less than 5 percent of the recipients are found to be on the rolls illegally. Most overpayments are the result of honest mistakes by recipients or welfare officials, and less than half of 1 percent of overpayments are referred for prosecution for fraud. In fact, many people who are eligible for welfare do not receive it.

Myth: Welfare is just a dole, a money handout.

Fact: Most welfare families also receive other social services—health care advice (including Medicaid) and financial, home, and employment counseling, as well as services to improve housing conditions and to help children continue in school.

Myth: The welfare rolls are full of able-bodied loafers.

Fact: Less than 1 percent of welfare recipients are able-bodied, unemployed males. These men are required by law to sign up for work or for work training in order to remain eligible for welfare. Nearly all unemployed adults of working age on welfare are mothers, most of them single heads of families. The majority of the heads of poor families are working. Many of them are poor because they have only part-time, seasonal jobs; others work full time, but still earn incomes below the poverty line. In the last decade, about 7 percent of the people actively looking for a job could not find one.

Source: Adapted from U.S. Department of Health, Education, and Welfare, *Welfare: Myths vs. Facts* (Washington, D.C.: U.S. Government Printing Office, 1972); and U.S. Bureau of the Census, *Current Population Reports: Characteristics of the Low-Income Populations,* Series P-23, No. 57 (Washington, D.C.: U.S. Government Printing Office, 1975).

policy that requires higher taxes or more government intervention in the private economy is vigorously opposed by powerful corporations, as well as by organizations of wealthy individuals whose interests are threatened by the welfare state.

Finally, suspicion of "government handouts" and antagonism toward the poor are pervasive in American culture. Survey after survey shows that the poor are thought to have weak characters and to be responsible for their own condition. In 1964, when the idealism of the War on Poverty was running high, the majority of Americans still saw "lack of effort" as the major cause of poverty (Free and Cantril, 1967, pp. 28–31). Interviews conducted in the 1970s found that four out of five respondents (including over 81 percent of whites and 78 percent of blacks in one study) agreed with the statement, "There are too many people receiving welfare who should be working" (Waxman, 1977, p. 72). Also reported were many instances of blaming the victim. For example:

> Slums remind me of people who don't give a damn. . . . You can't get rid of the slums by putting people in new buildings — it's people that make the slums.

> The bottom class is people who don't care how they live and don't care to change things. . . . There's usually some way to work out of the bottom if you want to. . . . The bottom is people who've just given up.

> They can't hold a job—they haven't picked up the right habits. . . . They usually aren't working—they don't like to. . . . They won't even look for work—they don't want it. (Coleman and Rainwater, 1978, pp. 194–98).

In a society based on the idea that everyone has an equal chance to succeed, the existence of inequality is justified by the belief that the poor are personally unwilling or unable to make the most of the unlimited opportunities that are available. According to the myth of the American dream, everyone who works hard gets ahead; there is no reason not to succeed except because of laziness or incompetence.

In what Michael Lewis has called the American *culture of inequality,* poverty is explained by the personal inadequacies or disabilities of the poor (1978). According to liberals, poverty is caused by lack of skills and other disadvantages; liberal remedies thus stress more education, job training, and family counseling programs for the poor. According to conservatives, poverty is caused by the moral failings and irresponsibility of individuals; conservatives want to cut back programs that spend public money on people who they believe are unwilling to help themselves. These beliefs prevent Americans from recognizing that the true causes of poverty are found, not in the personal qualities of the poor, but in the economy and social structure that deny them an equal chance. Far from presenting unlimited opportunities for success, American society actually offers certain groups very limited chances to have the kind of education, health, and employment that are necessary for a decent life.

Ending poverty is a practical possibility. Substantial progress has already been made toward providing minimal income, housing, education, and medical care for everyone in the United States. A relatively small amount of additional money would eradicate official poverty, and any serious attempt at tax reform would redistribute enough income to provide every American family with an adequate standard of living These remedies will not be put into effect however as long as American culture justifies inequality and the American economy promotes wide disparities in income. Moreover, recent cutbacks in government spending will lead to substantial reductions in eligibility for food stamps, welfare, and perhaps even Social Security retirement benefits. Should economic hard times continue and opposition to the claims of the deprived become even more intense, then a return to greater poverty is likely in the near future.

Summary

1. Absolute poverty, the lack of the food, clothing, and shelter necessary to sustain life, is extensive in the United States.

2. In 1978, the government's official poverty line was an unrealistically low estimate, according to which about 11.4 percent of the population or 25 million people are poor.

3. Half the median income has been suggested as a more accurate poverty line. If the relative definition of having less than the median income is used as the measure of poverty, 20 percent of Americans or 45 million people are poor.

4. Official figures show that poverty declined during the 1960s. Economic growth during this period brought a higher standard of living to all income groups, and new social welfare programs increased job opportunities and public assistance for the poor. However, the distribution of total income has not changed since the end of World War II.

5. Poverty profoundly affects an individual s life chances, or the opportunity to get a college education, good medical care, and a well-paying job. Compared with those better off, the poor pay more for the goods they buy, contribute proportionately more of their income to taxes, and are hit harder by inflation. They must also suffer the psychological cost of being considered worthless failures by the rest of society.

6. Poverty is concentrated in certain social groups: female-headed families, blacks, Hispanics, and Native Americans. Most of the chronically poor and unemployed live in central cities.

7. Theories of poverty try to explain why poverty persists in affluent societies. The culture of poverty theory holds that poverty is a way of life that negatively influences poor people's character and expectations. This theory has been criticized because the so-called cultural traits of the poor are more likely to be caused *by* poverty than be causes *of* it. Many find the culture of poverty theory to be a case of "blaming the victim" for social problems.

8. Functional theory finds social inequality to be inevitable and necessary to ensure that the most important positions in society are filled by the most qualified people. Herbert Gans shows the irony of this argument by illustrating how inequality benefits the non-poor at the expense of the poor.

9. A focus on economic factors suggests that the dual labor market prevents competition between workers in different sectors of the economy. Unemployment and underemployment are concentrated in the secondary market of badly paid, unskilled, and dead-end jobs.

10. The conflict theory of poverty finds that the poor lack the resources necessary to bargain for better jobs and services. Women and minorities are also up against the discriminatory hiring practices of powerful groups.

11. In 1975, the United States spent $286.5 billion on social welfare. Over two-thirds of the money went to all income levels through Social Security, veterans' pensions, and unemployment insurance. Cash welfare for the poor represents only 10 percent of government transfer payments.

12. Eliminating poverty is well within the power of the affluent United States. The American culture of inequality, however, justifies the continuation of poverty by finding its causes in the incompetence or incapacity of the poor themselves.

Suggested Reading

De Lone, Richard H. *Small Futures.* New York: Harcourt Brace Jovanovich, 1979.
Harrington, Michael. *The Other America.* New York: Macmillan, 1962.
Lewis, Michael. *The Culture of Inequality.* New York: New American Library/Meridian, 1978.
Ryan, William. *Blaming the Victim.* New York: Random House, 1976.
Stern, Philip. *The Rape of the Taxpayer.* New York: Random House, 1973.

References

Antonovsky, A. "Social Class, Life Expectancy and Overall Mortality." In P. Blumberg (Ed.), *The Impact of Social Class.* New York: Crowell, 1972.
Bagdikian, B.H. *In the Midst of Plenty.* Quoted in R.L. Hurley, *Poverty and Mental Retardation.* New York: Random House, 1969, p. 83.
Baskir, L.M., and W.A. Strauss. *Chance and Circumstance.* New York: Knopf, 1978.
Caplovitz, D. *The Poor Pay More.* New York: Free Press, 1967.
Caplovitz, D. *Making Ends Meet.* Beverly Hills, Cal.: Sage, 1979.
Coleman, R.P., and L. Rainwater. *Social Standing in America: New Dimensions of Class.* New York: Basic Books, 1978.
Congressional Budget Office. "Poverty Status of Families Under Alternative Definitions of Income," Background Paper No. 17 (June 1977).
Council of Economic Advisers Annual Report. Washington D.C.: U.S. Government Printing Office (February 1974), pp. 168–69.
Davidson, C., and C.M. Gaitz. "Are the Poor Different?" *Social Problems,* Vol. 22 (December 1974), pp. 229–45.
Davis, K., and W.E. Moore. "Some Principles of Stratification." *American Sociological Review,* Vol. 10 (April 1945), pp. 242–44.
De Lone, R.H. *Small Futures.* New York: Harcourt Brace Jovanovich, 1979.
Free, L.A., and H. Cantril. *The Political Beliefs of Americans.* New Brunswick, N.J.: Rutgers University Press, 1967.
Gans, H.J. *More Equality.* New York: Random House, 1973.
Gans, H.J. "What Can Be Done About Poverty?" *Dissent* (Winter 1981), pp. 40–42.
Giddens, A. *The Class Structure of the Advanced Societies.* New York: Harper & Row, 1975.
Hurley, R.L. *Poverty and Mental Retardation.* New York: Random House, 1969.
Keniston, K., and the Carnegie Council on Children. *All Our Children.* New York: Harcourt Brace Jovanovich, 1977.

Kerr, C. "The Balkanization of Labor Markets." In E.W. Bakke (Ed.), *Labor Mobility and Economic Opportunity.* Cambridge, Mass.: MIT Press/New York: Wiley, 1954, pp. 92–97.

Lewis, M. *The Culture of Inequality.* New York: New American Library/Meridian, 1978.

Lewis, O. *Five Families: Mexican Case Studies in the Culture of Poverty.* New York: Basic Books, 1959.

Lewis, O. *La Vida: A Puerto Rican Family in the Culture of Poverty—San Juan and New York.* New York: Irvington, 1966.

Lewis, O. *Anthropological Essays.* New York: Random House, 1970.

Mayer, A.J., and T.F. Hoult. "Social Stratification and Combat Survival." *Social Forces,* Vol. 34 (December 1955), pp. 155–59.

Morse, D. *The Peripheral Worker.* New York: Columbia University Press, 1969.

National Advisory Council on Economic Opportunity. *Critical Choices for the Eighties.* Summarized as "Facts We Dare Not Forget." *Dissent* (Spring 1981), p. 166.

Okun, A.M. *Equality and Efficiency.* Washington, D.C.: Brookings Institution, 1975.

Pechman, J.A., and B.A. Okner. *Who Bears the Tax Burden?* Washington, D.C.: Brookings Institution, 1974.

Rainwater, L. *The Family, Poverty, and Welfare Programs: Poverty, Living Standards and Family Well-Being,* Paper No. 12, Part 2. Washington, D.C.: U.S. Government Printing Office, 1973.

Rodgers, H.R., Jr. "Hiding Versus Ending Poverty." *Politics and Society,* Vol. 8, No. 2 (1978), pp. 254–55.

Ryan, W. *Blaming the Victim.* New York: Random House, 1976.

Thurow, L.C. "The Myth of the American Economy." *Newsweek,* February 14, 1977, p. 11.

Thurow, L.C. *The Zero-Sum Society.* New York: Basic Books, 1980.

U.S. Bureau of the Census. *Current Populations Reports,* Series P-60. Washington, D.C.: U.S. Government Printing Office (July 1975), pp. 17–18.

U.S. Bureau of the Census. *Current Population Reports: Consumer Income,* Series P-60, No. 114. Washington, D.C.: U.S. Government Printing Office (July 1978a).

U.S. Bureau of the Census. *Statistical Abstract of the United States.* Washington, D.C.: U.S. Government Printing Office, 1978b.

U.S. Bureau of the Census. *Current Housing Reports: Annual Housing Survey, 1977,* Series H-150-77. Washington, D.C.: U.S. Government Printing Office, 1979a.

U.S. Bureau of the Census. *Current Population Reports: Characteristics of the Population Below the Poverty Level, 1977,* Series P-60, No. 119. Washington, D.C.: U.S. Government Printing Office, 1979b.

U.S. Bureau of the Census. *Current Population Reports: Money Income and Poverty Status of Families and Persons in the United States, 1978* (Advance Report), Series P-60, No. 120. Washington, D.C.: U.S. Government Printing Office, 1979c.

U.S. Department of Health, Education, and Welfare. *Vital and Health Statistics,* Series 22, No. 14 (March 1972).

Valentine, C.A. "Conditions of Poverty Versus Culture of Poverty." In R.E. Will and H.G. Vatter (Eds.), *Poverty in Affluence.* New York: Harcourt Brace Jovanovich, 1970, pp. 135–40.

Waxman, C.I. *The Stigma of Poverty.* Elmsford, N.Y.: Pergamon, 1977.

Zeitlin, M., K.G., Lutterman, and J.W. Russell. "Death in Vietnam: Class Poverty, and the Risks of War." *Politics and Society,* Vol. III (Spring 1973), pp. 313–28.

Chapter Ten

Racial Inequality

**The History of Racism in the
 United States**

Native Americans

Black Americans

Mexican Americans

The Roots of Racism

Social Preconditions

Racist Ideology

Maintaining Racial Inequality

Prejudice and Discrimination

Institutionalized Racism

**Contemporary Racial Issues and
 Conflicts**

Actions

   Southern Protest

   Chicano and Pan-Indian Movements

   Urban Riots

Reactions

   Legislation

   Retrenchment

**The Dimensions of Racial Inequality
 Today**

In the twenty years since the Civil Rights Movement captured public attention in the United States, the attitudes of white people toward black people have changed dramatically. According to Harris polls conducted in the early 1960s and again in 1978, the percentage of whites who would be troubled if a black family moved in next door dropped from 51 to 27; the percentage who would be unhappy if their child brought a black child home to dinner fell from 42 to 10; the percentage who cared whether a black sat next to them at a lunch counter went from 20 to 6. In 1963, 31 percent of whites polled said they believed that blacks were inferior; by 1978, only 15 percent said they believed this. Indeed, the 1978 poll showed that most whites favored programs designed to eliminate racial inequality. By a majority of 71 to 21 percent, whites agreed that "after years of discrimination, it is only fair to set up special programs to make sure that ... minorities are given every chance to have equal opportunities in employment and education." Two-thirds supported affirmative action programs (setting aside places for qualified members of minority groups) in industry. The proportion of whites who felt that blacks were trying to move "too fast" dropped from 71 percent in 1966 to 33 percent in 1978. Prejudice toward blacks (and toward other minorities) has not disappeared, but it is fading (Louis Harris and Associates, 1978).

The puzzle is why, when prejudice has declined, when discrimination in housing, education, and employment has been outlawed, when government and private organizations have established affirmative action programs opening doors for minorities—why, then, does racial inequality persist? Why do blacks and members of other minorities still die younger, complete fewer years of school, and earn less over their lifetimes than the white majority does?

This chapter attempts to solve that racial puzzle. We begin, in the first section, by examining the history of racism in the United States, focus-ing on Native Americans, Mexican Americans, and black Americans. This overview enables us to suggest why racism develops in some societies and not in others. In the second section, we show how interacting economic, social, and historical forces turn differences between groups into racial divisions. Common sense suggests that racial inequality persists in a society because of prejudice and discrimination. In the third section, however, we look at theories of prejudice and discrimination and show that these attitudes alone do not account for the problem. Inequality persists because racism has been institutionalized. Efforts to close the racial gap have provoked conflicts of interest and of values that are not easily resolved, as we show in the fourth section. Is the "race problem" becoming a thing of the past, as many white Americans believe? In the final section, we measure the economic and social gaps that exist between whites and nonwhites in the United States today.

The History of Racism in the United States

Racism is the belief that members of an out-group (or out-groups) that are distinguished by physical appearance and ancestry are innately inferior. Racists maintain that a variety of socially significant characteristics and abilities are biologically determined. They attribute differences in culture, power, and status among groups to immutable genetic factors, not to social or historical circumstance. In a racist society, certain physical characteristics linked to ancestry are a prerequisite for full social acceptance. Color, which is an obvious trait, is often used as a dividing line. Here we will describe the impact of racism on three groups: Native Americans, black Americans, and Mexican Americans. But first, some definitions.

A biological definition of a *race* is a population that differs from other populations in the in-

A UNESCO Statement on Race

1. Scientists are generally agreed that all men living today belong to a single species, *Homo sapiens,* and are derived from a common stock, even though there is some dispute as to when and how human groups diverged from this common stock.

2. Some of the physical differences between human groups are due to differences in hereditary constitution and some to differences in the environments in which they have been brought up.

3. National, religious, geographical, linguistic, and cultural groups do not necessarily coincide with racial groups.

4. Broadly speaking, individuals belonging to major groups of mankind are distinguishable by virtue of their physical characters, but individual members, or small groups, belonging to different races within the same major group are usually not so distinguishable.

5. Studies within a single race have shown that both innate capacity and environmental opportunity determine the results of tests of intelligence and temperament, though their relative importance is disputed.

6. The scientific material available to us at present does not justify the conclusion that inherited genetic differences are a major factor in producing the differences between the cultures and cultural achievement of different peoples or groups.

7. There is no evidence for the existence of the so-called "pure" races. In regard to race mixture, the evidence points to the fact that human hybridization has been going on for an indefinite but considerable time.

8. We wish to emphasize that equality of opportunity and equality in law in no way depend, as ethical principles, upon the assertion that human beings are in fact equal in endowment.

Source: UNESCO Statement on Race and Race Differences (July 1952). Quoted in I.M. Lerner, *Heredity, Evolution and Society* (San Francisco: Freeman, 1968), p. 226.

cidence of some genes (Lerner, 1968, p. 223). In the past, anthropologists classified humankind into races on the basis of differences in pigmentation (skin color) and morphology (features and build). This approach created a number of anomalies, however. (For example, Melanesians resem- ble black Africans, who live half a world away.) Anthropologists today classify races in terms of genetically determined immunological and biochemical differences. This approach has revealed that there are no "pure" races in the biological sense. Human beings have interbred for countless years. But some genes are more frequent in certain populations—in certain races—than in others. A sociological definition of a *race* is a large number of people who see themselves, and are seen by others, as different because of their ancestry and physical appearance.* The emphasis in this definition is on the meaning that people attach to real or imagined differences. For example, central Africans assign people to the Tutsi and Hutu "races" partly on the basis of height. Although they have similar skin color and facial features, the Tutsi tend to be tall; the Hutu, short. In this country, we assign people to different races primarily on the basis of skin color and facial features, ignoring height. Both methods of classification have social consequences (van den Berghe, 1967, p. 12).

The history of the United States echoes with racial conflict. Many groups have encountered racial or ethnic prejudice and hostility in this country—the Irish, Italians, Chinese, Japanese, and Jews are a few of them. Against this panorama, the plight of Native Americans, black Americans, and Mexican Americans stands out. Racism has had a particularly cruel and long-lasting impact on these groups. Their histories differ, but they all have experienced decades of oppression and exploitation by whites, conflict with whites, and protest against their position (see Figure 10–1).

Native Americans

Native Americans are descendants of the Asian peoples who crossed the Bering Strait to Alaska at least 40,000 years ago—perhaps 100,000 years ago—and gradually moved across North and South America. Because of Columbus's error—on first landing in the Bahamas, he thought he had realized his dream of sailing around the world to East India—Native Americans were called "Indians." In fact, the diverse tribes and nations living in the Americas had no collective name for themselves. Long before Europeans discovered the two continents, hundreds of distinctive cultures had developed there, ranging from the mighty Maya, Inca, and Aztec empires of Central and South America to small bands of nomadic hunter-gatherers.

Native Americans and European settlers met on an equal footing in North America (Steinberg, 1981, pp. 13–16). Few European settlers would have survived their first winters without the protection, food, and skills the Native Americans gave them. Europeans were forced to recognize their hosts as independent nations and to negotiate with them for the purchase of land. Both the British and the French eagerly sought them out as trading partners and allies. This equality was short-lived, however. Early in the seventeenth century, the balance of power began to shift. Native Americans were soon outnumbered—and out-gunned—by the growing European population. Bows and arrows were no match for muskets. Accommodation gave way to almost two centuries of physical, social, and cultural conflict.

The heart of the conflict was the struggle for land. Typically, white settlers would push beyond the boundaries they had negotiated with one or another nation, provoking an attack, and the attack would be used as an excuse to "punish" the offending nation. Overpowered, Native Americans would cede a parcel of land in return for a promise that the territory they retained would never be threatened, and a solemn treaty would be signed. It would be only a matter of time, however, before the cycle of white encroachment, warfare, and dispossession repeated itself.

In 1830, Congress passed a Removal Act that allowed the President to deport all Native Ameri-

---

* An *ethnic group* consists of a large number of people who see themselves, and are seen by others, as different because of their *cultural heritage*. Members of an ethnic group usually come from the same part of the world, speak the same language, practice the same religion, and so on.

cans to an Indian Territory west of the Mississippi, on land whites considered uninhabitable. The justification given for removing Native Americans from their homeland was agricultural progress. The land was destined to be tilled. From the European perspective, Native Americans who hunted and collected wild food over wide expanses were not truly "using" the land. Theodore Roosevelt later wrote in *The Winning of the West* (1889–96): "This great continent could not have been kept as nothing but a game preserve for squalid savages" (p. 90). This racist characterization of Native Americans reflected public attitudes. In effect, the Removal Act legalized a military solution to white civilian pressure for land. In 1838, for example, some 12,000 Cherokee farmers were removed from their homes in Georgia at bayonet point, confined to a stockade, and then forced to march to Kansas in the dead of winter. An estimated 4,000 died on what the Cherokee called the "Trail of Tears." No sooner had Eastern tribes been transported westward than whites discovered riches there—especially gold. White migration to the West accelerated, and soon Western tribes, too, were in the way. The end of the Civil War freed soldiers to concentrate on "pacifying" Native Americans in the West.

In June 1876, Sioux warriors, led by Chief Crazy Horse, surprised and defeated General Custer's troops at Little Bighorn, in the Sacred Black Hills of Dakota. It was the Native Americans' last military victory. They were defeated once and for all in 1890, at Wounded Knee: An accidental shot provoked a shootout that left dead 300 of the 350 Native Americans, many of them unarmed women and children. "A people's dream died there," said Chief Black Elk. "There is no center any more, and the sacred tree is dead" (in Brown, 1970, p. 446). Of the estimated 1 to 1.5 million original inhabitants of North America, only 250,000 remained (Schaefer, 1979, p. 241). They were defeated not only in battle but also by imported diseases like measles and small pox, for which they had no immunity, and by the loss of hunting and fishing territories on which their way of life depended.

Even before the battle of Wounded Knee, the U.S. government had stopped negotiating with Native Americans and started legislating for them. The period of oppression—of unopposed domination—of Native Americans dates back to the 1870s. The reservation system established at that time in effect reduced the Native Americans to colonial status (Steinberg, 1981, pp. 18–20). Decisions were made and implemented by officials of the Bureau of Indian Affairs (BIA), most of whom were white political appointees. For the next half-century, BIA officials decided who could live on reservations, who could leave, whether to sell or lease tribal lands and other resources, what religions were permitted, and even which children would be sent to boarding schools. It was only in 1924 that Native Americans were given the right to vote, as a "reward" for their service in World War I.

Government policy toward Native Americans over the past century has vacillated between attempts to assimilate them into the larger society and attempts to preserve tribal traditions and social organization. The 1887 Allotment Act divided reservations into individual plots, with the unstated aim of promoting assimilation by weakening tribal authority. The Reorganization Act of 1934 reversed this policy, allowing Native Americans to adopt tribal constitutions, elect tribal councils and chairmen, and bargain with the government and other outsiders collectively, rather than as individuals. Policy shifted again in the 1950s. The controversial Termination Act of 1953 allowed tribes to vote on the question of terminating their special relationship as wards of the federal government. And the Voluntary Relocation Program of 1956 provided assistance to individual Native Americans who wanted to leave their reservations.

Figure 10–1
Landmarks in U.S. Race Relations

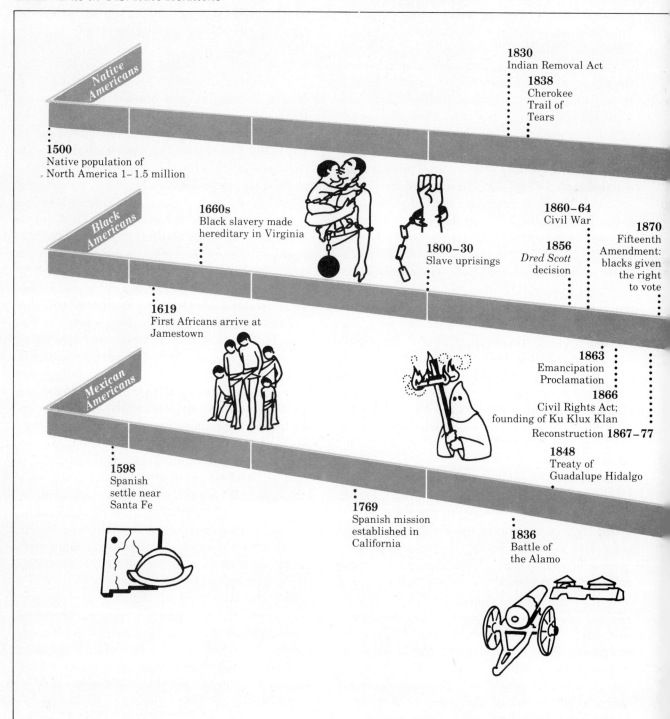

Native Americans

1830
Indian Removal Act

1838
Cherokee
Trail of
Tears

1500
Native population of
North America 1–1.5 million

Black Americans

1660s
Black slavery made
hereditary in Virginia

1800–30
Slave uprisings

1860–64
Civil War

1856
Dred Scott
decision

1870
Fifteenth
Amendment:
blacks given
the right
to vote

1619
First Africans arrive at
Jamestown

1863
Emancipation
Proclamation

1866
Civil Rights Act;
founding of Ku Klux Klan

Reconstruction **1867–77**

Mexican Americans

1848
Treaty of
Guadalupe Hidalgo

1598
Spanish
settle near
Santa Fe

1769
Spanish mission
established in
California

1836
Battle of
the Alamo

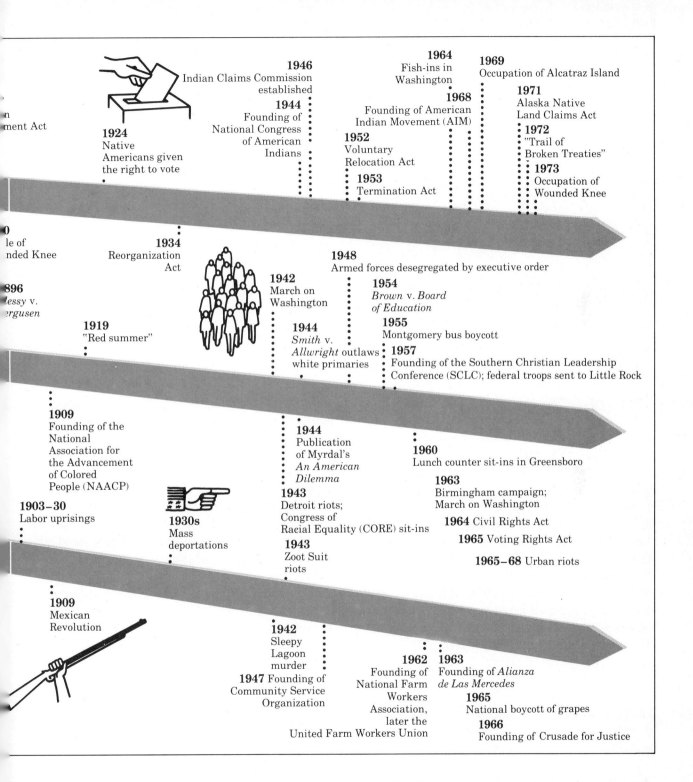

1924
Native Americans given the right to vote

1946
Indian Claims Commission established

1944
Founding of National Congress of American Indians

1964
Fish-ins in Washington

1968
Founding of American Indian Movement (AIM)

1952
Voluntary Relocation Act

1953
Termination Act

1969
Occupation of Alcatraz Island

1971
Alaska Native Land Claims Act

1972
"Trail of Broken Treaties"

1973
Occupation of Wounded Knee

...ment Act

...le of ...nded Knee

1934
Reorganization Act

1896
Plessy v. *Ferguson*

1919
"Red summer"

1942
March on Washington

1944
Smith v. *Allwright* outlaws white primaries

1948
Armed forces desegregated by executive order

1954
Brown v. *Board of Education*

1955
Montgomery bus boycott

1957
Founding of the Southern Christian Leadership Conference (SCLC); federal troops sent to Little Rock

1909
Founding of the National Association for the Advancement of Colored People (NAACP)

1903–30
Labor uprisings

1930s
Mass deportations

1944
Publication of Myrdal's *An American Dilemma*

1943
Detroit riots; Congress of Racial Equality (CORE) sit-ins

1943
Zoot Suit riots

1960
Lunch counter sit-ins in Greensboro

1963
Birmingham campaign; March on Washington

1964 Civil Rights Act

1965 Voting Rights Act

1965–68 Urban riots

1909
Mexican Revolution

1942
Sleepy Lagoon murder

1947 Founding of Community Service Organization

1962
Founding of National Farm Workers Association, later the United Farm Workers Union

1963
Founding of *Alianza de Las Mercedes*

1965
National boycott of grapes

1966
Founding of Crusade for Justice

Some of the "badlands" pawned off on Native Americans in the last century have proved rich in deposits of oil, gas, coal, and uranium. The Navajo of Window Rock, Arizona, shown here, have struck oil. But like Third World nations, Native Americans must turn to outsiders for the capital and technology to mine their resources.

Today, as in the past, conflict between white and Native Americans centers on land. Between 1887 and 1934, tribal holdings dropped from 138 million acres to 56 million, most of them marginal even for ranching (*The New York Times Magazine,* February 11, 1979, p. 32). Ironically, these "badlands" pawned off on Native Americans more than a century ago contain some of the nation's richest deposits of coal, uranium, and oil. Although the plot of the conflict remains much the same, the cast of characters has changed. Giant corporations armed with capital and technology have replaced settlers, who invaded with horse and plow; corporate lawyers have replaced the cavalry (Steinberg, 1981, p. 21).

Black Americans

The first Africans to set foot in North America arrived at Jamestown, Virginia, on a Dutch frigate in August 1619 (one year before the arrival of the *Mayflower*). They came as indentured servants, bound to a master who paid their passage to the New World for a specific number of years. After their period of service, they were free. Many whites came to the colonies under similar circumstances. But unlike the Africans, who were all captives, some European servants had voluntarily sold their labor for passage. Others were paupers or convicts who had been sentenced to the colonies. Unfree whites made up one-sixth of the colonial population of Virginia in this period (Fredrickson, 1981, pp. 59–60). The peculiar institution of slavery, which singled out blacks for permanent servitude and for cruel and unusual treatment, was not established by law until late in the seventeenth century. As slaves, Africans and their descendants had "no rights that a white man need respect" (*Dred Scott* v. *Sandford*). Conditions under slavery varied. Basically, it was a totalitarian system that combined exploitation and oppression. Under the law, slaves were treated as property, not as human beings. Slavery was rationalized on the grounds that blacks were "natural servants," unfit for freedom and citizenship.

Why did black slavery take hold in the South but not in the North? In part because it was profitable. The South had plenty of arable land and a good climate for agriculture, but a shortage of labor. High profits could be gained by using slaves as gang labor on large plantations to produce crops for export, like cotton and tobacco. Native Americans would have been difficult to enslave since they were at home on this continent and knew how to survive on their own. For them, escape would have been relatively easy. Moreover, industrialization in Europe had created more jobs and higher wages, so that fewer Europeans were desperate enough to sell themselves into indentured servitude across the sea. Once seized as the solution to an economic problem, slavery expanded rapidly. The number of blacks in Virginia grew from 300 in 1650 to 120,000 in 1750 (Pettigrew, 1976, p. 467). By 1860, the slave labor force comprised almost 4 million blacks (U.S. Bureau of the Census, 1918, p. 53).

Grade-school textbooks teach that the Civil War was fought in the name of racial equality, to free the slaves. This is at best a partial truth (Fredrickson, 1981, pp. 150-62). On the eve of the Civil War, very few white Americans believed in racial equality. Most Northern states had black codes, which severely restricted "free Negroes." Abolitionists were a small, unpopular minority. Indeed, rumors that abolitionists endorsed racial intermarriage touched off bloody race riots in Northern cities in the 1830s and 1840s. Abolitionists failed to arouse sympathy for blacks as human beings, but their contention that slavery gave the South an unfair economic advantage struck a responsive chord. Northerners may not have been concerned about racial equality, but they were concerned about economic equality between regions. This conflict came to the surface when Congress debated whether slavery would be permitted in new territories admitted to the union. Southerners insisted on it; Northerners were antagonized. Although they had been sympathetic to the Southerners' desire to preserve local traditions (including oppression of blacks), they began to see the South as an aggressive, expansionist "slave power." Thus, each region saw the other as a threat to its own way of life. From this perspective, the Civil War was an economic struggle between democratic, industrial states in the North and aristocratic, agricultural states in the South. The future of black slaves was almost a side issue.

The Emancipation Proclamation was signed in 1863, a year before the war ended. After the war, Northern troops remained in the South to oversee Reconstruction. In this period, a number of steps were taken to give blacks equal rights. The 1866 Civil Rights Act declared blacks citizens and gave the federal courts jurisdiction over cases arising from violation of their civil rights. The Fifteenth Amendment, ratified in 1870, gave blacks the right to vote. Freedman's Bureaus were established, and blacks were elected to public office for the first time. Racial equality proved elusive, however. Whites were able to subjugate blacks without actually owning them.

Reconstruction focused on political rights, not on economic issues. Contrary to a wartime rumor, the Freedman's Bureau did not provide each former slave with "forty acres and a mule." Most Southern plantation owners, left destitute by the war, were unable to pay wages for labor. Planters borrowed money from Northern banks in exchange for a share of their next crop; planters, in turn, advanced supplies to black sharecroppers in exchange for future wages. The endless cycle of borrowing and indebtedness chained blacks to the land that they had worked as slaves. Most of them were no better off materially as sharecroppers than they had been as slaves.

Toward the end of the century, when crop failures threatened to provoke an agrarian revolt in the South, blacks became scapegoats (Woodward, 1966). False rumors of atrocities committed by blacks diverted attention from crop failures and government scandals, providing a rationale for segregation. One by one, Southern states passed Jim Crow laws, which banned black citizens from restaurants, railroad cars, waiting rooms, and other public accommodations. Poll taxes, literacy tests (for blacks only), and white-only primaries excluded blacks from the political process. In Louisiana, the number of black voters was cut from 130,000 in 1896 to less than 1,400 in 1904 (Woodward, 1966, p. 68). The Supreme Court gave segregation its approval, declaring "separate but equal" facilities for blacks constitutional in *Plessy* v. *Ferguson* (1896). The segregation era has been called "the nadir of Black American fortunes" (Pettigrew, 1976, p. 469). It was an era of terrorism. According to one estimate, 5,000 black Americans were lynched between the 1880s and 1920s (Kitano, 1980, p. 133). By the end of the century, Southern states had reconstructed white supremacy and black servitude without the formal apparatus of slavery.

World War I increased demands on U.S. industries and also cut the flow of European immigrants, opening job opportunities in the North. Given conditions in the South, it is not surprising that blacks sought escape. Northern cities did not turn out to be the promised land, however. After the war, jobs were scarce. Returning soldiers saw blacks as unwelcome competition for jobs and living space. In a race riot in East St. Louis in 1917, thirty-nine blacks and nine whites were killed. Twenty-six riots followed in the "red summer" of 1919 (Schaefer, 1979, p. 1975). This pattern of migration and violent interracial conflict was repeated during World War II.

Black rebellion against oppression and exploitation dates back more than a century (McLemore, 1980, pp. 262–82). In 1811, 300 to 500 slaves, armed with pikes and hoes, marched on the city of New Orleans. Nat Turner and his band killed fifty-five white men, women, and children before Turner was arrested and hanged, in 1831. In 1909, "radical" blacks who refused to accept second-class citizenship under Jim Crow laws joined white liberals to from the National Association for the Advancement of Colored People (NAACP). In the 1920s, Marcus Garvey, who preached black separatism (the establishment of a separate black state on U.S. territory or in Africa), gained wide support among urban blacks. A. Philip Randolph, president of the predominantly black Brotherhood of Sleeping Car Porters, threatened mass demonstrations in Washington in the early 1940s, prompting President Franklin Roosevelt to sign an executive order establishing the Fair Employment Practices Commission. In short, black protest in the United States is not a modern phenomenon.

The systematic, often violent, oppression of blacks is part of this nation's history; its effects are still felt in the inequality of black Americans.

Mexican Americans

Mexican Americans are a diverse group of light- and dark-skinned, traditional and assimilated, rich and poor, recent immigrants to and long-term residents of North America. They are the descendants of the Spanish conquerors and the indigenous people of Latin America, who interbred more freely than did the Europeans and Native Americans in the North. Most Mexican Americans see themselves, and are seen by others, as members of a distinct racial and ethnic group.

The history of Mexican Americans begins with a Spanish settlement north of what is now Santa Fe, New Mexico, in 1598. Spanish colonization of California dates back to 1769, when Franciscan monks established the first of twenty-one missions in San Diego. What distinguished early Spanish communities from other European settlements in North America was their isolation. The small, scattered communities had few contacts with the outside world.

Early in the nineteenth century, however, large numbers of white settlers headed to the West, provoking armed conflict with Mexicans. Anglos (as the English-speaking settlers were called) succeeded in wrestling Texas from Mexican control in 1839; federal troops won much of the rest of the Southwest in the Mexican-American war in 1848; the remainder was purchased in 1853. In some ways, this period in Mexican-American history resembles the conquest of Native Americans. The West was won by force of arms. Spanish-speaking inhabitants did not choose to become part of the United States. Many of them remained neutral during the Mexican-American War, however, and after the war, more than 75,000 elected to stay in this country (Bahr, Chadwick, and Strauss, 1979, p. 56).

Under the Treaty of Guadalupe Hidalgo (1848), Mexican Americans were guaranteed full rights as citizens of the United States. In practice, however, they were soon robbed of their land and pushed into menial labor. Land grants made under the Spanish legal system were imprecise by Anglo standards. The emphasis in the Spanish or Mexican system was on agricultural products and livestock, not boundaries. The procedural rules in U.S. courts were Anglo; the judges and lawyers were also Anglo. Some Mexican Americans lost their land in court; others were forced to sell it in order to pay taxes. In the 1870s, the widespread use of inexpensive barbed wire, which enabled large landowners to shut out small ranchers, and innovations in irrigation and copper mining, both of which required large financial investments, accelerated the process of displacement in the Southwest. The discovery of gold in California in the 1840s and the opening of the railroads had accelerated the migration to the West. Between 1849 and 1890, countless Mexican Americans were forced from their mining claims by the new Anglo

Illegal Mexican immigrants have been in the headlines for decades. The photograph was taken in 1948. But many Mexican Americans had settled in the Southwest before there was a United States. From their point of view, "Anglos" were the unwelcome immigrants.

arrivals, who burned their camps and lynched resisters (Burkey, 1978, p. 228). Many Mexican Americans were reduced to low-paying unskilled labor on Anglo-owned farms, mines, and railroads.

The Mexican Revolution, which began in 1909, and the expansion of agriculture in the Southwest stimulated a new wave of immigration early in this century. The officially recorded number of Mexicans entering the United States grew from 25,000 in the first decade of the century to almost 500,000 in the 1920s (Grebler et al., 1970, p. 64). The actual number was probably much greater.

Emigration from Mexico differs in a number of ways from emigration from Europe and Asia. First, for Europeans and Asians, immigration to the United States is a momentous move: They must cross an ocean to get here. For Mexicans, immigration involves only a short trip and does not mean a sharp break with the past. The Southwest is geographically and, in many ways, culturally similar to Mexico. This affects the way permanent residents view Mexican immigrants. Today, as in the past, they are seen as foreigners who can easily go home if they dislike conditions here. Second, because there is no one port of entry, the Mexican border is difficult to patrol. The fact that many Mexican Americans are illegal immigrants means that they are in no position to insist on legal rights and equal treatment.

Government policy toward Mexican immigrants has been inconsistent at best. During World War I, the demand for "stoop" labor in the citrus, melon, and tomato industries grew, and Mexicans were welcomed—indeed invited. During the Great Depression, competition for jobs turned into hostility toward "foreigners," and thousands of U.S. residents of Mexican heritage (including an unknown number of naturalized citizens) were shipped back to Mexico. In the period 1931–32 alone, 200,000 Mexican Americans were deported (McLemore, 1980, p. 222). World War II, however, created a new manpower emergency, drawing thousands of immigrants from Mexico, as well as migrants from the Southwest, to the West Coast.

Hostility between Anglos and Mexicans flared during this period. Two incidents that occurred in Los Angeles illustrate the level of white prejudice toward Mexican Americans (Kitano, 1980, pp. 187–89). In 1942–43, newspapers printed rumors of a "crime wave" by Mexican-American youth gangs. The young people, who dressed in long coats with padded shoulders, high-waisted pants, and porkpie hats were known as "zoot suiters."

When a man was murdered at Sleepy Lagoon (the press's name for an abandoned gravel pit) in August 1942, the public was alarmed. Responding to pressure, the police arrested twenty-four Mexican-American youths. Seventeen were prosecuted in what was the largest mass trial for murder in this nation's history. All of them were eventually acquitted, but only after they had been held in prison for two years. Rumors about zoot suiters continued to make headlines. One night in the spring of 1943, some 200 sailors on leave descended on Mexican-American neighborhoods, stripped and beat residents, and ransacked bars and movie theaters. The attacks continued for almost a week, as the police stood passively by. The press reported the Zoot Suit Riot as if the Mexicans had been the aggressors. A Los Angeles police captain endorsed the racist motive for these incidents. Mexican Americans, he argued, are violent by nature. Whereas an Anglo youth fights with his fists, a Mexican "uses a knife or some lethal weapon. . . . [H]is desire is to kill, or at least let blood" (in McLemore, 1980, p. 226).

Mexican Americans have never accepted Anglo dominance passively. Resistance to United States' annexation of Mexican territory continued for seventy-five years after the 1848 Treaty of Guadalupe Hidalgo. *Guerrilleros* like Juan Cortina, who led armed raids on Anglo settlements to reclaim land from the whites, were heroes to Mexican Americans, but they were bandits to Anglos (Pettigrew, 1976, pp. 494–95). Mexican Americans struck the copper mines in Arizona in 1903 and again in 1916; they struck against their agricultural employers in California on numerous occasions in the 1930s (Burkey, 1978, pp. 278–79). After World War II, returning Mexican-American servicemen set up political organizations in California and Texas. The Chicano Movement led by Cesar Chavez in the 1960s is only the most recent expression of Mexican-American protest. The history of Mexican Americans in the United States is part of a pattern of racism.

The Roots of Racism

Racism is not the unique creation of Western colonial powers, as contemporary discussions of the topic often imply. Centuries ago, Cicero warned, "Do not obtain your slaves from the Britons, for the Britons are so stupid and so dull that they are not fit to be slaves." In the nineteenth century, Scottish missionary David Livingstone reported that black Africans were so repulsed by whites that women and children hid from them, and even dogs and chickens fled in terror (Schaefer, 1979, p. 17). But neither is racism universal. In many multiracial societies (for example, in Hawaii and Latin America), people do not regard their physical differences as proof of innate superiority. This is not to say that they regard one another as equals. Most look at other groups' customs and ways with disdain. "Members of all human societies have a fairly good opinion of themselves compared with members of other societies, but this good opinion is frequently based on claims to cultural superiority. . . . Only a few human groups have deemed themselves superior because of the content of their gonads" (van den Berghe, 1967, p. 12). Ethnocentrism (a belief in cultural superiority) may be universal; racism is not. Why does an ideology of biological inferiority and superiority develop in some societies but not in others?

Social Preconditions

The sociologist Pierre van den Berghe (1967, pp. 13–18) has identified the social conditions that have generally given rise to racism. First, a society must contain "sufficient numbers of two or more groups that look different enough so that at least some of their members can be readily classifiable" (p. 13). It is one thing for a small town to absorb one black family, for example; the arrival of several thousand black families is another. A concentration of people with a different way of life makes them noticeable. Second, physical differences are important, for they create more permanent group markers than cultural differences do. Distinctive physical attributes make people noticeable even if they adopt the ways of the dominant group. For example, a Roumanian immigrant who learns to speak English and discards traditional dress can disappear into a crowd. A Chinese immigrant who learns the language and dresses in American styles still looks Chinese. Third, groups must "be culturally different (or at least must have been so when they first met) and in a position of institutionalized inequality for the idea of inherent racial differences to take root" (p. 13). If the groups are culturally similar and meet as equals, people are not as likely to regard physical differences as socially meaningful.

Van den Berghe identifies four social situations that meet these conditions: a military conquest that enables the victor to establish political and economic domination over indigenous people; frontier expansion, with one group pushing another from its territory and killing off resisters; involuntary migration, with the dominant group importing captives for use as servants; and voluntary migration, with an alien group seeking economic opportunities or political refuge.

The presence in sufficient numbers of physically and culturally distinct groups in positions of inequality is a necessary but not a sufficient condition for the emergence of racism. There are many cases in which all of these conditions were met and racism did not develop. The Spanish conquest of the New World is an especially puzzling case. The oppression of Native Americans in Central and South America was as brutal as in the United States, if not more so. The United States and South and Central America have a common history of massive importation of African slaves, their employment in plantation agriculture, and eventual emancipation from slavery.

Yet an explicit doctrine of racial inequality did not develop in Latin America. It was easier for an African slave to obtain freedom in Latin American societies than it was in the United States, and intermarriage between Europeans and Native Americans was also more common in Latin America. Neither African nor Native American ancestry acquired the stigma that they had in North America. Why?

Van den Berghe suggests that racism solved a problem of cultural contradiction not only in the United States but in all the British colonies. The treatment of Native Americans, black slaves, and others stood in direct contradiction to Anglo-American ideals of freedom and equality for all. This contradiction was especially apparent in the United States, which justified its fight for independence from England on egalitarian grounds. "The desire to preserve both the profitable forms of discrimination and exploitation and the democratic ideology made it necessary to deny humanity to the oppressed groups" (van den Berghe, 1967, p. 18). If all men are created equal, then blacks and others must be less than men. Paradoxically, then, egalitarian ideals contributed to the rise of racism. In the aristocratic societies of colonial Latin America, there was no need to rationalize unequal treatment. Inequality was considered normal.

Racist Ideology

Western racism developed slowly. The seeds of racism were planted early in the colonial period but did not take root until the beginning of the nineteenth century. At first, treatment of Native Americans and black slaves was justified on religious grounds. Columbus, for example, saw the subjugation of Native Americans and the theft of their gold as his Christian duty. "Gold is treasure, and he who possesses it does all he wishes to in the world, and succeeds in helping souls into paradise" (Burkey, 1978, p. 64). Sixteenth- and seven-teenth-century Europeans drew a sharp distinction between "civilized Christians" and "heathen savages." The prevailing view was that civility was the original state of humankind. After the flood, however, some of Noah's descendants wandered astray, lost their awareness of God, and degenerated into a state of savagery. According to another version, barbarism resulted from the curse of Ham. Nonwhites had inherited a curse of God (Fredrickson, 1981, p. 10). From this perspective, the domination of indigenous people and the abduction of Africans were acts of charity and kindness. As increasing numbers of oppressed people were converted to Christianity, this position became difficult to maintain, however. Just as religious rationalizations began to lose their power, a new explanation of white supremacy was introduced: Social Darwinism.

The idea that the dominant group in a society is naturally superior and the poor naturally inferior was not conceived in the nineteenth century. But the publication of Charles Darwin's *Origin of Species* in 1859 seemed to give this view scientific backing. Darwin documented the evolution of species; he said nothing whatever about cultural evolution. Nevertheless, a number of social scientists—Herbert Spencer, William Graham Sumner, and others—used Darwin's concepts to explain social inequalities (Hofstader, 1959). Social Darwinists, as they were called, held that the dominant position occupied by whites in the nineteenth century was the product of natural selection and what Spencer called "survival of the fittest." Asians, Africans, and other non-Europeans were at an earlier or lower stage of evolution. Biological differences were believed to determine the "natural" capacities and destinies of the races. Over the next half-century, all kinds of group differences were traced to heredity—including poverty and crime, which had previously been viewed as moral defects. The role environment and opportunity play in shaping behavior was ignored.

The 1911 edition of the *Encyclopaedia Britannica* characterizes "the Negro" as follows:

. . . the negro would appear to stand on a lower evolutionary plane than the white man. . . . Mentally the negro is inferior to the white. . . . [T]he remark of F. Manetta, made after a long study of the negro in America, may be taken as generally true of the whole race: "the negro children were sharp, intelligent and full of vivacity, but on approaching the adult period a gradual change set in. The intellect seemed to become clouded, animation giving place to a sort of lethargy, briskness yielding to indolence. . . ." On the other hand negroes far surpass white men in acuteness of vision, hearing, sense of direction and topography. . . . For the rest, the mental condition is very similar to that of a child, normally good-natured and cheerful, but subject to sudden fits of emotion and passion during which he is capable of performing acts of singular atrocity. . . . (Vol. 19, pp. 344–45)

The idea that blacks suffer from arrested evolution was used to explain and justify their inferior position: Their alleged indolence justified whipping slaves; their supposedly primitive instincts made them akin to beasts of burden. Native Americans, Mexican Americans, Chinese immigrants, and others were alleged to have similar inherited, biological defects.

Modern science has rejected explicit biological theories of racial inequality. The main thrust of contemporary sociology has been to establish the social character of race and the overriding influence of the environment on personality and behavior. Yet, echoes of Social Darwinism linger. The "New Darwinists," as the sociologist Stephen Steinberg has called one group of contemporary theorists, substitute notions of cultural superiority and inferiority for biological explanations of racial inequality. According to this view, children inherit a set of immutable cultural traits from their parents, just as surely as if they were implanted in their genes. One group's cultural inheritance enables them to excel; another's con-

demns them to the bottom of the socioeconomic heap. New Darwinists revive the principle of the survival of the fittest, defined in cultural instead of biological terms: "[T]he underlying premise of the New Darwinism is that 'good' things come to those with the 'right' cultural values" (Steinberg, 1981, p. 80). This view obscures the external obstacles that hold a racial group down and puts the blame for racial inequality not on social institutions but on the victims themselves.

Maintaining Racial Inequality

The classic statement of the clash between democratic ideals and racial inequality is found in Gunnar Myrdal's *An American Dilemma* (1944). Myrdal described a vicious cycle of prejudice and discrimination: Because whites are prejudiced against blacks, they discriminate against them, denying them job opportunities, housing, equal education, and common dignity. Because blacks are discriminated against, they are poor, undereducated, and forced to maintain a lower standard of living. Their lower standard of living confirms the white population's prejudices. In Myrdal's words, "The Negroes' poverty, ignorance, superstition, slum dwellings, health deficiencies, . . . appearance, disorderly conduct, . . . and criminality stimulate and feed the antipathy of the whites for them" (p. 1066). Once established, prejudice and discrimination develop a momentum of their own, and racism may be institutionalized. In this section, we will analyze prejudice, discrimination, and institutionalized racism.

Prejudice and Discrimination

Prejudice is a negative or hostile attitude toward an entire category of people. (Racism is one form of prejudice; but negative attitudes may be based on cultural or economic explanations of group differences as well as on biological theories.) Prejudice is directed against individuals because they are members of a particular category. Individuals are avoided or rejected simply because the group with which they are identified is believed to have objectionable characteristics (Allport, 1954, p. 7). The word "prejudice" comes from the Latin word for prejudgment. Prejudgments are a necessary part of social life. They enable us to predict how others will behave, and to act accordingly. Prejudgment becomes prejudice when new, contradictory information does not alter a person's beliefs. Consider the statement "José does well in school, for a Chicano." José is the exception that proves the rule. His academic performance has not altered the speaker's low estimate of Chicano intelligence. Prejudice rests on *stereotypes*, or unexamined generalizations about a group and its members.

Why are some groups in a society more prejudiced than others? Why do some groups and individuals feel that maintaining racial boundaries is a matter of utmost importance? Why do some individuals accept derogatory stereotypes about racial groups while others reject them? Why is one member of a family prejudiced and another not? Here we will look at four theories of prejudice.

According to one theory, prejudice is rooted in personality: It performs a psychological function. Frustration-aggression theory (Dollard et al., 1939) suggests that when people's goals or desires are frustrated, they become aggressive. They want to strike out. The person or group that is causing the frustration (for example, the boss) may be too powerful to attack openly or directly, however. Blacks, Native Americans, Jews, and other racial groups provide a convenient and safe substitute target because they are not in a position to retaliate. Attacking a scapegoat has the cathartic effect of relieving aggression, and racial minorities are "safe goats" (Allport, 1958, p. 332).

A second theory linking prejudice and personality was developed in the aftermath of World War

II by Theodore Adorno and associates (1950). In an investigation of anti-Semitism, they found that people who were prejudiced against Jews were also prejudiced against blacks, liberals, intellectuals, sexual nonconformists, and others. Prejudice seemed to be associated with a number of other personality traits: the glorification of power; sexual repression; superstitiousness; obsessive conformity; a tendency to see things as either all good or all bad, all black or all white. The researchers labeled this psychological syndrome "the authoritarian personality" and traced its roots to early childhood. Simply put, people whose parents are intolerant and authoritarian become intolerant and authoritarian themselves: A harsh upbringing leads to harsh attitudes.

At best, psychological theories provide only a partial explanation of prejudice. They do not explain why frustration is displaced toward racial scapegoats rather than toward another powerless group, such as children or old people. They do not account for the fact that levels of prejudice vary from one society and from one region to another. If frustration always leads to aggression, one would expect scapegoats to strike back. Personality theories imply that prejudice is an expression of psychological disturbance. But can whole societies suffer from mental disorder?

Situational theorists take a different position, maintaining that prejudice, in many cases, is a matter of social adjustment (Pettigrew, 1976, p. 487). In contrast to personality theories, which explain prejudice as a crutch that helps maladjusted people limp through life, situational theory holds that prejudice is normal in societies in which racial bigotry is rewarded and racial tolerance punished. Prejudice reflects the social situations in which people find themselves; it does not reflect ingrained personality traits. Situational theory, then, helps to explain why people sometimes exhibit prejudice in one social setting but not in another. For example, two researchers (Lohman and Reitzes, 1952) found that white

Washington, D.C., students protest the Supreme Court ruling on school desegregation in 1954. Were these students psychologically disturbed, socially frustrated, or protecting their future jobs? Or were they simply conforming to the norms of that time and place?

members of an integrated union accepted blacks at work but rejected the idea of blacks as their neighbors.

Conflict theories emphasize the role prejudice plays in economic competition and class struggles (Wilson, 1980, pp. 4–9). According to the orthodox Marxist view, the capitalist (or ruling) class encourages racial prejudice in order to divide the working class into two hostile segments. Divisions within the working class weaken its bargaining position, making workers easier to control. In addition, racial prejudice and discrimination create a surplus pool of black laborers whom capitalists can hire if white workers demand too much. A variation on this theory traces prejudice to white workers' efforts to maintain their own position. By denying members of racial minorities the opportunities to develop and practice skills, higher-paid workers ensure that they will not be replaced or undercut by cheaper labor. According to the first view, prejudice is a capitalist device that blinds white workers to the interests they have in common with black workers. According to the second view, prejudice directly benefits higher-paid white workers.

The four theories of prejudice presented here are not incompatible. Conflict theory puts racial prejudice in social context. Situational theory

suggests why many well-adjusted people are prejudiced and why people select racial groups as scapegoats Personality theories explain why some individuals develop extreme racial prejudice or maintain racial prejudices in spite of social disapproval.

The term "prejudice" refers to attitudes; the term "discrimination" refers to actions. In a literal sense, discrimination means drawing distinctions on the basis of quality. To say that a person is discriminating is to say that he or she is selective. In the context of intergroup relations, however, *discrimination* is the intentional effort to restrict or require activities of selected groups (Burkey, 1978, p. 79). Members of racial or other groups may be denied voting rights, education, job opportunities, housing, public accommodations, and membership in clubs and other private organizations. In some cases, they are required to engage in activities that are not required of other people—to perform services (forced labor), obey curfew laws, wear a symbol of their inferior social status, or move to certain restricted areas. Discrimination ranges from the avoidance of intimate, primary relationships (especially marriage) to informal but customary agreements to exclude members of racial minorities (for example, from private clubs) to laws

Segregation in South Africa and in the American South

The term "segregation" came into common use in both South Africa and the American South at about the same time—in the early years of the twentieth century. South African white supremacists may in fact have borrowed the term from their American counterparts. But a close examination of the two modes of legalized discrimination reveals some major differences in how they worked and in the functions they performed. . . .

. . . The most important *spatial* aspect of white minority rule in twentieth-century South Africa has been the territorial division of the country on the principle of "possessory segregation" as originally mandated by the Native Land Act of 1913. This legislation prohibited Africans from purchasing land outside designated native reserves and even from entering into sharecropping arrangements in the "white" agricultural areas. . . . African laborers were needed on farms outside the reserves, but their status was to be that of contract wage laborers or labor tenants rather than sharecroppers or "squatters." . . .

Translating this form of "segregation" into an American context requires a counter-factual flight of imagination. Assume for a moment that the American Indian population had not been decimated and that the number of European colonists and immigrants had been much less than was actually the case—creating a situation where the Indians, although conquered, remained a substantial majority of the total population of the United States. After the whites had seized the regions with the most fertile land and exploitable resources, the indigenes were consigned to a fraction of their original domain. All one has to envision here are greatly enlarged versions of the current Indian reservations. Then suppose further that Indians were denied citizenship rights in the rest of the country but nevertheless constituted the main labor force for industry and commercial agriculture. . . .

specifically designed to isolate them physically and socially. In sixteenth-century Italy, for example, Jews were prohibited from owning real estate and confined by law to a walled ghetto. In the seventeenth century, the British prohibited Irish Catholics from opening or teaching in schools, entering the learned professions, producing or selling books, manufacturing or selling arms, or owning a horse worth more than five pounds. At one time or another, the Chinese in Thailand have been forbidden to fish in Thai waters; drive vehicles for hire; sell cloth to Buddhist monks; sell pork, tobacco, wine, or sugar; or collect birds' nests (for soup). In South Africa today, there are over 300 special laws that govern blacks—including curfews, a ban on a gathering of more than

Despite some superficial similarities, . . . the differences between Jim Crow and "native segregation" or "separate development" are . . . great, in terms both of underlying structures and patterns of historical development. . . . First, the southern mode, except on a local level, was directed at a minority rather than a majority. . . . Second, the Afro-American freedmen and their descendants were more influenced by white culture than the majority of twentieth-century black South Africans. A third difference was that southern blacks were theoretically citizens of a democratic nation and not conquered aliens. . . . Finally, blacks and whites in the South had never been geographically separated; hence there was no basis for employing the notion that each race had its own natural territories as a rationale for determining status by real or fictive location. . . .

The significance of all these differences can perhaps be summed up by stating that blacks of the post-emancipation era in the South were, despite all the discrimination and *de facto* or *de jure* segregation and disfranchisement, much more integrated into the white-dominated society and culture than most Africans have ever been in South Africa. . . .

Southern segregation, therefore, was an effort to establish and maintain a rigid caste division between racial groups that were inextricably involved in the same culture, society, economy, and legal system. "Native segregation," on the other hand, was an effort to perpetuate a post-conquest pattern of vertical ethnic pluralism that initially involved major cultural differences, divergent social institutions, and even separate legal codes governing Europeans and Africans.

Source: George M. Frederickson, *White Supremacy: A Comparative Study in American and South African History* (New York: Oxford University Press, 1981), pp. 241–52.

ten blacks for any purpose other than religious, and a law against educating blacks without government supervision (Burkey, 1978, pp. 80–89).

The relationship between prejudice and discrimination is not as straightforward as one might think. The two do not necessarily go together; people do not always practice what they preach. In a classic experiment, Richard La Piere (1934) traveled across the United States with a Chinese couple, stopping at 66 hotels and 184 restaurants and cafés. In spite of strong anti-Chinese prejudices at the time of the study, they were refused service only once. After the trip, La Piere wrote to all the proprietors of the establishments they had visited, asking whether they would accept "members of the Chinese race" as

Table 10-1
The Relationships Between
Prejudice and Discrimination

Four Relationships Between Two Social Variables

Prejudice	Discrimination	Four Personality Types
1 +	+	Active bigot (the restaurant owner in the Deep South)
2 +	−	Timid bigot (the same restaurant owner in the North)
3 −	+	Fair-weather liberal (the club president; the real estate agent)
4 −	−	All-weather liberal (the minister)

Source: Robert K. Merton, "Discrimination and the American Creed," in Robert MacIver (Ed.), *Discrimination and National Welfare* (New York: Harper & Row, 1949), p. 103.

customers. Over 90 percent of those who responded said that they would *not* serve Chinese.

La Piere's experiment illustrates a point made by Robert Merton in an essay entitled "Discrimination and the American Creed" (1949). The relationship between prejudice and discrimination is variable. Depending on the social situation, a prejudiced person may treat members of a minority as equals, or an unprejudiced person may practice discrimination.

To underscore this point, we go back about twenty-five years, to before the era of the Civil Rights Movement. Imagine a man who has been raised to have strong prejudices against blacks. He owns a restaurant in the Deep South and, almost without thinking about it, refuses to serve black customers. He is an "active bigot." One day this man sells his restaurant and opens one in New York City. He discovers that many of his potential customers are blacks and that he is expected to serve them. In this setting, discriminating against blacks is contrary to his self-interest, so he welcomes them to his restaurant. The man's feelings haven't changed, but his behavior has. Because of the social situation, he has become a "timid bigot." Imagine another man, who has been raised to consider all people equal, regardless of their race or religion. He becomes president of an exclusive club that accepts only white Anglo-Saxon Protestants. He may not be prejudiced himself, but he wants the social approval of other club members, and when Jews or Catholics apply for membership, he turns them down. He is a "fair-weather liberal," who discriminates to gain social rewards. Now imagine a black real estate agent during this period of overt discrimination. He is not prejudiced against his own people, but he shows black families homes only in black neighborhoods because he needs referrals from white agents, who would disapprove of his breaking neighborhood color lines. He, too, is a non-prejudiced discriminator; he discriminates to avoid social punishment. Imagine a fourth man, who is the minister of a white congregation in the Deep South. Most members of his congregation strongly oppose integration. He knows that if he openly expresses his views on racial integration, he is likely to lose his job. Nevertheless, he joins Civil Rights protest marches. This man's self-esteem depends on a broader reference group. He is an "all-weather liberal." These four possible relationships between prejudice and discrimination are shown in Table 10–1.

The key point in Merton's analysis is that both prejudice and discrimination derive from the social setting. Prejudices are acquired through socialization. Children develop their social identities in part by learning what kinds of people are not like them, what kinds of people are "outsiders." Discrimination reflects socialization and social control. Groups deliver social rewards and punishments for conformity and nonconformity. A person's self-esteem depends in part on group acceptance (primarily, though not necessarily, the groups with which he or she deals every day). Psychological explanations of prejudice tend to obscure the role of social forces. It implies that if people's attitudes changed, racial inequality would disappear. In fact, the problem is rooted in the social structure. Racial discrimination has been outlawed in most areas of public life in the United States. Although prejudice has not disappeared, it has declined significantly, as suggested at the beginning of this chapter. Yet racial inequality persists. How can this be?

Institutionalized Racism

The term *institutionalized racism* refers to established practices and policies that have the unintended consequence of restricting the opportunities of certain racial groups.* Discrimination is built into customs that, on the surface, seem to have nothing to do with race. As a result, inequality persists if people simply go about their lives in the usual way, not because of deliberate efforts to keep minorities in their "place."

Stokely Carmichael and Charles Hamilton distinguish between individual racism, which consists of overt acts by individuals or small groups, and institutionalized racism, which "originates in the operation of established and respected forces in society" (1967, p. 4). When white terrorists planted a bomb in a church in Birmingham, Alabama, killing five black children, it was an act of individual racism. When 500 black infants in that same city die each year because of inadequate food, shelter, and medical care, it is a function of institutional racism. When the home a

---

* The term is also used to refer to established, standardized, socially approved forms of discrimination. Here we use the term to refer only to unintentional discrimination.

black family purchases in a white neighborhood is vandalized, the family is a victim of individual racism. When low incomes, zoning laws, transportation policies, and other social factors confine tens of thousands of blacks to decaying inner cities, they are victims of institutionalized racism. Most Americans today condemn acts of individual racism (overt discrimination by individuals or small groups). But most are not even aware of institutionalized racism.

Examples of institutionalized racism are found in employment and banking procedures, education, housing, the criminal justice system, and current economic policies. Most jobs today have educational requirements, whether or not there is any proven relationship between a diploma and job performance. Because blacks and members of other minorities tend to complete fewer years of school than whites, they are automatically excluded from many jobs. The principle of seniority is firmly established in U.S. business and industry. Because nonwhites are likely to be the most recently hired — not because of overt prejudice or discrimination — they are likely to be the first fired. The seniority system tends to counteract the gains that minorities have made since enactment of the civil rights legislation of the 1960s.

Banks and insurance companies are businesses, run for profit. Decisions about whether to approve a mortgage or how much to charge for life insurance are based on statistical predictors. For example, many banks "red line" (exclude) neighborhoods that, according to their statistics, are high risks for mortgages. Banks may use ZIP codes as a guide in determining whether to grant a personal or business loan. By no design on the banks' part, the excluded neighborhoods often are predominantly nonwhite. Life insurance premiums are based on predictions of life expectancy. Because blacks have a shorter life expectancy than whites, they pay a higher premium for insurance. The statistics that financial institutions use may be colorblind, but the adverse consequences are discriminatory. Thus, the use of unbiased statistics tends to perpetuate inequality.

The perpetuation of racial discrimination is an unintended consequence of educational policies. Most schools use tracking, or ability grouping, to sort students of the same age into different class sections (Hurn, 1978, Chapter 6). Some evidence indicates that teachers assign students to different tracks on the basis of neatness, dress, general deportment, and information on the child's parents and background, as well as on demonstrated academic potential. As a result, a disproportionate number of black children are assigned to "slow" and non-academic tracks. Teachers are not necessarily exhibiting prejudice. Experience tells them that children from certain backgrounds who behave in certain ways are not likely to be good students. There is very little mobility in school tracking systems: Once a student is assigned to a "slow" track, the chances of moving up are small. Critics argue that ability grouping becomes a self-fulfilling prophecy. If teachers label certain students "stupid," they tend to view the behavior of those students as stupid. Moreover, in time, the students' performance will tend to confirm the teachers' prophecy. If a teacher seats students in the back of the room, gives them little instruction, and treats them as behavior problems, they may eventually fall behind other students, whatever their potential. In these ways, tracking may perpetuate racial inequality. Similarly, IQ and other tests may unintentionally discriminate against nonwhite youngsters. Critics argue that these tests give middle-class white children an unfair advantage by basing questions on material that is familiar to these youngsters and failing to measure the special knowledge and skills of minority children.

Housing policies also contribute to institutionalized racism. From 1935 to 1950, the handbook of the Federal Housing Administration (FHA) officially discouraged granting mortgages in racially integrated neighborhoods, on the grounds that such neighborhoods were unstable. Other, seemingly unrelated government policies have contributed to residential segregation and inequality: decisions to invest federal funds in highways rather than in mass transit, contributing to the growth of suburbs; subsidies for private home ownership, but not for communal or rental arrangements, with FHA and Veterans Administration mortgages; relatively high standards in housing codes, contributing to the "trickle-down process" (see Chapter 6); the hiring of people from the real estate industry to administer housing programs; and even urban renewal programs. When a suburban town votes to require a certain amount of land for each dwelling or to exclude low-income housing, institutionalized racism is reinforced. Disproportionate numbers of blacks have low incomes and are therefore excluded without there being any overt acts of discrimination.

The criminal justice system provides numerous examples of institutionalized racism. Only a small percentage of persons who commit crimes are arrested, and an even smaller percentage of persons arrested are tried and sent to prison. Police, prosecutors, judges, and prison officials exercise considerable discretion at each step along the route. Crime statistics show that nonwhites commit proportionately more violent and property crimes than whites do. (Whites commit more white-collar crimes, at greater financial cost, but society does not regard those as quite so serious.) In part because of statistics, police and prosecutors are more likely to arrest, charge, and prosecute blacks than whites. Often, there is a long delay between the charge and the trial. Whether a suspect remains in jail or goes free during this period often depends on the bail a judge sets and whether a professional bondsman considers the accused person a good risk. Often, the poor are denied bond because they lack collateral security or

Table 10–2
Blacks' Share of Public Assistance

Program	Percentage of Beneficiaries of Government Programs Who Are Black	Percentage of Reductions Proposed by the Reagan Administration
Social Security retirement and survivors' insurance	8.1%	6.0%
Medicare	9.3	2.0
Veterans' compensation and pensions	10.0	0
Supplemental security income	27.4	0
Aid to Families with Dependent Children	44.4	11.0
Food stamps	34.2	24.3
CETA public service jobs	33.0	90.8
Medicaid	34.9	5.0
Public housing	36.0	34.8
Social Security disability	14.9	7.2
Education for disadvantaged	34.5	*
Extended unemployment insurance	15.0	15.4

*Data not available.

Source: *The New York Times,* June 2, 1981, p. B11, based on data from various government and private sources.

cannot pay a premium. Because a larger percentage of minority group members are poor, nonwhites are more likely than whites to remain in jail. This, in turn, influences the willingness of minority group members to plead guilty and the chances of their being acquitted when they go to trial.

The cuts in the federal budget enacted in 1981 will also have a disproportionate effect on blacks. Although fewer than 12 percent of Americans are black, according to the 1980 census, a third or more of the people who receive food stamps or Medicaid or who live in public housing, and almost half of those who receive welfare, are black. Spending for these programs is being severely cut. On the other hand, blacks are underrepresented in the programs that have been included in the proposed "social safety net": Only 8 percent of Americans who receive Social Security

and about one tenth of Americans who receive veterans' compensation or who are on Medicare — the programs to be spared drastic cuts — are black (see Table 10–2). Because middle-class blacks have been denied jobs in private industry and have had difficulty obtaining financing for their own businesses, a disproportionate number of them work in public jobs, as teachers or postal workers, for example. As a result, cutbacks in the number of federal employees will have more impact on blacks than on whites. One of the unintended consequences of the budget cuts, then, will be to further entrench racial inequality.

In short, the problem is not in people's hearts and minds. Racism is built into the social system. Eliminating prejudice and discrimination will not eliminate racial inequality. The true dilemma is that unprejudiced, non-discriminatory policies and programs perpetuate inequality. The gap between blacks' and whites' life chances in this country is in part an unintended consequence of numerous established and respected norms and values. The myth of individual achievement—the belief that anyone who works hard can get ahead in America—blinds people to the impact of institutionalized racism. In the early days of the Civil Rights Movement, whites asked why individual blacks couldn't "pull themselves up by their own bootstraps." The answer is that because of institutionalized racism, blacks did not have bootstraps.

Contemporary Racial Issues and Conflicts

Minorities have never wholly accepted the status quo, as shown in the early histories of Native Americans, black Americans, and Mexican Americans. Only in the late 1950s and early 1960s, however, was discontent transformed into "a full-fledged protest movement, with the leadership, organization, resources, and popular base to mobilize and sustain a direct assault on racist structures" (Steinberg, 1981, p. 213). In this period, protest achieved political maturity. Here we will look at the actions that blacks and other groups took to upset the status quo and at government and public reactions.

Actions

Working through the courts, blacks won a number of victories in the fight against segregation in the 1940s. For example, white primaries, which effectively kept blacks out of political office, were declared unconstitutional in 1944. But the Supreme Court decision in *Brown* v. *Board of Education* (1954) was a turning point. The Court ruled that "separate educational facilities are inherently unequal," reversing the separate but equal doctrine set forth in the 1896 *Plessy* decision. (Later the principle of "separate cannot

be equal" was extended to public accommodations, employment, and housing.) In the *Brown* decision, the Court referred to social science research, suggesting that segregation was damaging to black children's self-esteem. In the words of Chief Justice Earl Warren, "To separate [black students] from others of similar age and qualifications because of race generates a feeling of inferiority as to their status in the community that may affect their hearts and minds in a way unlikely ever to be undone." The Court added that school desegregation must proceed with "all deliberate speed," an ambiguous phrase that seemed to invite delay.

Southern protest On December 1, 1955, Mrs. Rosa Parks was arrested in Montgomery, Alabama, for refusing to give her seat on a public bus to a white man. Word of the arrest spread, and black citizens rallied around a young Baptist minister, Martin Luther King, Jr. A boycott planned to last 1 day stretched to 381 days. The protest was a significant shift away from black Americans' reliance on NAACP court battles. Dr. King advocated "*active* nonviolent resistance to evil." He encouraged disobeying the law when the law was unjust but emphasized nonviolence and "willingness to accept suffering without retaliating" (King, 1963). The aim was to pressure whites to repeal segregation laws by creating civil disorder, economic hardship, and public shame.

Over the next decade, support for the Civil Rights Movement among conservative blacks and liberal whites grew. Throughout the South, boycotts, sit-ins, protest marches, and freedom rides were met with jail terms, mass arrests, police dogs, tear gas, mob violence, and in some cases, death. During the Montgomery bus boycott, for example, four black churches were bombed and Dr. King's home was set on fire. Violent reactions to the Civil Rights Movement only increased public support, however. In September 1957, the governor of Arkansas ordered the National Guard to prevent nine black students from entering Little Rock's Central High School. President Eisenhower sent federal troops to enforce the Supreme Court's desegregation order, and the troops remained in Little Rock for the full school year. In 1960, black college students in Greensboro, North Carolina, asked to be served at a Woolworth lunch counter, setting off a chain reaction of student sit-ins. When mass arrests failed to stop a Civil Rights campaign in Birmingham, Alabama, in 1963, Sheriff "Bull" Connor met protesters with clubs, high-pressure water hoses, and elec-

tric cattle prods. The spectacle of police attacking unarmed, unresisting men, women, and children was broadcast throughout the world. Later that year, an estimated 250,000 black and white Americans gathered in Washington, D.C., to hear Dr. King's most famous speech, "I have a dream. . . ."

Why did the Civil Rights Movement emerge in the late 1950s, and not sooner? The "great man" theory of history does not explain this timing. Dr. King was not the first charismatic leader to emerge from the black community. Mrs. Parks

A social problem becomes a social issue: In the early 1950s, most white Americans were not aware of the sometimes violent oppression of blacks in the South. Photographs like this one, showing a Birmingham police officer turning attack dogs on nonviolent protesters, awakened the national conscience.

was not the first individual to refuse indignities. (The Congress of Racial Equality, CORE, held sit-ins in the 1940s.) Steinberg (1981, pp. 213–14) argues that by the mid-1950s, the racial caste system in the South had become obsolete. Mechanization was replacing the agricultural system that had profited from large numbers of disenfranchised black sharecroppers. Freedom from the almost feudal constraints of the past, in turn, made black protest feasible. Other factors include the courtship of newly independent African nations during the cold war, making segregation of public accommodations in this country an international insult; the growing size and importance of the black vote in the North; and the *Brown* decision, which gave protest against segregation a new legitimacy.

Chicano and Pan-Indian Movements The black Civil Rights Movement provided a model for Mexican Americans, Native Americans, and other minorities, inspiring more than a decade of protest.

The best-known leader of the Chicano Movement is Cesar Chavez. In 1962, Chavez resigned from his job to organize California's Mexican-American migrant farm workers. Chavez succeeded in attracting the mass media, starting a national boycott of grapes in 1965, and winning contracts for the United Farm Workers Union (UFW) from about half of California's table-grape producers in 1970. Chavez was not the only Chicano leader during this period, and migrant labor was not the only Chicano issue. In Denver, Rodolfo ("Corky") Gonzales organized the Crusade for Justice to combat job discrimination and alleged police abuses and to seek better housing and education for urban Chicanos. In New Mexico, Reies Lopez Tijerina's militant *Alianza de Las Mercedes* seized part of the Kit Carson National Forest, which they felt had been stolen from the original Mexican-American settlers.

The different branches of the Chicano Movement were united in their demand for an end to Anglo discrimination, their desire for local control of local institutions, their assertion of the cultural distinctiveness of Mexican Americans, and their pride in their heritage. Earlier organizations, such as the Mexican American Political Association (MAPA), which was founded in California in 1958, had sought assimilation of Mexican Americans through conventional political channels. The Chicano Movement sought political and cultural autonomy by unconventional means. The results have been mixed. For example, Chavez won recognition for the UFW but then found himself battling with the Teamsters' union. Under pressure from the Chicano Movement, the federal government required schools to offer bilingual education, but the requirement has been challenged in the courts (Schaefer, 1979, pp. 290–94).

The first national organization to represent the many different Native American tribes, the National Congress of American Indians (NCAI), was founded in 1944. Like the NAACP and the MAPA, it has worked through traditional political channels, lobbying for Native American interests. In the 1960s, however, the NCAI was overshadowed by the more aggressive National Indian Youth Council and the American Indian Movement (AIM). AIM was founded in Denver in 1968 by Clyde Bellecourt and Denis Banks, with the immediate goals of monitoring police treatment of Native Americans and promoting educational reform and alcoholic rehabilitation programs. The organization came to national attention in 1969, when AIM took over the abandoned prison on Alcatraz Island in San Francisco Bay, claiming squatter's rights. In 1972, AIM helped to organize the "Trail of Broken Treaties," a march on Washington, D.C., which ended with a takeover of the Bureau of Indian Affairs. In 1973, AIM occupied the historic village of Wounded Knee for seventy days. In short, the Pan-Indian Movement adopted the politics of confrontation.

The underlying goals of the Pan-Indian Movement were to regain lands and rights granted under treaties signed with the U.S. federal government but ignored in practice and to regain local autonomy. Again, the results were mixed (Schaefer, 1979). For example, under pressure from the Alaskan Federation of Natives, Congress passed a bill granting the Aleuts, Inuits (or Eskimos), and other Native Americans ownership and control of 40 million acres of Alaskan land. The bill also provided them with a cash settlement of nearly $1 billion for land that traditionally was occupied by Native Americans but that the state had auctioned off when oil was discovered there. The Pan-Indian Movement itself has been torn by internal conflict, however—tribe against tribe, reservation dwellers against city dwellers, "full bloods" against "mixed bloods," conservatives against militants. Meanwhile, the movement for black rights, which had inspired the Chicano and Pan-Indian Movements, had taken another turn.

Urban riots The Civil Rights Movement changed black-white relations in the United States in two ways: It diminished not only legal but also extra-legal terror against blacks in the South, and it won full citizenship under the law for blacks. The impact of the movement on the North and the West was mixed, however. Blacks' victories heightened racial consciousness and raised the expectations of blacks in urban ghettos but did little to improve their daily lives.

In August 1965, a routine arrest for speeding touched off six days of burning, looting, and sniping in the Watts section of Los Angeles. It took 12,000 National Guardsmen and 2,500 city and county police one week to bring the Watts riot under control. Before the riot was over, 34 people were killed (28 of them black), 4,000 people were arrested, and some 200 buildings were destroyed. Property loss was estimated at $40 million. It was the first of three "long, hot summers" that shook

the nation. In 1967 alone, there were 257 riots in 173 cities, claiming 87 lives, injuring 2,500, and resulting in 19,200 arrests (Schaefer, 1979, p. 191).

The urban uprisings of the 1960s differed from earlier race riots in important ways. Prior to World War II, race riots were nearly always instigated by whites who were determined to enforce segregation. Most riots took the form of fights between white and black civilians over an area where one group (usually the whites) felt that the other group did not belong, such as a public beach. These earlier riots were interracial territorial contests. In contrast, the riots of the 1960s were instigated by blacks and confined to black neighborhoods. Violence was directed not at civilians and homes but at stores owned by whites and at symbols of white authority (law enforcement officers and firefighters).

The summers of 1965 through 1968 baffled most white Americans. The riots broke out at the end of a long period of struggle, when it seemed that the Civil Rights Movement had achieved many of its goals. Why were blacks rioting just when things were getting better? Common sense suggests that people take to the streets because the conditions under which they live are intolerable: We associate riots with poverty and oppression. People who are hungry and deprived of basic rights have little to lose. However, James Davies's studies (1969) of the French and American revolutions and other uprisings revealed an unexpected pattern. Davies found that in most cases, revolutions break out following a period of economic growth, not decline.

Davies suggests that people are most likely to rebel when a long period of rising expectations and economic gains is followed by a short period of economic reversal. Davies reasons this way: Extreme poverty and deprivation tend to lead to a sense of hopelessness and to apathy. People who expect little in life are not likely to rebel; they are preoccupied with daily survival. When the

The Detroit riot shown here was not an isolated incident. In the "long hot summer" of 1967, more than 150 American cities reported violent outbreaks. Riots broke out again in 1968 after Martin Luther King, Jr., was assassinated.

economic situation improves, however, people's expectations rise. The more progress people make, the more they hope for. They begin to think that a better standard of living is not only possible but probable. A sudden setback makes them fear they will lose the ground they have already gained, and the gap between their expectations and their actual situation becomes intolerable. They are being deprived of rights to which they feel entitled and of improvements they considered probable. The riots of 1965 through 1968 seem to fit this pattern. The economic situation of most black Americans had improved markedly in the 1950s. The victories of the Civil Rights Movement raised the expectations of the black community to a new

high. When expected changes failed to materialize, black ghettos exploded.

During the time of the urban riots, many white Americans wanted to believe that the riots did not reflect the feelings of the majority of black Americans. According to the "riff-raff" theory, the riots were caused by a small number of deviant youths. The typical rioter was pictured as an unemployed, uneducated juvenile delinquent or as a recent immigrant from the South who had not adjusted to city life. According to the "rabble-rouser" theory, the riots were led by small bands of black militants, perhaps tied to an international conspiracy, who were intent on overthrowing the U.S. system. The *Report of the National*

Advisory Commission on Civil Disorders (1968), known as the Kerner Commission Report, found all of these beliefs to be false. Although only about 20 percent of Watts residents had actively participated in the riots, another 30 percent had watched sympathetically from the sidelines. The majority of Watts residents (62 percent) saw the riot as a form of protest, not as a criminal act. Over half the people arrested during the Watts riot were twenty-five years old or older. Half of them had never been convicted of a crime. The typical rioter had been born and raised in Watts, had slightly more education than non-rioters, and was employed at least part time. What seemed to distinguish rioters from non-rioters was their conviction that they deserved better jobs and were being held back by racism. There was no evidence of a conspiracy in the Watts or in other riots. In addition, the Commission found that the violence was neither indiscriminate nor unrestrained, contrary to what the public believed. Attacks were directed at stores that sold inferior goods or charged excessive prices or both; homes, schools, and churches were untouched (Fogelson, 1971).

Reactions

The Civil Rights Movement captured national and international attention. The responses of the federal government and the public have gone through two phases: legislation and retrenchment.

Legislation In the 1960s, the government took a number of steps to eliminate overt discrimination (individual racism). The 1964 Civil Rights Act outlawed racial discrimination in public accommodations and in employment and denied federal funds to institutions that practiced discrimination. The 1965 Voting Rights Act outlawed literacy tests and gave the federal government the right to station poll watchers to oversee

implementation of the Act. A 1968 federal law made discrimination in housing illegal.

Meanwhile, the courts continued to struggle with school desegregation. Ironically, de facto segregation (segregation in fact) in the North turned out to be more problematic than de jure segregation (segregation by law) in the South. Although Northern and Western states had rarely passed specific laws requiring blacks and whites to attend separate schools, schools were nonetheless segregated because blacks and whites tended to live in separate neighborhoods. (Typically, blacks and other minorities were concentrated in inner cities; whites, in suburbs.) This raised two issues. First, was unintentional segregation against the law? Second, for purposes of desegregation, did the courts have the right to consider a city and its surrounding suburbs a single unit? In the early 1970s, the Supreme Court answered both questions in the affirmative. In a 1971 case in Charlotte, North Carolina, the Court approved of busing students across a large metropolitan region to achieve desegregation. In a 1973 case in Denver, the Court ordered desegregation of Northern schools, noting that "Hispanos" also suffered from segregation and must be included in the plan.

Partly in response to the riots of the late 1960s and the threat of national disorder and partly in response to the threat of prosecution under the new civil rights laws, private organizations and corporations took steps to reduce racial inequality. For example, in 1968 the Association of American Medical Colleges (AAMC) recommended that "medical schools must admit increased numbers of students from geographical areas, economic backgrounds and ethnic groups that are now inadequately represented" (in Dreyfuss and Lawrence, 1979, p. 19). The next year, the AAMC suggested that 12 percent of first-year places in medical schools be awarded to blacks by the 1975–76 academic year. This was one of many affirmative action programs created during this period. These programs were aimed at reducing institutionalized racism by giving minorities a limited amount of preferential treatment.

Retrenchment It was only a matter of time before the new laws and court decisions raised conflicts of interest and of values. The use of busing to achieve school desegregation conflicts directly with the concept of a neighborhood school, which is almost a sacred institution in the United States. Busing conflicts with the belief that families who work and make sacrifices in order to move to a neighborhood with good schools have a right to send their children to those schools. Opponents of mandatory busing argue that it forces parents to send their children to schools over which they have no control, that it causes children to lose time, and that it exposes youngsters to potential accidents en route to school. To complicate matters, research on the effects of school desegregation have produced conflicting findings (Bahr, Chadwick, and Strauss, 1979, p. 417). Some studies show that attending integrated schools boosts the academic performance of minority students; others do not. (No evidence indicates that integrating schools has a negative impact on white students.) Some researchers have argued that busing defeats the goal of the *Brown* decision by accelerating "white flight" to the suburbs (Coleman, Kelly, and Moore, 1975).

The busing controversy reached a peak in 1976, when buses were burned and black students were attacked in Boston. The incidents made headlines, but, in fact, major disturbances occurred in only a few of the districts in which busing was implemented, even in Boston (Bahr, Chadwick, and Strauss, 1979, p. 421). Most researchers conclude that white flight to the suburbs is caused by a fear of crime and violence in cities, by the movement of jobs to the suburbs, by the increase in construction in the suburbs, and by deteriorating inner-city services—not by busing and desegregation (Pettigrew and Green, 1976).

Whatever the facts, the Supreme Court has retreated from school busing. In 1974, the Court rejected a plan to merge inner-city and suburban school districts in Denver. Moreover, numerous anti-busing proposals were made in Congress throughout the 1970s.

Affirmative action programs conflict with the merit system, which holds that people should be awarded places in schools and jobs and should be given promotions solely on the basis of individual achievement. In 1977, for example, Allan Bakke sued the University of California at Davis on the grounds that he had been discriminated against because he is white. The Davis faculty had set aside sixteen places in its medical school for disadvantaged (primarily minority) students. Bakke argued that admitting people less qualified than he because they were members of minorities was a violation of his rights. (Ironically, Bakke sued under the 1964 Civil Rights Act.) The Supreme Court ruled that universities may use race as one criterion in admitting students but that strict racial quotas are unconstitutional. Bakke was admitted to the Medical School at Davis (Dreyfuss and Lawrence, 1979). In other cases, the Supreme Court has ruled that affirmative action is constitutional if it is based on an agreement between private parties (a company and a union, for example) or if it is designed to correct an "identifiable" pattern of discrimination but that companies are not required to make amends for discrimination that occurred before the 1964 Civil Rights Act. All of these are what lawyers call "limited decisions." They apply only to specific cases. The current Supreme Court has retreated from the Civil-Rights-activist position of the Warren Court (Pettigrew, 1976, pp. 472–73).

Underlying the busing and affirmative action controversies is a basic conflict in American values. On the one hand, our political system is based on the egalitarian ideal of one person, one vote. The election system, the separate judicial system, and periodic waves of reform are all aimed at ensuring political equality. On the other hand, our economic system is based on the theory that inequality is a necessary spur to progress. Our laissez-faire ideal holds that free competition among producers and free choice among workers and consumers are the best ways to allocate resources and effort. According to this view, economic inequalities provide necessary incentives for effort and rewards for enterprise. Today's racial problems reflect this "inherent conflict between the inegalitarian consequences of a liberal economy and the egalitarian ideal of a liberal political democracy" (De Lone, 1979, p. xi).

The Dimensions of Racial Inequality Today

According to the Harris poll cited at the beginning of this chapter, almost 60 percent of white Americans feel that blacks enjoy full equality in the United States today. Only a small minority of blacks (19 percent) agree. Indeed, the overwhelming majority of blacks feel that they are denied equal education, equal housing, and equal opportunity at work (see Figure 10–2). What are the facts? How do minority racial groups compare with whites?

The average white American born in 1978 can

Figure 10–2

Discrimination: Blacks' and Whites' Perspectives

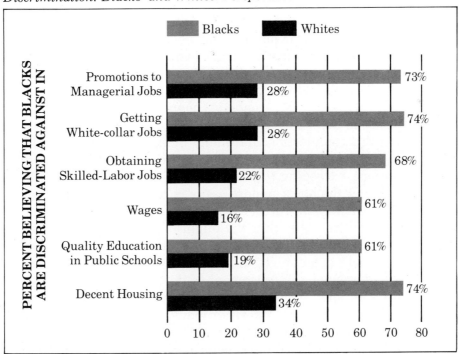

Source: Louis and Associates, *A Study of Racial Attitudes Toward Racial and Religious Minorities and Toward Women* (New York: The National Conference of Christians and Jews, November 1978), pp. iv–v.

Is the Significance of Race Declining?
Two Points of View

From William Julius Wilson, "The Declining Significance of Race"

Race relations in the United States have undergone fundamental changes in recent years, so much so that now the life chances of individual blacks have more to do with their economic class position than with their day-to-day encounters with whites. In earlier years the systematic efforts of whites to suppress blacks were obvious to even the most insensitive observer. Blacks were denied access to valued and scarce resources through various ingenious schemes of racial exploitation, discrimination, and segregation, schemes that were reinforced by elaborate ideologies of racism.

But the situation has changed. However determinative such practices were in the previous efforts of the black population to achieve racial equality, and however significant they were in the creation of poverty-stricken ghettoes and a vast underclass of black proletarians—that massive population at the bottom of the social class ladder plagued by poor education and low-paying, unstable jobs—they do not provide a meaningful explanation of the life chances of black Americans today. The traditional patterns of interaction between blacks and whites, particularly in the labor market, have been fundamentally altered. . . .

It would be shortsighted to view the traditional forms of racial segregation and discrimination as having essentially disappeared in contemporary America; the presence of blacks is still firmly resisted in various institutions and social clubs. However, in the economic sphere class has become more important than race in determining black access to privilege and power. It is clearly evident in this connnection that many talented and educated blacks are now entering positions of prestige and influence at a rate comparable to or, in some situations, exceeding that of whites with equivalent qualifications. It is equally clear that the black underclass is in a hopeless state of economic stagnation, falling further and further behind the rest of society. . . .

[I]t would be difficult to argue that the plight of the black underclass is solely a consequence of racial oppression, that is, the explicit and overt efforts of whites to keep blacks subjugated, in the same way that it would be difficult to explain the rapid economic improvement of the more privileged blacks by arguing that the traditional forms of racial segregation and discrimination still characterize the labor market in American industries. The recent mobility patterns of blacks lend strong support to the view that economic class is clearly more important than race in predetermining job placement and occupational mobility.

From Charles V. Willie, "The Inclining Significance of Race"

[A] study by the Survey Research Center of the University of Michigan that was published in the *New York Times* February 26, 1978, reported that 61 percent of all blacks in a nationwide poll believed that whites either don't care whether or not blacks "get a break" or were actively trying to keep blacks down. It would appear that neither the sentiment of blacks nor the facts of the situation are in accord with the analysis of Professor Wilson and his claim that "class has become more important than race in determining black life chances." . . .

If one assumes that there are not extraordinary biological differences between blacks and whites in the United States, then it is difficult to explain why the proportion of poor blacks with an annual income under $5,000 is two and one-half times greater than the proportion of poor whites. . . .

Among whites with only an elementary school education or less, 50 percent are likely to have jobs as service workers or laborers at the bottom of the occupational heap; but 80 percent of black workers with this limited education are likely to find work only in these kinds of jobs. . . .

I would like to introduce a counterhypothesis that the significance of race is increasing and that it is increasing especially for middle-class blacks who, because of school desegregation and affirmative action and other integration programs, are coming into direct contact with whites for the first time for extended interaction.

My case studies of black families who have moved into racially integrated neighborhoods and racially integrated work situations indicate that race for some of these pioneers is a consuming experience. They seldom can get away from it. When special opportunities are created, such as in the admissions programs, the minorities who take advantage of them must constantly prove themselves. . . . Try as hard as they may, middle-class blacks, especially middle-class blacks in racially integrated situations at this period in American history are almost obsessed with race. Many have experienced this adaptation especially in residential and work situations.

Source: William Julius Wilson, *The Declining Significance of Race* (Chicago: University of Chicago Press, 1978); Charles V. Willie, "The Inclining Significance of Race," *Society,* July–August 1978.

expect to live almost seventy-four years; the average black, Native, or Mexican American can expect to live a little more than sixty-eight years. The health risks of belonging to a minority racial group begin at birth. While 12 out of every 1,000 white babies will die in infancy, more than 22 black and more than 15 Native American babies of every 1,000 die in infancy (U.S. Commission on Civil Rights, 1978; U.S. Bureau of the Census, 1979).

The education gap between whites and the three racial groups examined in this chapter has narrowed in the last two decades. The percentages of black, Native, and Mexican Americans who have completed high school have increased. The percentages of blacks, Hispanics, and whites who go on to college are now nearly the same (whites, 24.6 percent; blacks, 24.1 percent; Hispanics, 22.6 percent). Still, members of all three minority groups have higher rates of non-attendance in high school than whites and are two to three times more likely to fall behind in school. While 34 percent of white males between the ages of twenty-five and twenty-nine had finished college in 1976, only 11 percent of black and Mexican-American males and a scant 8 percent of Native American males in that age group had done so. The statistics for females in the same age category are similar (U.S. Commission on Civil Rights, 1978).

Minority racial groups have made some economic gains in the last two decades—especially among college-educated blacks and Native Americans. The comparative economic situation for college-educated Mexican-American males actually worsened between 1960 and 1976. On average, black, Native, and Mexican-American wage earners still take home fewer dollars than do whites. In addition, there is some indication that gains made in the last two decades are fading. In 1953, the median income for black families was 56 percent of that for white families. This figure rose to 63 percent from 1964 to 1969, but fell

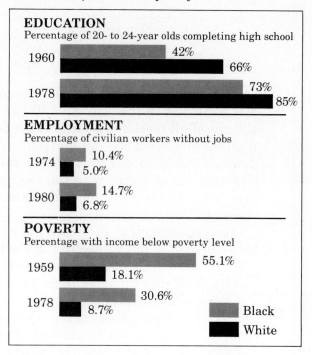

Figure 10–3
Indicators of Racial Inequality

EDUCATION
Percentage of 20- to 24-year olds completing high school

1960 — 42% / 66%
1978 — 73% / 85%

EMPLOYMENT
Percentage of civilian workers without jobs

1974 — 10.4% / 5.0%
1980 — 14.7% / 6.8%

POVERTY
Percentage with income below poverty level

1959 — 55.1% / 18.1%
1978 — 30.6% / 8.7%

Black
White

Source: Data based on figures from the U.S. Department of Commerce and the U.S. Department of Labor.

to 57 percent in 1980 (*The New York Times,* June 2, 1981, p. B11).

The most pronounced evidence of economic inequality is found in data on poverty. In 1976, while less than one white in ten lived below the government-established poverty line, the rate for black, Mexican, and Native Americans was at or above one in four (U.S. Commission on Civil Rights, 1978). Two years later, the situation for blacks worsened: 30 percent of black families or unrelated individuals were living below the poverty line (U.S. Bureau of the Census, 1980).

Black, Mexican, and Native Americans suffer from both unemployment and underemployment (not holding the same jobs as whites with comparable education). In 1960, the unemployment rate for blacks and Mexican Americans was double the rate for whites, while the rate for Native American males was three times that for white males. By 1976, the situation was no better for blacks or Mexican Americans, though Native American males had caught up with other minorities. The situation for minority teen-agers is even worse. While white males aged sixteen to nineteen had an unemployment rate of 5.9 percent in 1976, the rate for Native Americans was 35 percent, the rate for Mexican Americans was 24 percent, and the rate for black male teen-agers was almost 48 percent (U.S. Commission on Civil Rights, 1978).

While occupational advances have been made by minority workers, such as increases in the percentage of blacks holding white-collar jobs, the fact remains that many black, Mexican, and Native Americans are trapped in the "secondary market," in jobs that are not unionized, provide irregular or unstable employment, pay low wages, offer few benefits, and hold little promise of promotions, salary advances, or more desirable lives. Although some progress has been made, the gap between whites and nonwhites remains (see Figure 10–3).

Summary

1. For sociological purposes, race is defined as a large number of people who see themselves, and are seen by others, as "different" because of their ancestry and physical appearance. Racism is the belief that members of certain racial out-groups are innately inferior.

2. Although Native Americans and Europeans met on an equal footing, in time, the Native Americans were outnumbered and out-gunned by the white settlers, who appropriated their lands. Government policy toward Native Americans has vacillated between attempting to assimilate them into the larger society and attempting to preserve tribal traditions and social organizations.

3. The institution of black slavery—which defined blacks as property—developed gradually in the United States, in response to economic pressures. Although blacks were granted legal rights after the Civil War, most of them were no better off materially than they had been under slavery. Jim Crow laws that were passed at the turn of the century recreated black servitude without the formal apparatus of slavery. Informal social pressure restricted blacks in the North.

4. Mexican Americans are descendants of both early settlers whose land was annexed to the United States and more recent immigrants. Attitudes toward them have shifted as economic conditions in the Southwest have changed.

5. Racism is most likely to develop when many members of two or more culturally distinct groups, whose members look different enough to be identifiable, meet in a position of institutionalized inequality. In Western societies, racism was justified first on religious grounds, then on pseudoscientific grounds (by Social Darwinists).

6. Prejudice is a hostile attitude toward an entire category of people. It has been

traced to frustration, the authoritarian personality, situational factors, and economic competition and class conflict.

7. Discrimination, the deliberate attempt to restrict or require activities of selected groups, ranges from avoidance of primary relationships to formal policies of extinction. The relationship between prejudice and discrimination varies with the social setting.

8. Institutionalized racism results from established practices and policies that have the unintended consequence of restricting certain racial groups' opportunities. Changing people's hearts and minds—eliminating prejudice and discrimination—will not eliminate institutionalized racism.

9. The declining importance of sharecropping, the rising importance of the black vote, and the legitimacy provided by Supreme Court decisions set the stage for the Civil Rights Movement. Organized, active, nonviolent resistance to Jim Crow laws provided a model for other minority protest movements.

10. The urban riots of the late 1960s are best explained as blacks' response to rising expectations not being met by concrete improvements.

11. Efforts to implement Supreme Court decisions and civil rights legislation have provoked conflicts of interest and values, and some degree of retrenchment.

12. Despite progress, the gap between whites and nonwhites in the United States remains wide.

Suggested Reading

Brown, Dee. *Bury My Heart at Wounded Knee.* New York: Holt, Rinehart and Winston, 1970.
Fredrickson, George M. *White Supremacy.* New York: Oxford University Press, 1981.
Grebler, Leo, et al. *The Mexican-American People: The Nation's Second Largest Minority.* New York: Free Press, 1970.
Steinberg, Stephen. *The Ethnic Myth.* New York: Atheneum, 1981.
Wilson, William J. *The Declining Significance of Race,* 2d ed. Chicago: University of Chicago Press, 1980.

References

Adorno, T.W., et al. *The Authoritarian Personality.* New York: Norton, 1950.
Allport, G. *The Nature of Prejudice.* Reading, Mass.: Addison-Wesley, 1954.
Bahr, H.M., B.A. Chadwick, and J.H. Strauss. *American Ethnicity.* Lexington, Mass.: Heath, 1979.
Brown, D. *Bury My Heart at Wounded Knee.* New York: Holt, Rinehart and Winston, 1970.
Burkey, R.M. *Ethnic and Racial Groups.* Menlo Park, Cal.: Cummings, 1978.
Carmichael, S., and C. Hamilton. *Black Power.* New York: Vintage, 1967.
Coleman, J.S., S.D. Kelly, and J. Moore, "Trends in School Segregation: 1968–73." Washington, D.C.: Urban Institute Working Paper, 1975.
Davies, J.C. "The J-Curve of Rising Expectations and Declining Satisfaction as a Cause of

Some Great Revolutions and a Contained Rebellion." In H. Graham and T. Gurr (Eds.), *Violence in America.* New York: Bantam, 1969, pp. 547–76.

De Lone, R.H. *Small Futures.* New York: Harcourt Brace Jovanovich, 1979.

Dollard, J., L.W. Doob, N.E. Miller, O.H. Mowrer, and R.R. Sears. *Frustration and Aggression.* New Haven: Yale University Press, 1939.

Dreyfuss, J., and C. Lawrence III. *The Bakke Case: The Politics of Inequality.* New York: Harcourt Brace Jovanovich, 1979.

Fogelson, R.M. *Violence as Protest.* New York: Doubleday, 1971.

Fredrickson, G.M. *White Supremacy.* New York: Oxford University Press, 1981.

Grebler, L., et al. *The Mexican-American People: The Nation's Second Largest Minority.* New York: Free Press, 1970.

Harris, L., and Associates, Inc. *A Study of Attitudes Toward Racial and Religious Minorities and Toward Women.* New York: The National Conference of Christians and Jews (November 1978).

Hofstadter, R. *Social Darwinism in American Thought.* New York: Braziller, 1969.

Hurn, C. *The Limits and Possibilities of Schooling.* Boston: Allyn and Bacon, 1978.

King, M.L., Jr. *Why We Can't Wait.* New York: Mentor, 1963.

Kitano, H.H.L. *Race Relations,* 2d ed. Englewood Cliffs, N.J.: Prentice-Hall, 1980.

La Piere, R.T. "Attitudes Versus Action." *Social Forces,* Vol. 13 (1934), pp. 230–37.

Lerner, I.M. *Heredity, Evolution, and Society.* San Francisco: Freeman, 1968.

Lohman, J.D., and D.C. Reitzes. "Note on Race Relations in Mass Society." *American Journal of Sociology,* Vol. 57 (November 1952), pp. 240–46.

McLemore, S.D. *Racial and Ethnic Relations in America.* Boston: Allyn and Bacon, 1980.

Merton, R.K. "Discrimination and the American Creed." In R. MacIver (Ed.), *Discrimination and National Welfare.* New York: Harper & Row, 1949, pp. 99–126.

Myrdal, G. *An American Dilemma.* New York: Harper & Row, 1944.

Pettigrew, T.F. "Race and Intergroup Relations." In R.K. Merton and R. Nisbet (Eds.), *Contemporary Social Problems,* 4th ed. New York: Harcourt Brace Jovanovich, 1976, pp. 461–508.

Pettigrew, T.F., and R.L. Green. "School Desegregation in Large Cities: A Critique of the Coleman 'White Flight' Thesis." *Harvard Educational Review,* Vol. 46, No. 1 (February 1976), pp. 1–53.

Report of the National Advisory Commission on Civil Disorders. New York: Bantam, 1968.

Roosevelt, T. *The Winning of the West,* Vols. 1–4. New York: Putnam, 1889.

Schaefer, R.T. *Racial and Ethnic Groups.* Boston: Little, Brown, 1979.

Steinberg, S. *The Ethnic Myth.* New York: Atheneum, 1981.

U.S. Bureau of the Census. *Negro Population: 1790-1915.* Washington, D.C.: U.S. Government Printing Office, 1918.

U.S. Bureau of the Census. *Statistical Abstract of the United States, 1979.* Washington, D.C.: U.S. Government Printing Office, 1979.

U.S. Bureau of the Census, *Current Population Reports: Population Profile of the United States, 1979,* No. 350 (May 1980), p. 40.

U.S. Commission on Civil Rights, *Social Indicators of Equality for Minorities and Women.* Washington, D.C.: U.S. Government Printing Office, 1978.

van den Berghe, P.L. *Race and Racism.* New York: Wiley, 1967.

Wilson, W.J. *The Declining Significance of Race,* 2d ed. Chicago: Univ. of Chicago Press, 1980.

Woodward, C.V. *The Strange Career of Jim Crow.* New York: Oxford University Press, 1966.

Chapter Eleven

Gender Inequality

Explaining Gender Inequality

Biology Is Destiny

Learned Inequality

    Gender Socialization
    Mixed Sexual Identities
    Cross-Cultural Studies

Biology and Learning Reviewed

Prejudice

Institutionalized Sexism

Women and Inequality

Women and Families

Women and Education

Women and Work

Men: Dilemmas and Confusion

Responses to Inequality

Womanhood in America: A Brief History

The Women's Movement Today

Responses to Feminism

Johnny is a second-grader from a middle-class home. His family's income is a little above average: They have to watch their budget, but they are comfortable. Johnny enjoys school. His teachers describe him as an attentive student. Tests show that he has a slightly higher than average IQ score and reads a little above his grade level. Chris is a second-grader from an equally nice home. Like Johnny, Chris scores above average on tests, enjoys school, and is described by teachers as bright. Nevertheless, the two children can anticipate quite different futures. The chances are good that Johnny will enter college and graduate. He is slightly more likely than Chris to obtain a bachelor's degree and nearly three times as likely to earn a doctoral degree. There is a good chance that Chris will be unemployed or will work only part time for extended periods. At age forty, Johnny is thirteen times as likely as Chris to hold a job that puts him in the top income bracket. Chris probably will earn $6,000 less per year than Johnny. Most likely, both Johnny and Chris will get married and have one or two children. Estimating the odds of marital bliss is extremely risky, but it is possible to make some educated guesses (Tavris and Offir, 1977). Johnny will probably thrive on marriage. Although he might be the last to admit it, he will be healthier and happier married than he ever was single. In contrast, marriage may undermine Chris's mental and physical health, self-esteem, and actual achievements. Married or single, Chris is three to six times as likely as Johnny to suffer from severe depression at some point in life (Scarf, 1980). Still, Chris is much less likely to be the victim of a crime, to be shot at or sent to jail, or to become a drug addict or an alcoholic. Indeed, Chris probably will outlive Johnny by seven years.

Why do two children with similar socioeconomic backgrounds and roughly equal talents and skills face such different futures? Because Johnny is a boy and Chris is a girl. Such is the arithmetic of gender inequality.

In the first section of this chapter, we will look at different explanations of gender inequality. How much does biology contribute to the differences between men and women? How much does socialization contribute? Are girls and women victims of individual prejudice, or is sexism institutionalized? How unequal is the position of women in our society? In the second section, we will consider women's position in the family, in education, and in the economy. Next, we will examine the special problems that gender inequality creates for men: Being in a dominant position has disadvantages as well as advantages. We will trace the rise of feminism in the United States in the fourth section, and then, in the final section of the chapter, evaluate the responses to feminism, with an eye to future patterns.

Explaining Gender Inequality

Every known society recognizes and elaborates on sex differences (Rosaldo, 1974). Usually, boys and girls play different games. Men and women work at different jobs, wear different clothes and hair styles, and behave differently with members of the same and opposite sexes. Often, men and women are thought to have different needs, interests, perceptions, and temperaments. Often masculinity and femininity are conceived as opposites. Thus it is useful to distinguish between sex and gender. A person's *sex* is his or her biological identity and role in reproduction, as male or female. *Gender* is the set of behavior patterns, attitudes, and motivations that a culture defines as masculine or feminine. Put another way, sex refers to biological basics; gender, to social elaborations on basic sex differences.

Gender differences and gender inequality are not synonymous. The fact that men and women are different does not necessarily mean that one is inferior to the other. By themselves, gender differences are not a social problem. In Western societies, however, women have long been subordinate to men. They have not had equal economic, social, or political rights and responsibilities. Women have been, in Simone de Beauvoir's phrase, "the second sex" (1953). The question is whether gender inequality is universal, natural, or necessary. If female subordination is not natural and necessary, then this inequality is a social problem.

Biology Is Destiny

The idea that gender inequality is a direct reflection of biological sex differences has a long history. Plato, for example, argued that women were governed by their wombs, not by their brains. "The womb is an animal which longs to generate children," he wrote. "When it remains barren too long after puberty, it is distressed and sorely disturbed . . ." (in Tavris and Offir, 1977, p. 12). Applying theories from the physical sciences to human behavior (a favorite nineteenth-century pastime), the sociologist Herbert Spencer argued that women used up so much energy in reproduction that they had little left for intellectual and personal development (Rossi, 1977). According to this view, gender inequality is natural and inevitable. Women are men's biological inferiors.

In modern times, one of the most influential statements of biological determinism was made by the psychoanalyst Sigmund Freud. "Anatomy is destiny," he wrote, borrowing the phrase from Napoleon (Tavris and Offir, 1977). Unlike many of his contemporaries, Freud did not believe that female or male behavior is determined by instincts and hormones. Rather, he argued that the meanings people attach to anatomical differences shape personality. According to Freud, young girls are devastated by the discovery that boys have a penis and they do not. "When she makes a comparison with a playfellow of the other sex, she perceives she has 'come off badly' and she feels that this is a wrong done to her and a ground for inferiority" (1924, p. 178). Freud said that penis envy leaves "ineradicable traces on [girls'] development and formation of character" (1933). Women have a permanent sense of inferiority in relation to men and feelings of contempt for other women. They are driven to seek attention and praise to ease this early wound to their self-esteem (hence, female vanity and jealousy). The young girl's desires and disappointments are buried in the unconscious, but continue to influence her behavior throughout life. Ideally, according to Freud, the unconscious wish for a penis is replaced by the wish for a baby.

Freud's theory of penis envy came under sharp attack. The psychologist Karen Horney (1967) argued that women are envious of men's superior social position, not their anatomy, and that men are envious of women's role in the mysteries of childbirth, nursing, and motherhood. Freud himself amended his views many times. Nevertheless, for more than fifty years, in treating female patients, most mental health professionals saw their job as helping women to overcome "unnatural masculine strivings." This particular theory has fallen into disrepute in recent years, but the possibility that biology shapes behavior remains.

In an article entitled "A Biosocial Perspective on Parenting," the sociologist Alice Rossi (1977) put gender differences in evolutionary perspective. For 90 percent of human existence, our ancestors lived off the land as hunters and gatherers. Men hunted large game and defended the group from predators and human attacks—activities that require size, strength, good vision, and quick decisions. Women collected small game, fruits, and vegetables and cared for young children—activities that require endurance, persistence, patience, and manual dexterity. This sexual division of labor was an adaptation to the environments in which our ancestors lived. The residues of the selective pressures they experienced can be seen today, in men's larger size and, according to Rossi, in behavior patterns. Rossi cites maternal behavior as a case in point. Mother-infant interactions include a number of unlearned responses. Without thinking about it, most mothers cradle an infant in their left arm, and the infant is soothed by the mother's heartbeat. Women everywhere open their eyes wide, raise their eyebrows, exaggerate their expressions, and elongate their vowels when talking to infants—behavior that would seem bizarre in any other context and that women have difficulty repeating unless they are looking at a baby. Furthermore, an infant's crying stimulates the secretion of oxytocin in a mother's body, making her nipples erect for nursing. Rossi's point is that although a man can care for an infant (using bottles), infant care comes more naturally to a woman: Women have an "endocrinological advantage." Rossi believes that this is true for other activities as well: "A biosocial perspective does not argue that there is a genetic determination of what men can do compared to women; rather, it suggests that the biological contributions shape what is learned, and that there are differences in the ease with which the sexes can learn certain things" (p. 4). Men require compensatory training to care for young infants; women, compensatory training to do such things as serve in combat or work on construction crews. As Rossi discovered, this is not a popular view (Rossi et al., 1979). The biosocial perspective is considered to be anti-feminist.

Learned Inequality

A second explanation of gender inequality emphasizes the way in which children are raised. The infant is seen as a *tabula rasa,* or a blank slate. Nearly all significant differences between the sexes are the product of socialization. Children must be taught to think and behave like boys or girls. Thus, society, not biology, creates gender differences in personality and in behavior.

Socialization is the process whereby individuals learn the behavior, attitudes, and motivations that are culturally associated with their social identities of sex, class, ethnic group, and so on. Through socialization, people acquire an inner sense of right and wrong and an awareness of the external controls on behavior (laughter, criticism, ostracism, legal penalties, and so on). They learn cultural ideals (for example, a mother must always be patient with her child) and also the range of non-ideal behavior that people accept in practice. When socialization works, people regard the social limits on their behavior as right or at least as unavoidable. In most cases, cultural indoctrination is so thorough that people take the norms for granted, as though they were part of the natural order. Most sociologists put gender roles in this taken-for-granted category.

Gender socialization Gender socialization begins at birth, when a newborn baby girl is wrapped in a pink blanket and a newborn baby boy in a blue one. From the start, parents perceive males and females as different (Rubin, Provenzano, and Lurig, 1974). They describe boys as hefty and active, girls as delicate and sweet. Indeed, the first thing most adults ask about a baby is its sex: They do not know how to relate to an "it." In one study, mothers were observed playing with a six-month-old child (Will, Self, and Datan, 1974). Some were told the child was a girl; others were told the child was a boy. Mothers who thought that the child was a girl gave "her" a doll and said she was a "real girl," much sweeter than a boy would be. (The child was a boy.)

As a child grows, explicit gender training reinforces early, subtle messages. To simplify a bit, boys are given trucks and asked what they want to be when they grow up; girls are given dolls and asked whom they want to marry. Gender socialization includes training both sexes for incompetence. Boys are encouraged to be disinterested in child care and cooking; girls, to be inept at science and mathematics. Even when parents consciously try to raise children as equals, they may unconsciously pass on the sex-typed lessons they learned as children. For example, a mother may allow a little girl to cling to her skirt but "instinctively" (that is, because of her own training) tell a little boy not to be a "sissy."

How effective is gender socialization? Reviewing the literature, Eleanor Maccoby and Carol Jacklin (1974) found surprisingly few differences in parental treatment of children according to sex or in children's behavior (see Weitzman, 1979). There were some differences, however. Although roughly equal when they start school, during adolescence, girls tend to slip behind boys in mathematical ability, a difference that carries over into adulthood. At about age ten, girls begin to edge ahead of boys in verbal ability, an advantage they maintain at least through high school (Maccoby and Jacklin, 1974). Study after study shows that males are clearly more aggressive than females (Jacklin, 1977). This difference appears in early childhood and continues into adulthood. Boys play rough: They push, shove, hit, and yell much more often than girls do. Boys are somewhat more inclined than girls to resist or challenge their parents. Male adolescents and adults commit nearly all violent crimes. Males also are more likely than females to be victims of violence in childhood and in adulthood (Maccoby, 1980). There is also some evidence that females are more nurturant (more responsive to the needs) of babies and small children than males are (Maccoby, 1980).

Whether these differences are an expression of biological distinctions or gender socialization is

The dramatically different self-presentations of these men and women—the ways they dress and stand—illustrate the power of gender socialization. She may be drawing attention to her curves, but he dominates the conversation.

difficult to say. The data should not be taken too literally, for several reasons (Maccoby, 1980). First, in most studies, it is impossible to conceal the sex of the subjects. Hence, the results may be biased by what observers expect. Second, establishing that a sex difference exists may tell little about the origins of that difference. Researchers often run into the chicken-and-the-egg problem. For example, studies show that parents discipline boys more often and more harshly than they do girls and that boys are more rebellious than girls. But which comes first? Fathers are rougher with boys than with girls. Is this because boys enjoy rough handling (they are innately aggressive), or because fathers teach them to enjoy it (socialization), or is it for both reasons? Finally, these differences are only averages. Many individual girls are rebellious; many individual boys are good with their hands or with words. There is a great deal of variation within each sex and considerable overlap between the sexes. Indeed, the similarities between boys and girls and between men and women outnumber the differences.

Mixed sexual identities Studies of children whose sexual development has gone awry suggest that biology and socialization interact in complex ways. Because of genetic abnormalities or hormonal imbalances during the prenatal period, some infants' external genitals are ambiguous. In most such cases, doctors recommend raising the child as a girl, primarily because constructing a vagina surgically is easier than constructing a penis. John Money and Anke Ehrhardt (1972) have studied a number of such children and have found that they accept the label given to them, regardless of their genetic identity. In one case of normal seven-month-old twin boys, one twin's penis was accidentally burned off during circumcision. After much agonizing, the parents decided to follow the doctor's advice to approve a sex-change operation and thereafter raise that twin as a girl. When observed at age four, the girl was fussy about her appearance, but her brother didn't care at all about his. She enjoyed cooking and other feminine activities, which he ignored. Although tomboyish, she clearly thought of herself as a girl and expected to grow up as a woman. In this case, socialization as a girl canceled out most of the effects of male genes and male hormones combined.

Money and Ehrhardt's studies offer dramatic evidence that socialization *may* override biology. But the results should be viewed with caution. Only a small number of cases have been studied. In every case, the sex change was made at an early age. Thus, gender identification may be similar to imprinting in animals: The child's sexual identity can be established or changed only during a brief period in childhood. The parents of these children may have bent over backwards to teach them to be feminine. All of them have been or will be given female hormones during adolescence, so researchers will not have a chance to learn if socialization alone can maintain gender identity. Moreover, Money's own research indicates that biology has an impact on behavior: A number of genetically and anatomically normal girls who were accidentally exposed to overdoses of the male hormone androgen during prenatal development developed tomboyish builds and interests (Money and Ehrhardt, 1972).

Cross-cultural studies A second line of research on the importance of socialization in creating and maintaining gender differences are cross-cultural studies. As the anthropologist Margaret Mead (1935) pointed out, the characteristics that Westerners think of as masculine and feminine are by no means universal. There are many cross-cultural variations in the roles assigned to men and women. For example, the Toda of India consider housework a sacred task, which only men can handle. The Manus of New Guinea believe that men enjoy playing with babies much more than women do. In Iran, women are thought to be the cold and logical sex, and men emotionally unstable. In the Soviet Union, people expect a physician to be female. In some societies, women do the gardening or the weaving; in other societies, men monopolize these activities. In some societies, men wear skirts and women wear trousers.

In many cultures, it is considered insulting for a man to touch a woman in public, but normal and natural for men to demonstrate affection to each other. In 1981, however, the International Federation of Soccer urged national associations to discourage "the unmanly behavior of some football players who embrace, kiss and hug each other in an over-emotional fashion after scoring a goal."

Gender roles are highly variable, suggesting that many gender differences are socially created.

There are limits to variation, however (Rosaldo, 1974). Every known society recognizes differences in men's and women's manners and responsibilities. The division of labor by sex is found in almost all societies. Moreover, in every known society, a higher cultural value is placed on men's roles and activities than on women's. In parts of New Guinea, for example, women grow sweet potatoes and men grow yams, virtually identical vegetables; but yams are the prestigious food that is distributed at feasts. In Nigeria, Yuroba women dominate the markets and hence control the supply of food and cash, but feign obedience to their husbands and kneel to serve them. The female-dominated medical profession does not enjoy the prestige in the Soviet Union that the male-dominated medical profession has in the United States. In short, gender inequality appears to be universal, although the degree of female subordination varies.

Biology and Learning Reviewed

The fact that gender inequality is universal does not necessarily mean that it is inevitable, however. Throughout most of human existence, social survival depended on three major activities: reproduction, subsistence (acquisition or production of food), and defense (Sanday, 1974). Because women expended disproportionate amounts of energy on pregnancy and infant care, responsibility for subsistence and defense fell to men. This put men in a position to control strategic resources. Put another way, infant care confined women to the domestic sphere and freed men to pursue the broader associations that we call "society" (Rosaldo, 1974). Specialization enhanced survival. The division of labor by sex was an adaptation to environmental necessities.

In modern societies, many of the conditions under which this adaptation evolved no longer exist. Few jobs depend on brute strength today. In a service or post-industrial economy, most people work in offices, dealing with other people and with information. Even war is automated. At the same time, modern birth control devices have enabled women to limit and space the number of children they have (if any) with more accuracy than in the past. The possibility of becoming pregnant at any time need no longer dominate women's lives. Moreover, baby bottles and formulas allow someone other than a mother to care for small infants. Thus, the biological and environmental constraints on males and females have been weakened.

Prejudice

Gender inequality is in part the result of prejudice toward and discrimination against women. Notions of female inferiority are part of the cultural store of knowledge passed on through socialization. To some extent, masculinity is defined in opposition to femininity. When a boy is told not to act like a "sissy," for example, he is being told that part of being a boy is not acting like a "silly girl." In the extreme, this attitude takes the form of misogyny, or hatred of women. Some personality types may be predisposed toward viewing women as inferior. The glorification of male strength and power is part of the profile of the authoritarian personality, described in Chapter 10. But the social setting determines whether individual or group prejudice is translated into discriminatory behavior. Thus, in the locker room and in the board room, a man may be rewarded for bragging about sexual exploitation of women or joking about "women's libbers." In the kitchen or in the nursery, the same man may behave quite differently. With racial and ethnic prejudice, a line is drawn at intimate relationships. Few people cross this social barrier. With prejudice against women, intimacy and social distance coexist: Men who consider women inferior nevertheless marry and live with them. Fair-weather liberalism (treating women as equal in settings that reward

this) and timid bigotry (bowing to social pressure to treat women as equal, despite contrary views) may be the norm. But prejudice alone does not explain gender inequality.

Institutionalized Sexism

Attitudes about women have changed dramatically in the United States in recent years. In the early 1960s, 66 percent of women interviewed for one poll said that they thought the man in the house should make major family decisions. Questioned again in 1980, only 28 percent still felt that way. The percentage of women who support efforts to improve the position of women in our society has risen from 40 percent in 1970 to 64 percent in 1980. Three out of four Americans say they would be willing to vote for a woman candidate for President. Most husbands approve of their wives' having careers (*The New York Times*, January 11, 1980). But although attitudes have changed, the objective facts of most women's lives have not. Gender inequality persists. Why? Because of institutionalized sexism.

The term *institutionalized sexism* refers to established policies and practices that have the unintended consequence of restricting women's opportunities. Discrimination is the byproduct of customs that, on the surface, seem to have nothing whatever to do with sex or gender. No effort has to be made to keep women in their "place." Gender inequality will persist simply because people go about their lives as usual. For example, the custom of setting business hours from nine to five is not a plot against women. Yet, it prevents women who want to care for small children from holding full-time jobs and advancing in a career. The vesting system in pension plans, which requires an employee to work for the same company for a number of consecutive years in order to earn benefits, is not a plot against women. Yet it means that women who decide to have children lose equity. An examination of women's position in families, education, and the economy illustrates institutionalized sexism.

Women and Inequality

Gender inequality is rooted in the family and is reinforced by education and the economy. The three institutions are interrelated. Structured obstacles in one area handicap women in other areas. For example, the role of women in the family reduces their ability to function as equals to men in the workplace; inequality in the workplace, in turn, affects their role in the family.

Women and Families

Studies of the family reveal a persistent gap between egalitarian ideals and everyday realities. Both husbands and wives like to think of marriage and parenthood as equal partnerships. In practice, however, women do not have equal legal rights, financial resources, or power in the family. The cards are stacked against them. "[W]omen are *structurally* deprived of equal opportunities to develop their capacities, resources, and competence in competition with males" (Gillespie, 1971, p. 448).

Women's position in modern, Western societies is in part the result of changes in the structure of work and the family (Degler, 1980). In pre-industrial, colonial America, work life and family life were one and the same. Most people lived on family farms or worked in businesses that were family owned and operated. Women were part of the family work force. Industrialization removed work from the home, creating separate domestic and public spheres of activity. Women dominated the domestic sphere; men, the public sphere. As the importance of the public sphere grew, women's power and influence declined. In the mid-twentieth century, suburbanization added geographic separation to the social distance between the public and domestic spheres. More subtly, industrialization and modernization encouraged the growth of individualism, the pursuit of individual success. But the family still requires that, to some extent, a woman subordinate her individual interests to those of her husband and children. Thus, industrialization and modernization freed men—but not women—from family constraints.

As a result of these far-reaching social changes, "his and her" marriages are quite different. The traditional marriage contract included a number of hidden clauses that put women at a disadvantage. In large part, the law legitimized gender inequality (Gillespie, 1971, pp. 449–50). For example, until recently a husband had the legal right to force his wife to have sexual intercourse with him. (Today, six states allow a woman to bring charges against her husband for rape.) A husband was legally entitled to his wife's homemaking services. Legally she could not be paid for housework or child rearing. A wife was required by law to live in the home her husband established and to perform domestic chores (cooking, cleaning, child care). If he moved, she was required to move with him. In return, the husband was obligated to support her. But she had no legal right to a portion of his income and no legal voice in how he spent it. In recent years, all of these laws have been challenged in court; and, in many cases, they have been struck down. In some ways, however, behavior resembles these old laws more closely than it does the new rulings.

The Women's Movement has focused on getting women out of the house, into the paid work force, and, ideally, on the route to successful careers. A majority of married women do work outside the home today, as noted above. But for most working wives, a paying job does not mean liberation. Instead of holding one job (as homemaker), women now hold two. Working wives spend roughly thirty hours a week cleaning house, preparing and cleaning up after meals, doing laundry, shop-

Why Women Are Paid Less Than Men: A Public Debate

An Editorial by Economist Lester C. Thurow

In the 40 years from 1939 to 1979 white women who work full time have with monotonous regularity made slightly less than 60 percent as much as white men. Why?

Over the same time period, minorities have made substantial progress in catching up with whites, with minority women making even more progress than minority men.

Black men now earn 72 percent as much as white men (up 16 percentage points since the mid-1950's) but black women earn 92 percent as much as white women. Hispanic men make 71 percent of what their white counterparts do, but Hispanic women make 82 percent as much as white women. As a result of their faster progress, fully employed black women make 75 percent as much as fully employed black men while Hispanic women earn 68 percent as much as Hispanic men. . . .

"Discrimination against women" is an easy answer but it also has its problems as an adequate explanation. Why is discrimination against women not declining under the same social forces that are leading to a lessening of discrimination against minorities? In recent years women have made more use of the enforcement provisions of the Equal Employment Opportunities Commission and the courts than minorities. Why do the laws that prohibit discrimination against women and minorities work for minorities but not for women? . . .

While discrimination undoubtedly explains part of the male-female earnings differential, one has to believe that men are monumentally stupid or irrational to explain all of the earnings gap in terms of discrimination. There must be something else going on.

Part of the answer is visible if you look at the lifetime earnings profile of men. . . .

The decade between [age] 25 and 35 is when men either succeed or fail. It is the decade when lawyers become partners in the good firms, when business managers make it onto the "fast track," when academics get tenure at good universities, and when blue collar workers find the job opportunities that will lead to training opportunities and the skills that will generate high earnings.

If there is any one decade when it pays to work hard and to be consistently in the labor force it is the decade between 25 and 35. For those who succeed, earnings will rise rapidly. For those who fail, earnings will remain flat for the rest of their lives.

But the decade between 25 and 35 is precisely the decade when women are most apt to leave the labor force or become part-time workers to have children. When they do, the current system of promotion and skill acquisition will extract an enormous lifetime price.

This leaves essentially two avenues for equalizing male and female earnings.

Families where women who wish to have successful careers, compete with men, and achieve the same earnings should alter their family plans and have their children either before 25 or after 35. Or society can attempt to alter the existing promotion and skill acquisition system so that there is a longer time period in which both men and women can attempt to successfully enter the labor force.

Without some combination of these two factors, a substantial fraction of the male-female earnings differentials are apt to persist for the next 40 years, even if discrimination against women is eliminated.

Letters to the Editor in Response

To the Business Editor:

The reason women are paid less than men is because they continue to pursue careers in women-glutted fields.

Show me a woman garbage collector, and I'll show you a woman who makes $20,000 a year. Show me a woman web press operator and you can up the ante $5,000. Show me women electricians, roofers, tree-trimmers, mechanics and carpenters and I'll show you some well paid women!

MEREDITH A. TARNEY
Feminist and Writer
Whitefish Bay, Wis., March 9, 1981

To the Business Editor:

Professor Thurow misses the mark. People act to maximize their well-being; they do not necessarily act to maximize their money income. As people will forgo income for the sake of leisure, people will also forgo some income for the sake of maintaining esteem. Some men would suffer loss of self-esteem if their wive's earnings exceeded their own earnings. Hence, to them, earnings discrimination against women is rational.

DONALD L. CHAMPAGNE
Schenectady, N.Y., March 8, 1981

Source: Lester C. Thurow, "Why Women Are Paid Less Than Men," *The New York Times,* March 8, 1981; "Letters: Readers Dispute Why Women Earn Less," *The New York Times,* March 15, 1981.

ping, and caring for children (Vanek, 1974). This plus the hours that working wives spend on the job brings their total workweek to about seventy hours. One might think that when wives go to work their husbands would do more around the house. They do not. In the United States, the average husband devotes only a few hours a week to domestic chores (mostly shopping) (Pleck, 1977). As a result, husbands have an extra ten to fifteen hours free time each week (more than a day off) compared with wives. Typically, husbands spend their weekends resting and relaxing; wives spend them catching up.

Why don't husbands do more around the house? One survey (Robinson and Robinson, 1975) suggests their wives don't want them to. Only 19 percent of the women polled said they wanted more help from their husbands. Being a good homemaker is part of the traditional definition of femininity. Single women spend almost as much time doing domestic chores as do young, childless wives, and an hour or two more than single men (Tavris and Offir, 1977, p. 232). As a rule, wives do not work at as high-prestige jobs or earn as much as their husbands do. Apparently, many women are reluctant to give up their one area of exclusive expertise. When a husband does work around the house, his activity is defined as helping her out. She may thank him for washing the dishes, as if he were doing her a favor. Final responsibility for housekeeping is hers.

Final responsibility for young children also is the wife's. Again, the father often helps out. He watches the baby while the mother is shopping; takes the children to the park on Saturday; teaches them to throw baseballs and ride bicycles. The mother is responsible for seeing that the children eat regular meals, wear socks and mittens, do their homework, are polite to elders, and a thousand other details—responsibilities that require constant attention. If a child is sick, it is nearly always the mother who stays home from work. If the child is in a play at school, again it is usually the mother who attends. If a wife has no children and her career prevents her from cooking a three-course meal every night, people may excuse her. Failure to fill the role of mother is another matter. People do not excuse a mother for forgetting to provide dinner for her child. When a child is neglected, the mother is more likely to be blamed than the father. Being a working wife creates role overload. Being a working mother (especially one with young children) creates role conflict. In filling one role, a woman almost inevitably violates the other. In one mother's words, "You're either at work feeling like you should be home with your sick child or you're at home feeling like you should be at work" (in Ryan, 1979, p. 232).

Working mothers face two structural obstacles. The first is the small number of day-care centers. The United States is the only industrialized nation that does not have a national child-care program. There are only 1.6 million places in licensed day-care facilities for an estimated 7 million children under six years of age whose mothers work. The other 5.4 million youngsters are left with relatives or baby sitters or are left alone. (When Congress passed a $15 billion child-care program, President Nixon vetoed it on the grounds that government interference would threaten family life.) The second obstacle is inflexible work schedules. Most jobs require people to work nine to five (not including time spent commuting), five days a week. As a result, working mothers can meet the nonroutine responsibilities of child rearing only by taking time off. In other industrial nations, many parents are allowed to schedule work in ways that enable them to spend more time with children. In West Germany, for example, half of all white-collar workers have "flextime"; in the United States, only 6 percent have flexible hours (*Newsweek*, May 19, 1980).

What do husbands have to say about this? Apparently, a good deal. Studies of marital power focus on who decides what job the husband should take, where the family should go on vacation, which doctor should be called when someone is sick, and so on (Blood and Wolfe, 1960). Constantina Safilios-Rothschild (1970) distinguishes between two kinds of family power. *Orchestration power* refers to making important and infrequent decisions that determine family life style. The spouse with orchestration power sets family policy. He or she has final say about such things as choice of residence, but is not consumed by minor, everyday problems. *Implementation power* refers to frequent but less important decisions, such as what to serve for dinner or whether to let the children stay up late for a TV special. The spouse with implementation power makes countless everyday decisions within agreed-upon guidelines. The difference between orchestration and implementation power is the difference between deciding what kind of car to buy and what color the car should be. As a rule, husbands have the former power, wives the latter. Wives who work do seem to have more power than wives who do not. They are more likely to make decisions about financial matters and large expenditures than are wives who do not have their own income. They also seem to have more control over decisions about whether to have children (Bahr, 1974a, 1974b). Still, most families rest on a delicate *imbalance* of power.

Husbands' attitudes toward women's working vary by social class. Working-class husbands tend to have stronger objections to their wives' working than middle-class husbands do, but less power to stop them. One wife reported:

> My husband says I don't have to work, but if I don't we'll never get anywhere. I guess it's a matter of pride with him. It makes him feel bad, like he's not supporting us good enough. I understand how he feels but I also know that, no matter what he says, if I stop working, when the taxes on the house have to be paid there won't be any money if we didn't have my salary. (in Rubin, 1976, pp. 173–74)

Middle-class husbands support their wives' careers—up to a point. In the words of one male college student:

> I believe that it is a good thing for mothers to return to full-time work when the children are grown, provided the work is important and worthwhile. Otherwise, housewives get hung up with tranquilizers because they have no outlet for their abilities. A woman should want her husband's success more than he should want hers. Her work should not interfere with or hurt his in any way. (in Komarovsky, 1973, p. 881)

William Goode summed up the difference between the two: "Lower class men concede fewer rights *ideologically* than their women in fact *obtain,* and the more educated men are more likely to concede *more* rights ideologically than they in fact grant" (1963, p. 21). Whether a husband demands deference because he is a man and head of the family or because of his profession ("I've had a hard day at the office"), the effect on the distribution of power in the family is much the same.

Women and Education

More women than ever before are completing high school and earning college degrees today. In 1978, 47 percent of all bachelor's degrees and 48 percent of all master's degrees were awarded to women. If one looks at the kinds of degrees women earn, however, the picture changes. Men still dominate professional fields and physical sciences, the areas most likely to lead to well-paid employment. In 1978, men received 95 percent of the B.A.'s in engineering; almost 80 percent of the degrees in architectural, agricultural, computer, information, and physical sciences; and over 70 percent of the law degrees. In contrast, women dominated home economics, library science, health professions, foreign languages, fine and applied arts, and education—almost all of which are declining fields (Brown, 1979). In 1978, only 28 percent of Ph.D.'s were awarded to women. Girls get off to a good start in school. They do at least as well as boys in the early grades. Indeed, boys outnumber girls four to one in remedial reading classes (Maccoby, 1980, p. 210). By college, however, girls are falling behind. What happens during the years in between?

Studies of children in elementary school reveal a hidden curriculum. Even when teachers make a conscious attempt to treat boys and girls alike, nonconscious sexist ideology slips through. For example, two children are hammering nails at a workbench. The teacher walks over and says to the boy, "That's right, give it another whack." The teacher turns to the girl and says, "Here, let me help you" (Frazier and Sadker, 1973, p. 185). There are at least two messages here: Boys are self-reliant and girls need help; boys are expected to achieve and girls are praised just for trying. Another example comes from a sixth-grade class. Susie is picking on Scott, trying to kick him in the groin. When the angry boy turns and slaps her, the teacher calls out, "Scott, don't you know we *never* hit girls?" (Tavris and Offir, 1977, p. 162). Note that the teacher does not tell Scott that hitting is wrong; hitting a female is wrong. The hidden message is that girls are, by definition, weak and defenseless. How does this affect school performance? There is some evidence that with every year of school, girls become less willing to take intellectual risks and have a lower opinion of girls (Freeman, 1971).

Studies of children's books have revealed high levels of sex stereotyping (U'Ren, 1971; Weitzman, 1972; Women on Words and Images, 1972). Men and boys outnumbered women and girls eleven to one in prize-winning picture books. Boys were portrayed as fearless adventurers. They climbed mountains, battled monsters, and rescued helpless animals and girls. In contrast, girls were usually shown indoors, serving men or daydreaming. Women appeared as the wives of rulers, judges, and explorers—never as rulers, judges, or explorers themselves. Elementary-school readers listed 147 occupations for boys (including cowboy and astronaut), but only 26 for women (including witch and fat lady in the circus). In a number of children's books, women were ridiculed for being stupid and fearful. The overall message was clear: Not only are men more competent than women, they also have much more fun. Furthermore, the adult media reinforce gender stereotypes. In recent years, publishers have made an effort to reduce sex stereotyping. Interestingly, while some new books show women in what used to be considered male roles (as scientists, athletes, and the like), few books show the reverse (men as nurses, secretaries, and so on).

The hidden lessons of elementary school are repeated and reinforced in later grades. Many school systems assign high-school students to different tracks, or even different schools, according to their ability and career plans. One of the unintended consequences of tracking is sex segregation. Many more girls than boys choose to study typing; many more boys than girls study auto mechanics. There is some evidence that school counselors recommend that girls who choose nonconventional career goals be sent for psychological counseling (Thomas and Stewart, 1971). The sexes are segregated for sports, and boys' athletics receive considerably more money (and hoopla) than do girls'. Whereas most elementary-school teachers are female, most high-school teachers are male. Thus, just when girls are beginning to make decisions about their future, they have fewer role models than before.

Studies conducted in the early 1970s indicate that although women got better grades than men in high school, they were less likely to think they were capable of college work. Over 75 percent of the students who qualified for college but did not attend were female. Up through the 1960s, women were not admitted to some professional schools (for example, Harvard's business school

Table 11–1
Degrees in Dentistry, Medicine, and Law, by Sex

	Dentistry (D.D.S. or D.M.D.)			Medicine (M.D.)			Law (LL.B. or J.D.)		
	Number		Percentage	Number		Percentage	Number		Percentage
Year	Men	Women	to Women	Men	Women	to Women	Men	Women	to Women
1949–50	2,561	18	.6%	5,028	584	10%	*	*	*
1959–60	3,221	26	.8	6,645	387	5	9,010	288	3%
1968–69	3,376	32	.9	7,415	610	7	16,373	680	3
1977–78	4,623	566	11.0	11,210	3,069	21	25,457	8,945	26

* Data prior to 1954–55 are not shown because they lack comparability with the figures for subsequent years.
Source: National Center for Education Statistics, *Digest of Education Statistics 1980* (Washington, D.C.: U.S. Government Printing Office, 1980).

was all male until 1963) and were limited by quotas in others. With sex discrimination outlawed, the number of women in business, law, and medical schools has increased dramatically. Still, women have by no means caught up with men (see Table 11–1). Unequal education is one of the reasons why women do not earn as much or advance as far in their careers as men do—but it is only one reason.

Women and Work

Between 1900 and 1940, the percentage of married women in the work force more than doubled; between 1940 and 1970, it almost tripled (Stockard and Johnson, 1980). When we consider women and work, the extent of gender inequality becomes especially clear, for real dollars can be used to measure the gap between men and women.

In principle, women in the United States today can do anything they want to do. Sexual discrimination in employment is against the law. In practice, however, women are concentrated in a small number of low-paying, low-prestige, dead-end jobs. Although in recent years, women have established the right to equal pay for equal work and have entered previously all-male occupations (like that of firefighter), their position in the job market has changed very little (see Figure 11–1).

In 1979, women earned an average of fifty-nine cents for every dollar men earned—down from sixty-four cents in 1955 (statistics from U.S. Department of Labor, 1979, unless otherwise noted). While 48 percent of male workers earned $15,000 or more in 1979, 32 percent of women earned less than $7,000. Americans like to think that education is the key to success. This does not appear to be the case for women. Earning a bachelor's degree increases a man's annual income by an average of $2,500 but a woman's by less than $200. In 1977, women with four years of college earned less than men who had completed school only through the eighth grade. The income gap narrows a bit in skilled occupations but does not disappear. The median salary of women scientists, for example, was $4,100 less than that of men in the same fields in 1977.

Figure 11-1

The Earnings Gap: Median Income of Year-Round, Full-Time Workers, Fourteen Years of Age and Over

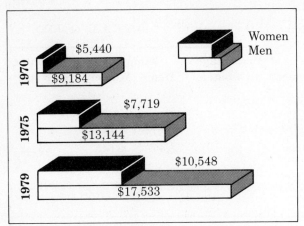

Source: U.S. Bureau of the Census, *Statistical Abstract of the United States, 1980* (Washington, D.C.: U.S. Government Printing Office, 1980), p. 463.

Unequal pay reflects continuing sex segregation. Women may be paid the same wage as men for the same job, but they rarely hold the same job. Although less rigid than in the past, the distinction between so-called men's jobs and women's jobs persists. Physicians, lawyers, judges, engineers, college educators, and architects tend to be men; elementary-school teachers, nurses, librarians, dieticians, and health technologists are usually women. The female boss is still an exception: 80 percent of all managers and administrators and 98 percent of top executives are men. Most of the women who entered the job market in recent years became office workers. Clerical work has become what domestic service was at the turn of the century: "a virtual ghetto of women workers" (Ryan, 1979, p. 228). Over 12 million working women in this country (one out of three) hold low-paying office jobs. In 1976, 98.5 percent of secretary-typists, 91 percent of bank tellers, 90 percent of bookkeepers, 88 percent of cashiers, and 74 percent of office-machine operators were women (U.S. Department of Labor, 1977, Table 8). These women were ill-paid, but not uneducated. Over 45 percent of female high-school graduates become secretaries, and one out of six female college graduates also becomes a secretary (Ryan, 1979, p. 228). Whatever field women go into, they usually occupy the low-level positions. In retail sales, for example, men sell most of the high-priced, commissioned items, while women sell low-priced goods over the counter.

The unemployment rate for women in the United States has been consistently higher than that for men. In 1978, 6 percent of women aged twenty and over could not find work, compared to 4.2 percent of men. In some fields, the difference is greater. For example, the unemployment rate for female sales workers is twice that for male sales workers. And actual female unemployment is probably higher than statistics indicate. Women are more likely than men to stop looking for work and thus may not appear in official statistics on unemployment.

Women in the United States are over-represented among the poor. Between 1966 and 1976, the number of female-headed families grew ten times as fast as the number of two-parent families, and almost half of all female-headed families live below the poverty line (Stockard and Johnson, 1980, pp. 33–34).

The rationalization of unequal work and pay for women rests on two assumptions. First, a woman is a "bad investment" for employers and colleagues because she is certain to quit her job when she gets married or when she has a baby. Second, women do not need to earn as much as men because most women are supported by a man (their father or husband). Women work for extra or supplemental income. What are the facts? Most women do become wives and mothers. Although women today wait a bit longer to get married, only 6 percent are single in their thirties, and

Sexual Harassment

Sexual harassment is best described as unsolicited nonreciprocal male behavior that asserts a woman's sex role over her function as worker. It can be any or all of the following: staring at, commenting upon, or touching a woman's body; requests for acquiescence in sexual behavior; repeated nonreciprocated propositions for dates; demands for sexual intercourse; and rape. These forms of male behavior frequently rely on superior male status in the culture, sheer numbers, or the threat of higher rank at work to exact compliance or levy penalties for refusal. The variety of penalties include verbal denigration of a woman sexually; noncooperation from male co-workers; negative job evaluations or poor personnel recommendations; refusal of overtime; demotions; injurious transfers and reassignments of shifts, hours, or locations of work, loss of job training; impossible performance standards and outright termination of employment. . . .

In May 1975 the Women's Section of the Human Affairs Program at Cornell University distributed the first questionnaire ever devoted solely to the topic of sexual harassment. . . .

There were 155 responses in all, and although they did not constitute a random sample of the population, the results were startling:

- 92 percent listed sexual harassment as a serious problem
- 70 percent personally experienced some form of harassment
- 56 percent of these reported physical harassment

It occurred among all job categories, ages, marital statuses, and pay ranges. . . .

Economic need, the structure of the workplace, and female sex-role conditioning are critical factors in the way women respond to sexual harassment. Because assertions of male dominance are socially sanctioned, because men normally hold higher rank at work, because work is a source of income, and because society trains women to be "nice," few women object to male invasiveness unless it is profoundly disturbing. However, when there are overt threats to job security coupled with requests for kissing, petting, fellatio, and intercourse, working women are faced with a somewhat insoluble dilemma. They want work but they also want, and deserve, freedom of choice in sexual intimacy.

Source: Lin Farley, *Sexual Shakedown: The Sexual Harassment of Women on the Job* (New York: McGraw-Hill, 1978).

Sexism in the Mass Media

. . . Since 1954, there has been relatively little change in the presentation of women according to the available statistical indicators. Then as now, only about 45 percent of the people presented on television have been women; about 20 percent of those shown as members of the labor force have been women. Men are shown as aggressors, women as victims. Symbolically subservient, policewomen who have been knocked to the floor by a bad buy are pulled from the floor by a good guy; in both cases, women are on the floor in relationship to men. Twenty-five years ago, as today, women on television were concentrated in the ghetto of situation comedy. They are and were, as the U.S. Commission on Civil Rights put it, "window dressing on the set."

That similarity between past and present is found elsewhere in the media. In the 1950s as now, the lives of women in women's magazine fiction have been defined in terms of men—husbands, lovers, or the chasm of male absence. Ads continue to portray women in the home and men outside it, although there are no systematic statistical comparisons of ads from twenty-five years ago with those of today. Voiceovers continue to be dominated by men; fewer than 10 percent use women's voices to announce station breaks, upcoming programs, and where to buy a product. . . .

. . . [T]he very underrepresentation of women, including their stereotypic portrayal, may symbolically capture the position of women in American society—their real lack of power, It bespeaks their "symbolic annihilation" by the media. . . . Just as representation in the media signifies social existence, so too underrepresentation and (by extension) trivialization and condemnation indicate symbolic annihilation.

Source: Gaye Tuchman, "Women's Depiction by the Mass Media," *Signs: Journal of Women in Culture and Society,* Vol. 4, No. 31 (1979), pp. 528–42.

only 5 percent plan to remain childless (Ryan, 1979, p. 230). A majority of married women (51 percent), however, work outside the home, including 43 percent of mothers with children under six years of age (a total of 5.5 million mothers with 7 million children) (see Figure 11–2). In most cases, women's incomes are vital to their families. Estimates are that only about 45 percent of jobs available today will comfortably support a family of four. Women's incomes (usually a third of total family income) protect families from poverty or from a severely lowered standard of living (Ryan, 1979, p. 231). Why, then, are women unequal in the workplace?

Figure 11–2
Percent of Married Women Who Work

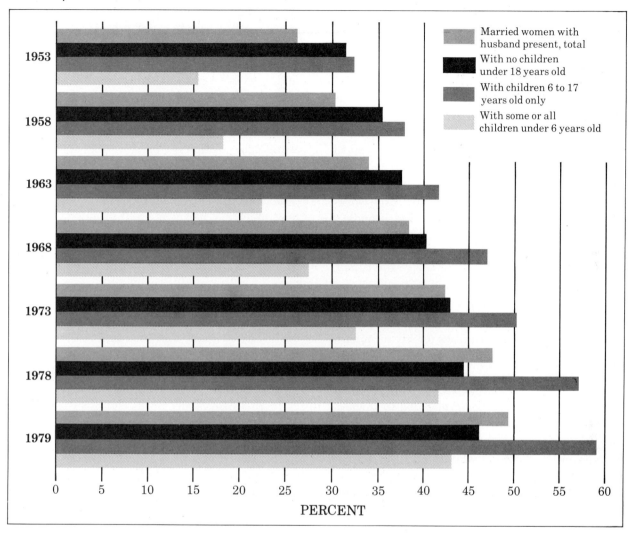

Source: U.S. Bureau of the Census, *Social Indicators III* (Washington, D.C.: U.S. Government Printing Office, December 1980), p. 329.

A number of explanations of gender inequality in the workplace have been proposed (Blau and Jusenius, 1976; Stockard and Johnson, 1980, pp. 35–45). The *overcrowding* hypothesis suggests that women are packed into certain areas of the workplace and that overcrowding lowers wages.

This hypothesis is based on the law of supply and demand. Simply put, if the supply of workers in a given field exceeds the demand, employers pay less. Women are, indeed, crowded into some occupations. But this hypothesis does not explain why men tend to have high wages and lower unemployment rates in traditionally female occupations, such as social work and teaching.

The *human capital* hypothesis suggests that women earn less than men because they have fewer resources to sell on the labor market. Because women have fewer years of education, less work experience, and higher turnover rates, they are worth less to employers. This hypothesis does not explain why women with advanced education and continuous work histories—women with a good deal of capital—do not do as well as men in the workplace.

The *dual labor market* hypothesis offers a third explanation. According to this view, the workplace is divided into a primary and a secondary market (see Chapter 7). The primary market is characterized by high wages, opportunities for advancement, good working conditions, and job security. There are a small number of entry-level jobs in the primary market, but long promotion ladders. The secondary market is characterized by low wages, few opportunities for advancement, poor working conditions, and job insecurity. There are many entry-level jobs in the secondary market, but promotion ladders are short or nonexistent. Women have been relegated to the secondary market—to such low-paying and unstable jobs as garment worker, beautician, waitress, laundry or dry-cleaning worker, and dressmaker (Baker, 1978, pp. 349–50).

Underlying all three hypotheses is the idea that prejudice and discrimination keep women in their "place." Women are crowded into certain occupations, perceived as having less capital than men, and relegated to the secondary market because of cultural stereotypes that portray women as incapable of performing "male jobs." The economy reinforces "the tendency for males to differentiate their activities from those of women's and devalue those roles" (Stockard and Johnson, 1980, p. 44). The process is circular. Because of cultural stereotypes, women are pushed into certain kinds of jobs, and these jobs (rather than something inherent in women's nature) lead them to act in ways that reinforce cultural stereotypes. The result is institutionalized sexism.

Rosabeth Kanter's analysis of the positions women occupy in corporations emphasizes structural inequalities. The worlds of men's work and women's work can be quite different. Consider secretaries. The structure of the corporate secretary's job differs from that of other workers in three basic ways. The first characteristic of the secretarial position is *status contingency:* A secretary's formal rank and salary reflect her boss's rank, not her own skills or the specific tasks she performs.* How much power she has depends on how much he has. On an informal level, how much people like and respect her may depend on their feelings toward her boss. The second characteristic is *principled arbitrariness:* Beyond certain basic requirements (mainly typing), there is no formal job description for the secretarial position and no objective criteria for evaluating performance. The company does not define a secretary's responsibilities as it does for other workers. How a secretary spends her time and whether she gets a raise usually is left to the boss's discretion. She is there to serve his needs, however arbitrary. Thus, her job may range from writing letters for her boss to watering his plants. The third feature of the ideal secretary-boss relationship is *fealty:* the secretary's loyalty and devotion to her boss. Ideally (from the boss's point of view), a secretary derives her primary rewards from their relationship. Ideally, she identifies her interests with his. The boss is able to let down his guard because he knows she will not "blow his cover." Secretaries are rewarded for fealty rather than for objective performance, often with symbolic rather than concrete rewards (praise and a windowed office rather than a raise and promotion). The formal tasks secretaries perform are routine (typing,

---

* Use of *he* for the boss and *she* for the secretary is deliberate.

The gender roles men and women have learned at home carry over into the workplace. The woman in the top photograph is no more uncomfortable serving her boss than she would be serving her husband or father; the men in the bottom photograph are not used to being lectured by a woman. Jobs also structure behavior. One of the women is a secretary; the other is an official of the Interstate Commerce Commission.

The Special Case of Minority Women

Does the structure of education, work, and the family place black (and other minority) women in double jeopardy? Are they discriminated against because of both race and sex? Is the position that women in minority communities occupy the same as or different from the position that women in white communities occupy?

Data on black women can be interpreted in different ways. The income gap between black men and women is considerably smaller than that between white men and women: in 1977, $2,400, compared with $6,400 (U.S. Department of Labor, 1979, Table 13). The 1970 census showed the percentage of women who were doctors (12.5 percent) or lawyers (11 percent) was higher in the black community than in the white community (Epstein, 1976, p. 442). Relative to men, black women are better off than white women. Viewed from a different angle, however, this advantage disappears. The actual number of black female professionals is very small: There were about a thousand black female lawyers and doctors in 1970. The average black woman receives less education, is more frequently unemployed, and has a lower-paying job than white women, black men, or white men. She is also more likely to be the official head of her household, though most black wives and mothers (75 percent) live with their husbands. (The ideas that black women run their families and that the black community is matriarchal are myths.)

Black women occupy an ambiguous position in American society (Lewis, 1972). They share common minority-group experiences with black men on the one hand and with white women on the other. But both of these potential allies are also potential enemies. Black men belong to the dominant male group; white women, to the dominant white group. As a result, their interests conflict.

In the early days of the Women's Movement, blacks kept their distance. It was difficult for black women to identify with many feminist issues. . . . Conditions that white feminists labeled sexist looked like privileges to black women. Quite simply, women who were forced to do domestic work in order to feed their children did not sympathize with women who protested the enforced dependency and idleness of the middle-class housewife. For a number of years, black women seemed to accept the role of bearing and rearing "warriors" for the Civil Rights struggle. When black men began to make visible (if token) progress, however, black women began to see more of their difficulties as the product of sexism.

answering the phone). In terms of skills, they are easily replaced. However, a secretary can protect her job by specializing in the boss: by learning his wants, needs, and interests and by making him dependent on her. The position of secretaries provides a clear illustration of how jobs shape people. In Kanter's words:

> Perhaps no other job category in the large corporation displays so vividly the constraints that give rise to characteristic behaviors, attitudes, and styles on the part of workers. In the case of secretaries, they were assumed to display the properties of "women as a group." But what they really displayed were the orientations of people whose strategies for achieving recognition and control were constrained by the social organization of their job. (p. 91)

Men in low-opportunity positions often behave like stereotypic women. They limit their aspirations, seek satisfaction outside work and in their families, put more energy into building sociable relationships at work than into the job itself, often interrupt their careers, and often daydream (Kanter, 1977, p. 161). This behavior reflects a worker's job, not his or her "psychology" or innate disposition.

Structural analysis also helps to explain why there are not more women managers in today's corporations. Managerial positions are surrounded by uncertainty: Things never go exactly as planned. Wherever there is uncertainty, someone has to make decisions, and that someone is the manager. Responsibility forces managers to rely on other people: Trust, commitment, and shared understandings and values are especially important. Social conformity becomes a substitute for certainty. In recruiting trainees, managers tend to "reproduce themselves in kind" (Kanter, 1977, p. 48). Women are seen as "different." Male executives feel that they do not understand women or do not know how to treat them in a work setting. They cannot engage women in such traditional masculine rituals as swearing, back-slapping, and girl watching. Going drinking with a female co-worker means something different from going drinking with a male co-worker (if it does not, the man may feel threatened). Top male executives are not likely to take on a female protégée, introduce her to the old-boy network, and sponsor her advance. A woman is too much of a risk: She may not work out; she may leave to have children. Because her future is uncertain, male peers are less likely to trust her with confidential information or undercover assistance. She may not be around to reciprocate. The organization man has help getting to the top; the organization woman is largely on her own.

Women who do gain top positions often find that they are *tokens*: People see them as representatives of a social category rather than as individuals (Kanter, 1977, Chapter 8). This has a number of repercussions. Because they are different, they are always in the spotlight. Everything they say or do is closely observed: Men watch to see how *as women* they fill their managerial role and how *as managers* they live up to images of womanhood. The presence of an outsider may cause members of the dominant group to exaggerate their own commonality—for example, prompting men to tell war stories or brag of sexual adventures. By offering acceptance as a reward, members of the dominant group may pressure the token to conform to its stereotypes. Token advances thus may reinforce stereotypes and perpetuate institutionalized sexism.

Men: Dilemmas and Confusion

Given the hard facts of sexual inequality, one would think that men, as men, "have it made." Males enjoy a variety of privileges and advantages, simply because they are male. The social system works in their favor. Or does it? Inevitably the attention given to women's problems in recent years has raised questions about the male role. Does sexism have negative consequences for men as well as for women? Does the dominant position exact its own kind of penalties?

On the average, men die earlier than women do (by about seven years). Men are more likely than women to have heart attacks and to suffer from psychosomatic disorders (ulcers, asthma, migraines). About three times as many men as women kill themselves; nearly fifteen times as many become alcoholics. Some of this difference is biological. Men are the weaker sex. (More males than females are lost in pregnancy, childbirth, and infancy.) Nevertheless, stress is a factor in all of the health problems mentioned. Where might excess stress come from? From the cultural demand that men conceal their emotions, from the achievement imperative, and from changing role requirements.

At one time or another, almost every male child in the United States is told, "Big boys don't cry." There is a taboo on men's expressing weakness or pain. Men are expected to be tough, competitive, rational, objective, emotionally inexpressive.

Showing tenderness or vulnerability is considered unmanly. Such trained inexpressiveness may create stress in two ways. Because men are taught to conceal inner feelings, they must constantly be on the alert. Other people, who might pry into their secrets, are a threat. Men develop a psychological coat of armor. They pay less attention to their own (and other people's) feelings and may not know when they (or others) are troubled. Constant wariness is one source of stress (Jourard, 1971, pp. 34–41). Difficulty in establishing intimate relationships is a second source of stress (Balswick and Peek, 1971). In effect, men operate under an emotional double standard. A man is expected to be cool and self-contained with everyone but his wife or lover. To have a meaningful love relationship he has to *un*learn the inexpressiveness he has practiced since childhood.

The role requirement of inexpressiveness carries over into father-child relationships. Traditionally, American fathers have been portrayed as distant and aloof (Fein, 1978). According to the prevailing stereotype, fathers are neither inter-

Does caring for small children come more easily to women than to men? Or have women excluded men from the nursery and the kitchen, to preserve their own areas of expertise?

ested in nor involved with newborn infants: They are less nurturant than mothers, happy to leave caretaking to mothers, and less competent than mothers in caring for a baby. In part because of this stereotype, there has been comparatively little research on father-infant interaction. One survey of first-time fathers indicated that they were surprised by the powerful impact the baby had on them. Another study showed that at four weeks, babies respond differently to their fathers than to strangers, even when the father is not the primary caretaker. Interestingly, fathers are more likely to touch and rock their infants when they are alone than when the mother is present. How involved they become in caring for a baby seems to depend on how involved their wives allow them to be.

The pressure to achieve is another source of stress for men. In most societies, work is central to a man's identity. In large part, economic success is the measure of the man. Masculinity is contingent on the ability to provide for a wife and children. Only a small number of jobs, however, allow men to live up to achievement standards (Walum, 1977). Men are supposed to be independent, but over 80 percent of American men work for somebody else. About 50 percent hold routine factory jobs that provide little intrinsic satisfaction (see Chapter 7). At any given time, millions of men are unemployed. The main reason men give for staying in a job they dislike is to provide for their families. At the same time, the job keeps them away from home. Paradoxically, then, the family keeps men working, but work keeps them from their family. The job competes with the family for a man's time, commitment, and loyalty (Pleck and Pleck, 1980, p. 430).

Like the female role, the male role is changing (Pleck, 1976). Change is one source of role strain. Role strain develops when people are subjected to contradictory demands and expectations. They do not know which of two conflicting sets of standards applies to a particular situation, or they attempt to fill both sets simultaneously. Are changing norms creating role strain for men today? Mirra Komarovsky's (1976) interviews of sixty male seniors at an Ivy League college provide clues. Komarovsky found that many gender stereotypes had broken down. The male students did not believe in notions of "female psychology." Although most thought that women were more emotional than men, they rejected the idea that men are more logical and women more artistic. Most said that they valued originality and intelligence in females as well as in males. But although ideological support for sharply different gender roles had weakened, the students had not given up their belief in male superiority. They were experiencing role strain. A number said that bright women made them feel insecure: "If a girl knows more than I do, I resent her" (in Komarovsky, 1973, p. 874). And many of those who said that they did not feel an intellectual relationship was a problem on dates indicated that they felt superior to their girlfriends or mentioned some weakness that offset a girlfriend's intellectual competence.

Komarovsky asked the students how they felt about wives' working. A number were "modified traditionalists." They expected their wives to work when they were first married, to leave their jobs when they had children, and then to return to work. This position was entangled in a web of contradictions, however. The students' values and preferences were at odds. "It is only fair to let a woman do her own thing, if she wants a career" one senior declared. He added, "Personally, though, I would want my wife at home" (in Komarovsky, 1973, p. 880). Most of the students interpreted equality of achievement between a husband and a wife as a defeat for the man. The conviction that there is no real alternative to a mother's care of young children helped students to reconcile their desire to have traditional wives with their belief that women should have equal career opportunities.

Komarovsky found that the college students were as ambivalent about their own roles as they were about changing definitions of femininity. They said that a real man should exhibit such traditionally masculine traits as aggressiveness, decisiveness, independence, and courage. He also should possess such traditionally feminine traits as patience, sensitivity, and artistic appreciation. Asked to describe themselves, many of the students expressed anxiety about being able to live up to role demands. They felt that their girl-friends expected them to be more self-assured, more responsible, and more emotionally supportive than they felt themselves to be. Women, they complained, "want it both ways." The students seemed to conceive of change in terms of role reversals. If a man gives up his dominant position in the family, his wife will be the boss. If a woman aggressively pursues a career, she will lose her traditionally feminine warmth and compassion. Although the students did not believe in innate sex differences, they did seem to think that a person had to be *either* masculine *or* feminine.

Responses to Inequality

Feminism—the doctrine that women have rights equal to those of men—is not a modern invention. In *A Vindication of the Rights of Women,* published in 1772, Mary Wollstonecraft had urged members of her sex to break out of their "gilt cages" and "acquire strength, both of mind and body." The First Women's Rights Convention in the United States took place in Seneca Falls, New York, in 1848. That July, three hundred people (mostly women) gathered to issue a Declaration of Sentiments, modeled on the Declaration of Independence. The Declaration began with the assertion that "all men and women are created equal" and went on to indict mankind for a "his-

tory of repeated injuries and usurpations" designed to "destroy woman's confidence in her own powers, to lessen her self-respect, and to make her willing to lead a dependent and abject life" (in Chafe, 1972, p. 5). In *The Subjection of Women* (1869), John Stuart Mill had argued, "What is now called the nature of woman is an eminently artificial thing—the result of forced repression in some directions, artificial stimulation in others." Here we will put the contemporary Women's Movement in the United States in historical perspective, to show what *is* new.

Womanhood in America: A Brief History

In colonial America, women had no legal rights to speak of (Chafe, 1977, Chapter 2; Ryan, 1979). Like slaves and children, women could not own property, make contracts, bring suit in court, or vote in elections. Their fathers, their husbands, and their sons were entitled to make all legal decisions for them. Practical necessity often undermined patriarchal norms, however. Separation of the sexes was a luxury few colonial families could afford. Women's skills and labor in tending animals, planting gardens, weaving cloth, making clothes, and preserving food were a necessary part of the colonial economy. Norms concerning a woman's "place" existed, and a few wealthy merchants may have installed their wives in drawing rooms. But the actual content of most women's lives contrasted sharply with the norms (Chafe, 1977, p. 20). "Adam's rib" was a favorite seventeenth-century expression for women, implying that they were vitally important to men.

Segregation of the sexes and establishment of a separate woman's sphere began in the mid-nineteenth century. Industrialization caused many jobs to be moved from the home to the factory and created a new class of managers, bureaucrats, and professionals. In the growing middle class, work was redefined as a male prerogative, and housekeeping and motherhood were idealized as female occupations. For the first time in the United States, behavior conformed to cultural ideals. Social realities reinforced social norms. Women continued to do a good deal of work in the home. But they were isolated from mainstream economic activities. They were also isolated from lower-class women, who provided the industrial economy with cheap labor (Chafe, 1977, Chapter 2; Ryan, 1979, Chapter 3).

Stimulated by the higher education provided in the new women's colleges and by social upheavals (the Civil War, the postwar waves of immigration), many middle- and upper-class women took up causes in the nineteenth century (Weitz, 1977, pp. 236–44; Ryan, 1979, Chapter 4). Women joined the call for the abolition of slavery. They founded the Women's Christian Temperance Union, which later claimed credit for Prohibition. In the latter part of the century, they worked in the Progressive Movement, establishing settlement houses in poor immigrant neighborhoods, lobbying for municipal health and sanitation codes, and fighting for children's rights.

In a sense, the feminist movement was a by-product of these other causes. Women's efforts to work in the abolition movement were often greeted with derision and contempt. In 1840, for example, women were denied entry to an anti-slavery conference in London. Churches in this country condemned outspoken female abolitionists as unnatural: "The appropriate duties and influence of women are unobtrusive and private" (in Chafe, 1977, p. 25). Stung by rejection, female activists began to identify with slaves and to fight for their own emancipation. "All I ask of our [brothers]," declared abolitionist Sarah Grimké, "is that they will take their feet from our necks, and permit us to stand upright on the ground which God has designed us to occupy" (in Chafe, 1977, p. 25).

Early feminists attacked the entire framework of assumptions that defined women's position in society. Even by today's standards, they seem radical. Elizabeth Cady Stanton, for example, declared women's suffrage a superficial issue. "[W]oman's chief discontent is not with her political, but with her social, and particularly her marital bondage," Stanton wrote in 1869 (in Chafe, 1977, p. 7). She went on, in the 1890s, to organize an effort to write a woman's Bible. Near the turn of the century, Charlotte Perkins Gilman argued that women could attain freedom only if they achieved economic equality with men and that this equality would come about only if child care and food preparation were institutionalized. Gilman advocated replacing families with communes. Others, notably Victoria Woodhull, expanded the concept of female emancipation to include free love and licensed prostitution. These early feminists were on the fringe of the radical movements of their day. In an age scarred by social disorder, they inspired widespread antagonism.

Over time, the forces of compromise prevailed. Radical feminists were replaced with a generation of female reformers—women like Carrie Chapman Catt and Jane Addams, who sought to minimize controversy. Whereas the early feminists attacked the foundations of sex differentiation, the new reformers exploited the notions of a woman's "place"—brilliantly (Chafe, 1977, pp. 13–15). They described society as the family in macrocosm and argued that women's experience in the home made them uniquely qualified to deal with human problems. They portrayed themselves as society's housekeepers. Focusing on the issue of suffrage, they argued that giving women the vote would "soften" political debate. In short, they sought to expand the traditional feminine role, but not to change it. By comparison to early feminist programs, the call for women's suffrage seemed tame. In 1918, President Woodrow Wilson declared women's suffrage "vital to the winning of the war" (in Chafe, 1972, p. 3). Finally, in 1920, the Nineteenth Amendment was ratified: The right to vote could no longer be denied on account of sex.

Passage of the Nineteenth Amendment did not, as its supporters had hoped, usher in an era of feminist reform. Women's new legal and political status did not change their social position. Indeed, the Nineteenth Amendment marked the beginning of almost fifty years of retrenchment. World War I had accentuated the differences between men, who went to war, and women, who kept the home fires burning. In winning the vote, the feminist movement lost its chief rallying point. Women did not vote as a bloc (feminists had underestimated the effects of class and ethnic differences among women), so politicians could safely ignore them. Social activism and reform went out of fashion in the 1920s (Ryan, 1979, Chapter 5). Concern with youth and appearance seemed to replace the ideals of purity and piety, but the position of women remained essentially the same. Then, in the 1930s, the Great Depression made the special problems of women seem minor.

World War II brought many women out of their homes and into factory jobs vacated by men. "Rosie the Riveter" was applauded for her contribution to the war effort, but after the war, she was encouraged to give up her job and go home. Many wartime industries closed. The Selective Service Act required employers to give returning veterans priority if they sought their old jobs. The last hired, women were the first fired. Moreover, the GI Bill enabled many veterans to go to college and move into managerial jobs, and Federal Housing Authority loans enabled many veterans to buy homes in the suburbs. For the first time in a long while, many women could afford to stay home and raise children. Thus, social policies that on the surface had nothing to do with women changed many women's lives.

Many women did not stay home, however. Between 1945 and 1946, 1 million women were laid off and 2.25 million quit their jobs. But nearly 2.75 million were hired during the same period, for a net decrease of 500,000. What is peculiar about the 1940s is that although unprecedented numbers of women joined the labor force, traditional attitudes toward a woman's "place" remained essentially unchanged (Chafe, 1972, pp. 184–90). Discrimination against women was widespread. For example, medical schools imposed a 5 percent quota on female admissions, and 70 percent of hospitals refused to take female interns. It seemed that most Americans accepted women's working outside the home as long as the situation was seen as temporary (a wartime job, or a job after the children were grown) and as long as the traditional division of labor, into men's and women's jobs, was maintained.

The Women's Movement Today

The revival of feminism is often traced to the publication of Betty Friedan's *The Feminine Mystique* in 1963 (Weitz, 1977, pp. 245–46). Friedan wrote about "the problem that has no name." She argued that the glorification of domestic values and the neglect of *self*-fulfillment for women in American society had created widespread discontent. In particular, Friedan attacked the "sexual sell"—the way that advertisers played on women's guilt about not being the perfect housewife or the perfect playmate as a means of selling products; the way educators and psychotherapists encouraged women to live vicariously through their husbands and children. Friedan's book was addressed to a mass audience and became a best seller. It helped to transform women's private troubles into a social issue, by giving the problem a name (the feminine mystique) and by suggesting who was responsible (advertisers, educators, psychotherapists).

The beginning of Women's Liberation? Popular wisdom holds that women "filled in" for men in the workplace during World War II but returned to being full-time housewives after the war was over. This was only partially true. The number of women working increased silently but steadily through the 1950s and 1960s.

Friedan was not the first writer to make these points. Simone de Beauvoir's *The Second Sex* (1949) was a classic. The question is why Friedan's book—and feminist ideals in general—caught on in the 1960s. William Chafe (1972) offers two basic reasons. First, the 1960s was a decade of generalized social reform. The Civil Rights campaign called national attention to prejudice against minorities, dramatized the immorality of discrimination, and provided a model for social action. Second, women's position in American society had already changed. By the end of the 1960s, 40 percent of American women (including many middle-class women and many wives) held jobs. Nearly half of adolescent girls were growing up with examples of working married women in their own homes (pp. 232–37). As Chafe puts it, "If women had been as oppressed as the feminists claimed, no amount of rhetoric could have aroused them from their captivity" (p. 234). Having started on the road to improvement, women felt their relative deprivation all the more keenly. The contemporary Women's Movement was a "revolution of rising expectations." Structural changes preceded and paved the way for changes in attitudes.

What transformed the social issue of women's rights into a social movement? A series of events in the 1960s brought women together, established networks of communication, and focused and sharpened their discontent (Freeman, 1973). In 1961, President Kennedy appointed a Commission on the Status of Women. The Commission's report, issued in 1963, documented the extent to which American women were denied rights and opportunities. Spotting an opportunity to repay political debts to women, many governors appointed similar state commissions. These commissions brought together politically knowledgeable and active women who might not have met otherwise. A network of like-minded women was established. The commissions also raised expectations: Surely something would be done. Then women experienced unexpected setbacks. In an effort to slow passage of the 1964 Civil Rights Act and thereby delay racial integration, the word "sex" was added to Title VII of the bill. Many officials considered the addition a joke—including the first director of the Equal Employment Opportunity Commission (EEOC), who called it a "fluke" that had been "conceived out of wedlock" (in Freeman, 1973). Women were outraged. When officials at the Third National Conference of Women's Commissions, in June 1966,

refused to recognize a motion supporting Title VII, twenty-eight participants met in Friedan's hotel room and founded the National Organization for Women (NOW). From the beginning, NOW focused on legal and economic rights, especially for career women. Much of the organization's early success was due to its members' skills in attracting media attention.

Meanwhile, a second branch of the Women's Movement was taking shape. The Civil Rights and Anti-War Movements had brought together many young, middle-class, college-educated women. In these movements, women learned to see most problems as political ones that could be solved through organized protest. They also learned strategies of confrontation. But within these movements, many women found that their "revolutionary brothers" expected them to perform such menial tasks as operating Xerox machines and making coffee. In the words of the black leader Stokely Carmichael, "the position of women in our movement should be prone" (in Chafe, 1972, p. 233). When women tried to introduce feminist issues at the 1967 Convention for New Politics, the chairman patted one woman on the head and said, "Cool down little girl" (Freeman, 1973, p. 801). Incidents like these provoked women to take action on their own behalf. Around the country, women formed consciousness-raising groups, which combined techniques of group psychotherapy with political explanations of female inequality. What the two branches of the Women's Movement had in common was a desire to end class treatment of women. Both of them fought the idea that because of their sex, women should automatically be expected to do housework, rear children, and serve as secretaries at meetings (Chafe, 1972, p. 238).

The similarities between the early feminist movements and today's Women's Movement are clear. Both developed in periods of social turmoil, which created possibilities for and expectations of sweeping social change: Slaves would be freed; immigrants would become full-fledged Americans. A century later, these dreams were revived and expanded: Full racial integration would be achieved; the war in Vietnam would be stopped. Because many women worked in these movements, communications networks were already established when events turned women's attention toward their own discontent. In both periods, women discovered that their own rights were being ignored while they were working for the rights of others (blacks, immigrants, war resisters).

Today's Women's Movement differs from the earlier feminist movement in several important respects, however (Chafe, 1977, Chapter 5). First, the early feminist movement developed on the fringe of society. The issues its leaders addressed were far removed from most women's experience and everyday concerns. The contemporary Women's Movement developed out of, and built upon, prevailing social trends. By 1960, many American women were already working outside their home, and many more women were joining the labor force. They knew that they received less pay than men did. They had struggled with balancing the demands of a job and the demands of child care and housekeeping. The Women's Movement spoke directly to their everyday experience. And in the 1960s, norms of sexual behavior were changing. The Women's Movement stressed the right of women to know their own bodies and use them as they saw fit. It addressed women's personal experiences. Second, most of the early feminists had come from a similar social class and background. The contemporary Women's Movement, however, attracted a diverse following. It was a grass-roots movement, with energy coming from the bottom, not the top. Finally, after its first, radical days, the early feminist movement focused on a single issue: women's suffrage. When this goal was achieved, public interest in women's

rights faded. The contemporary Women's Movement has addressed a wide range of issues: discrimination in employment, birth control and abortion, sexism in the classroom, lesbianism, the special problems of divorced and widowed women —to name a few. The contemporary movement thus avoided "the pitfalls of thinking there was any single answer to inequality or sex role stereotyping" (Chafe, 1977, p. 130).

Responses to Feminism

Women have made visible progress in the United States in recent years. The 1964 Civil Rights Act banned discrimination against women in hiring and promotion. In a landmark decision against the American Telephone and Telegraph Company (AT&T), the world's largest employer of women, the Equal Employment Opportunity Commission established the principle of equal pay for equal work. AT&T was required to pay $23 million in immediate pay increases, plus $15 million in back pay, to employees who had been denied promotions or were underpaid because of their sex or race. The 1974 Equal Credit Opportunity Act made it illegal to deny a person credit because of sex or marital status, giving married women new financial opportunities. Although the numbers are still small, a growing proportion of women are training for careers in business, law, medicine, and engineering. Women now attend such traditionally all-male institutions as Princeton and Yale Universities and the United States Military Academy. There are women clergy, women jockeys, and TV and telephone repairwomen. In 1981, a woman was appointed to the Supreme Court. Feminist issues reach a wide audience through such publications as *Ms.* magazine. Awareness of the oppressive features of traditional sex roles and of discrimination against women is widespread. Even language is changing. Textbooks now substitute *he or she* for the formerly omnipresent masculine pronoun, and *humankind* or *humanity* for *mankind.*

Just how many women have benefited from this national consciousness raising is questionable, however. Many of the breakthroughs in the sexual division of labor are only token changes. The number of women in the clergy, for example, is small. Equal pay for equal work does not address the problem of women's segregation in low-paying fields, such as clerical work. The principle of equivalent pay for equivalent men's and women's work has not gained support. Indeed, the gap between men's and women's income has increased in recent years. For most women, the freedom to work means having a routine, low-paying office or factory job, not a career. Whether public gains affect women's private lives is also questionable. Whatever else has changed, women still do most of the housework.

Surprisingly, perhaps, much of the opposition to women's liberation has come from women. *The Total Woman* (Morgan, 1973) and *Fascinating Womanhood* (Andelin, 1975) enjoyed considerable, although short-lived, success. Both books defend the traditional division of labor by sex with the argument that women have the best of both worlds: domestic power (as wives and mothers) plus male protection outside the home. A true woman, they maintain, lives to serve others. Her life revolves around her church, husband, children, and home. Her success as a woman is measured in terms of her family's happiness. Active, organized opposition to women's liberation has focused on the Equal Rights Amendment (ERA) and the abortion issue. Although Congress passed the ERA by an overwhelming majority in 1972, it may well not be ratified by the states within the time allotted. And although the U.S. Supreme Court declared existing anti-abortion laws unconstitutional (*Roe v. Wade,* 1973), Congress has restricted the use of public funds for abortions unless the mother's health is in danger, and further restrictions on abortion are introduced in each session.

In the 1960s and 1970s, feminists fought for the right of married women to work outside their homes. Today, feminists are fighting for the right of working women to bear and raise children. Whether they succeed will depend on changes in the structure of work and the family. In this country, jobs are not designed for people who have primary responsibility for small children, nor is the family designed to meet the needs of two adults who work full time. The United States lags behind other Western nations in family policy: This is the only Western country that does not provide universal maternal and child health care programs, maternity leave of three months or more, maternity benefits, job protection, and family allowances to supplement parents' earnings. France, a bastion of family centeredness and individuality, has an extensive nursery system, free kindergarten for children aged three to five (which 95 percent of them attend), and 200,000 licensed nannies. Sweden not only provides free day care but also pays 90 percent of the salary of a mother *or* father who stays home from a job to care for a baby for up to a year. In the United States, paternity leaves are rare; maternity leave is optional (a company may or may not guarantee a woman her job if she takes three months off); day-care centers can provide for only about one in five children of working mothers; and the only parents who receive family allowances are unemployed single mothers, under the welfare system.

The ultimate goal of the contemporary Women's Movement is not to eliminate sex differentiation but to remove institutional obstacles to gender equality. Because sexism is institutionalized, because it is woven into the fabric of social life in subtle and myriad ways, this goal proves elusive. Changes in gender roles would cause profound changes in many institutions. For example, if job opportunities for women improve, the birth rate might drop. This might help to solve problems of overpopulation and the environment, but it would exacerbate the problem of caring for the elderly in years to come. (The fewer babies women have, the fewer workers there will be to support the Social Security system in years to come.) Close analysis shows that social problems in different areas are often interconnected.

Summary

1. Sex is a biological identity and role in reproduction; gender is a set of behavior patterns, attitudes, and motivations that are defined by culture as masculine or feminine.

2. The biosocial perspective suggests that learning certain behavior (such as infant care or physical combat) may be easier for one sex than for the other.

3. A wide range of studies—of child rearing and early sex differences, of children with ambiguous sex identities, and of male and female behavior in other societies—indicates that socialization has at least as much impact on development as biology, and probably more. Many of the environmental conditions that promoted gender inequality no longer exist.

4. Prejudice alone does not explain why gender inequality persists. Sexism has been institutionalized; it is an unintended consequence of established social policies and practices.

5. Changes in work and in the family contributed to the emergence of "his and her" marriages. Wives still bear final responsibility for housekeeping and child rearing, even if they work; husbands still seem to wield more power than wives.

6. Although more women than ever before are finishing high school and college, the hidden curriculum, the hidden message in schoolbooks, tracking, and other forces push women into traditionally female, and less lucrative, fields.

7. Women are still concentrated in low-paying jobs and still earn less than men for equivalent work. Analysis of the role of secretaries suggests that the kind of jobs available to women reinforce stereotypes about female inferiority, providing a rationale for continuing discrimination.

8. The pressure to conceal emotions, the achievement imperative, and changing role requirements create special problems for men.

9. Feminism has a long history in the United States. The early feminist movement began on the fringes of the abolition movement, went through radical and reform stages, and ended with the ratification of the Nineteenth Amendment, which gave women the vote.

10. The general climate of social reform and the fact that many women had entered the work force raised women's expectations in the 1960s; preestablished communication networks gave women the organization to respond to insults and setbacks. The contemporary Women's Movement fit the times.

11. Responses to feminism have been mixed. Women have made gains in some areas, but limited change does not attack the underlying problem of institutionalized sexism.

Suggested Reading

Chafe, William Henry. *Women and Equality: Changing Patterns in American Culture.* New York: Oxford University Press, 1977.

de Beauvoir, Simone. *The Second Sex.* H.M. Parshley (Trans.). New York: Knopf, 1953.

Hoffman, Lois W., and F. Ivan Nye (Eds.). *Working Mothers: An Evaluative Review of the Consequences for Husband, Wife, and Child.* San Francisco: Jossey-Bass, 1974.

Maccoby, Eleanor E., and Carol N. Jacklin. *The Psychology of Sex Differences.* Stanford, Cal.: Stanford University Press, 1974.

Pleck, Elizabeth H., and Joseph H. Pleck. *The American Man.* Englewood Cliffs, N.J.: Prentice-Hall, 1980.

Rosaldo, Michelle Z., and Louise Lamphere (Eds.). *Women, Culture, and Society.* Stanford, Cal.: Stanford University Press, 1974.

Tavris, Carol, and Carole Offir. *The Longest War: Sex Differences in Perspective.* New York: Harcourt Brace Jovanovich, 1977.

References

Andelin, H. *Fascinating Womanhood,* rev. ed. New York: Bantam, 1975.

Bahr, S.J. "Adolescent Perceptions of Conjugal Power." *Social Forces,* Vol. 52 (1974a), pp. 357–67.

Bahr, S.J. "Effects on Power and Division of Labor in the Family." In L.W. Hoffman and F.I. Nye (Eds.), *Working Mothers: An Evaluative Review of the Consequences for Husband, Wife, and Child.* San Francisco: Jossey-Bass, 1974b, pp. 167–85.

Baker, S.H. "Women in Blue-Collar and Service Occupations." In A. Stromberg and S. Harkness (Eds.), *Women Working.* Palo Alto, Cal.: Mayfield, 1978.

Balswick, J.O., and C.W. Peek. "The Inexpressive Male: A Tragedy of American Society." *The Family Coordinator,* Vol. 20, No. 4 (October 1971), pp. 363–68.

Blau, R.O., and C.L. Jusenius. "Economists' Approaches to Sex Segregation in the Labor Market: An Appraisal." *Signs,* Vol. 1 (1976), pp. 181–200.

Blood, R.O., Jr., and D.M. Wolfe. *Husbands and Wives; the Dynamics of Married Living.* New York: Free Press, 1960.

Brown, G.H. *Degree Awards to Women: An Update.* Washington, D.C.: National Center for Educational Statistics, 1979.

Chafe, W.H. *The American Woman: Her Changing Social, Economic, and Political Roles, 1920-1970.* New York: Oxford University Press, 1972.

Chafe, W.H. *Women and Equality: Changing Patterns in American Culture.* New York: Oxford University Press, 1977.

de Beauvoir, S. *The Second Sex.* H.M. Parshley (Trans.). New York: Knopf, 1953.

Degler, C.N. *At Odds: Women and the Family in America from the Revolution to the Present.* New York: Oxford University Press, 1980.

Epstein, C.F. "Sex Roles." In R.K. Merton and R. Nisbet (Eds.), *Contemporary Social Problems,* 4th ed. New York: Harcourt Brace Jovanovich, 1976, pp. 415–56.

Fein, R.A. "Research on Fathering: Social Policy and an Emergent Perspective." *Journal of Social Issues,* Vol. 34, No. 1 (Winter 1978), pp. 122–35.

Frazier, N., and M. Sadker. *Sexism in School and Society.* New York: Harper & Row, 1973.

Freeman, J. "The Building of a Gilded Cage." *The Second Wave,* Vol. 1, No. 1 (Spring 1971).

Freeman, J. "The Origins of the Women's Liberation Movement." *American Journal of Sociology,* Vol. 78, No. 4 (1973), pp. 792–811.

Freud, S. "The Dissolution of the Oedipus Complex." In J. Strachey (Ed.), *The Standard Edition of the Complete Psychological Works of Sigmund Freud,* rev. ed., Vol. XIX. London: Hogarth, 1924, pp. 173–79.

Freud, S. "Femininity." In J. Strachey (Ed.), *The Complete Introductory Lectures on Psychoanalysis.* New York: Norton, 1966, pp. 567–99.

Friedan, B. *The Feminine Mystique.* New York: Dell, 1963.

Gillespie, O. "Who Has the Power? The Marital Struggle." *Journal of Marriage and the Family,* Vol. 33, No. 3 (1971), pp. 445–58.

Goode, W. *World Revolution and Family Patterns.* New York: Free Press, 1963.

Horney, K. *Feminine Psychology.* New York: Norton, 1967.

Jacklin, C.N. "Sex Differences and Their Relationship to Sex Equity in Learning and Teaching." Paper presented at the National Institute of Education, September 1977.

Jourard, S.M. *The Transparent Self.* New York: Van Nostrand, 1971.

Kanter, R.M. *Men and Women of the Corporation.* New York: Basic Books, 1977.

Komarovsky, M. "Cultural Contradictions and Sex Roles: The Masculine Case." *American Journal of Sociology,* Vol. 78, No. 4 (November 1973), pp. 873–84.

Komarovsky, M. *Dilemmas of Masculinity.* New York: Norton, 1976.

Lewis, D.K. "A Response to Inequality: Black Women, Racism, and Sexism." *Journal of Women in Culture and Society,* Vol. 3, No. 2 (Winter 1972), pp. 339–61.

Maccoby, E.E. *Social Development: Psychological Growth and the Parent-Child Relationship.* New York: Harcourt Brace Jovanovich, 1980.

Maccoby, E.E., and C.N. Jacklin. *The Psychology of Sex Differences.* Stanford, Cal.: Stanford University Press, 1974.

Mead, M. *Coming of Age in Samoa.* 1935; rpt. New York: Morrow, 1971.

Money, J., and A.A. Ehrhardt. *Man and Woman, Boy and Girl.* Baltimore: Johns Hopkins University Press, 1972.

Morgan, M. *The Total Woman.* New York: Pocket Books, 1973.

Pleck, E.H., and J.H. Pleck. *The American Man.* Englewood Cliffs, N.J.: Prentice-Hall, 1980.

Pleck, J.H. "The Male Sex Role: Definitions, Problems, and Sources of Change." *Journal of Social Issues,* Vol. 32, No. 3 (Summer 1976), pp. 155–64.

Pleck, J.H. "The Work-Family Role System." *Social Problems,* Vol. 24 (1977), pp. 417–27.

Robinson, N.H., and J.P. Robinson. "Sex Roles and the Territoriality of Everyday Behavior." Ann Arbor, Mich.: Survey Research Center. University of Michigan, unpublished manuscript, 1975.

Rosaldo, M.Z. "Woman, Culture, and Society." In M.Z. Rosaldo and L. Lamphere (Eds.), *Woman, Culture, and Society.* Stanford, Cal.: Stanford University Press, 1974.

Rossi, A.S. "A Biosocial Perspective on Parenting." *Daedalus,* Vol. 106, No. 2 (1977), pp. 1–32.

Rossi, A.S. et al. "Viewpoint: Considering a Biosocial Perspective on Parenting." *Signs: Journal of Women in Culture and Society,* Vol. 4, No. 4 (1979), pp. 695–714.

Rubin, J.Z., F.J. Provenzano, and Z. Lurig. "The Eye of the Beholder: Parents' Views on Sex of Newborns." *American Journal of Orthopsychiatry,* Vol. 44, No. 4 (1974), pp. 512–19.

Rubin, L.B. *Worlds of Pain: Life in the Working-Class Family.* New York: Basic Books, 1976.

Ryan, M.P. *Womanhood in America: From Colonial Times to the Present,* 2d ed. New York: New Viewpoints, 1979.

Safilios-Rothschild, C. "The Study of Family Power Structure." *Journal of Marriage and the Family,* Vol. 32 (1970), pp. 539–52.

Sanday, P.R. "Female Status in the Public Domain." In M.Z. Rosaldo and L. Lamphere (Eds.), *Woman, Culture, and Society.* Stanford, Cal.: Stanford University Press, 1974, pp. 189–206.

Scarf, M. *Unfinished Business: Pressure Points in the Lives of Women.* New York: Doubleday, 1980.

Stockard, J., and M.M. Johnson. *Sex Roles: Sex Inequality and Sex Role Development.* Englewood Cliffs, N.J.: Prentice-Hall, 1980.

Tavris, C., and C. Offir. *The Longest War: Sex Differences in Perspective.* New York: Harcourt Brace Jovanovich, 1977.

Thomas, A.R., and N.R. Stewart. "Counselor Response to Female Clients with Deviate and Conforming Career Goals." *Journal of Counseling Psychology,* Vol. 18, No. 4 (1971), pp. 352–57.

U'Ren, M.B. "The Image of Women in Textbooks." In V. Gornick and B.K. Moran (Eds.), *Woman in Sexist Society: Studies in Power and Powerlessness.* New York: Basic Books, 1971, pp. 218–25.

U.S. Department of Labor. *U.S. Working Women: A Data Book.* Washington, D.C.: U.S. Government Printing Office, 1977.

U.S. Department of Labor. *The Earnings Gap Between Men and Women.* Washington, D.C.: U.S. Government Printing Office, 1979.

Vanek, Joann. "Time Spent in Housework." *Scientific American,* Vol. 231 (November 1974), pp. 116–20.

Walum, L. *Dynamics of Sex and Gender.* New York: Random House, 1977.

Weitz, S. *Sex Roles: Biological, Psychological, and Social Foundations.* New York: Oxford University Press, 1977.

Weitzman, L.J. "Sex-Role Socialization in Picture Books for Preschool Children." *American Journal of Sociology,* Vol. 77, No. 6 (1972), pp. 1125–50.

Weitzman, L.J. *Sex Role Socialization.* Palo Alto, Cal.: Mayfield, 1979.

Will, J., P. Self, and N. Datan. 1974; Unpublished paper cited in C. Tavris and C. Offir, *The Longest War: Sex Differences in Prespective.* New York: Harcourt Brace Jovanovich, 1977, p. 173.

Women on Words and Images. *Dick and Jane as Victims: Sex Stereotyping in Children's Readers.* Princeton, N.J.: Women on Words, 1972.

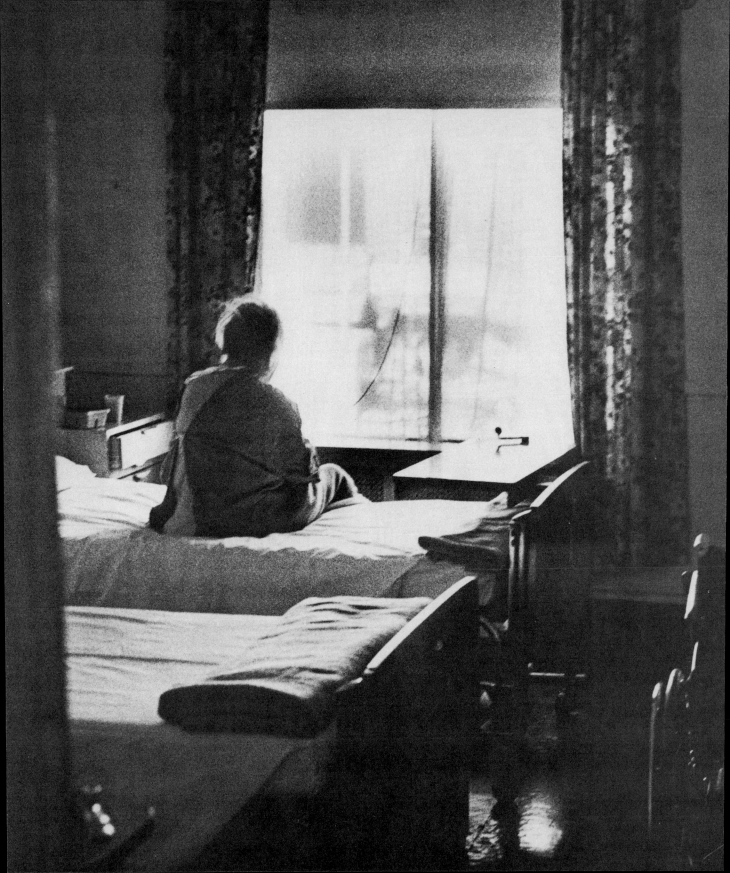

Chapter Twelve

Age Inequality

The Early Years: Childhood and Adolescence

Children's Rights

The History of Childhood
Competing Interests

Adolescent Turmoil

The Social Origins of Adolescence
The Social Problems of Adolescence

The Later Years

Attitudes Toward Aging and the Elderly
The Negative Consequences of Aging

Poverty and Underemployment
Housing Problems
Victimization of the Elderly

Problems and Prospects

Age and aging are biological facts. We begin to age the moment we are born. Nothing we do—no exercise program or diet—can accelerate or stop the clock. Age limits the social roles people are capable of playing. A three-year-old simply cannot be a wet nurse, a stevedore, or a brain surgeon. For different physiological reasons, these roles are also closed to ninety-year-olds. Thus, a certain amount of inequality is biologically determined.

The social meanings attached to age and aging extend well beyond the obvious physiological limitations, however. All societies put age to social use, elaborating on the biological facts of life. In Western societies, we divide the life cycle into stages: childhood, adolescence, young adulthood, middle and old age. Among other things, age determines whether you can vote or serve on a jury; whether you can legally drive a car, purchase cigarettes, buy beer, or get married; whether you are required to go to school or forced to retire. Murderers are not sent to prison if they are below a certain age; college students do not pay full tuition if they are over sixty-five (Riley and Waring, 1976, p. 357). Informal norms limit behavior further. For example, we consider adults who enjoy sexual relations to be normal. But a ten-year-old with an intense interest in sex is considered a problem child, and the thought of an eighty-year-old enjoying sex is embarrassing to many people. These concepts of age-appropriateness are social, not biological. There is a good deal of social pressure to "act one's age."

Formal and informal norms establish a system of age stratification. People are divided into separate and unequal strata according to their ages. The roles they are allowed and expected to play, the privileges they enjoy, are determined in part by their birthday. The inequalities that result go well beyond biological decrees.

This system of social stratification rests on *ageism:* the belief that denying people certain rights and responsibilities because of their age is biologically justified. In some ways, ageism is like racism and sexism. Age is an ascribed status. People have no control over it, and it is marked by physical characteristics that are difficult to change or disguise. Like racism and sexism, it affects all members of society and is woven into all social institutions. People are expected to act their age whether they are rich or poor, black or white, male or female, bright or slow. Age is used to define roles in the family, at school, at work, and at play. In some ways, however, age-linked status is different from race- and sex-linked status. Whereas race and gender are immutable (with the rare exception of sex change operations), a person's age keeps changing. People move from one stage in the life cycle, from one position in the age hierarchy, to the next, in sequence. No one escapes age stratification. Ageism is one form of discrimination that everyone experiences.

Socially constructed inequality explains only some of the social problems that are associated with age and aging. The succession of *cohorts,* or generations, also creates problems. Members of the same cohort have common experiences, which members of other cohorts do not share. Age cohorts move through history together. It is useful to think of the aging process as an escalator (Riley, Johnson, and Foner, 1972): Each cohort steps onto the escalator at birth and remains on the same step as the escalator moves from childhood to adolescence and on toward old age. The escalator keeps moving as new cohorts step on at the bottom and aged cohorts step off at the top. Historical events affect everyone on the escalator. But because of cohorts' relative positions on the escalator, events influence them differently. The Vietnam war, for example, affected everyone, but its impact on ten-, twenty-, thirty-, forty-, and fifty-year-olds was quite different. During the Great Depression, it was one thing to be a young adult, ready and eager to start a family, but another to be a child or an old person. The costs and advantages of being in a particular position on the escalator depend on historical circumstances.

The size of a cohort can make a significant difference. The 64 million infants born between 1946 and 1961—the so-called baby-boom generation—were by far the largest cohort in the nation's history (see Figure 12–1). Now in their twenties and thirties, members of this cohort make up a third of the U.S. population. Just as they crowded maternity wards, elementary schools, high schools, and colleges in years past, they are now pushing into the job and housing markets. The sheer size of this cohort created a marriage squeeze in the 1960s: Because women usually marry men a few years older than themselves and because there were more women in the baby-boom cohort than there were men in the preceding cohort, the number of women seeking husbands exceeded the number of eligible men. The marriage squeeze was one reason why in the 1960s, more women in the United States delayed starting a family and went to work—a change that has affected all of society. The high crime rates of the 1970s also resulted in part from the huge number of men in the crime-prone years (fifteen to twenty-four). If only because of its numbers, this cohort's experiences and opportunities at different ages are quite different from their parents' and children's experiences.

Because of its particular history, each cohort is in some ways unique—a fact that contributes to intergenerational conflict. Different encounters with history result in a "stratification of experience" (Mannheim, in Elder, 1975, p. 169). Value differences that result from parents' and children's different positions in the life cycle are compounded by value differences that result from their unique experiences. To some extent, parents try to socialize their offspring to an adolescence that existed twenty or thirty years before. Their children have difficulty imagining, for example, a world without television, fast food, or environmental consciousness.

Figure 12–1

The Baby Boom and Bust: U.S. Births from 1940 to 1980 (in millions)

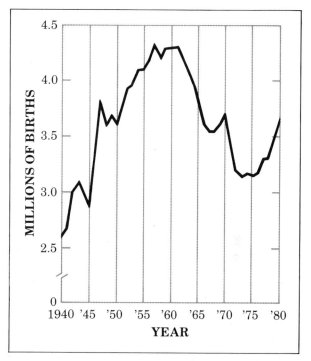

Source: U.S. Bureau of the Census, *Current Population Reports,* Series P-60 (Washington D.C.: U.S. Government Printing Office, 1981), and earlier issues.

In this chapter, we will examine social problems that result both from ageism and age stratification and from differences in the effects of history on different age cohorts. We focus on the two most disadvantaged strata in U.S. society—youth and old age. In the first section, we will look at the causes and consequences of changing attitudes toward children, and we will consider whether children are a privileged class in the United States. In the next section, we will put adolescence in sociological perspective and show how much of the turmoil of adolescence is socially structured. In the sections on the later years, we will look first at ageist attitudes and then at the special problems of growing old in a society that is designed for a young population. In the final section, we will consider solutions to the problems of age inequality, segregation, and conflict.

The Early Years: Childhood and Adolescence

Two recent rulings highlight a major source of controversy over the position of young people in U.S. society—the conflict between children's rights and children's needs. In July 1976, the U.S. Supreme Court held that children under the age of eighteen need not have parental consent in order to obtain an abortion (*Planned Parenthood* v. *Danforth*, 1976). This ruling reflected the movement toward granting young people the same rights as adults—in this case, the right to make their own decisions regarding reproduction. Also in 1976, in response to a complaint filed by Action for Children's Television, the Federal Trade Commission ruled that a drug company must stop advertising a "super-vitamin." The decision was based on the belief that "children are unqualified by age or experience to decide themselves whether or not they need or should use" the product (Stier, 1978, p. 46). One ruling views children as autonomous; the other views them as dependent. These conflicting views suggest that in American society, childhood and adolescence have become social issues.

Children's Rights

Contemporary child advocacy is part of the movement toward granting full rights to groups that have been discriminated against in the past (Feshbach and Feshbach, 1978). It is an extension of the fight against unequal treatment of blacks, women, and other minorities. Indeed, these groups used to be denied full rights in part because they were alleged to have childlike qualities. Children, like members of other minorities,

have been denied the right to vote, subjected to special laws (statutory laws that make it a crime for someone under eighteen to drink, smoke, or engage in other activities that are not illegal for adults), shut out of the labor market, and segregated (in schools). There is an important difference with children, however. Quite simply, they are not adults. They do not have the physical or intellectual skills, the experience, and the judgment of adults. But neither are they entirely helpless.

The history of childhood The emergence of childhood as a social issue took place barely a hundred years ago (Takanishi, 1978). The concept of childhood as a special and important stage in life did not exist during the Middle Ages (Ariès, 1962). Children were fully integrated into the adult world. They were put to work as soon as they were physically able. No one thought it necessary to protect them from the facts of life—from birth, death, and sex. There were no special children's games, stories, or social events. In fifteenth-century paintings, children of six and seven years of age are depicted as miniature adults, with the same physical proportions, the same style of dress, and the same facial expressions as grown-ups. The belief that children have special natures and needs can be traced to the sixteenth century. Renaissance thinkers portrayed the child as an innocent who required separation and protection from the adult world. By the eighteenth century, most upper-class families had accepted this view. Lower-class children, however, remained part of the adult world through most of the nineteenth century. Late in the nineteenth century in the United States, attitudes toward children began to change. A growing literature depicted children as the redeemers of society—the torchbearers to the civilization of the future. The saying "a little child shall lead them" captured this mood.

In the United States, the period from about

The Class of 1911, South Pittston, Pennsylvania. Until the 1930s there was no law against putting young children to work in the mines, factories, or fields.

1880 to 1914 has been described as the child-saving era (Takanishi, 1978). In this period, changing images of childhood were translated into organized efforts. In the years following the Civil War, industrialization, urbanization, and immigration caused profound and visible changes in U.S. society. The child-saving movement originated among members of the upper and middle classes, who were alarmed by the growing numbers of immigrant children who roamed city streets in unsupervised bands or who worked long hours as street peddlers and in factories. The reality of these children's lives contrasted sharply with the new image of childhood as a unique and formative period in life. The first juvenile court was established in Chicago in 1899, on the theory that children were not wholly responsible for their own behavior and should be rehabilitated, not punished. Judges were given far more discretion in juvenile courts than in adult courts. Child labor laws were passed. The public school system was expanded and education made compulsory. Campaigns promoted the use of clean (pasteurized) milk and the need to build playgrounds and establish fresh air camps for city children. The child-saving movement itself was professionalized, and many new specialized careers (such as pediatrics) were established.

It is tempting to see changes in attitudes toward and treatment of children as a steady march of progress. Children have received more and more rights, more enlightened care at home, and the services of more specialized agencies and professions. In fact, however, the child-saving era left a problematic legacy (Takanishi, 1978). Many late nineteenth- and early twentieth-century reforms created problems and are themselves subjects of contemporary reform. In 1907, Alfred Binet invented an objective measure of mental ability in an attempt to reform the arbitrary placement of children in institutions. Today, the use of intelligence tests based on Binet's model is highly controversial: Critics argue that these tests discriminate against minority children, whose experiences and vocabularies differ from those of middle-class children. The juvenile court system, designed to give young people special protection, is now being accused of depriving juveniles of basic rights. At the turn of the century, reformers advocated special classes for handicapped youngsters. Today, reformers maintain that segregation stigmatizes these children and advocate putting them into regular classrooms. Reformers fought for almost forty years for laws that would ban child labor. Today, the integration of school and work, especially for adolescents, is a major educational issue (Coleman et al., 1974). Thus, well-intentioned reforms created unanticipated problems for children and for society.

In recent times, the focus has shifted from children's needs to children's rights. Child liberationists, who would like to see children obtain the equal rights that blacks, women, and other minorities have been seeking, have joined child savers, who want the state to assume a broader role in intervening in the family on the child's behalf, on the debating platform. Current debate focuses on children's right to legal representation, informed consent to medical procedures and participation in research, normalizing the lives of handicapped children, and self-determination in custody disputes. Questions have been raised about adoption policies, child labor laws, compulsory schooling, school desegregation, intelligence testing, and consumer rights in education. Should children have the right to choose between parents in a divorce case? Should they have the right to obtain birth control information and devices? Should they have the right to decide whether to attend school or look for work? At what age are children capable of making responsible choices?

Competing interests One reason the issues of children's rights are so difficult to resolve is because they involve the often-competing interests of parents, children, and the state. In our society, parents have the right and the responsibility to raise their children as they see fit. Parental autonomy is firmly established in the law. Unless parents do something terribly wrong, no one has the right to take their children away from them, and children do not have the right to remove themselves from their parents' home. The doctrine of parental autonomy is based on the belief that the parent-child bond is special and inherently beneficial. At the same time, the state has the right and the responsibility to intervene if it decides that children are being abused or neglected. The doctrine of state responsibility dates back to the child-saving era. It is based on the belief that children are vulnerable and dependent and therefore require special protection. In addition, children themselves have rights in relation to their families and the state. The doctrine of children's rights is new, and it seems to be gaining popular support.

Often parents', children's, and state's rights conflict. Consider adoption. In most jurisdictions, children cannot be adopted without their biological parents' consent. As a result, many abandoned children are placed in temporary foster care rather than in permanent, adoptive homes. Should the state put parents' rights to their offspring ahead of children's rights to a family?

Who Defines "Neglect" and "Abuse"?

There is tension . . . in the definition of danger to children, and who defines it. Every state has some kind of child-abuse or -neglect law that confers broad authority on public agencies and courts to intervene in family life in the interests of children who are threatened by neglect or abuse by their parents. Under these laws, parents can be criminally prosecuted for their conduct and children can be removed from their homes. Very often no clear standards are stated as to what constitutes "neglect" or even "abuse." . . . All too often, an arrogant state legal apparatus invokes the doctrine that the parents are "neglecting" their children and removes the children without attempting to give the family the supportive help it needs—for example, the money to buy food, pay the rent, or pay the homemaker who could care temporarily for the children while the parent recuperates from illness or goes out to look for a job. Even conscientious social workers and court personnel often have no power to command the tangible resources that might help the family continue intact. All they have is the coarsest implement: removal of the child.

This means that well-intentioned and even not-so-well-intentioned courts and social workers, acting in the "best interests of the child," can impose their norms of morality and upbringing upon families. Families live differently from one another, they treat children differently, they expect different standards of behavior, and they punish differently. Most families accused of abuse and neglect are minority families with low incomes, often one-parent families. Judges and court personnel, on the other hand, generally come from quite another social, economic, and ideological world. Behavior that may be quite normal in another social milieu may be shocking to them in terms of their own, and as a result they can be too quick to condemn and not eager enough to invest time and attention in trying to help. Moreover, they can, ironically, be blind to the deficiencies in institutional alternatives to which they send children. Some juvenile judges have never visited the local orphanages, foundling homes, shelter homes, or detention facilities to which they consign children every week.

Source: Kenneth Keniston and the Carnegie Council on Children, *All Our Children: The American Family under Pressure* (New York: Harcourt Brace Jovanovich, 1978), pp. 186–87.

Should adopted children be allowed to know who their biological parents are? (Until recently, the files in most states were sealed.) Consider child abuse. In the United States, every state has the legal right to remove a battered child from his or her family for the child's protection. But to protect parents' rights, the burden of proof is on the state: It does not intervene in cases of suspected or potential family abuse, and there is no clear and absolute distinction between acceptable physical punishment and child abuse. Often a child is battered by a parent who had the idea of enforcing discipline. Why should parents be allowed to treat children in ways that would be considered criminal if the person were an adult? Should abused children be given a say in their own cases? Often youngsters want to return to the home in which they were abused.

The task of balancing such competing interests falls to the courts. In the landmark *Gault* decision (1967), the U.S. Supreme Court declared that "neither the Fourteenth Amendment nor the Bill of Rights is for adults only." It was the first time that the Court had affirmed the constitutional standing of minors. The case involved a fifteen-year-old who had been arrested for allegedly making obscene phone calls, and then held without his parents' being notified. Even though the complainant failed to appear at the hearing, the boy was sent to a reform school for the remainder of his minority (until age twenty-one). Two years later, in a case involving the right of high-school students to protest the Vietnam war by wearing armbands (*Tinker* v. *Des Moines,* 1969), the Supreme Court declared that under the Constitution, children are "persons." More recently, the Court noted, "Constitutional rights do not mature and come into being magically only when one attains the state-defined age of majority" (*Planned Parenthood* v. *Danworth,* 1976).

These rulings, however, are not part of a general movement toward granting equal rights to children as a class (Stier, 1978). Rather, the courts have granted certain children limited rights in a piecemeal fashion. For example, the *Gault* decision extended to juveniles the procedural rights normally given to adults in criminal proceedings, including notice of the charge, the right to counsel, the privilege to refuse to give self-incriminating testimony, and the right to cross-examine witnesses. But the courts have not given children equal rights with respect to search and seizure, grand jury indictments, trial by jury, release on bail, or public trials. The ruling in *Brown* v. *Board of Education* (1954), which banned segregated schools, has been interpreted as asserting that children have a basic right to education. In another ruling, however, the Court held that Amish parents have a right to prevent their children from attending high school, thus placing the parents' right to religious freedom above children's right to education (*Wisconsin* v. *Yoder,* 1972). Children's rights remain a gray area of the law. The contest between parents', children's, and the state's interests is far from decided.

Adolescent Turmoil

In industrial Western societies, adolescents are essentially marginal people. The term "marginal man" was coined by Robert C. Park to describe the dilemma of second-generation Americans who spoke one language and followed one set of cultural rules at home, but another in school or on the job, and who did not feel at home in either world. By analogy, adolescents have one foot in the adult world and one foot in childhood and do not feel entirely comfortable or accepted in either world. One minute, parents and teachers expect them to behave like adults; the next minute, they expect them to accept childish limitations on their behavior (curfews, classroom rules, and so on). Like immigrants, adolescents are new arrivals—not to a geographical territory, but to the social territory dominated by their elders. As the anthropologist Ruth Benedict pointed out (1938), adolescents in the United States face sharp discontinuities. American culture defines childhood and adulthood in terms of opposites. Children are supposed to play and act carefree; adults are expected to work and assume responsibilities. Children are supposed to be obedient; adults are supposed to be dominant. Children are supposed to be sexless; adults are supposed to be sexually competent and active. In order to become adults, adolescents face the task of *un*learning, or reversing, the behavior patterns they learned in childhood. Their position is at very least ambiguous. Many adolescents suffer from what Kurt Lewin called "uncertainty of belongingness" (in Brody, 1968).

The social origins of adolescence The adolescent is frequently described as an intellectual and emotional child with the body of an adult. This implies that teen-agers' troubles are the direct result of the physiological changes that occur at puberty. Cross-cultural studies show that sexual development does not necessarily create psychological conflicts (Mead, 1928). The transition from childhood to adulthood is not necessarily stormy. Puberty is a biological phenomenon, but adolescence as we know it is a social invention. In many traditional societies, young people assume the economic and social responsibilities of adulthood gradually. Children begin working as soon as they are physically able; no one stops them from playing sexual games. Hence, there are none of the sharp discontinuities that Benedict saw in American culture. With regard to occupation and life style, young people in traditional societies do not face the dazzling array of choices that young people in Western industrial societies face. They can assume that their lives will closely resemble their parents' lives. In a sense, their social identities are ready-made.

In some traditional societies, the age at which people are allowed to assume different rights and responsibilities is clearly defined. The move from one age-grade to the next is marked by rituals, changes in dress and residence, and so on. Thus, age-grades are stable and institutionalized. There is no question of where a person belongs—no "uncertainty of belongingness." In our society, there is. Young people can anticipate leading quite different lives than their parents led. Indeed, their parents may expect and pressure them to "get ahead in life." As a result, parents cannot serve as experienced guides to the future. Because of cohort-historical differences, adolescents are largely on their own in forming an identity.

In the United States, social concern for adolescents dates back to the middle of the nineteenth century (Demos and Demos, 1973, pp. 212–28). During this period, experts began to talk of a stage between childhood and adulthood and to describe youth as a critical transition period, during which an individual's character takes permanent shape. By implication, teen-agers were exceptionally vulnerable. Driven by "wild desires" and "restless cravings" from within, youth was presented with a host of "seductive temptations" from without. Early in the twentieth century, the psychologist G. Stanley Hall published a monumental work (1904) in which he characterizes adolescence as a period of inevitable "storm and stress." Hall recommended a moratorium on adult responsibilities for adolescents, so that they could work through their rebelliousness and establish independent identities.

A number of economic and social factors contributed to the institutionalization of adolescence as a special stage in life. The rapid industrialization and urbanization of American society in the late nineteenth and early twentieth centuries put an end to the tradition of family members working together as a unit. When the society was rural and agricultural, occupations passed from father to son, and one generation's experiences were much the same as those of the next. Industrialization greatly increased the number of specialized occupations and the years of training required to fill them. These changes created a gap between parents' and children's experiences and made the teen years a time for choosing an occupation. The teen years took on a new significance. Compulsory education and child labor laws widened the gap between generations, creating a separate world for children and adolescents.

The gap between adolescence and adulthood has steadily widened, for two reasons (Coleman et al., 1974, pp. 127–30). First, the number of years young people spend in school has increased. As a result, adolescents are segregated from people of different ages for an extended period, and this prolonged schooling results in prolongated dependency; adult responsibilities and accomplishments are withheld for an extended period. Outside school, adolescents have relatively few opportunities to interact with adults in work situations. Their relationships with adults tend to be specialized and limited. As a rule, adolescents do not get to know their teachers personally; they interact with them only in their role as teacher. They know their parents only as parents, not in their work roles. Moreover, they are segregated with peers of their exact age. They have few opportunities to develop relationships with younger children or with old people. (That families are small and siblings close together in age further limits contacts.) This segregation of adolescents contributes to the development of a distinctive youth culture. Many young people see themselves as "outsiders" who have little connection with the "system" or "establishment."

Second, the options available to adolescents have shifted. Young people may have more opportunities than their parents had to study, travel, and indulge their tastes for music, entertainment, and clothes. But young people have many fewer opportunities for employment. The option to do responsible work outside the home has been deferred to the end of an ever-increasing period of schooling. Adolescents may work after school or during summer vacations, but most challenging jobs now require a college, or even a graduate or a professional, degree. The gap between the kinds of jobs that are available to teen-agers and the kinds available to educated adults has widened.

The social problems of adolescence A number of problems that popular wisdom attributes to the "hot-bloodedness" of teen-agers in fact reflect social forces. In particular, the segregation of young people in schools and their exclusion from the labor market have a negative impact. Adolescents who do not do well in school or get along well with their families have few alternatives.

Consider runaways. Young people are expected to live in their parents' home until they are in their late teens or early twenties. Runaways violate the norms by leaving home early and without parental consent. In 1979, police took 164,400 into custody (*The New York Times*, July 21, 1981), but the actual number of runaways is probably much higher. The National Statistical Survey on Runaway Youth found that in 1975, 733,000 youths aged ten to seventeen ran away from home for at least one night (Opinion Research Corporation, 1976). The percentages of males and females were about equal. Children from low-income and single-parent homes were over-represented, but runaways came from the entire spectrum of American families. Most of the children did not go far from home (less than ten miles) or stay away for very long (less than three days). But 18 percent traveled fifty miles or more, and 16 percent were gone longer than a month.

Running away is not a passing fad; it is part of this nation's history (Libertoff, 1980). Many of the first immigrants to America were runaways. Labor was in short supply in the American colonies (unlike today). Shipping children to the colonies as indentured servants, bound to work until age seventeen or eighteen, was a convenient solution to the growing problem of street urchins and orphans in England's big cities. Once here, young people who found their positions as indentured servants or as apprentices intolerable solved the problem by running away. Colonial newspapers were filled with descriptions of runaways, who could be severely punished for their crime. (One of the most illustrious runaways in our history was Benjamin Franklin, who escaped apprenticeship to an older brother in Boston by talking his way onto a ship bound for New York City.) Later, the Revolutionary War and Civil War and the Western frontier provided escape hatches. In the late nineteenth and early twentieth centuries, the big city, with its promise of factory jobs, became a magnet for farm children; and during the Great Depression, bands of runaway youngsters roamed the nation. Runaways faded from national consciousness in the 1940s and 1950s but returned with the counterculture youth movement of the 1960s. "It was a new consciousness . . . drawing together all the freaky, hip, unhappy, young, happy, curious, criminal, gentle, alienated, weird, frustrated, far-out, artistic, lonely, lovely people to the same place at the same time" (Rubin, 1970, p. 56). What was different about the runaways of the 1960s was that so many of them came from comfortable middle- and upper-class homes.

Studies conducted in the 1970s identified three types of runaways (Nye, 1980). Perhaps 20 percent of them were running *to* something. They had positive reasons for leaving home: They sought adventure, new people, new places, and new experiences. In a sense, they were victims of the cloistering of young people in school, where they do not learn what it is like to work at a menial job or survive on the streets. They accepted the media's idealized image of the world out there and went looking for their dream. About 75 percent of runaways were running *from* something. They were escaping conflict with parents, rejection and alienation at school. Often they talked in terms of relative deprivation or injustice. They were receiving more trouble (lectures, restrictions, punishment) than they felt they should re-

ceive or more than other young people received. A third group (roughly 5 percent of runaways) were "pushouts." They wanted to leave home, but they did not think that the adult world offered anything better than what they had. Their parents would have liked to be rid of them but found no socially acceptable (or legal) way in which to unload them. These parents and youths lived "in a state of mutual alienation, rejection, and conflict" (Nye, 1980, p. 291).

What are the consequences of running away? The social costs are high. In 1978, Congress appropriated $11 million for programs for runaways (Nye, 1980, p. 293). Robberies, assaults, drug pushing, prostitution, and other criminal behavior add millions of dollars to this price tag. To estimate the cost to individuals, one group of researchers compared young people who had run away twelve years earlier to their siblings who had not run away (Olson et al., 1980). Only a small number of former runaways were located and interviewed, but the results of the survey suggest that the runaways suffered from compound social disabilities. Many had been labeled "dumb," "lazy," or "troublesome" at an early age and had responded by staying away from school, ignoring homework, and becoming detached or hostile in school—thereby worsening their problems. Entering the world of work proved to be difficult for the former runaways. Less than half of them were regularly employed. Whereas their siblings had pursued a single line of work with evident success, they had moved from one dead-end job to another and were frequently fired. Middle-class runaways especially felt a deep sense of failure. In young adulthood as in childhood, the former runaways had had troubled relationships with their parents. They felt a lingering sense of bitterness, as if they were still getting the short end of the stick. The former runaways traced conflict with parents back to conflict over school performance. Their parents traced it back farther, describing these young people as having been difficult to get along with as babies. The former runaways' relationships with members of the opposite sex seemed to recreate these conflicts: "[D]emands made by spouses seemed much like those they faced earlier in the family of origin: find a better job, make more money, 'wear a suit and tie,' do this, do that. To the runaway each new demand . . . revived old feelings that the runaway did not measure up" (Olson et al., 1980, pp. 180–81). All of the former runaways, but none of their siblings, had had run-ins with the law for offenses ranging from being drunk and disorderly to assault and battery. Ironically, the young people who most wanted independence – those who ran away – were found to be less free: Because they lacked skills, education, and on-the-job training, they had become more dependent on their parents than were their conforming siblings.

Juvenile delinquency, like the problem of runaways, can be linked to adolescents' peculiar position in the social structure. In the 1960s and 1970s, juvenile crime rates climbed steadily, then leveled off. Juveniles account for 22.5 percent of all arrests recorded by law-enforcement agencies and for almost 39 percent of arrests for serious crimes (murder, rape, robbery, aggravated assault, burglary, larceny, motor vehicle theft, and arson) (*The New York Times,* July 24, 1981, p. B4). More serious and violent crimes are committed by young people – especially young urban male members of minorities – than by any other age group. Rising juvenile crime rates reflect population changes. Because there are proportionately more young people in the population today, there are more arrests of juveniles. But this is only part of the explanation. Adolescents in the United States do seem to be prone to crime. Arrest rates accelerate after age ten, peak in the late teens, and decline gradually over the remaining stages of the life cycle (see Figure 12–2).

High juvenile crime rates have added another voice to the chorus that is debating the position of young people in American society. During the child-saving era, juveniles were given a special status under the law. The creation of a special juvenile court system was based on the belief that young people should not be fully accountable for their actions and that young offenders should be treated and cared for rather than punished. Certain special legal restrictions were placed on young people during this period. Juveniles are required by law to obey their parents and other authorities, to attend school, to observe curfews, and the like. This special legal position for young people has been questioned in recent years from both the political right and the political left. As noted above, child liberationists argue that the system that is designed to protect young people in fact penalizes them for being young. According to this view, both the juvenile court system and statutory laws deny young people basic rights. At the same time, however, the public is asking for protection *from* violent youthful offenders and for "adult" punishments for serious crimes. Thus, society is faced with contradictory goals: protecting juvenile offenders and protecting their victims (Empey, 1978, p. 138).

Why are adolescents crime-prone? We will discuss theories of crime and violence in detail in Chapter 14. One theory in particular, however, applies to adolescents (Merton, 1938). Teen-agers and adults have many of the same goals; they experience many of the same culturally conditioned desires. But legitimate opportunities for earning money, getting a job with potential for advancement, and starting a family are denied teen-agers. For each generation, the age at which the opportunities for success become available has been postponed a little more. Opportunities have shifted, so that young people remain segregated for a longer period. The result is a high level of anomie, or normlessness. Adolescents respond to the gap between goals and legitimate means of attaining them by seeking illegitimate means of achieving conventional goals and by redefining

Figure 12-2

Arrest Curve by Age

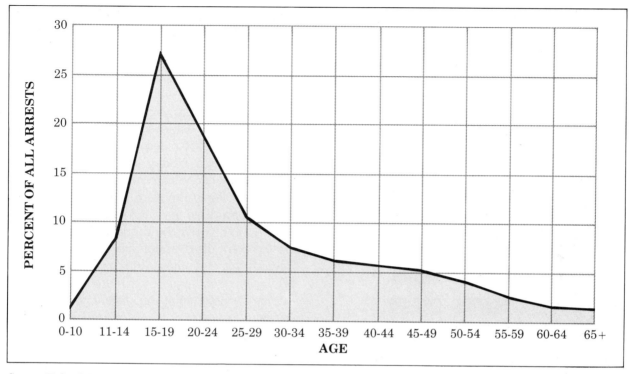

Source: Federal Bureau of Investigation, *Uniform Crime Reports* (Washington, D.C.: U.S. Government Printing Office, 1973), pp. 128–29.

success in terms that often violate adults' norms. Thus, adolescent turmoil may be explained, not as an expression of internal confusion, but as a response to external socially structured frustrations and ambivalence.

The Later Years

The population of the United States is growing older—a phenomenon the media call the graying of America. In 1900, 3 million Americans were sixty-five or older; today, 23 million are, and this number will probably double early in the next century. Over half of the nation's elderly are over age seventy-three. The seventy-five-plus category is growing faster than any other age group. The proportion of older people in the United States is also growing. In 1900, one in thirty persons was over sixty-five; today one in ten is. If current trends continue, in the next century, one in five will be over sixty-five. The median age is rising (see Figure 12–3).

There are two basic reasons why the population is growing older: increases in life expectancy and decreases in the birth rate. Reductions in infant mortality, better nutrition, and improved health care have all contributed to a dramatic increase in life expectancy. A male born in 1920 could expect to live to age fifty-four; a female, to age fifty-six. Today, life expectancy for males has reached seventy-two years; for females, eighty-one years.

Figure 12–3

The Graying of America: Median Age of the U.S. Population, 1970-2030

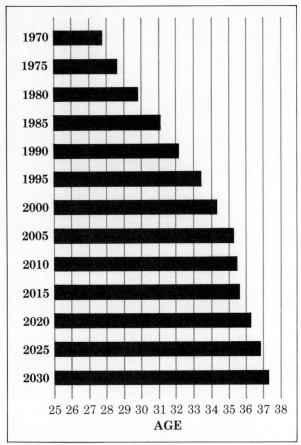

Source: U.S. Bureau of the Census, *Statistical Abstract of the United States, 1977* (Washington, D.C.: U.S. Government Printing Office, 1977).

At the same time, the birth rate has declined. In the late 1940s and in the 1950s (the baby-boom years), the average woman in the United States had three or four babies; today, she has one or two. The number of children aged thirteen and under in the United States actually dropped by nearly 8 million in the 1970s. Improved contraception and legal abortions, the Women's Movement, and changes in life style (especially women's working) all contributed to the current baby bust. With the lower birth rate, the proportion of Americans over the age of sixty-five increases every year. Already, there are as many white-haired Americans as there are black Americans.

Social change has not kept pace with demographic change. Our social system is designed for a younger population. In the 1950s, the nation geared up for the baby-boom generation. Not only were thousands of schools built each year, but teachers' colleges and graduate programs also were expanded. Suddenly there were more trained teachers than were needed. The medical system specialized in infectious and acute diseases that threaten the young and middle aged, not in chronic diseases that affect the aged. Today there are too many hospital beds (primarily used for the young and middle aged) and too few home-nursing services (what the elderly need). Our retirement and Social Security systems are designed for a society in which only a small percentage of the population reaches old age. The problem is that there is a sociocultural lag: The age of the population is changing faster than ideas, behavior, and social institutions are changing, and we have not developed the social apparatus for dealing with the special problems of the elderly. Thus, part of the problem is cultural: a question or norms, values, and beliefs. And part of the problem is structural: The economic system (the distribution of income), the organization of families, and even the way we build cities and suburbs are not designed for a graying population. Let us look first at the cultural side of the problem.

Attitudes Toward Aging and the Elderly

American culture places a high value on youth. Every year, millions of dollars are spent on products that are claimed to delay or disguise the ef-

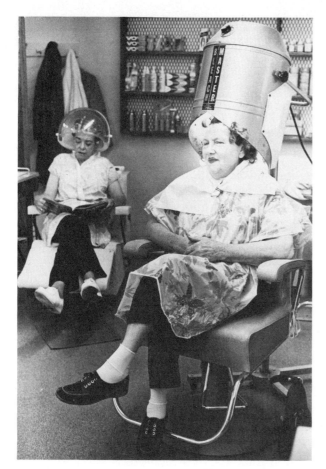

Americans spend millions of dollars in the ultimately vain attempt to preserve youth. In other cultures, the wrinkles of age are thought to be quite beautiful.

fects of aging (face creams, hair dyes, vitamins, exercise programs). We like to think of ours as a young nation, as an energetic, innovative, forward-looking society (all qualities we associate with youth). We tend to think of aging as a process of physical, mental, and social deterioration, beginning at about age thirty. Americans do not have positive images of the elderly. A recent Harris poll indicated that most people in this country think of old people as isolated, ill,

narrow-minded, inefficient, and intellectually impaired (Harris and Associates, 1975). Negative stereotypes of old age have a direct impact on the quality of life. Not only do they influence the way younger people perceive and treat the elderly, but they also influence the way the elderly see themselves.

Perhaps the most damaging stereotype of older people relates to work. Intellectual ability, like physical strength, is thought to decline with age.

The Double Standard of Aging

People in industrial societies are haunted by numbers. They take an almost obsessional interest in keeping the score card of aging, convinced that anything above a low total is some kind of bad news. In an era in which people actually live longer and longer, what now amounts to the latter *two-thirds* of everyone's life is shadowed by a poignant apprehension of remitting loss.

The prestige of youth afflicts everyone in this society to some degree. Men, too, are prone to periodic bouts of depression about aging—for instance, when feeling insecure or unfulfilled or insufficiently rewarded in their jobs. But men rarely panic about aging in the way women often do. Getting older is less profoundly wounding for a man, for in addition to the propaganda for youth that puts both men and women on the defensive as they age, there is a double standard about aging that denounces women with special severity. . . . Men are "allowed" to age, without penalty, in several ways that women are not.

This society offers even fewer rewards for aging to women than it does to men. Being physically attractive counts much more in a woman's life than in a man's, but beauty, identified, as it is for women, with youthfulness, does not stand up well to age. Exceptional mental powers can increase with age, but women are rarely encouraged to develop their minds above dilettante standards. Because the wisdom considered the special province of women is "eternal," an age-old, intuitive knowledge about the emotions to which a repertoire of facts, worldly experience, and the methods of rational analysis have nothing to contribute, living a long time does not promise women an increase in wisdom either. The private skills expected of women are exercised early and, with the exception of a talent for making love, are not the kind that enlarge with experience. "Masculinity" is identified with competence, autonomy, self-control—qualities which the disappearance of youth does not threaten. Competence in most of the activities expected from men, physical sports excepted, increases with age. "Femininity" is identified with incompetence, helplessness, passivity, noncompetitiveness, being nice. Age does not improve these qualities. . . .

To be sure, the calender is subject to some variations from country to country. In Spain, Portugal, and the Latin American countries, the age at which most women are ruled physically undesirable comes earlier than in the United States. In France it is somewhat later. French conventions of sexual feeling make a quasi-official place for the woman between thirty-five and forty-five. Her role is to initiate an inexperienced or timid young man, after which she is, of course, replaced by a young girl. (Colette's novella *Chéri* is the best-known account in fiction of such a love affair; biographies of Balzac relate a well-documented example from real life.) This sexual myth does make turning forty somewhat easier for French women. But there is no difference in any of these countries in the basic attitudes that disqualify women sexually much earlier than men.

Aging also varies according to social class. Poor people look old much earlier in their lives than do rich people. But anxiety about aging is certainly more common, and more acute, among middle-class and rich women than among working-class women. Economically disadvantaged women in this society are more fatalistic about aging; they can't afford to fight the cosmetic battle as long or as tenaciously. Indeed, nothing so clearly indicates the fictional nature of this crisis than the fact that women who keep their youthful appearance the longest—women who lead unstrenuous, physically sheltered lives, who eat balanced meals, who can afford good medical care, who have few or no children—are those who feel the defeat of age most keenly. Aging is much more a social judgment than a biological eventuality. Far more extensive than the hard sense of loss suffered during menopause (which, with increased longevity, tends to arrive later and later) is the depression about aging, which may not be set off by any real event in a woman's life, but is a recurrent state of "possession" of her imagination, ordained by society—that is, ordained by the way this society limits how women feel free to imagine themselves.

Source: Susan Sontag, "The Double Standard of Aging," *Saturday Review,* September 23, 1972. Copyright 1972 Saturday Review, Inc.

Studies conducted ten and twenty years ago support this view. Recent, more exacting studies, however, do not (Baltes and Schaie, 1974). Not only did these studies find no evidence of a decline in intelligence with age, but they found systematic increases in intelligence. A person's crystallized intelligence (accumulated skills and knowledge) and visualization (ability to organize visual materials) continue to improve into the seventies; cognitive flexibility (the ability to shift from one way of thinking to another) remains stable over the years; only visuomotor flexibility (coordination) declines slightly.

Nevertheless, negative stereotypes can become self-fulfilling prophecies (Merton, 1968). If the elderly accept the negative stereotypes of the effects of age on intelligence, they are less likely to seek intellectual challenges—less likely to read, enroll in a class, or debate their youngers. For lack of exercise and information, their intellectual powers may, in fact, decline, thus fulfilling the prophecy. The same is true for other stereotypes. Only a small percentage of older people become senile, lose their sight and hearing, find they have nothing to do in retirement, lose interest in friends, lose interest in sex, want to live with their grown children, or become financially dependent on their children. But many Americans believe these myths to be true. As a result, ordinary lapses in memory such as people have at all ages may be taken as signs of senility. Given the competition for jobs, housing, and other valuables in our society, it is convenient for young and middle-aged adults if old people do believe that they are enfeebled and so withdraw from activities.

The Negative Consequences of Aging

Ageism is not the only source of problems for the elderly in the United States. The growing size of the cohort that is over sixty-five years of age creates problems for which there are no historical precedents. More people than ever before live beyond age sixty-five. When a relatively small percentage of the population lived to a ripe old age (3 percent in 1900), the nation could afford to revere the elderly. Old people were scarce and special. When 10 or 20 percent of the population lives beyond age sixty-five (the projection for the early twenty-first century), the situation changes. Rather suddenly, old people begin to compete with younger people for income and living space. The expectation that most people will retire gracefully at age sixty-five and spend their golden years in a rocking chair, waiting for visits by grandchildren, is unrealistic. One-tenth of the population cannot be put on the shelf and brought out for family holidays. Unless the nation adjusts to the new demographic profile, many Americans can look forward to spending the last ten, twenty, or even thirty years of their lives in relative or absolute poverty, inadequate housing, and fear.

Poverty and underemployment In 1900, two out of three men sixty-five and over held jobs; today, only one out of four does. The percentage of older women who work has increased, but the percentage is still small—about 10 percent (Butler, 1975, p. 68). There is little question that older workers are discriminated against. In 1965, the U.S. Department of Labor estimated that 50 percent of available job openings were closed to applicants over the age of fifty-five. Indeed, 25 percent of the job openings were closed to applicants over the age of forty-five. The 1967 Federal Age Discrimination Act, which bans age discrimination in hiring, firing, pay, and other terms of employment (except for specified occupations, such as airline pilot), may have eased the situation somewhat. However, proving that a company has refused to hire or promote someone solely because of his or her age is difficult, and counting the number of workers who have been subtly pressured out of their jobs also is difficult. We do know that men who lose their jobs when they are between the ages of forty-five and sixty-five stay unemployed longer than do younger workers (Schulz, 1976, pp. 54–56).*

Most Americans expect to stop working in their later years, but there is considerable debate about the age at which a person should retire and about whether retirement should be mandatory or flexible and voluntary. Although the age for mandatory retirement has been raised from sixty-five to seventy, debate continues. Supporters of mandatory retirement argue that it assures everyone of equal treatment. Opponents argue that chronological age is an arbitrary measure of ability and that mandatory retirement discriminates against competent, able older workers. Supporters argue that a fixed retirement age opens opportunities for jobs and promotions to young people. Opponents ask why young people have more right to a job than elderly people have. Supporters argue that younger workers are more productive than older workers. Opponents point out that with the exception of certain physically demanding and time-paced jobs, older workers have been found to perform as well as their juniors. Indeed, considerable evidence shows that older workers are more dependable than younger workers and have fewer absences and accidents (Harris and Cole, 1980, pp. 249–50).

If present trends continue, mandatory retirement may become an academic issue. Between 1964 and 1974, the number of American workers who chose to retire before the age of sixty-five tripled. Moreover, not all workers are told when to retire. About fifty-four of every one hundred wage and salary workers in the United States are subject to mandatory retirement. Of these, thirty

retire before they reach the required age. Of the twenty-four still working, ten are willing to retire at sixty-five, and four are unable to continue working. Of the ten who are willing and able to work, three find jobs. Thus, only seven of every one hundred workers are actually forced to retire. Who continues working beyond the age of sixty-five? Managers, proprietors, and people in sales, service, and agriculture—occupations with high levels of self-employment and part-time job opportunities. The most common reasons given for retirement are deteriorating health and pension benefits (Schulz, 1976, p. 55).

Retirement almost always means a sharp drop in income. The median income of elderly families is about half that of families whose members are under sixty-five. The median income of elderly people who live alone or with non-relatives is about two-fifths that of older couples. The proportion of older people living below the poverty line has been dropping steadily for over a decade. Nevertheless, the numbers are high. If one counts the elderly people who are near poor, who are poor but live with relatives whose incomes are above the poverty line, and who are institutionalized, about 7 million people aged sixty-five and over live below or near the poverty line. Elderly blacks are about three times as likely to be living in poverty as elderly whites, with elderly black women at the bottom of the scale (Harris and Cole, 1980, pp. 321–24).

Most older people in the United States are not living in absolute poverty. Indeed, the average age of millionaires in the United States is sixty (Harris and Cole, 1980, p. 324). Nevertheless, most retired Americans experience relative deprivation. They are poorer than they were before they retired. And most of them live near the edge financially. A serious or chronic illness or a sharp downward turn in the economy would push them beyond their means, forcing them to become dependent on their families or on government aid. One retiree described it this way:

---

*Women now between the ages of forty-five and sixty-five are less likely than others to have worked full time most of their lives and more likely to become discouraged about looking for work. As a result, they are underrepresented in unemployment data.

I don't is a most accurate description of the older adult living in retirement. I don't entertain. I don't go out with friends. I don't eat in restaurants. I don't go to movies. I don't buy new clothes. I don't ride subways and buses. I don't buy cake. I don't eat a lot. I don't take care of my health like I should. I don't, I don't, I don't. (Quoted in Fitzpatrick, 1975, p. 131)

Seventy percent of older individuals and 50 percent of older couples depend on Social Security for at least half their income (see Table 12–1). Social Security was designed during the Great Depression to give workers old-age insurance. Over the years, benefits were extended to dependents and survivors, and disability insurance and Medicare were added to the program. The basic benefits under Social Security are based on a worker's

average earnings over a period of years. In 1979, the maximum monthly benefit for a worker retiring at age sixty-five was $553.30; the minimum, $121.80; and the average, $283. Since 1972, payments have been adjusted each year for cost-of-living increases. The basic benefit is paid to workers retiring at age sixty-five. It is reduced for people who claim Social Security benefits at age sixty-two (the minimum age) and increased slightly for those who do not collect until after age seventy-two. There is also an earnings ceiling on Social Security. In 1980, the benefit for someone between sixty-five and seventy-two years of age was reduced $1 for every $2 he or she earned over $5,000. (After age seventy-two, there is no earnings ceiling.) Couples are treated as a unit under Social Security. In 1979, the maximum benefit to a married couple was $278 less than the maximum benefits to two single individuals.

The Social Security system was created when the proportion of older people in the United States was smaller than it is today. It is not a savings plan that sets aside a portion of younger workers' earnings for their future retirement. Rather, Social Security transfers money from the younger working population to the older retired population by means of a payroll tax. In 1945, there were thirty-five wage earners for every recipient; today there are only three (see Figure 12–4). To maintain benefits, the government has raised both the tax rate and the amount of income taxed. In 1945, the basic tax rate was 1 percent of the first $3,000 of earned income. The most any worker had to pay was $30 a year. In 1981, the basic tax rate was 6.65 percent of the first $29,700, and the most any worker paid was $1,975.05 a year. Even so, the fund is running short. The combination of high unemployment rates and prolonged schooling reduces the number of workers contributing to the system; the growing trend toward early retirement adds to the number of people drawing benefits, further burdening the system. When the baby-boom gen-

Table 12–1
Income Sources for Older Americans

	Percentage with Income from Designated Source	
Income Source	Family	Unrelated Individual
Social Security and railroad retirement	90.9%	90.1%
Personal assets (interest, dividends, rent)	64.4	53.8
Wages or salary	41.7	13.5
Private, military, and federal employee pensions	35.7	22.9
Veterans, unemployment, and workmen's compensation	12.3	8.6
Supplementary security income	8.4	13.9

Source: National Council on the Aging, Inc., *Fact Book on Aging: A Profile of America's Older Population* (Washington, D.C., 1978), p. 56.

Figure 12-4
The Social Burdens of Aging

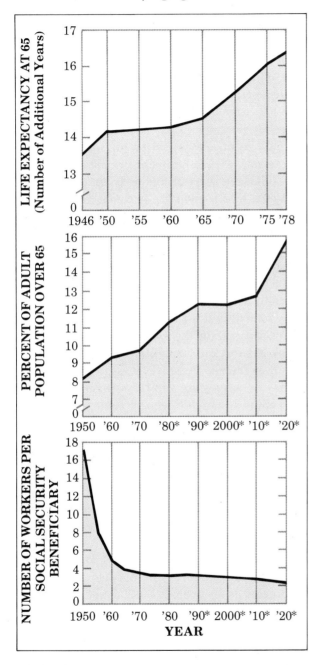

Source: Data from National Center for Health Statistics; U.S. Bureau of the Census; Social Security Administration, 1981.

eration reaches retirement age, the system may well buckle. Will tomorrow's young workers be willing to contribute even more of their earnings to support an ever-increasing cohort of retirees? Social Security pits generation against generation and may well create a political division between the old and the young.

Social Security was not designed to provide a full retirement income. Most retirees who depend entirely on Social Security find their incomes reduced by more than half. For some retired people, private pension plans make up some of the difference, but pensions have certain built-in problems. First, most private pension plans are not adjusted for increases in the cost of living. (At 12 percent annual inflation, a $10,000-a-year pension would shrink to $1,037 in twenty years.) Second, a person must work a specific number of consecutive years to become eligible, and the amount received in retirement depends on how much the worker earned and how long he or she was employed. Workers who change employers, work part time, or have low earnings are penalized. In particular, those women who leave full-time jobs to bear and raise children are penalized. Third, only about 50 percent of male workers and 35 percent of female workers in the United States are covered by private pension plans. The rest must live on savings and Social Security (Schulz, 1976, p. 160).

Housing problems Most older Americans do not live, or want to live, with their children. Over 70 percent of Americans age sixty-five and older own their own homes—a higher percentage than among younger people—and 85 percent of elderly homeowners have paid off their mortgages. Fourteen out of twenty people over sixty-five live in a family setting—usually a husband-wife household with no other relatives. Four in twenty live alone or with non-relatives. One in twenty (5 percent of the elderly) is institutionalized, usually after age eighty. The image of older Americans

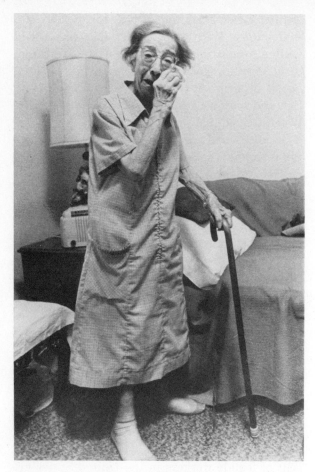

At age eighty, Mrs. Eva Charzak is informed that she has one month to vacate the apartment where she has lived for the last thirty-seven years.

being abandoned to lonely rooms or to nursing homes or living as unwanted guests in their children's homes is greatly exaggerated—though these situations do exist.

Statistics on homeownership do not tell the full story, however. Estimates put the number of elderly people in the United States who live in inadequate housing at 4 to 6 million, or 20 to 30 percent (Butler, 1975, pp. 108–14; Carp, 1976, in Barrow and Smith, 1979, p. 21). Some residences do not have indoor flush toilets, hot showers, or

adequate heat, and some of the elderly cannot afford maintenance, repair, and tax costs for their homes. Elderly people may find that they cannot climb stairs or use the bathtub in the home they bought in their youth. They may not be able to get from their home to shopping centers or to a doctor's office without assistance. Thus, housing is inadequate, both in that it is deteriorating and in that it does not serve the special needs of the elderly. Because the number of old people is growing, and because most old people want to live independently, these problems are magnified.

Residential segregation adds to the housing problems of the elderly. A comparatively high percentage of older people in the United States live in rural areas and in central-city districts. In the sunbelt states, the elderly are segregated largely by choice (La Gory, Ward, and Mucatel, 1980). Most of them moved to the sunbelt after retirement and chose to live with "their own kind." They were drawn to the South by the lower cost of living, special housing for retirees, and the promise of leisure and sociability (a retirement life style). In the North, however, segregation of the elderly is largely involuntary. Older people are left behind in cities when the young move to the suburbs. The elderly cannot keep up with the succession of neighborhoods (described in Chapter 6). Often homeownership locks the elderly into decaying neighborhoods. Selling the small, low-priced homes they bought years ago would not provide them with the funds necessary to purchase or rent housing more suitable for old people or nearer their relatives.

In their isolation, older Americans resemble children and adolescents. While young people are segregated from people of other ages in school, older people tend to be segregated from people of other ages in their own homes (as well as in retirement communities and nursing homes). People of other ages are working or in school most of the day. Hence, old people associate mostly with other old people. Limiting contacts between generations tends to perpetuate negative stereotypes and ageism. The simultaneous segregation of the young and old, in particular, limits their opportunities to learn from one another.

Victimization of the elderly Many older people in the United States are locked into their homes by fear. The elderly count crime as their most serious personal problem—ahead of income, housing, and even health (Harris and Associates, 1975). In fact, the elderly are the least victimized of any age group. Their children and grandchildren are far more likely to become victims of violent or property crimes. Why, then, are the elderly so fearful? A number of reasons combine (Yin, 1980). First, the media tend to give more attention to crimes against the elderly than to routine crimes committed against younger people. And older people tend to discuss crime more than young people do: Each older person knows someone who knows someone (and so on) who was victimized. Second, older people tend to be less involved in their neighborhoods than younger people are. So many of the people they encounter are strangers that they do not know whom to fear or whom to turn to for help when they are suspicious. Finally, older people worry about their ability to recover from injury. Crime exacts a higher price from the elderly in terms of physical injuries and economic losses. Among the elderly, fear of crime may be a greater problem than crime itself. The more fearful people are, the more likely they are to stay at home. Worrying about crime causes them to limit their activities. Isolation, stress, and anxiety reduce the quality of life for many of the elderly.

The elderly are especially vulnerable to two types of crime: fraud and family violence. Older people often fall prey to such swindles as phony dating and marriage brokerage, vanity publishers, land frauds (especially retirement communities), mail-order fraud, investment fraud, useless health aids, and medical quackery (Barrow and Smith, 1979, pp. 243–55). Since many older people live on fixed incomes, they welcome the chance to make extra or easy money. Many are lonely. Confined to their home while everyone else is at work or school, they welcome the chance to talk to the door-to-door salesperson. And many older people are naive. They may not have as much education as younger people, not keep up with the news, and lack the confidence and know-how to ask questions. Physical disabilities contribute to their vulnerability. Impaired hearing may cause them to misunderstand; poor eyesight may make the fine print on a contract illegible. Finally, people in poor health may be desperate to try anything that promises relief or cure. It is difficult to say how many older people fall victim to fraud. Police do not require victims to state their age, and many are ashamed to admit that they have been swindled and so do not report the crime.

The idea that someone would swindle or mug an older person is troubling; that a family member would physically abuse an aging parent is almost unthinkable. Like child and wife abuse, abuse of elders was a hidden problem until quite recently. But data collected by the U.S. House Select Committee on Aging indicate that this is "far from an isolated and localized problem involving a few frail elderly and their pathological offspring" (1981, p. xiv). Estimates are that one in twenty-five older people in the United States, or about 1 million, become victims of family violence each year. The rate of abuse of the elderly is almost as high as the rate of child abuse, but cases are far less likely to be reported. Many victims are confined to their homes, dependent on their abusers, and ashamed. Abuse of elders ranges from neglect to direct assault (Steinmetz, 1978). Caretakers may tie an old person to a bed or chair while they are out shopping, give extra medication or alcohol to "ease discomfort" (that is, to make him or her more manageable), use or threaten violence to get an old person to sign over a Social Security check or change his or her will, or in some cases, beat an old person to death. The victims are most likely to be very old (age seventy-five or older), female, and dependent on others for their care and protection. The abuser is usually a son or daughter of the victim and usually is experiencing compound stress — alcoholism, drug addiction, marital problems, or chronic financial difficulties in addition to the burden of caring for an aging parent (U.S. House Select Committee on Aging, 1981).

There are a number of parallels between elder abuse and child abuse. Often adults who abuse their parents were victims of child abuse. In other words, elder abuse is part of the battered child syndrome. It occurs most often in families in which violence is the normative response to conflict and frustration. Elder abuse can be seen as an exaggeration of both the widespread social approval of violence in American society and negative attitudes toward the elderly. But the presence of an aging parent creates special problems. Often, middle-aged couples take in an elderly parent just when they are launching their own childen and the wife has gone back to work. Should she then stay home to care for the parent, or should she pay someone while she goes to work? Either way, she will lose some of her freedom and independence as well as some of her income. Conflicts between the demands of growing children and the demands of an aging parent may add to financial and emotional stress. If the couple is paying for college tuition bills, as well as expensive medical care for the older person, the financial burden is even heavier. Often, the caretakers are not prepared to cope with the needs of a parent whose health is deteriorating. They lack nursing skills and do not know how to find help. The elderly person may react to loss of control over the basic tasks of daily living (bathing, dressing, and so on) by becoming extremely demanding or extremely withdrawn — behavior

the caretaker may not understand. A sudden increase in an old person's needs and demands, usually because of illness, may precipitate violence. Finally, while the number of people who live to an age where they require care is increasing, family size has been decreasing, so that there are fewer middle-aged children to care for elderly parents. If current trends continue, many parents will be dependent on their children for almost as long as their children were dependent on them. Thus, the graying of America is causing unanticipated changes in the life cycle and in the relations between generations. In some families, the empty-nest stage, after children leave home, is being replaced by a nursing-home stage, when a parent comes to stay.

Problems and Prospects

Three central themes emerge from this chapter. First, both the young and the old in the United States are excluded from the workings of society (Riley and Waring, 1976). Because of their age, they are denied opportunities for economically productive, socially valued roles. Members of both age groups live in enforced dependency. Both are segregated from people of other ages. Furthermore, prolonged schooling and early retirement have lengthened the periods of age segregation. Second, the age structure of the population and the age structure of social roles are often out of balance. Sometimes there are too many people in a given cohort for the roles allotted to its stage in the life cycle; sometimes there are too few. There may be more young people ready for high school than there are classrooms to receive them, for example, or more people reaching age seventy-five than there are services to provide for their needs. Or there may be too few pregnant women to support existing maternity wards and baby industries. One part of the system may generate needs and desires that the next part cannot satisfy. For example, college education may create aspirations for challenging work that the job market cannot satisfy, so that many young people will be overqualified for and unhappy with their jobs. Third, because of their positions in the age stratification system and the roles allotted to them, members of succeeding generations have different, often competing interests. Discrimination, the cohort-role mismatch, and special interests lead not only to age inequality but also to conflicts between generations.

The obvious solution to these socially structured inequalities would be to eliminate age as a criterion for distributing roles; that is, declare that no one is too young or too old to hold a job, vote in elections, play with dolls, get married, and so on. As Matilda Riley and Joan Waring point out, this might create more problems than it solves (1976, pp. 399–400). If no one could be denied a job because of age, other criteria would have to be established for allocating scarce and desirable positions. If physical stamina and up-to-date education were used as criteria, a new set of age inequalities would be established. Middle-aged and older workers would be pushed out of their jobs by the healthy, well-educated cohort of young people. If experience were used as the main criterion, the elderly would preempt jobs now held by middle-aged and young workers. If financial need were the standard, middle-aged people with teen-aged children would be given almost all jobs. The different levels of the age stratification system are interconnected. As a result, changes that benefit people in one stage of the life cycle have negative consequences for people in other stages. One generation's solution is another's problem (Merton and Nisbet, 1976, pp. 9–10).

While abolishing age-grading would be problematic, modifications in the current system might reduce age inequalities, age segregation, and age conflict. Riley and Waring recommend a more flexible distribution of education, work, and leisure. Today, the young have a near-monopoly on education; the middle aged, on work; the elderly, on leisure. Young people might be given opportunities for productive work in addition to self-development through education—for example, work-study programs. Middle-aged workers might be given more opportunities for leisure—for example, year-long sabbaticals or regular four-day weekends. Social Security might be redesigned to encourage the elderly to work or study part time.

Changes in the direction of age flexibility are already taking place. It no longer shocks us to hear of a twenty-five-year-old being elected mayor, a seventy-year-old attending college, or a fifty-five-year-old man becoming a father for the first time or starting a second family. The internal signals and external social pressures that tell us we are too young or too old to go to school, get married, hold a job, or retire are not as compelling as they once were. Still, the twenty-five-year-old mayor and the seventy-year-old student are exceptions to the rule of age stratification.

Summary

1. Ageism (the belief that denying people certain rights because of their age is biologically justified) and cohort-historical differences create special problems for the young and the old in American society.

2. The idea that childhood is a special stage in life and that children are inherently different from adults is relatively new.

3. At the turn of the century, changing attitudes toward children stimulated the child-saving movement, which emphasized state responsibility for children's needs; today, the child liberation movement emphasizes children's rights in relation to their families and the state.

4. The adolescent stage of life is the result of social changes that opened a gap between parents' and children's experiences and opportunities. In recent years, age segregation and shifting opportunities have widened this generation gap.

5. The special problems of adolescence, such as running away and juvenile delinquency, can be explained in terms of the ambiguous position that teenagers occupy in American society.

6. The elderly in the United States today are victims of a sociocultural lag: The number and proportion of older people is changing faster than are ideas, behavior, and social institutions.

7. Negative stereotypes of the older person's work abilities can become self-fulfilling prophecies.

8. The increasing number of people who depend on Social Security for at least part of their income may lead to generational conflict.

9. Segregation of the elderly is an unintended consequence of housing patterns.

10. Although fear of crime may be exaggerated among the elderly, they are especially vulnerable to fraud and family violence.

11. A redistribution of education, work, and leisure across the life cycle might reduce age inequality and generational conflict.

Suggested Reading

Ariès, Philippe. *Centuries of Childhood: A Social History of Family Life.* R. Baldick (Trans.). New York: Knopf, 1962.

Blythe, Ronald. *The View in Winter: Reflecting on Old Age.* New York: Harcourt Brace Jovanovich, 1979.

Coleman, James S., et al. *Youth: Transition to Adulthood.* Report of the Panel on Youth of the President's Science Advisory Committee. Chicago: University of Chicago Press, 1974.

De Lone, Richard. *Small Futures: Children, Inequality, and the Limits of Liberal Reform.* New York: Harcourt Brace Jovanovich, 1979.

Harris, Diana K., and William E. Cole. *The Sociology of Aging.* Boston: Houghton Mifflin, 1980.

Riley, Matilda W., Marilyn Johnson, and Anne Foner (Eds). *Aging and Society: A Sociology of Age Stratification,* Vol. 3. New York: Sage, 1972.

References

Ariès, P. *Centuries of Childhood: A Social History of Family Life.* R. Baldick (Trans.). New York: Knopf, 1962.

Baltes, P.B., and K.W. Schaie. "The Myth of the Twilight Years." *Psychology Today,* March 1974, pp. 35–40.

Barrow, G., and P. Smith. *Aging, Ageism and Society.* St. Louis: West, 1979.

Benedict, R. "Continuities and Discontinuities in Cultural Conditioning." *Psychiatry,* Vol 1, No. 2 (1938), pp. 161–67.

Brody, E.B. *Minority Group Adolescents in the United States.* Baltimore: Williams and Wilkins, 1968.

Butler, R.N. *Why Survive? Being Old in America.* New York: Harper & Row, 1975.

Coleman, J., et al. *Youth: Transition to Adulthood.* Report of the Panel on Youth of the President's Science Advisory Committee. Chicago: University of Chicago Press, 1974.

Demos, J., and V. Demos. "Adolescence in Historical Perspective." In M. Gordon (Ed.), *The American Family in Social-Historical Perspective.* New York: St. Martin's Press, 1973.

Elder, G.H., Jr. "Age Differentiation and the Life Course." *Annual Review of Sociology,* Vol. 51 (1975), pp. 165–90.

Empey, L.I. *American Delinquency.* Homewood, Ill.: Dorsey, 1978.

Feshbach, N.D., and S. Feshbach. "Toward an Historical, Social, and Developmental Perspective on Children's Rights." *Journal of Social Issues,* Vol. 34, No. 2 (1978), pp. 1–7.

Fitzpatrick, B. "Economics of Aging." In M. Spencer and C. Dorr (Eds.), *Understanding Aging: A Multidisciplinary Approach.* New York: Appleton-Century-Crofts, 1975, pp. 105–33.

Hall, S.G. *Adolescence: Its Psychology and Its Relation to Physiology, Anthropology, Sociology, Sex, Crime, Religion, and Education.* 1905; rpt. New York: Arno, 1970.

Harris, D.K., and W.E. Cole. *The Sociology of Aging.* Boston: Houghton Mifflin, 1980.

Harris, L., and Associates. *The Myth and Reality of Aging in America.* Washington, D.C.: National Council on Aging, 1975.

La Gory, M., R.A. Ward, and M. Mucatel. "Patterns of Age Segregation." Albany: State University of New York, unpublished paper, 1980.

Libertoff, K. "The Runaway Child in America: A Social History." *Journal of Family Issues,* Vol. 1, No. 2 (1980), pp. 151–64.

Mead, M. *Coming of Age in Samoa.* New York: Morrow, 1928.

Merton, R.K. "Social Structure and Anomie." *American Sociological Review,* Vol. 3 (1938), pp. 672–82.

Merton, R.K. *Social Theory and Social Structure.* New York: Free Press, 1968.

Merton, R.K., and Nisbet, R.A. (Eds.) *Contemporary Social Problems,* 4th ed. New York: Harcourt Brace Jovanovich, 1976.

Nye, F.I. "A Theoretical Perspective on Running Away." *Journal of Family Issues,* Vol. 1, No. 2 (1980), pp. 274–99.

Olson, L., et al. "Runaway Children Twelve Years Later: A Follow-Up." *Journal of Family Issues,* Vol. 1, No. 2 (1980), pp. 165–88.

Opinion Research Corporation. *National Survey on Runaway Youth.* Princeton, N.J., 1976.

Riley, M.W., M. Johnson, and A. Foner (Eds.). *Aging and Society: A Sociology of Age Stratification,* Vol 3. New York: Sage, 1972.

Riley, M.W., and J. Waring. "Age and Aging." In R.K. Merton and R.A. Nisbet (Eds.), *Contemporary Social Problems,* 4th ed. New York: Harcourt Brace Jovanovich, 1976, pp. 357–410.

Rubin, J. *Do It.* New York: Simon & Schuster, 1970.

Schultz, J.H. *The Economics of Aging.* Belmont, Cal.: Wadsworth, 1976.

Steinmetz, S.K. "Battered Parents." *Society,* Vol. 15 (July/August 1978), pp. 54–55.

Stier, S. "Children's Rights and Society's Duties." *Journal of Social Issues.* Vol. 34, No. 2 (1978), pp. 46–58.

Takanishi, R. "Childhood as a Social Issue: Historical Roots of Contemporary Advocacy Movements." *Journal of Social Issues,* Vol. 34, No. 2 (1978), pp. 8–28.

U.S. House of Representatives Select Committee on Aging. *Elder Abuse: An Examination of a Hidden Problem.* Washington, D.C.: U.S. Government Printing Office, 1981.

Yin. P.P. "Fear of Crime Among the Elderly: Some Issues and Suggestions." *Social Problems,* Vol. 27, No. 4 (1980), pp. 492–504.

PART FIVE

Private Troubles, Public Issues

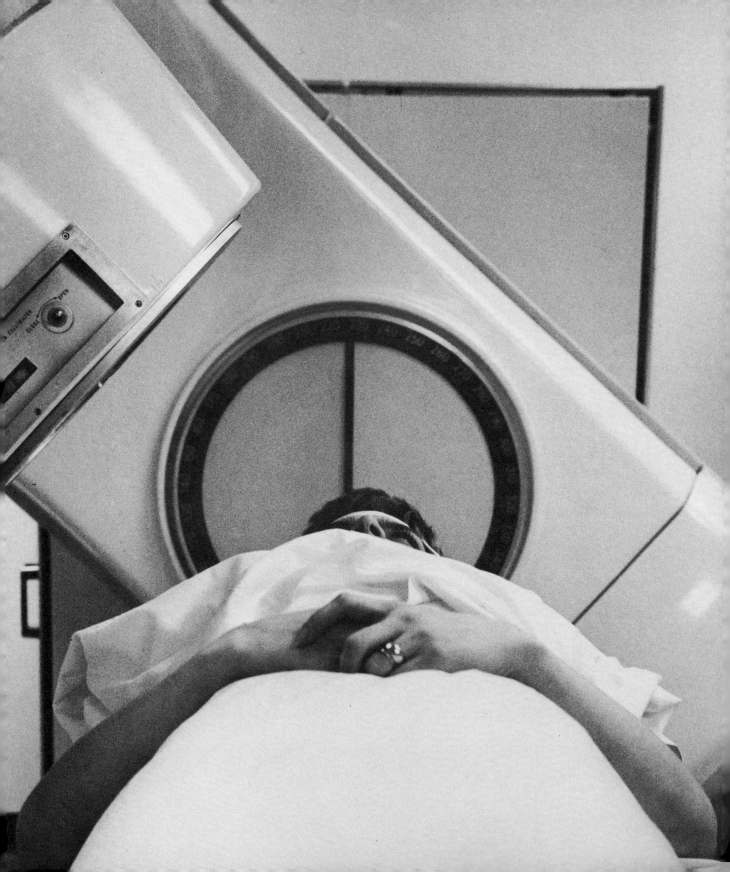

Chapter Thirteen

Physical and Mental Health

Physical Disorders

The Medical Establishment

  The AMA

  Blue Cross

  Medical Centers

  Professional Autonomy and Social Control

Escalating Costs

  Physicians

  Hospitals

  Alternative Financing Systems

Poverty, Old Age, and Health

Mental Disorders

The Medical Model

  The Freudian Influence

  The Mental Hospital

The Social Model

  Mental Disorders and Social Class

  Mental Disorders and Labeling

The Community Mental Health Movement

  Deinstitutionalization and the Drug
    Revolution

  Community Mental Health Centers

**Health Care: Toward an Uncertain
  Future**

Advancing Medical Technology

The Politics of Health Care

Preventive Care: Whose Responsibility?

By almost any measure, Americans are leading longer, healthier lives today than ever before. A baby born in the United States in 1900 had a life expectancy of forty-seven years. Today the average is seventy-three years. Diseases that once killed thousands of Americans each year have been controlled and, in some cases, eliminated. Epidemics of smallpox, cholera, leprosy, and malaria used to be routine. No longer. As late as 1960, poliomyelitis swept the country every summer. In 1954, 18,000 cases of this dread childhood disease were recorded; in 1975, only 6 (Brown, 1979, p. 224). Even measles is disappearing. Modern medicine has, indeed, produced miracles. Over a quarter of a million Americans are able to lead active lives because of techniques in open-heart surgery that were not available thirty years ago. Drugs that control hypertension save an estimated 2 million lives a year. New medical technology has saved the lives of tens of thousands of Americans with kidney disease, tuberculosis, and Parkinson's disease. Many battles in the war against cancer have been won. The survival rate for nine common forms of cancer has increased steadily, thanks to improved diagnosis and treatment.

Treatment of the mentally ill has changed even more dramatically. In 1955, there were 550,000 patients in U.S. mental hospitals — more than the total number of patients hospitalized for all physical ailments (Clausen, 1976). Seventy-five percent of all persons with mental disorders were institutionalized. In 1975, fewer than 200,000 Americans were confined to mental hospitals, and three out of four persons receiving mental health care were being treated as outpatients (The President's Commission on Mental Health, 1978). The major explanation can be given in a single word: drugs. Before drugs, mental wards were crowded with catatonic patients frozen in rigid postures; delusionary patients hugging the walls in nameless fear; hallucinatory patients pacing hour after hour, talking to their voices. Violent patients who attacked staff for reasons known only to themselves were confined to padded cells, strapped to beds, or wrapped in wet sheets. Very few would ever be released. Staff members watched their charges from behind protective shields (Berger, Hamburg, and Hamburg, 1977, p. 263). After drugs were introduced, the staff had little to fear. Patients could enjoy television, ping-pong, and pool. Most were in the hospital only for a temporary stay (usually three weeks), until drugs took effect. Mental hospitals were not only happier places; they were being emptied out.

Yet close examination of health and health care in the United States reveals a paradox. Although this country has the most advanced medical technology and the most sophisticated medical facilities of any nation on earth, Americans are not the healthiest people in the world. Far from it. As many as 33,000 American babies die from preventable causes each year. Twenty-five years ago the United States had the eighth lowest infant mortality rate among industrial nations. By 1975, its ranking had dropped to fifteenth. Over the last twenty-five years, the United States has slipped from third to sixth in female life expectancy for industrial nations; from sixth to a poor sixteenth in male life expectancy. Scandinavian men are twice as likely as American men to survive middle age (ages forty to fifty) and, on the average, live five years longer. Thus although health statistics for the United States improve each year, this country is slipping behind most European nations, and some non-European nations, in its ability to keep its people healthy and alive (Kotelchuck, 1976, pp. 6–10). According to the President's Commission on Mental Health (1978), only about 7 million of the 20 to 30 million Americans who need mental health care receive it. Many of the people released from mental hospitals on drugs have nowhere to go. About two-thirds of the patients admitted to hospitals today have been there before (Sheehan, 1981).

Advances in medical care have proven to be a

mixed blessing. The federal government estimates that 150,000 deaths each year are "iatrogenic," or physician-induced. A study at the Yale-New Haven Hospital suggested that as many as one in five hospital patients is made ill by their treatment (Blumenthal and Fallows, 1973). In 1974, surgeons performed an estimated 2.4 million unnecessary operations; 11,900 of their patients died as a result (House Committee on Interstate and Foreign Commerce, 1976). Every year, about 1.5 million Americans are admitted to hospitals because they had adverse reactions to drugs their physicians prescribed (*U.S. News & World Report,* June 10, 1975). The "miracle drugs" that have enabled so many mental patients to return to the community can have negative side effects, ranging from dangerously high blood pressure to involuntary and irreversible muscle spasms (Sheehan, 1981). Health care can be dangerous to your health.

The disappointing health record in the United States today can be traced to two underlying problems: differential access to medical treatment and overmedicalization. All Americans do not have equal access to medicine. The distribution of health and health care in the United States is as uneven as the distribution of cars, housing, and other consumer goods (Blumenthal and Fallows, 1973). For example, the infant mortality rate for nonwhites is almost twice as high as that for whites (24.2 per 1,000 for nonwhites compared to 14.2 per 1,000 for whites in 1978, according to the U.S. Bureau of the Census), in part because of inadequate prenatal care. Schizophrenia is more prevalent in the lower class than the upper class (Srole, 1978). Whereas most low-income mental patients are treated in clinics, where they may or may not see a therapist, high-income mental patients usually see a private psychiatrist regularly. The government and private insurance companies absorb some of the high cost of medical treatment. But many Americans are "too rich for Medicaid, too poor for Blue Cross, and too young

for Medicare" (Ehrenreich and Ehrenreich, 1971, p. 5). Thirty million have no health insurance whatever. And the majority of those who do are only covered for hospital expenses. A simple visit to the doctor, costing between fifteen and fifty dollars, "requires a careful calculation of whether the illness or the bill will be more painful" (Blumenthal and Fallows, 1973). The average American can only afford physical or mental health care in an emergency.

The second underlying problem is overmedicalization. The term *medicalization* refers to labeling a condition or behavior a symptom of illness that requires, and ought to be given, medical attention. For example, at the turn of the century, most American women had their babies at home, with the assistance of a midwife and family members. In the 1920s or thereabout, pregnancy and childbirth were medicalized. Pregnant women were treated as though they were ill. Childbirth was transferred to hospitals and treated almost as a surgical procedure, complete with anesthesia.

In recent decades, Americans have become increasingly dependent on the health care establishment. "All kinds of problems now roll to the doctor's door, from sagging anatomies to suicides, from unwanted childlessness to unwanted pregnancy, from marital difficulties to learning difficulties, from genetic counseling to drug addiction, from laziness to crime . . ." (Kass, in Fox, 1977, p. 10). Overmedicalization has contributed to the rising cost of health care and to unnecessary, sometimes harmful, treatment. For example, some physicians now believe that the routine use of anesthesia during childbirth is harmful to the infant. Overmedicalization also has cost Americans some personal and societal loss of control. For many years, fathers were banned from almost all delivery rooms in the United States, and many mothers were rendered unconscious. Individuals rely on physicians to interpret symptoms and to manage treatment, ced-

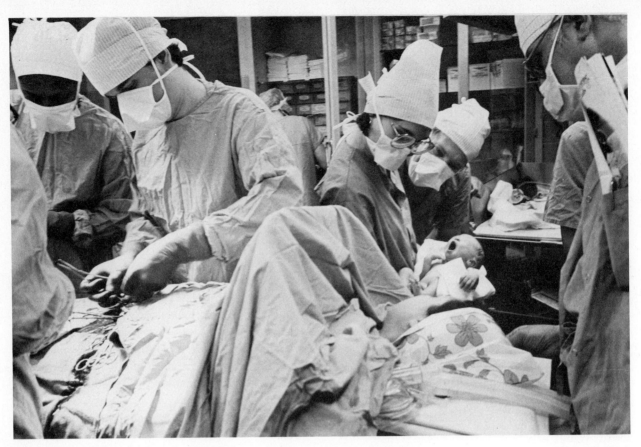

The medicalization of childbirth. The increasing use of Caesarian sections has become a social issue. Critics argue that physicians perform more Caesarians than are medically necessary because this procedure allows them to schedule births at convenient times, to charge more than they do for natural births, and perhaps to avoid being sued for accidents occurring during natural births.

ing personal autonomy. For example, few women will question a doctor's decision to perform a Caesarean section (an expensive procedure that causes some discomfort), although women's groups are questioning the widespread use of this procedure. On the societal level, reliance on professional treatment has given enormous power to medical practitioners, who exercise a monopoly over the specialized knowledge and technology of health care. Medicalization has tended to obscure the social origins of many health problems. It has

contributed to the emphasis on cure and relative neglect of prevention. Physicians are more interested in, and patients more impressed by, open-heart surgery than preventive diet and exercise programs.

In the first section of this chapter, we consider treatment of physical disorders. Health care is big business in the United States today. We trace the growth of the medical establishment, explain why the cost of health care has risen so high, and describe the impact of the current health care system on the poor and elderly. In the second half of the chapter, we look at the treatment of mental disorders. We trace the history of modern views and treatment of mental disorders, show what sociologists have contributed to their understanding, and consider the consequences of today's "drug revolution" in the treatment of mental illness. In the final section, we suggest what the future may bring. Differential access to health care and overmedicalization are themes that run throughout the chapter.

Physical Disorders

We begin this section with a short story. In August 1964, author Norman Cousins (1979) returned from a trip to Moscow with a slight fever and body aches. At first he suspected general fatigue and "jet lag." As the week progressed, however, his condition grew worse. His neck was stiff; he found it difficult to move his arms, then his legs. He called his physician, who sent him directly to the hospital for tests. In the hospital, his condition deteriorated. He could barely move, his jaws locked, a grave rash spread over his body, and the pain was intense. Cousins was put on painkillers and other unidentified drugs. Experts were called in to diagnose symptoms in different parts of his body.

Up to this point, there is nothing unusual about Cousins's story. When Americans feel poorly, they consider it only natural to consult a physician. Medical intervention is considered the appropriate remedy for all physical (and psychological) troubles. If the problem is serious, we expect to be sent to specialists and perhaps to the hospital. Cousins was unusual for two reasons. First, he did not have to worry as much about the cost of medical treatment as other Americans do. Second, although not a physician, he had written about medical subjects for many years and was not hesitant to question his doctors' diagnosis and

treatment. The experts informed him that they weren't sure, but he seemed to have a disease of the connective tissues (a disease related to arthritis). He was literally coming unstuck. The prognosis was poor.

What Cousins did next may come as a surprise. With the collaboration of his personal physician, Cousins set out to cure himself. He took himself off the drugs his doctors had prescribed (one of which turned out to be producing a rash); he substituted laughter for painkillers (Marx brothers films, reels from Candid Camera, and joke books); and he moved himself from the hospital to a hotel. In Cousins's words, "I had the fast-growing suspicion that a hospital is no place for a person who is seriously ill. . . . One of the incidental advantages of the hotel room, . . . was that it only cost about one-third as much as the hospital. The other benefits were incalculable. I would not be awakened for a bed bath or for medication or for a change of bed sheets or for tests or for examinations by hospital interns. The sense of serenity was delicious" (1979, p. 40). Slowly, his body began to recover.

Cousins's description of his experience in *Anatomy of an Illness* (1979) was an instant best seller. He had touched a raw nerve. Teams of specialists have replaced family doctors in the United States; hospitalization has, to some extent, replaced home care; the cost of medical treatment keeps rising; and doubts about the quality of medical care are rising almost as fast as the costs. The entire system of health care seems out of control. To understand the problem, we must explore how it developed.

The Medical Establishment

The health care system in the United States did not develop according to any preconceived plan. Today's health industry is the product of changing technology, reorganizations of health services, and vested interests.

The AMA In 1849, when the American Medical Association (AMA) was founded, the medical profession was still in its infancy (Brown, 1979, Chapter 2). At that time, only three American universities offered formal medical education (University of Pennsylvania, Harvard, and Dartmouth). Most physicians acquired training as apprentices, "learning by doing." The medical profession was not very popular in this period. Physicians still relied on such methods as lancing, bleeding, blistering, and purging (inducing severe vomiting). The "cures" were unpleasant and often lethal. As late as 1880, physicians had only a few reliable medicines: quinine for malaria, mercury for syphilis, and digitalis for heart disease. When sick or injured, most Americans used home remedies or called on lay healers. Medical licensing laws were largely ignored.

The AMA played a central part in changing the role of physicians in American society. From the beginning, the AMA insisted that the practice of medicine was a *profession* — an occupation requiring intense training and expertise, and dedicated to the welfare of its clients. This professional stance gave doctors a claim to autonomy. It established physicians' right to set standards for themselves and to recruit, train, and police their own members. In its original code of ethics, the AMA set down the principle of obeying doctors' orders. Lacking expertise, patients should never question medical treatment.

As the nineteenth century progressed, a number of medical schools were established in this country, and many would-be physicians went to study in Europe, where they discovered "scientific medicine." (Bleeding and blistering were hardly scientific.) European physicians had adopted the new germ theory of disease. They viewed medical treatment essentially as an engineering problem (attacking and/or building defenses against germs). The treatments they prescribed were grounded in research, not tradition and folk remedies. Most important, they were achieving results (primarily because of discoveries in bacteriology and anesthesia).

Scientific medicine soon spread to the United States. New treatments and the training needed to apply them justified the AMA's claim that physicians were professionals. Medical schools added research to their curricula. By the turn of the century, scientific medicine had largely replaced the art of healing. Working through the AMA, physicians established a monopoly over health care. Traditional healers were largely discredited.

The early twentieth century was the era of the family doctor. Physicians gained in prestige — and income. Most treated patients in their own homes and were considered part of the family. As the pace of technological development picked up, however, more and more doctors also practiced in hospitals. Hospitals not only provided doctors with the latest equipment; they also offered large numbers of patients on whom to practice. (Originally created as charity homes where the poor could receive care, hospitals had begun to attract middle-class patients as well.) The growth of hospitals led to the growth of health insurance, particularly Blue Cross.

Blue Cross Blue Cross has been described as "the child of the Depression and the American Hospital Association (AHA)" (Law, 1974). The basic idea came from Dr. Justin Ford Kimball of Baylor University, Dallas, Texas. When Kimball discovered piles of unpaid bills in the university's hospital accounts, he came up with the idea of having teachers pay in advance for hospitalization at the rate of fifty cents a month. The 1,250 teachers who enrolled in the program were covered for twenty-one days of hospital care. The year was 1929. As the Great Depression set in, many hospitals found that they were unable to collect money for their bills and joined the Blue Cross program. From the 1930s on, the AHA worked to obtain a special tax rate for Blue Cross and to limit competition from other insurance companies. (Typically, state law requires an insurance company to establish agreements with the majority of hospitals in the area to be covered, and the AHA influences an individual hospital's decisions.) As physicians established a monopoly over diagnosis and treatment, so Blue Cross established a near-monopoly over hospitalization.

When Blue Cross began issuing contracts to employers as well as private individuals, enrollments climbed. Health insurance became a major issue in collective bargaining, with labor supporting Blue Cross. As employment and wages rose during World War II, so did the enrollments in Blue Cross. Private commercial companies made inroads on the health insurance market in the 1950s. In the early 1960s, Blue Cross recovered by convincing the federal government to allow it to administer Medicare.

Medical centers In the 1950s, medical centers (medical schools and affiliated institutions) began to emerge as a major force in the medical establishment. This was the period in which America fell in love with science (an affair that is only now cooling). The government began to pour millions of dollars into biomedical research. Although reluctant to expand enrollments and flood the market with doctors, medical schools were ready and willing to accept research grants. This was also the period of increasing specialization in the practice of medicine. The more specialized a physician, the more he or she needs to be in communication with other physicians. "A specialist can no more function in isolation than his organ specialty (eyes, chest, gut, etc.) can function in isolation" (Ehrenreich and Ehrenreich, 1971, p. 31). Hospitals bring specialists together. Just as physicians need hospitals, so hospitals need medical schools, to supply them with the best interns and residents, equipped with the latest scientific knowledge.

In the 1960s, research funds began to dry up.

Attention was shifting to the war in Vietnam and the "war on poverty." So were funds. Medical schools obtained a reprieve when the nation "discovered" a shortage of doctors (the poor weren't being treated) and passed the first health manpower bill. The bill provided financial aid for medical education (Behn and Sperduto, 1979). Grants in their pockets, medical schools began to establish affiliations with neighboring hospitals, expanding their territory and patient population. Johns Hopkins Medical College, Harvard Medical School, and others became the hubs of giant medical centers. In effect, entire communities became teaching hospitals for students and researchers. And this put medical centers in an ideal position when the federal government began to supplement the millions spent on research with millions for Medicare and Medicaid. Quite simply, medical centers had the patients that the government wanted to reach.

The medical establishment thus has been decades in the making. The AMA, the AHA, Blue Cross, and most recently, medical centers have all played major roles in its development. There are two basic cultural reasons why these groups have been able to control health care services and expand (Waitzkin and Waterman, 1974, pp. 88–89). The first is the belief in medical expertise—the idea that only doctors and related professionals have the technical knowledge to decide which programs and facilities are needed. The second is the helping ideology—the belief that doctors and hospitals are public-spirited. It is difficult to argue with physicians who claim new hospital beds and equipment are needed, difficult to say "no" to a research project that might save lives.

A number of sociologists characterize the organization of health care in the United States today as a "medical-industrial complex" (borrowing President Eisenhower's warning of a military-industrial complex). According to this view, power over health care is concentrated in the hands of a small number of organizations that are united by common interests and a web of financial and personal ties (Waitzkin and Waterman, 1974, Chapter 5). The medical-industrial complex has its own power elite. The government hires consultants from the health insurance industry; executives of medical supply companies sit on the boards of hospitals and medical schools; physicians advise hospitals, insurance and pharmaceutic companies. They exchange personnel. Moreover, the AMA depends on income it receives from drug companies that advertise in its journal. In large part, physicians depend on advertisements for information about new medications. Hospitals depend on insurance companies for patients' fees. Insurance companies depend on hospitals—and so on.

Professional autonomy and social control The medical profession has enormous authority (that is, legitimate power) in American society today. Physicians have a legal monopoly over health care. They have sole authority to prescribe drugs and to perform surgery. Perhaps more significantly, physicians have the legal authority to decide whether a person is genuinely sick or malingering, whether an individual is fit or unfit to exercise his or her rights.

The medical profession's power over individuals is most obvious in cases where the courts ask psychiatrists to decide whether a person is mentally capable of standing trial. Physicians cannot force adults to accept medical treatment for most physical ailments, but they can force parents to allow their children to receive treatment. These are perhaps extreme cases. Physicians also have the power to decide whether a worker will be paid, or a soldier punished, for taking time off. A doctor's note can temporarily exempt a student from taking an exam. Family approval for one's staying in bed all day may depend on being pronounced ill by a physician.

The medical profession acts as an agency of *social control.* Physicians decide whether individuals who violate norms are to be blamed or exempted. They decide whether the violator will be given punishment or treatment. As agents of social control, physicians have a high degree of autonomy. The medical profession is largely self-regulating. Advanced medical technology creates an aura of mystery around the practice of medicine that few lay people feel competent to challenge. Moreover, the medical profession's sphere of authority has grown steadily in recent decades, as more and more troublesome forms of behavior have been medicalized.

What are the social consequences of overmedicalization? Defining problem behavior as illness tends to remove an issue from public debate (Conrad, 1975). It becomes a matter for doctors, who control diagnosis and treatment, to discuss among themselves. Medicalization permits the use of forms of social control that wouldn't be accepted otherwise, such as psychoactive drugs or surgery. (Using these treatments without consent in prisons, to change behavior, would be considered highly unethical—a form of torture.) When behavior is defined as a symptom of illness, people tend to locate the causes and potential for cures in individual patients, ignoring the social circumstances in which the behavior developed and continues to function. Medicalization also can be a way of dismissing behavior, silencing people, and rationalizing their confinement to hospitals where they can't be seen and won't create problems. (This has indeed been the case with mental illness, as we will show later in this chapter.)

Escalating Costs

Overmedicalization has caused the price of health care to skyrocket. This country spends more on health care than on national defense, housing, or transportation. In 1980, the total U.S. medical

Medicine and Deviance: "The Sick Role"

As Talcott Parsons suggested three decades ago (1951), illness is a form of deviance. On first reading, this may be puzzling. (What do a man who has the flu and, say, a man who robs banks have in common?) But follow Parsons's reasoning. When people are sick, they do not fill their usual social roles—as students or workers, active family members, and so on. Sick people violate social norms—take time off from school or work, stay in bed all day, expect others to care for them, perhaps "pop pills." Indeed, how do people decide they are sick? In some cases, a disability is obvious. But in others, people "realize" they are sick because they aren't following their usual social routines or because they're "acting funny" (see Twaddle, 1969).

The difference between illness and other forms of deviance—the crucial difference—is that we consider the person's behavior involuntary. We do not blame someone who is sick for failing to conform to ordinary expectations (even if they brought the illness on themselves by smoking or staying out in the cold). "It's not their fault." Moreover, we do not expect sick people to cure themselves through an act of will. We don't insist that they "pull themselves together" or "shape up." Thus, we don't hold sick people responsible either for bringing on their condition or for correcting it.

Sickness confers a legitimate exemption (in varying degrees, depending on the illness) from everyday obligations. This exemption is conditional, however. A sick person *is* obliged to want to get well, to seek competent help, and to cooperate with attempts to bring about a cure. In our society, this means putting oneself "in doctor's hands."

Note that the role Parsons is describing does not depend on an actual invasion of the body by bacteria or an actual injury. A person playing this role may or may not be physically sick. Some individuals fake illness ("malingerers"); others ignore symptoms and discomfort and carry on ("stoics"); most people do one or the other on occasion. Adopting the sick role is a decision made by an individual (or people around the person) *and* his or her physician. The latter—the physician's contribution—is a key point.

Figure 13- 1

National Health Expenditures, 1940 to 1990

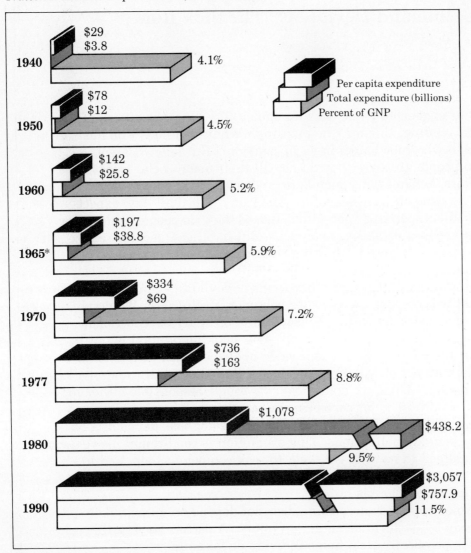

*Year Medicaid and Medicare introduced
Source: U.S. Department of Health, Education, and Welfare, *Social Security Bulletin*,
Vol. 43, No. 7 (July 1978), Table 1.

bill came to $244.6 billion, or $1,078 for each man, woman, and child. The average adult American works one month every year just to pay for the medical system. Over the last decade, the cost of health care has risen faster than any other commodity except perhaps energy. Medical costs accounted for almost $1 of every $10 spent in 1980, compared to $1 of every $20 in 1960 (see Figure

13–1). Why has the cost of medical care skyrocketed? Where are our health dollars going?

Physicians Physicians' fees explain part of the high cost of health care. In 1980, medical doctors charged this nation $45 billion for their services.

Before World War II, physicians earned about two and a half times as much as other full-time workers. Today, with their incomes more than five times the national average, physicians are the highest-paid occupational group in the country (Brown, 1979, p. 2). One reason for the increase is specialization. Physicians who develop expertise in a particular field of medicine command higher fees than general practitioners. A generation ago, over half the physicians practicing in the United States were general practitioners. Today, six out of seven physicians are specialists. In the 1970s, malpractice suits and insurance pushed doctors' fees still higher. A physician who spent about $4,700 for malpractice insurance in 1970 paid $14,000 or more for the same coverage in 1975 (*Time,* March 24, 1975, p. 62). These costs are passed along to the consumer—that is, to the patient.*

Doctors *fees* are only part of the story, however. Physicians raise health costs in other ways. For example, the only legal way to obtain antibiotics or other restricted drugs is through a physician. Estimates are that U.S. physicians write 2.5 billion prescriptions a year, at a cost of more than $5 billion to patients (*U.S. News & World Report,* June 18, 1975, p. 61). More significantly, physicians decide who requires hospitalization, what kind of treatment they will receive, and how long they will stay. Visiting a doctor's office is a matter of individual discretion. The choice of whether to suffer through an illness or to seek treatment is up to the individual. But hospitalization is not entirely voluntary. Relatively few individuals feel competent to overrule a doctor who recommends hospitalization. In addition, the risk of malpractice suits may push doctors toward hospitalization. Given a choice between trusting their own judgment and verifying their observations with sophisticated tests, doctors are likely to "play it safe" by ordering the patient into the hospital. Thus, physicians add more to health care costs than their actual bills suggest.

Hospitals Hospital costs have contributed far more to rising health costs than have doctors' fees (see Figure 13–2). In 1980, hospitals billed patients for $97.3 billion (U.S. Department of Health and Human Services, 1980). This country spends five times as much on hospital care today as it did in 1965. Some of the rise in hospital costs can be attributed to increases in wages and salaries for hospital workers, and some to increases in the cost of goods and services that hospitals buy (thermometers, bedpans, laundry, and so on). The biggest increase, however, is the result of changes in the *kind* of services that hospitals provide, or the "intensification" of hospital care. The use of laboratory tests, X-rays, and the like rose steadily during the 1970s. So did the use of new and sophisticated technology, such as the CAT scanner and heart-bypass surgery (U.S. Department of Health, Education, and Welfare, 1978, p. 11). The equipment is extremely expensive. And sophisticated equipment and procedures require highly trained—and highly paid—employees, in increasing numbers (see Table 13–1).

There is no doubt that open-heart surgery (to pick one example) saves lives. There are questions, however, about how much sophisticated equipment is really necessary. Because physicians, hospitals, and patients all want the most advanced technology, there is a good deal of over-

---

*With hospitals as well as doctors purchasing coverage, malpractice insurance has become a $500 million business. Consumers pay the cost, but only about 15 percent of this money is returned to consumers as awards for damages. Most of it goes to lawyers and insurance companies (Bodenheimer, 1976).

Table 13-1
The Cost of Advanced Medical Care

	Small, General Hospital (70 beds)	Large, Specialized Hospital (700 beds)
Facilities	Postoperative recovery rooms	Intensive care unit
	Premature nursery	Open-heart surgery facilities
	Blood bank	Postoperative recovery room
	Physical therapy department	X-ray therapy
	Occupational therapy department	Cobalt therapy
	Full-time pharmacist	Radium therapy
	Dental services	Radioisotopic facility
	Emergency department	Histopathology laboratory
	Psychiatric emergency department	Blood bank
	Social work department	Electroencephalography
	Family planning service	Physical therapy department
		Inhalation therapy department
		Full-time pharmacist
		Dental services
		Renal analysis
		Inpatient services
		Emergency department
		Psychiatric emergency department
		Social work department
		Rehabilitation services
		Outpatient unit
		Home care program
		Hospital auxiliary
		Organized outpatient department
Total services	11	24
Staff	2.5 persons per bed	5 persons per bed
Overall costs	$25,000 per year, per bed	$40,000 per year, per bed
Employee payroll*	$15,714 per year, per bed	$25,600 per year, per bed

*Reflects need for more highly trained personnel in large hospitals
Source: W.R. Rosengren, *Sociology of Medicine: Diversity, Conflict, and Change* (New York: Harper & Row, 1980), Table 3-1, pp. 64–67.

Figure 13–2

The Distribution of U.S. Health Expenditures, 1980 (total: $244.6 billion)

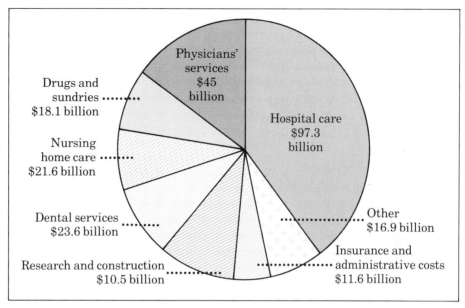

Physicians' services $45 billion

Drugs and sundries $18.1 billion

Hospital care $97.3 billion

Nursing home care $21.6 billion

Dental services $23.6 billion

Research and construction $10.5 billion

Other $16.9 billion

Insurance and administrative costs $11.6 billion

Source: Department of Health and Human Services, 1981.

lap in equipment. For example, in 1972, 800 U.S. hospitals were equipped to perform open-heart surgery. A third of these hospitals had never performed these operations; another third used the facility fewer than twelve times a year. Yet, new units continued to be built (Blumenthal and Fallows, 1973). Physician specialization and the use of sophisticated technology — two offshoots of overmedicalization — boost the cost of health care.

Alternative financing systems Hardly anyone who enters the hospital pays the bill out of their own pocket today. In 1977, 94 percent of hospital costs were paid by "third parties" — that is, by private health insurance companies (such as Blue Cross), company health plans, and government programs (primarily Medicare and Medicaid)

(U.S. Department of Health, Education, and Welfare, 1978). Third parties — especially private insurance — have indirectly encouraged physicians and patients to use expensive hospital facilities rather than outpatient or preventive medical services. Most *private insurance* policies cover only the cost of hospitalization. In the mid-1970s, nearly 160 million Americans had private health insurance policies, but 55 percent had no coverage for visits to a doctor's office (Bodenheimer, Cummings, and Harding, 1976, pp. 79–80). This means that if a doctor performs X-rays, blood tests, and the like in his or her office, the patient pays out of pocket. If the same tests are performed in a hospital, the insurance company pays most of the bill. Hence, both doctors (who are sure of being paid) and patients (who don't feel they're paying) may favor hospitalization. Of course, patients pay for insurance, but they would pay this cost anyway, whether or not they were sick. Moreover, in many cases, health insurance premiums—like income taxes—are deducted from paychecks. They don't *feel* like an added expense.

Medicare (a federal program administered through Social Security, which covers Americans who are sixty-five years old or over) and *Medicaid* (a federal and state program for reimbursing doctors and hospitals who treat the nation's poor and disabled) have also raised health costs. It is only a slight exaggeration to say these programs wrote the medical profession a blank check. The day these bills were passed, millions of people who could not have paid for health care the year before became "available" for treatment. From 1950 to 1965, the overall cost of health care in this country rose 7 to 8 percent a year. Since 1966, when Medicare and Medicaid went into effect, health expenditures have been rising 10 to 12 percent a year. Less than a year after the birth of Medicare, the federal government had to raise Social Security taxes by 25 percent. In 1967, the government estimated that providing Medicaid to forty-eight states would cost $2.25 billion a year. Although only thirty-seven states participated, the actual bill came to $3.54 billion (Hodgson, 1976). Both systems were abused. The Social Security Administration estimates that in the first five years of its existence, Medicare was overcharged $27 million by doctors, hospitals, and nursing homes (*U.S. News & World Report,* June 16, 1975, p. 51).

One program for correcting this situation, already being tried, is the creation of *health maintenance organizations* (HMOs). With HMOs, patients pay a set yearly fee which entitles them to whatever medical services they require, from checkups to major surgery. Doctors affiliated with HMOs are paid salaries, not fees for service, and in some programs receive a bonus if they succeed in reducing treatment costs. HMOs have three basic goals. The first is to improve health by encouraging doctors and patients to focus on preventive care. The second is to discourage unnecessary hospitalization and overuse of sophisticated, expensive treatments. The third is to reduce costs, by improving health and reducing hospitalization. It is debatable how successful HMOs like the Kaiser Permenante Group in California or the Health Insurance Program in New York have been in achieving these goals (see Mechanic, 1976, pp. 85–98). Participants complain of long delays and red tape in making appointments, difficulties in obtaining emergency service, and unattended health problems (Waitzkin and Waterman, 1974, pp. 104–05). There is evidence, however, the HMOs reduce hospitalization rates by as much as 20 percent (Blumenthal and Fallows, 1973).

A wide range of *national health insurance* (NHI) programs have been proposed over the past ten years. Some would offer federal health insurance on a voluntary basis to whoever wanted coverage; others would make health insurance mandatory. Some would establish a new health agency to oversee health care; others would subsidize existing medical services and insurance plans. A number include plans for HMOs (see Margolis, 1977). A major criticism of NHI proposals is that, like Medicare and Medicaid, national health insurance would encourage overtreatment and overcharging, driving costs higher. Other criticisms focus on the legendary inefficiency of federal bureaucracies and the inadvisability of allowing nonphysicians to supervise health care. On the positive side, NHI could lay the foundation for centralized planning and better distribution of services. It would transfer some of the cost of medical care from the sick to the healthy— much as Social Security transfers some of the cost of old age from the elderly to younger, working people. Ideally, NHI would reduce inequalities in health care.

Both NHI and HMOs are controversial. There is general consensus on one point, however. Health care has become a major industry in the United States. Indeed, the private practice of medicine is the most profitable small business in the country; drug companies, hospital supply companies, health insurance, and even nursing homes are among the most profitable big businesses (Ehrenreich and Ehrenreich, 1971, pp. 21–22). Would national health insurance or the creation of health maintenance organizations take power away from the medical-industrial complex? Not necessarily. The manifest goals of NHI and HMOs, as indicated above, are to improve the quality of health care and to reduce costs. A latent goal, however, is to further expand medical empires, according to Howard Waitzkin and Barbara Waterman (1974). They believe this is already happening.

For example, in the early 1970s, a number of medical centers (Harvard, Yale, Johns Hopkins, and others) "jumped on the HMO bandwagon." Why would they support programs designed to *reduce* the need for sophisticated hospital treatment (the medical center's specialty)? HMOs are a source of institutional prestige, putting them in the forefront of community and preventive medicine. They are also a source of funds. (Typically, HMOs budget more for low-income than for middle-income participants, on the grounds that the risk of illness or injury is greater among the poor. The poor, of course, also bring in government funds.) Blue Cross and other insurance companies are backing selected NHI proposals and experimenting with HMOs. Why? If NHI-HMO proposals become law, they can claim to have the most experience and best apparatus for administering new programs.

According to Waitzkin and Waterman, the problem with current proposals for reforming health care in the United States is that they leave power in the hands of those who provide health services (physicians, hospitals, etc.), rather than in the hands of health care consumers (the patients).

Poverty, Old Age, and Health

The disappointing health record in the United States is in large measure a reflection of poor health among disadvantaged groups. Studies of the lowest-income groups reveal higher infant mortality rates, higher overall mortality rates, and a greater incidence of both infectious and chronic diseases (Kitagawa, 1972). The health gap between white and black Americans, a higher percentage of whom are poor, stands out. The mortality rate for nonwhite infants is nearly twice that for white babies (*The New York Times,* January 13, 1976, p. 1). Life expectancy for black males is six years shorter than for white males in the United States (U.S. Department of Health, Education, and Welfare, 1975).

This health gap is the result of poverty, not of biological racial differences. Studies also show that the higher the level of education, the lower the mortality rate. A study of whites revealed that the mortality rate for men with less than a high-school education was 64 percent higher than that for men with four years of college or more. For women, the difference was 105 percent (Kitagawa and Hauser, 1973, pp. 12–14). The poor are more likely to suffer ill health during their lifetimes. About 30 percent of Americans with incomes of $3,000 or less are disabled, compared to 8 percent with incomes of $10,000 or more. People with incomes of $5,000 or less spend 50 to 60 percent more time confined to bed or hospitals than do wealthier Americans (U.S. National Center for Health Statistics, 1974, p. 7). Demographer Evelyn Kitagawa (1972) estimates that if all Americans had had the same standard of living and health care in 1960 as whites age twenty-five and older with one year of college education, 17 percent of deaths among whites and 36 percent of deaths among nonwhites would not have occurred. Put another way, 292,000 deaths in 1960 were preventable. Indirectly, these deaths were caused by a lower standard of living and poor health care.

Poor children suffer health disadvantages even before they are born. As many as a third of the women who give birth in public hospitals received no prenatal care (Kennedy, 1976). Many are malnourished, resulting in low birth weights. The chances of death in the first years of life are much higher for poor children, especially poor black children. As they grow up, poor children do not have adequate diets. Inadequate childhood nutrition is associated with lifelong health problems, especially mental retardation. Estimates are that 90 percent of children diagnosed as "marginally retarded" come from poor families and have no organic brain damage (De Lone, 1979, p. 12). Poor children are exposed to such environmental hazards as rat bites and lead poisoning—a major health problem in spite of publicity campaigns (De Lone, 1979, p. 13). Many are also exposed to such "social hazards" as high crime rates and drug abuse. Many receive little or no medical attention. Even if they do receive medical attention, their health is much worse than other children's. A study of 1,178 Mississippi children receiving Medicaid revealed a total of 1;301 major health problems, including anemia, poor eyesight, untreated cardiac anomalies, parasites, and cavities. Children in a low-income Chicano community in Los Angeles had four times as much amebic dysentery as the national average and twice as many cases of measles, mumps, and tuberculosis (De Lone, 1979, pp. 12–13).

Childhood health problems carry over into adulthood, where the combination of a low standard of living and a low standard of health care continues to operate. Medicaid and other programs provide health care payments for many of the nation's poor, but the quality of care is not up to standard. Often the only medical attention the poor receive is through hospital clinics and emergency rooms, which do not provide continuing, comprehensive care. Very few poor Americans have a doctor of their own, whom they see regularly and who knows their medical history. There are fewer doctors in the urban ghettos and rural areas where most of the poor live. Moreover, the stress of coping with poverty day in, day out, may itself contribute to poor health (Rainwater, 1974).

Elderly Americans, poor and non-poor, are also disadvantaged when it comes to health care. Health care for Americans sixty-five years old and over has improved under Medicare. The federal government now takes care of almost 70 percent of their medical bills, and older citizens are using the health care system more than they did in the past (Hammerman, 1974). Many problems remain, however.

Most of the benefits of modern medicine have gone to the young. Although the life expectancy of a baby born in the United States has increased forty-seven years since the turn of the century, the life expectancy of Americans age sixty-five has increased by only three years (U.S. National Center for Health Statistics, 1974, p. 7). Fewer than half of American medical schools have courses in geriatrics or gerontology (*U.S. News & World Report,* April 24, 1978, p. 57). The medical system tends to be crisis-oriented (Hammerman, 1974). Physicians and hospitals are better equipped to deal with acute conditions than with the chronic diseases of old age (arthritis, impairments of vision and hearing, heart conditions). Many older Americans have trouble getting to a doctor or clinic, even if someone else pays the bill. Perhaps 15 percent are housebound because of physical ailments; for another 15 percent, going outdoors is extremely difficult (Hammerman, 1974). And many have no one at home to care for them if they are sick. There is evidence that the most frightening health problem of old age—senility—is often

Medicaid and Medicare give the poor and the elderly access to medical care. But the care they receive is often impersonal. Patients may wait hours to see a physician and never see the same one twice.

misdiagnosed and mistreated. Estimates are that 20 to 40 percent of institutionalized older people could live at home if they were given help with housekeeping, personal care, and transportation. As things stand, many of the physiological and social problems of the elderly are unattended (see Chapter 12).

Mental Disorders

In 1978, the President's Commission on Mental Health estimated that at any given time, about 15 percent of the U.S. population needs some form of mental health care. In 1976, expenditures for mental health care reached $17 billion (12 percent of all health costs). Each year, between 750,000 and 1.2 million people see psychiatrists in private offices or clinics, as outpatients (Na-

tional Institute of Mental Health, 1973). A description of leading mental disorders appears in Table 13–2. Here we want to focus on changing ideas about the causes of mental disorders and their impact on treatment. We begin with a history of the idea of mental illness and the medicalization of mental disorders. We then look at the emergence of a social model and demedicalization.

The Medical Model

The idea that people can become *mentally* ill is comparatively new. Up through the nineteenth century, people with mental disorders were believed to be possessed by demons. As such, they were a clear danger to the community. Religious leaders took it upon themselves to exorcise the offending spirits through moral lectures, prayer, or

Mental Disorders and Old Age

An estimated 1 to 1.6 million older Americans suffer from chronic organic brain syndrome, the scientific name for senility. Most younger people consider senility the inevitable consequence of old age and assume little can be done to correct memory loss, confusion, and other symptoms of senility. Indeed, the former Department of Health, Education, and Welfare (HEW) took this position. Medicare does not cover the cost of psychiatric care for older persons diagnosed as senile on the assumption "that those symptoms attributable to chronic brain syndrome condition are not expected to remit."

Professor Monica D. Blumenthal, head of the University of Pittsburgh's geriatric psychiatry clinic, considers HEW's position a crime (*The New York Times,* January 27, 1980, p. 20E). "We know now that it is not naturally a part of old age to feel depressed, slide into apathy, or lose one's cognitive capacities. . . . But where senility occurs, to exclude treatment from Medicare coverage is a crime against the elderly."

Blumenthal estimates that only fifty of every one hundred patients labeled senile are actually suffering from chronic organic brain syndrome. About twenty are suffering from hardening of the arteries; about thirty, from overdoses of medication for maladies such as high blood pressure, metabolic disorders, diabetes, and other physical ailments whose symptoms masquerade as senility. The most common mental disorder among the elderly is depression, which takes the form of inability to sleep, loss of appetite and weight, slowness of body functions, assorted aches and pains, and loss of the ability to concentrate. Depression in the elderly can be treated with counseling and with antidepressant drugs. Although there is no known cure for the fifty patients actually experiencing senility, it is possible to improve the quality of these older persons' lives by teaching them how to orient themselves, keep track of their possessions, and the like.

In Blumenthal's view, the fact that most senile and pseudo-senile Americans are given custodial care instead of treatment is only part of the problem. Few psychologists are interested in the elderly, so that little research is being done in the area of geriatric mental disorders.

if these failed, by starving the person, boring holes in their head, flogging, or burning. An uncounted number of men and women were locked up during this period. Parents took their children to "lunatic asylums" on holidays, to show them what happened to people who consorted with the devil. The chained inmates were put on exhibition, like animals in a zoo. (The most famous lunatic asylum was Bedlam, in England.) Other people whom we would consider mentally ill today lived more or less contentedly in villages and towns, where they were known as "imbeciles" or "crackbrains," and provided a source of local entertainment (Rosengren, 1980, p. 33).

Ideas about the insane changed only slowly. Phillippe Pinel unchained the inmates at La Bichêtre in Paris in 1792. In England, William Tuke unleashed the inmates of Bedlam. A century later, schoolteacher Dorothea Dix began a crusade to grant rights to the insane in the United States. All three led humanitarian movements based on changing values, not on new discoveries about mental disorders. The notion of mental *illness* had begun to grow—in part because Emil Kraepelin had discovered that one type of insanity was caused by the disease syphilis (Altrocchi, 1980, pp. 20–24). The concept of mental illness, however, did not take hold until the early twentieth century. The man most responsible for a medical model of mental disorders was Sigmund Freud.

The Freudian influence Freud's theories about the causes and cures of mental disorders grew from his work with people who had physical disorders for which there was no physiological explanation (hysterics, they were called). Freud worked first with hypnosis, gradually developing the technique of psychoanalysis, which one patient dubbed "the talking cure." Through hundreds of hours of analysis of patients—and hundreds more of introspection—Freud came to the conclusion that virtually all mental disorders result from powerful aggressive and sexual impulses that people experience as children but consider unacceptable as adults (for example, the desire to kill a parent). Most individuals develop mechanisms for defending themselves from these impulses and the shame and guilt they induce. (They may consciously suppress or unconsciously repress the thought, deny the feeling, project it onto others, and the like.) Freud believed that mild disorders, or neurotic behavior, result from a person constructing overly elaborate and only partly effective defense mechanisms. Severe disorders, or psychotic behavior, represent a breakdown of defense mechanisms.

Freud focused on psychological processes, not physiological processes. His theories, however, contributed to the growth of a medical model of mental disorders. Just as physicians act on the assumption that symptoms (e.g., fever) are caused by underlying diseases (e.g., an infection), so he believed that psychological symptoms (e.g., hysterical blindness) are caused by underlying conflicts (hostility toward a parent or spouse that the patient cannot bear to "see") (Altrocchi, 1980, p. 25). The physician's job is to uncover and treat the underlying disease; the psychoanalyst's or therapist's is to uncover and treat the underlying conflict. The idea that people who behave abnormally are mentally *ill* follows naturally from this theory.

The term "medical model" does *not* refer to biological explanations of mental disorders. There is growing evidence that genetic and biochemical factors play a role in mental disorders. For example, relatives of schizophrenics—particularly identical twins—are more likely to develop this disorder than are other members of the population (Heston, 1970). There is some evidence of biochemical disorders among schizophrenics (Antelman and Caggiula, 1977; Gunne et al., 1977). But, if genetic or biochemical disorders were the sole cause of mental disorders, they would be found in 100 percent of the cases. They are not.

Table 13–2
Leading Mental Disorders

Psychoses

Schizophrenia. This term applies to a variety of disorders characterized by disorganized thoughts and perceptions, unusual emotional responses, and social withdrawal. The world looks different to schizophrenics; their conversation is difficult to comprehend. Schizophrenia is the most common diagnosis for severe mental disorders. Every year about 6 of every 1,000 Americans are treated for schizophrenia. Nearly half of the beds in psychiatric wards and hospitals are occupied by schizophrenics. In most cases, schizophrenia appears in young adulthood. (Kramer, 1976)

Affective (or Mood) Disorders. *Manic* states—bursts of wild elation during which an individual is hyperactive and talks incessantly, hatching grandiose plans—belong in this category. So does severe *depression*—intense feelings of guilt, unworthiness, and discouragement that render a person indifferent to whatever might happen. In some cases, individuals go through *manic-depressive cycles,* shifting from one state to the other. An estimated 2 to 4 percent of Americans experiences one of these disorders in their lifetimes. Close to 7 million are immobilized by spells of depression each year. The frequency of affective disorders increases with age. Two to three times as many women as men experience mood disorders. (Altrocchi, 1980, pp. 436–61)

Neuroses

Because neurotic behavior is usually treated outside hospitals, or not at all, precise data on these disorders are impossible to obtain. However, anxiety and depression seem to be the most common neuroses. (Hilgard, Atkinson, and Atkinson, 1979, Chapter 15; Altrocchi, 1980)

Anxiety Reactions. "Free-floating" fear in the absence of any discernible threat or danger, often taking the form of heart palpitations, breathlessness, jitters, chest pains, dizziness, headaches, and/or chronic exhaustion.

Depression. Feelings of sadness that are out of proportion to the event that inspired them and persist beyond the usual recovery time. Often the person is unable to make decisions or take interest in people and events.

Obsessive-Compulsive Reactions. *Obessions* are persistent, unwelcome thoughts that an individual cannot push out of his or her mind. *Compulsions* are irrational, irresistible urges to perform certain acts in a ritualistic fashion.

Phobias. Intense fear of situations (being in a small, closed room), objects (snakes), or specific kinds of people (doctors) that are way out of proportion to the danger these present.

Conversion Reactions. Physical symptoms (such as loss of sensation in part of the body or blindness) that have no underlying organic cause. The experience is real, however; the person isn't faking. (Conversion reactions are distinct from psychosomatic illnesses, such as ulcers, which are organic disorders brought on by stress.)

Thus, genetics and biochemistry are only part of the answer. Further explanation is necessary, and the medical model is one attempt to supply that explanation.

The medical model was not meant to be taken literally. Rather, the idea was to treat mental disorders *as if* they were diseases (Sarbin, 1969). Mental illness is a metaphor. Freud recognized the limitations of a medical model. Many of his followers did not, however. Gradually, the "as if" was forgotten. A literal version of the medical model came to dominate psychiatry.

The mental hospital Acceptance of the medical model had a direct impact on the treatment of mental disorders. William R. Rosengren illustrates this by contrasting conditions at Worcester State Hospital in Massachusetts before and after it was run by medical professionals (1980, pp. 332–41).

In the 1830s, Worcester became a center for moral therapy. Moral therapy was based on the belief that the insane were basically normal people who had "lost their reason" because of severe stress and misfortune. The goal of moral therapy was to provide pleasant, communal living conditions where reasonable behavior could be encouraged. In other words, treatment consisted of benign resocialization.

At Worcester, "guests" lived close to superintendents (local people who acted as helpers) and superintendents' families. The words "patient" and "inmate" were never spoken. Guests attended lectures, engaged in such healthful activities as picnics, and entertained visitors freely. They were also expected to work. Mild punishments were given out for misbehavior. Guests continued to wear their street clothes. They were allowed to mingle with members of the opposite sex. They were even allowed to use knives and forks at meals—something never permitted in lunatic asylums of an earlier day or the mental hospitals of days to come.

Worcester's records suggest that moral therapy produced remarkable recovery rates. Over 60 percent of the individuals admitted to Worcester "recovered their reason" and were discharged. A follow-up study conducted more than thirty years later indicated that 48 percent had remained well; fewer than 30 percent experienced a severe relapse. By the time this study was conducted, however, moral therapy had been abandoned. Why?

Financial support for Worcester and similar institutions was eroding steadily. One reason may have been ethnic prejudice. In the 1830s and 1840s, the population of Worcester was culturally homogeneous. Guests and superintendents came from the same communities and shared the same basic values. In the 1850s, waves of immigrants came to this country's shores—and to its treatment centers. By the turn of the century, Worcester and other state hospitals were filled with Irish, Italians, Scandinavians, and Germans, and a new diagnostic category was invented: "foreign insane pauperism." The growing number of mental patients made personal relationships difficult to sustain. A final reason for the demise of moral therapy was medicalization. Moral communities were slowly being taken over by medical professionals and transformed into mental hospitals. By the turn of the century, Worcester was well on its way to becoming what Erving Goffman (1961) has called a total institution.

Goffman compares the giant state mental hospitals that emerged at the beginning of this century to monasteries, military boot camps, and prisons. Mental hospitals are *total institutions* "in the sense that the inmate lives all the aspects of his life on the premises in the close company of others who are similarly cut off from the wider world" (1961, p. 191). Through the first half of this century, the doors and gates of mental hospitals were locked. The mentally ill were segregated from other members of society (not to mention members of "the relevant sex").

The residents of mental hospitals were "patients," not guests, and as such, they were obliged to obey staff orders. Goffman characterizes the experience of being in a state hospital as a series of "mortifications." Upon entry, patients were deprived of their personal clothing, private possessions, toilet articles, and the like—the things people outside the hospital use to reinforce their personal sense of identity—and were given standard hospital issue. Once inside, they were deprived of privacy. Typically, they slept in open wards and used communal bathrooms. Every moment of the day, they were under the surveillance of staff. They were also deprived of the right to make decisions for themselves. Every hour of the day was scheduled. They were expected to do as they were told, however arbitrary the command, however meaningless the activity. In effect, they were treated like children—bad children.

These state mental hospitals were essentially custodial institutions. In other words, they were designed more to protect society from the mentally ill and the mentally ill from themselves than to offer treatment. Many were located in remote areas and understaffed. Treatment depended on the availability of personnel and on prevailing notions about what worked (e.g., whether shock therapy was "in" or "out"). So-called back wards were created for patients who were considered utterly hopeless.

Only in 1975, in the *Donaldson* case, did the Supreme Court rule that persons confined to mental hospitals have a legal right to treatment. In that landmark case, the Court ruled in favor of a former patient who had been committed to a Florida mental hospital and involuntarily kept there for fifteen years. Kenneth Donaldson had received no treatment during this period; his petitions for release had been turned down repeatedly by the courts. When finally released in 1971, Donaldson sued hospital officials for damages. The Supreme Court supported his suit, ruling that a person cannot be involuntarily confined unless he is proven dangerous to himself and/or others (a diagnosis of mental illness alone is not enough) and that if a person is committed to a mental institution, he or she is entitled to treatment.

In short, up through the 1970s, the history of treatment of mental disorders is one of increasing medicalization, to the point where doctors were given the authority to deny a person virtually all rights. In recent years, however, the medical model has been questioned.

The Social Model

The medical model emphasizes the internal dynamics of mental disorders. The social model directs attention away from individual psyches, toward the social environment and the roles people play. How do social factors affect mental disorders? (Is there something about society that "drives people mad"?) Who is most likely to suffer from mental disorders (what categories of people)? Who decides who is mentally ill and who is mentally well? What are the consequences? In seeking answers to these questions, sociologists arrived at a new model of mental disorders.

Mental disorders and social class In the 1930s, two sociologists at the University of Chicago, Robert Faris and Warren Dunham (1938), launched the sociology of mental disorders with a study of residents of Chicago's psychiatric hospitals. Faris and Dunham found that a high percentage of mental patients came from the inner city. The rates of mental disorder increased steadily as one moved from stable, upper-middle-class suburbs in toward the decaying slums of the center city, with their poor and highly mobile populations. They concluded that urban poverty was a major factor in the genesis of mental disorders.

By today's standards, Faris and Dunham's research is not terribly sophisticated. Nevertheless, they did uncover evidence that social factors play a role in mental disorders, suggesting that both the psychiatrist's couch and the hospital corridor were in need of sociological investigation (Rosengren, 1980, pp. 310–15). And this laid the foundation for a social model of mental disorder.

A study of psychiatric patients in New Haven, Connecticut, conducted in 1950–51 by the sociologist August B. Hollingshead and the psychiatrist Frederick C. Redlich (1958), confirmed suspicions about social class and mental disorder. Hollingshead and Redlich collected data on outpatients as well as hospital inmates. They, too, found an inverse relationship between mental disorder and social class: The highest rates of mental disorder were found in the lower classes. A significantly higher percentage of the poor suffered from severe mental disorders, were hospitalized for the disorders, and remained in a mental institution for an extended period or returned after being released. (A follow-up study conducted ten years later confirmed these class differences [Meyers, Bean, and Pepper, 1965]).

Hollingshead and Redlich were also interested in the question of how people come to the attention of mental health professionals. They found that the poor and the affluent arrived at the psychiatrist's office by quite different paths. By and large, members of the upper class knew something about psychiatric treatment. They viewed frustration, unhappiness, and abnormal behavior as psychological problems and believed that something could and ought to be done. In most cases, the decision to seek psychiatric care was made by the individual and his or her family. Members of the lower class were more inclined to tolerate high levels of abnormal behavior and to attribute their problems to bad luck, laziness, meanness, or physical ailments. They feared that seeking psychiatric care would mean that they, or a member of their family, would be "taken away." In most cases, the poor were referred to psychia-

trists by police, the courts, or other social agencies. Thus, members of the upper class were induced to seek help in "more gentle and 'insightful' ways." For the lower class, referral was "direct, authoritative, compulsory, and at times, coercively brutal. . . ."

The most ambitious study of social factors and mental disorders conducted to date is the Midtown Manhattan Study, conceived in the early 1960s by the psychiatrist Thomas A.C. Rennie (Srole, 1978). For this project, researchers interviewed a cross section of nearly 1,700 residents of a section of Manhattan. This enabled them to gather data on people who were *not* being treated for mental disorders, as well as on those who were, and thus estimate the overall incidence of mental disorders. Respondents were asked such questions as whether they had ever had a "nervous breakdown" or sought psychiatric help, whether they had difficulties with interpersonal relationships, and whether they got headaches or stomach pains when they were emotionally upset. Their responses were later evaluated by a team of psychiatrists.

The results of the Midtown Manhattan Study came as a shock (see Figure 13–3). Less than 19 percent of those interviewed were rated mentally "well." Fifty-eight percent were suffering from mild to moderate disorders; 23 percent were not able to function adequately—including many who were not receiving any form of mental health care. The results indicated that not only are mental disorders more common and more severe among the lower classes but also that the poor are far less likely to be treated for mental disorders, and when they are treated, they are less likely to recover. Seventy-two percent of former mental patients in the upper class functioned well on the outside, compared to only 32 percent in the lower class.

The rates of mental disorders revealed by the Midtown Manhattan Study are not unique to New York City or even to modern times. Histori-

Figure 13–3

Incidence of Mental Disorders: Midtown Manhattan Study

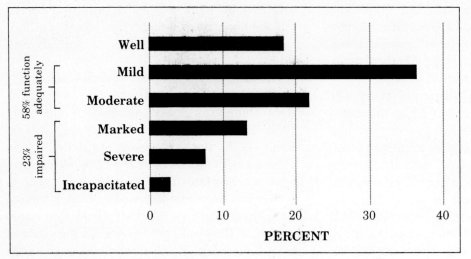

Source: Data from L. Srole et al., *Mental Health in the Metropolis: The Midtown Manhattan Study,* rev. ed. (New York: New York University Press, 1978), p. 197.

cal research shows that the rate of hospitalization for mental disorders in Massachusetts, for example, was about the same in 1850 as it was in 1950 (Rothman, 1971). Mental disorder is not a modern, urban problem, as Faris and Dunham had believed (see Clausen, 1976, pp. 118–20).

The relationship between social class and mental disorders is well established. The question is, why does this relationship exist? Is low economic status one of the causes of mental disorders or one of the consequences? Is the higher incidence of mental disorders among the poor the result of social causation (does life in the lower class produce abnormal behavior) or the result of social selection (do mentally disturbed people drift into the lower classes because of their disorders)? The Midtown Manhattan Study researchers believed both play a part. On the one hand, individuals suffering from mental disorders may be unable to maintain their social position and slide downward. On the other hand, economic insecurity, overcrowding, poor physical health, and the in-

ability to plan for tomorrow may bring out mental disorders (see Kohn, 1972). There is a third possibility, however—namely that what to middle- and upper-middle-class researchers and psychiatrists appears to be abnormal behavior may in fact represent "normal" or adaptive strategies for coping with stressful living conditions (Dohrenwend and Dohrenwend, 1974). According to this view, the higher incidence of mental disorders in the lower classes in part reflects the middle-class biases of mental health researchers and professionals. (This is the main criticism of the Midtown Manhattan Study.)

Mental disorders and labeling A second sociological approach to the study of mental disorders focuses on who decides that certain behavior is a sign of mental disorder, that certain people need treatment, and why.

All definitions of abnormal behavior reflect prevailing norms and values. Psychiatric judgments about what is "appropriate" are not made in a scientific vacuum. They are delivered at a particular time in a particular society by people who are part of that society. Numerous studies have shown that psychiatric diagnosis can be a highly subjective procedure. At best, independent psychiatrists agree on their diagnosis of the same patient only 60 percent of the time (Conover, 1972, p. 168). (Agreement among physicians on the diagnosis of physical disorders is also low!) One problem is that psychiatrists use different terms to describe the same behavior; another, that they weigh symptoms differently. Studies that compared American and British psychiatrists' diagnoses (reported in Conover, 1972) are particularly revealing. Using the same case material, American psychiatrists in one study reported twice as many symptoms as British psychiatrists did. (By British standards, they overdiagnose.) The two groups also disagree on what kinds of behavior they consider symptomatic. Americans tend to focus on signs of inactivity—apathy, indecisiveness, and dependence. In contrast, the British tend to focus on signs of overactivity—excitement, elation, grandiosity. Thus, not only do psychiatrists disagree, their diagnoses seem to reflect cultural norms about what is appropriate.

Given the subjective factors in psychiatric diagnosis, there is always a danger that the label "mentally ill" will be used as an instrument of social control. In the U.S.S.R., for example, political dissidents have been confined to mental institutions and "treated" with mind-altering drugs. In the United States, during the early days of the Civil Rights Movement, several black Americans who rebelled against the tradition of racial discrimination in the South were sent to mental institutions for observation. People couldn't understand what was "wrong with them" (Coles, 1970). In both situations, authorities medicalized political behavior. Critics of the medical model argue that this is often the case.

Thomas Scheff (1966) has maintained that vir-

tually all of the people diagnosed as mentally ill are victims of the status quo. People in all societies categorize violations of the norms or rules as sins, crimes, ignorance, poor manners, and the like. There is always, however, a residue of violations for which people have no explicit name, for the simple reason that most people consider the violations unthinkable. (Examples would be talking out loud to oneself or fondling oneself in the full hearing or view of other people.) Unnamed violations of norms are lumped together in a residual category. In some societies, residual deviance is considered a sign of possession by demons; in ours, it is considered mental illness.

Scheff argues that all people engage in residual deviance on occasion. Children go through stages in which they throw tantrums, invent fantasy playmates, and develop intense fear of the dark. Compulsions, depression, and hallucinations (with or without drugs) are common experiences among adults. In most cases, no one pays much attention (the experience is rationalized or denied), and the behavior goes away. In some cases, however, the behavior is not ignored. The individual is labeled mentally ill, setting off what Scheff sees as a chain reaction.

Mental illness is a stigma in our society. Once a person is so labeled, people tend to reinterpret his or her behavior in terms of the diagnosis. The individual is brought to the attention of professionals whose *job* it is to identify symptoms of mental disorder. In subtle ways, they may reward the individual for conforming to their diagnosis. The person's attempts to resist or to change may be punished. (A Civil Rights worker who argued with the psychiatrist was described as "resistant" to psychological insights.) Eventually the stigmatized individual may find it easier to conform to cultural stereotypes of mental illness than to reassert his or her sanity. Scheff compares the mentally ill to actors who have been type-cast against their will, but who eventually give up seeking other kinds of roles.

Being Sane in Insane Places

An experiment conducted by D.L. Rosenhan (1973) supports labeling theory. Eight sane people (including three psychologists, a pediatrician, a psychiatrist, a painter, and a housewife) had themselves voluntarily committed to mental hospitals. In their admissions interviews, each faked a single symptom: They said that they had heard voices telling them something like "empty," "hollow," and "thud." Otherwise, they answered all questions truthfully. All were admitted to hospitals and held for an average of nineteen days.

Once in the hospital, Rosenhan's colleagues behaved normally. When asked, they said they felt fine and did not hear voices. Daily visitors found the pseudo patients somewhat nervous about their new surroundings at first but otherwise in good shape. A number of patients guessed that they were impostors. But, not one staff member discovered the hoax. After their release, their records were labeled "schizophrenia in remission."*

Why weren't the pseudo patients detected? Rosenhan suggests several reasons. First, contacts between patients and staff were rare. (Nurses entered the wards an average of eleven or twelve times per shift; doctors, only six or seven times.) The staff members seemed to keep themselves segregated, as if their patients' disorders were contagious. When they did walk through the wards, they often acted as if patients were invisible. Patients' attempts to initiate conversation were usually futile. (In one case, a pseudo patient approached a doctor, excused himself, and asked when he would be given ground privileges. The doctor replied, "Good morning, Dave. How are you today?" and moved on, not waiting for an answer.) Finally, Rosenhan suggests that once a person is diagnosed as mentally ill, the meaning of his or her behavior is determined by the diagnosis. Normal behavior is labeled "symptomatic." (For example, all of the pseudo patients kept notes. One staff member entered this in the records as "patient engages in writing behavior.") Rosenhan doesn't blame the staff. From their point of view, it is much more dangerous to misdiagnose illness than health. Although the experiment included only eight pseudo patients, it does give pause.

* Later the procedure was reversed. The staff of a teaching hospital was told that one or more pseudo patients would seek admission over the next three months. Staff members identified forty-three pseudo patients; psychiatrists, twenty-three. To Rosenhan's knowledge, no pseudo patient had applied.

Thomas Szasz (1960) has argued that the very notion of mental illness is a myth. In his words, "Our adversaries are not demons, witches, fate or mental illness. We have no enemy whom we can fight, exorcise, or dispel by 'cure.'" What we do have are *problems in living*—whether these be biological, economical, political, or sociopsychological . . ." (p. 118). The medical model implies that the problem lies deep in the individual's psyche and can be understood and treated without considering the social context in which the problems developed. This is extremely convenient, argues Szasz, for it absolves both individuals and society from dealing directly with problems in living. Instead, troubled people can be handed over to doctors.

Both Scheff and Szasz believe that mental disorder does not reside in the individual or the individual's behavior. It is ascribed to the person by others. People are diagnosed as mentally ill, not so much because they are deviant (everyone is on occasion), but because they are unable to resist or evade labeling. Their behavior reflects the role into which they have been cast. In effect, the label creates the disorder.

The evidence does not support an extreme version of labeling theory, however. In one long-term study of males labeled schizophrenic (Clausen and Huffine, 1975), a third of the men had led normal lives in the fifteen to twenty years since they had left the hospital. The label had not stuck. Another third had been able to function with periodic treatment as outpatients. Only a third had had recurring difficulties. At first, the admission that an individual was disturbed did create a crisis for most patients and their families, provoking more seriously disturbed behavior in the patient. In the long run, however, the label "mentally ill" enabled many patients and their families to reinterpret past behavior in a more hopeful light. Now they had an explanation for unusual behavior. Moreover, the rejection many

expected to encounter when released from the hospital failed to materialize.

Few social scientists today accept the idea that mental disorder is nothing more than a myth, a label applied to people whose behavior we do not like and would rather not see (though it can be used this way). But the idea that mental illness derives in part from social causes is gaining widespread acceptance. In the words of one clinical psychologist, "we now think that abnormal behavior often develops not only from . . . inner conflicts but from difficulties between one person and another or between an individual and society" (Altrocchi, 1980, p. 25). This moderate view has supported the community mental health movement.

The Community Mental Health Movement

The last ten years have witnessed a revolution in the treatment of mental disorders. Hospital walls are crumbling. The changes taking place today are the result of both changing attitudes toward mental illness (acceptance of the social model) and new technology.

Deinstitutionalization and the drug revolution For the first half of this century, the rate of committing people to state mental hospitals climbed at a more or less steady rate of 2 percent a year. In 1956, for the first time in history, the number of mental patients dropped, and it has continued to drop (see Figure 13–4). The main reason, as we have indicated, is drugs.

The drug revolution began in the early 1950s when doctors discovered that a new drug for tuberculosis, isoniazid, sent elderly patients dancing along hospital corridors. This led to the creation of a series of antidepressants (e.g., Elavil) that alleviate insomnia, despair, listlessness, and suicidal impulses in as many as 70 percent of

Figure 13–4

Inpatient and Outpatient Care for Mental Disorders, 1955 and 1975

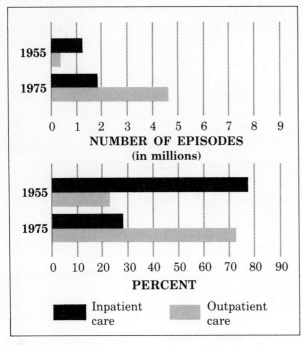

Source: U.S. Bureau of the Census, *Social Indicators III* (Washington, D.C.: U.S. Government Printing Office, December 1980), p. 68.

individuals experiencing severe depression. At about the same time, another group of doctors discovered that phenothiazines (e.g., Thorazine), originally created to reduce stress during surgery, reduce disordered thought. (Exactly why, no one knows.) Phenothiazines enable about 70 percent of patients diagnosed as schizophrenic to function in the outside world. The third major psychoactive drug, lithium carbonate, was first used in the United States in about 1970. A simple salt, lithium prevents hyperactive, manic episodes and the depression that often follows. These drugs are the main reason why so many people who would have been hospitalized ten or fifteen years ago are now back in the community.

Drugs brought a new optimism to the mental health field. At last, doctors could do something for severely disturbed patients. The widespread use of drug therapy has begun to create controversy, however. Long-term treatment often produces negative side effects. About 40 percent of people taking phenothiazines develop involuntary muscle spasms and twitches; antidepressants may raise a person's blood pressure to a dangerously high level. Moreover, none of the new drugs eliminates or cures mental disorders. They merely relieve symptoms. If for one reason or another, a person stops taking the medication, the symptoms reappear.

Drugs freed hundreds of thousands of people from mental wards. Whether the massive release of mental patients in the 1970s was wise is an open question, however. Many former patients have few resources to cope with life outside the hospital. Between 1975 and 1979, New York State hospitals discharged 83,659 adults from its mental hospitals (including about 40,000 in New York City). About 4,000 have been placed in homes to help them adjust. But an estimated 20,000 live alone in run-down, single-room occupancy hotels (*The New York Times,* November 18, 19, 20, 1979). Chicago has a thirty-block "psychiatric ghetto." The hospital's responsibility for mental patients ends the day they are discharged. Former patients receive help only if they voluntarily apply to community health centers, and many do not. This has created a "revolving door syndrome": Patients are discharged, fail to connect with agencies that might help them to live on their own, eventually stop taking their medicine, end up back in the hospital, where they are treated with drugs, released, and the cycle begins again. Critics argue that however well-intentioned, the current policy of deinstitutionalization fails to take into account that many of these individuals' problems are social, not mental. This brings us to a second "revolutionary front" in mental health care.

The miracle drugs of the 1960s enabled mental hospitals to release tens of thousands of mental patients. But not all continue taking their medications outside the hospital or remain in contact with community mental health agencies. How many lose touch, no one knows.

Community mental health centers In the early 1960s, President John Kennedy, encouraged by recent social science findings, declared "obsolete the traditional methods of treatment which imposed on the mentally ill a social quarantine, a prolonged or permanent confinement in a huge, unhappy mental hospital where they were out of sight and forgotten" (in Rosengren, 1980, p. 349). In 1963, Congress passed the Community Mental Health Center Act, which laid the groundwork for shifting mental health care from state hospitals to small, decentralized, neighborhood centers.

The community mental health movement was based on the conviction that removing people from their family and friends, home and community created as many problems as it solved. The original community mental health plan was ambitious (Smith and Hobbs, 1966). Ideally, the community center would provide twenty-four-hour emergency service; create flexible inpatient and outpatient services (including day-care and night-care centers); implement preventive programs; offer education and consultation; and involve nonprofessionals from the community. The key to community health centers is the emphasis on providing troubled individuals with *social support*. The emphasis is on developing strategies for coping with problems in living, not on treating inner conflicts.

To date, only 725 of a planned 1,500 community centers are actually in operation (The President's Commission on Mental Health, 1978). Some have been blocked because of lack of funds, others because of community opposition to locating mental health facilities in "our neighborhood." Nevertheless, these centers provide services to as many as 90 million people (counting former and potential mental patients and their families). Moreover, they are supplemented by a variety of public and private alternative support services: homes for runaway children and battered wives, hotlines for rape victims and potential suicides, and so on. Thus, the social model of mental disorder is being put to work.

Health Care: Toward an Uncertain Future

The World Health Organization summarized much of what we have discussed in this chapter when it defined health as "a state of complete physical, mental, and *social* well-being" (emphasis added). How healthy will Americans be in the year 2000? What advances will medical science produce? How will the politics of health care shape our future? Who, ultimately, is responsible for our physical, mental, and social well-being?

Advancing Medical Technology

Thirty or forty years ago, medicine was a relatively simple science. The chemical structure of genes was still a mystery. Drugs like streptomycin and phenothiazine had yet to be discovered. Medical hardware was crude. Much has changed in the last thirty years, and much will change. Among other advances, futurologists predict that there will be extensive transplantation of limbs and organs, and ultimately organ regeneration; reduction of hereditary defects, choice of sex of offspring, even cloning; more reliable drugs to control not only mood, perception, personality, and alertness but also memory and intelligence; brain-computer links; and the prolongation of youthful vigor (Carlson, 1975, pp. 119–21).

Advances in medical technology can be expected to create situations for which there are no clear norms or values. Indeed, this has already happened. The invention of machines to prolong life (to revive the heart and maintain respiration) made it necessary for us to redefine death. An ad hoc committee of doctors, lawyers, philosophers, and historians took on this challenge, convening at Harvard in the mid-1960s. The "Harvard definition" of death focuses on awareness, movement, and brain wave activity. The case of Karen Ann Quinlan, who fell into a coma on April 15, 1975, and never recovered, brought this issue to a head. Doctors thought Ms. Quinlan was being kept alive by respirators. Her parents and priest argued in court that she would not have wanted to live in a vegetative state, that the right to death is as sacred as the right to life, and they ultimately won their case. (As of this writing, Ms. Quinlan is still alive. Even though the respirator was disconnected, she is still comatose.) (Reiser, 1977)

Advances in medical technology force difficult choices. For example, when kidney dialysis machines first became available, the demand greatly exceeded the supply. Who should decide which of the thousands of people with fatal kidney failures will live or die? How should they make this decision? A committee of physicians and laymen and women at the Seattle Artificial Kidney Center was applauded on one side and attacked on the other when a reporter revealed they were considering not only medical suitability but also age, sex, marital situation, and overall "social worth." With the help of a lawyer, one elderly gentleman presented his case so forcefully that he was admitted, but a prostitute was rejected (Fox and Swazey, 1974).

Advances in medical technology also force trade-offs. The decision to invest funds in one form of technology is a decision to save some lives but lose others. The cost-effective approach suggests investing money where it will save the most lives. According to this perspective, the estimated $200,000 a year it will cost to treat a single dialysis patient in 1985 would be better spent preventing nine or ten deaths from cancer and the $1 billion it will cost to treat 5,000 dialysis patients would be better spent fighting air pollution (Carlson, 1975, pp. 125–26). But again, who should make these decisions? Should physicians? (By and large, physicians have made these decisions in the past.) The more advanced medical science becomes in the treatment of mental and physical disorders, the more quandaries we will face.

The Politics of Health Care

In other nations, health care is a right guaranteed by law. In Great Britain, for example, every citizen can obtain virtually free medical care simply by registering with a general practitioner. British general practitioners own or rent their own offices and equipment, but are paid by the government on a per capita rate arrived at through negotiation with physician representatives. Specialists in Great Britain are salaried staff members of hospitals that are owned and operated by the government. The entire British National Health Service is funded through general taxes (Anderson, 1972).

Medical care is also a guaranteed right in the People's Republic of China (Sidel, 1975). The health care system in China reflects planned decentralization and deprofessionalization. In 1965 (the latest data available), there was 1 physician for about every 5,000 Chinese citizens, compared to about 1 per 1,000 in Western nations. But, these doctors are backed up by several hundred thousand physicians' assistants who have the equivalent of a high-school education in modern medicine, and by over a million Red Medical Workers—farmers and factory workers who have received three to six months' training in basic physical examination, the administration of modern and traditional medicine, injections, acupuncture, and in health education. Traditional healers have not been discredited in China, as they were in the West, but have been integrated into the system. They are trained in basic modern medicine, and modern physicians study their techniques. The Red Medical Workers run clinics in their own communities; physicians and their assistants are assigned to urban posts and rural teams on a rotating basis. Health care was decentralized and deprofessionalized in China in part to bring medical care to a vast, dispersed population, in part to demystify medicine. (According to one doctor, a major problem in China has been convincing people that poor health is not "fixed in heaven," that there are remedies.) The system also depends on mass participation. Literally everyone takes part in regular campaigns to disseminate information about birth control, immunize children, rid neighborhoods of pests, and the like.

The growing demand for health care rights in the United States has collided head-on with the medical profession. The medical establishment claims that deprofessionalization and decentralization of health care, as in China, or socialization, as in Great Britain, will reduce the quality of health care. Do we want "barefoot doctors"? Do we want a federal bureaucracy behind medical care? Critics argue health maintenance and national insurance programs will not improve either the quality or the distribution of health care, but will only bring us more of the same. Two major obstacles to change in this country are the lingering belief that the doctor-patient relationship should be a private one (even though most medical care is delivered in depersonalized clinics and hospitals today) and the belief that "the doctor knows best."

Preventive Care: Whose Responsibility?

Perhaps the most serious consequence of over-medicalization is that individuals surrendered to the medical establishment responsibility for their own health. This, in turn, led to an emphasis on reactive medicine, to the neglect of preventive health care. In 1975, Rick Carlson wrote:

> We deserve the medical care we get. . . . We freely choose to live the way we do. We choose to live recklessly, to abuse our bodies with what we consume, to expose ourselves to environmental insults, to rush frantically from place to place, and to sit on

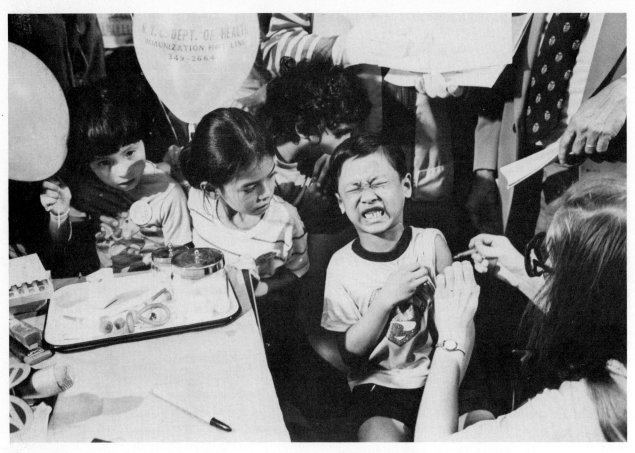

Preventive medical care is beginning to receive as much popular support as reactive care, for adults as well as children.

our spreading bottoms and watch paid professionals exercise for us. . . . Today few patients have the confidence to care for themselves. The inexorable professionalization of medicine, together with reverence for the scientific method, have invested practitioners with sacrosanct powers, and correspondingly vitiated the responsibility of the rest of us for health. (pp. 44, 142)

Attitudes are changing, however. Many Americans are coming to believe that good health is as much the product of a good life and a good society as of expert medical care.

Physicians, too, are changing. In *Doing Better and Feeling Worse* (1977), physician John H. Knowles states, unequivocally, "The health of human beings is determined by their behavior, their food, and the nature of their environment" (p. 57). By extension, the health of human beings is *not* determined by their doctors. Knowles argues that the physician's primary goal should be preventive, not reactive, medicine. Knowles specifies such activities as vaccinating children against infectious diseases, detecting diseases such as breast cancer early so they can be treated, preventing diseases already in progress (such as diabetes) from worsening and providing health education. Beyond this, he believes, health is in the hands of individuals and of society.

Knowles cites evidence that common sense and good habits can do more to prolong life than the best medical care. For example, a forty-five-year-old man adds eleven years to his life expectancy if he eats three regular meals a day (including breakfast but excluding snacks); exercises moderately two or three times a week; sleeps seven or eight hours a night; and avoids gaining weight, smoking, and drinking (except in moderation). At age sixty-five, someone who follows all of these rules can be as healthy as a thirty-five-year-old who ignores them. Knowles also cites social actions that have produced concrete improvements in health, including the lowering of speed limits during the oil embargo (a 40 percent reduction in automobile accidents), the Surgeon General's 1964 report on smoking (10 percent of the male population stopped smoking over the next ten years), and self-help programs for diabetics and heart patients. Knowles believes that "99 percent of us are born healthy and made sick as a result of personal misbehavior and environmental conditions" (p. 58). Judging by the number of joggers and ex-smokers, the environmental and consumer protests, many Americans agree that health is a matter of individual and social responsibility, not medical intervention.

We do not know enough about the causes of mental disorders to prevent them. But we do know enough to identify populations at risk and crisis points in individual's lives (the death of a loved one, loss of a job, divorce); to train lay persons (clergy, teachers, hospital workers) in the identification of mental disorders; and through early detection and treatment, to reduce suffering (Altrocchi, 1980, Chapter 15).

Summary

1. The United States has the most advanced medical technology in the world, but we have fallen behind other industrial nations. Two of our problems are differential access to health care and overmedicalization.

2. Overmedicalization is in part the result of the development of a professionalized establishment that is insulated from outside social controls. The growth of the American Medical Association, Blue Cross, and medical centers contributed to this process.

3. Physician specialization and the use of increasingly sophisticated technology, funded by third parties, have pushed the cost of health care skyward. Health maintenance organizations and national health insurance might help to reverse this trend.

4. The poor are exposed to special health hazards that indirectly cause many preventable deaths each year. Many of the health problems of the elderly (such as senility) are misdiagnosed and mistreated.

5. The medicalization of mental disorders can be traced to humanitarian movements in the eighteenth and nineteenth centuries, to Freud's theory of unconscious motivations, and to the transformation of "moral communities" into "total institutions."

6. The medical model focuses on the internal dynamics of mental disorders; the social model focuses on the impact of the social environment on mental health.

7. The social model grew out of research that showed both the incidence and treatment of mental disorders is unevenly distributed through society.

8. Labeling theory emphasizes the social forces that lead people to define certain individuals as mentally ill, and the consequences of this labeling.

9. In recent years, changing attitudes and revolutionary new drugs have greatly reduced the number of patients confined to mental hospitals. Deinstitutionalization is being questioned, however, for many former patients do not stay in contact with community mental health centers.

10. In the future, advanced technology may raise difficult moral questions; the growing demand for health rights (such as the right to death) may clash with professional control of medicine; and preventive care and personal responsibility for health may bring about some demedicalization.

Suggested Reading

Brown, E. Richard. *Rockefeller Medicine Men: Medicine and Capitalism in America.* Berkeley, Cal.: University of California Press, 1979.

Goffman, Erving. *Asylums.* New York: Doubleday/Anchor, 1961.

Knowles, John H. *Doing Better and Feeling Worse: Health in the United States.* New York: Norton, 1977.

Lear, Martha Weinman. *Heartsounds.* New York: Pocket Books, 1980.

Rosengren, William R. *Sociology of Medicine: Diversity, Conflict, and Change.* New York: Harper & Row, 1980.

Sheehan, Susan. "A Reporter at Large: The Patient." *The New Yorker,* May 25, June 1, June 8, June 15, 1981.

Srole, Leo et al. *Mental Health in the Metropolis: The Midtown Manhattan Study,* rev. ed. New York: New York University Press, 1978.

References

Altrocchi, J. *Abnormal Behavior.* New York: Harcourt Brace Jovanovich, 1980.

Anderson, O.W. *Health Care: Can There Be Equity?* New York: Wiley, 1972.

Antelman, S.M., and A.R. Caggiula. "Norepinephrine-Dopamine Interactions and Behavior." *Science,* Vol. 195 (1977), pp. 646–53.

Behn, R.D., and K. Sperduto. "Medical Schools and the 'Entitlement Ethic.'" *The Public Interest,* Vol. 57 (Fall 1979), pp. 48–68.

Berger, P., B. Hamburg, and D. Hamburg. "Mental Health: Progress and Problems." In J.H. Knowles (Ed.), *Doing Better and Feeling Worse: Health in the United States*. New York: Norton, 1977, pp. 261–76.

Blumenthal, D., and J. Fallows. "Health: The Care We Want and Need." *Washington Monthly* (October 1973).

Bodenheimer, T. "The Malpractice Blow-up: Fighting over the Carcass." In D. Kotelchuck (Ed.), *Prognosis Negative: Crisis in the Health Care System*. New York: Vintage, 1976, pp. 419–24.

Bodenheimer, T., S. Cummings, and E. Harding. "What People Get from Health Insurance." In D. Kotelchuck (Ed.), *Prognosis Negative: Crisis in the Health Care System*. New York: Vintage, 1976, pp. 78–81.

Brown, E.R. *Rockefeller Medicine Men: Medicine and Capitalism in America*. Berkeley, Cal.: University of California Press, 1979.

Carlson, R.J. *The End of Medicine*. New York: Wiley, 1975.

Clausen, J.A. "Mental Disorders." In R.K. Merton and R. Nisbet (Eds.), *Contemporary Social Problems*, 4th ed. New York: Harcourt Brace Jovanovich, 1976, pp. 103–39.

Clausen, J.A., and C.L. Huffine. "Sociocultural and Social-psychological Factors Affecting Social Responses to Mental Disorder." *Journal of Health and Social Behavior,* Vol. 61, No. 4 (December 1975), pp. 405–20.

Coles, R. "A Fashionable Kind of Slander." *Atlantic,* Vol. 226, No. 5 (November 1970), pp. 53–55.

Conover, D. "Psychiatric Distinctions: New and Old Approaches." *Journal of Health and Social Behavior,* Vol. 13, No. 2 (June 1972), pp. 167–80.

Conrad, P. "The Discovery of Hyperkinesis: Notes on the Medicalization of Deviant Behavior." *Social Problems,* Vol. 23 (October 1975), pp. 12–21.

Cousins, N. *Anatomy of an Illness as Perceived by the Patient* New York: Norton, 1979.

De Lone, R.H. *Small Futures.* New York: Harcourt Brace Jovanovich, 1979.

Dohrenwend, B.P., and B.S. Dohrenwend. "Social and Cultural Influences on Psychopathology." *Annual Review of Psychology,* Vol. 25 (1974), pp. 417–52.

Ehrenreich, J., and B. Ehrenreich. *The American Health Empire: Power, Profits, and Politics.* New York: Vintage, 1971.

Faris, R.E.L., and H.W. Dunham. *Mental Disorders in Urban Areas*. Chicago: University of Chicago Press, 1938.

Fox, R.C. "The Medicalization and Demedicalization of American Society." In J.H. Knowles (Ed.), *Doing Better and Feeling Worse: Health in the United States.* New York: Norton, 1977, pp. 9–22.

Fox, R.C., and J. Swazey. *The Courage to Fail* Chicago: University of Chicago Press, 1974.

Goffman, E. *Asylums.* New York: Doubleday/Anchor, 1961.

Gunne, L.M., L. Lindström, and J. Terenius. "Naxoxone-induced Reversal of Schizophrenic Hallucinations." *Journal of Neural Transmissions,* Vol. 40 (1977), pp. 13–19.

Hammerman, J. "Health Services: Their Success and Failure in Reaching Older Adults." *American Journal of Public Health,* Vol. 64 (March 1974), pp. 253–56.

Heston, L. "The Genetics of Schizophrenia and Schizoid Disease." *Science,* Vol. 167 (1970), pp. 249–56.

Hilgard, E.R., R.L. Atkinson, and R.C. Atkinson. *Introduction to Psychology,* 7th ed. New York: Harcourt Brace Jovanovich, 1979.

Hollingshead, A.B., and F. Redlich. *Social Class and Mental Illness.* New York: Wiley, 1958.

House Committee on Interstate and Foreign Commerce. *Cost and Quality of Health Care: Unnecessary Surgery.* Washington, D.C.: U.S. Government Printing Office, 1976.

Kennedy, E.M. Address to the National Council of Organizations for Children and Youth, Bicentennial Conference on Children. Washington, D.C., February, 3, 1976.

Kitagawa, E.M. "Socioeconomic Differences in Mortality in the United States and Some Implications for Public Policy." In C.F. Westoff and R. Parke, Jr. (Eds.), *Demographic and Social Aspects of Population Growth,* Vol. 1. Washington, D.C.: Commission on Population Growth and the American Future, 1972, pp. 85–110.

Kitagawa, E.M., and P.M. Hauser. *Differential Mortality in the United States.* Cambridge, Mass.: Harvard University Press, 1973.

Knowles, J.H. (Ed.). *Doing Better and Feeling Worse: Health in the United States.* New York: Norton, 1977.

Kohn, M.L. "Class, Family, and Schizophrenia: A Reformulation." *Social Forces,* Vol. 50, No. 3 (March 1972), pp. 295–304.

Kotelchuck, D. (Ed.). *Prognosis Negative: Crisis in the Health Care System.* New York: Vintage, 1976.

Kramer, M. Paper presented at the second Rochester International Conference on Schizophrenia. Rochester, N.Y., May 1976.

Law, S. *Blue Cross: What Went Wrong?* New Haven: Yale University Press, 1974.

Margolis, R.J. "National Health Insurance—The Dream Whose Time Has Come." *The New York Times Magazine,* January 9, 1977, pp. 12–13ff.

Mechanic, D. *The Growth of Bureaucratic Medicine.* New York: Wiley, 1976.

Meyers, J.K., L.L. Bean, and M.P. Pepper. "Social Class and Psychiatric Disorders: A Ten-Year Follow-up." *Journal of Health and Social Behavior* (Summer 1965), pp. 74–79.

National Institute of Mental Health. "Patient Care Episodes in Psychiatric Services." *Statistical Note 92.* Washington, D.C., 1973.

Parsons, T. *The Social System.* New York: Free Press, 1951.

President's Commission on Mental Health. *Report to the President from the President's Commission on Mental Health,* Vol. 1. Washington, D.C.: U.S. Government Printing Office,.1978.

Rainwater, L. "The Lower Class: Health, Illness, and Medical Institutions." In L. Rainwater (Ed.), *Inequality and Justice.* Chicago: Aldine, 1974, pp. 179–87.

Reiser, S.J. "Therapeutic Choice and Moral Doubt in a Technological Age." In J.H. Knowles (Ed.), *Doing Better and Feeling Worse: Health in the United States.* New York: Norton, 1977, pp. 47–56.

Rosengren. W.R. *Sociology of Medicine: Diversity, Conflict, and Change.* New York: Harper & Row, 1980.

Rosenhan, D.L. "On Being Sane in Insane Places." *Science,* Vol. 179 (1973), pp. 250–59.

Rothman, D.J. *The Discovery of the Asylum.* Boston: Little, Brown, 1971.

Sarbin, T.R. "The Scientific Status of the Mental Illness Metaphor." In S.G. Plog and R.B. Edgerton (Eds.), *Changing Perspectives in Mental Illness.* New York: Holt, Rinehart and Winston, 1969, pp. 9–31.

Scheff, T.J. *Being Mentally Ill: A Sociological Theory.* Chicago: Aldine, Atherton, 1966.

Sheehan, S. "A Reporter at Large: The Patient." *The New Yorker,* May 25, June 1, June 8, June 15, 1981.

Sidel, V.W. "Medical Care in the People's Republic of China: An Example of Rationality." *Archives of International Medicine,* Vol. 135 (July 1975), pp. 916–26.

Smith, M.B., and N. Hobbs. "The Community and The Community Mental Health Center." *American Psychologist,* Vol. 21, No. 6 (June 1966), pp. 499–509.

Srole, L. et al. *Mental Health in the Metropolis: The Midtown Manhattan Study,* rev. ed. New York: New York University Press, 1978.

Szasz, T. "The Myth of Mental Illness." *American Psychologist,* Vol. 15 (February 1960), pp. 113–18.

Twaddle, A.C. "Health Decisions and Sick Role Variations: An Exploration." *Journal of Health and Social Behavior,* Vol 10 (June 1969), pp. 105–15.

U.S. Department of Health, Education, and Welfare. *Health, United States 1975.* National Center for Health Statistics, 1975.

U.S. Department of Health, Education, and Welfare. "National Health Expenditures." *Social Security Bulletin,* Vol. 41, No. 7 (July 1978).

U.S. National Center for Health Statistics. *Limitation of Activity and Mobility Due to Chronic Conditions, United States – 1972,* Series 10, No. 96. Rockville, Md., 1974.

Waitzkin, H., and B. Waterman. *The Exploration of Illness in Capitalist Society.* New York: Bobbs-Merrill, 1974.

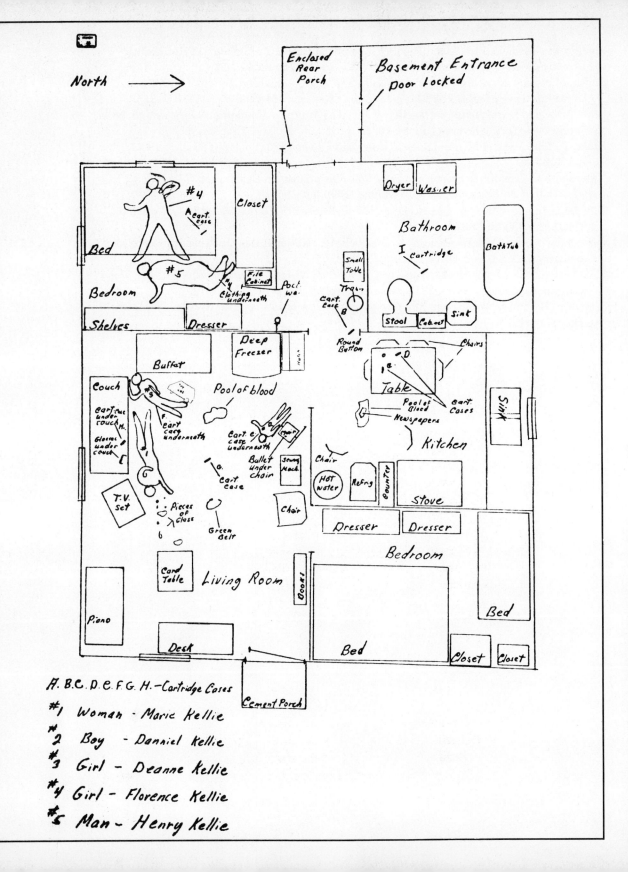

North ⟶

Enclosed Rear Porch

Basement Entrance
Door Locked

Dryer   Washer

Bathroom

Closet

Bed

#4   Cart. case

#5

File Cabinet

Clothing underneath

Bedroom

Shelves   Dresser

Deep Freezer

Buffat

Pool of blood

Couch

Cart. case under couch

Gloves under couch

Cart. case underneath

Cart. case underneath

Bullet under chair

Sewing Mach.

T.V. Set

Pieces of glass

Cart. case

Green Belt

Card Table   Living Room

Piano

Desk

Cement Porch

Bath Tub

Small Table

Trash

Cart. case B

Stool   Cabinet   Sink

Round Button

Cart. Cases

Table

Pool of Blood

Newspapers

Chairs

Kitchen

Sink

Chair

Hot Water   Refrig.   Counter

Stove

Dresser   Dresser

Bedroom

Bed

Doors

Bed

Closet   Closet

A. B. C. D. E. F. G. H. – Cartridge Cases

#1 Woman – Marie Kellie

#2 Boy – Daniel Kellie

#3 Girl – Deanne Kellie

#4 Girl – Florence Kellie

#5 Man – Henry Kellie

Chapter Fourteen

Crime and Violence

Criminal Behavior

What Is a Crime?

Patterns of Crime

The Costs of Crime

Measuring Crime

The Extent of Crime

   Uniform Crime Reports

   National Crime Survey

Perpetrators and Victims

Causes of Violence

Biological Explanations

Psychological Explanations

Social-Psychological Explanations

   Social Learning

   Differential Association

Sociological Explanations

   Social Disorganization

   Violence and Anomie

   Opportunity Structures

   Culture and Violence

The Criminal Justice System

The Police

The Courts

Prisons

Capital Punishment

Deterrence Considered

The Social Roots of Crime and Violence

One evening two teen-agers decided to take a walk in West Los Angeles. No one was safe that night, they told themselves. The first person they met was Philip Lerner, who was walking his infant in a stroller. They let him pass. At the next intersection, they stopped Arkady and Rachel Muskin. The couple handed over eight dollars and two watches, then fled with their lives. Two elderly Chinese women were not so lucky. One of the teen-agers pulled out a gun and killed both of them. A few blocks later, they stopped three people out for a stroll, took a watch and a few dollars, and without a single word, fatally shot one of them. They met seventy-six-year-old Leon Ocon in front of a drive-in restaurant. When he began to argue with them, the teen-agers shot him, too, then climbed into their car and drove away. All the killings had taken place in plain view, on the public street. All of the victims were strangers to the killers (*Newsweek,* March 23, 1981, p. 46). Incidents like this, reported in the mass media, seem to be changing the way Americans live.

"Fear of crime is slowly paralyzing American society," a national survey on fear of crime reports (The Figgie Report, 1980). Four out of ten Americans are afraid of being assaulted, robbed, raped, or murdered in their homes or on the streets where they live and work. City dwellers, women, and blacks are the most apprehensive. In many cases, their fears are based on first-hand information. People who know someone who was held up in an armed robbery in the last two years are almost twice as likely to express a high level of fear as those who do not—and one in five have personal knowledge of a violent crime. Nine out of ten people questioned keep the doors to their homes locked. More than half dress plainly to avoid attracting the attention of criminals. Two in ten say concern for personal safety keeps them from going places and doing things they might otherwise do. A national poll reported that a majority of Americans have little or no confidence in the ability of the police to protect them (*News-*

week, March 23, 1981). Over half say that they keep guns for personal safety.

Are these fears realistic? This chapter examines the evidence. The first section describes the range of crimes and suggests why violent crimes, in particular, have become a social issue. The second section explains how crime and crime rates are measured. The third section, on who commits violent crimes, lays the groundwork for the question of why. Are certain kinds of people biologically or psychologically predisposed to violence? (Are some people "born criminals"?) Do certain kinds of experiences teach people to be violent? Or are the opportunities and incentives to violence built into the social system? The fourth section, on the criminal justice system, examines the efforts society has made to reduce the incidence of violent crime.

Criminal Behavior

Teen-agers demand money at gunpoint. A thief cracks a safe. A senator accepts a free vacation from an oil company. A drug manufacturer does not release the results of studies that show one of its products has harmful side effects. An executive pads her expense account. A clerk helps himself to office supplies. A man beats his wife. An unmarried teen-age girl has an abortion. A private country club rejects a black family's application for membership. A journalist fabricates information in a newspaper article. A group of factory workers bet on the outcome of Sunday's football game. Which of these are crimes?

What Is a Crime?

The law distinguishes between two types of illegal activities (Sykes, 1978, pp. 46–48). The civil law deals with *torts* (from the Latin word for twisted or crooked) or wrongs against individuals—such things as defamation of character,

Fear of a sudden, violent assault by a stranger is changing the way many Americans live.

trespassing, and negligence. Criminal law deals with wrongs against society—including physical violence, infringement on property rights (as in theft), and actions that are claimed to endanger health, morals, or public safety (from prostitution to treason). The legal proceedings in civil and criminal cases are quite different. In criminal cases, the state initiates action: The police make an arrest, bring charges, and so on. The state reserves the right to press charges regardless of the desires of the person who has been wronged. In civil cases, private citizens initiate court action by filing suit. If the parties to a dispute reach an agreement outside of court, the state drops the

matter. The rules of evidence are stricter in criminal than in civil cases. In criminal cases, the state must prove a defendant guilty "beyond a reasonable doubt." Evidence that an individual committed an illegal act is not enough; the state must also prove *intent* to commit a crime. In civil cases, a "preponderance of evidence" is sufficient. Criminal cases lead to conviction or acquittal; civil cases, to a finding or judgment. In civil cases, the emphasis is on compensating the victim of a wrongdoing or adjusting conflicting interests. The state plays the role of impartial referee. In criminal cases, the emphasis is on prosecuting the wrongdoer, and the state plays two roles, prosecutor (who must gather and present evidence) and judge.

There is no universal agreement about what should or should not be considered a crime. For example, some Americans equate abortions with murder; others see banning abortions as a crime against women. Some Americans consider gambling immoral. Many think it is wrong to discriminate against people because of their race or religion. Each of the activities listed above violates some group's norms, or rules for behavior, but not all are crimes. It is not a crime to have an abortion in the United States today, though it has been in the past. It is not a crime for a private club to practice discrimination, though it is a crime for the owner of a public restaurant, an employer, a landlord, or a real estate agent to do so. It is not a crime for a journalist to make up a story, although it is considered unethical. It is a crime, however, for a witness to lie in court. Littering and double-parking are illegal, but we do not consider someone who drops a candy wrapper on the street or parks illegally a "criminal."

Patterns of Crime

Legal analysis of crime focuses on the wrong that has been done and the right that has been violated. Sociological analysis focuses on the social context in which crime takes place. Sociologists study the patterns of crime in a society, public attitudes toward different crimes, the offender's background and social standing, the relationship between criminal and victim, the meaning attached to the act by participants, onlookers, and peer groups, and whether the crime is a departure from the person's usual behavior or part of a way of life. In the course of such investigations, sociologists have discovered a variety of social patterns associated with different types of crimes.

In cases of *violent crime,* the offender and the victim usually come from similar socioeconomic backgrounds, live in the same area, and are of the same race. Often, they know each other—intimately. Between 20 and 40 percent of all murders can be traced to family quarrels (National Commission on the Causes and Prevention of Violence, 1969, p. 218). Violent crimes involve a direct confrontation between the criminal and victim and direct bodily harm to the victim. Most murders and assaults are unscheduled ("unpremeditated") events that take place during leisure time, not working hours (Luckenbill and Sanders, 1977, pp. 112–24). Often violence erupts in public. Typically, one party threatens or feints violence to demonstrate that he or she cannot be ridiculed, challenged, cheated, or pushed around. If the other responds in kind, violent threats may reach a point of no return. Thus, death or injury usually result from a pattern of interaction between the criminal, victim, and often an audience.

Over 90 percent of the major crimes reported to police are *property crimes*—such as pickpocketing, shoplifting, car theft, and burglary. Here, unlike in violent crimes, the offender avoids direct confrontation with the victim. The lack of interaction may lessen the offender's sense of doing "real" harm. Not seeing the person whose property you are taking may make it easier to repress or ignore the meaning of the behavior (Sykes, 1978, pp. 93–94). *White-collar crime*—price fixing, false advertising, bribery of government officials, and other crimes committed for the benefit of a business or corporation—differs from other property crimes in several ways (Sutherland, 1949; Geis and Meier, 1977). For example, white-collar offenders are often highly respected, otherwise conforming members of their communities. In part because of this, they are able to escape being labeled as "common criminals" by themselves or others. White-collar criminals are seldom arrested or prosecuted. If convicted, they are usually given probation and fines instead of being sent to prison. Offenders rationalize their crimes as being "accepted business practice." The term "white-collar crime" may also be used to describe illegal acts committed in the course of work for personal gain, not corporate profits—such things as embezzling funds, accepting kickbacks, padding expense accounts, and employee shoplifting (Sykes, 1978, pp. 103–08).

The Watergate scandal that forced President Richard Nixon from office in 1976 brought *political crime* to national attention. There are at least two different types of political crimes: illegal acts designed to make a political point or to bring about political change (for example, an illegal sit-in or a military coup) and acts that involve the misuse of office by people in government for political purposes (such as illegal wiretapping or firing someone who reveals government corruption) (Sykes, 1978, Chapter 6). Often the line between these two types of political crime blurs, however. For example, some political observers see the criminal behavior of the White House staff during the Watergate scandal as an attempt to use political office for personal gain. Others believe they acted in the conviction that national security is far more important than constitutional restrictions on the use of government power.

Edwin Schur (1965) coined the term *crimes without victims* to describe such things as the illegal use of drugs, public drunkenness, illegal gambling, homosexuality, prostitution, pornography, and other sex offenses. What distinguishes these crimes in Schur's view is that they injure no one, except perhaps the offender. The offenders are condemned, not because they harm innocent people, but because they violate the social norms of those who have the power to enforce the law. Prostitution, for example, violates the social definition of sexual behavior as an expression of love. Gambling violates the work ethic by enabling people to "get something for nothing" (to make money without working). Laws against these activities are extremely difficult to enforce. The main reason is that there is no injured party, no complainant who will bring charges or give evidence in court. This puts the police in the position

of protecting people from themselves, indirectly creating opportunities for police violations of civil liberties. Many Americans feel that this is an abuse of power; that the government has no business telling adults what they can or cannot do in private. Moreover, the fact that these activities are illegal may push people who occasionally experiment with drugs or engage in homosexual behavior into "deviant careers." For example, someone who takes drugs (primary deviance) may be forced to steal (secondary deviance) because laws against drugs push up the price. Someone who is discovered in a homosexual relationship may find that heterosexuals shun him or her and drift into a homosexual life style.

The Costs of Crime

Different types of crimes entail different costs. Some crimes cause direct harm to individuals and society. The man whose wallet is stolen, the family whose house is looted, the consumer who overpays, the saloonkeeper who "buys protection" from organized crime all suffer direct financial losses. The woman who is raped, the store owner who is beaten up by robbers, the pedestrian who is hit by a drunken driver suffer physical injury. The cost of crime in the United States, estimated in 1967 dollars, is shown in Table 14–1 (Sykes, 1978, p. 26, Table 1). Note that the "price tag" for murder is reckoned in terms of the victims' lost earnings. Note also that illegal goods and services take almost twice as much money from the legitimate economy as all other crimes combined. Many crimes also cause indirect harm. The emotional cost must be taken into account. These include the shock and pain of the victims, the hurt and dislocation felt by their families and acquaintances, and general feelings of insecurity. From this perspective, violent crime "costs more" than other types of crime.

When people talk about the crime problem they are usually thinking about holdups and shoot-

Table 14–1
The Costs of Crime

Type of Crime	Estimated Cost Per Year in Dollars (Millions)
Crimes of Violence	
Willful homicide	750
Assault	65
Crimes Against Property	
Arson	100
Vandalism	210
Burglary	450
Larceny	196
Embezzlement	200
Unreported business theft (retail trade)	1,300
Auto theft	140
Fraud	1,300
Forgery	64
Robbery	60
Illegal Goods and Services	
Gambling	7,000
Narcotics	350
Loansharking	350
Prostitution	225
Illicit alcohol	150
Other	
Tax fraud	100
Driving under the influence of alcohol	1,800

Source: President's Commission on Law Enforcement and Administration of Justice, *Task Force Report: Assessment of Crime* (Washington, D.C.: U.S. Government Printing Office, 1967).

ings, or "crime in the street." In terms of dollars lost, crimes against business cost the nation far more than robberies do. (Businesses lose an estimated $40 billion a year from thefts by customers and employees [*U.S. News & World Report,* February 21, 1977]). Many more Americans are hurt or killed in accidents in their homes or cars than during muggings. Why is the public more alarmed by street crime? With auto accidents, there is usually no intent to harm. Someone was careless, even reckless, but the person did not mean to cause injury. With crimes against business, the costs are hidden from the public. Stores routinely raise the price of goods to consumers by 1 to 2 percent to cover losses to theft, but this "crime tax" does not appear on the consumer's bill. In contrast, muggings involve a direct, intentional confrontation between the criminal and victim, and cause direct, visible harm.

The impersonality of muggings compounds the fear of injury and loss. "What harms us most . . . [is the] threat of some sudden, unpredictable, savage assault upon our own body by a stranger—a faceless, nameless, fleet-footed figure who leaps from the shadows, strikes us with his fists, an iron pipe, or a switch-blade knife, and then vanishes . . ." (Hunt, 1972). Crimes of passion—assaults or murders that occur during quarrels among intimates—have a history and a motive. People can understand why they happened. The victim knows why he or she was involved. Violence at the hands of strangers seems random. It exposes the frailty of the social order. Every day each of us encounters numerous strangers. Our ability to go about our business as usual depends on the ability to make certain assumptions about how these strangers will behave. The social order requires some degree of predictability. Muggings undermine trust in social interaction. They have no history and often no clear motive. (The victim hands over his money, but is shot anyway.) They are impossible to predict and difficult to guard against. (You can avoid someone who is angry at you, but you cannot avoid strangers.) Victims of muggings, like victims of natural disasters, often feel

Organized Crime

The mass media have made organized crime as familiar as cowboys to Americans. Most familiar is the Mafia. The question is whether this secret organization, rooted in a Sicilian tradition of violence, held together by ethnic solidarity, and operating outside the law, exists in fact or only in fantasy. Social scientists disagree on this point. The sociologist Donald Cressey (1969), who served on the President's Commission on Law Enforcement and Administration of Justice on Organized Crime, has argued that organized crime is big business in the United States today. Cressey described a nationwide network of twenty-four crime "families," linked by understandings and obedience, that controlled almost all illegal and some legal gambling (a $50-billion industry in 1969), monopolized loan-shark operations, dominated the narcotics import business, controlled perhaps $10 billion in legal enterprises (such as vending machines), and had infiltrated labor unions and government. The anthropologist Francis Ianni (1972), on the other hand, is one of those who argue that most of the "evidence" of a national, ethnically based crime organization comes from assertions by government officials. In Ianni's view, crime families operate on the local level, but there is no national conspiracy, and kinship is more important than fear and coercion in holding families together. He adds that the myth of the Mafia tends to hold Italian Americans back from entering legitimate businesses. Whether the Mafia exists, or ever existed, in this country is not conclusively known. What is clear is that some crime, such as the drug traffic, is organized on a local, if not regional or national level. Organized crime causes both direct harm, as in a "gangland slaying," and indirect harm, as in the loss of profits to legitimate businesses. While some organized crime depends on public demand for commodities, such as pornography, drugs, and gambling, other activities of organized crime, such as extortion, hijacking, and the protection racket, are "services" that the public could well do without.

that the world is no longer a safe place. The cost of these crimes must be reckoned in terms of threats to the social order as well as in emotional and economic losses. Compared with other crimes, the number of muggings may be small. But the threat of a sudden, direct, yet depersonalized attack is especially frightening.

Measuring Crime

In the spring of 1981, a major magazine reported "a plague of violent crime" (*Newsweek*, March 23, 1981). Is this description accurate? How many murders, rapes, robberies, and assaults are committed in the United States each year? Is the rate

Table 14–2
Violent Crimes in the U.S., 1979

Type of Crime	Known to Police (UCR)		Victimization (NCS)	
	number	rate/100,000	number	rate/100,000
Murder	21,460	9.7	*	*
Rape**	75,990	35.5	192,000	110
Robbery	466,880	212.1	1,116,000	630
Aggravated assault	614,210	279.1	1,769,000	990
Total violent crimes	1,178,540	5,521	5,351,000	32,600

*Of all crimes, murder is the least likely to be hidden from law enforcement officials. Hence, NCS does not collect data on murders.
**Forcible rapes, not including statutory rape (sexual intercourse with a consenting minor).
Source: *National Crime Survey Report,* "Criminal Victimization in the U.S.," September, 1980, p. 2; *Uniform Crime Reports, 1979* (Washington, D.C.: U.S. Government Printing Office, 1980), p. 37.

of violent crime rising? Who commits most crimes of violence?

The Extent of Crime

There are two official sources of data on crime in the United States: the *Uniform Crime Reports* and the *National Crime Survey.*

Uniform Crime Reports The FBI began collecting data on crime from local law enforcement agencies in 1930. Fifteen thousand police departments covering 98 percent of the population participate in the program today. The results are published each year in the *Uniform Crime Reports*

(UCR). The UCR includes data on the number of crimes reported to or uncovered by police; the number of arrests; the age, sex, race, and ethnic origins of people arrested; and the number of offenders turned over to the courts for trial (cleared by arrest). To determine whether crime is increasing slower, faster, or at the same pace as the population, the FBI also calculates crime rates—that is, the number of crimes reported per a specific population of 100,000 persons. The numbers and rates of violent crimes recorded in 1979 are shown in Table 14–2. That year, a violent crime was committed every 27 seconds; an assault, every 51 seconds; a robbery, every 68 seconds; a rape, every 7 minutes; a murder, every 24 minutes. In 1979, 5,521 in every 100,000 Americans were victims of violent crime according to FBI calculations.

The UCR has a number of built-in limitations (Sykes, 1978, pp. 75–78). First, local law enforcement agencies vary in their legal definitions of crime, procedures for gathering information, and care in keeping records. What is considered aggravated assault in one place may be simple assault in another. Second, politics may influence police records. Local law enforcement agencies may record fewer index crimes than actually were reported to hide an increase in crime, or inflate figures to win public support for an increase in the police budget. Third and most significant, the UCR reports only on crimes and criminals *known to the police*. Only a small fraction of the crimes committed each year are ever reported to police, and only a fraction of these are cleared by arrest. In 1967, the National Opinion Research Center (NORC) conducted a random survey of 10,000 households for the President's Commission on Law Enforcement and Administration of Justice. This survey suggested that there were three times as many rapes, twice as many assaults, and 50 percent more robberies than the UCR had recorded that year (p. 17). Why weren't these crimes reported? The most frequent reason given in the NORC survey was the belief that the police could not do anything about the crime, followed by the desire to protect an offender who was a relative or friend, fear of retaliation, and fear the police would uncover something about the victim. In addition, only 21 percent of reported crimes were cleared by arrest in 1978. The UCR's profile of offenders describes those who were caught — the "least successful" criminals in the nation.

National Crime Survey To collect data on unreported offenses, the Department of Justice launched the *National Crime Survey (NCS)* in 1973. The NCS collects data on victimization from a representative sample of approximately 60,000 American households. Once selected, a household remains in the survey for three years. Family members over twelve years of age are interviewed every six months during this period. The NCS collects information about the victim, the nature of the crime (if one occurred), the extent of injury or economic loss, the relationship between the criminal and the victim, and the characteristics of the criminal. Interviewers also ask whether a crime was reported and if not, why not. According to the NCS, over 100,000 rapes, 600,000 robberies, and 1,000,000 assaults were not reported in 1979.

The NCS, too, has certain built-in limitations (Booth, Johnson, and Choldin, 1977). Especially in low-income neighborhoods, people may refuse to participate. Those who do may not report all crimes to the interviewer. (In one study, only 74 percent of people known to have reported crimes to the police told an interviewer about the incidents.) They do not always remember exactly when a crime took place, and so may inflate the statistics for a six-month period. And the sample does not include transients and tourists, who may be particularly vulnerable to crime. Nevertheless, the NCS does indicate that there is far more violent crime in the United States today than appears in the UCR. Combined NCS data on property and violent crime suggest that one in three U.S. households was victimized by violent or property crime in 1979–80.

Perpetrators and Victims

Who commits violent crimes? Who is most likely to be victimized? In a classic study of criminal violence, the sociologist Marvin Wolfgang (1958) analyzed official data on 588 murders committed in Philadelphia between 1948 and 1952. Wolfgang found that young black males were the most frequent offenders *and victims* during that period. Interracial violence was not as frequent as is popularly believed. UCR figures from the 1970s

Is the Crime Rate Increasing?

It depends on whose statistics one chooses to rely on. In the 1960s, UCR statistics indicated that the crime rate (especially the rate of violent crime) was climbing (Sykes, 1978, pp. 142–45). Between 1956 and 1968, the UCR showed that murder increased 52 percent; rape, 71 percent; aggravated assault, 82 percent; and robberies, 143 percent. According to the UCR, the violent crime rate continued to climb in the 1970s. Between 1970 and 1978, murders and robberies reported to the police increased 23 percent; aggravated assault, 69 percent; and rape, 85 percent (UCR, 1979, p. 37). The greatest increases in crime were found not in the big cities of the Northeast but in smaller cities in the Southwest. In 1979, for example, the crime rate rose 5 percent in New York City; 20 percent in Albuquerque, New Mexico (*The New York Times,* October 28, 1979, pp. 1, 64). Thus, according to the UCR, there was an increase in reported crime in the 1970s. The NCS data on victimization suggest a different picture, however. If one goes by reported victimization, there was no crime wave in the 1970s (see figure below). According to the NCS, it seems that the wave of violent crime has been exaggerated.

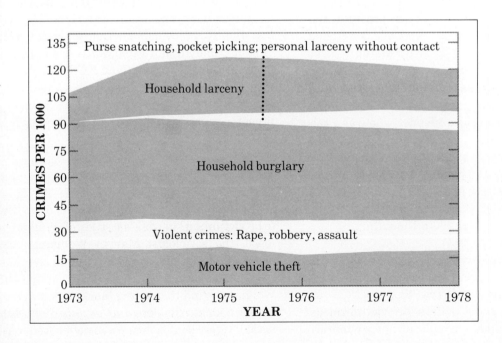

Table 14–3
Arrests for Violent Crimes by Age, Sex, and Race, 1979

	Age	Sex		Race	
Type of Crime	% under 18	% male	% female	% white	% black
Murder	9	86	14	49	48
Rape	16	99	0.8	50	48
Robbery	31	93	7	41	57
Aggravated assault	49	88	12	61	37
Total violent crimes	20	90	10	54	44

Source: *Uniform Crime Reports, 1979* (Washington, D.C.: U.S. Government Printing Office, 1980), pp. 198–200.

tell a similar story (see Table 14–3). Crime rates vary by sex, race, social class, and age.

Whatever their age, race, or social class, males are far more prone to committing violent crimes (indeed, all crimes except prostitution) than females are. According to UCR data for 1979, male arrests outnumbered female arrests by five to one (UCR, 1979, p. 186). There are signs that this pattern is changing slightly. While arrests of males for violent crimes increased 50 percent between 1967 and 1979, arrests of females rose by more than 70 percent. Even so, males are responsible for 90 percent of violent crimes.

In the years studied by Wolfgang, blacks made up 18 percent of the population of Philadelphia, but 75 percent of those arrested for murder and 73 percent of their victims were black. Nationwide data indicate blacks are still over-represented. In 1979, 48 percent of those arrested for violent crimes and 45 percent of the victims — but only 12 percent of the population — were black. Interpreting these statistics is problematic, however. First, much higher percentages of black than white Americans are poor, unemployed,

crowded into inner cities, and divorced or separated. The higher crime rate for blacks reflects these interacting factors, as well as the social consequences of race. Second, there is some evidence that police are more likely to arrest blacks than whites. (Remember, only about a third of crimes are cleared by arrest.) Jerome Skolnick, who conducted a field study of police, found that officers "identify certain kinds of people as symbolic assailants, that is, as persons who use gesture, language and attire that the policemen recognize as a prelude to violence" (1966, p. 45). In Skolnick's view, the police tend to see blacks as symbolic assailants and therefore to arrest and book them more often. Third, overall crime rates conceal a wide range of variations within groups and changes over time. The Irish, for example, were once considered a "criminal class." As a general rule, crime rates are highest among newly arrived ethnic groups (such as Latin American immigrants today) and those with a long history of conflict and deprivation (blacks and Native Americans). There are exceptions to this rule, however. For example, crime rates seem to be

Who is hurt by violent crime? Black Americans are much more likely than whites to be held up, beaten, robbed, or murdered in the United States today.

rising among Orientals, who have been in this country for generations (Cohen and Short, 1976, p. 62).

Official statistics have consistently shown an inverse relationship between social class and crime—that is, the highest crime rates are found in the lower class. In recent years, however, the class-crime connection has been questioned on two grounds. First, lower-class offenders are more likely to become statistics. When middle-class people have violent fights, it is likely to be in the privacy of their suburban homes. The poor are more visible. When low-income people fight, the neighbors hear everything. If they call the police, and the police make an arrest, the argument becomes a statistic. Second, definitions of serious crimes are class-biased. Robbery and assault are given more weight than white-collar crimes (even though unsafe products, for example, may cause as many injuries). However, victimization surveys and self-reports (crimes that subjects report unofficially to an interviewer) do confirm the UCR conclusion that rates of violent crime are highest in the lower class (Braithwaite, 1981).

Wolfgang found that the typical murderer in Philadelphia was young (age twenty to twenty-five) and that the victim was only a few years older (age twenty-five to thirty-nine). UCR data indicate this is still true. Teen-agers and young adults are more likely than members of other age groups to commit or to become victims of violent crime. Indeed, the age at which people enter the crime statistics has fallen. In 1977, eighteen- and nineteen-year-olds appeared in the statistics as often as twenty-one-year-olds. Between 1970 and 1979, the violent crime rate for people under eighteen increased by 40%; that for people eighteen years old and over, by 50.2%. This figure includes a 55 percent decrease in the murder rate, a 59.7 percent increase in aggravated assault, and a 32.7 percent increase in robberies committed by young people (UCR, 1979, p. 190). Data on young criminals may be inflated somewhat. At least two victimization surveys indicate thirty-five-year-olds are as likely to physically attack another person, or to be attacked, as young people (Stark,

1975). It may be that young people are more likely than older adults to fight in public and that police view them as "symbolic assailants" and arrest them more often.

Causes of Violence

What makes people violent? Why are some sections of the country, some neighborhoods, and some groups more violent than others? There are no simple answers to these questions. Here we will look at four approaches, beginning with biology.

Biological Explanations

The idea that some people are violent "by nature" dates back to the nineteenth century. Building on Charles Darwin's theory of human origins, Cesare Lombroso popularized the notion that some criminals were throwbacks to an earlier stage of human evolution. One can tell these "born criminals," Lombroso asserted, by the shape of the jaw, the size of the ears, the primitive cast of the features, and numerous other signs that Lombroso called "stigmata." In this century, William Sheldon hypothesized that the restless energy of heavy, muscular, athletic types predisposed them to juvenile crime and delinquency. There is no evidence that facial features or body types are linked to violent crime, as critics of these theories quickly pointed out, although there is a real possibility that people of some body types are more readily chosen for certain types of activities (occupation, crime, sports).

Current biological research focuses on genetic abnormalities, neurological disturbances, biochemical imbalances, and the interaction of chemicals with physiological properties of the body that influence behavior (Mednick et al., 1981). To date, there is no evidence that certain people are "born

criminals" (no evidence of genetic predisposition). There are documented cases of violence caused by brain dysfunctions (Mark and Ervin, 1970), but these account for only a fraction of murders, rapes, and assaults, There *is* abundant evidence linking alcohol to violent crime in the United States. Often, both the attacker and the victim have been drinking (National Commission on the Causes and Prevention of Violence, 1969). But this does not necessarily prove cause and effect. Our culture associates alcohol with loss of emotional control: People may drink to excuse themselves from responsibility for what they anticipate will be a violent confrontation. In other cultures, drunkenness is common, but violence is exceedingly rare (Paddock, 1975).

Psychological Explanations

One school of psychological theories of violence is rooted in Freud's theory of personality development, which captured scientific and public attention in the United States in the early part of this century. According to Freudian theory, human infants are born with a host of primitive, aggressive instincts. A *normal* baby is a greedy, self-centered, domineering, hedonistic, amoral being, devoid of feelings for others. Gradually, however, these primitive instincts (called the *id* by Freud) are brought under control by the *ego* (the rational and realistic part of the self) and the *superego* (the portion of the self that upholds norms and values, acquired primarily from parents).

The aggressive urges of infancy do not disappear as the person matures, however. They remain just below the surface of consciousness, engaging the ego and superego in a continuing struggle. Ideally, the ego and superego "win": When violent urges are aroused, the superego creates feelings of anxiety and guilt that inhibit their expression. Unacceptable impulses are channeled into socially approved activities (such as a career or sport). In some cases, however, this "taming" process is incomplete, and the inner controls on behavior are weak. Freud believed the development of a strong superego depends on a child's relationship with the same-sex parent. If a boy's father is unfair and untrustworthy, for example, the boy's superego will be much the same. His own ideas of right and wrong and internal guards will vacillate as his father's did, allowing impulses from the id to break through (Sykes, 1978, pp. 288–89). This, in brief, is the psychoanalytic explanation of crime and violence. "We are all, in this view, born criminals. We do not learn to become criminals; rather some of us learn to control the criminality with which we are afflicted, while some do not" (Cohen and Short, 1976, p. 70).

Psychologists have long debated whether, in extreme cases, faulty socialization may lead to a "psychopathic personality"—to an absorption with gratifying one's own needs so total that a person feels no guilt or remorse about injuring other people. As described in the literature, psychopaths lack both inner and outer controls on behavior. They are unable to identify with other people; they cannot put themselves in the place of the subject of a violent impulse and therefore cannot restrain themselves. They act impulsively, without regard for the consequences of an action. Whether this personality type exists in fact, or merely in clinical lore, is debatable.

Psychological explanations of violence have a number of limitations. First, the reasoning tends to be circular. Why did John abuse his child? Because he is disturbed. How do we know he is disturbed? Because he beat up his child. Second, if we knew that certain personality traits were linked to violence, how could we tell which came first? For example, does paranoia (irrational fears) cause a person to become violent, or do violent encounters cause a person to become paranoid? Third, unconscious motivations do not lend themselves to empirical inquiry. Psychoanalytic

explanations of violence are based on detailed case histories of individuals under treatment, not systematic research. The analysis of a patient's problem depends on theoretical interpretations and clinical intuitions. Attempts to use personality tests to identify a predisposition to violence have not been consistent (Monahan, 1981). Finally, psychological theories may help to explain why a particular individual committed a particular crime. They do not explain changes in the rate of violent crime or variations among groups and social categories.

Social-Psychological Explanations

Social-psychological explanations of violence form a link between psychological and sociological theories. Whereas biological and psychological explanations suggest violence comes from inside a person, social-psychological theories emphasize the social environment. Whereas the former maintain that violence is instinctive in some or all people, social-psychological theories hold that violent behavior is learned. As one theorist puts this, "Some of the elementary forms of physical violence can be perfected with minimal guidance, but most aggressive activities—dueling with switchblade knives, sparring with opponents, engaging in military combat, or indulging in vengeful ridicule—entail intricate skills that require extensive social learning" (Bandura, 1973, p. 61).

Social learning There are two basic ways in which people learn: through reinforcement (rewards and punishments) and through modeling (following other people's examples). The theory of reinforcement assumes that people learn directly from experience, repeating behavior that has brought rewards in the past and avoiding behavior that has invoked punishment. For example, if a mother praises her daugher for defending herself on the playground (positive reinforcement),

Part of "becoming a criminal" is learning norms and values that approve of criminal acts, associating with people who hold these norms, and having opportunities to learn special skills like fighting with switch-blade knives.

the child is likely to fight back the next time she is challenged. Similarly, if she finds that she can get a toy by hitting another child, she is likely to do it again. Conversely, if she is strongly reprimanded for punching a playmate (negative reinforcement), she *may* not try it again. We emphasize "may." There is some evidence that attention is a reward in itself, even if the attention is punitive. In one experiment, nursery-school teachers found it was more effective to praise cooperative behavior and *ignore* aggressive behavior than to use punishment (Brown and Elliot, 1965).

People also learn indirectly through modeling: by observing how other people handle situations and whether these models are rewarded or punished for their behavior. Albert Bandura and associates demonstrated the modeling of aggressive behavior in a series of experiments with preschool-aged children (Bandura and Walters, 1963, pp. 61–63). Children were shown a film of an adult physically and verbally attacking a Bobo

doll. After the film, the youngsters were put through a mildly frustrating situation and left alone in a room with an identical doll. Many attacked the doll, imitating the adult model almost exactly. Only a few children who had not seen the film took out their frustrations on the doll. What this suggests is that parents who hit a child because the child hit the boy next door may be modeling the very behavior they want to discourage (the use of physical force). The following description of the Watts riot of 1968 (described in Chapter 10) shows one adult serving as an aggressive model for a crowd of onlookers:

Without conscious thought of his action, he darted into the street and hurled the empty pop bottle in his hand toward the last of the department's black-and-white cars. Striking the rear fender of Sgt. Rankin's car, it shattered, and it was as if in that shattering the thousand people lining the street found their own release. . . . Rocks, bottles, pieces of wood and iron—whatever missiles came to hand—were projected against the sides and windows of the bus and automobiles that, halted for the past 20 minutes by the jammed street, unwittingly started through the gauntlet. . . . It was 7:45 P.M. . . . [T]he Los Angeles uprising had begun. (Conot, 1967, p. 29)

These examples suggest how people learn violent behavior. The question is: Why do some people learn to be violent, while others learn to be peaceable? Edwin Sutherland's theory of differential association attempts to answer this question.

Differential association Sutherland (1939) sought to explain all kinds of criminal behavior, not just violence. He argued that whether an individual leads a respectable, law-abiding life or engages in criminal behavior is a matter of differential associations with other people—that is, it is determined by the frequency, intensity, duration, and primacy of the person's associations.

In a heterogeneous nation like the United States, there are many different social groups, each with its own norms and values. Some groups encourage law-abiding behavior; others, criminal and perhaps violent behavior. In Sutherland's view, individuals are likely to engage in criminal or violent behavior if they are exposed to more pro-criminal than anti-criminal norms and values for an extended period, or if they often find themselves in situations that reward criminal and violent behavior. It is a matter of exposure and the balance of "good" and "bad" influences. In association with criminals, a person learns motivations, attitudes, and rationalizations of criminal behavior, as well as specific techniques for stalking a victim to mug, using a knife, and the like. He or she learns to define criminal behavior in positive terms.

Sociological Explanations

Sutherland's theory of differential association raises two questions: Why do pro-criminal, pro-violence norms and values develop in the first place? Why do they take hold in some groups but not in others? For sociologists, the answer lies in the social structure, not in psychological processes.

Social disorganization In the early 1900s, most sociologists attributed high crime rates in the United States to social disorganization. Rapid industrialization and urbanization, cultural dislocations among immigrants to the nation and migrants to cities, and the weakening of neighborhood and family ties had left individuals socially isolated. According to this view, small, stable communities provide individuals with a consistent set of cultural standards. Norms have the authority of tradition. They are reinforced by relatives and neighbors with whom the individual has intimate, face-to-face, lifelong relationships. In contrast, rapidly changing social systems confront the individual with numerous inconsistencies. Different groups' norms compete and clash. One group may reward the ability to get along with people; another group, violent response to any challenge. One group may reward hard work; another, "easy living." Impersonal relationships displace relationships with kin and neighbors, but do not entirely replace them. Casual acquaintances do not have the influence that kin or close friends have. Groups that once claimed the individual's allegiance and conformity (especially the family) may be destroyed or lose their significance. This social isolation releases individuals from constraints on behavior. At the same time, the social structure offers opportunities and incentives for nonconformity. According to this view, high rates of crime and violence are symptoms of "social pathology" (in everyday language, a "sick society").

In the 1940s and 1950s, the social disorganization view came under attack. Critics like C. Wright Mills (1943) argued that this "explanation" of crime was little more than a value-laden rejection of modern society; an expression of nostalgia for the rural, small-town life many sociologists had left behind. In saying that crime had resulted from the breakup of families and neighborhoods, sociologists had ignored the impact of larger social forces. Moreover, they had ignored the fact that crime also exists in stable, respectable communities (white-collar crime), as well as in urban ghettos.

Violence and anomie In "Social Structure and Anomie" (1938), Robert Merton dealt with the larger social forces. How does the social structure pressure certain people into nonconforming (sometimes criminally violent) behavior? Merton reasoned as follows: People's motivations are determined in large part by the goals their culture sets for them. In the United States, a high value is placed on material success, on the accumulation and display of wealth. (Other cultures place a higher value on holiness, for example, or on prowess in war.) Culture also prescribes the legitimate means for achieving these goals. According to American standards, wealth is the reward for hard work and talent. The definition of success is more or less the same for everyone in the United States. But everyone does not have equal access to legitimate means for achieving success. There are sharp differences in the opportunities available to members of different ethnic and racial groups and to different classes. A gap between cultural goals and institutionalized means leads to anomie, or a breakdown in norms. People tend to do whatever "works," leading to high levels of crime. In other societies, inequalities are just as great as they are in the United States, but different classes of people have goals more in keeping with their perceived opportunities. Anomie is less likely in such societies. Merton suggests that failure is doubly painful in a society like ours. Not only is a person denied the goods, services, and prestige that money can buy, but the individual, not the system, is blamed for the failure. Just as Americans admire the self-made man, so they condemn the loser.

Merton identifies five ways in which individuals adapt to this situation (as described in Chapter 1). Conformists accept culturally approved goals and means for achieving them. Innovators pursue culturally approved goals by socially disapproved methods. They cut corners, lie, steal, or do whatever is expedient. Ritualists are so compulsive about following cultural guidelines that they lose sight of the goals. Playing by the rules becomes an end in itself. Retreatists withdraw from social involvement, abandoning both goals and means. Rebels reject both the goals and the means their culture prescribes, substituting new ones.

The theory of anomie applies most directly to white-collar and property crimes. It can also help to explain rates of violent crime, however. In many cases, violence is innovative: the illegitimate use of force to obtain things the culture deems valuable. In other cases, violence is an act of rebellion (a terrorist attack); a form of retreatism (in suicide); or ritualism (soldiers blindly obeying orders to shoot unarmed civilians). The key point in Merton's essay is that high rates of crime and violence are the product of a particular kind of social system—one that pressures individuals into seeking goals they have no legitimate means of achieving.

Opportunity structures Richard Cloward and Lloyd Ohlin (1960) expand on the theory of anomie. The social structure not only provides differential (unequal) access to legitimate opportunities; it also provides differential access to *illegitimate* opportunities. Everyone in our society does not have equal opportunities to observe models of a gang fight, for example, or to learn and practice the use of switchblade knives, iron pipes, and so on. How people adapt to anomie depends on their opportunities. At least one reason why few suburban, middle-class men and women become pimps or prostitutes or hired guns is that they lack opportunities to learn the techniques and rationales of these activities. When individuals fail, or anticipate failure, in achieving success by socially approved means, and when they blame the failure on the social system rather than on themselves, they seek the support of others in similar positions. If their social environment offers illegitimate opportunities, they are likely to take them. Thus, in Cloward and Ohlin's view, an individual's response to anomie depends on his or her location in both the legitimate and illegitimate opportunity structures. The combination of failure at legal routes to success and access to illegal routes breeds crime.

Culture and violence Merton and Cloward and Ohlin focus on the reasons why individuals violate norms. Albert Cohen (1959) expands this theory to explain the existence of delinquent and criminal subcultures. Cohen sees subcultures as "collective solutions to problems characteristic of certain locations in the social system" (Cohen and Short, 1976, p. 76). Why are the rates of delinquency among working-class boys higher than among middle-class boys? Cohen explains as follows: Males of all social levels in America are measured by the same standards. They judge themselves, and are judged by others, in terms of their potential academic, occupational, and economic value, how closely their dress and speech resemble those of men at the top, and so on. But their working-class origins put them at a systematic disadvantage. They are less likely to perform well according to these criteria than are middle-class youngsters and are more likely to suffer blows to their self-esteem. One solution to this problem is to band together, reject middle-class norms and values, and collectively develop their own standards. Delinquent subcultures in the United States substitute contempt for property (expressed in theft and vandalism) for middle-class respect for property, a readiness for aggressive action for restrained behavior, a demand for immediate gratification for a willingness to save and wait. In effect, the delinquent subculture takes mainstream culture and turns it upside down.

Marvin Wolfgang and Franco Ferracuti (1967) studied subcultures that approve and even demand violence in central cities in the United States and in other countries—Colombia, Mexico, Italy, and India. In the groups they studied, violence was a way of life, a tradition handed down from one generation to the next. Men in these communities are quick to take offense. A slight push or a derogatory comment about a man's family or his age is perceived as a challenge. And the norms demand that a man respond to such challenges with physical aggression. Failure to respond forcefully is likely to be met with ridicule and punishment. "Men must demonstrate their 'valor' or face a loss of prestige and estrangement from political and social life. Homicide is justified and even prescribed" (Wolfgang and Ferracuti, 1967, p. 282). Wolfgang and Ferracuti do not attempt to explain how such subcultures come into being. Rather, they describe social settings in which individuals are unable or unwilling to rely on the formal legal system to settle disputes. Each is individually responsible for the defense of his person and property. Some theorists maintain that the lower-class community as a whole in the United States has a long-established tradition of its own that "demands" a violent response to certain situations and accepts many forms of illegal behavior (Miller, 1958).

Looking at American society as a whole, some sociologists (Straus, Gelles, and Steinmetz, 1980) conclude that approval of violence is not a subcultural phenomenon. Violence is part of our national heritage and is woven through our culture. "Men murdered themselves into this democracy," D.H. Lawrence wrote of America (in Silberman,

Gun Control: A View from Abroad

The United States is the only country in the world whose constitution gives citizens the right to carry guns. In Britain, even police do not carry guns (with a few exceptions). In France, all guns must be registered and all gun owners licensed. In West Germany, only members of established hunting clubs are allowed to own guns. In Japan, only the police, soldiers, and some competitive marksmen are permitted to own pistols. In the Netherlands, permits are required for all firearms. The attempted assassination of President Ronald Reagan in 1981 elicited this reaction from one British editor:

America presents the chequered spectacle of so much gentle churchgoing and so much blood. The main reason for America's swiftly rising murder rate of about 10 per 100,000 (nearly 10 times the British rate) is not the innate violence of America's frontier tradition, nor even the admitted problem that a mobile, unhomogenous and too divorce-prone society creates rootlessness among too large a minority of its drifting young. The main reason lies in a rectifiable failure by its politicians: the republic has not written sensible laws to controls its guns. . . .

The usual underestimates say there are about 55 million handguns lying around in American homes (plus 90 million rifles and shotguns), and that about 2 million of those particularly-lethal-because-concealable handguns are sold across shop counters every year. The gun that shot the president was sold by a Dallas pawnshop to a psychiatrist's patient who had been expelled from a party of neo-Nazis because he seemed even to them to be too violence-prone. The president's fellow Americans, who are not shielded by brave agent McCarthy, are being shot to death by handguns at an average rate of one every 50 minutes. This uncontrol is justified by the age-old (i.e., barbarous) eighteenth-century right granted to every American to bear arms with which to defend himself against Red Indians and King George; but the real trouble is that the subjection of even handguns to anything like Britain's effective gun registration laws would cause political outcry among the more conservative owners of all of America's 145 million guns. . . .

The handgun threatens chiefly the lowest in the land in the ghettos, and the highest in it when assassination (which is an imitative crime) comes horridly into fashion. The pointers suggest a grim period of criminal violence in America may lie ahead.

Source: "Now Wake the Brave," *The Economist*, April 4, 1981, pp. 10–11.

1978, p. 21). Since colonial times, Americans have turned to physical force when other means of achieving their goals failed. Murder rates were as high in the 1850s as they are today in the nation's cities, or higher. Vigilantism thrived on the frontier. Feuds between settlers and Native Americans, cowboys and farmers, Hatfields and McCoys carried on for generations. Outlaws like the James brothers became national heroes. Between 1882 and 1930, as many as 2,000 blacks were killed by lynch mobs. Armies of strikers and company police clashed in the late nineteenth and early twentieth centuries. Gangster Al Capone became the symbol for an era. This nation's fascination with firearms is embedded in the language. We describe a coward as "gun-shy," a forthright person as a "straight-shooter," someone who is impulsive as "going off half-cocked." Surveys conducted for the National Commission on the Causes and Prevention of Violence suggest that many Americans (50 percent) agree "that justice may have been a little rough-and-ready in the days of the Old West, but things worked better than they do now with all the legal red tape." And over 40 percent of those surveyed said they owned firearms (Stark and McEvoy, 1970). In short, Americans see violence as a means to an end, and even as a form of expression (an end in itself). Given this cultural backing, high rates of violent crime should not be surprising.

The criminologist Gresham Sykes summarizes sociological theories of crime and violence this way:

> In most instances, criminal behavior is not simply a wild outburst of anger, a compulsive act beyond control, an unthinking response to a deprivation, or the delayed expression of childhood traumas. Instead . . . crime is often the pursuit of goals widely understood and accepted; and, as such, it is frequently permitted or condoned—if not actually demanded—by the norms of certain social groups. Crime, that is to say, may often not be the act of a person whom society has failed to socialize, but may be instead the behav-

ior of a person who has absorbed society's norms all too well. It is this illumination of the age-old puzzle of criminal behavior that the sociological perspective has helped to provide. (1978, p. 283)

The Criminal Justice System

What can be done to reduce the incidence of violent crime in the United States? Much of the public has lost faith in the ability of the criminal justice system to control crime (see Table 14–4). Many people feel the police, courts, and prisons are not doing their job—but there is little agreement about what that job is.

There are a number of different rationales for the arrest and imprisonment of criminals (Sykes, 1978, pp. 480–95). The concept of *retribution* dates back at least to biblical times. When a crime is committed, the moral order is disturbed. If harmony is to be restored, this wrong must be righted. The state has a moral duty to punish wrongdoers. A second rationale for the punishment of criminals is *vengeance*. People who resist temptations to violate the law need to feel their self-denial has meaning. Forcing criminals to pay for their violations is a collective expression of the desire for revenge. The notion of *deterrence* is more utilitarian. The state attempts to prevent or reduce crime by appealing to individuals' self-interest. When someone is punished for breaking the law, that person is less likely to break the law again (special deterrence). Moreover, the threat of punishment prevents most people from breaking the law in the first place (general deterrence). In effect, the state punishes Peter to keep Paul honest. *Incapacitation* is a fourth rationale. The state protects innocent, law-abiding citizens by isolating criminals in prisons. The fifth rationale is *rehabilitation*. According to this view, the purpose of incarceration is not punishment but therapy. The state takes responsibility for curing criminals.

Table 14-4
Public Assessment of the Criminal Justice System
(*by a sample of 1,030 people interviewed in 1981*)

How much confidence do you have in the police to protect you from violent crime?

A great deal	15%
Quite a bit	34%
Not very much	42%
None at all	8%
Don't know	1%

How much confidence do you have in the courts to sentence and convict criminals?

A great deal	5%
Quite a bit	23%
Not very much	59%
None at all	11%
Don't know	2%

Leaving aside those cases in which there is a murder, how do you feel a criminal who carries a gun when committing a crime should be sentenced?

Life in prison	15%
5 to 10 years added to sentence	51%
Sentence should be the same as with no gun	20%
Depends on circumstances	8%
Don't know	6%

Are you in favor of or opposed to the death penalty for persons convicted of murder?

Favor	65%
Opposed	24%
Don't know	11%

Do you approve or disapprove of these alternatives for dealing with crime?

	Approve	Disapprove	Don't know
Allowing the police to stop and search anybody on suspicion	48%	50%	2%
Allowing the police to wiretap the telephone of anyone they suspect	30%	67%	3%
Allowing the police to search a home without a warrant	13%	86%	1%
Encouraging citizens to carry defensive weapons such as Mace	65%	32%	3%

Source: Data from *Newsweek,* March 23, 1981, pp. 50, 52. The *Newsweek* Poll, © 1981 Newsweek, Inc.

In public discussions of the criminal justice system, the emphasis has shifted from rehabilitation—the hope of the 1960s and early 1970s—to deterrence. *If* there were enough police on the streets, *if* there were fewer restrictions on police, *if* the courts weren't backlogged, *if* the penalties imposed on convicted criminals were severe enough, *if* prisons were better staffed, *if* we brought back the death penalty (used it more often), the "epidemic" of violent crime would be halted. So the arguments go. Are police presence, court action, and punishment—especially the

Although white-collar and political crimes cost the nation much more than robberies and burglaries do, the people who commit them are often given fines and suspended sentences. Former U.S. Attorney General John Mitchell, who was convicted of crimes related to Watergate and sent to prison, was an exception.

death penalty—effective deterrents to violent crime? If not, why not? In attempting to answer these questions, we will show how the different branches of the criminal justice system operate. We will also suggest how the overlapping and sometimes conflicting goals of retribution and vengeance, incapacitation and rehabilitation, complicate the issue of deterrence.

The Police

The police system in the United States is highly decentralized, with some 15,000 federal, state, and local law enforcement agencies ranging in size from one- or two-man police forces in rural areas to New York City's 28,012-person force (UCR, 1979, pp. 238–46). The police are responsible for maintaining order (the first rationale for arresting and imprisoning criminals), enforcing the law, and performing a variety of public services.* Police become involved in the criminal justice system when officers observe a crime firsthand, when they uncover a crime in the course of investigating "suspicious circumstances," or when private citizens register a complaint. Most crimes are brought to police attention by the victim, neighbors, relatives, business competitors, or (especially with narcotics) informers. Once a crime is reported, police are responsible for the investigation of the crime and the arrest and interrogation of suspects.

Perhaps 50 percent of all crimes never come to official attention (see Figure 14–1). Some complaints are ignored because the police do not judge them to be serious. Others are dropped because they are considered civil, not criminal complaints. And others are abandoned because prosecutors conclude they will not be able to gather enough evidence for a conviction. Most crimes are not solved Sherlock-Holmes-style, through detective work. They are solved because the victim knows the offender, a witness comes forward, or in rare instances, the police themselves have witnessed the crime. This is why the clearance rate for violent crimes, in which the victim and offender often know one another, is

---

* According to one study (Wilson, 1968, p. 18), police spend almost 40 percent of their time on service calls (assisting with accidents, rescuing animals, and the like), 30 percent on maintaining order (dealing with gang fights, family quarrels), and only 10 percent on law enforcement.

higher than it is for property crimes.* Moreover, many people believe the police are too limited in their ability to investigate crimes and interrogate suspects. They cannot make a search without a warrant or "probable cause"; they must read a suspect his or her Miranda rights (You have the right to remain silent . . .). Nonetheless, police do exercise considerable discretion in deciding which crimes to investigate, which suspects to arrest, and what testimony to give in court.

Would increased police presence be a deterrent to crime? The most thorough study of this question was launched in Kansas City, Missouri, in 1972 (Kelling et al., 1974). The city's fifteen police beats were randomly divided into three groups. In the first group, all cars were taken off patrol, and officers were instructed to respond only to complaints. In the second group, patrols were continued at the usual level of one car per beat. In the third, patrols were increased to two or three times their usual level. The experiment lasted a year. Kansas City police found that increasing or decreasing patrols had virtually no effect on the number of crimes recorded, the number of arrests, or the fear of crime among citizens. A natural experiment was conducted in New York City. In 1965, the number of police on the subways was doubled in response to a rise in the crime rate. Robberies declined at first, but after a year began to climb to the old level (Wilson, 1975, pp. 86–87). Although the benefits of increased police presence seem small, the costs are high. According to one estimate, it cost almost $35,000 to prevent a single felony through increased police patrol of the subways (Conklin, 1981, p. 412).

Would increasing the arrest rate deter crime? Probably. But ironically, increasing arrests might *reduce* the certainty and severity of punishment.

---

*In 1979, the percentages of crimes cleared by arrest were: murder, 73%; aggravated assault, 60%; forcible rape, 48%; robbery, 25%; burglary, 15%; larceny, 19%; motor vehicle theft, 14%—for a total of 20% (UCR, 1979).

Figure 14–1
The Criminal Justice Funnel

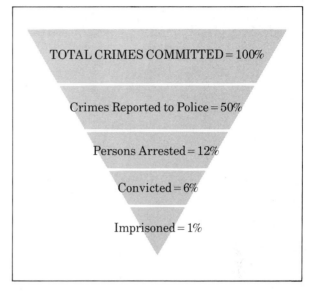

J.A. Humphrey and M.E. Milakovich, *The Administration of Justice* (New York: Human Sciences Press, 1981), p. 129.

As things stand, the courts are backlogged and the prisons are badly overcrowded. If the police stepped up arrests, the courts would be forced to give more convicted criminals probation and to give those who were sent to jail shorter sentences.

The Courts

Like the police system, the court system in the United States is decentralized. There are state and federal court systems, each with its own types of courts, its own geographical jurisdiction, and its own laws. Within each system, courts are arranged hierarchically. For example, trial courts may be at the bottom; appellate courts, which review decisions, at the top. The court system is responsible for charging suspected criminals, bringing them to trial, deciding penalties for convicted criminals, and interpreting the federal or state laws.

There are three principal actors in the criminal courts: the prosecutor (or district attorney), the defense attorney, and the judge. The prosecutor, who represents the state, is in some ways the most powerful of the three. It is the prosecutor who decides whether or not to bring a case to trial and what charges to press. Only a small number of the cases brought to the prosecutor's office are tried. In some cases, charges are dropped because of insufficient evidence. Other cases are resolved through plea bargaining: The defendant waives the constitutional right to trial in exchange for a lesser charge or for the promise of a more lenient sentence (a promise that can only be made off the record). In effect, the prosecutor acts as judge and jury in such cases. According to one study, over 90 percent of convictions are the result of plea bargaining rather than prosecution, and over a third of the defendants had originally pleaded not guilty (Newman, 1966). Plea bargaining is probably a necessity and is sanctioned by the U.S. Supreme Court. Estimates are that if only 10 percent of the defendants who now plead guilty demanded a trial, the number of trials on already overcrowded court calendars would increase by 100 percent (Sykes, 1978, p. 358). Most prosecutors are elected to office and see the position as a stepping stone to a political career. As a result, they are likely to prefer plea bargaining to trial (where they risk losing in public) and to bring defendants to trial only when they expect to win or when the public demands a trial (Sykes, 1978, pp. 413–15).

In our adversarial justice system, the burden of proof rests on the prosecutor. A defendant is assumed innocent until proven guilty. The defense attorney is responsible for showing there is a "reasonable doubt" that a client is guilty as charged. Since 1963, states have been required to provide an attorney for felony defendants (and in some states, for misdemeanor defendants) who cannot afford one themselves. About 60 percent of felony defendants and about 50 percent of mis-

demeanor defendants rely on public attorneys (Silverstein, 1965, pp. 8–9). The low pay, low prestige, and heavy caseloads of court-appointed attorneys do not always ensure the best representation.

If a case is brought to trial, the judge acts as a referee, deciding what is and is not admissible evidence. In most jurisdictions, the judge is also responsible for sentencing defendants who are found guilty. In making this decision, the judge usually takes into account the person's arrest record and social history (employment, family relationships, and so on). The legislature may set outer limits for penalties, but like the police and prosecutors, judges exercise a good deal of discretion.

Sentencing policies have provoked heated debate in recent years. On the one hand, there are those who cite the fact that most serious crimes are committed by repeaters and argue that judges are too lenient. On the other hand, there are those who cite examples of quite different penalties imposed for the same crime and argue that sentencing is too arbitrary. One possible solution to both complaints is mandatory sentences: legislating nonnegotiable sentences for specific crimes, specific categories of criminals (such as repeaters), or dangerous aspects of crime (such as carrying a gun). Proponents argue, first, that this would take more criminals off the streets (incapacitation) and second, that certainty of punishment would be a more effective deterrent than current procedures. Would mandatory sentences, in fact, deter crime? According to one study (Petersilia and Greenwood, 1978), the prison population would have to be increased by 3 to 10 percent to achieve only a 1 percent reduction in the crime rate through incapacitation. This relatively small benefit would be enormously costly. With nearly 400,000 federal and state inmates in 1980, U.S. prisons already are badly overcrowded. A 1 percent reduction in crime rates through incapacitation would add 30,000 prisoners to this population; a 15 percent reduction, perhaps 150,000 additional prisoners. It costs about $30,000 to build a single new prison cell and about $2,000 per cell to operate prisons (Lieber, 1981, p.26). In 1973, when New York State imposed mandatory sentences for certain narcotics offenses, the number of sentences actually declined, apparently because more severe penalties made judges and juries reluctant to find defendants guilty (*The New York Times*, September 5, 1976).

Prisons

Less than half of the people the courts find guilty receive active sentences sending them to jail or prison; the remainder are given probation or suspended sentences. And most of those who are sent to prison are eligible for parole after having served about a quarter of their actual sentences (Humphrey and Milakovich, 1981, pp. 127, 134). Even so, on any given day, about half a million Americans are confined to jails, detention centers, or prisons. The number of federal prisoners jumped from 196,000 in 1973 to 314,000 in 1980 (Lieber, 1981, p. 26). The capacity of prisons has not increased as rapidly, however. Cells designed for one prisoner now hold two, three, or more.

Prison officials are assigned a number of different, and difficult, tasks in the United States (Sykes, 1978, pp. 502–17). They are responsible, first, and foremost, for keeping convicts behind bars (incapacitation). They are expected to maintain internal order and to control large numbers of people who often have long histories of disorderly, violent behavior. Prisons exact retribution, or deliver punishments. The "pains of imprisonment" include loss of freedom of movement, interrupted relationships with family and friends, loss of autonomy, involuntary celibacy, and "forced association with other criminals for prolonged periods of time under conditions of severe deprivation" (Sykes, 1978, p. 525). At the same time,

prisons are expected to rehabilitate, or reform, convicts and to provide education and, in some cases, therapy.

Do prison sentences act as a special deterrent to violent crime? (Are individuals who have been imprisoned less likely to break the law again?) Do prison sentences act as a general deterrent? (Do people who are tempted to break the law refrain because they fear the consequences?) Both questions are difficult to answer. A number of social scientists have argued that a prison sentence may encourage rather than discourage crime by exposing people to a criminal subculture. In prison, a person who has committed only one crime may learn new techniques for breaking the law and, perhaps more significant, new rationales for a criminal life style. Statistics comparing recidivism rates of people who have been given probation to those given prison sentences suggest that prison is not an effective special deterrent. Recidivism rates are higher for those sent to prison. These data must be viewed with caution, however (Sykes, 1978, pp. 561–63). Society is not willing to experiment with crime. Judges send high-risk criminals to prison and give low-risk criminals probation. The higher recidivism rates among the former prisoners may result from the characteristics that sent them to prison in the first place, not from the impact of prison life and the inmate subculture. To learn whether prison sentences act as a general deterrent, researchers would have to identify "potential criminals," find out how aware they are of the penalties for various crimes, whether they believe they would be caught, and so on—a near-impossible task.

Capital Punishment

The one sure way to incapacitate convicted criminals and prevent recidivism is capital punishment. The rationale for the use of the death penalty in Western societies comes from the biblical formula "an eye for an eye," and, by extension, a life for a life. Murder is not the only crime that has been punishable by death in the United States, however. In the seventeenth century, stealing grapes was a capital crime in Virginia; striking a parent was a capital crime in New York. Until the mid-1960s, kidnapping, rape, treason, actions that resulted in mass injury and death (such as train wrecking), and capital perjury (giving false testimony that led to the execution of an innocent person) were all punishable by death (Finkel, 1967).

The death penalty first became a social issue in the United States in the 1840s when executions were public and frequently disorderly (Espy, 1980). The spectacle of fights, shootings, thefts, and other crimes "in the shadow of the gallows" provoked a groundswell of opposition to capital punishment. The issue faded during the Civil War but was revived when the electric chair was introduced in 1890. Much of the public found the new method of execution inhumane. The pendulum swung back during World War I when fear of subversion and talk of a crime wave brought the death penalty back into favor. After the war, support for executions faded. The percentage of Americans who supported use of the death penalty dropped from 62 percent in 1946 to 42 percent in 1966. In 1972, the U.S. Supreme Court declared that the arbitrary and capricious way the death penalty had been applied violated the constitutional ban on "cruel and unusual punishment" (*Furman* v. *Georgia*). In the South, for example, the death penalty for rape had been imposed mostly when the rapist was black and the victim white (Wolfgang and Riedel, 1975) (see Figure 14–2). Since 1972, however, thirty-five state legislatures have passed new capital punishment statutes; the Supreme Court has ruled that laws establishing clear standards for capital punishment *are* constitutional (*Gregg* v. *Georgia*); and public support for the death penalty has

revived. In 1980, 65 percent of those polled favored capital punishment for people convicted of murder (*Newsweek,* March 23, 1981, p. 52). Four convicted murderers have been executed in recent years.

Obviously, capital punishment is an effective incapacitator: It deters those who are executed. The question is whether the threat of execution acts as a general deterrent, restraining "potential murderers." Supporters of the death penalty argue that any sane person would conclude that the cost of taking another human being's life outweighs the benefits. The publicity given executions reminds people of the costs. Opponents argue that the death penalty has the opposite of the effect intended. According to this view, "capital punishment brutalizes society because executions show that lethal violence is an appropriate response to those who offend" (Bowers and Pierce, 1980, p. 453). Executions devalue life, providing potential murderers with a model. Instead of identifying with the person who has been executed, the potential murderer may identify the executed criminal with someone who has betrayed or disgraced him and take that person's punishment into his own hands. Executions convey the message that violent retribution is legitimate. The fact that executions are performed by duly appointed officials on duly convicted criminals may seem an irrelevant detail.

The evidence for and against capital punishment is far from clear. One researcher has calculated that each execution performed in the United States between 1933 and 1967 saved eight lives (Ehrlich, 1975). Others have concluded that in the month following executions during this period, there was an average of two *additional* murders (Bowers and Pierce, 1980). Researchers comparing the murder rates in neighboring states, one of which had the death penalty and one of which did not, and murder rates in the same state before and after the death penalty was

Figure 14-2

The Geographic and Social Distribution of Executions, 1930–1978

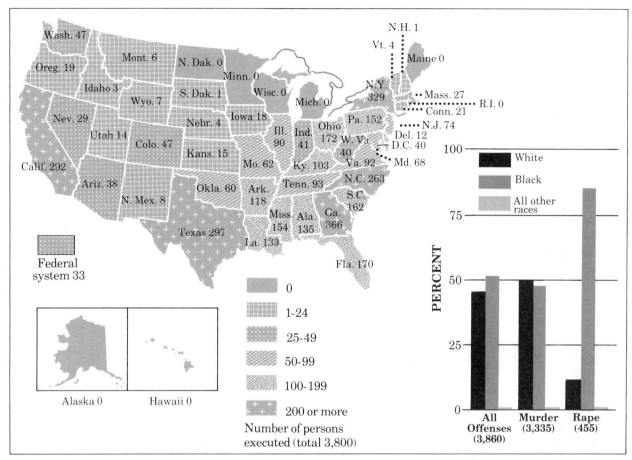

Source: U.S. Department of Justice, Law Enforcement Assistance Administration, National Criminal Justice Information and Statistics Service, *Capital Punishment, 1978* (Washington, D.C.: U.S. Government Printing Office, December 1979), p. 9.

in use, have not found significant reductions in homicide (Gibbs, 1979). Moreover, innocent people convicted of capital crimes and sentenced to execution also increase the costs of having capital punishment. This is not to say that the death penalty has no effect, but that the effects are unknown.

Deterrence Considered

What general conclusions can be drawn about these efforts to deter crime and violence? The theory of deterrence is based on the assumption that human beings are rational creatures who carefully think through the consequences of their behavior and that people stop to calculate costs (or risks) and benefits before acting. This may be true of people who are contemplating an instrumental crime like theft. But it does not describe spontaneous, emotional crimes, such as a violent outburst of rage that leads to murder. Many assaults and murders are "crimes of passion" rather than "crimes of calculation." Stiff penalties are not as likely to deter such crimes.

Let us assume for the moment that people do, in fact, weigh the consequences of their actions in advance. The cost of breaking the law would depend not only on the severity of the penalty but also on the certainty of punishment and on the actual risk of being caught, tried, convicted, and sentenced. Public discussions of crime control tend to focus on the severity of punishments. The courts, it is argued, are too lenient. Support for the death penalty is based, in part, on the assumption that the harsher the penalty, the more effective it will be as a deterrent. In fact, research suggests that while certainty of punishment is a moderate deterrent, severity alone has little impact (Antunes and Hunt, 1973). Indeed, severe punishment may increase rather than decrease recidivism rates. The social stigma attached to prison sentences, the difficulties of returning to a normal life after an extended stay in prison, and heightened feelings of alienation and injustice may make a person more likely to violate the law. Simply put, punishment breeds resentment. Someone who already bears the stigma of a criminal record, and who cannot get a job because of this, has little to lose.

The Social Roots of Crime and Violence

In the final analysis, the criminal justice system fails to reduce crime because it does not attack the root causes of crime and violence in the social

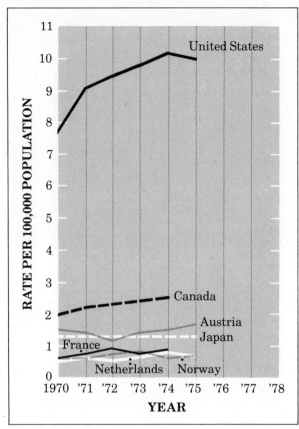

Figure 14-3
Comparative Homicide Rates, 1970-1975

Source: U.S. Bureau of the Census, *Social Indicators III* (Washington, D.C.: U.S. Government Printing Office, December 1980), p. 235.

structure. All evidence points to the fact that crime is rooted in poverty, unemployment (particularly among the young), inequality, family isolation, cultural ambiguity on the subject of violence, social pressures to exhibit material success, and other elements of the social structure. Attempting to reduce crime by sentencing convicted criminals to prison is like trying to rid a lawn of dandelions by snapping off the tops. The roots remain in the soil and the weed springs back. So it is with violent crime. The root causes remain in the social structure; new criminals appear; recidivism rates are high.

It is useful to compare the United States, which has one of the highest violent crime rates, to Japan, where crime rates are comparatively low (Conklin, 1981, pp. 484–90) (see Figure 14–3). What is different about Japan? Unemployment rates in Japan are comparatively low. Most Japanese work for the same company all of their lives, and most companies take responsibility for the social welfare of their employees. Japanese culture places a higher value on commitment and attachment to the family than on individualism and the private pursuit of material success. Even in large cities, neighborhoods tend to be tightly knit communities. The gap between the wealthiest and poorest members of Japanese society is not as great as it is in this country. Material expectations are not so high. As a result of these combined factors, the Japanese have a higher stake in conformity. They are more attached to the social order in the sense of caring a great deal about the good opinion of others. They are more committed to their families, jobs, and neighborhoods, for they invest a good deal of their time, energy, and their reputations in those settings. If they break the law, they risk losing the investment they have made in conventional behavior (Hirschi, 1969).

The observation that crime is rooted in the social structure is sometimes dismissed as useless. It implies that without massive social transformations, the crime problem is insoluble. Comparatively small steps could be taken to increase commitment to conformity, however (Conklin, 1981, pp. 487–90). For example, paroled convicts might be required to work in the communities where they reside (restoring buildings, working with youngsters, or whatever their talents suggest). This might give them a greater investment in the community. The family is the basic source of attachment to the social order. Instead of taking an abused child out of the family or sending a delinquent teen-ager to training school, both of which break up the family, programs could be designed to assist family members in meeting responsibilities (a guaranteed income, day-care centers so parents would be guaranteed time off, classes in child development and child rearing). A "car library" for teen-agers, a system for borrowing automobiles, might reduce their temptation to gain the status of driving a car by stealing one. The underlying goal of programs like these would be to increase individuals' personal stakes in conformity to the law.

Summary

1. Types of crime can be distinguished in terms of whether they cause direct or indirect harm, whether they are isolated acts or part of a career, the relationship between the criminal and the victim, the way the public perceives the crime and the criminal, and the way the criminal sees him- or herself.

2. Violent crime not only causes physical injury and, in some cases, financial loss but also threatens the social order.

3. The Department of Justice's *National Crime Survey,* which measures victimization, indicates many crimes are not reported to the police and recorded in the FBI's *Uniform Crime Reports.*

4. Young, black, low-income males are the most frequent offenders *and* victims.

5. Biological factors account for only a small fraction of violent crimes, if that. Psychological explanations suggest violent criminals have not acquired inner controls on behavior. Social-psychological explanations emphasize outer controls and the role of learning and differential associations in violent crime.

6. Sociological explanations trace violent crime to social disorganization, a gap between cultural goals and legitimate means of achieving them, illegitimate opportunity structures, and cultural support of violence.

7. The criminal justice system gives police considerable discretion. Only a fraction of crimes reported to police are cleared by arrest.

8. The principal actors in the criminal courts are the prosecutor, the defense attorney, and the judge. Only a fraction of people arrested for crimes are convicted and sent to prison.

9. In addition to incapacitating convicted criminals and maintaining internal order, prison officials are assigned the tasks of punishing and rehabilitating offenders.

10. Research on capital punishment has produced contradictory findings. Some studies indicate that the threat of execution causes a slight reduction in violent crime; other studies, that it causes a slight increase. Certainty of punishment may have more impact than severity.

11. Crime rates are high, in part, because the criminal justice system does not deal with the root causes of crime and violence in the social structure.

Suggested Reading

Cloward, Richard A., and Lloyd E. Ohlin. *Delinquency and Opportunity: A Theory of Delinquent Gangs.* New York: Free Press, 1960.

Cressey, Donald R. *Theft of the Nation: The Structure and Operations of Organized Crime in America.* New York: Harper & Row/Colophon, 1969.

Geis, Gilbert, and Robert S. Meier (Eds.) *White-Collar Crime: Offenses in Business, Politics, and Professions,* rev. ed. New York: Free Press, 1977.

Schur, Edwin M. *Crimes Without Victims.* Englewood Cliffs, N.J.: Prentice-Hall, 1965.

Wilson, James Q. *Thinking About Crime.* New York: Basic Books, 1975.

References

Antunes, G., and A.L. Hunt. "The Impact of Certainty and Severity of Punishment on Levels of Crime in America." *Journal of Criminal Law and Criminology,* Vol. 64 (1973), pp. 486–93.

Bandura, A. *Aggression: A Social Learning Analysis.* Englewood Cliffs, N.J.: Prentice-Hall, 1973.

Bandura, A., and R.H. Walters. *Social Learning and Personality Development.* New York: Holt, Rinehart and Winston, 1963.

Booth, A., D.R. Johnson, and H.M. Choldin. "Correlates of City Crime Rates: Victimization Surveys versus Official Statistics." *Social Problems,* Vol. 25, No. 2 (December 1977), pp. 187–97.

Bowers, W.J., and G.L. Pierce. "Deterrence or Brutalization: What is the Effect of Execution?" *Crime and Delinquency,* Vol. 26 (October 1980), pp. 453–84.

Braithwaite, J. "The Myth of Social Class and Criminality Reconsidered." *American Sociological Review,* Vol. 46, No. 1 (1981), pp. 36–57.

Brown, P., and P. Elliot. "Control of Aggression in a Nursery School Class." *Journal of Experimental Child Psychology,* Vol. 2 (1965), pp. 103–07.

Cloward, R.A., and L.E. Ohlin. *Delinquency and Opportunity: A Theory of Delinquent Gangs.* New York: Free Press, 1960.

Cohen, A.K. *Delinquent Boys.* New York: Free Press, 1955.

Cohen, A.K., and J.F. Short, Jr. "Crime and Juvenile Delinquency." In R.K. Merton and R. Nisbet (Eds.), *Contemporary Social Problems,* 4th ed. New York: Harcourt Brace Jovanovich, 1976, pp. 47–100.

Conklin, J.E. *Criminology.* New York: Macmillan, 1981.

Conot, R. *Rivers of Blood, Years of Darkness.* New York: Bantam, 1967.

Cressey, D.R. *Theft of the Nation: The Structure and Operations of Organized Crime in America.* New York: Harper & Row/Colophon, 1969.

Ehrlich, I. "The Deterrent Effect of Capital Punishment: A Question of Life or Death." *The American Economic Review,* Vol. 65 (June 1975), pp. 397–417.

Epsy, M.W., Jr. "Capital Punishment and Deterrence: What Statistics Cannot Show." *Crime and Delinquency,* Vol. 26 (October 1980), pp. 537–44.

The Figgie Report on Fear of Crime: America Afraid. Part I: The General Public. Willoughby, Ohio: A-T-O, Inc., 1980.

Finkel, R. "A Survey of Capital Offenses." In T. Sellin (Ed.), *Capital Punishment.* New York: Harper & Row, 1967, pp. 22–31.

Geis, G., and R.F. Meier (Eds.). *White Collar Crime: Offenses in Business, Politics, and Professions,* rev. ed. New York: Free Press, 1977.

Gibbs, J.P. "Assessing the Deterrence Doctrine." *American Behavioral Scientist,* Vol. 22, No. 6 (July/August 1979), pp. 653–77.

Hirschi, T. *Causes of Delinquency.* Berkeley, Cal.: University of California Press, 1969.

Humphrey, J.A., and M.E. Milakovich. *Administration of Justice: Law Enforcement, Courts, and Corrections.* New York: Human Sciences Press, 1981.

Hunt, M. *The Mugging.* New York: New American Library, 1972.

Ianni, F.A. *A Family Business.* New York: Russell Sage, 1972.

Kelling, G.L., T. Pate, D. Dieckman, and C.E. Brown. "The Kansas City Preventive Patrol Experiment." In S. Halleck (Ed.), *The Aldine Crime and Justice Annal 1974.* Chicago: Aldine, 1975.

Lieber, J. "The American Prison." *The New York Times Magazine,* March 8, 1981, pp. 26–35ff.

Luckenbill, D.F., and W.B. Sanders. "Criminal Violence." In E. Sagarin and F. Montanino (Eds.), *Deviants: Voluntary Actors in a Hostile World.* Glenview, Ill.: Scott-Foresman, 1977, pp. 88–156.

Mark, V.H., and F.R. Ervin. *Violence and the Brain.* New York: Harper & Row, 1970.

Mednick, S.A., et al. "Biology and Violence." Paper presented at the Philadelphia Workshop on Criminal Violence, January 30, 1981.

Merton, R.K. "Social Structure and Anomie." *American Sociological Review,* Vol. 3 (1938), pp. 672–82.

Merton, R.K., and R. Nisbet. *Contemporary Social Problems,* 4th ed. New York: Harcourt Brace Jovanovich, 1976.

Miller, W. "Lower Class Culture as a Generating Milieu of Gang Delinquency." *Journal of Social Issues,* Vol. 14, No 3 (1958), pp. 5–19.

Mills, C.W. "The Professional Ideology of Social Pathologists." *American Journal of Sociology,* Vol. 49 (September 1943), pp. 165–80.

Monahan, J. *The Clinical Prediction of Violent Behavior.* Rockville, Md.: U.S. Department of Health and Human Services, 1981.

National Commission on the Causes and Prevention of Violence. *Crimes of Violence,* Staff Report, Vol. 12. Washington, D.C.: U.S. Government Printing Office, 1969.

Newman, D.J. *The Determination of Guilt or Innocence Without Trial.* Boston: Little, Brown, 1966.

Paddock, J. "Studies on Antiviolent and 'Normal' Communities." *Agressive Behavior,* Vol. 1 (1975), pp. 217–33.

Petersilia, J., and P.W. Greenwood. "Mandatory Prison Sentences: Their Projected Effects on Crime and Prison Populations." *Criminology,* Vol. 69 (1978), pp. 604–15.

Schur, E.M. *Crimes Without Victims.* Englewood Cliffs, N.J.: Prentice-Hall, 1965.

Silberman, C.E. *Criminal Violence, Criminal Justice.* New York: Random House, 1978.

Silverstein, L. *Defense of the Poor in Criminal Cases in American State Courts.* Chicago: American Bar Foundation, 1965.

Skolnick, J. *Justice Without Trial.* New York: Wiley, 1966.

Stark, R. *Social Problems.* New York: Random House, 1975.

Stark, R., and J. McEvoy III. "Middle Class Violence." *Psychology Today,* Vol. 4 (November 1970), pp. 52–65.

Straus, M.A., R.J. Gelles, and S.K. Steinmetz. *Behind Closed Doors.* Garden City, N.Y.: Doubleday/Anchor, 1980.

Sutherland, E. *Principles of Criminology.* Chicago: Lippincott, 1939.

Sutherland, E.H. *White-Collar Crime.* New York: Holt, Rinehart and Winston, 1949.

Sykes, G.M. *Criminology.* New York: Harcourt Brace Jovanovich, 1978.

Uniform Crime Reports (UCR), 1976. Washington, D.C.: U.S. Government Printing Office, 1977.

Uniform Crime Reports (UCR), 1979. Washington, D.C.: U.S. Government Printing Office, 1980.

Wilson, J.Q. *Varieties of Police Behavior.* Cambridge, Mass.: Harvard University Press, 1968.

Wilson, J.Q. *Thinking About Crime.* New York: Basic Books, 1975.

Wolfgang, M. *Patterns in Criminal Homicide.* Philadelphia: University of Pennsylvania Press, 1958.

Wolfgang, M., and F. Ferracuti. *The Subculture of Violence.* London: Tavistock, 1967.

Wolfgang, M., and D. Riedel. "Rape, Race and the Death Penalty in Georgia," *American Journal of Orthopsychiatry,* Vol. 45, No. 4 (1975), pp. 658–68.

Chapter Fifteen

Sexual Behavior

Sex and Society

Instincts or Social Learning?

Variations in Sexual Conduct

Sexual Attitudes and Behavior in the United States

   The Victorian Influence
   Science "Discovers" Sex
   A New Morality?

Adolescent Sexuality

Teen-age Pregnancy

Venereal Disease

Marital and Extramarital Sexuality

The Sociology of Sexuality

   Learning Sexual Roles
   Sexual Dysfunction

Alternatives to Monogamous Sexuality

   The (Clandestine) Affair
   Sex and Divorce

Commercialized Sex

Pornography

   The Legal Dilemma
   The Public Concern
   The Future of Pornography

Prostitution

   An Industry in Decline
   Contrasting Views of Prostitution

Homosexuality

Problems of Definition

Becoming Homosexual

   The Homosexual "Condition": Biological and Psychological Explanations
   The Homosexual Role: Learning Theory

The Politics of Homosexuality

   Gay Liberation

A False Dichotomy

Social Problems and Social Issues

Sex is serious business for Americans. Like income and race, it provides a criterion for judging a person's worth. Americans often evaluate people in terms of their choice of sexual partners. If they have what we consider to be too many sexual encounters, we call them promiscuous; if they have too few, we call them prudes. If they prefer their own sex, we label them queer. If money is exchanged for sexual behavior, we call it prostitution. "[T]he presumed proficiency, style and attitudes of the participants, too, reflect on their general moral character" (Cavan, 1976, pp. 57–58). (Americans are not alone in these beliefs.)

Like other serious matters, sex is controversial (see Table 15–1). Few readers will be surprised to find a chapter on sexual behavior in a social problems textbook. There is little agreement, however, about where the problem lies. Is American society today too permissive with regard to sexual behavior, or too restrictive? Are variations on traditional, heterosexual, one-to-one sexual relations normal expressions of human sexuality, or are they pathological conditions that should be treated and cured? Has scientific investigation of sexual behavior established a foundation for healthier attitudes, or has science taken the mystery, and some of the joy, out of sex? Are Americans today sexually liberated or sexually obsessed?

Changing norms and disagreement over the consequences of change have made sexual conduct a major social issue. In the first section of this chapter, we put today's controversy into perspective by examining cross-cultural and historical variations in sexual behavior. This section illustrates the link between people's private lives and the public issues, between sex and society. In the second section, we consider adolescent sexuality. Are teen-agers' experimentations with sex harmful? If so, why? In the section on marital and extramarital sexuality, we trace the social origins of what appear to be private troubles, including sexual dysfunction. Then we turn to com-

mercialized sex. Pornography and prostitution are both social issues: They arouse public concern and controversy. But are they social problems? Do they cause actual harm? In the final section, we examine myths about homosexuality and their consequences.

Sex and Society

The sociological approach to the study of sex focuses on the ways that the groups to which people belong and the society and times in which they live influence their attitudes, their behavior, and even their feelings. People tend to think of sex in intimate, private terms. They are inclined to look for psychological or biological explanations of sexual puzzles. The idea that society is a silent partner in bed, as well as in other public arenas like work and government, is a radical departure from common views of sex. It takes sociological imagination (Mills, 1959) to see that sex, like other forms of behavior, is guided at least in part by norms. This section sets the stage for alleged sexual problems by showing that sexual norms vary from culture to culture and change over time.

Instincts or Social Learning?

Is sexual behavior instinctive? Or do human beings acquire sexual preferences and styles in the same way they acquire other tastes and skills—say, for a particular kind of cooking, or for sports —through learning?

The Grand Valley Dani of West New Guinea are an interesting case. The anthropologist Karl Heider (1976) spent two and a half years as a participant-observer among the Dani. He returned from the field convinced that hardly anyone would believe what he found. The Dani are not interested in sex. Like many other traditional people, the Dani observe a postpartum taboo: Sexual relations between a husband and wife are forbid-

Table 15-1
Attitudes Toward Sexuality*

	What Is Your Opinion if a (Boy/Girl) Sixteen–Nineteen Has Sexual Intercourse with a (Girl/Boy) Without Love?	If An Unmarried Adult (Man/Woman) Has Sexual Intercourse with a (Woman/Man) When They Love Each Other?	If a Married Person Has Sexual Intercourse with Some-one Other than the Marriage Partner?	What Is Your Opinion of Sex Acts Between Two Persons of the Same Sex When They Have No Special Affection for Each Other?	When They Love Each Other?
Always wrong	51.7%	31.5%	72.7%	77.7%	70.2%
Almost always wrong	19.4	14.0	14.3	8.4	8.4
Wrong only sometimes	19.6	22.2	10.7	6.3	7.2
Not wrong at all	5.0	28.7	2.1	5.6	11.4
Don't know	4.0	3.5	0.4	1.6	2.2
No answer	0.1	—	0.1	0.1	0.3
	99.8	99.9	99.8	99.7	99.7

*Based on 3,018 interviews.
Source: Eugene E. Levitt and Albert D. Klassen, Jr., "Public Attitudes Toward Homosexuality: Part of the 1970 National Survey by the Institute for Sex Research," *Journal of Homosexuality* (Fall 1974), p. 31.

den after the birth of a child.* In most cultures, the postpartum taboo extends one, perhaps two,

*Anthropologists see the postpartum taboo as an adaptation to an environment in which protein is scarce and people do not have modern birth control devices. By nursing, a mother can provide a baby with adequate nourishment during the early, crucial years of development. But she would not be able to feed two or three babies at the same time. Nursing may also delay conception.

years. The Dani abstain from sex for four to six years. As far as Heider could tell, the taboo was never violated. Siblings were invariably spaced at least four years apart. How do the Dani enforce the taboo? Does some terrible punishment await offenders? No. Indeed, the question of enforcement puzzled them. When pressed, they speculated that the ghosts might be angry if a couple embraced too soon. But they do not take their ghosts very seriously: They treat them more like bothersome in-laws than like powerful forces. Heider found no evidence that husbands or wives engaged in extramarital or homosexual affairs or in masturbation during the long taboo period. Perhaps most surprising, Heider found no evidence of unhappiness or strain because of sexual abstinence. One possible explanation is that something is biologically or genetically wrong with the Dani. Nothing is wrong. They are as healthy and well-nourished as related, neighboring tribes whose members are quite active sexually.

The idea that an entire group of people are not very interested in sex and do not mind going years without it is difficult to accept because it runs counter to our culture's ideas about the nature of human sexuality. The sociologist Erich Goode has listed six American "tenets of faith" regarding sexuality (1978, p. 301): (1) Sexual behavior is biologically determined. Our sexuality is an expression of innate drives, or "animal instincts." (2) The sex drive is an extremely powerful force, analogous to hunger and thirst, and demands fulfillment. (3) Sex plays a central role in everyone's life; many apparently unrelated activities and objects symbolize or stand in for sex. (4) Unless checked, our animalistic sexual urges could destroy not only our own lives but the entire social structure. (5) The need for sexual expression is constant. (6) Sexuality, as described here, is universal. All people go through the same stages of sexual development; "behavior, organs and thoughts mean pretty much the same thing to everyone everywhere." Thus, Americans tend to assume that every human being has a natural, heterosexual destiny, which can be twisted only as a result of early, traumatic experiences. We tend to label some sexual activities and feelings natural and others unnatural.

Goode rejects all of the above. With Heider, he argues that Americans believe in an innate sex drive because that is what our culture teaches.

Dani culture teaches a quite different view of sexuality, and Dani attitudes and behavior reflect that. In other words, human sexual expression is the product of social learning. What we do in bed (or, for that matter, out of bed) is dictated by our imaginations, our relationships, and our culture, as well as by our chemistry. We are born with the potential for sexual arousal, but what form it takes depends on learning. In Goode's words, "We have no sexual 'instinct.' We have a sexual drive— or even better, a sexual *appetite*—which can be turned off, minimally potentiated, or strongly stimulated . . ." (p. 303).

Variations in Sexual Conduct

Cross-cultural studies document an almost infinite variety of human sexual behavior (Ford and Beach, 1951). Cultures differ in their views of who is an acceptable partner for sexual activities. Some cultures restrict premarital and/or extramarital sex; other cultures do not. The approved list may or may not include members of an older or a younger age group, members of different ethnic groups or religions, members of one's own extended family or clan,* or members of one's own sex. Stimulating oneself sexually may or may not be acceptable. On the South Pacific island of Lesu, for example, women masturbate openly, sitting down and bending their right leg so that the heel of the foot presses against the genitalia. In Lesu, no shame is attached to masturbation. Women learn the technique as small girls, by watching their mothers, sisters, and neighbors (Powdermaker, 1933, pp. 276–77).

Styles of attraction and seduction also vary cross-culturally. People learn to consider some

---

*With the exception of a small number of royal families known from history, the taboo against incest is universal. There is a great deal of variation, however, in who is considered family and thus is subject to the incest taboo and in the severity with which the taboo is enforced (see Chapter 8).

physical characteristics attractive and others un-attractive; they learn who is supposed to take sexual initiative and how. In some cultures, attractiveness is measured in terms of the shape of a person's eyes or ears; in other cultures, in terms of external genitalia. In American society, thin long-legged, big-bosomed blond women are idealized. In other cultures, only babies are interested in breasts, and fat is considered beautiful (Hyde, 1979, p. 19).

Sexual relations are also variable. Culture establishes the appropriate time, place, frequency, and technique for sexual activities. Natives of the island of Inis Beag, off the coast of Ireland, consider it more than enough for a husband and wife to have sexual intercourse once or twice a month. The Aranda of Australia make love, sleep a bit, make love, sleep, and make love again—three to five times a night—every night. When the African Thonga first encountered Europeans, they could not believe that the whites kissed, "eating each other's saliva and dirt" (Hyde, 1979, p. 18).

Although the details vary, all cultures set standards for sexual conduct. Norms govern the who, what, where, when, and why of sex (Gagnon, 1977, Chapter 1). In some societies, the reason people give for sexual activity is love; in other societies, the satisfaction of a physical need. Which purpose receives the stamp of approval varies not only from one culture to another but over time. American culture is a good illustration of this.

Sexual Attitudes and Behavior in the United States

In *Patterns of Sexual Behavior* (1951), a classic survey of 190 societies, the anthropologist Clelland Ford and the psychologist Frank Beach concluded that America was one of the most sexually restrictive societies in the world. How much have behavior and attitudes changed in the past thirty years? Did the 1960s bring about a sexual revolution?

The Victorian influence The sexual conventions of the first half of the twentieth century have their roots in Victorian England. To the Victorians, the only socially approved reason for sexual activity was procreation. Sex for pleasure, or even for love, was condemned. The reproductive act was thought disgusting. Victorians layered medical advice on top of Judeo-Christian ethics: Masturbation (a nonreproductive act) was not only sinful but was dangerous to one's health. Victorians elevated the double standard to the level of a natural law: They believed that men regrettably have strong sexual impulses, whereas women "(happily for them) are not very much troubled with sexual feelings of any kind." (Acton, in Marcus, 1966, p. 31). Respectable women submitted to their husbands' sexual demands only out of a sense of duty. Even veiled references to sex were taboo among Victorians. Polite people simple did not discuss sex.

How many Victorians actually lived by these standards is debatable. Official attitudes toward sexual behavior reflected the standards of a growing middle class, which placed a high value on thrift, saving, and investment (Gagnon and Henderson, 1975). Women were expected to "save" themselves for marriage; a woman who gave up her virginity prior to marriage was "damaged property." The Victorian euphemism for ejaculation was "spend"—and a prudent man did not spend too much. In practice, however, prostitution and pornography were widespread. An estimated 40,000 prostitutes worked the streets of London in the 1880s. (Gagnon, 1977, p. 2). Pornographers drew vivid pictures of copulation in every conceivable combination and position (Marcus, 1966, pp. 283–84). In short, the Victorian era was characterized by a good deal of ignorance about human sexuality and an equal amount of hypocrisy.

Victorian standards of sexual conduct were welcomed—indeed, championed—in the United States. Here as in England, norms kept sexuality

Following an age-old custom, an admiring patron slips money into the dancer's costume. A decade ago "everyone knew" that women did not enjoy watching a man strip or looking at nude male pinups. Have women changed or are they coming out into the open?

hidden. Late in the nineteenth century, however, science began to turn on the lights. Scientific discoveries were both a cause and an effect of changing sexual norms.

Science "discovers" sex Sigmund Freud was among the first to break the taboo against talking or writing openly about sex. He went so far as to argue that *libido,* the sex drive or instinct for sex, plays a central role in human existence. Freud shocked his contemporaries by suggesting that sexual urges do not appear suddenly in puberty but are present from birth. He argued that many, if not most, psychological problems could be traced to the clash between biological sexual urges and cultural restraints on sexual expression. He saw the sex drive as a dangerous force, but one that could be channeled into creative, socially valuable activities such as science or art (through a process called sublimation). Libido, he maintained, is the driving force of civilization as well as the source of much human discontent.

Although Freud was considered a radical in his day, he remained the Victorian gentleman in many ways. He believed that heterosexual intercourse was the natural aim and object of sexual desire (though he believed that all people have some homosexual impulses). He believed that women are not as highly sexed as men and that ultimately all mature women want to have children. He stressed the importance of the nuclear family (parents and children living together), both to the social order and to individual psychological development. At the same time, he maintained that the individual, the family, and, indeed, society run on the sexual fuel of libido.

The evidence for this view consists of case studies of people—usually troubled individuals—who came to Freud for analysis or treatment. Whether their childhood memories, dreams, and longings were typical of all human beings everywhere is debatable. But there is no debating the influence Freud had on sexual attitudes. It was he who made talking about sex and studying sex respectable.

The next breakthrough in the scientific investigation of sex came in 1948, with the publication of Alfred C. Kinsey and his associates' *Sexual Be-*

havior in the Human Male, followed by Kinsey and Paul Gebhard's *Sexual Behavior in the Human Female,* published in 1953. In 1938, Indiana University asked Kinsey to teach a course on sex and marriage that would include sexual advice for students. Finding virtually no scientific information on sexual behavior in the library, Kinsey began to interview students and colleagues at the university. One thing led to another, and over the next eighteen years, Kinsey and his co-workers questioned 5,300 American men and 5,940 women about their sex lives. Where Freud had theorized, Kinsey quantified. His findings shocked the nation. It seemed that Americans (like Victorians) honored strict sexual norms more in word than in deed (Tavris and Offir, 1977, pp. 63–71). About half of the married men and a quarter of the married women interviewed had had sexual intercourse with someone other than their spouse. Women turned out not to be as asexual as moralists had hoped: Many women became sexually aroused and had orgasms. But by and large, men had richer sexual fantasies and more frequent and varied experiences, with more partners. How much variety was quite a surprise. Although only 4 percent of the men were exclusively homosexual, by age forty-five nearly 37 percent had had at least one homosexual experience leading to orgasm.

Kinsey's methods have been both praised and criticized. Kinsey relied exclusively on volunteers, who may have been more willing to experiment with and talk about sex than the "average" American. Although he made every effort to interview a wide variety of social types (from divinity students to convicted sex offenders), his sample was not representative of the population as a whole. Young, white, Protestant, well-educated Midwesterners were overrepresented. His interview strategy, however, is well regarded. Interviewers memorized a basic set of 350 questions. They spoke to the subjects in plain English (for example, using the term "masturbation" rather than the euphemism "touching yourself"). To discourage embarrassment and under-reporting, they asked direct questions ("When did you start masturbating?" instead of "Have you ever masturbated?") A number of subjects were re-questioned eighteen months or more after their first interview, and husbands' and wives' responses were compared.

Kinsey's major contribution to changing sexual norms was in showing that "normal" men and women engage in a wide variety of sexual activities. He showed people who suffered private guilt for what they thought were unusual or perverse sexual fantasies and behaviors that they were not alone. Despite the many pages of charts and statistics, Kinsey's books were instant best sellers, and polls showed that most of the American public generally approved of the research.

In the last decade of his life, Kinsey, with his associates at the Institute for Sex Research, began filming sex live (Pomeroy, 1972, pp. 172–78). This research was never made public, however. The direct observation of sexual behavior fell to the obstetrician-gynecologist William Masters and his associate, Virginia Johnson. Their book, *The Human Sexual Response* (1966), was a third landmark in sex research. Masters and Johnson focused on physiology of sex, rather than psychology of sexual behavior (as Freud did) or its incidence (as Kinsey did). Over twelve years, they observed more than 300 women and 300 men, ranging in age from eighteen to eighty-nine, in more than 10,000 cycles of sexual arousal and orgasm. They invented devices for photographing and measuring response to sexual stimulation. Ultimately, they were able to diagram a sequence of physiological changes: excitement (the blood flows to organs and tissues, causing them to swell); plateau (body muscles tense, the heart beats faster, breathing is heavy); orgasm (intense, rhythmic contractions and, in males, ejaculation); and resolution (return to the unaroused state).

Like Kinsey, Masters and Johnson relied on volunteer subjects. They observed sexual behavior only in the laboratory. Their procedures, too, have raised questions: What kind of people would participate in sex experiments? Are they representative? Does sexual behavior in a laboratory accurately reflect behavior in private? Possibly not. Masters and Johnson, however, were interested in physiology, and they approached their subject within the limitations imposed on any medical research that involves human beings.

Masters and Johnson's most influential contribution was in their description of female sexual responses. Previous discussions of female sexuality were based on speculation—largely by men. Indeed, women's views of their own sexual responses were based on men's interpretations. Masters and Johnson supplied facts: They found that women not only have orgasms, but that they may have multiple orgasms. They also found that females' orgasms are usually triggered by direct stimulation of the clitoris or indirect stimulation during intercourse, not by contact between the penis and the vaginal wall.* Women's responses tended to be more variable than men's, but on the whole, Masters and Johnson found that women and men were more alike than different. In *Human Sexual Inadequacy*, published in 1970, Masters and Johnson reported what they had learned about barriers to sexual satisfaction from their work as sex therapists. They suggested that the leading causes of sexual dysfunction were ig-

norance about sexuality and performance anxiety, or fear of failure.

Like the Kinsey reports, Masters and Johnson's books were instant best sellers. They were published during a period when attitudes toward sex in the United States were changing, partly as a result of scientific investigation. Freud made talking about sex respectable, even chic. Kinsey made other people's private sex lives public. And Masters and Johnson described in clinical terms what happens when a man or women is sexually aroused and experiences orgasm.

A new morality? Nudity and explicit sex acts are portrayed openly on movie screens today. Respectable magazines print advice for unmarried couples who live together. Gay men and women have not only "come out of the closet"; they have organized. Fifteen or twenty years ago, all of this would have been unthinkable. The theory of social disorganization (see Chapter 1) suggests that sudden, dramatic change is disruptive, for individuals and for society. Specifically, this approach suggests that a breakdown in the traditional norms that regulate behavior causes strain for individuals. Before examining this possibility, we must determine whether the 1960s did, in fact, bring a new morality. Have the sexual attitudes and behavior of Americans changed radically, or have they simply come out into the open? Do signs of change reflect the experiments of a small but visible minority or the attitudes of the majority (Hunt, 1974, pp. 5–15)?

In the early 1970s, the Playboy Foundation commissioned an independent research firm to resurvey the territory explored by Kinsey in the 1940s and 1950s. The results were analyzed and reported by Morton Hunt in *Sexual Behavior in the 1970s* (1974). Hunt's report was not an exact replication of the Kinsey surveys. Researchers used written questionnaires. These provide total anonymity, something not possible in personal interviews, but make it difficult to detect evasion

---

*The idea that women have two different kinds of orgasms, clitoral and vaginal, had been the subject of intense debate. Freud maintained that young girls have orgasms by stimulating the clitoris, but that mature women have vaginal orgasms through heterosexual intercourse. The myth of the vaginal orgasm gave men the biological right to dominate women in sex as in other activities. According to this view, a woman needs a man in order to have a perfect and total orgasm. If she is not satisfied by what satisfies him (intercourse), something is wrong with her. Masters and Johnson laid these myths to rest (see Lydon, 1970).

or bragging. In some respects, however, the sample was more representative of the population as a whole than Kinsey's survey was, though this survey, too, relied on volunteer subjects. Nevertheless, the two surveys invite comparison.

Hunt reported that attitudes and behavior had, indeed, changed since Kinsey's surveys were published (see Table 15–2). On the whole, Americans today are more tolerant of sexual variations, particularly with regard to premarital sex. Fewer people believe that most men want to marry virgins or that men should always take the sexual initiative. Fewer people believe that masturbation, oral-genital sex, and homosexuality are wrong. There is little evidence of mass promiscuity, however. Hunt found that sex continues to have deep emotional significance for most Americans and that most sexual activity takes place within a committed relationship. (The sociologist Ira Reiss [1967] calls the new standard "permissiveness with affection.") In addition, Hunt reported that change is most evident among the young. Past researchers found that attitudes toward sex were linked to social class: Greater sexual permissiveness was associated with higher education, a higher occupational level, and religious and political liberalism. Today, age is the best predictor of sexual attitudes. For example, whatever their socioeconomic status, women under twenty-five are three-and-one-half times as likely as women over fifty-five to think that premarital sex leads to better and more stable marriages. Hunt also reported that married couples are more creative in bed today than they were in Kinsey's day. He concluded, "[D]uring the past generation a major—and permanent—reevaluation of sexual attitudes has been occurring throughout our society . . ." (p. 27).

Whether these changes add up to a sexual revolution is debatable, however. In the 1920s, there was a great deal of talk about free love. Associations were formed to promote open marriage, swinging, and other experiments that people today

think of as recent inventions. In the 1930s, some marriage manuals suggested that good sex is crucial to happy marriages. Although the language has changed, many of today's popular books on sex are simply pouring new findings into old bottles (Gordon and Shankweiler, 1971). Most of them still imply, for example, that the man is in charge and that he is responsible for satisfying his partner as well as himself. Thus today's sexual norms might be most accurately described as the product of evolution, not revolution—that is, as the product of gradual, partial change, not of sudden, dramatic change (Moneymaker and Montanino, 1978).

How liberating have these changes been? Today's preoccupation with sex may cause as much unhappiness as yesterday's repression of sex. Certainly, ignorance about human sexuality was not bliss. But knowing the facts may have created new pressures. People who worried that they were the only ones "doing it" may have been replaced by people who worry they are the only ones *not* "doing it." Either way, the result is pluralistic ignorance: People do not know what others think and do or that their troubles are shared. The new norms tend to focus on orgasms, not on general pleasure. Orgasms are a product, and Americans strive to produce as many orgasms as possible. This is a revival of the Protestant work ethic, whereby "[nothing should be] enjoyed for its own sake except striving" (Slater, 1973). Sex is work, and Americans work to be successful at sex. The "discovery" of female orgasms has complicated the situation (Lydon, 1970). The ability to bring a woman to orgasm has become a measure of a man's sexual prowess. This puts pressure on both the man and the woman to perform. In bed, couples compete with mythical rivals and new standards of ecstasy: "If a woman has been assured that she will, should, and must see colored lights, feel like a breaking wave, or helplessly utter inarticulate cries, then she is apt to consider herself or her husband at fault when

Table 15–2
Changes in Sexual Behavior

| | Kinsey (1948, 1953) | | Hunt (1974) | |
	Men	Women	Men	Women
Masturbation:				
at least once	92%	58%	94%	68%
by age 13	45%	15%	63%	33%
Premarital Sex Acceptable:				
for man only		8%	75%	55%
for both sexes		22%	60%	41%
Engaged in Premarital				
Intercourse by Age 25	71%	33%	97%	67%
Marital Sex:				
frequency per week*				
age 16–25	2.45		3.25	
26–35	1.95		2.55	
36–45	1.40		2.00	
46–55	0.85		1.00	
55+	0.50		1.00	
frequency of male-on-top position	75%		35%	
frequency of oral-genital sex				
respondents with high-school education	15%	48%	56%	58%
respondents with college education	44%	55%	66%	72%
Engaged in Extramarital Intercourse:				
under age 25	39%	8%	32%	24%
25–34	38%	19%	41%	21%
35–44	34%	20%	47%	18%
45–54	31%	20%	38%	12%
55+	30%	20%	43%	15%

*Ages adjusted.
Source: A.C. Kinsey, W.B. Pomeroy, and C.E. Martin, *Sexual Behavior in the Human Male* (Philadelphia: Saunders, 1948); A.C. Kinsey and P.H. Gebhard, *Sexual Behavior in the Human Female* (Philadelphia: Saunders, 1953); M. Hunt, *Sexual Behavior in the 1970s* (Chicago: Playboy, 1974), pp. 77, 115–16, 191, 198, 202, 258, 261.

these promised wonders do not appear" (Hunt, 1962, p. 319). The same applies to men and to couples who feel that they ought to be creative. In part, then, the sexual revolution is one of rising expectations: People expect more from their sex lives, and they feel deprived if their experience does not meet their higher expectations.

Sexual norms and sexual conduct have crisscrossed. The gap between norms and behavior—combined with changing, often conflicting, standards—has created not only private troubles but also social issues. The controversy over adolescent sexuality, to which we now turn, is a case in point.

Adolescent Sexuality

Sexuality may be one of the most pressing concerns of and about adolescents (Chilman, 1978, p. 6). That is, both teen-agers and their parents worry about adolescent sexual activity. Parents tend to assume that young people today are far more sophisticated and more active sexually than they themselves were in their youth. But, by and large, the new willingness to discuss sex openly has not been extended to adolescents. Young people learn about sexuality in much the same way their parents did—from their friends and from books and magazines, but only rarely from their parents or from sex education courses (Hunt, 1974, p. 122). In one survey (Haas, 1979, p. 173), 75 percent of adolescents said that their parents had distorted images of their sexual activity. In short, what adolescents think about sexuality and how they behave are mysteries to most adults.

Adults' attitudes toward adolescent sexuality illustrate the unevenness of the supposed sexual revolution. On the one hand are adults who think teen-agers' sexual activity is natural and healthy. On the other hand are adults who feel that adolescent sexuality is not only wrong but harmful. This view is based on the belief that early sexual activity has a negative effect on psychological development. According to this view, adolescent sexuality is a social problem, in and of itself.

The evidence is mixed. In societies where casual premarital sexual affairs among adolescents are culturally approved (for example, in Samoa [Mead, 1961]), young people have few problems with sex. In American society, however, physical intimacy has strong emotional overtones. Sex is not play for American teen-agers. Many of them say that sexual intercourse is "okay" for people their age only if they are in love. And many adolescents lack skills with emotional involvements. Research indicates that some adolescents have benefited from permissive sexual norms. They are more honest and open with their partners and have a better-informed and more natural approach to sex. But other adolescents report feelings of conflict or guilt as a result of sexual activity. They feel exploited or rejected, and they realize too late that they have got in over their heads emotionally (Sorenson, 1973). Moreover, many American teen-agers are ill-equipped to deal with the possible consequences of sexual activity, in part because adults do not provide them with information or equipment. With norms changing, adolescents may be getting the message "do anything you want as long as you don't let us know and as long as you don't get pregnant or contract venereal disease." How serious are the consequences of adolescent sexual activity in the United States?

Teen-age Pregnancy

Since the mid-1960s, the percentage of young people in the United States who engage in premarital intercourse has climbed steadily. A third or more adolescents today "go all the way" by age eighteen. The average age of first sexual experience is sixteen. By age nineteen, only one in twenty males and three in ten females have not

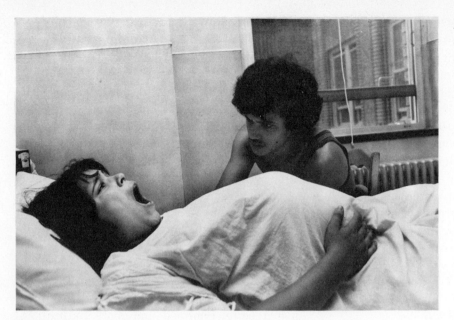

had intercourse (*Teenage Pregnancy,* 1981). By far the greatest change in behavior has occurred among white females. Between 1967 and 1974, the rate of premarital intercourse for white males rose 50 percent; the rate for white females rose 300 percent (Chilman, 1978). The double standard seems to be fading.

Not all adolescents who have sexual relations conceive children. But it seems that only a small percentage of sexually active teen-agers use birth control devices regularly (Dryfoos and Heisler, 1978, p. 224). Estimates are that less than 50 percent of teen-agers use contraceptives the first time they have sexual intercourse, and only 20 percent use them regularly (Chilman, 1978). There are a number of reasons for this. One survey indicated that many adolescent girls believe (falsely) that they are not pregnancy risks. Some think that they are too young to get pregnant; some think that they have sex too infrequently or that they know what time of the month is unsafe. A few sexual experiences that do not result in pregnancy may convince them that, magically, they are protected.

Although most adolescents think that boys ought to take responsibility in sexual relations, birth control is often left to the girls. The social and personal costs of using contraception, however, may override the benefits for a girl (Luker, 1975). Using birth control regularly means that a girl must come to terms with her own sexuality. She must give up the fantasy that sex is spontaneous. Being prepared may earn her a reputation of being promiscuous (especially on a first date). And to acquire contraceptives, she must admit to a doctor or pharmacist that she is sexually active. Thus she pays in terms of her modesty and her sexual innocence. A number of structural barriers also keep young people from using birth control. Some states require that unmarried females under the age of eighteen have parental consent in order to obtain contraceptives. Birth control clinics may be too close to home (creating the risk of being seen) or too far away to get to. They may offer services only during hours when adolescents must be in school or at home, their services may cost more than a teen-ager can afford, and they may not respect confidentiality. In 1977, 367,000 fifteen- to nineteen-year-old girls had legal abortions. Although abortions are generally safe, the fact that many teen-age girls wait longer than older women (because they do not recognize or admit the symptoms of pregnancy or because they fear their parents' reactions) makes them a greater risk (Baldwin, 1980).

In a report to the Department of Health, Education, and Welfare, Catherine Chilman (1978) pointed out that the main objection to making birth control information and contraceptives available to adolescents is the belief that doing so will encourage sexual activity. In fact, most teen-agers do not seek birth control until they have been having sexual intercourse more or less regularly, and then many of them cannot obtain the contraceptives they need. Thus, the belief that it is wrong for young people to be sexually active makes adolescents reluctant to ask about contraceptives and makes adults reluctant to provide them.

Traditionally, any young woman who became pregnant would get married if she could. The number of forced ("shot gun") marriages seems to be declining, however, particularly among white adolescents. According to one estimate, the proportion of out-of-wedlock conceptions that were "legitimized" by marriage dropped from 65 percent to 35 percent between 1960 and 1970. When confronted with pregnancy, as many teen-age girls—perhaps more—choose single parenthood as choose marriage (Baldwin, 1980). One reason may be that the chances of a teen-age couple being able to support themselves and a child, much less complete their educations, are slim: The number of jobs available to adolescents has decreased, and the years of schooling required to get a good job have increased steadily since World War II. In one study of unwed mothers, half the women said that they did not want to marry their child's father because they did not feel he could fulfill the roles of husband and father. Forced marriages have also declined because being a wife and a mother are not the only socially accepted roles for women in American society today. Many more women than before are staying in school, going on to college, and pursuing careers. Finally, there may now be less stigma attached to being a single parent or an "illegitimate" child than there was in the past.

Increased sexual activity, irregular use of birth control devices, and a decline in forced marriages all contribute to the high rate of out-of-wedlock births to teen-age girls. Although teen-agers constitute only 18 percent of the females in the United States who are capable of becoming pregnant, they account for 46 percent of out-of-wedlock births and over 30 percent of abortions. In 1978, over 1.1 million teen-agers became pregnant, and 554,000 teen-agers gave birth. Only 17 percent of the babies born to teen-agers were conceived after marriage. Thirty-eight percent of teen-age pregnancies were terminated with abortions, 22 percent resulted in out-of-wedlock births, and the rest were miscarried (*Teenage Pregnancy*, 1981).

What are the consequences of births to teen-agers? Much research suggests that adolescents are high risks as parents. Childbearing during adolescence can have negative consequences for the health of both the mother and the child. In the long run, a birth during adolescence diminishes a woman's life chances. More immediately, the rates of both serious complications in pregnancy and low birth weights (associated with infant mortality and with mental retardation) are higher for adolescent mothers than for older mothers. Poor diet or poor prenatal care explains some of the health problems; the physical immaturity of the adolescent mother explains others.

As of 1975, schools receiving federal funds were prohibited from excluding students because of pregnancy. Yet pregnancy and motherhood are major reasons why girls leave school. Child care responsibilities interfere with a young single mother's ability to get a job and advance in an occupation. (In New York City, an estimated one-half of unwed teen-age mothers live in households that receive public assistance.)

In addition, there is some evidence of a high risk of child abuse among teen-age parents (Bolton, 1980). Unrealistic expectations for the child and a general lack of knowledge about parenting, combined with isolation from friends and family, can increase the usual frustrations of being a new parent. These frustrations may be taken out on the child. Of course, not all single adolescent mothers have health problems or make poor parents, but the risks do exist.

Venereal Disease

The evidence of teen-age sexual activity raises concerns about venereal diseases (VD). Like sex itself, VD has long been a taboo subject in the United States. Venereal diseases are named after the Roman goddess of love, Venus. VD is caused, not by sexual intercourse, but by germs that are transmitted from one person to another through sexual contact. (It is theoretically possible—but extremely unlikely—to contract venereal disease by touching an object. The germs do not usually survive outside the human body for more than a few minutes.) The most common forms of venereal diseases are gonorrhea, syphilis, and herpes.

Gonorrhea is transmitted through sexual intercourse. Within three to eight days of contracting this disease, males feel a frequent desire to urinate, and urination may be painful; women may develop a vaginal discharge. These symptoms go away by themselves, but the person remains infectious. If untreated, gonorrhea may cause sterility in women and, over time, may damage the joints and the heart in both sexes. The disease almost always can be cured with high doses of penicillin or other antibiotics.

Syphilis is usually transmitted through sexual

contact (including kissing, in some cases), but can also pass directly through the skin (especially where there is a cut or scratch). The first symptom of syphilis—a painless sore, usually in the genital area—appears about three weeks after the disease is contracted. The sore goes away by itself. If untreated, the person remains contagious, and secondary symptoms will appear a few weeks, or even months, later. A rash may be accompanied by a mild fever and aches (symptoms often mistaken for the flu). These, too, disappear, and the disease goes into a latency stage. The person has no symptoms and is not contagious, but the syphilis bacteria remain in the body. Over time, they can cause severe damage to the heart, blood vessels, eyes, spinal cord, and brain, causing mental disorders and, eventually, death. If detected and treated with penicillin or other antibiotics, syphilis can be eliminated.

Unlike gonorrhea and syphilis, which are bacterial infections, herpes is caused by a virus. One type of herpes causes cold sores; another type causes blisters in the genital area, which develop into small, painful ulcers and may be accompanied by headaches and fever. The ulcers heal in a matter of weeks but may reappear at any time. While herpes is active, the person is contagious. No one knows precisely how the herpes virus is transmitted from person to person. (Most people are probably exposed to one or the other form of herpes; many people, however, are resistant.) To date, there is no known cure.

No one knows how many Americans have contracted venereal disease. Many people do not recognize the symptoms or do not seek treatment, and many private doctors do not report all of the cases they treat. About a million cases of gonorrhea are reported each year, but the actual number of cases may be three times that many (Kolata, 1976). About 25,000 new cases of syphilis are reported each year, but as many as 500,000 more Americans are not being treated (Chiappa and Forish, 1976). Estimates are that 300,000 people contract herpes each year. The incidence of venereal disease seems to be rising, particularly in the case of gonorrhea among fifteen- to twenty-nine-year-olds. Indeed, the chances of a sexually active young person being infected with gonorrhea before age twenty-five are about fifty/fifty (Millar, 1972). Why, if venereal diseases are treatable (with the exception of herpes), is their incidence increasing? There are technical, psychological, and social obstacles to the control of these diseases (Offir, 1982, Chapter 8).

The technical reasons have to do with the nature of the diseases themselves. Many people do not experience symptoms and unknowingly pass the disease on to others. (About 80 percent of women and 5 to 20 percent of men who have gonorrhea have no symptoms; 90 percent of women and 40 to 60 percent of men who have syphilis have no symptoms.) People do not develop a natural immunity to gonorrhea and syphilis as they do to chicken pox or German measles—there is no limit to the number of times a person can contract these diseases, and in some cases, diagnostic tests do not identify them.

Psychological obstacles to the control of venereal disease include embarrassment and guilt, which prevent many people from seeking treatment. Venereal diseases are stigmatized: Only "dirty" or "promiscuous" people are supposed to get such diseases, and most people do not put themselves in these categories. (Before World War II, the Army treated the contraction of venereal disease as a crime.) As we saw in the case of birth control, it may be particularly difficult for teen-agers to admit their sexual activity to a doctor or to some other health official, and this may prevent their getting treatment.

Additional obstacles are social. Americans have taken the attitude that the best way to treat venereal disease is to ignore it. We have not invested heavily in anti-VD campaigns. In 1974, for example, the government spent about $52 million on VD control, compared to $84 million to build one B-1 bomber (Boston Women's Health Book Collective, 1976). There is no journal of venereal disease and no medical specialty in the United States. Despite talk of a VD epidemic, there has been no national campaign offering free, anonymous tests, as there have been for other diseases. There are no VD marathons on television. Obstacles are particularly great for teen-agers because of opposition to practical, explicit sex education. High rates of venereal disease are in part the result of ignorance and shame: Studies show that most teen-agers know little about the causes, symptoms, cures, and long-term consequence of untreated venereal disease (Hayes and Littlefield, 1976).

The social problems relating to teen-age sexuality are part structural, part cultural. The prolonged period of education that is required in industrial societies like the United States has widened the gap between the age at which young people reach biological sexual maturity and the age at which they legitimize sexual activity through marriage. The number of years during which a young woman may conceive a child out of wedlock has increased, while the opportunities—the life chances—for a woman who has a child during adolescence have decreased. Changing norms have led adolescents to consider sex outside marriage "okay." But adults who believe it is wrong for adolescents to be sexually active have made it difficult for teen-agers to acquire information about the risks of pregnancy and venereal disease and to find information about how to protect themselves.

Marital and Extramarital Sexuality

From all available evidence, the increase in premarital sexual activity has not dampened our enthusiasm for marriage. Compared with Americans in the past, Americans today wait somewhat longer before getting married. But 80 to 90 percent of Americans do get married, and if their first marriages do not work, most try again (Gagnon, 1977, p. 191). In our society, marriage remains the most widely approved setting for sexual activity. How, then, have changing norms affected marital sexuality?

The Sociology of Sexuality

Concern about marital sexuality is relatively new. Two or three generations ago, "nice women" (the kind men married) were not expected to delight in sexual activity. If a man was satisfied very quickly, so much the better for his patient wife. In fact, this may still be the case in some lower- and working-class marriages (Rainwater, 1964; Komarovsky, 1967). Norms and behavior have changed, but in marital sexual conduct, as in premarital sexual conduct, change has proceeded unevenly. Old norms linger. (For example, as we will see, Masters and Johnson have found that a high percentage of couples with sexual troubles still observe the taboo on talking openly about sex.) New norms have raised expectations: Sex *ought* to be fun; couples *should* experiment; wives *should* enjoy sexual relations as much as their husbands do, and so on. Hunt's survey indicated that married couples today make love more often and are more imaginative and playful in their lovemaking than couples were in the past. But "like all liberated people, we are more discontented now than we were before our lot began to improve" (Hunt, 1974, p. 197). When women did not expect to enjoy sex, for example, lack of orgasms did not feel like deprivation. But expectations have risen. To complicate the situation, a husband and wife may enter the marriage bed with quite different expectations.

Learning sexual roles The term *sexual role* describes socially patterned expectations, rights, and obligations regarding sexual behavior.* In our society, males and females are assigned different sexual roles. That is, Americans are raised with the assumption that the sexual attitudes and behavior of males are different from those of females.

The differences between men's and women's feelings about sex reflect both anatomy and culture, as John Gagnon and William Simon have detailed (1973). For boys, the unmistakable signs of sexual arousal—erection and ejaculation—appear in early adolescence. By age thirteen or fourteen, nearly all boys have experienced orgasms, sometimes through nocturnal emissions ("wet dreams"), but more often through masturbation. Biology focuses boys' attention on their genitals. Masturbation encourages them to have explicitly sexual fantasies. And the masculine role may lead them to be aggressive in seizing sexual opportunities and to brag to other boys. Among themselves, many adolescent American boys complain about being "horny," compare the girls they know in purely physical terms, and speculate about how "far" a girl will go. They may report their conquests in detail. For most boys, sexual experience is a source of status. Sexual prowess is linked to self-esteem. Biology and social learning combine to make American males achievement oriented in sexual conduct.

While boys are training for sex, girls are training for romance. Female bodies and learning experiences are different from those of males. Anatomy hides the center of female sexual arousal (the clitoris). Many fewer adolescent girls than boys masturbate or engage in explicitly sexual fantasies. Culture prohibits girls from talking about what they look like or how they feel "down there." Girls' talk often focuses on clothes, parties, flirtations, and what it is like to fall in love. Girls may

---

* Note the distinction between *sexual* role and *gender* (or *sex*) role, which refers to expectations regarding the entire range of masculine and feminine behavior (see Chapter 11).

discuss a boy's looks, but not the size of his sexual organs; they may describe being touched, but not touching. For many girls, the biggest turn-on is making themselves the object of male desire, the recipient of male attention. Even today, sexual experience is not necessarily a source of status for girls. (A girl is supposed to worry about her reputation, not build one.) First experiences with necking and petting produce diffuse sensations that girls may not identify as sexual for some years to come. Girls' fantasies tend to be more emotional than erotic.

Different sexual roles reflect and magnify biological differences. Typically, American men are trained for physical sex, but not for tenderness; American women are trained for love and affection, but not for physical sex. It may take time for a male to learn to time his sexual responses in ways that please a woman and for a female to discover her responses and accept her sexuality (Gagnon and Henderson, 1975, pp. 38–39). Yet, American norms say sex should be spontaneous. People do not like to think that sex, like tennis or arithmetic, requires knowledge, skill, and practice (Gagnon, 1977, p. 192). As a result, many married couples find that their sexual relationship falls short of their expectations.

Sexual dysfunction Sexual dysfunction in marriage is a clear example of a social issue (not only different norms for men and women but changing cultural rules for sex) creating private troubles. The term *sexual dysfunction* refers to a person's inability to experience satisfaction in sexual relations. No one knows how many American married couples find their sex lives unfulfilling. Masters and Johnson (1970) believe that half the adults in this country experience sexual dysfunction at some time. This figure seems high, but the Kinsey and Hunt surveys do indicate that 10 to 20 percent of married men and women are not totally happy about their sexual relationship. (Whether people define less-than-perfect sex as a problem is

another story. For example, a woman who experiences orgasms through manual stimulation but not during intercourse may or may not feel that she has a problem.)

In *Human Sexual Inadequacy* (1970), Masters and Johnson identified a number of types of sexual dysfunction. The most common problems for men are erectile dysfunction (not getting or maintaining an erection) and premature ejaculation (ejaculating too soon, although how soon is too soon is largely subjective); the most common problem for women is not having orgasms some or all of the time.* Masters and Johnson reject the widely held belief that sexual dysfunction is a symptom of underlying psychological problems. They argue that sexual dysfunction, like sexual functioning, is learned behavior—and can be unlearned. They reject the belief that sexual dysfunction is an individual problem (a private trouble, in the sociologist C. Wright Mills's phrase). Often the problem lies in the way a husband and wife relate to one another, in their different expectations. In other words, Masters and Johnson believe that the sexual roles imposed by culture are largely responsible for sexual dysfunction.

In a high percentage of the 790 cases reported in Masters and Johnson's book, fear of sexual failure created a self-fulfilling prophecy. For example, a husband is tired and does not respond to his wife. Failure to perform on this occasion makes him worry that it might happen again. The next time they attempt sex, the husband is so anxious that he does not get an erection. This convinces him that his condition is irreversible and sets off a cycle of fear and failure. The prophecy is fulfilled. Masters and Johnson report that observing and judging one's own behavior instead of en-

---

* Less common problems include retarded ejaculation, or not having orgasms, in men; vaginismus, or uncontrollable contraction of the vaginal muscles, for women; and painful intercourse, for both sexes.

joying sex, as well as lack of communication, ignorance of effective methods of sexual stimulation, and past painful or guilty experiences are also common causes of sexual dysfunction. Masters and Johnson's treatment of sexual dysfunction combines education in sexual processes with homework assignments designed to discourage goal-oriented sexual performance; they attempt to turn work into play (Kaplan, 1974).

Alternatives to Monogamous Sexuality

In the 1970s, the traditional Judeo-Christian ethic of marital fidelity came under attack. Advocates of open marriage (O'Neil and O'Neil, 1972) argued that limiting oneself to a single sexual partner from marriage until death was unnatural and unhealthy. According to this view, marital fidelity tends to destroy—not preserve—marriage. Sexual freedom provides an escape valve for the tension of incompatible sexual roles. Thus, a social issue developed as to whether extramarital sexual behavior was a problem or a solution. There is little concrete evidence that extramarital sexual activity is harmful—or that it is beneficial. What is clear is that traditional norms of marital fidelity may clash with new norms of sexual liberation.

The (clandestine) affair Hunt (1974) reported that 40 to 45 percent of men and about 20 percent of women have had *affairs*—extramarital sexual relations that they hid from their spouse. These figures are almost identical to those Kinsey reported in the late 1940s and early 1950s. The only significant change is among women under age twenty-five, who seem to be catching up with men their own age. Hunt attributes this to the new emphasis on sexual equality: "The change is not a radical break with the ideal of sexual fidelity, but a radical break with the double standard" (1974, p. 263). Extramarital sex has not gained wide ac-

ceptance, however. Over 80 percent of the people questioned by Hunt said that they or their mate would object to an extramarital affair.

The evidence suggests that very few people have affairs in the traditional sense of a passionate, irresistible but impossible love relationship that goes on for years, despite the individuals' attempts to forget one another (Gagnon, 1977, p. 219). In most cases, extramarital sex is sporadic, furtive, and hurried. Because of guilt about deceiving one's spouse and fear of detection, most affairs are no more pleasurable than is marital sex. In fact, Hunt reports that extramarital sexual encounters are more inhibited than marital relations: Lovers are less likely to use nonconventional positions, and women reportedly have orgasms less regularly with lovers than with their husbands (pp. 275–76).

What this suggests is that sex is not the only, or the primary, reason why people have affairs. The psychic rewards—a renewed feeling of personal desirability; the illusion of recapturing one's youth; the excitement of doing something forbidden; the excitement of conquest; or the taking of revenge against one's mate—seem to outweigh the physical delights.

Estimates are that about 2 percent of married couples experiment with *swinging*—that is, a married couple having sex with another person or with other couples with the full knowledge and participation of all parties (Hunt, 1974; Spanier and Cole, 1975). Swinging seems to be a middle- and upper-middle-class phenomenon. Most participants are ordinary, otherwise conventional married couples. Ideally, swinging offers sexual excitement and variety without emotional involvement, thus protecting a marriage. Early studies suggested that swinging promotes sexual equality. More recent research, however, suggests that swinging involves sexual exploitation of women. According to recent studies, many wives participate only because their husbands insist; they find the experience unpleasant or humiliating; and far from becoming enthusiasts, they are quick to drop out (Denfield, 1974).

Sex and divorce Perhaps the most common alternative to monogamous sex is divorce and a return to a single life style or remarriage. How many people seek divorce because of sexual troubles within their marriage—or because of sexual attractions outside their marriage—is impossible to say. Sexual dysfunction or disinterest may be a cause or a consequence of marital unhappiness, or both. Over half the divorced men and women in the Hunt (1974) survey said extramarital affairs played a part in their decision to separate, but only a part (p. 268). Much postmarital sexual activity, like most premarital sexual activity, is part fun, part preparation for marriage.

Divorce may solve some problems and create others. Divorced people often find that they are as awkward about making dates, as worried about a date's sexual expectations, and as restricted in sexual opportunities (particularly if they have children) at age forty as they were at sixteen (Gagnon, 1977, pp. 230–32). Learning to relate to new sexual partners is one of many role adjustments that accompany divorce.

The investigation of marital and extramarital sexuality illustrates the social origins of what seem to be very private troubles. Today's preoccupation with sexuality and pressures to perform sexually within marriage contribute to sexual dysfunction. So do the different sexual roles for men and women. The clash between norms of marital fidelity and sexual liberation make alternatives to monogamous sexuality a social issue.

Commercialized Sex

Sex is not only serious business for Americans; it is also big business. In the last ten to fifteen years, pornography and prostitution have come out into the open. Profits from the sale of sex are estimated in billions of dollars (Sheehy, 1973, p. 4). In the past, debate over commercialized sex focused on moral and legal issues (Offir, 1982, Ch. 13). Those who sought to suppress pornography and prostitution saw their opponents as immoral libertines and smut peddlers who threatened the entire social order. Those who favored a free-market economy for sex saw their opponents as uptight reactionaries who threatened the freedom of expression that is guaranteed in the Bill of Rights. If you knew a person's religious and political convictions, you could predict his or her views on commercialized sex. Today, however, the issues seem to be more complex. Conservatives accept sexual references in the media that would have been unthinkable a few years ago. Liberals, too, have begun to rethink their position. Does freedom of expression include the right to show children in pornographic films? Or to show women in bondage?

Pornography

Pornography refers to books, pictures, movies, and live shows that are designed specifically to arouse sexual interest. (The term comes from the Greek word for prostitution, *porneia,* and literally means "to describe prostitution.") By age eighteen, about 80 percent of American males and 70 percent of females have seen or read explicit sexual materials. In one survey, 40 percent of adult men and 26 percent of adult women said that they had been exposed to pornography within the preceding two years. The most frequent patrons of pornographic bookstores and cinemas are middle-aged, middle-class, married white men (*Report of the Commission on Obscenity and Pornography,* 1970). Pornography has created both a legal dilemma and a public concern.

The legal dilemma The legal debate over pornography in the United States dates back to 1873, when Congress passed the Comstock laws, which

The Business of Sex

The sex trade, by tradition man and woman's oldest business, has become a multibillion-dollar business with the characteristics of many conventional industries—a large work force, high-salaried executives, brisk competition, trade publications, board meetings, sales conventions.

The sex industry includes a broad range of activities: small outlets traditionally associated with hard-core pornography; prostitution; sexually explicit material appearing in newspapers, magazines, books, television shows and movies; video devices and tapes and disks that are heavily dependent on sex for commercial value; items, like vibrators, bought for sexual gratification.

It is a rapidly growing, still immature industry, a significant part of New York and the nation's economy. . . .

Sex activities that a few years ago would have been regarded as pornographic are now accepted as commonplace.

Highly explicit sex shows are seen on cable television across the country. Mass-circulation newspapers and magazines regularly run sex advice stories that a few years ago editors would have given no thought to printing or that readers would have demanded be removed. Television is rife with stories containing sexual themes and jokes.

Sexual devices and literature can regularly be charged to Visa or Mastercard accounts, and people can join clubs that play over the telephone provocative statements and sounds, including sexual coaching.

Major companies often use sensuous or explicitly sexual themes as a selling point in advertisements. The advertising industry is using teen-age models and models not yet in their teens to pose, often in seductive fashion, for a wide variety of products. . . .

No one knows for sure what the exact amount is, or, because much of the sex industry remains underground, what the nation's total sex expenditures might be. . . .

But the $5 billion estimate represents twice as much as Americans spend on breakfast cereal each year, about one-fifth of what they spend on fresh fruits and vegetables, a fourth of what they donate to their churches.

About 100,000 people are employed in legal parts of the industry, and tens of thousands more are employed in its illegal sectors.

Source: *The New York Times*, February 9, 1981, pp. B1, B6.

The issue with pornography is where to draw the line. Most Americans strongly disapprove of using children in pornography. But when does a photograph of a nude child stop being artistic or cute and become pornographic? Is showing adult women or men in bondage any less exploitative?

were named for a man who led a forty-year crusade against pornography. The law banned the mailing of any "obscene, lewd, lascivious, indecent, filthy or vile article, matter, thing, device or substance"—including birth control devices and information on abortion. Many state and local governments passed similar ordinances, with little opposition.

The pornography issue resurfaced in 1933 in a court case concerning James Joyce's novel *Ulysses.* At first banned in the United States because of certain sexually explicit passages, the novel was later accepted on the grounds of its literary merit. In 1957, in *Roth* v. *United States,* the Supreme Court attempted to clarify the issue. The Court declared that obscenity is not protected under the First Amendment, which guarantees freedom of expression, but went on to say that not all sexual material is obscene. A work was considered obscene only if "to the average person, applying contemporary community standards, the dominant theme of the material as a whole appeals to prurient interest." This did as much to confuse the issue as to clarify it. What does "prurient interest" mean? Does it mean any sexual interest, or only "perverted" interest? Subsequent decisions attempted to clarify this point. In a 1966 case involving the erotic classic *Fanny Hill*, three Supreme Court justices—there was no majority opinion—declared a work to be obscene if it was "patently offensive" and "utterly without redeeming social value." In a 1973 decision, *Miller* v. *California*, the Supreme Court changed "utterly without redeeming social value" to "[lacking] serious literary, artistic, political, or scientific value" and emphasized local community standards. This is where the matter stands today.

The Supreme Court has avoided making a clear definition of obscenity. "I know it when I see it," Justice Potter Stewart declared in 1964 (*Jacobelis* v. *Ohio*). By ruling that not all explicit sexual material is obscene, the Court opened the door to pornographic entrepreneurs. By ruling that the sale of sexual material that lacks "serious value" or violates "community standards" is illegal, the Court also opened the door to moral entrepreneurs—people who make it their business to enforce their own standards (Becker, 1963). Reliance on community standards means that a film can be shown in Kansas City, Missouri, but banned across the river, in Kansas City, Kansas. Thus people who write erotic books or produce erotic films cannot know whether they are breaking the law until they are—or are not—arrested, a situation that violates the legal principle of due process (Offir, 1982, Ch. 13).

The public concern Underlying the legal debate is the basic question of whether pornography harms or corrupts people who are exposed to it. Does the explicit portrayal of sex acts "deprave

Figure 15-1

The Incidence of Sex Offenses (Excluding Incest) Reported in Denmark, 1948-1970

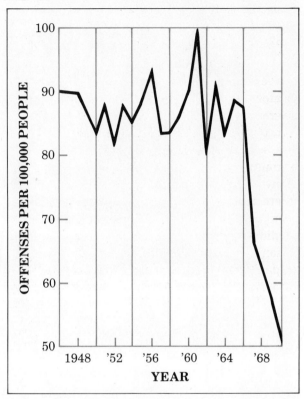

Source: B. Kutchinsky, "The Effect of Easy Availability of Pornography on the Incidence of Sex Crimes: The Danish Experience," *Journal of Social Issues*, Vol. 29 (1973).

and corrupt" the beholder? Does pornography teach people to perform sex acts they might not consider otherwise? Does it create or encourage sex criminals?

In 1967, Congress appointed the National Commission on Obscenity and Pornography to study the traffic in pornography and its impact on individuals. In its 1970 report, the Commission concluded:

Exposure to erotic stimuli appears to have little or no effect on already established attitudinal commitments regarding either sexuality [sexual behavior] or sexual morality. . . . [There] is no evidence to date that exposure to explicit sexual materials plays a significant role in the causation of delinquent or criminal behavior among youths or adults. (pp. 29, 32)

For example, the Commission's research indicated that convicted sex offenders have no more interest in pornography than other adults do. In fact, the convicted sex offenders tended to report less sexual experience, directly or vicariously (through pornography), than other men did. Many of them came from repressed backgrounds, where sex was taboo, and were largely ignorant about sexual matters. Violence, but not sex per se, did arouse them (pp. 30–32). But were these prisoners telling the truth, or were they covering up past behavior and fantasies in order to "look good"?

Denmark provided the Commission with a natural experiment on pornography's impact on sex crimes. Denmark responded to a wave of hardcore materials in the 1960s by legalizing the sale of pornographic books and magazines to persons sixteen years old and older in 1967; movies and pictures in 1969. The incidence of sex crimes dropped after legalization. This finding suggests that pornography acts as a safety valve, releasing tensions that might otherwise be expressed in dangerous, antisocial behavior (see Figure 15–1, Table 15–3).

The results of the Danish experiment must be examined with care (Kutchinsky, 1973). The fact that crime rates dropped the year pornography was legalized does not prove that one event caused the other. For example, the rates of passive sexual offenses (exhibitionism, peeping, and verbal indecency) may have dropped because attitudes changed, not because pornography was

Table 15–3
Sex Offenses Against
Females in Copenhagen*

	Year			
Offenses	1959	1964	1969	Decrease 1959–1969
Rape	32	20	27	16%
Exhibitionism	249	225	104	58
Peeping	99	61	20	80
Coitus with minors	51	18	19	63
Verbal indecency	45	43	13	71
Other offenses against women	137	103	60	56
Other offenses against girls	282	204	87	69

* Based on police records.
Source: B. Kutchinsky, "The Effect of Easy Availability of Pornography on the Incidence of Sex Crimes: The Danish Experience," *Journal of Social Issues,* Vol. 29 (1973).

available. Perhaps Danish women began to consider exhibitionists as pathetic, not dangerous, and no longer reported them to the police. The decline in child molesting suggests that men approach children largely because they cannot find adult partners. In this case, pornography may provide an alternative, socially more acceptable outlet for sexual tension. Rape did not decrease nearly as much as other sex crimes, suggesting that it may be primarily a violent crime, not a sexual crime, and that pornography is not a substitute for violence. The Danish experiment does not provide data on sex acts that are not reported as, and may not be viewed as, sex crimes—for example, a man forcing his wife in sex acts against her will (Finkelhor and Yllo, 1980). Finally, Denmark is a small, homogeneous society with a highly literate, relatively affluent population, a comprehensive social welfare system, and a generally low crime rate. Conclusions based on Denmark's experiences do not necessarily apply to the United States (Gagnon, 1977, pp. 358–59; Luria and Rose, 1979, pp. 403–05).

Although the Commission on Obscenity and Pornography considered the benefits of sex education, it did not explore the potential benefits of pornography. For example, some sex therapists find that explicit portrayals of sex are useful in the treatment of sexual dysfunctions. Carefully chosen pornography provides information and models of sexual behavior. It may also encourage fantasies and allow people to become aroused in a situation in which they are released from responsibilities and the pressures of sexual victory or defeat and in which they do not have to perform (Gagnon, 1977, p. 357). On the other hand, pornography may arouse new fears and make viewers feel more pressure to perform.

The future of pornography Much of the opposition to pornography is directed, not at the portrayal of sexual activities in books and movies, but at the way in which they are portrayed. By emphasizing anatomy over emotion, aggressiveness over compassion, pornography presents a distorted image of sexual intimacy. Pornography reinforces stereotypes—in most cases, male stereotypes. Typically, women are depicted as willing servants of male desire or as shy, inhibited creatures that men can turn into sexual slaves simply by turning them on. Many books and films imply that women secretly enjoy being initiated into forbidden pleasures, if not being brutalized.

Feminist groups, such as Women Against Pornography, have led the opposition to pornography. These groups make a distinction between obscenity (the portrayal of sexual activities that involve one person using, entrapping, deceiving, overpowering, or hurting another) and erotica (the portrayal of sexual activities in which all partners are equal, willing, and responsible participants and no one is victimized). They have also called attention to the number of films and magazines that link sex and violence.

Does pornography degrade women? Does evidence of forced sex in marriage indicate that men are learning about new and varied sex acts from pornography and demanding that their wives perform them? The answers to these questions await further research. At best, the evidence published since the report of the Commission on Obscenity and Pornography is inconclusive. Pornography is likely to remain a social issue in years to come. As Gagnon and Simon (1973) have pointed out, pornography is arousing largely because it deals with forbidden sex. Virtually all pornographic films and books at least hint at prostitution, adultery, group sex, incest, and other illicit activities. In pornography, the rule is, if the activity is conventional, the setting is not (people are shown having sex with the wrong partners, at the wrong times and places, for the wrong reasons); or if the setting is conventional, the activity is not (a married couple is shown playing slave and master, for example).

Prostitution

A *prostitute* is someone who sells sexual services without emotional attachment. The customer purchases only the act, nothing more. Both men and women engage in prostitution. Here we will consider female prostitution, which is far more common than male prostitution.

Female prostitution is often characterized as the world's oldest profession. This is true and not true. The role prostitutes play in our society is quite different from that of the *Hetairae* of ancient Greece (educated, respected women who entertained aristocrats with music and conversation as well as with sex), of the temple priestesses of ancient India (who served gods as well as men with their bodies), or even of the Victorian streetwalker (often sentimentalized as a "fallen dove"). Today, a few high-priced call girls have become celebrities—Xaviera Hollander, for example. But in the minds of most Americans, prostitutes are less than respectable.

An industry in decline While the pornography industry has expanded and diversified in recent decades, achieving a degree of respectability, prostitution seems to be on the wane. Precise figures are hard to come by, but nearly 70 percent of the white males Kinsey interviewed in the 1940s had had some experience with prostitutes. In those days, young men frequently acquired their sexual initiation from prostitutes. According to Hunt's survey (1974), this is no longer the case. Hunt found that less than half as many men under thirty-five as over thirty-five have had sex with a prostitute. The proportion of men initiated into sexuality by prostitutes has dropped from about 19 percent to 7 percent (Hunt, 1974, pp. 144–45).

The decline of prostitution reflects a number of interrelated social changes. First, the percentage of American women who engage in nonmarital intercourse has increased. Thus, going to a prostitute today can be seen as a sign that a man has failed with women other than prostitutes. Second, the number of men who never marry has declined. Third, behavior and attitudes about sexuality within marriage have changed. Experimentation in the marriage bed has become more acceptable and more common. Perhaps most important, the chaste women who saves herself for marriage and behaves "properly" in bed is no longer idealized. This is not to say that promiscuity has replaced chastity. Women who engage in sexual acts indiscriminately—for money rather than for love or even pleasure—are still looked down upon.

Contrasting views of prostitution Despite repeated crackdowns on streetwalkers, call-girl rings, and massage parlors, prostitution has shown a remarkable ability to survive. Why?

Some sociologists—notably Kingsley Davis (1937)—believe that prostitution is not only inevitable but functional. In Davis's view, prostitution is an outgrowth of the family on the one hand and social stratification on the other. There will always be a demand for impersonal, noncommittal sex—for example, from men who are away from home or who live in an all-male environment; who cannot ask their wives or lovers to perform certain sex acts; and from men who cannot find partners because they lack the requisite social skills or are deformed. By filling the needs of these men, prostitution helps to preserve families. Our system of social stratification then provides women with a reason to become prostitutes. In Davis s words: "Since the economic means are distributed unequally between classes but female attractiveness is not, some women of lower economic means can exploit their attractiveness for economic gain." Davis adds, "It is economically and politically foolish to punish a large number of society's productive and otherwise orderly members [that is, the customers] for a vice that injures no one" (1976, p. 247).

Becoming a Streetwalker

In her study of prostitutes, Nannette Davis asked the women she interviewed how they had come to be streetwalkers. Most had been initiated into sexuality at an early age (at about thirteen). For some, sex with older men was a source of prestige. Some associated sexual activity with freedom (escape from their families); some, with security (male companionship). A number of the prostitutes came from unstable, disreputable, destitute families. Almost all of them had been labeled as troublemakers by their parents, neighbors, and teachers. Many of them had been sentenced to juvenile institutions. Thus, they had been isolated from conventional associations early in life.

Typically, these girls drifted from casual sex into their first act of prostitution. Some were encouraged by friends in the life who made them feel there was no reason not to accept money from strangers. Some were recruited or drafted by a pimp, who promised to take care of them. Some were attracted by "the glamour and the game of it." They started for kicks. At that point, they did not think of themselves as prostitutes. Most of them zigzagged between trying to establish a conventional life style (returning home, getting a regular job) and "turning tricks." They lived in fear of being discovered. But they were also learning on the job—learning how to let men know that they were available, how to set and collect fees, how to talk about and perform a variety of acts, how to spot the police, and so on.

The women began to think of themselves as prostitutes, however, only when they were forced to—for example, when a woman's pimp stopped talking like a lover and began demanding that she work, or when she was arrested and labeled a "common prostitute" in court. From then on, the women began to associate less and less with conventional people, who condemned them, and more with other hustlers, who supported them. Their identities and associations changed. They became immersed in the subculture of prostitution, which rationalized—indeed, glorified—their occupation: "Society needs us." "Johns [customers] are suckers anyway." "How many other women can make $200 a night?"

Source: Based on Nannette J. Davis, "Prostitution: Identity, Career, and Legal-Economic Enterprise," in J.M. Henslin and E. Sagarin (Eds.), *The Sociology of Sex: An Introductory Reader* (New York: Schocken Books, 1978).

The New Masseuse

Paul Rasmussen and Lauren Kuhn's study of women who engage in sex for money in massage parlors presents a somewhat different picture from Davis's study on prostitutes. (In the parlors studied by Rasmussen and Kuhn, masturbation, fellatio, and intercourse were available as extras on a sliding scale of about $10 to $30 above the basic rate for a massage.) By and large, the masseuses interviewed did not defend their work as vehemently as streetwalkers defend theirs. Nor did they express the contempt for their customers and society that Davis found among streetwalkers. Most of the women said they had taken the job because the working conditions and the pay (as much as $36,000 a year) were good. Many of them enjoyed the job. "It's exciting doing something that just about everyone else thinks is wrong," one woman told the researchers. Although they realized that people look down on what they do, they did not accept the label of "common prostitute." Masseuses neutralized the social stigma attached to their work activities by invoking new sexual norms: The body is a source of pleasure and should be used for pleasure.

Rasmussen and Kuhn suggest several reasons why masseuses are able to neutralize the label "prostitute" and maintain a more positive self-image. First, the massage parlor provides the woman with a front—the illusion that she is working in an establishment that offers relaxation, not sex. A masseuse has a semi-legal status. Technically, all she does is give massages. If a customer asks for sexual action, he, not she, is breaking the law, even if she agrees to it. Second, she can accept or reject customers. If she dislikes a man, she can refuse to provide anything more than a massage. This gives her not only more freedom of choice but also the ability to tell herself that she is abiding by the new ethic—"if you like the person and it feels good, do it." Third, working in a massage parlor is safer than working on the streets. If a customer becomes violent, other people are close by. And because a masseuse does not offer sex directly, she is not subject to arrests. She also is less vulnerable to exploitation by pimps and others than are streetwalkers. Rasmussen and Kuhn suggest that massage parlors may represent a shift in attitudes toward sex for money. In addition, massage parlors may represent a reorganization in the sale of sexual services.

Source: Based on Paul K. Rasmussen and Lauren L. Kuhn, "The New Masseuse: Play for Pay," *Urban Life,* Vol. 5, No. 3 (October 1976).

Others see prostitution as part of a persistent pattern of sexual exploitation of women. According to this view, prostitution does injure someone —the prostitute. Prostitutes are victims of economic exploitation (by pimps and others), social-psychological abuse (through labeling), and frequently, physical abuse (by pimps, police, and customers). Prostitution thrives on the double standard: In most states, it is a crime for a woman to rent her body, but not for a man to hire it. Prostitution is grounded in cultural notions of women as sexual objects—if not, as in Victorian days, as sexual property. A former prostitute, now with a doctorate in psychology, explained prostitution this way: "[T]here's a special indignity in prostitution, as if sex were dirty and men can only enjoy it with someone *low*. . . . It involves a type of contempt, a kind of disdain, and a kind of triumph over another human being" (in Millet, 1973, pp. 57, 58).

To the extent that prostitution victimizes the women who make it their occupation, it is a social problem. A number of sociologists (e.g., Schur, 1965) believe that the problem exists only because the law makes it a crime, forcing prostitutes into criminal social networks, and because negative attitudes isolate prostitutes from conventional social networks. Certain counties in Nevada have legalized houses of prostitution. Oregon and New York have made it a crime, punishable by up to a year in jail and a $1,000 fine, for a man to pay a woman for sexual services. Research would show whether the legalization of prostitution or the equalization of laws would increase or decrease patronage of prostitutes, whether it would improve working conditions and reduce exploitation of prostitutes.

Homosexuality

At different times, Americans have characterized homosexuality as a sin, a perversion, a crime, a mental illness, and, most recently, a distinctive way of life. The Kinsey reports (1948, 1953) had a significant impact on the public perception of homosexuality. Kinsey found that sexual contacts between members of the same sex were far more common than anyone had imagined. Among some segments of the population, this finding caused disbelief and then alarm ("What if my friend, my neighbor, my child's teacher has had homosexual experience?"). To others, Kinsey's findings provided relief ("I m not alone"). But data on homosexual activity did little to change the widespread and lingering beliefs that homosexuals are different and homosexuality is abnormal.

Problems of Definition

The word "homosexual" comes from the Greek *homo,* meaning "same" (not from the Latin *homo,* meaning "man"). In everyday conversation, people apply the term "homosexual" to a wide range of feelings and behavior among members of the same sex. For example, a girl is attracted to other girls in early adolescence, has her first homosexual love affair at age nineteen, and remains exclusively homosexual thereafter. A married man has brief, secret, anonymous sexual contacts with men in public baths and lavatories (Humphreys, 1975) but remains committed to his wife and family. Another man or woman has fantasies of sexual relations with members of the same sex but never acts on these fantasies. Assigning all of these individuals to a single category, that of homosexual, stretches the term to the point of meaninglessness.

One definition of homosexuality classifies people according to their behavior. Anyone who actually engages in homosexual acts is defined as a homosexual. This includes people who engage in transitory or situational homosexuality—for example, adolescents who experiment with a member of the same sex and then lead exclusively heterosexual lives, or men and women who usually are heterosexual but engage in homosexual activities in prison. A second definition focuses on sexual preferences. Thus, people who have a pattern of choosing members of the same sex as sexual partners when members of the opposite sex are available are defined as homosexuals. Both of these definitions are problematic. People's sexual preferences may change. For example, in Kinsey's sample, only half the men who were exclusively homosexual for as long as three years remained so throughout their lives (1948, p. 651).

Kinsey argued that these definitions fail because they assume that a person is *either* a homosexual *or* a heterosexual. In Kinsey's view, there are no homosexual people, only homosexual acts; and there are no heterosexual people, only heterosexual acts. He stated: "The world is not divided into sheep and goats.... Only the human mind invents categories and tries to force facts into separate pigeon holes" (1948, p. 639). Kinsey described human sexuality as a continuum, with exclusive heterosexuality at one end, exclusive homosexuality at the other, and many variations in between. He located people along the continuum in terms of the relative frequency with which they engaged in hetero- or homosexual acts (see Figure 15–2).

Where on Kinsey's scale do most Americans fall? Precise figures are not known. The best estimates are that about 75 percent of American men and 85 percent of women are exclusively heterosexual; about 2 percent of men and 1 percent of women are exclusively homosexual; and about 25 percent of men and 15 percent of women have

Figure 15–2
The Sexual Continuum

	0 Exclusively Heterosexual	1 Mostly Heterosexual	2 Heterosexual with Substantial Homosexual Experience	3 Equal Heterosexual and Homosexual Experience	4 Homosexual with Substantial Heterosexual Experience	5 Mostly Homosexual	6 Exclusively Homosexual
Kinsey, 1953*							
Men Single 53-78% Married 90-92%	18-42%	13-38%	9-32%	7-26%	5-22%	3-6%	
Women Single 61-72% Married 89-90%	11-20%	6-14%	4-11%	3-8%	2-6%	1-3%	
Hyde, 1979		SOME HOMOSEXUAL EXPERIENCE					
Men 75%				25%			2%
Women 85%				15%			1%

*Range reflects age, whether individual is single or married, and other factors.

had experience with homosexuality in varying amounts (Hyde, 1979, p. 334). Although the percentage of exclusive homosexuals seems to be small, the numbers are significant. Between 6 and 7 million Americans consider themselves homosexuals (and as many as 80 million Americans have had some experience with homosexuality). Homosexuals come from all walks of life, all ethnic groups, all races, and all religions (Hooker, 1957, 1958). Their life styles and loves are as varied as those of heterosexuals. Still, three out of eight Americans claim, "I know one when I see one" (Levitt and Klassen, 1974).

In this section, we will use the term *homosexuality* to refer to sexual behavior involving members of the same sex. We will use the term *homosexual* to refer to people who have adopted the social role of homosexual—that is, people who accept the cultural notion that a person is either a homosexual or a heterosexual, who consider themselves (and are considered by significant others) homosexual, and who engage almost exclusively in homosexual relations.*

Becoming Homosexual

A central question in the minds of many Americans is: Why do people become homosexual? Most Americans think of being homosexual as a condition—as a more or less fixed trait within a person (Levitt and Klassen, 1974). Some people believe the condition to be caused by biological factors. Most people believe it to be caused by psychological factors which may or may not be overcome. In contrast, sociologists see being homosexual as a role that people learn to play, much as they learn other social roles (those of student, parent,

and so on). What is the evidence for these different views?

The homosexual "condition": biological and psychological explanations If being homosexual is seen as a condition, the logical step is to look for its underlying causes. A number of researchers have investigated possible biological explanations, but with little success. There is no reliable evidence that homosexuals are anatomically different from heterosexuals or that individuals inherit a genetic predisposition for homosexuality (Money, 1970). Although slight imbalances in sex hormones have been found in some studies of homosexuals, the findings are inconsistent (Rose, 1975). As far as we know, then, homosexuals are not "born that way."

Researchers have also looked to childhood experiences for psychological explanations of homosexuality. Some theorists have suggested that homosexuals are seeking the love they never received from their same-sex parent (Wolff, 1971; Bieber, 1976). Other theorists have hypothesized that the parent of the opposite sex was overprotective, seductive, and jealous, making the individual fearful of heterosexual entanglements (Bieber et al., 1962). Still others point to early sexual traumas. However, most psychological theories of homosexual development are based on studies of individuals who sought psychotherapy and therefore may not represent homosexuals in general. Psychologists are trained to look for problems that occurred in early development, and, in many cases, they find them. Current research indicates that the kinds of relationships and early experiences that have been cited as explanations of homosexuality are just as common among exclusive heterosexuals (Bell and Weinberg, 1978). Like heterosexuals, homosexuals may come from happy or unhappy homes, have good or bad experiences growing up, and find their first sexual encounters frightening or exciting.

---

*Later we will consider research on *bisexuals,* people who do not accept the belief that homosexuality is an either/or condition and who engage in sexual relations with both men and women.

Future research may reveal that certain biological or psychological factors predispose individuals to choose sexual partners of the same sex. It is extremely unlikely, however, that research will uncover a single, underlying cause of the varied types of behavior our culture classifies as homosexual.

The homosexual role: learning theory For sociologists, the key questions are: How do people learn homosexual behavior? How do they learn a homosexual role? What makes people decide that they are homosexuals?

Learning theory teaches that most behavior patterns are the result of rewards and punishments for past behavior. For example, if a rat is rewarded with a food pellet each time it accidentally presses a bar (that is, if bar pressing is reinforced), it learns to press the bar when it is hungry. Although human behavior is much more complex, the same principle applies. People repeat behavior that brought pleasure in the past and avoid behavior that brought pain.

Learning theory suggests a number of life experiences that might reinforce homosexual behavior (Offir, 1982, Ch. 8). For example, if a young person has his or her first orgasm during sex play with a member of the same sex, he or she may try to repeat the experience and, if it proves rewarding time after time, may develop a preference for the same sex. A child who is sent to an all-boys or all-girls school may find numerous opportunities for sexual gratification with members of the same sex, but few with members of the opposite sex. A girl who is extremely tomboyish or a boy who is exceptionally delicate may be labeled as homosexual at an early age and may be excluded from the conversations and activities in which other youngsters learn heterosexual behavior. An extremely unpleasant encounter with a member of the opposite sex may "teach" a young person to avoid such encounters in the future. Learning theory suggests that a person's sexual orientation

depends on the accumulation of, or balance between, pleasant and punishing experiences.

Like psychological theories, learning theory has a number of shortcomings. One is the chicken-and-the-egg problem. Did early, pleasurable encounters with members of the same sex teach a child homosexual preferences, or did the child seek these experiences and find them pleasurable because he or she already had homosexual feelings? Second, no special or unique pattern distinguishes homosexuals. Many children have homosexual experiences, attend all-boys or all-girls schools, or have unpleasant heterosexual experiences and grow up to be heterosexual. Learning theory does not explain why individuals react differently to such experiences. Finally, our culture offers countless rewards for heterosexual behavior and almost as many punishments for homosexual behavior. From the time they are young, children are inundated with images of heterosexual love. Children themselves use the terms "fag" and "queer" as ultimate insults. For a child not to learn that society punishes homosexuals would be extremely difficult. All the social pressures move in one direction, toward heterosexuality. The puzzle is why some people do not take these loud, insistent lessons to heart and become homosexual in spite of them.

In the final analysis, we simply do not know what leads one person to engage in homosexuality, another to avoid it; what leads one person to adopt a homosexual life style and identity, another to enjoy a homosexual experience but go on to lead a heterosexual life. In all likelihood, there are many developmental paths leading to homosexuality.

The Politics of Homosexuality

In other societies and at other times, homosexuality has been praised or ignored, expected or at least accepted. In classical Greece, for example, emotional and erotic relationships between young

Coming Out

At what point does a person identify himself or herself as a homosexual and begin to explore the homosexual community? Barry Dank interviewed and observed male members of an urban homosexual community. None of the men made the transition from straight to gay alone. They had to learn the role. As Dank points out, people who become homosexual do not undergo anticipatory socialization as children—that is, they are not usually presented with opportunities to learn about the role and to practice in advance. Most of them do not have role models to study. One subject told Dank, "I guess I was like everybody else [who is homosexual] and thought I was the only one in the world. . ." (p. 182).

If a person hears anything about homosexuals in his or her early years, it is likely to be negative—for example, that they are effeminate, obsessed with sex, and particularly attracted to young men and boys (McIntosh, 1968). Coming out requires overcoming—or unlearning—such negative stereotypes.

Most of Dank's subjects began to consider a homosexual identity only when they found themselves in a social context that provided knowledge about and support for homosexuality. One man described his first visit to a gay bar: "I said to myself . . . not all gay men are dirty men or idiots, silly queens, but there are just some normal-looking and acting people, as far as I could see. I saw gay society and I said, 'Wow, I'm home'" (p. 187). From other gays, a person learns ways of expressing and explaining his sexual feelings to himself and to others. The gay community provides both insulation from social stigma and a social network that reinforces a positive homosexual identity. For some (but not all) homosexuals, coming out marks the beginning of a slow process of detachment from many heterosexual associations. The gay identity becomes central.

In Dank's view, the homosexual role is not an example of secondary deviance (a response to labeling by others). Rather, it is a question of opportunities: The decision to come out depends on social support.

Source: Based on Barry Dank, "Coming Out in the Gay World" *Psychiatry*, Vol. 34 (May 1971), pp. 180–97.

boys and older men were idealized (and relations between husbands and wives were considered regrettable necessities). Reportedly, Plato's male student Alexis of Iion was also his lover (Dover, 1979). In modern Western societies, and especially in America, homosexuality is stigmatized.

The term "stigma" comes from the ancient Greek custom of cutting a mark on the bodies of traitors, criminals, and slaves so that respectable citizens could recognize and avoid them. Thus a stigma is a sign that a person is disgraced and need not be treated with respect (Goffman, 1963).

Attitudes toward homosexuality and homosexuals have become somewhat more tolerant in recent years. In Hunt's survey (1974), for example, almost half the respondents said that sexual acts — including homosexual acts — between consenting adults should be legal. But tolerance is not acceptance. In a 1977 Gallup poll, 65 percent of respondents said that they did not think homosexuals should be allowed to be teachers, 54 percent did not want homosexuals admitted to the clergy, and 44 percent would exclude homosexuals from the medical profession. The legalization of homosexual relationships between consenting adults was opposed by 57 percent of the respondents. Homophobia (fear of homosexuals) is more often directed toward males than females. It is difficult to say why this is. The fact that male homosexuals are more numerous and more visible than female homosexuals, the belief that sex between two women is not "real" sex, the higher value our culture places on the male role, and traditional warnings about spilling the seed may all contribute to the greater fear of and hostility toward male homosexuals (Offir, 1982, Ch. 8).

Fear and hatred of homosexuality have turned a social issue into a social problem. A range of formal and informal social controls are used to "protect" heterosexuals and to punish or reform homosexuals. Although homosexuality itself is not illegal in the United States, homosexuals are frequently prosecuted under sodomy statutes (laws against oral and anal sex), which are virtually never applied to heterosexual couples. At various times, homosexuals have been prayed for, thrown into prison, and referred for psychiatric treatment. (Until 1974, the American Psychiatric Association included homosexuality in its official list of mental disorders.) Each year, the military gives 2,000 to 3,000 less than honorable discharges because of homosexuality. Persons so discharged are not eligible for full benefits and may be refused civilian jobs (Williams and Weinberg, 1971).

In 1957 in England, the Wolfenden Committee recommended that homosexual behavior between consenting adults in private be legalized. The Committee reported that it had found no evidence that laws prohibiting homosexuality reduce the incidence of homosexuality or that changing the laws would increase the number of "conversions." The Committee also reported that it had found no evidence that adult homosexuals attempt to seduce children any more often than adult heterosexuals do. In 1969, the Task Force on Homosexuality of the U.S. National Institute of Mental Health made similar recommendations. The Task Force noted that while laws do not seem to prevent homosexuality, they do contribute to stress and mental problems in homosexuals (in part by opening the door to blackmail).

Ten years after the Wolfenden Report, the British Parliament acted on its recommendations. In the United States, however, change has been uneven.

Gay liberation On June 27, 1969, the New York City police launched what they assumed would be a routine raid on the Stonewall Inn, an after-hours gay bar. Instead of allowing themselves to be evicted as usual, bar patrons held their ground, taunting police. The next night, thousands of gays and gay rights sympathizers organized a protest march on police stations. It was the first open rebellion of its kind.

In the decade since, gay periodicals, gay churches, gay businesses and professional services, and gay campus organizations have proliferated under the rallying cry of "We are everywhere." The movement for homosexual rights has borrowed some techniques from the Civil Rights

Movement of the 1960s (demonstration and protest), some from mainstream America (fund-raising dinners for political candidates). Gays have made some progress. Thirty-six municipalities, seven counties, and the states of California and Pennsylvania have adopted statutes that prohibit discrimination against homosexuals. In addition, thirty-six states have repealed statutes that made sodomy a crime. However, gay rights bills have been voted down in popular referenda in some places—for example, in 1977 in Dade County,

Despite the number of demonstrators who turn out for Gay Freedom Day, homosexuals are denied jobs in the State Department, treated unequally in child custody suits, and subjected to other forms of discrimination.

Florida, where Anita Bryant launched a campaign against homosexuals. The U.S. Civil Service Commission announced in 1975 that it would not deny a person employment solely because of his or her sexual orientation, but the F.B.I., the C.I.A. and the State Department still deny employment to gays (on the grounds that they are vulnerable to blackmail). Moreover, homosexuals from foreign countries may still be barred from entering the United States. In this country, the Gay Liberation Movement has made the most gains in East and West Coast cities.

A False Dichotomy

To a degree, the Gay Liberation Movement has endorsed the belief that homosexuals are different. Homosexuals, like heterosexuals, tend to view homosexuality as a condition or trait—and for much the same reason (McIntosh, 1968). If homosexuality is a character trait, then it is more or less fixed—people either do or do not have it. Just as this belief deters people from drifting into homosexuality, "so it appears to foreclose on the possibility of drifting back into [heterosexuality] and thus removes the element of anxious choice" (McIntosh, 1968, p. 178). It keeps the boundaries safe for those who consider themselves homosexuals and for those who consider themselves heterosexuals.

In some societies, there is no such division of humankind into two kinds of people, heterosexuals and homosexuals. Youngsters may be expected to form homosexual attachments before beginning their heterosexual life styles. Or, as in ancient Greece, men are expected to enjoy both homosexual and heterosexual activities at every stage of life. There is a good deal of homosexual behavior in such societies, but there are no homosexuals. Their cultures have not established a separate homosexual role, as ours has.

Establishing two distinct categories and roles for homosexuals and heterosexuals tends to become a self-fulfilling prophecy. The belief that homosexuals are different and that a person is either heterosexual or homosexual creates a social environment that limits people's options, pushing them into behavior that seems to confirm the original (false) belief. In fact, exclusive homosexuals represent a minority of those people with some experience in homosexuality, in our society and in others. However, most people feel pressured to choose one camp or the other. Hence, the fears that homosexuality is "contagious" and that contact with homosexuals is "contaminating" may be self-fulfilling.

Bisexuals — people who do not accept the exclusive homosexual role and who engage in sexual relations with both men and women — are no more welcome in the homosexual community than they are in the heterosexual community, judging by Philip Blumstein and Pepper Schwartz's interviews of eighty bisexual women (1976). Often, lesbian friends ridiculed them as fence sitters. Their heterosexual inclinations were ignored or discounted as signs of emotional immaturity or emotional cowardice (just as homosexual inclinations are in the straight world). These women were seen as lesbians who refused to commit themselves to their "true nature."

Why did these women become bisexual? Some of them had had early homosexual experience, adopted a lesbian identity, and later embarked on a heterosexual relationship. Blumstein and Schwartz suggest that they were drawn by the social rewards of heterosexuality: They wanted the financial security of having a husband, and they wanted children and respectability. Some of them had been active heterosexuals who experimented with homosexuality and took their experiments seriously. Blumstein and Schwartz identify two sources of social support for women who move toward bisexuality. The first is the sexual revolution, which encourages experimentation. A number of the women described threesomes, in which a man had encouraged them to explore another

woman's body (often for the man's titillation). A second source of support is the Women s Movement, which encourages female solidarity and intimacy and brings women together in groups from which men are excluded.

Social Problems and Social Issues

This chapter offers clear illustrations of the complex interplay between social issues (acts or conditions that arouse public concern and debate) and social problems (acts or conditions that prove harmful).

Homosexuality, for example, is a social issue. While there is no evidence that homosexuality causes harm, the fact that it is stigmatized in our society clearly harms individuals who are sexually attracted to members of their own sex. In this case, a social issue creates a social problem.

With adolescent sexuality, the relationship between the issues and the problems is more complex. In a society that does not provide many job opportunities for adolescents and in which parents are expected to take sole responsibility for their children, pregnancy and motherhood are problems for teen-agers. Our society limits a girl's opportunities to be a proper mother and may therefore harm her child. Part of the problem derives from the fact that many adults are reluctant to provide adolescents with information about sexuality, birth control, and venereal disease. The issue exacerbates the problem.

With pornography, the relationship between social issues and problems is even more complex. Crusades against any form of erotic expression provoked defenders of free speech to take an extreme position, so that matters of degree were overlooked. In the same breath, people attacked — or defended — the novel *Ulysses* and brutal, sadistic films, as if there were no difference between them. The question of potential harm was obscured. With pornography as with prostitution, conflicting norms and confusing laws have helped to create a criminal underworld in which women especially may be victimized.

Thus in dealing with human sexuality, issues and problems are intertwined.

Summary

1. Cross-cultural variations suggest that many sexual skills and preferences are not the expression of innate drives, but the product of social learning.

2. Scientific investigation (by Freud, Kinsey, and Masters and Johnson) has contributed to bringing sexuality out in the open. A "play ethic" seems to have replaced the Puritan sexual norms of the nineteenth and early twentieth century.

3. Adult ambivalence toward adolescent sexuality and misinformation among adolescents are two contributing factors in the high rates of teen-age pregnancy, out-of-wedlock births, and venereal disease.

4. Many seemingly private troubles in marriage—different sexual norms for men and women, performance pressures (which may lead to sexual dysfunction), and the clash between norms of fidelity and sexual liberation—are social in origin.

5. The legal debate over pornography (centering on the question of freedom of expression) is complicated by the lack of clear research findings on whether exposure leads people to use sex in harmful ways.

6. Prostitution may be seen as a necessary social safety valve or as a form of exploitation of women, who are doubly victimized when prostitution is illegal and stigmatized.

7. Sexual preference is best seen as a continuum, with exclusive heterosexuality at one end and exclusive homosexuality at the other. A homosexual is someone who adopts the social role and identity of homosexual and engages almost exclusively in same-sex relations.

8. Neither biology, psychology, nor social learning theory provides a complete explanation of homosexuality. As with heterosexuality, there are probably many developmental paths.

9. The belief that homosexuality is an either-or condition functions as a self-fulfilling prophecy; bisexuality is distrusted by both homosexuals and heterosexuals.

Suggested Reading

Bell, Alan P., and Martin, S. Weinberg. *Homosexualities: A Study of Diversity Among Men and Women.* New York: Simon & Schuster, 1978.

Brown, Howard. *Familiar Faces, Hidden Lives: The Story of Homosexual Men in America Today.* New York: Harcourt Brace Jovanovich, 1976.

Chilman, Catherine S. *Adolescent Sexuality in a Changing American Society: Social and Psychological Perspectives.* Washington, D.C.: U.S. Department of Health, Education, and Welfare, 1978.

Gagnon, John H. *Human Sexualities.* Glenville, Ill.: Scott, Foresman, 1977.

Henslin, James M., and Edward Sagarin (Eds.). *The Sociology of Sex: An Introductory Reader.* New York: Schocken Books, 1978.

Humphreys, Laud. *Tearoom Trade: Impersonal Sex in Public Places.* Chicago: Aldine, 1975.

Kaplan, Helen S. *The New Sex Therapy.* New York: Brunner/Mazel, 1974.

Pomeroy, Wardell B. *Dr. Kinsey and the Institute for Sex Research.* New York: Harper & Row, 1972.

Wiseman, Jacquelin P. (Ed.). *The Social Psychology of Sex.* New York: Harper & Row, 1976.

References

Baldwin, W.H. "Adolescent Pregnancy and Childbearing—Growing Concerns for Americans." *Population Bulletin,* Vol. 31, No. 2 (January 1976), pp. 3–34.

Becker, H.S. *The Outsiders.* New York: Free Press, 1963.

Bell, A.P., and M.S. Weinberg. *Homosexualities: A Study of Diversity Among Men and Women.* New York: Simon & Schuster, 1978.

Bieber, I. "A Discussion of Homosexuality: The Ethical Challenge." *Journal of Consulting and Clinical Psychology,* Vol. 44 (1976), pp. 163–66.

Bieber, I., et al. *Homosexuality: A Psychoanalytic Study of Male Homosexuals.* New York: Basic Books, 1962.

Blumstein, P.W., and P. Schwartz. "Bisexual Women." In J.P. Wiseman (Ed.), *The Social Psychology of Sex.* New York: Harper & Row, 1976, pp. 154–62.

Bolton, F.G., Jr. *The Pregnant Adolescent: Consequences of Premature Parenting.* Beverly Hills, Cal.: Sage, 1980.

Boston Women's Health Book Collective. *Our Bodies, Our Selves.* New York: Simon & Schuster, 1976.

Cavan, S. "Talking About Sex By Not Talking About Sex." In J.P. Wiseman (Ed.), *The Social Psychology of Sex.* New York: Harper & Row, 1976, pp. 57–63.

Chiappa, J.A., and J.J. Forish. *The VD Book.* New York: Holt, Rinehart and Winston, 1976.

Chilman, C.S. *Adolescent Sexuality in a Changing American Society: Social and Psychological Perspectives.* Washington, D.C.: U.S. Department of Health, Education, and Welfare, 1978.

Dank, B. "Coming Out in the Gay World." *Psychiatry,* Vol. 34 (May 1971), pp. 180–97.

Davidson, G.C. "A Discussion of Homosexuality: The Ethical Challenge." *Journal of Consulting and Clinical Psychology,* Vol. 44, No. 2, pp. 157–62.

Davis, K. "The Sociology of Prostitution." *American Sociological Review,* Vol. 2, No. 5 (1937), pp. 744–55.

Davis, K. "Sexual Behavior." In R.K. Merton and R. Nisbet (Eds.), *Contemporary Social Problems,* 4th ed. New York: Harcourt Brace Jovanovich, 1976, pp. 220–61.

Davis, N.J. "Prostitution: Identity, Career, and Legal-Economic Enterprise." In J.M. Henslin and E. Sagarin (Eds.), *The Sociology of Sex: An Introductory Reader.* New York: Schocken Books, 1978.

Denfeld, D. "Dropouts from Swinging." *Family Coordinator,* Vol. 23 (1974), pp. 45–49.

Dover, K.J. *Greek Homosexuality.* Cambridge, Mass.: Harvard University Press, 1979.

Dryfoos, J.G., and T. Heisler. "Contraceptive Services for Adolescents: An Overview." *Family Planning Perspectives,* Vol. 10 (July–August 1978), pp. 223–33.

Finklehor, D., and K. Yllo. *Forced Sex in Marriage: A Preliminary Report.* Paper presented at the Annual Meeting of the American Sociological Association, New York, N.Y., 1980.

Ford, C.S., and F.A. Beach. *Patterns of Sexual Behavior.* New York: Harper & Row, 1951.

Gagnon, J.H. *Human Sexualities.* Glenville, Ill.: Scott Foresman, 1977.

Gagnon, J.H., and B. Henderson. *Human Sexuality.* Boston: Little, Brown/Time Maga-back, 1975.

Gagnon, J.H., and W. Simon. *Sexual Conduct: The Social Sources of Human Sexuality.* Chicago: Aldine, 1973.

Goffman, E. *Stigma.* Englewood Cliffs, N.J.: Spectrum, 1963.

Goode, E. *Deviant Behavior: An Interactionist Approach.* Englewood Cliffs, N.J.: Prentice-Hall, 1978.

Gordon, M., and P.J. Shankweiler. "Different Equals Less: Female Sexuality in Recent Marriage Manuals." *Journal of Marriage and the Family,* Vol. 33, No. 3 (August 1971), pp. 459–66.

Hass, A. *Teenage Sexuality: A Survey of Teenage Sexual Behavior.* New York: Macmillan, 1979.

Hayes, J., and J.H. Littlefield. "Venereal Disease Knowledge in High School Seniors." *Journal of School Health,* Vol. XLVI (November 1976), pp. 546–47.

Heider, K.G. "Dani Sexuality: A Low Energy System." *Man,* Vol. 11, No. 2 (June 1976), pp. 188–201.

Hooker, E. "The Adjustment of the Male Overt Homosexual." *Journal of Projective Techniques,* Vol. 21 (1957), pp. 18–31.

Hooker, E. "Male Homosexuality and the Rorschach." *Journal of Projective Techniques,* Vol. 22 (1958), pp. 33–54.

Humphreys, L. *Tearoom Trade: Impersonal Sex in Public Places.* Chicago: Aldine, 1975.

Hunt, M. *Her Infinite Variety.* New York: Harper & Row, 1962.

Hunt, M. *Sexual Behavior in the 1970s.* Chicago: Playboy, 1974.

Hyde, J.S. *Understanding Human Sexuality.* New York: McGraw-Hill, 1979.

Kaplan, H.S. *The New Sex Therapy.* New York: Brunner/Mazel, 1974.

Kinsey, A.C., W.B. Pomeroy, and C.E. Martin. *Sexual Behavior in the Human Male.* Philadelphia: Saunders, 1948.

Kinsey, A.C., and P.H. Gebhard. *Sexual Behavior in the Human Female.* Philadelphia: Saunders, 1953.

Kolata, G.B. "Strategies for the Control of Gonorrhea." *Science,* Vol. 192, No. 4236 (1976), p. 245.

Komarovsky, M. *Blue-Collar Marriage.* New York: Vintage, 1967.

Kutchinsky, B. "The Effect of Easy Availability of Pornography on the Incidence of Sex Crimes: The Danish Experience." *Journal of Social Issues,* Vol. 29 (1973), pp. 163–81.

Lemert, E.M. *Social Pathology.* New York: McGraw-Hill, 1951.

Levitt, E.E., and A.D. Klassen, Jr. "Public Attitudes Toward Homosexuality: Part of the 1970 National Survey by the Institute for Sex Research." *Journal of Homosexuality,* Vol. 1, No. 1 (1974), pp. 29–43.

Luker, K. *Taking Chances: Abortion and the Decision Not to Contracept.* Berkeley, Cal.: University of California Press, 1975.

Luria, Z., and M. Rose. *Psychology of Human Sexuality.* New York: Wiley, 1979.

Lydon, S. "The Politics of Orgasm." In R. Morgan (Ed.), *Sisterhood Is Powerful.* New York: Vintage, 1970, pp. 197–205.

McIntosh, M. "The Homosexual Role." *Social Problems,* Vol. 16, No. 2 (1968), pp. 182–92.

Marcus, S. *The Other Victorians: A Study of Sexuality and Pornography in Mid-Nineteenth-Century England.* New York: Basic Books, 1966.

Masters, W.H., and V.E. Johnson. *Human Sexual Response.* Boston: Little, Brown, 1966.

Masters, W.H., and V.E. Johnson. *Human Sexual Inadequacy.* Boston: Little, Brown, 1970.

Mead, M. *Coming of Age in Samoa.* New York: Dell, 1961.

Millar, J.D. "The National Venereal Disease Problem." *Epidemic Venereal Disease: Proceedings of the Second International Symposium on Venereal Disease.* St. Louis: American Social Health Association and Pfizer Laboratory, 1972.

Millet, K. (Ed.). *The Prostitution Papers.* New York: Avon Books, 1973.

Mills, C.W. *The Sociological Imagination.* New York: Oxford University Press, 1959.

Money, J. "Sexual Dimorphism and Homosexual Gender Identity." *Psychological Bulletin,* Vol. 74 (1970), pp. 425–40.

Moneymaker, J., and F. Montanino. "The New Sexual Morality: A Society Comes of Age." In J.M. Henslin and E. Sagarin (Eds.), *The Sociology of Sex: An Introductory Reader.* New York: Schocken Books, 1978, pp. 27–40.

Offir, C. *Human Sexuality.* New York: Harcourt Brace Jovanovich, 1982.

O'Neil, N., and G. O'Neil. *Open Marriage: A New Lifestyle for Couples.* New York: Avon Books, 1972.

Pomeroy, W.B. *Dr. Kinsey and the Institute for Sex Research.* New York: Harper & Row, 1972.

Powdermaker, H. *Life in Lesu.* New York: Norton, 1933.

Rainwater, L. "Marital Sexuality in Four Cultures of Poverty." *Journal of Marriage and the Family,* Vol. 26, No. 4 (November 1964), pp. 457–66.

Rasmussen, P.K., and L.L. Kuhn. "The New Masseuse: Play for Pay." *Urban Life,* Vol. 5, No. 3 (October 1976), pp. 271–92.

Reiss, I. *The Social Context of Sexual Permissiveness.* New York: Holt, Rinehart and Winston, 1967.

Report of the Commission on Obscenity and Pornography. New York: Bantam, 1970.

Rose, R.M. "Testosterone, Aggression, and Homosexuality: A Review of the Literature and Implications for Future Research." In E.J. Sacher (Ed.), *Topics in Psychoendocrinology.* New York: Grune & Stratton, 1975.

Sheehy, G. *Hustling.* New York: Delacorte Press, 1973.

Slater, P.E. "Sexual Adequacy in America." *Intellectual Digest* (December 1973), pp. 432–35.

Sorenson, R.C. *Adolescent Sexuality in Contemporary America.* New York: World, 1973.

Spanier, G.B., and C.L. Cole. "Mate Swapping: Perceptions, Value Orientations and Participation in a Midwestern Community." *Archives of Sexual Behavior,* Vol. 4, No. 2 (1975), pp. 143–59.

Tavris, C., and Offir, C. *The Longest War: Sex Differences in Perspective.* New York: Harcourt Brace Jovanovich, 1977.

Teenage Pregnancy: The Problem That Hasn't Gone Away. New York: Alan Guttmacher Institute, 1981.

Williams, C.J., and M.S. Weinberg. *Homosexuals and the Military: A Study of Less Than Honorable Discharge.* New York: Harper & Row, 1971.

Wolff, C. *Love Between Women.* New York: Harper & Row, 1971.

Chapter Sixteen

Drug Use

Drugs and Their Effects

Depressants

Stimulants

Hallucinogens

Drug Use: The Contemporary Scene

Patterns of Drug Use

Explaining Drug Use

The Social Control of Drug Use

The Politics of Drug Control

Drug Laws and Their Consequences

   Intolerance
   Tolerance

The Drug Problem in Perspective

Most Americans regard heroin use as the nation's number one drug problem. The image of the depraved junkie, leading a life of crime and squalor, preying on society, enslaved to an insatiable habit, is imprinted on the public consciousness. The Supreme Court described the "horrors of addiction" this way: "To be a confirmed drug addict is to be one of the walking dead. . . . The teeth have rotted out, the appetite is lost, and the stomach and intestines don't function properly. . . . Good traits of character disappear and bad ones emerge. . . . Nerves snap; vicious twitching develops. Imaginary and fantastic fears blight the mind and sometimes complete insanity results. . . . Such is the torment of being a drug addict; such is the plague of being one of the walking dead" (*Robinson* v. *California,* 1962). Every recent President has sounded the alarm. "If we cannot destroy the drug menace in America," declared President Nixon, "then it will surely destroy us. . . . The problem has assumed the dimensions of a national emergency" (in Goldberg, 1980, p. 32). In the last decade alone, the nation spent $6 billion on drug treatment and law enforcement (The Drug Abuse Council, 1980, p. 4).

At the same time, millions of Americans regularly use three substances we do not ordinarily think of as drugs: the caffeine in coffee and soft drinks, the nicotine in cigarettes, and alcohol. By any scientific or medical definition, all three are drugs. In addition, as many as 25 million Americans have tried marijuana and 10 million are said to use it regularly (The Drug Abuse Council, 1980, p. 1). And millions more regularly use stimulants, sedatives, tranquilizers, and hallucinogens for nonmedical purposes.

In this chapter, we will look at the use of both illicit (illegal) drugs and licit (legal) drugs in the United States today. Changing and often inconsistent norms about who should or should not be allowed to use drugs, which drugs, and under what circumstances have made drug use a major social issue. To assess the drug problem, we have to put the issue into perspective. Certain drugs and certain patterns of drug use are more harmful than others. Are the norms governing use of a specific drug consistent with the known hazards? Are we too intolerant of some drugs, too tolerant of others? What are the individual and social costs of both tolerance and intolerance? In the first section of this chapter, we examine the pharmacological effects of some of the most feared drugs (like heroin) and some of the nation's "favorite" drugs (like alcohol). What do these drugs do to people? What do they do for people? Next we look at contemporary patterns of drug use. Different social categories (teen-agers, housewives) use different drugs in different ways. The question is why. In the third section, we explore the politics of drug control. We identify the special interests behind drives to control some drugs and "decontrol" others. We also point out unanticipated consequences of efforts to control drug use. In the final section of the chapter, we suggest that popular ideas and public policies may obscure the problems underlying drug use, hampering attempts to deal with these problems.

Drugs and Their Effects

A *drug* is any chemical substance that changes physiological and/or psychological functioning. Our specific concern in this chapter is with *psychoactive drugs:* chemicals that alter people's moods, perceptions, thinking, and/or behavior. What immediate effect does a drug have on people? What are the known consequences for a person's health of using the drug?

Depressants

People take the drugs classified as depressants to reduce tensions, to forget their troubles, to obtain relief from failure or loneliness. The effects of

Figure 16-1

Alcohol Levels in the Blood
(After drinks taken on an empty stomach by a 150-lb. person)

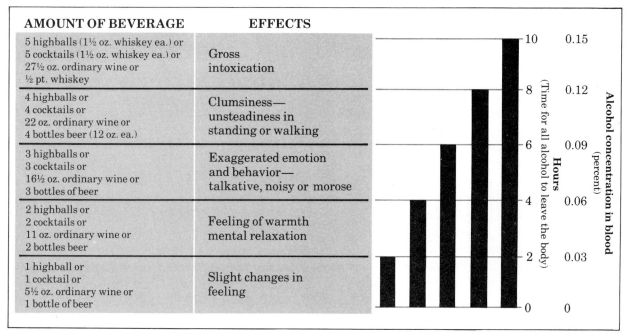

AMOUNT OF BEVERAGE	EFFECTS
5 highballs (1½ oz. whiskey ea.) or 5 cocktails (1½ oz. whiskey ea.) or 27½ oz. ordinary wine or ½ pt. whiskey	Gross intoxication
4 highballs or 4 cocktails or 22 oz. ordinary wine or 4 bottles beer (12 oz. ea.)	Clumsiness— unsteadiness in standing or walking
3 highballs or 3 cocktails or 16½ oz. ordinary wine or 3 bottles of beer	Exaggerated emotion and behavior— talkative, noisy or morose
2 highballs or 2 cocktails or 11 oz. ordinary wine or 2 bottles beer	Feeling of warmth mental relaxation
1 highball or 1 cocktail or 5½ oz. ordinary wine or 1 bottle of beer	Slight changes in feeling

Source: *Time* magazine, in J. Fort and C.T. Cory, *American Drugstore: A (Alcohol) to V (Valium)* (Boston: Little, Brown, 1975), p. 32.

these drugs are short-lived, so that people have to keep taking them to maintain the feeling of calm.

The most frequently used drug in Western societies is *alcohol*. One or two drinks lead to feelings of warmth and relaxation (see Figure 16–1). Another round, and inhibitions are lowered. Feelings of inadequacy and self-criticism may fade. Sensitivity to outside stimuli, judgment, learning, and memory are reduced. Emotions and behavior may become exaggerated. Some people become extremely talkative; others become morose and withdrawn. A fourth or fifth round impairs motor coordination: Speech is slurred and the drinker is unsteady on his or her feet. With continued drinking, some people fall into a stupor (they "black out"); others become confused, agi-

tated, and violent. Thus, the effects of alcohol are contradictory. "At various dose levels and phases of the drinking cycle it may depress or stimulate, tranquilize or agitate" (Brecher, 1972, p. 245). The effects depend on the social context—on the individual's health and mood, why he or she is drinking, where and with whom, and what the drinker expects based on past experiences.

Occasional, moderate drinking has few ill effects save hangovers. (What precisely causes a hangover and how to cure it are not known.) Immoderate drinking is a different story. Death from overdose of alcohol is not unknown, although most people "black out" before they consume enough to impair breathing and heart rate. Long-term, heavy use of alcohol is a proven health risk (Coleman, 1976, pp. 417–19). Alcohol contains calories but no nutrients. Heavy drinkers who do not eat may have peripheral nerve degeneration due to malnutrition. Prolonged heavy drinking can cause irreversible brain damage: The cerebral cortex shrinks and waste products accumulate in the brain. Heavy drinkers have a one in ten chance of developing cirrhosis (irreversible scarring and hardening of the liver). People who drink heavily over a long period of time, then attempt to stop, may go through *delerium tremens* (the DTs): a state of panic accompanied by sweating, trembling, and hallucinations (often of animals crawling over one's body) that lasts from three to six days. The death rate from convulsions or heart failure during the DTs is about 10 percent. In addition to these health problems, alcohol is implicated in perhaps 30 percent of suicides, 40 percent of homicides, and 70 percent of all fatal traffic accidents (Brecher, 1972, p. 263).

Why some people can drink occasionally with no problem, whereas some become psychologically dependent (they do not feel comfortable without alcohol and are preoccupied with the next drink) and some physiologically dependent (they cannot have one drink without going on a spree or cannot stop without withdrawal symptoms) is not known. Estimates are that 10 to 12 percent of drinkers (5 million Americans) become "alcohol addicts" (Brecher, 1972, p. 245).

Not long ago, alcohol was frequently prescribed as a "nerve tonic" or sedative. This role has been taken over by barbiturates (phenobarbital, Nembutal, Seconal), sleeping pills (or hypnotics, such as Quaalude), and most recently by the minor tranquilizers (meprobamate, Librium, Valium). Whereas our culture defines alcohol as a social drug, these drugs are considered medicines. People usually take them in the privacy of their bathrooms, not among friends at a bar or a party. Moreover, the effects are not as obvious. (You cannot detect Seconal or Valium on a person's breath.) Hence, someone can use high doses without anyone else knowing.

Barbiturates (from the synthetic drug barbital) were developed around the turn of the century as a sleeping medication. The immediate effects of barbiturates are similar to those of alcohol: The user feels relaxed or "mellow" and therefore can fall asleep. Strong doses may lead to slurred speech, an unsteady gait, and impaired judgment and memory. Barbiturates are dangerous to health in two ways. If a person takes barbiturates every night for several weeks, they become ineffective (National Institute on Drug Abuse, 1977). The user develops a *tolerance* for the drug and must take stronger and stronger doses to relax and fall asleep. However, people do not become "tolerant" in the sense of being able to take larger doses without risk of heart or lung failure (as is the case with heroin and the opiates). As a result, it is fairly easy to take a lethal overdose of barbiturates. Second, the combination of barbiturates and alcohol is synergistic: Each intensifies the effects of the other. The result can be lethal. Every year, some 27,000 Americans die from accidental or suicidal overdoses of barbiturates (Altrocchi, 1980, p. 535). Taking barbiturates can lead to physiological dependence and, as with alcohol, withdrawal can be dangerous (Coleman, 1976, pp. 445–46).

Today barbiturates are being replaced to some extent by Miltown (meprobamate), Librium, and Valium—called *minor tranquilizers* to distinguish them from the major tranquilizers used to treat severe mental disorders (see Chapter 13). The immediate effects of tranquilizers are similar to those of barbiturates, although they do not make people quite as drowsy. They are not thought to cause physiological dependence, though they may lead to psychological dependence. People who have used high doses for some time may experience the same withdrawal symptoms as with barbiturates and alcohol. Death from overdose is rare, but none of these drugs

Helping Alcoholic Women

"I couldn't stop drinking" said Diane, brushing away her long dark hair with a hand that still trembled. "I tried everything from dumping drinks down the sink to moving to a dry county, but it didn't help."

One day at a dingy unemployment center she noticed a handwritten sign advertising an unusual program for alcoholic women. The center, sponsored by the Women's Alcoholic Coalition, a nonprofit group of recovering alcoholics, child care workers and alcoholism counselors, uses a feminist approach to help women stop drinking. Since she enrolled in the program four months ago, Diane has been sober. She has reconciled with her husband and plans to go back to college in the fall.

Diane is one of 10 women currently enrolled in the free program. They receive individual and group counseling, vocational guidance and an education in nutrition, physical fitness and money management five days a week for up to six months. Since the center opened in October, 60 women have participated, most of them single mothers of young children.

"Traditional treatment programs are usually ineffective for alcoholic women because they don't take into consideration the special needs of women," said Pam Miller, program director. "Unlike male alcoholics who come to the attention of police and legal authorities by getting into fights, women drink quietly and alone at home. Frequently the only ones who know that the woman has a drinking problem are the children because physicians, clergymen and welfare workers ignore it." . . .

Helping women overcome their conditioning to please others is an important part of the center's approach. "Unlike other treatment programs, we have a feminist approach that stresses that women have choices and that they can achieve what they want in terms of a career or family life without turning to alcohol to deaden the pain that comes from denying their own needs. . . .

"Society's image of an alcoholic is still a gray-haired man with a wine bottle hanging out of his pocket," Miss Miller said. "Nobody wants to admit that the attractive mother of young children or the busy career woman has a drinking problem, so women don't get the help they need."

Source: Sharon Johnson, "Help for the Alcoholic Woman: Stressing the Feminist Approach," *The New York Times,* June 14, 1980.

have been in use long enough for their long-term health effects to be known. Although tranquilizers are useful in treating muscle spasms and *petit-mal* epilepsy, most prescriptions are written by family doctors (not psychiatrists) for patients who complain of "bad nerves" (Cant, 1976). And because people usually obtain them with a prescription, tranquilizers enjoy medical legitimacy.

Heroin and other opium derivatives (morphine, codeine) are also depressants. No one knows for sure how many Americans use this drug. Estimates are that there are about 350,000 heroin addicts in the United States today (compared with an estimated 15 million alcoholics). Heroin was introduced at the turn of the century as a cure for morphine addiction. Physicians soon discovered that heroin is stronger and faster-acting than morphine and that it is just as likely to lead to tolerance and physiological dependence. The immediate effects of heroin are variable. Some users experience a "rush" that they compare to a sexual orgasm in the first sixty seconds after injecting heroin; some feel a wave of nausea. Some get "high." They relax; awareness of bodily needs (for food or sex) and of outside demands fades; they feel euphoric. Others say the drug simply makes them feel normal again. This lasts for four to six hours, after which the user needs another dose to feel normal or high again (Coleman, 1976, p. 436). Most users become physiologically dependent on heroin. They develop a craving for it and become physically ill (experience withdrawal symptoms) without it. No one knows exactly why this happens. One possibility is that heroin and other opiates interfere with the body's production of its own painkillers, so that when the drug is withdrawn users feel pain that nonusers do not feel (Pert and Snyder, 1973). It takes about a month of steady use to become physiologically dependent on heroin, but months—even years—to overcome cravings for this drug.

Heroin itself is not as dangerous a drug as most people imagine. There is no question that it is ad-

dictive and that withdrawal can be painful and frightening. But it is far less dangerous than withdrawal from alcohol or barbiturates, which may cause death. The death rate among heroin users is more than twice the national average (Valliant, 1970). But death from heroin overdose is rare. It would take enormous quantities of heroin to actually kill someone. In most heroin-related deaths, doctors suspect other causes, such as drug impurity (Brecher, 1972, Chapter 12). Continued use of heroin has few known ill effects on health (in sharp contrast to alcohol and tobacco). The emaciated bodies, sallow complexions, and rotting teeth popularly associated with heroin addiction are not side effects of the drug itself. They result from the fact that heroin is illegal and expensive. Many heroin addicts use money they might otherwise spend on food, clothing, and shelter to buy drugs. Their poor health is in large part the result of impoverishment.

Studies of the use of heroin and related drugs raise interesting questions. Some patients who are given morphine in the hospital do not get "high." In this setting, the opiate is socially defined as a medicine; these patients simply feel better. It is estimated that only 7 percent of soldiers who used heroin regularly in Vietnam continued when they returned home (Robins, 1974). They had used the drug in one setting and did not feel a pressing need for it in another. Of course, the heroin they used in Vietnam may have been chemically different from the heroin sold in the United States. But it does seem that the effect of heroin, like that of other drugs, depends in part on the social setting.

Stimulants

A second group of psychoactive drugs are the stimulants people take to overcome fatigue and depression. Stimulants temporarily increase alertness and stamina. However, the extra energy people expend while using these drugs can lead to exhaustion when their effects wear off. (Users may "crash.")

When Columbus discovered America, he also discovered tobacco, which Native Americans had used for centuries. The taste for tobacco spread rapidly through Western societies, first in the form of snuff, then as chewing and pipe tobacco, and in this century as cigarettes (Brecher, 1972, Chapter 23). The active ingredient in tobacco, *nicotine,* has paradoxical effects. Smokers report that cigarettes help them to remain alert and to think and work more effectively. (Among other things, nicotine stimulates the heart.) At the same time, they say smoking relaxes them. (This may be because the repetitive, habitual activities of lighting up, inhaling, and so on are relaxing.)

The ill effects of cigarette smoking are well documented in reports of the Surgeon General (U.S. Department of Health, Education, and Welfare, 1979). Cigarettes are one of the most harmful substances people use regularly and the leading cause of preventable death in the United States today. Estimates are that cigarettes cause more than 300,000 deaths a year. Smoking greatly increases the risks of lung cancer, heart disease, and chronic bronchitis and emphysema. A thirty- to thirty-five-year-old who smokes about two packs a day can expect to die eight or nine years earlier than a nonsmoker of the same age. Smokers spend 30 to 40 percent more days at home sick than nonsmokers do. Babies born to women who smoke tend to be underweight and are more likely to become victims of "sudden infant death syndrome." There is some evidence that involuntary smoking (breathing other people's smoke) is a health risk. For example, children whose parents smoke are more likely to have bronchitis or pneumonia in the first year of life. The earlier in life people begin to smoke, the longer they smoke, the more they smoke, and the greater the risks.

Per capita consumption of cigarettes in the United States has declined in the years since the first Surgeon General's report—from 4,345 cigarettes in 1964 to 3,965 in 1978 (over half a pack a day for every adult). As many as 29 million Americans have quit smoking, but millions of others have started (including teen-agers). People become psychologically and perhaps physiologically dependent on cigarettes. Estimates are that two years after they quit, as many as 75 percent of former smokers have taken up the habit again (Brecher, 1972). Most go back to smoking 20 to 30 cigarettes a day (the number it takes to keep a steady supply of nicotine in the bloodstream). Partially abstinent smokers are in a state of "chronic withdrawal" (U.S. Department of Health, Education, and Welfare, 1979, p. 32).

Amphetamines are synthetic stimulants known popularly as "speed." The earliest amphetamine was marketed in the 1930s in a nasal spray. Users discovered they could get "kicks" from ingesting amphetamines before scientists did. During World War II, amphetamines were given to both Allied and German soldiers in pill form to relieve fatigue. Civilians soon discovered them, and amphetamines became popular among night workers, truck drivers, students, and athletes. Their ability to suppress appetite was discovered later, and millions of pills were prescribed for dieters. The most controversial use of amphetamines is for hyperactive children whom, for unknown reasons, the drugs calm (Coleman, 1976, pp. 446–47).

Amphetamines reduce hunger and fatigue, lift depression, and increase alertness and activity. Do people become dependent on amphetamines? Not always (Brecher, 1972, Chapter 36). Some people find that moderate doses remain effective for years, without causing withdrawal symptoms. Others quickly develop tolerance and take larger and larger doses. High doses of amphetamines can result in heightened blood pressure, enlarged pupils, rapid and confused speech, trembling, and sleeplessness. Prolonged use may lead to malnutrition. The combination of strong doses and continued use has been linked to a temporary psychosis, characterized by paranoid delusions, and to suicide, homicide, and other acts of violence (Coleman, 1976, p. 447). Moreover, heavy users often take barbiturates to counteract the effects of amphetamines, doubling the drug risk.

Cocaine, like nicotine, is a Native American drug. The Incas and their descendants in the Andean highlands chewed the leaves of the coca plant for centuries, apparently without becoming addicted. Cocaine is an extract of the plant, however, and therefore more powerful (Petersen and Stillman, 1978a). Sniffed, swallowed, or injected, cocaine produces general feelings of alertness and euphoria. High doses or prolonged use may inflame nasal passages, increase the heartbeat and blood pressure, and in rare cases, lead to death from cardiovascular collapse. Too little is known about cocaine to say what percentage of people develop tolerance for and dependence on the drug. What is known is that like alcohol, cocaine has become a social drug in recent years; users rank it first among recreational drugs; indeed, it has become a "status drug."

Hallucinogens

Hallucinogens are a third group of psychoactive drugs that induce changes in perception, thought, and feelings. People who take hallucinogens experience things in different and unusual ways, almost as if they were dreaming.

One of the most potent hallucinogens is *LSD* (lysergic acid diethylamide). A dose smaller than a grain of salt induces hallucinations. First used as a research tool because it was thought to mimic psychosis, LSD was tried as an aid to psychotherapy, a cure for alcoholism, and a painkiller for terminal cancer patients in the 1950s (Ashley, 1975). LSD began to be used for recreational ("mind expanding") purposes in the early 1960s. Within forty minutes to an hour after taking LSD, people begin to experience an inten-

sification of sensory perception, loss of control over their thoughts and emotions, and feelings of depersonalization and detachment, as if they were watching themselves from a distance. (Their pupils may dilate and their body temperature rise.) Some LSD users say things never looked or sounded or smelled so beautiful; some have terrifying visions. Some experience extraordinary mental lucidity; others become horribly confused. The effects are highly variable, even for the same person. No two LSD "trips" are alike.

The chief dangers of LSD in the public mind are "bad trips" (extremely unsettling experiences that may lead to mental breakdowns, violence, and perhaps suicide) and "flashbacks" (spontaneous recurrences of hallucinations long afterward). Only a small number of such cases has been verified, however. How many actually occur is unknown. Surprisingly little research has been done on the effects of LSD. One researcher suggests several reasons why (Zinberg in Ashley, 1975, p. 62). The early association of LSD with madness and later association with the "psychedelic freak scene" of the 1960s put a stigma on research. A "society preoccupied with rationality and control" fears altered states of consciousness. Finally, it is difficult to "do neat, beautifully controlled and objectively measurable studies" on a drug whose effects depend on the users' subjective state.

The most commonly used hallucinogen in the United States today is *marijuana* ("grass" or "pot"). A comparatively mild hallucinogen, marijuana is often used like alcohol, for relaxation and intoxication. Many marijuana smokers report feelings of relaxation; heightened enjoyment of food, music, and sex; disruptions in short-term memory and sense of time (not remembering why or when you got up from a chair); and on occasion, dreamlike hallucinations. Some users become euphoric; some become suspicious, anxious, or depressed. But given wide differences in the quality or strength of the drug and the amount used, the similarities of experience are remarkable. It

No drug is completely safe. Los Angeles police used a shark net to capture this young man who had taken "angel dust"; he was too dangerous to approach.

may be that users' expectations shape their experiences. (Some people say they have to learn to recognize the signs of being high.)

How dangerous is marijuana? It has been reported that marijuana interferes with the body's immune response, affects endocrine function (especially levels of the male hormone testosterone and sperm count), causes brain damage, and leads to chromosome damage. But these reports in the press have been based on inconclusive and questionable research. Some users do have an "acute panic anxiety reaction" to marijuana: They forget that what they are experiencing is temporary and drug-induced. And long-term, heavy use of marijuana may damage the lungs and lead to tolerance and withdrawal symptoms if use is suddenly discontinued. But because marijuana is used primarily as a social drug in the United States, not as an "everyday"

drug like cigarettes and coffee, this is rare. A 1977 report of the Secretary of Health, Education, and Welfare asserted that "intermittent ingestion [of marijuana] rarely constitutes a health or social hazard." Nevertheless, there are still many more questions than answers about its effects.

Recently, a third hallucinogen, *PCP* (phencyclidine or "angel dust"), has appeared on the black market. Distributed legally as a veterinary agent to immobilize animals, PCP is easily synthesized from readily available materials. Very small amounts have been linked to disorganized thoughts, speech disturbances, agitation, and hostility. Larger doses (5–10 milligrams) may lead to vomiting, coma, or convulsions. In part because PCP obtained "on the street" is often adulterated, little is known about its long-term effects on health (Petersen and Stillman, 1978b).

Two themes emerge from this survey of drugs

and their effects. First, not one of these drugs is entirely predictable. It is impossible to say that chemical A always leads to experience X or behavior Y. Some people become buoyant and talkative when they are drinking; some, sad and withdrawn. Some people develop a tolerance for and dependence on amphetamines; some do not. The same person may experience ecstatic visions on one LSD trip, a waking nightmare on another. The effects of a drug in part reflect the drug user's mental "set" (his or her emotional state and expectations) and the setting (the people, place, and occasion). Thus, although barbiturates have similar chemical effects to alcohol, they are solitary, secretive drugs that people justify taking because they got them with a doctor's prescription. As a result, the effects seem different from the effects of alcohol. Cocaine has acquired a reputation as a sociable, high-status drug. People expect to have fun with it; to feel clever and elated. The second point is that not one of these drugs is without risks. The available evidence suggest that cigarettes and alcohol produce the greatest harm. Yet these are the most socially acceptable drugs in America today. Indeed, most people do not think of tobacco and alcohol as "drugs."

Drug Use: The Contemporary Scene

Who takes drugs that they know are harmful to their health and that they know may even be addictive? Who risks arrest for the effects of illegal drugs? Why? In the early 1970s, many Americans believed the "drug problem" was confined to urban ghettos, inner-city high schools, and the "hippie" enclaves of college campuses. Today, we know that the nonmedical use of drugs is widespread. Nevertheless, drug use is not evenly distributed through society. Different kinds of people take different kinds of drugs. The first step in answering the question of why people take drugs is to determine who takes which drugs.

Patterns of Drug Use

Studies of drug use reveal clear demographic patterns (Kandel, 1980, pp. 244–46). Although sex differences have declined somewhat in recent years, many more men than women use illicit drugs and drink heavily. This difference appears in adolescence: Almost twice as many high-school males as females smoke marijuana every day. In adulthood, men and women seem to use different drugs for the same purposes. Men are more likely to turn to alcohol when under stress; women are more likely to go to a doctor for a prescription. Drug use varies with location: More people drink heavily and take prescription or illegal drugs in cities and suburbs than in rural communities. (The smallest differences are for cigarettes.) Drug use also varies by race. A larger percentage of whites than blacks smoke, drink, take psychoactive pills, and use marijuana. But heroin use is more common among blacks than among whites. Among ethnic groups, Native Americans have the highest rates of drug use; Chinese Americans the lowest. Overall, unemployed persons have the highest rates of use of all drugs except marijuana. Variations by sex, location, ethnic background, and socioeconomic status do not compare with variations by age, however.

Young adults, age eighteen to twenty-five, take more legal and illegal drugs, more often, than any other age group in the population (Kandel, 1980, p. 246). In a survey conducted by the National Institute on Drug Abuse (Fishburne, Abelson, and Cisin, 1979), two out of three young adults said they had used an illicit substance. A third reported using hallucinogens, cocaine, or heroin; a third, using marijuana only. By comparison, only one in five older adults reported using illicit drugs. Rates of drug use among adolescents and young adults climbed in the 1970s. In 1967, fewer than 5 percent of college students and 2 percent of the general population had experimented with marijuana; by 1977, 64 percent of college students

An Anti-smoking Campaign Aimed at Children

Addiction to cigarettes often starts at a young age, as a social pastime or a means of asserting rebelliousness. It therefore makes sense to focus anti-smoking efforts on children and adolescents before the smoking habit becomes regular; but by now, it seems abundantly clear to specialists that the traditional "scare" tactics warning youngsters of the diseases they risk in old age do not work very well. Youthful time horizons extend only a few days or weeks and, at any rate, peer pressures to start smoking are usually far heavier than adult pressures to resist it for health reasons. . . .

[Dr. Russell V. Leupker, a cardiologist at the University of Minnesota] and others are experimenting with a new approach based on the notion that children respond best to demonstrations of the immediate physiological effects of smoking and to peer pressure. It was in such a program that 3,000 seventh graders in 13 New York City and Long Island schools were recently immersed. Devised by Dr. Gilbert J. Botvin, a psychologist at the Cornell Medical College in New York, this object lesson uses machines to illustrate the elevated carbon monoxide level in smokers' breath, to show increased hand tremors, pulse rate and blood pressure, and lowered skin temperature experienced by smokers.

Youngsters who might not be impressed by figures released by the Federal Trade Commission . . . showing carbon monoxide levels in cigarettes may be more responsive to the show-and-tell message. "Most kids of 12 think of themselves as immortal," said Dr. Nathan Maccoby, a psychologist at Stanford's Institute for Communications Research who has pioneered in these techniques. "But if you tell a girl her face will wrinkle from smoking, or tell kids that they will not do well on the basketball court, you might have some effect."

Most of the demonstrations include what Dr. Botvin calls "life skills training," in an effort to give children the skill and strength to resist procigarette peer pressures. The children are taught how to cope better with anxiety and the tensions of boy-girl relations and, perhaps most important, how to ask and refuse favors gracefully. . . .

It is too early to say if these techniques work, but preliminary results are encouraging.

Source: Robert Reinhold, "Of Smoking, Children, and a Deep Belief in Immortality," *The New York Times,* May 10, 1981, p. 20E.

Figure 16–2

Smoking, Drinking, and Age (percentages of a sample of 7,224 people)

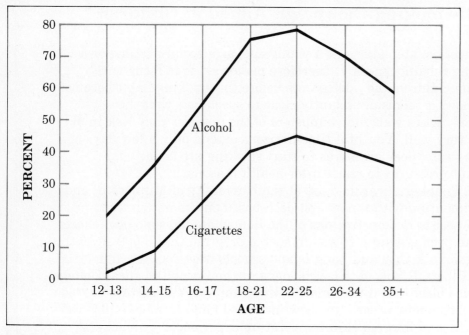

Source: P.M. Fishburne, H.I. Abelson, and I. Cisin, *National Survey on Drug Abuse: Main Findings: 1979* (Rockville, Md.: National Institute on Drug Abuse, 1979), p. 89.

and 25 percent of the general population had done so (Johnson, 1973; Abelson, Fishburne, and Cisin, 1977). Surveys indicate that while smoking cigarettes declined in the general population in the 1970s, it increased among teen-agers. In 1977, 22 percent of twelve- to seventeen-year-olds said they had smoked during the last month, compared with 17 percent in 1971. The percentage of sixteen- to seventeen-year-olds who reported drinking in the preceding month rose from 35 percent in 1971 to 52 percent in 1977 (Abelson, Fishburne, and Cisin, 1977, Tables 80 and 77). In 1979–80, however, regular cigarette smoking and marijuana use among high-school seniors seemed to decline (Bachman, Johnston, and O'Malley, 1981, pp. 7–9). But the age at which they had their first cigarette, drink, or other drug experi-

ence declined. Almost twice as many high-school seniors said they had tried marijuana in eighth grade or below in 1979 as in 1975 (Johnston, Bachman and O'Malley, 1979).

A close look at the data reveals that the kinds of drugs people use and their reasons for using them change over the life cycle. People tend to take different drugs at different ages. In particular, the use of illicit drugs (as opposed to socially accepted and medically prescribed drugs) changes (see Figure 16–2). The nonmedical or recreational use of illicit drugs is highest among eighteen- to twenty-five-year-olds. People in this age range are most likely to use illegal drugs (marijuana, LSD, cocaine, heroin) and also most likely to take other psychoactive drugs for "fun" (tranquilizers, stimulants, barbiturates). After age twenty-five, the recreational use of illicit drugs drops off. The medical use of drugs (prescription tranquilizers, sleeping medicines, and so on) picks up, however. Adults (over 26) are more likely to use licit drugs and to give their reason for taking drugs as medicinal. Intensive use of two socially tolerated drugs, nicotine and alcohol, peaks in young adulthood (as does illicit drug use), then gradually declines among people thirty-five and older. (See Table 16–1.)

Explaining Drug Use

Why do people take drugs? Why do some young people experiment with a drug once or twice while others become regular users? Why do adults continue taking drugs they know to be harmful?

There are no simple answers to these questions. An individual's vulnerability to drugs is the result of complex, interacting factors (Jaffe, 1980).

Table 16–1
Drug Use by Age and Sex* (percentages, based on a sample of 4,594 people interviewed)

Age	Used During Past Month			Used During Past Year					
				Psychoactive Nonmedical			Psychoactive Medically Prescribed		
	Cigarettes	Alcohol	Mari-juana	Stimu-lants	Seda-tives	Tran-quilizers	Stimu-lants	Seda-tives	Tran-quilizers
12–13	10	13	4	–	–	–	1	3	3
14–15	22	28	15	3	2	2	1	5	8
16–17	35	52	29	8	4	7	1	6	5
18–21	51	71	31	11	10	10	3	4	10
22–25	45	70	24	11	6	6	4	8	12
26–34	47	70	12	3	2	4	6	7	18
35–49	45	61	2	–	–	1	3	8	19
50+	34	44	1	–	–	–	2	11	20
Youth (12–17 years, N = 1,272)									
Male	23	37	19	5	3	4	2	4	5
Female	22	25	13	3	2	2	1	6	6
Adult (18 years and over, N = 3,322)									
Male	47	67	30	4	3	4	2	8	12
Female	35	50	19	1	1	2	5	10	23

*N = 4,594

Source: H.I. Abelson, P.M. Fishburne, and I. Cisin, *National Survey on Drug Abuse: 1977. Vol. I: Main Findings* (Princeton, N.J.: Response Analysis, 1977), and secondary analyses of data tape.

Genetic constitution, overall health, diet, and life style may make a person especially vulnerable or resistant to the effect of certain drugs (just as health and genetic factors make some individuals allergic to penicillin). Personality type, family structure, and peer group influences play a part. Cultural norms and values also have an impact. No one of these factors alone explains why some people develop hazardous patterns of use. Rather, the explanation depends on the interaction of many factors. (For example, exposure to a particular social environment might tip the scale in favor of drug use for someone with a particular personality type and genetic constitution but not for someone with the same genetic constitution but a different personality.) A complete explanation of drug use is beyond the scope of this chapter. Here we want to focus on sociological factors. We are concerned not with why one individual takes drugs, but with why the *rate* of drug use varies from one social group to another. In other words, we are concerned with social vulnerability to drugs.

The sociologist Charles Winick (1980) identifies three factors that contribute to high rates of drug use: access to drugs, role strain, and disengagement from prohibitions on their use. The first is obvious. Rates of drug use depend in part on legitimate or illegitimate opportunities (see Chapter 1). The term "role strain" refers to the difficulties people feel in meeting role obligations. Role strain may develop when people are taking on new roles or being tested for adequacy in a role, when obligations are ambiguous or inconsistent, or when a role makes contradictory demands on a person. Role strain alone does not explain vulnerability to drugs, however. Access to drugs and role strain must be combined with disengagement from prohibitions on drug use, so that the group is insulated from social pressures to abstain and warnings against drug use are deflected.

All three conditions are found among adolescents. Teen-agers are particularly vulnerable to role strain in Western societies. They have lost the role of child, but are not yet allowed to assume the role of adult. In effect, they are on trial for an extended period. In addition, adolescence is a time when young people must adjust to changes in their bodies, establish themselves in peer groups with little help from parents and other adults, and face the possible futures, real and imaginary, that are open to them. They have to make decisions about sex, friends versus family, school and college and work. Adolescents are also disengaged from social pressures against drug use. High-school students do not consider experimental or moderate use of drugs as harmful as their parents do, and the adolescent subculture insulates them from parental pressures to abstain. Finally, they have relatively easy access to drugs. The data on drug use support Winick's theory. Illicit drug use picks up at the point at which young people are most likely to experience role strain—at the age when they can legally quit school and go to work. Above-average rates of drug use are found among high-school students whose low grades and truancy records suggest they are disengaged from school and who spend most evenings out, suggesting they are disengaged from their families (Bachman, Johnston, and O'Malley, 1981).

A similar kind of social vulnerability to drugs is found among college students (Winick, 1974, pp. 3–13). Illicit drugs are readily available on most college campuses. A minority of college students strongly disapprove of the recreational use of drugs. Disillusionment with conventional life styles (especially during the Vietnam war years), anxiety about the future (career decisions, plus dwindling job opportunities in recent years), and competition with other students who have the same goals may create role strain. Research shows that liberal arts students are more likely to use illicit drugs than engineering students, who have made a career commitment; students who live off campus, more likely than those living on campus or with their families (Marra et al., 1967).

Rates of drug use are high among jazz and rock musicians, who tend to have liberated attitudes toward drugs and who work in places where drugs are readily available. Role strain is constant for jazz musicians—because of the uncertainty of employment, the musical demand for improvisation, and changing musical styles. Drug use has peaked among jazz and rock musicians in periods when musical styles were changing—during the transitions in jazz from Dixieland to swing (1930–35), from swing to bop (1945–49), and from jazz to rock (1954–58); this also happened during the transitions in rock music from rhythm and blues to British sounds (the early 1960s), to folk rock (the mid-1960s), and to "glitter rock" (the early 1970s) (Winick, 1960). Likewise, rates of drug use are higher among physicians and nurses than among pharmacists and veterinarians, even though all have easy access to drugs. Physicians and nurses are more likely to experience role strain because of such factors as life-and-death decisions and constantly changing technology.

Heroin use among American soldiers in Vietnam is an interesting case (Robins, 1974). Estimates are that 35 percent of U.S. soldiers in Vietnam tried heroin at least once, and 20 percent were "strung out" on heroin (physiologically dependent). Follow-up studies indicate that only 7 percent continued using heroin in the United States. In other words, 93 percent "kicked the habit." Why did they use heroin in Vietnam? Why did they stop? Winick's three-part theory suggests this. (1) Heroin was readily available in Vietnam, for about $2.50 a quarter gram. (2) Soldiers were disengaged from proscriptions on heroin use (many Americans and Vietnamese used the drug). (3) Boredom, homesickness, fear, the ambiguity of our role in Vietnam, the lack of a clearly defined front in the war, and strong opposition to the war in the United States all con-

tributed to role strain. For American soldiers, Vietnam was both boring and dangerous. On their return to the United States, soldiers found that heroin was not only difficult to obtain but also expensive (about $500 a quarter gram), there were many formal (legal) and informal proscriptions on using it, and role strain could be relieved by taking off their uniforms. Significantly, very few American officers used heroin in Vietnam. Officers had as easy access to heroin as soldiers. In contrast to soldiers, however, they were subject to strong proscriptions on using it. (Most were career officers: A heroin record would have jeopardized their future in the Army.) And officers were not as likely to experience role strain. (Most were volunteers who saw service in Vietnam as an opportunity to get ahead in the Army.)

Winick's theory also helps to explain what has been called "the hidden addiction" (Moffitt and Chambers, 1970): the quasi-legitimate use of prescription barbiturates, tranquilizers, and amphetamines. The people who use these drugs tend to be older, better educated, and more "respectable" (middle class) than other drug users (Goode, 1972, p. 155). They begin to use these drugs comparatively late in life, in a medical or quasi-medical context, to treat anxiety, tension, and sleeplessness. These drugs are readily available with a doctor's prescription. The fact that they are considered "medicine" insulates users from norms against becoming dependent on drugs. They do not think of themselves, nor are they seen as "junkies." "[T]he depressed housewife, the harried businessman, the exhausted long-haul truck-driver, the ambitious athlete, the anxious student cramming for an exam" say they use drugs to help them achieve practical, socially approved goals (Goode, 1972, p. 137). All of these people are likely to experience role strain—the housewife because of changing and conflicting standards for females, the businessman because "success" is an ever-receding goal, and so on.

With adults, the key question is not so much

Alcohol and Family Problems—A Poll

Currently, 22 percent of adult Americans say their homes are troubled by alcohol-related problems, nearly double the 12 percent recorded in 1974. At the same time, however, alcohol as a source of family problems seems to have leveled out since 1978, when the figure was 24 percent.

In the latest survey, women are almost twice as likely to perceive family problems related to the use of alcohol as are men. Of particular concern is the fact that slightly more persons under 30 years of age told Gallup interviewers that alcohol had caused trouble in their families than did persons 30 and older.

A somewhat higher proportion of alcohol-related problems is reported by persons from blue-collar than from white-collar households. Survey participants whose formal education ended at the high-school level or earlier were also more apt to cite an alcohol-related family problem than the college-educated segment of the population.

Following is the question asked and the trend since 1950:
"Has liquor ever been a cause of trouble in your family?"

Percent saying yes	
1981	22%
1978	24
1976	17
1974	12
1966	12
1950	14

Source: George Gallup, "Gallup Poll," *The Providence Sunday Journal,* February 8, 1981, p. A-5.

why people start taking drugs as why they continue. In particular, why do adults persist in using alcohol and nicotine (the drugs of choice for adults in the United States)? The answer rests in three different kinds of drug dependency. People are *psychologically dependent* if they rely on a drug to achieve or maintain a certain mood, way of thinking, or behavior pattern; if they feel unable to attain or maintain a desired state without the drug; and if they become preoccupied with it.

People are *physiologically dependent* when their body tissues require the drug. Users do not feel or function normally without it, and discontinuing use produces withdrawal symptoms. Either or both types of dependence play a role in heavy, habitual use of alcohol and nicotine. People use these drugs compulsively to alleviate physical or emotional discomfort. A third factor enters into the use of these drugs, however. *Social dependence* is the need to use alcohol or another drug to meet social expectations (Clausen, 1976, p. 197). College students "get smashed" because they want to be accepted by their peers; factory workers line up glasses on a bar because they want to demonstrate their masculine capacity; business executives order a martini or two before lunch because the situation requires it—not because they feel a physiological or psychological need for a drink. Rather, they are socially dependent on alcohol. Just as there are norms prohibiting alcohol in certain situations, there are norms prescribing or requiring alcohol in others.

What is harmful about dependence? Preoccupation with a drug consumes time and energy, so that a person's other activities and relationships may be compromised, disrupted, or damaged. The drug comes first (Altrocchi, 1980, pp. 522–24). Dependence on a drug magnifies harmful physiological effects. But dependence, like other effects of a drug, is at least partially a matter of social definition.

The Social Control of Drug Use

Attitudes toward drugs and drug use vary across cultures and over time. Drugs that are considered harmful and evil in one culture are seen as benign or even beneficial in another. Drugs that are socially acceptable to one generation are outlawed by the next. Why do social definitions of drugs change? What are the social consequences of making certain drugs (but not others) illegal and branding the people who use or distribute them as criminals? The history of opium in the United States provides clues.

Nineteenth-century America has been described as a "dope fiend's paradise," with some justification (Brecher, 1972, pp. 3–20). It was as easy to purchase opium then as it is to buy aspirin today. The narcotic was available from physicians (many of whom dispensed opium directly), on the shelves of pharmacies, groceries, and general stores, and from mail-order catalogues—all for a reasonable price. Countless patent medicines included opium or morphine (an opium derivative). Ads for Ayers Cherry Pectoral, Mrs. Winslow's Soothing Syrup, Darby's Carminative, Godfrey's Cordial, and others filled magazines and billboards. Opium was frequently prescribed as a cure for alcoholism (much as methadone is used as a substitute for heroin today) and as a tranquilizer. (Indeed, the word "tranquilizer" was coined in 1821 by Thomas de Quincey in *Confessions of an English Opium Eater.*) Mild doses were recommended for "women's problems," from menstruation to menopause. Morphine was introduced during the Civil War as a painkiller, and heroin was introduced at the turn of the century as a substitute for morphine.

Estimates are that 2 to 4 percent of the American population was dependent on these narcotics at the turn of the century (Duster, 1970, pp. 7–9). In contrast to today, most nineteenth-century narcotics users were women (in part because people frowned on women drinking alcohol or smoking tobacco). While today 85 percent of narcotics users are under age thirty, in the last century, most were middle-aged (forty-five to fifty years old). Unlike today, using narcotics was "an aristocratic vice." Opium users tended to be better educated and better off than alcohol users.

Many nineteenth-century Americans considered the use of opium immoral, as many thought dancing, smoking cigarettes, gambling, and recreational sex were immoral. But they did not think of narcotics as a social menace. "Wives did

America at the turn of the century has been described as a "dope fiend's paradise." But the men and women photographed in an opium parlor in New York's Chinatown did not think of themselves, nor were they seen by others, as "dope fiends."

not divorce their addicted husbands or husbands their addicted wives. Children were not taken from their homes and lodged in foster homes or institutions because one or both parents were addicted. Addicts continued to participate fully in the life of the community. Addicted children and young people continued to go to school, Sunday school, and college (Brecher, 1972, pp. 6- 7). Dependence on opium was considered a medical problem. There was no more stigma attached to a person's needing narcotics in the nineteenth century than there is to a diabetic's needing insulin today. The addict was looked on with pity, not fear and hatred. The use of alcohol and tobacco was far more troubling to nineteenth-century Americans than the use of narcotics was. By the 1920s, however, the narcotics user had become a hardened criminal, a moral degenerate, a thrill seeker in the public mind. An illness had become an evil. How did this change come about?

The Politics of Drug Control

The emergence of narcotics as a social issue has been traced in part to a small number of "moral entrepreneurs" (Becker, 1963, pp. 147–63). *Moral entrepreneurs* are individuals who make it their business to see that their notions of right and wrong earn popular approval and are enacted into law. Moral entrepreneurs are absolutists who are convinced that nothing will be right in the world until the evil they have identified is corrected. The Right Reverend Charles Brent, Episcopal Bishop of the Philippines, was an example. When the United States took over the Philippines at the end of the Spanish-American War, it inherited a political problem: the opium traffic. Two wars had been fought over the opium trade in the nineteenth century (largely because the Chinese objected to the British shipping "cut-rate" opium from India to China). American missionaries complained that opium was ruining the Chinese people; American merchants, who didn't trade opium, claimed it was hurting business. Like other men of his time, Brent felt that Westerners had a moral obligation to protect non-Christians, even from their own traditions and against their will. He shouldered "the white man's burden." Brent called for international regulation of the opium trade with missionary zeal. President Theodore Roosevelt agreed, and conferences were held first in Shanghai in 1909 and then in The Hague in 1911 and 1912. Dr. Harvey Wright was another moral entrepreneur. Alerted to the "opium menace" when he served on the Shanghai Commission, Wright applied his considerable energies to the drug situation here at home. With Dr. Harvey Washington Wiley and journalist Samuel Adams, he led a crusade against patent medicines to Congress.

The anti-narcotics campaign became a rallying point for "nativists" (those who believed America was for Americans only). Up to the turn of the century, there had been only one exception to the legal tolerance of opium in this country (Brecher, 1972, pp. 42–43). In 1875, San Francisco had passed an ordinance prohibiting the smoking of opium in "dens." The law was designed not to eliminate opium, but to outlaw a particular use of opium. Smoking opium was a Chinese custom, brought to this country by laborers who worked on the railroads. (Opium helped them to ease the pain of hard labor and increase work capacity.) When the railroad work was over and the Chinese drifted to cities, they were met with intense prejudice and were labeled as the "yellow peril." San Francisco's anti-opium ordinance was part of a pattern of discrimination. Dr. Wright used anti-Chinese sentiments in much the same way Bishop Brent used the notion of the white man's burden—to promote his own ideas of moral danger.

In 1914, Congress responded with the Harrison Act. The Act had three central provisions: First, anyone involved in the production or distribution of narcotics was required to register with the federal government and keep a record of all transactions. Second, anyone who sold or purchased narcotics was required to pay a sales tax (locating enforcement of the Act in the Treasury Department). Third, unregistered persons who wished to purchase narcotics had to obtain a prescription from a doctor, and prescriptions could be given only for "legitimate medical use." (The last provision turned out to be a sleeper, as we'll explain below.) The aim of the Harrison Act was not to stop the sale of narcotics, but to control it. Congress was more concerned with honoring commitments made at the international conferences than with narcotics *per se*. The Act passed with little fanfare. Narcotics had not aroused public concern as yet. Some people were for the bill, some opposed, but the great majority of Americans didn't care one way or the other (Dickson, 1968, pp. 148–49). This would soon change.

The immediate effect of the Harrison Act was to create an instantaneous clientele for physicians. Thousands of law-abiding narcotics users who had previously purchased over-the-counter drugs lined up outside doctors' offices (Duster, 1970, p. 15). With so many new patients, many doctors didn't have time to examine each individual and simply handed out prescriptions. "Narcotics mills" attracted the attention of the moral entrepreneurs, the press, and ultimately the courts. Between 1919 and 1922, the Supreme Court handed down a series of decisions that transformed the medical problem of narcotics dependence into a criminal problem. The Court declared, first, that maintaining a person's habit (giving him or her enough of a drug to remain comfortable) was not "a legitimate medical use" of narcotics; later, that narcotics prescriptions were illegal no matter what the doctor's intention. Over the next twenty-five years, some

25,000 physicians would be arraigned on charges of selling narcotics. Nearly 3,000 would serve prison sentences and thousands more would lose their licenses (Goode, 1972, p. 191). The problem of narcotics addiction was transferred from physicians to police.

Donald Dickson (1968) traces the criminalization of narcotics to the activities of the Federal Narcotics Bureau,* a branch of the Treasury Department created by the Harrison Act. It was the Narcotics Bureau that issued a sensationalistic report in 1919 claiming that narcotics were a threat to public health and morals, that use was directly connected to crime, and that addiction was on the rise, especially among children. It was also the Narcotics Bureau that persuaded the Supreme Court to delete the medical exception from the Harrison Act and proceeded to gather evidence for the arrest of physicians and narcotics users. Dickson argues that the Narcotics Bureau acted, not out of moral zealotry (like Bishop Brent and Dr. Wiley), but in bureaucratic self-interest.

All bureaucracies are concerned with their own survival. All devote some of their resources, not to making a profit or carrying out a congressional mandate, but to bureaucratic survival and growth. (To simplify, bureaucrats are as concerned with keeping their jobs as with doing their jobs.) Federal agencies are no exception. In some ways, they are unique, however. On the one hand, federal agencies are better equipped to deal with the public than other organizations. People are more likely to believe statements made by federal agencies than those made by private companies or groups. They have easy access to the press. And they can put pressure on their critics (in effect, use coercion). On the other hand, federal agencies are especially vulnerable. With private organizations, the decision to expand, to go on as before, to disband, or to change policies rests within the organization. With federal agencies, these decisions are made by Congress, the President, or the courts. To survive, a federal agency must convince the public and Congress that it serves a useful purpose (ideally, a necessary function) and that it is uniquely qualified for the task.

Dickson argues that these bureaucratic considerations outweighed moral concerns in the Narcotics Bureau's campaign against drugs. In stirring up fear and hatred of narcotics and narcotics users, the Bureau was furthering its own cause. As written, the Harrison Act gave the Bureau a limited scope of operations—mainly registering dealers and collecting taxes. The Bureau seized on the medical exception and, through propaganda and court action, greatly expanded its range as a law enforcer. It actively promoted the Marijuana Tax Act in 1937 (Becker, 1963, pp. 135–46). For example, the Bureau furnished "data" for articles in the American Medical Association's journal *Hygeia* that linked marijuana to "crime, bestiality, and insanity" (Reasons, 1975). In effect, the Federal Narcotics Bureau created a need for a narcotics bureau by criminalizing opiates and marijuana and scaring the public.

The politics of drug control is guided by the sometimes visible, sometimes invisible hands of organized interests. The Federal Narcotics Bureau's campaigns against opiates and marijuana succeeded, in part, because there was little organized opposition. Most marijuana is grown outside the United States. And most marijuana users in the 1930s were Mexican-American laborers who had little or no political clout. Today, however, marijuana has become a "middle-class drug." Eleven states have decriminalized marijuana possession, and in all but two remaining states, possession has been reduced from a felony to a misdemeanor (Anderson, 1981). Organized interests explain why other, potentially more harmful drugs have *not* been subjected to strict

---

*Since 1970, the Bureau of Narcotics and Dangerous Drugs

Marijuana—Big Business in California

On tracts hidden away in the mountains and forests of the northern coastal counties and in containers arranged boldly on big-city backyard patios, California seems abloom with marijuana these days. Though cultivating marijuana is a felony, the weed is plentiful and profitable. Indeed, except for cattle, milk and cotton, marijuana earns more than any agribusiness, more than $1 billion annually. In no other state is more marijuana smoked and produced, authorities say. . . .

Some northern California communities have come to depend on the crop. In Gaberville, a little town in Humboldt County where new businesses have opened and the growers have made political allies and gained financial clout, the townsfolk don't talk to strangers about the area's crop. "Don't need no publicity," said Ted Kogan, a nine-year resident of the area. . . .

Except for the state's raids on growers, little has been done to rid California of the crop. Prosecutions are rare and difficult, since the fields are seldom owned by the grower and, unless a grower is caught during harvesting in the fall, possession is often hard to prove. The marijuana isn't easy to find. Many fields are tucked away in rugged state parks. Some growers cultivate as many as 50 small plots.

In addition, marijuana growers have become a new sort of folk hero in California. Hiding out in the mountains and deserts, they are often romanticized as refugees from the cities who have eked out a life in the wilderness fighting poachers, lawmen and the elements. Of course, many growers are nothing of the sort, but rather practical businessmen and blue collar workers.

Growing even one marijuana plant is a felony in California, even though possession of an ounce is but a misdemeanor, an offense about as serious as a traffic ticket. Pro-marijuana groups are trying to change the law. They would like to see cultivation for personal use legalized. Alaska is the only state which has such a law.

Source: Pamela G. Hollie, "California Marijuana Farms Yield a Billion-Dollar High," *The New York Times,* July 13, 1980.

social controls. Corporate interests have fought to limit restrictions on the use of alcohol and tobacco, tranquilizers and amphetamines. Consider tobacco.

Studies linking smoking to cancer began to appear in the early 1960s (Sobel, 1978, pp. 182–239). Maurine Neuberger, wife of an Oregon senator and heavy smoker who died of lung cancer at age forty-eight, spearheaded the anti-cigarette campaign in Congress when she was elected to her husband's former seat. Neuberger and supporters faced a coalition of powerful, skilled opposition groups: the tobacco industry, senators from tobacco-growing states, and civil libertarians (who oppose all restrictions on personal freedom). Anti-cigarette forces succeeded in pressuring President Kennedy to appoint the Surgeon General's Advisory Commission, which in time led to the requirement that a health warning be printed on cigarette packs. But if one compares this warning with the ban on narcotics, or even the requirement for a prescription, it was a limited victory. When lawyer John Banzhaf III wrote to WCBS-TV in New York asking for equal time to respond to cigarette commercials on TV, then pursued the matter in the courts, he ran into still more opposition, this time from the mass media. Broadcasters argued that a ban on cigarette ads would sharply reduce their incomes and set a dangerous precedent: Anyone could demand equal time — environmentalists who were opposed to automobile ads, and so on. Banzhaf won in court (for a time, broadcasters were required to balance cigarette commercials with anti-smoking ads) and then in Congress, which banned cigarette ads from TV altogether. But again, it was a limited victory. Virginia Slims, for example, circumvented the new law by funding a women's tennis tournament. (Even though they do not advertise cigarettes directly, the name "Virginia Slims" appears on TV.)

In much the same way, the drug industry has protected its profits on amphetamines and tranquilizers by opposing strict controls (Graham, 1972). Numerous studies have shown that many more of these pills are produced each year than are medically necessary or can be obtained through legal prescriptions. But the drug companies are organized and the opposition to drugs is diffuse. To fight controls on its stimulants and depressants, the pharmaceutical company Hoffman-LaRoche reportedly paid its Washington lawyers three times the amount of money in the annual budget of the Senate committee that was investigating drug controls (Graham, 1972, p. 22). Laws controlling drug use are more a reflection of these special interests than of the physical and social hazards of the drugs themselves. As a general rule, the drugs used by the least powerful members of society are the most harshly and frequently repressed.

Drug Laws and Their Consequences

Drug laws in the United States today reflect this competition among different interest groups — including federal, state, and local law enforcement agencies. Until recently,* the federal government handled the problem one drug at a time. The result is a patchwork of laws, or more accurately a "crazy quilt." The enforcement of laws and severity of penalties bears little relationship to the actual or potential hazards of the drugs in question. What are the consequences of banning certain drugs and of allowing others to be distributed more or less freely? In other words, what are the consequences of official tolerance and intolerance of drugs?

---

*The 1970 Comprehensive Drug Abuse Prevention and Control Act places drugs into five categories or schedules, according to their presumed potential hazards. Each category is treated differently. However, assignment to one category or the next is a political process and does not necessarily conform to the evidence.

Intolerance The available evidence suggests that the punitive approach to the drug problem is at best ineffective, and may create as many problems as it solves. Banning certain drugs and treating users as criminals has not stopped (or even diminished) the use of illicit drugs. In the more than half-century since the Harrison Act was passed, the number of narcotics users in the United States has more than doubled. Even allowing for population growth, the percentage of Americans who use opiates is greater today than it was in 1914 (The Drug Abuse Council, 1980, pp. 66–67). Why?

The Harrison Act and enforcement policies divided narcotics users into three distinct groups (Goode, 1972, pp. 192–96). The first are middle-class drug users. When the Harrison Act banned over-the-counter drugs, these people went to their physicans for prescriptions (usually barbiturates). Precisely the same categories of people who used opiates in the nineteenth century use barbiturates and tranquilizers today: primarily nervous, unhappy, middle-aged, middle-class white women who feel they can solve emotional problems with a drug. The law did not stop these people from taking drugs; it merely changed the drug on which they depend. A second group of narcotics users were helped by legislation. When opiates were taken off the open market, they discontinued use. These were the least dependent group to begin with. The third group of narcotics users are "street addicts." Unable to purchase narcotics legally, these people became dependent on the black market and automatically became part of the criminal underworld. Thus, the law created a whole new class of criminals that had not existed before. The link between crime and addiction, a rumor before 1914, was forged after 1914.

In subtle, unanticipated ways, the Harrison Act may have encouraged narcotics use. Prior to 1914, opium users had no more in common than cigarette smokers, alcohol drinkers, or even diabetics (who depend on a drug) have today. "Addicts did not display any social cohesion or loyalty as a group; they possessed no lore concerned with the acquisition and administration of drugs, no ideology elaborating the qualities of various drug highs, no justification for using drugs, no rejection of the nonaddict world" (Goode, 1972, p. 195). Legislation and law enforcement, in effect, created the drug subculture. Today, narcotics users have their own language; special connections related to drugs; distinctive norms, values, and rituals. They are a special group. This subcultural identity gives narcotics users recruiting power. To become a member of the group, one must use drugs.

The Harrison Act also led to a rise in criminal activity among narcotics users. Anti-drug laws created a black market economy for drugs, inflating the price of narcotics. Nobody knows exactly how many crimes are committed to obtain money for heroin and other drugs (The Drug Abuse Council, 1980, p. 83). A number of studies suggest that the link between crime and heroin use is exaggerated in official statistics. For example, in the early 1970s, New York State estimated that addicts commit crimes totaling $6.5 billion a year. However, New York City police found that although the city has a high rate of addiction, less than 5 percent of its reported crimes against persons (robberies, muggings, and murder) were committed by heroin users (The Drug Abuse Council, 1980, pp. 84–85). Nevertheless, few people can afford heroin on their salaries alone.

Why hasn't the law been more effective in suppressing narcotics? There are several, interrelated reasons. First, buying, selling, and using narcotics are sometimes thought of as crimes without victims—or more precisely, crimes without complainants (The Drug Abuse Council, 1980, pp. 69–72). The victim plays a key role in most police work. It is he or she who initiates an investigation by making a complaint, provides evidence, and testifies in court. In drug

The final connection in the drug traffic.

enforcement, police usually have to work without victims or complainants. Everyone involved conspires to hide evidence. As a result, narcotics officers usually work under cover—a hazardous, time-consuming, and frequently unrewarding occupation. More than 75 percent of arrests for drug violations are "spontaneous": Police stumble upon evidence in the course of other work.

Second, narcotics production is international in scope. Growing opium is a traditional and legal occupation in many parts of the world (especially the Near East, India, and Southeast Asia). Most opium is grown for licit, medicinal use (primarily as codeine). The illicit heroin market in the United States accounts for only 2 percent of world

production (Holahan and Henningsen, 1972, p. 256). Attempts to limit opium production abroad have met with little success. On the one hand, when the U.S. or another government offers to buy the opium crop, black market purchasers increase their prices and production increases. On the other hand, banning the production of opium deprives local farmers of a valuable cash crop. In some places, people have been growing opium for centuries, use the plant for fodder and fuel as well as for a painkiller, and could not earn as much with a substitute crop (The Drug Abuse Council, 1980, p. 78). In any case, worldwide production is not within the control of the U.S. government.

Third, the trade in illicit heroin is an exceptionally profitable business (Brecher, 1972, pp. 90–100). Opium poppies can be cultivated almost anywhere. All that is required is a pool of surplus labor willing to be hired for a short period of intensive work harvesting the opium. To be marketable in the United States, morphine must be extracted from the opium and converted to heroin —relatively simple, inexpensive procedures. (Equipment for a heroin laboratory costs roughly $700 and can be fit on the back of a truck.) It takes about 25 pounds of pure heroin a day to supply 250,000 addicts. Of course, the laws against importing heroin increase the risk. But the odds favor the importer. The United States imports about 100 million tons of all goods each year. For U.S. Customs officials to locate the 4 to 5 tons of heroin needed to maintain a quarter of a million users would be like finding a needle in a haystack. About 4 million people enter the United States each week. One of these 4 million could carry a day's supply of heroin for the entire addict population on his or her person; two or three could fit a week's supply into ordinary luggage. In fact, few smugglers are caught. (In 1970, for example, Customs officials estimate that almost 7,000 pounds of heroin were smuggled into the country; only 311 pounds were confiscated.) Pure heroin is cut and diluted many times before it reaches consumers. At every step along the route to the black market, profits increase (see Figure 16–3). In 1970, an importer who bought a kilogram of heroin in Europe for $5,000 could sell it to a "connection" in the United States for $20,000. Street dealers, at the bottom of the heroin pecking order, could make as much as $1,000 a week, tax-free. To be sure, the heroin business is risky. But for every dealer who is arrested or retired, there are many applicants to fill the place. In addition, the law helps a small number of importers to maintain oligopolistic control of the market. When newcomers appear, they can be exposed to the police. Finally, the demand for heroin is relatively inelastic. Heroin does not seem to obey the laws of supply and demand: Demand does not go down very much when prices rise (Brecher, 1972). (The same is true for alcohol and cigarettes.)

This is not to say that the narcotics laws have had no impact whatever. It is impossible to known how many narcotics users there would be in the United States today if drugs were freely available. One reason for widespread dissatisfaction with drug policies is that they have been oversold by public officials (The Drug Abuse Council, 1980, p. 67). People do not expect the laws against burglary to stop all burglaries, yet people do seem to expect laws against narcotics to wipe out the heroin market. Nevertheless, the costs of enforcing these laws seem to outweigh the benefits. The chief benefits of current narcotics laws include the arrest of distributors, the channeling of users into treatment programs, and some containment of the spread of dangerous drugs. The list of costs is much longer: "money outlays for enforcement; such side effects as the stigma of arrest, the risk of impure drugs and associated health hazards, the creation of a black market, a potential rise in non-drug crime rates, and the risk of police corruption; the alienation of many segments of society; selective enforcement patterns . . . ; reduction of personal freedom; hostility between police and community" (The Drug Abuse Council, 1980. p. 93). These costs do not result from the use of the drug heroin, but rather from the laws that make this particular drug a crime.

Tolerance Tranquilizers and barbiturates, alcohol and tobacco are not distributed freely in the United States today. A person must have a prescription to purchase the former and must be a certain age to obtain the latter. Both alcohol and tobacco are taxed. In general, however, the law and the public are tolerant of these drugs. Users are not stigmatized. Why are these drugs tolerated? What are the consequences of drug tolerance?

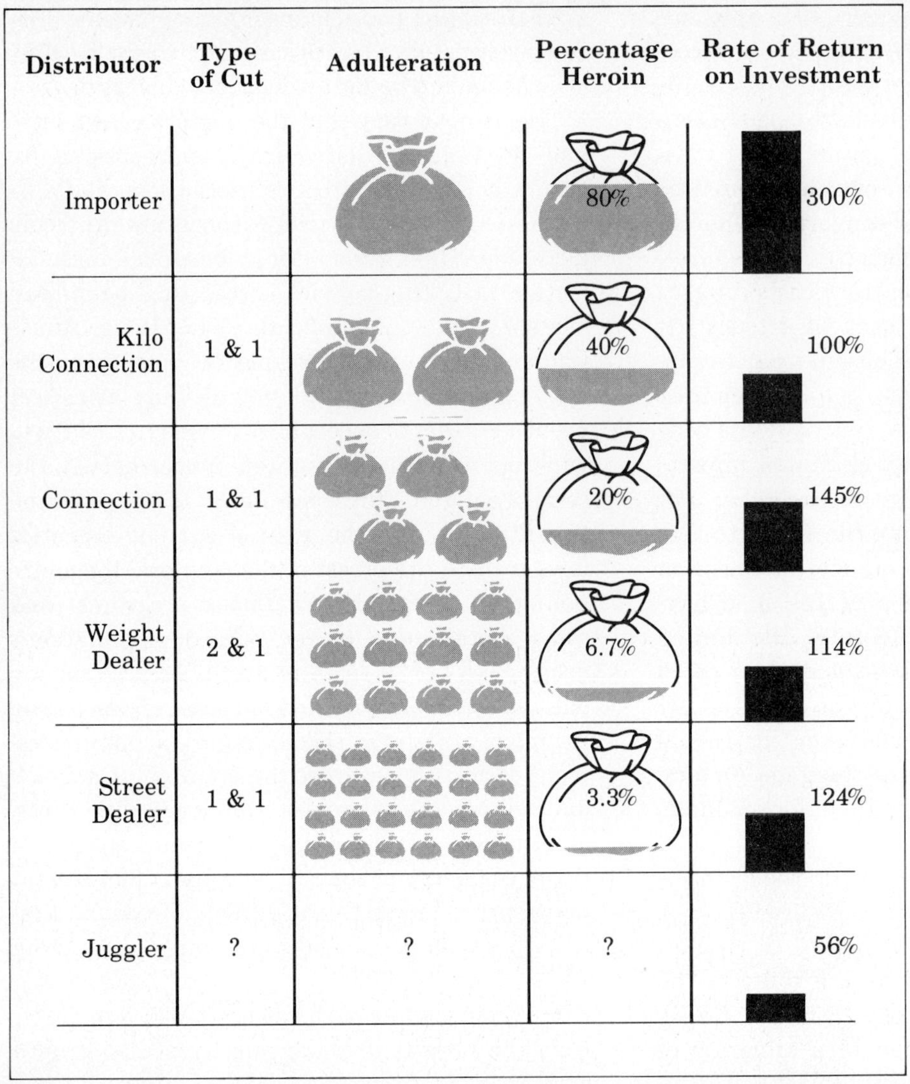

Distributor	Type of Cut	Adulteration	Percentage Heroin	Rate of Return on Investment
Importer			80%	300%
Kilo Connection	1 & 1		40%	100%
Connection	1 & 1		20%	145%
Weight Dealer	2 & 1		6.7%	114%
Street Dealer	1 & 1		3.3%	124%
Juggler	?	?	?	56%

Figure 16–3

The Heroin Market: Chain of Supply, Adulteration Process, and Profit

Source: E.M. Brecher and the Editors of Consumer Reports, *Licit and Illicit Drugs* (Boston: Little, Brown, 1972), p. 99.

The twentieth century has witnessed three "revolutions" in pharmacology that have increased the use of psychoactive drugs and social tolerance of these drugs. The first was the invention of vaccines and antibiotics that control or cure such formerly lethal diseases as diphtheria, polio, and measles. These "miracle medicines" helped to establish the notion that drugs are good for you in the West. The second revolution took place in the early 1950s when drugs for treating mental disorders (the major tranquilizers) became available. For the first time, doctors had alternatives to hospitalization, straitjackets, psychosurgery, electric shock, and years of psychotherapy (see Chapter 13). The major tranquilizers were part of a wave of drugs that acted on the mind (including barbiturates and hallucinogens). The third pharmacological revolution produced convenience drugs. Birth control pills are an example. Women who take "the pill" are not trying to cure physical illness or to change their mood. They are altering their bodies "for convenience and pleasure" (Fort and Cory, 1975, p. 18). Amphetamines, tranquilizers, and sedatives may also be used as convenience drugs—drugs that enable people to stay up, go to sleep, or forget anxieties whenever it is convenient. With each revolution, the number of people who take drugs and their reasons for taking drugs expanded.

The legitimacy of using chemical substances to relieve symptoms of distress has been firmly established in Western cultures. In "The American Way of Drugging," for example, Arnold Bernstein and Henry Lennard (1973) point out that about 60 percent of the patients whom physicians see in their offices or clinics have "nonspecific complaints." After an average examination of fourteen minutes, two-thirds of them leave with a prescription, and one-third of these are for psychoactive drugs. In the authors' view, these people seek medical help because they are "lonely, depressed, anxious, dissatisfied or unhappy. They are troubled because they find it difficult or impossible to measure up to prevalent social prescriptions concerning what one ought to get out of life. They are not as popular, successful, sweet smelling, thin, vigorous or beautiful as they have been led to believe that they ought to be or deserve to be" (p. 16).

Tolerance of drugs is costly. Americans spend billions of dollars on licit drugs each year. In 1970, physicians wrote 230 million prescriptions for psychoactive drugs—more than one bottle of pills for every man, woman, and child in the country. Drug companies produced 5 billion doses of tranquilizers, 5 billion doses of barbiturates, and 3 billion doses of amphetamines (Bernstein and Lennard, 1973, p. 14). The doses consumed each year greatly exceed their therapeutic uses. Moreover, licit drugs have hidden costs. No drug is completely safe (as described in Chapter 13). All have side effects—side effects that are compounded if a person takes more than one medication.

The American drugstore. Taking pills to fix whatever is wrong with us has become part of our way of life.

Table 16–2
Economic Costs of Alcohol Misuse and Alcoholism

	Billions of Dollars*
Lost Production	$9.35
Health and Medical	8.29
Motor Vehicle Accidents	6.44
Alcohol Programs and Research	0.64
Criminal Justice System	0.51
Social Welfare System	0.14
Total	$25.37

*In 1971 dollars.
Source: U.S. Department of Health, Education, and Welfare, *Alcohol and Health* (Rockville, Md.: National Institute on Alcohol Abuse and Alcoholism, 1974), p. 50.

Legal tolerance of drugs reflects vested interests in drug promotion, as well as public demand for medication. Ads for prescription drugs in medical journals frequently exaggerate the therapeutic uses of a drug and play upon physicians' emotions (like any other ad). Drug companies follow up ads with visits by company salesmen and with free samples. Incentives to "push" prescription drugs are built into the medical marketplace. To maximize profits on a given drug before new drugs make it obsolete, a company has to encourage usage. In principle, the use of a drug is limited by the incidence of the disease for which it is intended. In practice, this is not necessarily so. A "generous" definition of the symptoms a drug alleviates can promote usage. This is particularly true for psychoactive drugs. Just as law enforcement agencies have a vested interest in campaigns against illicit drugs, so drug companies have a vested interest in promoting and expanding the use of licit drugs. The same is true for the alcohol and tobacco industries.

Americans spent $20 billion on alcohol and $10.5 billion on cigarettes in 1970. Each year, the average American drinker consumes two and a half gallons of whiskey, two and a quarter gallons of wine, and twenty-eight gallons of beer (Keller and Gurioli, 1976, pp. 3–5). Indirectly, alcohol costs the nation much more than $20 billion. The federal government estimates that the country spends an additional $25 billion each year on alcohol-related problems. This figure includes lost production because of problem drinking, medical treatment for alcohol-induced health problems, loss of life and property in car accidents, costs to the criminal justice system (for arrests for drunkenness, disorderly conduct, and so on), and the price of social-welfare services (the support of people who cannot work because of alcohol) (U.S. Department of Health, Education, and Welfare, 1974) (see Table 16–2). Moreover, in addition to the health hazards from smoking tobacco mentioned earlier in the chapter, cigarettes are implicated in 75 percent of home, apartment, and hotel fires (Fort and Cory, 1975, p. 42). In short, both tolerance and intolerance of drugs are costly.

The Drug Problem in Perspective

What do people mean when they talk of drug abuse? As a rule, this label is automatically applied to any use of illicit drugs like heroin, but rarely used in discussions of the excessive or indiscriminate, nonmedical use of licit drugs. People do not ordinarily refer to smoking as "drug abuse," for example. To be sure, some drugs are more dangerous than others. But the distinction between licit and illicit drugs in the public mind and in the law is arbitrary. In the words of the Drug Abuse Council, a privately funded research institute, "The rigidity imposed by this classification creates unnecessary difficulties in addressing contemporary drug problems. Such classification often reflects solely the question of *social acceptability* and has nothing to do with potential health hazards or demonstrated risks to life or property from the drug in question" (1980, p. 149, emphasis added). Most parents would be far more upset to learn their sons or daughters had smoked marijuana than if they learned that they had smoked cigarettes, even though the known health hazards of tobacco are much greater. It is our view that the public and lawmakers alike tend to overestimate the harmful misuse of illicit drugs and to underestimate the harmful misuse of licit drugs.

Public discussion of the drug problem is cast in terms of different types of drugs. Different types of drug *use* are rarely mentioned. This, too, is misleading. Just as there are differences between a person who has an occasional glass of wine or beer, a social drinker, a problem drinker, and an alcoholic, so there are differences between swallowing, sniffing, smoking, or injecting heroin, amphetamines, or barbiturates. The emphasis on particular drugs in public discussions tends to obscure these differences. The National Commission on Marijuana and Drug Abuse (1973) identified five distinct types of drug-using behavior, each of which poses a different set of risks:

Experimental — short-term, non-patterned trial of one or more drugs, motivated primarily by curiosity or a desire to experience an altered mood state.

Recreational — occurs in social settings among friends or acquaintances who desire to share an experience which they define as both acceptable and pleasurable. Generally, recreational use is both voluntary and patterned and tends not to escalate to more frequent or intensive use patterns.

Circumstantial — generally motivated by the user's perceived need or desire to achieve a new

and anticipated effect in order to cope with a specific problem, situation, or condition of a personal or vocational nature. This category would include the use of stimulants for work-related tasks, and the use of sedatives or stimulants to relieve tension or boredom.

Intensive — drug use which occurs at least daily and is motivated by an individual's perceived need to achieve relief or maintain a level of performance.

Compulsive — consists of a patterned behavior at a high frequency and high level of intensity, characterized by a high degree of dependency, such as with chronic alcoholics, heroin dependents, and compulsive users of barbiturates. (pp. 93–99)

These patterns describe both licit and illicit drug use. Focusing on patterns of use, rather than on the drugs themselves, helps us to distinguish use from misuse and to identify gradations of use and misuse. In our view, the compulsive, nonmedical use of many licit drugs may be more harmful than the circumstantial, recreational, or experimental use of many illicit drugs. The problem lies in the user's behavior, as much as in the chemical properties of drugs.

Current drug policies are both unrealistic and costly. Psychoactive drugs have been used in almost every known society. To hope that drugs can be eliminated by strict law enforcement is unrealistic at best. The price we pay for enforcing laws against certain drugs is high in terms of "social dissension, confusion, and misunderstanding" — not to mention dollars (The Drug Abuse Council, 1980, p. 152). A national drug policy that deals with both licit and illicit drugs and is based on the different *ways* drugs are used, not the alleged properties of the drugs themselves, holds promise. Such a policy would treat drugs as a public health problem, not as a criminal matter. However, public health measures will not address the underlying question of what leads people to seek meaning, relief, or escape through psychoactive substances, or to use drugs in ways that endanger their own and other people's well-being. Hazardous use of drugs is, in the end, a symptom of more basic social problems.

Summary

1. Drug use may lead to psychological or physiological dependence, tolerance and overdose, indirect as well as direct damage to health. The effects of drugs vary from individual to individual and from one social situation to the next. None is without risks.

2. Drug use follows demographic patterns. Americans take different drugs at different stages in the life cycle. Use is heaviest among young, white, adult males.

3. The combination of access to drugs, role strain, and disengagement from prohibitions on drug use increases social vulnerability to drugs.

4. Attitudes toward drug use in the United States have varied. The emergence of drugs as a social issue can be traced to the activities of moral entrepreneurs, especially the Federal Narcotics Bureau that was created in 1919.

5. Drug laws have had unanticipated consequences, including the creation of a drug subculture and a black market. They are difficult to enforce because drug use is a "crime without complainant," production of drugs is international in scope, and the business is extremely profitable.

6. Revolutions in pharmacology helped to establish the legitimacy of using chemicals to avoid distress in the United States. Americans spend billions of dollars each year on licit drugs.

7. The tendency to confuse social unacceptability with physiological harm, and to focus on the chemical properties of drugs rather than on the way they are used, confuses public discussions of the drug problem.

Suggested Reading

Anderson, Patrick. *The True Story Behind NORML and the Politics of Marijuana.* New York: Viking, 1981.

The Drug Abuse Council. *The Facts About Drug Abuse.* New York: Free Press, 1980.

Goode, Eric. *Drugs in American Society.* New York: Knopf, 1972.

Musto, David. *The American Disease.* New Haven: Yale University Press, 1965.

Sobel, Robert. *They Satisfy: The Cigarette in American Life* (Garden City, N.Y.: Doubleday/ Anchor, 1978).

Winick, Charles, (Ed.). *Sociological Aspects of Drug Dependence.* Cleveland, Ohio: CRC Press, 1974.

References

Abelson, H.I., P.M. Fishburne, and I. Cisin. *National Survey on Drug Abuse: 1977. Vol. I: Main Findings,* Princeton, N.J.: Response Analysis, 1977.

Altrocchi, J. *Abnormal Behavior,* New York: Harcourt Brace Jovanovich, 1980.

Anderson, P. *The True Story Behind NORML and the Politics of Marijuana.* New York: Viking, 1981.

Ashley, R. "The Other Side of LSD." *The New York Times Magazine,* October 19, 1975, pp. 40ff.

Bachman, J.G., L.D. Johnston, and P.M. O'Malley. "Smoking, Drinking and Drug Use Among American High School Students." *American Journal of Public Health,* Vol. 71, No. 1 (January 1981), pp. 59–69.

Becker, H.S. *Outsiders.* New York: Free Press, 1963.

Bernstein, A., and H.L. Lennard. "The American Way of Drugging." *Society,* Vol. 10, No. 4 (May/June 1973), pp. 14–25.

Brecher, E.M., and the Editors of Consumer Reports. *Licit and Illicit Drugs.* Boston: Little, Brown, 1972.

Cant, G. "Valiumania." *The New York Times Magazine,* February 1, 1976, pp. 34–44.

Clausen, J.A. "Drug Use." In R.K. Merton and R. Nisbet (Eds.), *Contemporary Social Problems,* 4th ed. New York: Harcourt Brace Jovanovich, 1976, pp. 142–78.

Coleman, J.C. *Abnormal Psychology and Modern Life,* 5th ed. Glenville, Ill.: Scott, Foresman, 1976.

Dickson, D.T. "Bureaucracy and Morality. An Organizational Perspective on a Moral Crusade." *Social Problems,* Vol. 16, No. 2 (Fall 1968), pp. 143–56.

The Drug Abuse Council. *The Facts About "Drug Abuse."* New York: Free Press, 1980.

Duster, T. *The Legislation of Morality.* New York: Free Press, 1970.

Fishburne, P.M., H.I. Abelson, and I. Cisin. *National Survey on Drug Abuse: Main Findings, 1979.* Rockville, Md.: National Institute on Drug Abuse, 1979.

Fort, J., and C.T. Cory. *American Drugstore: A(Alcohol) to V(Valium).* Boston: Little, Brown, 1975.

Goode, E. *Drugs in American Society.* New York: Knopf, 1972.

Goldberg, P. "The Federal Government's Response To Illicit Drugs, 1969–1978." In The Drug Abuse Council, *The Facts About "Drug Abuse".* New York: Free Press, 1980, pp. 20–62.

Graham, J.M. "Amphetamine Politics on Capitol Hill." *Transaction,* Vol. 9, No. 3 (January 1972), pp. 14ff.

Holahan, J.F., and P.A. Henningsen. "The Economics of Heroin." In *Dealing With Drug Abuse: A Report to the Ford Foundation.* New York: Praeger, 1972, pp. 255–99.

Jaffe, J.H. "Genesis of Drug Abuse and Dependence." In A.G. Gilman, L.S. Goodman, and A. Gilman (Eds.), *The Pharmacological Basis of Therapeutics,* 6th ed. New York: Macmillan, 1980, pp. 534–84.

Johnson, B.D. *Marijuana Users and Drug Subcultures.* New York: Wiley, 1973.

Johnston, L.D., J.G. Bachman, and P. O'Malley. *1979 Highlights: Drugs and the Nation's High School Students.* Rockville, Md.: National Institute on Drug Abuse, 1979.

Kandel, D. "Stages in Adolescent Involvement in Drug Abuse." *Science,* Vol. 190, No. 4217 (November 28, 1975), pp. 912–14.

Kandel, D.B. "Drug and Drinking Behavior Among Youth." *Annual Review of Sociology 1980,* Vol. 6 (1980), pp. 235–85.

Keller, M., and C. Gurioli. *Statistics on Consumption of Alcohol and on Alcoholism.* New Brunswick, N.J.: Rutgers Center of Alcohol Studies, 1976.

Marra, E.F., et al. *Intoxicant Drugs: Survey of Student Use, Role and Policy of the University.* SUNY at Buffalo Committee on Drugs and the Campus, Buffalo, 1967.

Moffitt, A.D., and C.D. Chambers. "The Hidden Addiction," *Social Work,* Vol. 15, No. 3 (1970), pp. 54–59.

National Commission on Marijuana and Drug Abuse. *Drug Abuse in America,* 2d report. Washington, D.C.: U.S. Government Publishing Office, 1973.

National Institute on Drug Abuse. *Sedative-Hypnotic Drugs: Risks and Benefits.* Rockville, Md., 1977.

Pekkhanen, J.P. "Drug-Law Enforcement Efforts." In The Drug Abuse Council, *The Facts About "Drug Abuse."* New York: Free Press, 1980, pp. 63–95.

Pert, C.B., and S.H. Snyder. "Opiate Receptor: Demonstration in Nervous Tissue." *Science,* Vol. 179 (1973), pp. 1011–14.

Petersen, R.C., and R.C. Stillman (Eds.). "Cocaine: 1977." *National Institute on Drug Abuse Research Monograph,* 13. Rockville, Md. Department of Health, Education, and Welfare, 1978a.

Petersen, R.C., and R.C. Stillman (Eds.). "Phencyclidine (PCP) Abuse: An Appraisal." *National Institute on Drug Abuse Research Monograph,* 1. Rockville, Md.: Department of Health, Education, and Welfare, 1978b.

Reasons, C. "The Addict as a Criminal: Perpetuation of a Legend." *Crime and Delinquency,* Vol. 21, No. 1 (1975), pp. 19–27.

Robins, L.N. *The Vietnam User Returns.* Final Report Special Action Office, Monograph Series A, 2. Washington, D.C.: U.S. Government Printing Office, 1974.

Sobel, R. *They Satisfy: The Cigarette in American Life.* Garden City, N.Y.: Doubleday/ Anchor, 1978.

U.S. Department of Health, Education, and Welfare. *Alcohol and Health.* Rockville, Md.: National Institute on Alcohol Abuse and Alcoholism, 1974.

U.S. Department of Health, Education, and Welfare. *Smoking and Health: A Report of the Surgeon General.* Washington D.C.: U.S. Government Printing Office, 1979.

Valliant, G.E. "The Natural History of Narcotic Addiction." In M. Greenblatt and E. Artman (Eds.), *Seminars in Psychiatry,* Vol. 2 (1970), pp. 486–98.

Winick, C. "The Use of Drugs by Jazz Musicians." *Social Problems,* Vol. 7 (1960), p. 240.

Winick, C. (Ed.). *Sociological Aspects of Drug Dependence.* Cleveland, Ohio: CRC Press, 1974.

Winick, C. "A Theory of Drug Dependence Based on Role, Access to, and Attitudes Toward Drugs." In D.J. Lettieri, M. Sayers, and H.W. Pearson (Eds.), *Theories on Drug Abuse: Selected Contemporary Perspectives.* National Institute on Drug Abuse Research Monograph, 30. Rockville, Md.: National Institute on Drug Abuse, 1980, pp. 225–35.

Acknowledgments and Copyrights

Box Credits

1-2(pp. 12–13)   From Robert H. Lauer, "Defining Social Problems: Public and Professional Perspectives," *Social Problems,* Vol. 24 (October 1976), pp. 122–30. Reprinted with permission of The Society for the Study of Social Problems and the author.

1-4(pp. 32–33)   From Melvin L. Kohn, "Looking Back – A 25-Year Review and Appraisal of Social Problems Research, *Social Problems,* Vol. 24, No. 1 (October 1976), pp. 94–112. Reprinted with permission of The Society for the Study of Social Problems and the author.

2-1(p. 41)   From Robert K. Merton, "Notes on Problem-Finding in Sociology," in Robert K. Merton, Leonard Broom, and Leonard S. Cottrell, Jr. (Eds.), *Sociology Today: Problems and Prospects* (New York: Basic Books, 1959), pp. xv–xvi. Copyright © 1980 by Basic Books, Inc. By permission of Basic Books, Inc., Publishers, New York.

2-2(pp. 52–53)   From Frederick Mosteller, "Innovation and Evaluation," *Science,* Vol. 211, No. 4485 (February 1981), pp. 881–82. Copyright © 1981 by The American Association for the Advancement of Science.

2-3(p. 56)   From Morris Janowitz, "Disarticulation," *The New York Times,* April 26, 1981, op-ed. © 1981 by The New York Times Company. Reprinted by permission.

2-4(p. 61)   From John Glass, "Renewing an Old Profession," *American Behavioral Scientist,* Vol. 22, No. 4 (March/April 1979), pp. 513–30. Reprinted with permission of the publisher, Sage Publications, Beverly Hills, and the author.

3-1(pp. 78–79)   From Julian L. Simon, "Resources, Population, Environment: An Oversupply of False Bad News," *Science,* Vol. 208 (June 1980), pp. 1435–36. Copyright © 1980 by the American Association for the Advancement of Science.

and South African History by George M. Fredrickson. Copyright © 1981 by Oxford University Press, Inc. Reprinted by permission.

10-3(pp. 346–47)   Reprinted from William Julius Wilson, *The Declining Significance of Race,* by permission of The University of Chicago Press. Copyright © 1978 by The University of Chicago Press.
From Charles V. Willie, "The Inclining Significance of Race." Published by permission of Transaction, Inc., from *Society,* Vol. 15, No. 5. Copyright © July/August 1978 by Transaction, Inc.

11-1(pp. 362–63)   From Lester C. Thurow, "Why Women Are Paid Less Than Men," *The New York Times,* March 8, 1981, and "Letters: Readers Dispute Why Women Earn Less," *The New York Times,* March 15, 1981. © 1981 by The New York Times Company. Reprinted by permission.

11-2(p. 369)   From Gaye Tuchman, "Women's Depiction by the Mass Media," *Signs: Journal of Women in Culture and Society,* Vol. 4, No. 3 (1979), pp. 528–42. Reprinted with permission of The University of Chicago Press.

11-3(p. 372)   From Lin Farley, *Sexual Shakedown: The Sexual Harassment of Women on the Job* (New York: McGraw-Hill, 1978). Reprinted with permission of McGraw-Hill Book Company.

12-1(p. 397)   From Kenneth Keniston and The Carnegie Council on Children, *All Our Children,* copyright © 1977 by Carnegie Corporation of New York. Reprinted by permission of Harcourt Brace Jovanovich, Inc.

12-2(pp. 406–07)   From Susan Sontag, "The Double Standard of Aging," *Saturday Review,* September 23, 1972. Copyright © 1972 by Saturday Review, Inc. Reprinted with permission.

14-3(p. 477)   From "Now Wake the Brave," *The Economist,* April 4, 1981, pp. 10–11. Reprinted by permission.

15-1(p. 512)   From William Serrin, "Sex Is a Growing Multibillion Business," *The New York Times,* February 9, 1981. © 1981 by The New York Times Company. Reprinted by permission.

16-1(p. 537)   From Sharon Johnson, "Help for the Alcoholic Woman: Stressing the Feminist Approach," *The New York Times,* June 14, 1980. © 1980 by The New York Times Company. Reprinted by permission.

16-2(p. 543)   From Robert Reinhold, "Of Smoking, Children, and a Deep Belief in Immortality," *The New York Times,* May 10, 1981. © 1981 by The New York Times Company. Reprinted by permission.

16-3(p. 548)   From George Gallup, "Gallup Poll: Alcohol Abuse Problems Affect One Out of Every Five Families," *The Providence Sunday Journal,* February 8, 1981. Reprinted by permission of The Gallup Poll.

16-4(p. 553)   From Pamela G. Hollie, "Marijuana Farms Yield a Billion-Dollar High," *The New York Times,* July 13, 1980. © 1980 by The New York Times Company. Reprinted by permission.

Table Credits

2-1(p. 68)   From D. Granberg and B.W. Granberg, "Abortion Attitudes, 1965–1980: Trends and Determinants," *Family Planning Perspectives,* Vol. 12, No. 5 (September/ October 1980). Reprinted with permission from *Family Planning Perspectives,* Vol. 12, Number 5, 1980.

12-1(p. 410)   Table "Income Sources for Older Americans" from *Fact Book on Aging* published by The National Council on the Aging, Inc. Reprinted by permission.

13-1(p. 432)   Table 3.1 "Typical Facilities in Small and Large Hospitals" (p. 65) from *Sociology of Medicine* by William R. Rosengren. Copyright © 1980 by William R. Rosengren. Reprinted by permission of Harper & Row, Publishers, Inc.

15-1(p. 495)   From Eugene E. Levitt and Albert D. Klassen, Jr., "Public Attitudes Toward Homosexuality: Part of the 1970 National Survey by the Institute for Sex Research," *Journal of Homosexuality* (Fall 1974), p. 31. Reprinted by permission of Haworth Press, Inc.

15-3(p. 515)   From B. Kutchinsky, "The Effect of Easy Availability of Pornography on the Incidence of Sex Crimes: The Danish Experience," *Journal of Social Issues,* Vol. 29, No. 3 (1973), p. 166. Reprinted by permission of Plenum Publishing Corp., and the author.

Figure Credits

1-1(p. 28)   Table within figure reprinted with permission of Macmillan Publishing Co., Inc., from Robert K. Merton, *Social Theory and Social Structure,* enlarged edition (New York: The Free Press, 1968), p. 194. Copyright © 1968, 1967, by Robert K. Merton.

2-1(p. 43)   Illustration from *Behind Closed Doors* by Murray A. Straus, Richard J. Gelles, and Suzanne K. Steinmetz. Copyright © 1980 by Richard Gelles and Murray A. Straus. Reprinted with permission of Doubleday and Company, Inc.

3-2(p. 82) and **3-3**(p. 83)   From J. van der Tak, C. Haub, and E. Murphy, "Our Population Predicament: A New Look," *Population Bulletin,* Vol. 34, No. 5 (Washington, D.C.: Population Reference Bureau, Dec. 1979), pp. 5, 6. Reprinted by permission of Jean van der Tak, Director, Public Information Programs, Population Reference Bureau.

3-5(p. 89)   From R.G. Ridker and W.D. Watson, Jr., *To Choose a Future: Resources and Environmental Problems of the United States, A Long-Term Global Outlook.* Published for Resources for the Future, Inc., by The Johns Hopkins University Press. Reprinted by permission.

4-1(p. 130)   From *Newsweek,* July 14, 1980, p. 32. Copyright 1980 by Newsweek, Inc. All Rights Reserved. Reprinted by Permission.

6-3(p. 209)   Chart "Detroit and Case in Point" from *The New York Times,* August 24, 1980, Week in Review. © 1980 by The New York Times Company. Reprinted by permission.

15-1(p. 514)   From B. Kutchinsky, "The Effect of Easy Availability of Pornography on the Incidence of Sex Crimes: The Danish Experience," *Journal of Social Issues,* Vol. 29, No. 3 (1973), p. 164. Reprinted by permission of Plenum Publishing Corp., and the author.

Photo Credits

Page
2 © Erika Stone/Peter Arnold, Inc.
4 Wide World Photos
7 Wide World Photos
14 UPI
25 © Paul S. Conklin

Page
29 (top) Culver Pictures; (bottom) Library of Congress
38 © Sybil Shelton/Peter Arnold, Inc.
44 © Bettye Lane

Page
46 © Abigail Heyman/Archive Pictures
50 © Steve David/Sullivan Associates
67 (both) Bettye Lane

Index of Names

Abeles, R.P., 220
Abelson, H.I., 542, 544, 545
Abravanel, M.D., 187, 211
Adams, S., 551
Addams, J., 379
Adler-Karlsson, G., 147
Adorno, T.W., 330
Alexander, Y., 139
Allport, G., 330
Altrocchi, J., 439, 440, 447, 453, 536, 549
Andelin, H., 384
Anderson, O.W., 451
Anderson, P., 552
Angell, R.C., 140
Antelman, S.M., 439
Antonio, R.F., 22
Antonovsky, A., 294
Antunes, G., 486
Arad, R.W., 127, 128
Ariès, P., 394
Artman, E., 564
Ashford, N.A., 240, 242, 243
Ashley, R., 540
Atkinson, R.C., 47, 440
Atkinson, R.L., 47, 440
Ayres, R.U., 88, 116

Babbie, E.R., 45, 50
Bachman, J.G., 544, 546
Bagdikian, B.H., 296
Bahr, H.M., 325, 344
Bahr, S.J., 365
Baker, K., 71
Baker, S.H., 371
Bakke, A., 344

Bakke, E.W., 313
Baldick, R., 417
Baldwin, W.H., 505
Balswick, J.O., 376
Baltes, P.B., 408
Bandura, A., 472, 473
Bane, M.J., 257, 258, 260, 262, 263, 269
Banks, D., 340
Banks, W.C., 59
Banzhaf, J. III, 554
Barber, R.J., 167
Bard, M., 278
Barnet, R.J., 25, 88, 89, 91, 92, 93, 106, 124, 127, 133, 135, 136, 156, 157, 224, 237, 238
Barnett, H.J., 79
Barrow, G., 412, 413
Baskir, L.M., 294
Beach, F.A., 496, 497
Beale, C.L., 190
Bean, L.L., 443
Becker, H.S., 28, 29, 514, 550, 552
Behn, R.D., 427
Bell, A.P., 522
Bell, D., 180, 226, 227-28, 229, 244
Bell, G.D., 251
Bellecourt, C., 340
Benedict, R., 399
Bennett, L.A., 51
Berg, I., 156
Berger, P., 422
Berger, P.L., 35
Bernstein, A., 559
Bieber, I., 522
Binet, A., 396
Bird, C., 160

Black Elk, 319
Blau, R.O., 370
Blauner, R., 233
Blood, R.O. Jr., 365
Blumberg, P., 312
Blumenthal, D., 423, 433, 434, 438
Blumstein, P.W., 527
Blythe, R., 416
Bock, P.G., 136
Bodenheimer, T., 433
Bolton, F.G. Jr., 506
Booth, A., 467
Booth, K., 117
Boraiko, A.A., 101, 103
Botvin, G.J., 543
Bourlag, N., 90
Bourne, R., 275
Bowers, W.J., 484
Boyd, G., 134
Braithwaite, J., 470
Braverman, H., 228-29
Brecher, E.M., 535, 536, 538, 539, 549, 550, 551, 557, 558
Bremer, A., 275
Brent, C., 550, 551
Brezhnev, L., 131
Brody, E.B., 399
Bronfenbrenner, U., 256
Broom, L., 41
Brown, C.E., 490
Brown, D., 319
Brown, E.R., 422, 426, 431
Brown, G.H., 366
Brown, H., 528
Brown, L.R., 78, 80
Brown, M., 100

Brown, P., 473
Bruce-Briggs, B., 219
Bruhn, J.G., 251
Bryant, A., 526
Bumpass, L.L., 261
Burkey, R.M., 325, 326, 328, 331, 333
Burt, Sir C., 54–55
Butler, R.N., 408, 412
Button, A., 275

Caggiula, A.R., 439
Campbell, A.K., 215, 216
Cant, G., 538
Cantril, H., 310
Caplan, N., 58, 60
Caplovitz, D., 295
Caplow, T., 125
Capone, A., 478
Carlson, H., 245
Carlson, R.J., 450–51
Carmichael, S., 335, 382
Carns, D.E., 220
Carter, H., 263
Carter, J.E., 178, 190
Catt, C.C., 379
Caudill, H.M., 5, 9, 18, 22, 24, 25, 26, 30
Cavan, S., 494
Cecelski, E.W., 76, 89, 91, 93, 95, 103, 105
Chadwick, B.A., 325, 344
Chafe, W.H., 378, 379, 380, 381, 382, 383
Chafin, D., 25
Chambers, C.D., 547
Champagne, D.L., 363
Chavez, C., 326, 340
Chernicky, P., 51
Chiappa, J.A., 506
Chilman, C.S., 503, 504, 505
Chinoy, E., 235
Chirot, D., 31, 92, 119, 122, 124, 132–33
Choldin, H.M., 467
Cincin-Sain, B., 211, 212, 213
Cisin, I., 542, 544, 545
Clark, K., 209
Clausen, J.A., 422, 444, 447, 549
Cleveland, H., 117
Cloward, R., 27
Cloward, R.A., 475, 476
Cobb, S., 154, 167, 242
Cohen, A.K., 470, 472, 476
Cohen, J.S., 182
Cole, C.L., 160, 510
Cole, W.E., 409
Coleman, J.C., 536, 538, 539, 540
Coleman, J.S., 62, 194, 209–10, 344, 396, 400

Coleman, R.P., 299
Coles, R., 288, 445
Commoner, B., 97, 98, 100, 102
Conklin, J.E., 481, 487
Connally, J., 167
Conot, R., 489
Conover, D., 445
Conrad, P., 428
Cortina, J., 326
Cory, C.T., 535, 559, 560
Coser, L.A., 23, 24
Cottrell, L.S. Jr., 41
Cousins, N., 425
Crandall, R., 51, 54, 69
Crazy Horse, 319
Cressey, D.R., 26, 465
Cummings, M., 160
Cummings, S., 433
Curtis, H., 108

Dadzie, K.K.S., 132
Dank, B., 524
Darwin, C., 328
Datan, N., 356
Daum, S.M., 251
Davidson, C., 300
Davidson, G.C., 529
Davidson, K.M., 157, 159
Davidson, T., 271
Davies, J.C., 341
Davis, F.J., 35, 71
Davis, K., 301, 517
Davis, N.J., 518
Degler, C.N., 361
de Beauvoir, S., 66, 355, 381
De Lone, R.H., 294, 297, 345, 416, 436
Demos, J., 399
Demos, V., 399
Denfeld, D., 511
Dentler, R.A., 206
De Quincey, T., 549
Deutsch, K.W., 116
Dickson, D.T., 551, 552
Dickson, P., 246, 248
Dieckman, D., 490
Diener, E., 51, 54, 69
Dinitz, S., 47
Disraeli, B., 289
Dix, D., 439
Dohrenwend, B.P., 444
Dohrenwend, B.S., 444
Dollard, J., 330
Dollenmayer, J.A., 215, 216
Dolman, A.J., 112, 113, 115, 122, 124, 125, 127
Donaldson, K., 442

Doob, L.W., 351
Dorr, C., 417
Dover, K.J., 524
Downs, A., 205, 216–17
Dreyfuss, J., 343, 344
Dryfoos, J.G., 504
Duke, J.T., 23
Dullea, G., 269
Dulles, J.F., 117
Duncan, G.J., 268
Dunham, H.W., 442, 444
Durkheim, E., 194
Duster, T., 549, 551

Edgerton, R.B., 456
Ehrenreich, B., 423, 427, 435
Ehrenreich, J., 423, 427, 435
Ehrhardt, A.A., 358
Ehrlich, A.H., 90, 91
Ehrlich, I., 484
Ehrlich, P.R., 90, 91
Elder, G.H. Jr., 393
Elliot, P., 473
Empey, L.I., 402
Engels, F., 23
Epstein, C.F., 374
Erikson, K.T., 5, 6, 8, 9, 10, 15, 21, 22, 24, 25, 27
Ervin, F.R., 471
Espenshade, T.J., 263, 267
Espy, M.W. Jr., 484
Etzioni, A., 256
Evans, R. Jr., 86

Fallows, J., 150, 423, 433, 434
Faris, R.E.L., 442, 444
Farley, L., 372
Farley, R., 62, 63
Farson, R., 269
Fein, R.A., 376
Ferracuti, F., 476
Feshbach, N.D., 394
Feshbach, S., 394
Finger, S.M., 139
Finkel, R., 484
Finkelhor, D., 278, 279, 516
Fischer, C.S., 194, 195, 198, 199, 200, 201, 220
Fishburne, P.M., 542, 544, 545
Fitzpatrick, B., 410
Fleetwood, B., 211
Fogelson, R.M., 343
Foner, A., 392
Ford, C.S., 496, 497
Ford, D., 76

Ford, G., 131
Forish, J.J., 506
Fort, J., 535, 559, 560
Fox, J.R., 170
Fox, R., 80
Fox, R.C., 423, 450
Franklin, B., 401
Frazier, N., 366
Fredrickson, G.M., 322, 328, 333
Free, L.A., 310
Freedman, J.L., 200, 203
Freeman, J., 366, 382
Freud, S., 355, 439, 441, 471, 498
Friedan, B., 380, 381, 382
Friedman, M., 151
Friedman, R., 151

Gagnon, J.H., 497, 508, 509, 510, 511, 516
Gaitz, C.M., 300
Galbraith, J.K., 151
Gamson, W.A., 117
Gans, H., 63, 196, 198, 214, 301, 303
Gardner, J.W., 174, 178–79
Garson, B., 236
Garvey, M., 324
Gebhard, P.H., 499, 502
Geis, G., 462
Gelles, R.J., 42, 43, 44, 51, 270, 271, 272, 273, 274, 275, 278, 476
Gibbs, J.P., 485
Giddens, A., 303
Gil, D.G., 270
Gillespie, O., 361
Gilman, A., 563
Gilman, A.G., 563
Gilman, C.P., 379
Glass, J., 61
Glazer, N., 205, 207
Glick, P.C., 260, 262, 263, 264
Goffman, E., 441, 525
Goldberg, P., 534
Golden, H.H., 188
Goldwater, B., 167
Gonzales, R., 340
Goode, E., 496, 547, 552, 555
Goode, W.J., 257, 264, 365
Goodell, H., 251
Goodman, L.S., 563
Gordon, M., 417, 501
Gornick, V., 388
Graham, H., 351
Graham, J.M., 554
Granberg, B.W., 67, 68
Granberg, D., 67, 68
Grebler, L., 325

Green, M.J., 156, 158, 159, 163, 175, 176, 178
Green, M.R., 283
Green, R.L., 62, 344
Greenblatt, M., 564
Greenwood, P.W., 482
Greer, S., 199
Grimké, S., 379
Gruenberg, B., 236
Gunn, S.D., 51
Gunne, L.M., 439
Gurioli, C., 560
Gurr, T., 351

Haas, A., 503
Haas, J., 242
Haffner, S., 271
Hall, G.S., 399
Halleck, S., 490
Hamburg, B., 422
Hamburg, D., 422
Hamilton, C., 335
Hammerman, J., 436
Haney, C., 59
Hardin G., 119, 143
Harding, E., 433
Hareven, T.K., 283
Harkness, S., 386
Harrington, M., 18, 57, 289
Harris, D.K., 409
Harris, L., 282, 316, 405, 413
Harris, M., 90
Harrison, H., 103
Haub, C., 82, 83, 84, 85, 86, 88, 90
Hauser, P.M., 220, 435
Hauser, R.E., 129
Hawkins, R.B. Jr., 215, 216
Hawley, A.H., 215
Hayes, J., 507
Heer, D.M., 83
Heider, K.G., 494, 496
Heilbroner, R., 78, 165
Heisler, T., 504
Helfer, R.E., 282
Hellmann, D.C., 121
Henderson, B., 497, 509
Henningsen, P.A., 556
Henslin, J.M., 518
Herbers, J., 190
Hess, E.H., 51
Heston, L., 455
Heyerdahl, T., 100, 101, 102
Hiestand, D., 238
Hightower, J., 156, 157
Hilgard, E.R., 47, 440
Hinkle, G.J., 40

Hinkle, L.E., 243
Hinkle, R., 40
Hirsch, F., 78, 89
Hirschi, T., 489
Hobbs, N., 449
Hobbs, P.V., 103
Hofferth, S.L., 261
Hoffman, L.W., 261, 262, 386
Hofstadter, R., 328
Holahan, J.F., 556
Hollander, X., 517
Hollie, P.G., 553
Hollingshead, A.B., 443
Holsti, O.R., 128
Hooker, E., 522
Hoover, J.E., 172
Horney, K., 355
Horowitz, I.L., 119, 122, 124, 125
Hoult, T.F., 294
House, J., 154
Huffine, C.L., 447
Hughes, E.C., 30
Humphrey, J.A., 481, 483
Humphreys, L., 520
Hunt, A.L., 486
Hunt, M., 464, 500, 501, 502, 503, 508, 510, 511, 517, 525
Hurley, R.L., 312
Hurn, C., 351
Hyde, J.S., 497, 522

Ianni, F.A., 465

Jacklin, C.N., 357
Jacobs, J., 201
Jaffe, J.H., 545
Janowitz, M., 56, 60
Jefferson, T., 159
Johnson, B.D., 544
Johnson, D.R., 467
Johnson, L.B., 57, 163, 211
Johnson, M., 392
Johnson, M.M., 367, 368, 370, 371
Johnson, S., 537
Johnson, V.E., 499–500, 508, 509, 510
Johnston, L.D., 544, 546
Jourard, S.M., 376
Joyce, J., 513
Jusenius, C.L., 370

Kagan, J., 283
Kahn, H., 79
Kandel, D., 542
Kanter, R.M., 45–47, 54, 60, 230, 235, 245, 371, 375
Kaplan, H.R., 231

Kaplan, H.S., 510
Kasarda, J.D., 191
Keller, M., 560
Kelling, G.L., 481
Kelly, J.B., 268–69
Kelly, S.D., 62, 210, 344
Kemp, G., 127, 128
Kempe, C.H., 278
Kendall, M., 86
Keniston, K., 293, 306, 307, 397
Kennedy, E.M., 436
Kennedy, J.F., 175, 382, 449, 559
Kennedy, R.F., 175
Kerr, C., 141, 249, 302
Keynes, J.M., 164
Kimball, J.F., 426
King, M.L. Jr., 175, 338, 339
Kinsey, A.C., 498–99, 502, 520, 521
Kirschner, C., 62
Kitagawa, E.M., 435
Kitano, H.H.L., 324, 326
Kitsuse, J.I., 65
Klare, M.T., 112
Klassen, A.D. Jr., 495, 522
Knoedel, J., 90
Knowles, J.H., 452–53
Kohn, M.L., 32, 444
Kolata, G.B., 506
Komarovsky, M., 70, 365, 377, 378, 508
Kommers, D.P., 146
Korb, L.J., 166, 167
Kornhauser, A., 243
Kotelchuck, D., 422
Kraar, L., 136
Kraepelin, E., 439
Kramer, M., 440
Kriesberg, L., 115
Kristol, I., 146
Kuhn, L.L., 519
Kutchinsky, B., 514

La Gory, M., 412
Lamphere, L., 388
Lancaster, J., 52–53
La Piere, R.T., 333–34
LaRossa, R., 51
Larsen, O.N., 64
Lauer, R.H., 13
Lave, L.B., 168
Law, S., 426
Lawrence, C. III, 343, 344
Lawrence, D.H., 476
Lazarus, R.A., 51
Lear, M.W., 456
Lemert, E.M., 30, 530
Lendler, E., 193, 194

Lennard, H.L., 559
Lerner, I.M., 317
Lerner, P., 460
Lettieri, D.J., 564
Leupker, R.V., 543
Levitt, E.E., 495, 522
Lewin, K., 399
Lewis, D.K., 374
Lewis, M., 310
Lewis, O., 196, 198, 299, 300
Libertoff, K., 400
Lieber, J., 483
Lieberson, S., 166, 167
Lincoln, A., 83
Lind, J., 53
Lindstrom, L., 455
Lipset, S.M., 152
Littlefield, J.H., 507
Livingstone, D., 327
Loescher, G.D., 146
Lohman, J.D., 330
Loizos, P., 271
Lombroso, C., 471
Loomis, C.P., 220
Lopez Tijerina, R., 340
Love, W.T., 100
Lucas, R., 241
Luckenbill, D.F., 462
Luker, K., 504
Luria, Z., 516
Lurig, Z., 356
Lutterman, K.G., 294
Lydon, S., 500, 501

Maccoby, E.E., 357, 366
Maccoby, N., 543
MacIver, R., 351
Malthus, R.T., 90
Mancini, P.K., 187, 211
Manis, J.G., 15
Manning, B., 117, 118
Marcus, S., 497
Margolis, R.J., 434
Mark, V.H., 471
Marra, E.F., 547
Martin, C.E., 502
Martin, J.P., 282, 283
Martin, R., 152
Marx, K., 23, 232, 233, 294
Mason, K.O., 261
Massie, R., 181
Masters, W.H., 499–500, 508, 509, 510
Maurer, A., 275
Mayer, A.J., 294
McEvoy, J., 270, 274
McEvoy, J. III, 42, 478

McGregor, D., 244
McIntosh, M., 524, 526
McLemore, S.D., 324, 326
Mead, M., 264, 358, 399, 503
Meadows, D.H., 78
Mechanic, D., 434
Mednick, S.A., 471
Meier, R.F., 462
Merton, R.K., 11, 15, 20, 27, 28, 41, 65,
    171, 219, 282, 334, 387, 402, 408, 415,
    455, 475, 476, 529, 563
Mesarovic, M., 90
Meyers, J.K., 443
Michels, R., 172
Micklin, M., 146
Milakovich, M.E., 481, 483
Milgram, S., 51
Mill, J.S., 378
Millar, J.D., 507
Miller, L.B., 127
Miller, N.E., 351
Miller, P., 537
Miller, W., 476
Millet, K., 520
Mills, C.W., 5, 176, 474, 494, 509
Mintz, M., 182
Mire, J., 246
Mjasnikov, A., 242
Modigliani, A., 117
Moffitt, A.D., 547
Monahan, J., 472
Money, J., 358, 522
Moneymaker, J., 501
Montanino, F., 490, 501
Moore, B.C. Jr., 181
Moore, J.A., 62, 210, 344
Moore, K.A., 261
Moore, W.E., 301
Moran, B.K., 388
Morgan, D., 107
Morgan, J.N., 281
Morgan, M., 384
Morgan, O., 118
Morgan, R., 531
Morris, R.N., 199
Morrison, A., 60
Morse, D., 303
Morse, N.C., 246
Mosteller, F., 53
Mowrer, O.H., 351
Mucatel, M., 412
Müller, R.E., 133, 135, 136, 156, 157
Mulvihille, D.J., 201
Murphy, E., 82, 83, 84, 85, 86, 88, 90
Mushanga, T.M., 271
Muskin, A., 460

Muskin, R., 460
Musto, D., 562
Myrdal, G., 57, 329

Nader, R., 158, 159, 163, 236
Neuberger, M., 554
Newberger, E.H., 271, 275
Newman, D.J., 482
Nimkoff, M.F., 257
Nisbet, R., 11, 15, 20, 65, 219, 282, 351, 387, 415, 455, 489, 529, 563
Nixon, R.M., 64, 463, 534
Norton, A.J., 262, 263, 264
Novak, J., 79
Nye, F.I., 261, 401
Nyerere, J., 135

Ocon, L., 460
Odum, E.P., 107
Offir, C., 354, 355, 364, 366, 499, 507, 511, 514, 523, 525
Ogburn, W.F., 21
Ohlin, L., 27, 59
Ohlin, L.E., 475, 476
Okner, B.A., 295, 307
Okun, A.M., 291, 307
Olsen, M., 146
Olson, L., 401, 402
O'Malley, P.M., 544, 546
O'Neil, G., 510
O'Neil, N., 510
Orlov, Y., 131
Orr, D.W., 146, 147

Paddock, J., 471
Pagels, E., 129
Paige, J., 58
Palen, J.J., 186, 193
Palley, H.A., 194, 204, 207
Palley, M.L., 194, 204, 207
Palmore, E., 243
Park, R.C., 398
Park, R.E., 195
Parke, R. Jr., 456
Parkinson, M., 220
Parks, R., 338
Parshley, H.M., 386, 387
Parsons, T., 179, 429
Pasamanick, B., 47, 49, 50, 51, 54
Pate, T., 490
Pavalko, R., 233
Paykel, E.S., 265
Pearson, H.W., 564
Pearson, J.S., 240, 242
Pechman, J.A., 295, 307
Peck, C.W., 376

Pekkhanen, J.P., 564
Pepper, M.P., 443
Perrow, C., 76, 103, 104
Pert, C.B., 538
Pertschuk, M., 157, 159
Pestel, E., 90
Petersen, R.C., 540, 541
Petersilia, J., 482
Peterson, B., 10
Pettigrew, T.F., 62, 322, 324, 326, 330, 344
Pierce, G.L., 484
Pinel, P., 439
Pleck, E.H., 377
Pleck, J.H., 364, 377
Plog, S.G., 456
Pole, J.R., 168
Pomeroy, W.B., 499, 502
Powdermaker, H., 496
Provenzano, F.J., 356

Quinlan, K.A., 450

Radbill, S.X., 270
Raine, J.W., 21
Rainwater, L., 293, 299, 436, 508
Randolph, A.P., 324
Rasmussen, P.K., 519
Ravitch, D., 210
Ray, J.L., 119, 126, 140, 141, 143, 157
Reagan, R., 57, 477
Reasons, C., 552
Reddaway, P.B., 131
Redlich, F., 443
Reinhold, R., 543
Reiselbach, L.N., 182
Reiser, S.J., 450
Reiss, A.J., 54
Reiss, I., 501
Reiss, I.L., 264
Reitzes, D.C., 330
Rennie, T.A.C., 443
Revelle, R., 91
Rhinesmith, S.H., 141
Richards, T., 63
Ridker, R.G., 76, 88, 89, 91, 93, 95, 103, 105
Riedel, D., 484
Rigler, D., 274
Riley, M.W., 392, 414, 415
Ritzer, G., 226
Robertson, A.H., 131
Robins, L.N., 538, 547
Robinson, E., 103
Robinson, J.P., 364
Robinson, N.H., 364

Rock V.P., 215
Rodgers, H.R. Jr., 304, 306
Rogers, W., 175
Roman, P.M., 243
Roosevelt, F.D., 162, 324
Roosevelt, T., 319, 551
Roper, B.W., 141
Rosaldo, M.Z., 354, 359
Rose, M., 516
Rose, R., 242
Rose, R.M., 522
Rosenau, J.N., 134
Rosengren, W.R., 432, 439, 441, 443, 449
Rosenhan, D.L., 446
Rosenthal, D.B., 187
Rosow, J.M., 249, 251
Ross, H.L., 264
Rossi, A.S., 259, 355, 356
Rothman, D.J., 444
Rothschild, E., 250
Roy, M., 283
Rubin, J., 401
Rubin, J.Z., 356, 365
Rubin, L.B., 365
Rubington, E., 20
Rubinowitz, L.S., 217
Rule, J.B., 64
Russel, J.W., 294
Rutledge, A., 83
Ryan, M.P., 364, 368, 369, 379, 380
Ryan, W., 300

Sacher, E.J., 531
Sadker, M., 366
Safilios-Rothschild, C., 365
Sagarin, E., 490, 518
Sakharov, A., 131
Salamon, L.B., 171, 172
Sampson, A., 145
Samuelson, P.A., 151
Sanday, P.R., 359
Sanders, W.B., 462
Sarbin, T.R., 441
Sawhill, I.V., 264
Sayers, M., 564
Scarf, M., 354
Scarpatti, F.R., 47
Schaefer, R.T., 319, 324, 327, 340, 341
Schaie, K.W., 408
Schattschneider, E.E., 176
Scheff, T.J., 445, 447
Scherer, K.R., 200, 201
Schlesinger, A.M., 220
Schnaiberg, A., 104, 105
Schnore, L.F., 220
Schultz, J.H., 409, 411

Schur, E.M., 65, 463
Schwartz, B., 218
Schwartz, P., 527
Schwirian, K.P., 203
Scott, R.A., 40
Sears, R.R., 351
Self, P., 356
Seligman, J., 158, 159, 163
Sellin, T., 489
Sennett, R., 220
Shankweiler, P.J., 501
Sheehan, S., 422, 423
Sheehy, G., 511
Sheldon, W., 471
Sherrill, R., 112, 156, 158, 160, 161, 167, 169
Shore, A.R., 40
Short, J.F. Jr., 470, 472, 476
Sidel, V.W., 451
Siberman, C.E., 476
Silverstein, L., 482
Simmel, G., 119, 194
Simon, J.L., 79
Simon, W., 508, 516
Simon, W.E., 169
Singer, M.R., 134
Singh, B., 139
Skolnick, A., 257
Skolnick, J., 469
Slater, P.E., 501
Slocum, W., 231
Smigel, E.O., 251
Smith, A., 122, 155
Smith, M.B., 449
Smith, M.P., 217
Smith, P., 412, 413
Snyder, S.H., 538
Sobel, R., 554
Solomon, A.P., 207
Sontag, S., 407
Sorenson, R.C., 503
Sorokin, P.A., 256
Soroos, M.S., 143, 146
Spanier, G.B., 510
Spector, M., 65
Spencer, H., 328, 355
Spencer, M., 417
Sperduto, K., 427
Spinetta, J.J., 274
Sprey, J., 23
Srole, L., 220, 423, 443, 444
Stalin, J., 124
Stambaugh, R.J., 60
Stanton, E.C., 379
Stark, R., 42, 270, 274, 470, 478
Stein, B.A., 245
Steinberg, S., 319, 322, 329, 338, 340

Steinmetz, S.K., 42, 43, 44, 270, 271, 274, 275, 278, 413, 476
Stellman, J.M., 251
Stephens, D.W., 278
Stern, G.M., 6, 7
Stern, P.M., 165
Stewart, N.R., 366
Stewart, P., 514
Stier, S., 394, 398
Stillman, D., 152
Stillman, R.C., 540, 541
Stockard, J., 367, 368, 370, 371
Stouffer, S.A., 242
Strachey, J., 387
Straus, M.A., 42, 43, 44, 270, 271, 274, 275, 278, 476
Strauss, J.H., 325, 344
Strauss, W.A., 294
Street, D., 220
Stromberg, A., 386
Sumner, W.G., 328
Sutherland, E.H., 26, 462, 474
Swazey, J., 450
Sykes, G.M., 460, 462, 463, 467, 468, 472, 478, 482, 483
Szasz, T., 447

Takanishi, R., 394, 395, 396
Tarney, M.A., 363
Tavris, C., 354, 355, 364, 366, 499
Taylor, L., 271
Terenius, J., 455
Terkel S., 233, 234
Thayer, G., 175
Thomas, A.R., 366
Thompson, K.W., 134
Thurow, L.C., 96, 150, 173, 174, 291, 295, 296, 362, 363
Tinbergen, J., 112, 113, 115, 122, 124, 125, 127
Tobin, G.A., 220
Toffler, A., 31
Tönnies, F., 194
Trice, H.M., 243
Tuchman, G., 369
Tuke, W., 439
Tumin, M.M., 201
Turner, N., 324
Tussing, A.D., 305
Tuve, G.L., 96
Twaddle, A.C., 429

U'Ren, M.B., 366

Vacca, R., 78
Valentine, C.A., 300
Valliant, G.E., 538

Van den Berghe, P.L., 318, 327, 328
Van der Tak, J., 82, 83, 84, 85, 86, 88, 90
Van de Walle, E., 90
Vanek, J., 364
Van Ettinger, J., 112, 113, 115, 122, 124, 125, 127
Vatter, H.G., 313
Veblen, T., 171
Vidich, A.J., 179

Waitzkin, H., 427, 428, 434, 435
Waldheim, K., 15
Walker, L.E., 277
Wallerstein, J.S., 268–69
Walters, R.H., 473
Walton, J., 220
Walton, R., 248
Walum L., 377
Wamsley, G.L., 171, 172
Ward, R.A., 412
Waring, J., 392, 414, 415
Warren, E., 338
Wasserstein, B., 181
Waterman, B., 427, 428, 434, 435
Watson, J.B., 256
Watson, N., 233
Watson, W.D. Jr., 88, 89
Waxman, C.I., 310
Weaver, P., 146
Weber, M., 152, 170, 194, 230
Weinberg, M.S., 20, 522
Weiss, C.H., 55, 62
Weiss, R.S., 246, 258, 264, 265, 267, 268
Weitz, S., 379, 380
Weitzman, L.J., 357, 366
Weitzman, M.S., 258
Weller, J.E., 5, 10, 22
West, S.G., 51
Westin, A.F., 51
Westoff, C., 73
Westoff, C.F., 456
Wheeler, S., 63
White, W.H. Jr., 236
Wilensky, H.L., 236
Wiley, H.W., 551
Will, J., 356
Will, R.E., 313
Williams, C.J., 531
Willie, C.V., 347
Wilson, C., 158
Wilson, J.Q., 480, 481
Wilson, W., 379
Wilson, W.J., 331, 346, 347
Winch, R., 257
Winick, C., 546, 547
Wirth, L., 195, 196, 198, 199
Wise, D., 160

Wiseman, J.P., 529
Wolf, S., 242, 243
Wolfe, D.M., 365
Wolff, C., 522
Wolff, K.H., 146
Wolfgang, M., 467, 469, 476, 484
Wollstonecraft, M., 378
Woodhull, V., 379
Woodward, C.V., 324

Woodwell, G.M., 100
Wriggins, W.H., 136, 137
Wright, H., 551
Wurdock, C., 63

Yankelovich, D., 172, 231, 261
Yin, P.P., 413
Yllo, K., 516

Yu, F.T.C., 73

Zeitlin, M., 294
Zimbardo, P.G., 59
Zimmerman, J.F., 215, 216
Zinberg, N.E., 63, 540
Zito, J.M., 198, 199, 200, 201
Zuckerman, H., 54

Index of Subjects

Abortion: politics of, 65–69; teen-age, 504–05

Abscam, 175

Abused children, 271–72, 276, 397

Abused wives, 276–77; learned helplessness, 276

Accidents, at work, 240–42

Acid rain, 100

Addiction, and drug laws, 555–57

Adolescence: and age inequality, 398–403, and crime, 402, 470; and drug use, 542–44; institutionalization of, 399–400; role strain and drug use, 546–47; and runaways, 400–02; sexuality, 503–07; social origins of, 399–400

Adoption, and children's rights, 396–98

Affair, clandestine, 510–11

Affirmative action, 11, 60, 344

AFL-CIO, 175

Age: and divorce, 264; and drug use, 542–45; and unemployment, 239

Age cohorts, 392–93

Aged. *See* Aging; Elderly

Age inequality, 390–418; and adolescence, 398–403; and childhood, 394–98; and later years, 403–14

Ageism, 392

Agent Orange, 100, 101

Aging: attitudes toward, 404–08; double standard of, 406–07; negative consequences, 408–14

Agriculture Department, 171

Aid to Families with Dependent Children (AFDC), 305–07

Air pollution, 99–100; costs, 158

Alcohol, 534–37; and family problems, 548; social costs of, 560; and women, 537

Alianza de Las Mercedes, 340

Alienation, 21–22; and job satisfaction, 231–36

Allotment Act (1887), 319

American Indian Movement (AIM), 340

American Medical Association (AMA), 175, 426

American Telephone and Telegraph Company (AT&T), 248, 383

Amnesty International, 142

Amphetamines, 539–40

An American Dilemma (Myrdal), 57, 329

Andean Pact, 137

Angel dust, 541

Anomie, 27; and violence, 475

Anonymity, in cities, 199

Anti-War Movement, 382

Appalachia: alienation in, 21–22; Buffalo Creek disaster, 5–10, 104–05; conflict perspective on, 24–26; cultural lag in, 21; deviance and moonshine in, 26–30; history of, 8–10; mining in, 24–26

Arms: global build-up of, 113–14; in Middle East, 130

Asia Foundation, 140

Association of American Medical Colleges (AAMC), 343

Association of Clinical Sociologists, 61

Association of Southeast Asian Nations (ASEAN), 137

Authoritarian personality, and prejudice, 330

Authority, vs. power, 152

Automation, of production, 237–38

Baby-boom generation, 393

Back-to-the-city movement, 211–12

BaderMeinhoff, 139

Barbiturates, 536–37, 544, 547, 557, 559

Battered children, 271–72, 276, 397

Battered wives, 276–77

Beatrice Foods Co., 157

Bedlam, 439

Biology, and gender inequality, 355–56

Biosocial perspective, the, 355–56

Birth control, and teen-age pregnancy, 504

Birth rate, 81–82

Bisexuality, 527

Black Elk, Chief, 319

Black lung disease, 25

Blacks: aging and poverty, 409; and Civil Rights Movement, 338–40; and crime, 467–69; enslavement of, 322–23; and equality, 297–98; and racism, 322–24; segregation in South vs. South Africa, 332–33; and significance of race, 346–47; and unemployment, 238–39; and urban riots, 341–43; women, and gender inequality, 374

Black separatism, 324

Blue-collar workers, 233–36

Blue Cross, 426–27

British National Health Service, 451

Brotherhood of Sleeping Car Porters, 324

Brown v. *Board of Education,* 168, 209, 338, 398

Buffalo Creek, West Virginia: case study of destruction of, 5–10; risk at, 104–05

Buffalo Mining Co., 5, 7, 104

Bureaucracy: government, 169–72; revitalizing, 245

Bureau of Indian Affairs (BIA), 319, 340

Bureau of Public Roads, 204

Business. *See* Corporations; Workplace

Business Roundtable, 175

Busing, and desegregation, 343

Campaign contributions, and special interest groups, 175

Cancer, job-related, 240–43

Capitalism, 155–59

Capital punishment, 483–85

Cash assistance, and poverty, 305–07

Central cities, 191–92

Charter 77, 131

Chicano Movement, 340

Child(ren): anti-smoking campaign aimed at, 543; and divorce, 268–69; family violence toward, 271–72, 276, 397; poverty and health, 436; responsibility in family for, 364; rights of, 394–98; sexual abuse of, 278–80; and working mothers, 262

Child abuse, 271–72, 276, 397

Childhood: and age inequality, 394–98; the history of, 394–96

Child labor laws, 395

Child neglect, defining, 397

China: enigma of, 120–21; family planning in, 84, 86; health care in, 451

Chronic organic brain syndrome, and old age, 438

Cigarettes, 539, 542, 543, 557, 561; anti-smoking campaign aimed at children, 543; ban on TV smoking ads, 554; and corporate interests, 554, 560

Cities: bringing middle class back to, 214; central, 191–92; crime in, 201–02; and crowding, 200, growth, 186–89; locking poor into, 202–11; quality of life in, 198–201; revitalization, 211–17; sunbelt, 192–94; in transition, 189–94

Civil Rights Act: of 1866, 323; of 1964, 168, 209, 343, 382, 383

Civil Rights Movement, 168, 338–40; and urban riots, 341–42; and Women's Movement, 381, 382

Civil War, and racial equality, 323

Clandestine affair, 510–11

Class, 23; and crime, 300, 470; and family violence, 274; and mental disorders, 442–44

Clean Air Act (1970), 100

Clinical sociology, 61

Club of Rome, 78, 125, 142

Coal, 95; mining of in Buffalo Creek; 5–6, 9; in the 1980s, 31, 96

Coalitions, Third World, 137–38

Coal Mine Health and Safety Act (1969), 7

Cocaine, 540, 541, 544

Codeine, 538

Cohorts, 392–93

Cold War, 166–67

Coleman Report, 209–10, 216

Collective identity, *Gemeinschaft,* 194

Collective power, 179

Commercialization, and food supply, 92

Commission on Law Enforcement and the Administration of Justice, 59, 467

Commission on Obscenity and Pornography, 64, 516

Commission on the Causes and Prevention of Violence, 59

Commission on the Status of Women, 382

Commodity coalitions, Third World, 137

Commons, tragedy of, 119

Community action, 163

Community Mental Health Center Act (1963), 449

Community mental health centers, 449

Community mental health movement, and mental disorders, 447–49

Comprehensive Drug Abuse Prevention and Control Act (1970), 554

Comstock laws, 511–13

Conference of Women's Commissions, 382

Conflict Tactics Scale, 42–44

Conflict theory: of prejudice, 331; and social problems, 22–26

Conformists, 28; and anomie, 27, 475

Conglomerates, 157

Consumers: protection laws, 169; sovereignty and corporations, 158–59

Consumption patterns, 87–90

Control groups, 49

Convention for New Politics, 382

"Core societies," 119

Cornucopian Thesis, 78–79

Corporations: power of, 152–59; transnational, 133–36, 157; women in, 45–47, 60

Councils of Governments (COGs), 215–16

Courts, and criminal justice system, 481–83

Crazy Horse, Sioux Chief, 319

Crime: and addiction, 555; and adolescence, 402–03; in cities, 200–01; and class, 300, 470; costs of, 463–65; and crowding, 202–03; extent of, 466–67; measuring, 465–71; and the mass media, 63–64; organized, 465; patterns, 462–63; perpetrators and victims, 467–71; rate of, 468; social roots, 486–87; in sunbelt cities, 193–94; in U.S. and Japan, 487; without victims, 463

Criminal behavior, 460–65

Criminalization, of narcotics, 552

Criminal justice system, 478–80; and capital punishment, 483–85; and courts, 481–83; and deterrence, 485–86; and institutionalized racism, 336–37; and police, 480–81; and prisons, 483

Cross-cultural variations, 19

Crowding: and behavior in cities, 200; and crime, 202–03; and gender inequality in workplace, 370–71

Crusade for Justice, 340

Cultural lag, 21

Culture, 19; of inequality, 307–10; of poverty, 299–301; and violence, 476–78

Current reserves, energy, 93

DDT, 101–03

Death rate, 82

Declaration of a New International Economic Order, 137

Declaration of Sentiments, 378

De facto segregation, 343

Defense attorney, 482

Defense spending, and government, 166–68

Deinstitutionalization, and drug revolution, 447–48

De jure segregation, 343

Delirium tremens (DTs), 536

Delinquency, juvenile, 402

Demand, creating, 159

Demographic arithmetic, 81–83
Demographic transition, 85–86
Demography, 81
Dependent variable, 49
Depletion allowance, 165
Depressants, 534–38, 542, 547–62
Depression; and old age, 438; and drugs, 547
Desegregation, of schools, 343
Determinist view: of crime in cities, 200; of urban experience, 195–98
Deterrence: and criminal, 478; and criminal justice system, 485–86
Deviance: and illegitimate opportunities, 27; and medicine, 429; and moonshine, 26–30; residual, 445
Differential association: and deviance, 26–27; differential opportunities, and, 27; and violence, 474
Disarticulation, 56
Discrimination: in employment, 238–39; and racial inequality, 329–35
Disinvestment, in metropolitan housing, 205
Disorganization, social, 20–22; and violence, 474–75
Distribution, vs. supply, food, 91–93
District attorney, 482
Divorce, 262–69; and age of marriage, 264; changes in rates of, 263–64; impact on children, 268–69; mitigating economic impact, 266–67; and religion, 265; and residence, 264; and separation distress, 265; and sex, 511; and working wives, 261
Donaldson case, 442
Doubling time, population, 82
Dred Scott v. *Sandford,* 322
Drug(s), 534; dependence on, 548–49; depressants, 534–38; hallucinogens, 540–42; licit and illicit, 534, 560–62; and job satisfaction, 243; social dependence on, 549; stimulants, 538–40; and treatment of mental disorders, 422–23; 447–48. *See also* Drug use
Drug laws, and consequences, 554–60
Drug revolution, and deinstitutionalization, 447–48
Drug use: circumstantial, 561; compulsive, 561; contemporary, 542–49; control of, 549–60; experimental, 561; explanations of, 545–49; intensive, 561; problem in perspective, 560–62; recreational, 561; social control, 549–60. *See also* Drug(s)

Dual labor market, 302–03; and gender inequality at workplace, 371
Dysfunction, sexual, 509–10

East India Co., 133
East vs. West: competition for natural resources, 127–29; conflict over human rights, 129–32
Ecology: laws of, 97–98; and sociology, 80–81; and sociology of survival, 105–06
Economic security, and government, 160–66
Economy: and government, 164–65; and mental health, 154; post-industrial, 226–29
Ecosphere, 80
Ecosystems, 98
Education: and divorce, 265; and institutionalized racism, 336; and poor in cities, 208–11; and poverty, 294, 297; and women, 365–67
Ego, 471
Elderly: attitudes toward, 404–08; and health, 435–37; and mental disorders, 438; and poverty, 298; victimization of, 413–14
Emancipation Proclamation, 323
Employment: discrimination in, 238–39; and urban exodus, 191–92
Employment opportunities, and poverty, 297
Energy: consumption of, in First and Third Worlds, 88, 89; costs and profits, 96–97; problems, and clash of special interests, 173–74; resources, 93–97
Energy Department, 171
Enlightened patriotism, 140–41
Environment: allocation of risk, 103–05; at risk, 97–103
Environmental Movement, 168
Environmental Protection Agency, 101, 171
Equal Credit Opportunity Act (1974), 383
Equal Employment Opportunity Commission (EEOC), 168, 382, 383
Equal Rights Amendment (ERA), 384
Ethics, of research, 51–55
Ethnic group, 318n
Ethnocentrism, 327
European Common Market, 137
Evaluation research, 59
Experiment, as research tool, 47–51
Experimental drug use, 561

Experimental group, 49
Exurban migration, 190

Factory, global, 224–26
Fair Employment Practices Commission, 324
Fallout, technological, 98–103
Family: in Appalachia, 21–22; developing, 257–59; and divorce, 262–69; as dying, 256–57; female-headed, and poverty, 296–97; life in cities, 199; violence in, 42–45, 270–78; women in, 361–65
Family planning, 84
Family problems, and alcohol, 548
Family violence, history of, 270–271
Famine, in Africa, 76
Fealty, in secretary's job, 371
Fear of failure, and sexual dysfunction, 509–10
Federal Age Discrimination Act (1967), 408
Federal Bureau of Narcotics and Dangerous Drugs, 63
Federal Employment Act, 239
Federal Highway Trust Fund, 204
Federal Housing Act (1949), 204, 207
Federal Housing Administration, 172, 336
Federal Housing Authority, 207
Federal Mogul Corp., 152
Federal Register, 169
Federal Reserve System, 164
Federal Trade Commission, 394
Fees, physicians, 431
Feminism, responses to, 383–85
Fertility, speeding decline of, 83–86
Fertility rate, 81
Field study, as research tool, 45–47
Fifteenth Amendment, 323
Fire, in substandard housing, 205–06
First Amendment, 513
First World, 119, 122, 125–32, 139
Flex-time, 244, 246
Food: consumption of in First and Third Worlds, 88; supplies vs. distribution, 91–93
Food production: commercialization of, 92; mechanization of, 93
Freedmen's Bureaus, 323
Frustration-aggression, and prejudice, 330
Fulbright Program, 140
Furman v. *Georgia,* 484

Gambling, 463
Gault decision, 398
Gay Liberation Movement, 525–26
Gemeinschaft, 194
Gender, vs. sex, 354–55
Gender inequality, 354–61; and biology, 355–56; and institutionalized sexism, 360–61; learned, 356–60; and men, 375–78; and prejudice, 360; and responses to feminism, 383–85; and women, 361–75; and Women's Movement, 378–83
Gender roles, cross-cultural variations in, 358–59
Gender socialization, 356–58
General Electric Co., 237
General Motors Corp., 152, 159
Gentrification, of cities, 211–13
Gesellschaft, 194
G.I. Bill, 380
Global division of labor, 31
Global factory, 224–26
Globalization, of interests, 117–19
Gonorrhea, 506, 507
Goods, change to services from, 226–27
Government: as bureaucracy out of control, 169–72; and economy, 164–65; growth, 160–69; and individual, 161; inefficiency of, 170–71; metropolitan, 215–16; power of, 159–72; and pressure politics, 172–79
Great Britain, health care in, 451
Great Depression, and rise of big government, 160–63
Great Society program, 163
Great Transformation, 194–95
Greenhouse effect, 103
Green Revolution, 90–91, 93
Gregg v. *Georgia,* 484
Ground pollution, 100–01
Group-77, 137
Growth rate, of population, 82
Guadalupe Hidalgo, Treaty of, 325
Guerrilleros, 326
Gulf & Western, 157
Gulf Oil Corp., 136
Gun control, 477

Hallucinogens, 540–42, 544, 546, 552, 553
Harrison Act (1914), 551, 552, 555
Head Start, 163
Health: and mining, 24–25; and poverty, 293–94

Health care: and medical technology, 450–51; politics of, 451; preventive, 451–53
Health insurance: escalating costs of, 428–35; national, 434–35; private, 433–34
Health Insurance Program, 434
Health maintenance organizations, 434–35
Hearst, Patricia, 138
Helsinki Agreement, 131
Heroin, 538; attitudes toward, 534; and drug laws, 556–57; economics of, 556–57
Herpes, 506, 507
Hidden addiction, 547
Highways, and poor in cities, 203–04
Hispanic Americans, and poverty, 297. *See also* Mexican Americans
Homophobia, 525
Homosexuality, 520–27; biological explanations of, 522–23; definition of, 520–22; learning of role, 523; politics of, 523–26
Hooker Chemical Co., 100–01
Hospitals, costs of care in, 431–33
House Select Committee on Aging, 413
House Select Committee on Lobbying Activity, 175
Housing: and elderly, 411–13; and institutionalized racism, 335, 336; and poor in cities, 204–08
Housing and Community Development Act (1974), 217
Human rights: East-West conflict over, 129–32; UN Declaration of, 15–17
Hyde Amendment, 68

Id, 471
Identity, collective, *Gemeinschaft,* 194
Implementation power, in family, 365
Incapacitation, of criminals, 478
Incest, 278–80
Income: and divorce, 264–65; women vs. men, 367–68
Income distribution, 291–92
Independent variables, 48
Individual: and government, 161; in society, 19–20
Industrial democracy, 246–48
Industry, migration, 237–38
Inequality: culture of, 307–10; learned, 356–60; North-South, 132–33; and women, 361–75. *See also* Age inequal-

ity; Gender inequality; Racial inequality
Infant mortality rate, 422
Informed consent, and research, 54
In-kind aid, and poverty, 307
Inner cities, 191–92; and urban revitalization, 211–13
Innovators, 28; and anomie, 27, 475
Insane asylums, 439
Instinct, and sexual behavior, 494–96
Institutions, 19
Interdependence: *Gesellschaft,* 194; nations in age of, 116–19
Interests: clash, and pressure politics, 173–74; globalization, 117–19
International Confederation of Free Trade Unions (ICFTU), 142
International conflict, 115–16
International Council of Scientific Unions, 142
International Federation of Airline Pilots, 142
International Metalworkers Federation, 142
International order, toward, 138–44
International relations: East vs. West, 126–32; nations in age of interdependence, 116–19; North vs. South, 132–38; structure of, 119–26
Intimacy, and family violence, 274
Intolerance, and drug laws, 555–57
Irish Republican Army, 139
Isolation, and stress, in cities, 198–200

Jacobelis v. *Ohio,* 514
Japanese Red Army, 139
Jim Crow laws, 324
Job enrichment, 248
Jobs, and urban exodus, 191–92
Job satisfaction: and alienation, 231–36; and mental health, 243–44
Judges, 482–83
Juvenile court, 395
Juvenile delinquency, 402, 470

Kaiser Permanente Group, 434
Kerner Commission Report, 343
Knowledge: research in generating, 42–55; utilizing, 55–64

Labeling: and deviance, 27–30; and mental disorder, 444–47

Labor market: dual, 229–30, 302–03; global, 237; primary vs. secondary, 229–30
Laissez faire, 155, 162
Law of the Sea, UN Conferences on, 129
Lead poisoning, in substandard housing, 206
Learned helplessness, of abused wives, 276
Learned inequality, 356–60
Learning theory, and deviance, 26–27
Legislation, and racial conflict, 343–45
Libido, 498
Lifeboat ethic, 143
Life chances, and poverty, 293
Life expectancy, 403–04, 422
Lillies in the pond, riddle of, 80–81
Lilly (Eli) Co., 169
The Limits of Growth, 78, 142
Limits Thesis, 76–78
Little Bighorn, battle of, 319
Litton Industries, 238
Lobbying, and pressure politics, 174–79
Love Canal, 100–01
Loyalties, nationalization of, 116–17
LSD, 540, 542

Manager, plight of, 236
Marijuana, 540–41, 544, 545, 552; as big business in California, 553
Marijuana Tax Act (1937), 552
Market domination, 156–57
Massage parlors, 519
Masseuse, 519
Massey-Ferguson, 157
Mass transit, and poor in cities, 204
Master position, 30
Masturbation, 508
Material culture, 19
Media: distortions, 63–64; sexism in, 369
Medicaid, 307, 433, 434
Medical care, costs of, 428–35
Medical centers, 427–28
Medical establishment, the growth of, 425–28
Medical-industrial complex, 427–28
Medicalization, 423–25
Medical model, of mental disorders, 437–42
Medical profession, autonomy and social control, 428
Medical technology, and health care, 450–51
Medicare, 307, 433, 434
Megalopolis, 188, 189

Men, and gender inequality, 375–78; and housework, 364; and role strain, 377
Mental disorders: and class, 442–44; and community mental health movement, 447–49; and deinstitutionalization, 447–48; and drugs, 422–23, 447–48; and labeling, 444–47; medical model, 437–42; and old age, 438; and social class, 442–44; social model, 442–47
Mental health: and economy, 154; and job satisfaction, 243–44
Mental health centers, community, 449
Mental hospital, 441–42
Mentally ill, treatment of, 47–51
Metropolitan areas, and urban revitalization, 213–17
Metropolitan communities, 189
Metropolitan government, 215–16
Metropolitanism, 215
Mexican-American Political Association (MAPA), 340
Mexican Americans: Chicano Movement, 340; immigration policy toward, 326; inequality and, 297, 347–49; and racism, 324–25; and zoot suit riots, 326
Midtown Manhattan Study, 443–44
Migration: exurban, 190; of industry, 237–38
Military establishment, and government, 166–68
Military lobby, 175
Miller v. *California,* 514
Miners, and accidents at workplace, 240–42
Mining, in Appalachia, 24–26
Minorities, and poverty, 297–98
Minority women, 374
Minor tranquilizers, 536, 538
Mobil Oil Corp., 159
Momentum factor, population, 83
Monopolies, 156
Montgomery Ward, 159
Moonshine, and deviance, 26–30
Moral entrepreneurs, 29–30, 550–51
Morality, new, 500–03
Moral therapy, 441
Morphine, 538
Mt. Vernon Center for Community Mental Health, 192
Mugging, 464–65
Multinational corporations. *See* Transnational corporations.

Narcotics Bureau, 552
Narcotics mills, 551
Nations: in age of interdependence, 116–

19; three worlds of development, 119–26
National Advisory Commission on Civil Disorders, 211
National Association for the Advancement of Colored People (NAACP), 324
National Clearing House for Drug Information, 63
National Commission on Marijuana and Drug Abuse, 561
National Commission on Obscenity and Pornography, 514–15
National Congress of American Indians (NCAI), 340
National Crime Survey (NCS), 467, 468
National Energy Act (1977), 178
National health insurance, 434–35
National Highway Traffic Safety Administration, 168, 171
National Indian Youth Council, 340
Nationalism, 116–17; resurgence of, 118–19
Nationalization, of loyalties, 116–17
National Organization for Women (NOW), 382
National Rifle Association, 175
National Welfare Rights Organization (NWRO), 303
Native Americans: government policy toward, 319; and inequality, 297, 347–49; Pan-Indian Movement, 340–41; racism, 318–22
Natural resources: depletion at Buffalo Creek, 9; East-West competition for, 127–29
Neighborhoods: in cities, 196–98; revitalization, 212–13
New Darwinists, 329
New Deal, 163
Nicotine, 539
Nineteenth Amendment, 380
No-fault law, divorce, 263
Non-Aligned Nations, 137
Nonmaterial culture, 19
Nonrenewable resources, 93–96
Norm(s), 19; and family violence, 274–75
Normal accident, 103
North vs. South: economic inequality and, 132–33; Third World strategies, 136–38
Nuclear club, 113
Nuclear family, 258
Nuclear power plants, 95–96
Nuclear Regulatory Commission (NRC), 104
Nuclear war, effects of, 114

Obsolescence, planned, 159
Occupational hazards, 240–41
Occupational Safety and Health Act (1970), 243
Occupational Safety and Health Administration (OSHA), 168
Oceans: and competition for natural resources, 127–29; pollution of, 100
Office of Economic Opportunity, 163
Oil depletion allowance, 165–66
Old Age. *See* Elderly
Oligopoly, 155–57
Opium, 549–51
Opportunity structures: and deviance, 27; and violence, 475–76
Orchestration power, in family, 365
Organization: parallel, 245; transnational, 141–43
Organization of African Unity (OAU), 137
Organization of Petroleum Exporting Countries (OPEC), 96, 122, 137
Organized crime, 465
Overcrowding, and gender inequality in workplace, 370–71
Overmedicalization, 423–25; social consequences of, 428

Palestine Liberation Army (P.L.O.), 138
Pan-Indian Movement, 340–41
Parallel organization, 244, 245
Parallel pricing, 156
Parents, family violence toward, 273
Patriotism, enlightened, 140–41
Pay, men vs. women, 362–63
PCP, 541
Peace Corps, 140
Penis envy, 355
Pentagon, 170
Personality theory of prejudice, 330
Pesticides, 101–03
Petit-mal epilepsy, 538
Pharmaceutical industry, and drug use, 554
Pharmacology, revolutions in, 558–59
Photochemical smog, 100
Physical disorders, 425; and escalating costs of care, 428–35; and medical establishment, 425–28; and poverty and old age, 435–37
Physicians, fees, 431
Pivotal power, 126
Planned obsolescence, 159
Planned Parenthood v. *Danforth,* 394, 398
Plant shutdowns, 152–53
Plea bargaining, 482

Plessy v. *Ferguson,* 324
Police: and criminal justice system, 480–81; and victimless crime, 463
Political crime, 463
Political economy, 151
Political power: of corporations, 159; and violence, 176–77
Politics: of drug control, 550–54; of health care, 451; of homosexuality, 523–26; pressure, 172–79; of social problems, 65–69
Pollution: air, 99–100; ground, 100–01; water, 100
Poor, 287–313. *See also* Poverty
Popular Front for the Liberation of Palestine (P.F.L.P.), 138
Popular Movement for the Liberation of Angola (MPLA), 136
Population: age pyramids, 82; and future demands, 81–86; and starvation in Africa, 76
Population growth: and demographic transition, 85–86; momentum factor in, 83; in Third World, 83, 85–86
Pornography, 511–16; legal dilemma of, 511, 514; President's Commission on Obscenity and, 64, 514–16
Post-industrial economy, 226–29
Poverty: and aging, 408–11; culture of, 299–301; economics of, 301–03; explanations of, 298–304; and health, 425–27; penalties of, 293–96; amid plenty, 290–93; and power, 303–04; and racial inequality, 348–49; remedies and obstacles, 304–10; research into, 33; and social welfare programs, 304–07; victims of, 296–98
Poverty line, 290–91
Power: vs. authority, 152; collective, 19; of corporations, 152–59; of government, 159–72; and poverty, 303–04
The Power Elite (Mills), 176
Practitioners, and sociology, 55
Pregnancy, teen-age, 503–06
Prejudice: and discrimination, 331–35; and gender inequality, 360; Marxist view of, 331; and racial inequality, 329–35; situational theory of, 330–31
President's Commission on Law Enforcement and Administration of Justice, 59, 467
President's Commission on Obscenity and Pornography, 64, 516
President's Commission on Population Growth and the American Future, 58, 61, 64

Pressure politics, 172–79
Preventive health care, 451–53
Price leadership, 156
Principled arbitrariness, secretary's job, 371
Prisons, and criminal justice system, 483
Privacy: and family violence, 274; and poverty, 303; and research, 42–44, 51, 54
Pro-Choice Movement, 69
Production: automation of, 237–38; treadmill of, 105
Profits and costs, energy, 96–97
Prohibition, 29–30
Propaganda by deed, terrorism as, 138–39
Property crime, 462
Prosecutor, 482
Prospective reserves, energy, 93
Prostitution, 463, 517–20; economics of, 517; functional view of, 517; learning the role of, 518
Psychoactive drugs, 534
Psychological explanations: of homosexuality, 522–23; of violence, 471–72
Psychological theory of prejudice, 330
Public Health Service, 239
Public housing, 207
Public interest, and pressure politics, 179
Public policy makers, and sociology, 55
Public rights, and government, 168–69

Quadruple bind, 41
Quality of life, in cities, 198–201
Quasi-primary relationships, cities, 196

Rabble-rouser theory, of urban riots, 342
Race: biological definition of, 316–17; significance of, 346–47; sociological definition of, 318; UNESCO statement on, 317
Race relationships, research into, 33
Race riots, 324, 341–43, 473–74
Racial conflict, contemporary, 338–44; reaction to, 343–45
Racial inequality: dimensions, 345–49; maintaining, 329–38
Racial segregation: and urban education, 209–10; and urban housing, 207
Racism: and black Americans, 322–24; history, 316–27; ideology of, 328–29; institutionalized, 335–38; and Mexican Americans, 324–27; and Native Americans, 318–22; social preconditions for, 327–29

Radio Free Europe, 140
Rebels, 28; and anomie, 27, 475
Recidivism, 483
Recreational drug use, 561
Recycling, and ecosystems, 98
Red Cross, 142
Red lining, and institutionalized racism, 335
Red Medical Workers, 451
Reform, of workplace, 244–48
Regional coalitions, Third World, 137
Regional poverty, 298
Rehabilitation, of criminals, 478
Reinforcement, and social learning, 472–73
Removal Act (1830), 318–19
Renewable resources, 96
Replication, 49
Report of the National Advisory Commission on Civil Disorders, 216, 342–43
Representative sample, 44
Research: ethics of, 51–55; innovation and evaluation, 52–53; into social problems, 32–33
Resegregation, of urban schools, 210
Residential segregation, of elderly, 412
Resources: energy, 93–97; food supplies, 90–93; global, 90–97
Response rate, in surveys, 44
Responsiveness, of government, 171–72
Retreatists, 28; and anomie, 27, 475
Retrenchment, and racial conflict, 344
Retribution, against criminals, 478
Revitalization, of cities, 211–17
Riff-raff theory, of urban riots, 342
Rights, of children, 394–98
Right-to-Life Movement, 67–69
Riots, urban, 324, 341–43, 473–74
Ripple effect, of plant shutdowns, 152–53
Rising expectations, theory of, 343–44
Ritualists, 28; and anomie, 27, 475
Robinson v. California, 534
Robots, on assembly line, 237
Roe v. Wade, 67, 384
Roles, 20; gender, 356–58; sexual, 508–09
Role strain: and drug use, 546–47; men, 377
Roth v. U.S., 513
Runaways, 400–02

Saab, 246
Safety: and mining, 24–25; and the workplace, 240–43
Sample, 44

Sampling error, 44
Sanctions, 19
Scapegoats, and prejudice, 330
School busing, 209, 210
Science, and sex, 498–500
Second World, 119, 122–24
Secretary, structure of job, 371, 375
Segmentation, in cities, 195
Segregation: in South vs. South Africa, 332–33; in urban housing, 207; of urban schools, 209–10
Selective Service Act, 380
Self-fulfilling prophecy: labeling, as 30; negative stereotype of aging as, 408; social issue as, 18; urban exodus and, 201
Self-interest, and capitalism, 155
Self-realization, ethic of, 264
Self-selection, and urban life styles, 198
Senate Government Operations Committee, 152
Senility, and old age, 438
Serrano v. Priest, 210
Services, change from goods to, 226–27
Sex; business of, 512; commercialized, 511–20; and divorce, 511; vs. gender, 354–55; and science, 498–500; and society, 494–503
Sexism: institutionalized, and gender inequality, 360–61; in media, 369
Sex-role differentiation, research into, 32
Sex segregation: and tracking in schools, 366; at work, 368
Sexual abuse, of children, 278–80
Sexual attitudes, and behavior, 497–503
Sexual behavior: and attitudes, 497–503; commercialized sex, 511–20; conduct, 496–97; homosexuality, 520–27; social learning and, 508–09; social problems and social issues, 527–28; variations, 496–97
Sexual dysfunction, 509–10
Sexual harassment, of women at work, 372
Sexual identities, mixed, 358
Sexuality: adolescent, 503–07; American tenets, 497; marital and extramarital, 507–11; sociology of, 508–10
Sexual roles, learning, 508–09
Shale, 95
Sherman Anti-Trust Act (1890), 156, 163
Siblings, family violence toward, 273
Sick role, 429
Silicosis, 25
Situational theory, of prejudice, 330–31

Smog, 99–100
Snowbelt cities, decline of, 189, 194
Social acceptability, 561
Social action, and social problems, 65–69
Social class. See Class
Social control: of drug use, 549–60; and medical profession, 428
Social costs, of running away, 401–02
Social Darwinism, 328–29
Social disorganization, 20–22; and violence, 474–75
Social engineering, 60
Social institution, family as, 256
Social insurance, 304–05
Social issues: identifying, 11–15; sexual behavior as, 527–28
Socialization, 20, 356; and family violence, 274; gender, 356–58
Social learning: and sexual behavior, 494–96; and violence, 472–74
Social model, of mental disorders, 442–47
Social origins, of adolescence, 399–400
Social preconditions, of racism, 327–28
Social problems: of adolescence, 400–03; identifying, 15–18; in 1980s, 30–34; public perspectives on, 12–13; research into, 32–33; sexual behavior, 527–28; and social action, 65–69; theoretical approaches, 20–30
Social-psychological explanations, of violence, 472–74
Social roots, of crime and violence, 486–87
Social Security, 304, 410–11; and health care, 434
Social Security Act (1935), 163
Social Security Administration, 434
Social stratification, and poverty, 301
Social support, 449
Social system, 19
Social welfare programs, 304–07
Society: individual in, 19–20; and sex, 494–503
Sociocultural lag, and the age structure, 404
Sociological explanations, of violence, 474–78
Sociological frame of reference, 18–20
Sociological imagination, 4–5; and Buffalo Creek disaster, 7–9
Sociologist: and clinical sociology, 61; quadruple bind of, 41; responsibilities, 69
Sociology: clinical, 61; and ecology, 80–81; obstacles to use, 62–64; research in

generating knowledge, 42–55; of sexuality, 508–10; and social problems, 40; of survival, 105–06; uses and users, 55–62

South: Civil Rights Movement in, 338–40; segregation of blacks in, 332–33. *See also* Appalachia

Special interests, and pressure politics, 173–79

Spouses, family violence toward, 272–73

Stagflation, 151

Standard Metropolitan Statistical Areas (SMSAs), 188

State of the Globe, 142

Status: of individual in society, 19–20; master, 30

Status contingency, secretary's job, 371

Stereotypes, and prejudice, 330

Stimulants, 538–40

Stonewall Inn, and Gay Liberation, 525

Street addicts, 555

Streetwalker, becoming, 518

Stress, and isolation, in cities, 198–200

Strip cities, 188

Subcultural view: of crime in cities, 200–01; of urban experience, 198

Subcultures, 19

Suburbs: growth of, 187, 189; problems of, 192; opening up to city's poor, 216–17; zoning regulations in, 207, 217

Suffrage, for women, 379–80

Sunbelt cities, 192–94

Superego, 471

Supplementary Security Income, 305, 307

Supply-side economics, 165

Surgeon General's Advisory Commission, 539, 554

Survey, as research tool, 42–45

Survival, sociology of, 105–06

Swinging, 510–11

Symbionese Liberation Army, 138–39

Syphilis, 506, 507

Systems thinking, and global perspective, 141

Tar sands, 95

Technological fallout, 98–103

Technology, medical, and health care, 450–51

Teen-age pregnancy, 503–06

Television, cigarette advertising ban, 554

Termination Act (1953), 319

Terrorism, international, 138–39

Theory X, 244, 246

Theory Y, 244, 246

Third World, 119, 124–25; strategies in dealing with North, 136–38; weapons sales to, 112

Three Mile Island nuclear accident, 76, 103–04

Three worlds, in turmoil, 125–26

Tinker v. *Des Moines,* 398

Tobacco industry, and cigarette use, 554

Tokenism, 375

Tort, 460–61

Total institutions, 441–42

Tracking, and sex segregation in schools, 366

Traffic Safety Act (1966), 158

Tragedy of commons, 119

Trail of Broken Treaties, 340

Trail of Tears, 319

Trained incapacity, 171

Tranquilizers, minor, 536, 538

Transnational corporations, 157; and North-South inequality, 133–36

Transnational organizations, 141–43

Transportation, and poor in cities, 202–04

Transportation Administration, 171

Treadmill of production, 105

Treatment, of mentally ill, 47–51

Triad, 125

Trickle-down process, housing, 205, 336

Truman Doctrine, 166

Truth-in-Lending Act (1968), 169

Truth in Packaging Act (1966), 169

Tupamaros, 139

Unanticipated consequences, 202

Underemployment, and aging, 408–11

Unemployment, 236–39; and dual labor market, 302–03; in 1930s, 160; women vs. men, 368

Unemployment insurance, 304–05

Uniform Crime Reports (UCR), 466–67, 468

Unintended consequences, 211

United Farm Workers' Union, 303, 340

United Nations: Conference on Trade and Development (UNCTAD), 137; Conferences on the Law of the Sea (UNCLOS), 129; and global perspectives, 140; UNESCO statement on race, 317; Universal Declaration of Human Rights, 15–17

Universal coalitions, Southern nations, 137

Universal Declaration of Human Rights, 15–17

Uranium, 95; mining hazards, 240–41

Urban America, in transition, 189–94

Urbanization, 186–89

Urban League, 303

Urban poor: and education, 208–11; and housing, 204–08; and transportation, 202–04

Urban renaissance, 211–13

Urban renewal, 207

Urban riots, 324, 341–43, 473–74

Urban transportation, history of, 202–04

Variables, 48–49

Venereal disease (VD), and adolescent sexuality, 506–07

Vengeance, against criminals, 478

Veterans Administration, 207, 336

Victims: of family violence, 276–77; and perpetrators of crime, 467–71; of poverty, 296–98

Victimization, of elderly, 413–14

Victimless crime, 463

Victorian influence, on sexual attitudes and behavior, 497–98

Vietnam War, heroin use by soldiers, 547

Violence: and anomie, 475; biological explanations of, 471; causes of, 471–78; and culture, 476–78; in family, 42–45, 270–78; and gun control, 477; and political power, 176–77; psychological explanations of, 471–72; social-psychological explanations of, 472–74; social roots of, 486–87; sociological explanations of, 474–78

Violent crime, 462

Voluntary Relocation Program (1956), 319

Volvo, 246–48

Voting Rights Act (1965), 343

War on Poverty, 298

Watergate, 463

Water: pollution, 100; supplies, 76–77

Watts riot, 473–74

The Wealth of Nations (Smith), 155

Welfare: dual system, 305; government programs, 163; myths about, 308–09

White-collar crime, 462–63

White-collar workers, 233–36

White House Conference on Families, 254–55

Wife abuse, victims of, 276–77

Wisconsin v. *Yoder,* 398

Wolfenden Committee, 525

Women: alcoholic, 537; in corporations, 45–47, 60, 371–75; divorce and remarriage rates of, 263; and education, 365–67; in families, 361–65; family violence toward, 272–73, 276–77; as heads of families, and poverty, 296–97; minority, 374; and pay, 362–63; and prostitution, 463, 517–20; and social reform, 379–80; suffrage for, 379–80; and unemployment, 239; and work, 367–75; working wives and mothers, 260–62

Women Against Pornography, 516

Women's Alcoholic Coalition, 537

Women's Christian Temperance Movement, 379

Women's Movement, 66; history of, 378–80; responses to, 383–85; today, 380–83

Women's Rights Convention, 378

Worcester State Hospital, 441

Work: alienation and job satisfaction, 231–36; and discontents, 230–39; health hazards and, 240–43; post-industrial, 227–29; theories of, 244–48; and women, 367–75

Work ethic, 230–31

Workplace: accidents in, 240–42; changing, 224–30; danger, disability, and death at, 239–44; discrimination in, 238–39; global factory, 224–26; organizational response to hazards in, 240–41; in post-industrial economy, 226–29; reforming, 244–48; and unemployment, 236–39; unhealthy, 242–43

Works Progress Administration (WPA), 163

World Confederation of Labor (WCL), 142

World Council of Churches, 142

World Federation of Trade Unions (WFTU), 142

World Fertility Survey, 83, 86

World Health Organization, 450

World Order Models Project (WOMP), 142

World Population Conference, 86

Wounded Knee, battle of, 319

The Zero-Sum Society (Thurow), 173

Zero population growth, 82–83

Zoot suit riot, 326

A 2
B 3
C 4
D 5
E 6
F 7
G 8
H 9
I 0
J 1